STARTING POINTS

D1441633

STARTING POINTS

A Sociological Journey

Lorne Tepperman

OXFORD
UNIVERSITY PRESS

OXFORD

UNIVERSITY PRESS

8 Sampson Mews, Suite 204, Don Mills, Ontario M3C 0H5
www.oupcanada.com

Oxford University Press is a department of the University of Oxford.
It furthers the University's objective of excellence in research, scholarship,
and education by publishing worldwide in

Oxford   New York

Auckland   Cape Town   Dar es Salaam   Hong Kong   Karachi
Kuala Lumpur   Madrid   Melbourne   Mexico City   Nairobi
New Delhi   Shanghai   Taipei   Toronto

With offices in

Argentina   Austria   Brazil   Chile   Czech Republic   France   Greece
Guatemala   Hungary   Italy   Japan   Poland   Portugal   Singapore
South Korea   Switzerland   Thailand   Turkey   Ukraine   Vietnam

Oxford is a trade mark of Oxford University Press
in the UK and in certain other countries

Published in Canada
by Oxford University Press

Copyright © Oxford University Press Canada 2011

The moral rights of the author have been asserted

Database right Oxford University Press (maker)

First Published 2011

All rights reserved. No part of this publication may be reproduced,
stored in a retrieval system, or transmitted, in any form or by any means,
without the prior permission in writing of Oxford University Press,
or as expressly permitted by law, or under terms agreed with the appropriate
reprographics rights organization. Enquiries concerning reproduction
outside the scope of the above should be sent to the Permissions Department
at the address above or through the following url:
www.oupcanada.com/permission/permission_request.php

You must not circulate this book in any other binding or cover
and you must impose this same condition on any acquirer.

Every effort has been made to determine and contact copyright holders.
In the case of any omissions, the publisher will be pleased to make
suitable acknowledgement in future editions.

Library and Archives Canada Cataloguing in Publication

Tepperman, Lorne, 1943–
Starting points : a sociological journey / Lorne Tepperman.

Includes bibliographical references and index.
ISBN 978–0–19–542998–5

1. Sociology—Textbooks. I. Title.

HM586.T44 2011   301   C2010-907709-1

Cover image: A J James/Getty

This book is printed on permanent (acid-free) paper ∞
which contains a minimum of 10% post-consumer waste.

Printed and bound in the United States of America
2 3 4 — 14 13 12

Contents

From the Publisher   xv
Preface   xxiii

1   Introducing Sociology

Chapter Outline   3
Everyday Observations   4
Ways of Looking at Sociology   6
    Functional Theory   6
    Critical Theory   8
    Symbolic Interactionism   8
    Feminist Theories   9
    Postmodern Theories   10
Classic Studies: *Suicide*   12
    Modern Functionalism   14
    Functions of Deviance and Conformity   14
    The Functions of Conflict   17
    Critical Theory   17
    Conflicts over Power and Authority   19
Classic Studies: *The Vertical Mosaic*   20
    Modern Critical Theories   21
Classic Studies: *Stigma*   22
    Key Ideas of Symbolic Interactionism   23
    Social Constructionism   25
People Are Talking About Anthony Giddens   26
New Insights   27
Chapter Summary   29
Critical Thinking Questions   30
Recommended Readings   30
Websites   31

2 Material Settings

Chapter Outline   33
Everyday Observations   34
Ways of Looking at Population   35
    Functionalism   35
    Critical Theory's Approach to Malthus   36
Ways of Looking at Urban Life   37
    Functionalism   37
    Critical Theory   38
    Symbolic Interactionism   38
Ways of Looking at the Environment   39
    Functionalism   39
    Critical Theory   39
    Symbolic Interactionism   39
    Feminist Theory   40
Classic Studies: *The Limits to Growth*   40
    Why Demography?   42
    Population Trends Reveal a Society's History   44
    World Population   45
Classic Studies: *Risk Society: Towards a New Modernity*   49
    The Natural Environment   50
    Location, Location, Location   53
    Buildings and Cityscapes   54
    Urbanization   54
    Built Environments   56
People Are Talking About Manuel Castells   57
New Insights   59
Chapter Summary   61
Critical Thinking Questions   62
Recommended Readings   62
Websites   63

3 Social Structures

Chapter Outline   65
Everyday Observations   66
Classic Studies: *Outsiders*   67
    Identity, Roles, and Role-Sets   68
    Role Conflicts and Role Strains   74
Classic Studies: 'The Sociology of Secrecy and of Secret Societies'   75
    Dyads, Triads, and Small Groups   76
    Teams, Bands, and Gangs   77
    Cliques, Networks, and Small Worlds   79
People Are Talking About Michel Foucault   83
New Insights   86
Chapter Summary   89

Critical Thinking Questions   90
Recommended Readings   90
Websites   91

4   Culture

Chapter Outline   93
Everyday Observations   94
Ways of Looking at Culture   96
    Functionalism   96
    Critical Theory   97
    Symbolic Interactionism   98
    Cultural Studies Perspective   98
    The Production of Culture Perspective   99
    Language: A Key Cultural Realm   101
Classic Studies: *The Protestant Ethic and the Spirit of Capitalism*   104
    The Importance of Values: The Case of Religion   106
    Cultural Integration, Ethnocentricism, and the Mass Media   107
Classic Studies: *Theory of the Leisure Class*   109
People Are Talking About Pierre Bourdieu   110
    Cultural Variation   113
    Cultural Change   115
    Canadian Culture   116
    A Global Culture?   119
New Insights   119
Chapter Summary   121
Critical Thinking Questions   122
Recommended Readings   122
Websites   123

5   Gender Relations

Chapter Outline   125
Everyday Observations   126
Ways of Looking at Gender   127
    Functionalism   127
    Critical Theories   127
    Symbolic Interactionism   127
    Social Constructionist Approaches   128
    Types of Feminist Sociology   128
Classic Studies: *The Sociology of Housework*   129
    Gendered Socialization   131
    Mass Media   132
    The Beauty Standard   134
    Conflict between the Sexes   135
    The Gendering of Crime   136
Classic Studies: *Men and Women of the Corporation*   137
    Gender Influences in the Workplace   138

The Earnings Gap   139
    Gender and Immigration   141
Classic Studies: *The Double Ghetto*   142
    At Home: Women's Second Shift   143
    Gender Influences on Health   144
    Conflict Between the Sexes   146
People Are Talking About Dorothy Smith   147
New Insights   149
Chapter Summary   151
Critical Thinking Questions   152
Recommended Readings   152
Websites   153

6   Sexuality

Chapter Outline   155
Everyday Observations   156
Ways of Looking at Sexuality   158
    Functionalism   158
    Critical Theory   158
    Symbolic Interactionism   159
    Feminism   160
    Postmodernism   161
Classic Studies: *The Social Organization of Sexuality*   163
    The Sexual Double Standard and (Other) Changing
        Trends in Sexual Behaviour   164
    Marital Infidelity   166
Classic Studies: *The Sociology of Prostitution*   167
    Pornography   167
Classic Studies: *American Gay*   169
    Homosexuality and Heteronormativity   170
    Homophobia   173
    Paraphilia   175
People Are Talking About Judith Butler   177
New Insights   179
Chapter Summary   180
Critical Thinking Questions   181
Recommended Readings   181
Websites   182

7   Racial and Ethnic Groups

Chapter Outline   185
Everyday Observations   186
Ways of Looking at Racial and Ethnic Groups   186
    Functionalism   186
    Critical Theory   187

Symbolic Interactionism   188
Structural Theory   188
Classic Studies: *Social Distance*   189
The History of Racial and Ethnic Relations   191
The History of Immigration Policy   193
Immigration in the Twenty-first Century   195
Classic Studies: *The Polish Peasant in Europe and America*   197
Inter-Ethnic Interaction   198
Multiculturalism   201
Multiculturalism and Aboriginal Peoples   203
Multiculturalism and French Canadians   203
Classic Studies: *An American Dilemma: The Negro Problem
and Modern Democracy*   205
Racialization   206
Prejudice and Discrimination   207
Abuse and Violence   208
People Are Talking About Edward Said   210
New Insights   212
Chapter Summary   213
Critical Thinking Questions   214
Recommended Readings   214
Websites   215

8 Age Groups

Chapter Outline   217
Everyday Observations   218
Ways of Looking at Age Groups   220
Functionalism   220
Critical Theory   220
Symbolic Interactionism   221
Feminist Theories   222
Classic Studies: *Centuries of Childhood*   222
Youth: A Time of Risk-taking   224
Age Group Relations   225
Changing Age Relations   226
Classic Studies: *Children of the Great Depression*   227
Relations between Young and Old   229
Age in School and the Workplace   230
Classic Studies: *Mean Streets: Youth Crime and Homelessness*   231
Age and Crime   233
Age and Mental Health   233
Age and Physical Health   234
Abuse and Violence   236
People Are Talking About Karl Mannheim   237
New Insights   239
Chapter Summary   241
Critical Thinking Questions   242
Recommended Readings   242
Websites   243

9 Classes and Workplaces

Chapter Outline   245
Everyday Observations   246
Ways of Looking at Class and Work   247
    Functionalism   247
    Critical Theory   248
    Feminist Theories   249
    Symbolic Interactionism   249
    Social Constructionism   249
Classic Studies: *Labor and Monopoly Capital*   250
    Labour and Classes   251
    The Organization of Work Today   253
Classic Studies: *The Division of Labor in Society*   255
    Alienation and Collective Action   256
    Unions   256
    The Culture of Poverty   259
Classic Studies: *White-Collar Crime*   261
    Modern Forms of Capitalism   263
    The Relationship Between Class and Health   264
    Social Class and Crime   266
People Are Talking About Gerhard Lenski   266
New Insights   269
Chapter Summary   271
Critical Thinking Questions   272
Recommended Readings   272
Websites   273

10 Regions, Nations, and Empires

Chapter Outline   275
Everyday Observations   276
Ways of Looking at Regions, Nations, and Empires   277
Classic Studies: *The Modern World-System I: Capitalist
        Agriculture and the Origins of the European World-Economy
        in the Sixteenth Century*   278
    Networks of Dependency   280
    Differentiating between Nations, Regions, and Empires   282
    A Global Economy   282
    Blurring Social Distance through Technology   284
Classic Studies: *The Manifesto of the Communist Party*   285
    Conflict in Society   287
    International Politics and Discrimination   290
    International Violence and War   291
    Terrorism   291
People Are Talking About Immanuel Wallerstein   294
New Insights   297

Chapter Summary   299
Critical Thinking Questions   300
Recommended Readings   300
Websites   301

11   Families and Socialization

Chapter Outline   303
Everyday Observations   304
Ways of Looking at Family Life   305
    Functionalism   305
    Critical Theories   306
    Symbolic Interactionism   306
Ways of Looking at Socialization   307
Classic Studies: *World Revolution and Family Patterns*   308
    The Idea of 'Family'   312
    Socialization   315
Classic Studies: *The Authoritarian Personality*   317
    Gender Socialization   320
    Racial and Ethnic Socialization   321
    Class Socialization   322
People Are Talking About Arlie Hochschild   324
New Insights   326
Chapter Summary   329
Critical Thinking Questions   330
Recommended Readings   330
Websites   331

12   Schools and Formal Education

Chapter Outline   333
Everyday Observations   334
Ways of Looking at Education   335
Classic Studies: *The Academic Revolution*   336
    Educational Inequalities   339
Classic Studies: *The Adolescent Society*   341
    Ability Grouping or Streaming   343
    Segregation or Distance in Schools   344
Classic Studies: *Crestwood Heights*   347
    Abuse or Violence in Schools   349
    The Integrating Power of Schools   352
People Are Talking About James S. Coleman   354
New Insights   357
Chapter Summary   358
Critical Thinking Questions   360
Recommended Readings   360
Websites   361

13 Churches and Religion

Chapter Outline   363
Everyday Observations   364
Ways of Looking at Religion   366
Classic Studies: *The Elementary Forms of Religious Life*   367
    Definitional Problems   369
    Religion in Canada Today   370
    Religion vs. Science: The Debate of the Modern Era   376
Classic Studies: *Civilization and Its Discontents*   379
    The Idea of Secularization   380
    Civil Religion   382
    New Religious Movements   383
    Religion in the Schools?   384
People Are Talking About Robert Bellah   385
New Insights   388
Chapter Summary   391
Critical Thinking Questions   392
Recommended Readings   392
Websites   393

14 Media and Mass Communication

Chapter Outline   395
Everyday Observations   396
Ways of Looking at Mass Media   397
Classic Studies: *Deciding What's News*   398
    Media Ownership   400
    Canadian Content   401
    Media and Politics   403
    Global Media   404
Classic Studies: *Material Girls: Making Sense of Feminist*
    Cultural Theory   405
    The Cultural Studies Perspective   406
    Media Representation of Disadvantaged Groups   408
    Media Portrayal of Women and Gender   408
    Homogenization and Niche Marketing   411
    Media, Conflict, and Crime   412
    Media and the Construction of Social Problems   414
People Are Talking About Jean Baudrillard   414
New Insights   417
Chapter Summary   419
Critical Thinking Questions   420
Recommended Readings   420
Websites   421

15 Politics and Ideologies

Chapter Outline   423
Everyday Observations   424
Ways of Looking at Politics   425
Classic Studies: *The First New Nation*   426
   Political Science and Political Sociology   427
   Political Authority   428
   The State   430
   Gender and the State   433
   Politics in Canada: A Primer   434
Classic Studies: *Discipline and Punish: The Birth of the Prison*   438
   The Political Role of Ideology   440
   Ideologies and Publics   441
   Ideologies and Action   442
People Are Talking About Jürgen Habermas   443
New Insights   446
Chapter Summary   448
Critical Thinking Questions   450
Recommended Readings   450
Websites   451

16 Social Movements and Voluntary Associations

Chapter Outline   453
Everyday Observations   454
   Interdependence: The Real State of Nature   454
Classic Studies: *Improvised News: A Sociological Study of Rumor*   458
   Voluntary Associations and Sociability   460
   The Benefits of Voluntary Associations   461
   People Control One Another Informally   462
Classic Studies: *The Civilizing Process*   464
Ways of Looking at Social Movements and Voluntary Associations   465
Classic Studies: *Symbolic Crusade*   468
   Changing Causes of Social Movement Formation   470
   Social Movements in a Globalized World   472
People Are Talking About Charles Tilly   474
New Insights   476
Chapter Summary   478
Critical Thinking Questions   480
Recommended Readings   480
Websites   481

Glossary   482
References   488
Photo Credits   512
Index   513

From the Publisher

Starting Points: A Sociological Journey provides a comprehensive introduction for students delving into the fascinating world of sociology for the first time. Each chapter explores a central topic in sociology through discussions of real-life examples, classic and contemporary studies, and major theories and perspectives. With a fresh, engaging approach, the text takes students through the many factors that influence social relationships—from individual needs, characteristics, and interpretations to group dynamics and hierarchies to culturally established norms, institutions, and ideologies.

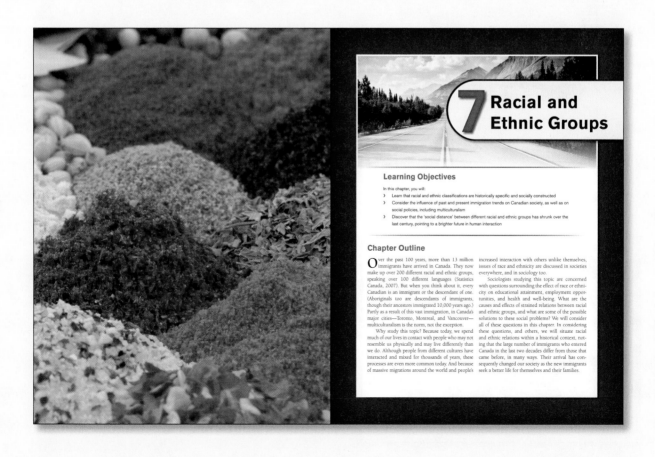

Key Features

Robert Merton, a key figure in developing this perspective, argued in his classic work *Social Theory and Social Structure* (1957) that **social institutions** perform both manifest and latent functions. *Manifest functions* are those that are intended and easily recognized; *latent functions* are unintended and often hidden. Education, for example, is intended to provide students with the knowledge, skills, and cultural values that will help them to work effectively in society. Both the school and its participants—students, teachers, parents, and others—formally recognize these **roles**. At a latent level, however, education also works as a regular 'babysitter' for young children and teenagers not yet ready to take full-time jobs; it also works as a 'matchmaker', a place where older high school and university students can meet and mingle with potential lovers or marriage partners.

Or consider another example—one of the classic ideas in sociology introduced by French sociologist Émile Durkheim. The manifest function of crime—law-breaking—is usually to benefit the lawbreaker: a robber, thief, embezzler, or the like. But Durkheim notes that crime is universal (found everywhere, at all times), so perhaps it serves a latent function for society. It actually does, he says: crime, by mobilizing popular sentiment, helps clarify the social boundaries for proper behaviour. In this way, it strengthens social solidarity, which every society needs.

These latent functions, as important to society as the intended ones, are considered latent because they are not the intended results (e.g., of educators or criminals), nor are they typically admitted to be such. When did you last hear school administrators, students, or parents admit that public school is a daycare service?

This distinction is important because it helps us understand, from the functionalist standpoint, how every social institution has a 'purpose'. The emphasis on the interconnection of society's parts, and how these parts support one another, usefully highlights how they also influence one another. This approach helps us understand why changes in one part of society bring about changes in other parts—for example, why changes in family life, such as increasing divorce and single-parenthood, have important, usually unconscious and unintended consequences for work and education.

Functionalists also characteristically explain social problems by focusing on the failure of institutions to fulfill their roles during times of rapid change. This view of social problems holds that sudden cultural shifts disrupt traditional values and common ways of doing things. By this reckoning, industrialization and urbanization in North America a century ago caused a sharp increase in social disorganization, leading to an upsurge of crime, mental illness, poverty, unsanitary living conditions, and environmental pollution. As we will see, there are other sociological explanations of the same phenomena.

French sociologist Émile Durkheim (see, e.g., 1964 [1893], 1964 [1897], 1965 [1912]) introduced the term *anomie*, or 'normlessness', to reflect the condition

This image of police restraining a protester during a riot illustrates what can happen when social control and norms break down, a condition of Anomie.

microsociology
The study of the processes and patterns of personal interaction that take place among people within groups.

sociological imagination
An approach to sociology that situates the personal experiences of individuals within the societal context in which these experiences occur.

social institution
One kind of social structure, made up of a number of relationships (i.e., stable patterns of meaningful orientations to one another). People use institutions to achieve their intended goals, as students use schools, or patients use hospitals.

role
The expected pattern of interaction with others.

Margin definitions clarify

essential concepts and terms to help students build their vocabularies.

Everyday Observations

Population size matters, so consider this example. Emily took her first subway ride while visiting her sister in the city. Coming from a small town, she was not used to the crowds of people and the noise (not to mention the smell) of the subway station. While she and her sister were waiting for the subway to arrive, Emily admired the interesting artwork along the wall. However, while doing so she noticed something scurrying in the dark corners of the tracks. Suddenly, the train came roaring into the station, blowing cold, stale air into her face. Emily stood back a little, startled by the speed of the subway and intensity of the wind. When the doors of the subway opened, people quickly pushed and shoved past her, fighting for a place inside. By the time she was able to wrestle her way through, Emily was pressed tightly against other passengers. She looked at her sister anxiously, who smiled back and simply said 'It's always busy at rush hour.'

If you grew up in a rural area, you likely know that urban life is different from rural life. Many factors play into the differences. First, the populations of cities are much larger and denser than those of small towns or villages. Second, the technologies that are central to city life, such as subways or other forms of rapid transit, are unlikely to be found in a rural area or a small town, since they were developed to deal with large populations,

The subway has enabled people to travel across the city in large numbers at inexpensive prices.

'Everyday Observations'

boxes introduce students the chapter's central topic by discussing a familiar situation from everyday life.

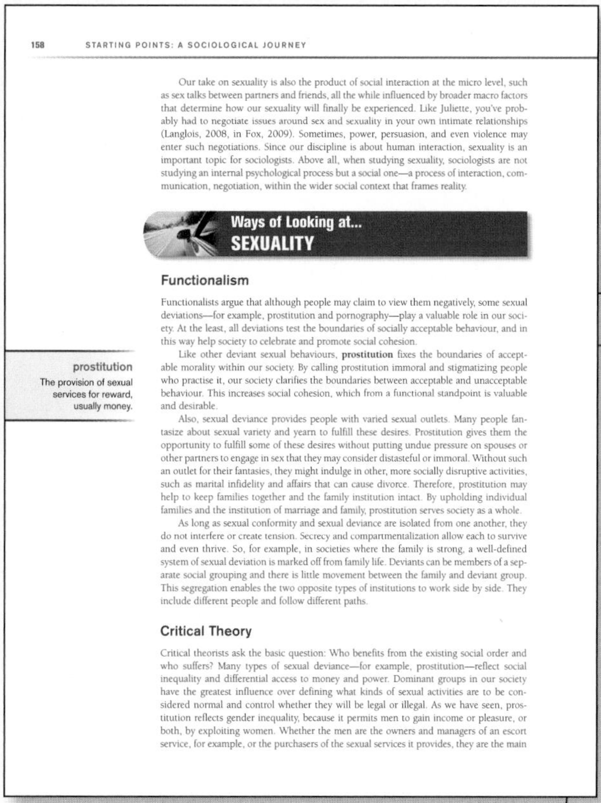

158 STARTING POINTS: A SOCIOLOGICAL JOURNEY

Our take on sexuality is also the product of social interaction at the micro level, such as sex talks between partners and friends, all the while influenced by broader macro factors that determine how our sexuality will finally be experienced. Like Juliette, you've probably had to negotiate issues around sex and sexuality in your own intimate relationships (Langlois, 2008, in Fox, 2009). Sometimes, power, persuasion, and even violence may enter such negotiations. Since our discipline is about human interaction, sexuality is an important topic for sociologists. Above all, when studying sexuality, sociologists are not studying an internal psychological process but a social one—a process of interaction, communication, negotiation, within the wider social context that frames reality.

Ways of Looking at... SEXUALITY

Functionalism

Functionalists argue that although people may claim to view them negatively, some sexual deviations—for example, prostitution and pornography—play a valuable role in our society. At the least, all deviations test the boundaries of socially acceptable behaviour, and in this way help society to celebrate and promote social cohesion.

Like other deviant sexual behaviours, **prostitution** fixes the boundaries of acceptable morality within our society. By calling prostitution immoral and stigmatizing people who practise it, our society clarifies the boundaries between acceptable and unacceptable behaviour. This increases social cohesion, which from a functional standpoint is valuable and desirable.

prostitution
The provision of sexual services for reward, usually money.

Also, sexual deviance provides people with varied sexual outlets. Many people fantasize about sexual variety and yearn to fulfill these desires. Prostitution gives them the opportunity to fulfill some of these desires without putting undue pressure on spouses or other partners to engage in sex that they may consider distasteful or immoral. Without such an outlet for their fantasies, they might indulge in other, more socially disruptive activities, such as marital infidelity and affairs that can cause divorce. Therefore, prostitution may help to keep families together and the family institution intact. By upholding individual families and the institution of marriage and family, prostitution serves society as a whole.

As long as sexual conformity and sexual deviance are isolated from one another, they do not interfere or create tension. Secrecy and compartmentalization allow each to survive and even thrive. So, for example, in societies where the family is strong, a well-defined system of sexual deviation is marked off from family life. Deviants can be members of a separate social grouping and there is little movement between the family and deviant group. This segregation enables the two opposite types of institutions to work side by side. They include different people and follow different paths.

Critical Theory

Critical theorists ask the basic question: Who benefits from the existing social order and who suffers? Many types of sexual deviance—for example, prostitution—reflect social inequality and differential access to money and power. Dominant groups in our society have the greatest influence over defining what kinds of sexual activities are to be considered normal and control whether they will be legal or illegal. As we have seen, prostitution reflects gender inequality, because it permits men to gain income or pleasure, or both, by exploiting women. Whether the men are the owners and managers of an escort service, for example, or the purchasers of the sexual services it provides, they are the main

'Ways of Looking at . . .'

sections examine significant topics from a variety of theoretical approaches, giving students a well-rounded understanding of each issue.

CHAPTER 6 SEXUALITY 159

beneficiaries of this sex industry. Though some men serve as paid gigolos—that is, male prostitutes—they are a minority we will ignore here, since the vast majority of prostitutes are women who provide sex for men.

In the end, prostitution is often just about poverty. Typically, women (and occasionally men) who resort to prostitution lack access to legitimate means of earning the money they need. This is obvious in the enormous numbers of prostitutes in the developing countries. There, poverty marginalizes many women and forces them to earn money by selling their bodies, often to affluent tourists. In our own society, prostitution recruits less-educated and socially disadvantaged women.

Symbolic Interactionism

Sexual norms and values change over time for a variety of reasons, especially through the social (and sexual) interaction between individuals. This change occurs with a rewriting of rules and restrictions on sexual behaviour, which take the form of **sexual scripts**. One of the dominant sexual scripts of our society is that of the sexually assertive man and the passive or resistant woman who is expected to desire sex much less than her sexual partner, or at least to be less forthcoming in expressing these desires. In practice, many couples rewrite these scripts to reflect their own personal tastes and needs.

sexual scripts
The guidelines that describe socially acceptable ways of behaving when engaging in sexual activities.

As more people come to know and accept varieties in the sexual behaviour of others, they come to admit the acceptability and 'normality' of behaviours formerly considered abnormal, thus supporting new 'rules' of sexual behaviour. In this way, some kinds of sexual deviance—including homosexuality, sex changes, cross-dressing, and fetishism—have become increasingly accepted sexual practices in the general population.

Interaction with members of minority groups—including minority sexual groups—also makes members of the majority more accepting of deviance. Thus, people who live in communities where they are likely to meet many homosexuals are more accepting of homosexuality. Large cities and large, heterogeneous social networks both broaden a person's sexual understanding in this way. Familiarity breeds understanding, so friendship or contact with known homosexuals is important to mitigating homophobia.

Further, the symbolic interactionist approach is useful in studying the socialization of prostitutes, their entry into this line of work, and how they develop strategies to deal with 'johns' (customers) and 'pimps' (managers). Prostitution has its own language, professional ethics, ways of exercising control and working around formal authority, and so on.

Finally, the interactionist approach is useful in studying the social construction of social problems around sexual activity. So, for example, sociologists in this tradition would be interested in tracking public discourse around changes in prostitution or pornography, including increased public demands for policing and prosecution. Equally, they would be interested in studying public views about changes in the age of initiation into sexuality. So, for example, there was a recent public outcry in Ontario against the government's stated plan to introduce more specific knowledge about sexual behaviour to elementary school children. Some critics argued that doing so would encourage earlier initiation into sexual activity, leading to risk-taking that was immature and premature. But would such public education create a problem or solve a problem? And how do such matters of public debate get resolved? These are both interesting questions for social constructionists.

Sex Trafficking occurs all around the world, but it is most common in countries such as Thailand where large numbers of women and children live in poverty. Seen here, Mukta is a child prostitute who was sold into slavery by her father, a common and desparate solution for poverty-stricken families.

CHAPTER 8 AGE GROUPS 231

ignore this rule of thumb often find themselves organizationally blindsided by misinformation or false information, rumours, or gossip. A failure to learn from older subordinates may derail or at least slow down their careers.

Francis Ianni's classic book, *A Family Business* (1972), the ethnographic study of an American crime family, provides another interesting example of the age-versus-experience problem. In organized crime, success means millions of dollars in revenue and failure can mean death or imprisonment, so members of the 'crime family' are keenly aware of organizational problems related to authority and succession. Here's the kind of problem they need to consider: Should they take advice from nephew Donny, the bright young whippersnapper with an economics degree from MIT but little experience or standing in the 'family'? Or should they take advice from Uncle Vito, the high-ranking 'capo', not too bright but a tough, responsible, and reliable leader in times past? True, it's Vito's 'time' to rule, but Donny has more up-to-date ideas about marketing, competition, and legitimate business. Remember, a wrong decision can be costly—even, fatal.

Classic Studies
Mean Streets: Youth Crime and Homelessness

Not only the elderly experience problems of deprivation. Consider the problems that young people face when they live on the streets, as revealed in a classic study by John Hagan and Bill McCarthy.

The primary goal of Hagan and McCarthy's study *Mean Streets: Youth Crime and Homelessness* (1997) was to examine how and why youths leave home for life on the street. The study sheds light on the daily toils and survival strategies of nearly 500 street kids in Toronto and Vancouver. In *Mean Streets*, the authors go against most current criminological research on youth crime which 'has been almost exclusively based on the work of 'school criminologists', academics whose work is based on the self-reports of young people living at home' (Piliavin, 1998: 414). Thus, the authors are focusing on a particularly deprived, crime-ridden group of young people.

The study first identifies the risks facing youth who come to live on the street. Street kids' problems have often begun at home with parental abuse and neglect, often in impoverished neighbourhoods where their parents may suffer unemployment. Many of the youth, especially boys, have suffered from violent outbursts by parents depressed or angered by a low or insecure income. Eventually, their schoolwork starts to slip, and a combination of poor grades and conflict with parents and school administration leads many of the youth to drop out of school. But too little social capital and poor skills limit the choices of these youth after leaving home and school, so the street is all that's left.

Why do youth subsequently turn to criminal behaviour after leaving home? The authors say it is because they cannot meet their basic daily needs like food, shelter, and clothing, so for them crime is a survival strategy. The authors note that hunger leads to

Despite Canada's relative economic prosperity, approximately one third of the homeless population in Canada is comprised of adolescents.

'Classic Studies' sections

outline groundbreaking studies that have shaped our understanding of major sociological questions, promoting critical thinking by providing examples of practical applications of theory.

criminal paraphilia include necrophilia (a sexual attraction to corpses), pedophilia (a sexual attraction to young children who have not yet reached puberty),bestiality (or zoophilia: a sexual attraction to animals), and lust murder (taking sexual pleasure from the commission of a murder).

Pedophilia is probably one of the most common criminal paraphilias in our society today. Two-thirds of molested children are girls, usually between the ages of 8 and 11, giving the lie to a common prejudice that pedophilia is a feature of male homosexuality. Most pedophiles are men, it is true, but their victims are usually female, and there are also cases of women having unwanted sexual contact with young boys. Note, then, that pedophiles are rarely people who commonly practise homosexuality with other consenting adults. Pedophiles, whether homosexual or heterosexual, are people who gain their sexual pleasure from people who are below the age of consent. Pedophilia is a form of violent domination, while homosexuality is not. While many pedophiles seduce and abuse strangers, far more commonly they seduce and abuse the children of family and friends.

As is evident, the world of sexualities is complex and in need of theorizing. That is the role that Judith Butler has, for many people, come to play.

People Are Talking About . . .
JUDITH BUTLER

Judith Butler was born in Cleveland in 1956. She studied philosophy at Yale University, where she received her bachelor's degree in 1978 and completed a doctoral dissertation in 1984, called *Subjects of Desire: Hegelian Reflections in Twentieth-Century France*. She lectured at various universities before becoming a professor of comparative literature at the University of California, Berkeley, and is a leader in the field of sexuality and gender.

Her most famous works are *Gender Trouble: Feminism and the Subversion of Identity* (1990); *Bodies That Matter: On the Discursive Limits of 'Sex'* (1993), *The Psychic Life of Power: Theories of Subjection* (1997), and *Undoing Gender* (2004). Butler's work centres around the idea that gender is not innate, but is derived from a narrative based on patriarchal culture. Thus gender consists in signs imposed via the psyche and internalized.

Gender Trouble is considered the most influential of Butler's works. In it, she tries to separate identity from the notion that human gender is binary—that one is either male or female. Feminists uncritically accept this notion, and thus mistakenly view women as a homogenous group having traits and interests in common. Through an account of patriarchal culture that assumes clear-cut masculine and feminine genders built on 'male' and 'female' bodies, sex-as-destiny seems inescapable. By erecting a 'natural' binary for sex, binaries for gender and heterosexuality are likewise constructed as natural. In this way, heterosexuality becomes 'essential' and normal, providing a basis for sexually limiting heteronormativity.

In her biography, Janet Borgerson (in Scott, 2006: 50) notes that, for Butler, 'Identities form over time [via iteration] and through repeated performances of socially constructed characteristics and appropriate gestures and signs . . . but if typical iterations elide, alter and shift, then the previously recognized definitive category—the apparent ideal—may be altered . . . opening up possibility for diverse gestures and characteristics, demonstrating contingency and allowing change over time.'

Thus Butler tries to deconstruct the 'grand narratives,' found in psychoanalysis and other fields, which together promote the notion that genders are unitary categories. To overcome this and other essentialisms, Butler suggests that genders be multiplied in what she calls subversive 'gender trouble', and that gender and identity be 'free-floating'—linked not to inherent characteristics but to performance. In this way, gender does not cause performance, but performance defines gender—an important aspect of so-called queer theory.

'People Are Talking About . . .'

boxes introduce students to individuals who have shaped—and continue to shape—the world of sociology.

New Insights

In the new sociological approaches, we see a wide variety of new political actors within the global system. Ironically, national identities—fragile and endangered—emerge despite the monopolistic policies of global dominance, according to Duman (2007). Nation-states, as modern political forms, have tried to create strong national identities by dissolving regional, ethnic, and class subidentities. However, postmodern forces, using the same strategy, have undermined this effort to construct ideological uniformity. The result is a fragmentation of national identity, and a weakening of social order through the increased emphasis on individuals and cultural subgroups. In short, Duman says, national identities may be impossible within the present-day world.

Edensor (2006) disagrees, however, suggesting that the similar daily lives and routines of citizens form a national identity, even without overarching ideologies and heroic acts. He claims that local time and space provide a more powerful basis for identity than global citizenship. This may help to explain why transnational entities have trouble gaining recognition and loyalty. Consider the European Union (EU), a relatively new political body (Hulsse, 2006). It has a complex organization, with multi-dimensional layers—much more sophisticated than the relatively homogenous nation-states that make it up. Yet people have been slow to give their loyalty to the EU, or to see themselves as meaningfully linked to this new identity. Hulsse claims the EU is perceived simply as another large nationalistic postmodern entity.

People have trouble imagining new transnational or global meanings, just as they have trouble celebrating global diversity. Kimura (2007) notes that, for the most part, international 'cultural heritage' projects assign cultural-historical meaning to largely unknown objects in other countries, in attempts to integrate them into an existing (universal) value system. However, these efforts do little more than feed a mild interest in 'ruins' and ecological beauty-spots. Neither competes strongly against the consumerism and waste of capitalist society.

Many would assign the problems of a globalized world to economic or political factors. However, modern citizenship is in crisis for cultural reasons too (Herera and Soriano Miras, 2005). States around the world face problems that are both internal and external. Usually, the internal problems arise from issues around political and cultural legitimacy, social regulation, resources and costs. The external problems, on the other hand, derive from global economic forces like recession, demographic changes like aging, and difficulties in managing social groups and social strata that are unconnected to the state: for example, multinational corporations.

The very idea of transnational or global citizenship works against the modern nation-state, in that it steers people away from national values and concerns. This leads us to ask: Is it possible to re-launch 'citizenship' as a basis for democracy, and if so, how? Doing so will likely require us to re-imagine citizenship as a complex of rights and duties that extend across national borders. In this sense, they will re-imagine civic life in terms of universal goals and universal rights. Devising this new global citizenship will, in some people's minds, be the key to a postmodern democratic state in the future.

And if the postmodern world ever comes to understand itself in a postmodern way, global cities will play a large role in this process. The reason is that, as Nisanci (2007) points out, in the context of postmodernism and globalization, cities will become the focus of democratic citizenship, just as they are (and will be) the nexus of culture, politics, and economy. Cities can play an important emancipatory (democratic) role under particular

---

'New Insights' sections

summarize contemporary research studies, describe where the research is headed, and explain how the findings can help us better understand our own lives.

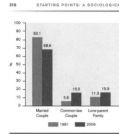

318 STARTING POINTS: A SOCIOLOGICAL JOURNEY

Figure 11.1 Family Structure, Canada, 1981 and 2006

Source: Human Resources and Skills Development Canada (2007).

Another change in marriage is the recognition of same-sex married couples, first enumerated in the 2006 Census after the legalization of gay and lesbian marriage in July 2005. In this tabulation, same-sex couples represent about 0.6 per cent of all couples in Canada. Of these same-sex couples, 16.5 per cent were married, and 83.5 per cent were cohabiting. Most same-sex married spouses are men, and relatively few live with children. Living with children under 24 years of age was more common among women (16.3 per cent) than among men (2.9 per cent). Half of the enumerated same-sex couples live in Canada's three largest metropolitan areas: Montreal (18.4 per cent), Toronto (21.2 per cent), and Vancouver (10.3 per cent) (Statistics Canada, 2006). Table 11.1 shows the distribution of same-sex couples by province. The percentage of same-sex couples in Canada is similar to that observed in other Western countries such as New Zealand and Australia.

Also, as Goode might have predicted, with the decline in marriage rates over the last few decades, single-parent families have increased from 11 per cent to 16 per cent, and cohabiting couples have increased from 6 per cent to 15 per cent (Human Resources and Skills Development Canada, 2007). As Figure 11.2 shows, cohabiting couples are especially common in Quebec, where one-quarter of all common-law families in Canada live.

Another well-known trend discussed by Goode is the increased rate of relationship dissolution (including divorce) in Canada and other developed countries. In part, this reflects the increased prevalence of cohabiting unions: cohabiting couples are more likely to break up than are married ones, especially for people under the age of 30 (Statistics Canada, 2006b, 2007a). In general, cohabiting unions also last for a shorter time than do legal marriages. In 2006, most people who broke up a cohabiting union had been together for only four years, compared to 14 years for the average marital breakup.

Keep in mind, however, that it is hard to accurately record cohabiting breakups, since these breakups are not documented as frequently or systematically as separations

One World, Many Societies

BOX 11.1

Age at Marriage

Marriage is a social process that forms families. The age at which people marry, however, differs between societies, for many reasons. One CBC report tells of recent marriage trends in Canada: Statistics Canada researchers say that both men and women are increasingly older when they first marry. In 2000, first-time brides were on average 31.7 years old, while grooms were 34.3. Compare these ages to those of 1980: 25.9 and 28.5. Statistics Canada suggests two reasons for the change—women's improving career opportunities, and a growing number of people living in common-law relationships.

According to UNICEF, brides tend to be much younger outside North America. In sub-Saharan Africa and South Asia, most girls are married young, as are many of those of traditional cultures in the Middle East, North Africa, and other parts of Asia. Families may view the husband as his wife's guardian. This is often the case in conflict-ridden Northern Uganda, where a girl will be married to a man in the militia to protect her, and often her family as well, from attack.

Sources: Adapted from CBC News (2005); UNICEF (2001).

'One World, Many Societies'

boxes highlight various social issues from around the globe and show how insights gleaned from international sources can illuminate our own lives and choices.

260 STARTING POINTS: A SOCIOLOGICAL JOURNEY

In 2007, Canadian-born magnate Conrad Black was tried and convicted of fraud in the United States. He was granted bail and released in 2010 after serving part of the sentence in a Florida prison.

in a Mexico City slum. The values and norms of this culture include a short-sighted view of the future, an impulsive or hedonistic attitude that lacks self-discipline, a failure to participate in mainstream culture, and a tendency to accept marginalized status —to hang back in the shadows.

Lewis found that many of these urban poor, like the Sanchez family, come from rural backgrounds that provided little in the way of coping skills. Without kin or social supports, let alone a social welfare net, in the city they struggle to understand an otherwise chaotic social world. Most lack the skills to attain better lives in better communities. So,

Media Distortion

BOX 9.2

Media Representations of the Working Classes

Think of the working-class characters you see on television—do they seem stereotyped? Social researchers such as Richard Butsch, in his article 'Ralph, Fred, Archie and Homer: Why Television Keeps Recreating the White Male Working-Class Buffoon', find that working-class men and women are under-represented in television series. When working-class men do appear, they are portrayed as unintelligent, irresponsible 'clowns'. The wives of these male characters rarely work outside the home, unlike the middle-class women seen on TV, who have not only jobs but careers.

Barbara Ehrenreich, in her article 'The Silenced Majority', finds that working-class issues are largely ignored in news and current affairs programming, and that when they are covered, it is middle-class white professionals who give 'expert' opinion on the topic. A study by the City University of New York showed that over two years, the US Public Broadcasting System devoted almost ten times as much prime-time programming to middle- and upper-class issues as it did to issues affecting the working class. And in mainstream news coverage, according to the Institute for Alternative Journalism, and Fairness and Accuracy in Reporting, union and labour issues, such as strikes, which are primarily working-class actions, either go unreported or are covered in a negative way.

Source: Adapted from Media Awareness Network (N.d.).

'Media Distortion'

boxes show how the media construes controversial sociological issues and suggest ways in which our interpretations of these issues are affected by media coverage.

'Point/Counterpoint'

boxes highlight contrasting viewpoints on current debates, giving students a basis from which they can develop their own informed opinions.

End-of-chapter critical thinking questions

invite students to synthesize what they have read and form their own opinions on key sociological issues. Lists of recommended readings and websites provide excellent starting points for further research and study.

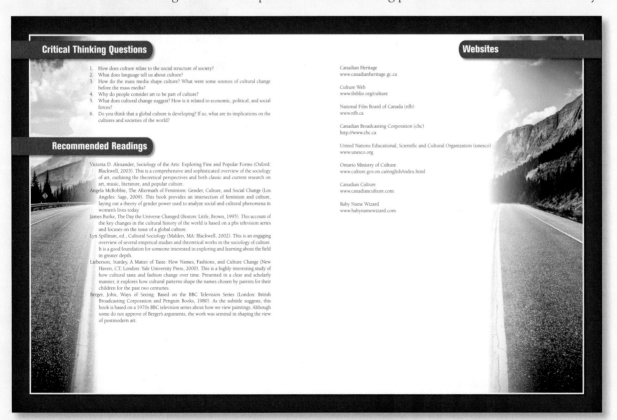

Extensive Online Ancillary Package.

For instructors: an instructor's manual, a test generator, and PowerPoint slides.
For students: a study guide and a variety of video clips.

COMPANION WEBSITE

Lorne Tepperman

Starting Points
ISBN 13: 9780195429985

Inspection copy request

Ordering information

Contact & Comments

About the Book

Starting Points is a text that is truly a reflection of its title in that it provides a solid starting point for introductory university-level students delving into the world of sociology for the first time. The text builds on concepts and theories introduced at the beginning of each chapter, moving from historical figures and founding principles to the most current research, literature, and key sociologists in the discipline today. By examining the social trends and phenomena that occur in Canada and around the world, the text provides a comprehensive examination of why studying sociology is important and its application to daily life.

Instructor Resources

You need a password to access these resources. Please contact your local Sales and Editorial Representative for more information.

Student Resources

Preface

About seven years ago, David Stover, a longtime publishing friend and now president of Oxford University Press, asked me to think about writing an introductory textbook for sociology students. He liked an introductory textbook I had co-written in the 1980s and thought it might be time for me to revisit the topic, realizing that I might have picked up some new ideas about how to approach it. That was, in essence, the starting point for this book.

Over the next few years, I tried several times to get going in earnest, each time writing an experimental chapter on one of sociology's key topics. But I couldn't seem to get out of neutral. Each attempt felt dead to me, because I hadn't come up with an interesting way to organize the book.

Inspiration finally hit on an flight from Toronto to Taiwan, when—with plenty of time for reflection—I finally figured out how to write the book. I would write an introductory textbook that talked about sociology as an empirical discipline. It would be a book about data collection and data analysis—practical topics, not grand theory. And it would celebrate the greatest sociological achievements, from the founders onward. I felt (I still do) that sociologists too often ignore the findings of earlier generations, so that the discipline appears to have scarcely moved forward. I wanted to tell new readers how the field had started, how it had progressed, and where I thought it was heading.

But I realized that writing a 500-page book from scratch was too big a journey to make in one trip. I needed to get there in shorter excursions. I persuaded David to let me write a short introduction to sociology aimed at general readers as well as students, and publishable in its own right; the product of that effort, called *The Sense of Sociability*, appeared in the spring of 2010, close to a year after I'd finished writing it. My hope was that I could build a full-size textbook on the chassis of this shorter work.

And so, with the aid of the short book, a plan for expanding it, and materials from my introductory lectures (Sociology 101), in the summer of 2009 work began on the full-length introductory text. The trouble was that the resulting book differed too radically from other textbooks in the field. Reviewers asked for more discussion of postmodern and critical perspectives, which meant more emphasis on modern research and a bit less on classic research.

I received good directions from my developmental editor, Allison McDonald, who helped me find a more conventional roadmap for the manuscript while at the same time preserving its distinctive features. I was also assisted by an advisory team of undergraduate students, headed by Nina Gheihman and, later, Hilary Killam. One of the peculiarities of textbooks is that they are almost always written with no input from the people who actually have to buy and read them—the students themselves. Perhaps that's why texts are all too often dismissed by students as 'boring' or 'out of touch'. But who better to consult on the suitability of the material and the approach to it than these recent graduates of introductory 'soc' courses. The insights I took from the study group's contributions had a great influence on many aspects of this textbook.

The resulting textbook is quite different from anything I've written before. It's not exactly the book I had imagined on the flight to Taiwan, but book writing sometimes works this way. As planned, the book talks about both classic and modern figures. It also calls attention to the role of empirical research in sociology, as I had hoped. I have learned a lot in writing this book, and I know much more about postmodernism and critical theory than I knew when I started. That's good—every book should be a learning experience for the author, as well as for the reader.

Starting Points has also reminded me just how great a force the sociological imagination can be. I hope readers of the book will come away with a similar sense of awe and appreciation for the sociological enterprise. Please let me know if you do.

Lorne Tepperman
University of Toronto
June 2010

Acknowledgements

As I mentioned in the preface, this book's journey has been slow and collaborative. My thanks go first to David Stover, president of Oxford University Press, for repeatedly urging me to write a book that would turn out to be harder and take longer to write than either of us imagined. Acquisitions editor Nancy Reilly's encouragement helped me get the wheels in motion. Thanks go next to developmental editor Allison McDonald, a fine editor with a great sense of humour, for cajoling me endlessly to lengthen and shorten, fix and change the book you are finally reading. Thanks go finally to Leslie Saffrey who edited the copy; and to Steven Hall, who oversaw the final formatting and cleanup, which meant taming a great mass of textual and visual information. Your work is much appreciated.

I want to give special thanks to my research assistant Nina Gheihman, who worked with me throughout this project. Nina played a key role in helping to transform my small, friendly book *The Sense of Sociability* into a large and authoritative academic book with appropriate referencing and learning aids. Under my supervision, Nina filled gaps in the research, edited and rearranged my written materials, and supervised other assistants who helped to prepare the book for publication. Nina even gave the page proofs a close and careful reading, to help catch the inevitable errors and omissions. It was a great pleasure working with Nina, and we continue to work together on other projects, even as I write these words. In the later stages of the project I received invaluable support from Hilary Killam and excellent feedback from the advisory team of work–study students, which included Balsam Attarbashi, Pam Bautista, Roxy Chis, Anita Feher, Len Liu, Cathy Long, Brianna Sykes, Cindy Yi, Jason Jensen, and Sarah Fox. Some of these students—Hilary, Balsam, Cathy, Len, Jason, and Sarah—have now graduated and gone on to bigger things. The others will continue their studies at the University of Toronto. I hope to work with them all again.

I am grateful also to the many reviewers who pushed us to improve the book and make it timelier. Your thoughtful comments and suggestions were greatly appreciated. In addition to those who provided anonymous feedback, I would like to recognize the following individuals:

> Christopher J. Fries, University of Manitoba
> Leanne Joanisse, McMaster University
> Abdolmohammad Kazemipur, University of Lethbridge
> C. Barry McClinchey, University of Waterloo
> Erin Steuter, Mount Allison University
> Ann Travers, Simon Fraser University

About the Author

Lorne Tepperman is professor of sociology at the University of Toronto. He holds a PhD from Harvard and a certificate in population studies from Princeton. Apart from serving as visiting professor of Canadian studies at Yale, he has spent his career at U of T, from which he graduated with an honours BA in 1965. He was chair of the university's sociology department from 1997 to 2003 and served a term as president of the Canadian Sociological Association. He has also received the CSA's Distinguished Contribution Award.

1 Introducing Sociology

Learning Objectives

In this chapter, you will:

> Come to understand the main competing approaches of sociology and see how they can be fused together to give us an understanding of society

> Learn about the history and development of sociology as a social scientific discipline

Chapter Outline

No one knows when sociology really began. Some would say it began when French thinker Auguste Comte invented the term *sociologie* in the early nineteenth century. Others would say it began millennia earlier, perhaps in the fifth century BCE when Greek philosopher Plato wrote his famous book, *The Republic*, which imagined the perfect society. Others still might suggest that sociology was a direct result of the so-called European Enlightenment of the eighteenth century, featuring the rise of science, skepticism about religious belief, and generalized doubt about political tradition. Most would say, however, that sociology emerged 200 years ago in response to new social problems that arose from industrialization, urbanization, and political revolution. People then needed new ways to think about the social problems they were experiencing, and new ideas about the best, most rational ways to organize society.

Two social revolutions were especially important for the growth of sociology. The Industrial Revolution changed people's lives by drawing them into harsh urban conditions and new kinds of exploitive, impersonal economic relationships. The French Revolution, which overthrew the monarchy, convinced people throughout the Western world that new social and political arrangements were possible and should be developed. Both revolutions gave scholars the impetus to study social change and social problems.

In this new social ferment, scholars started to develop theories about how people might live in 'post-revolutionary' societies. Three figures of particular importance were Karl Marx, Émile Durkheim, and Max Weber. They were among the first to question how the social world works and how people live together in societies. In this chapter, we will look closely at their work, and see how sociology has evolved to become the discipline that it is today.

We will also see that sociologists take several main approaches—the so-called 'paradigms' of sociology—which lead them to ask somewhat different questions. Viewing sociology from this 'multiple paradigms approach' helps us see the exciting variety in sociological research. However, this approach is sometimes confusing. So, to minimize confusion, this book will show, through a 'fusion approach', that there is an agreed-upon body of sociological knowledge,

Statues of Karl Marx and Friedrich Engels in Berlin, Germany. Marx is considered to be one of the founders of modern sociology.

stretching back nearly 200 years. This approach will help you learn the contours of that knowledge by downplaying the differences between paradigms.

However, before we go ahead with the 'fusion', let us spend a little while considering the three main sociological approaches or paradigms. We will note their points of difference before we concentrate on their fusion—how sociologists bring them together for a complete picture of the sociological discipline.

The key thing you will learn is that present-day sociology is deeply concerned with how we know what we know: how we view and judge different pictures of reality. All sociologists today grapple with the real challenge that our relationship to the world is mediated through symbols, assumptions, and culture. No one can be a perfect reader of the outside world. How any person views the world is, in large part, determined by his or her position in society. We all bring our personal, socially-determined viewpoints to the task of social analysis. Depending on what views we bring to the task—including what we want out of life and what we know about how to get it—our interpretations of the same material world will radically differ, one from another.

This insight is over a century old. Ultimately, it comes down to us from one of sociology's founders, Max Weber, and throughout this book we will see it reflected in the work of Karl Mannheim, Dorothy Smith, Michel Foucault, Edward Said, and others. In fact, we cannot get around this 'epistemological' problem when we do sociology, no matter how hard we try. All present-day sociologists look for ways to do useful, insightful work, but they are all aware of this 'elephant in the room' of social science. So we have to go into the job with our eyes open.

Everyday Observations

Some people have terrible table manners—they eat with their mouths open, make a lot of noise chewing, splatter food all over the people sitting near them, wipe their mouths on their sleeves, and so on. But the surprising thing is how many people have good table manners, and this was not always so. People have not always agreed on table manners—or 'etiquette'—and many people simply ignored them. One ate with one's hands, or a knife and a piece of bread (no fork or spoon). An interesting piece of sociology shows that the historical development of good manners, or etiquette, in Western societies required the rise of nation-states and middle-class homes. We will talk about the reasons for this development later on, but for now, it is worth noting that, in different societies and at different times in history, people do things differently. They have different rules about behaviour and tolerate different ways of behaving. This theme will recur throughout this chapter and this book.

Have you ever wondered why people in the United Kingdom drive on the left side of the road while North Americans drive on the right? Or why in some societies, it is considered bad manners to look someone in the eye when speaking to them, while in others, people are suspicious if you don't look them in the eye? Why in some societies, women walk behind men, while in other societies, they walk ahead of or beside them? Where there are social differences, sociologists look for explanations: reasons why *we* do things *this* way and *they* do things *that* way. **Sociology** and the other social sciences arose out of a desire to explain such differences, and to find patterns in people's social relations.

The historical growth of international trade and exploration fed this desire. Whenever people have met other civilizations, they have wondered about them, and in turn reflected on their own **societies**. Even Herodotus—the world's first historian (484–425 BCE)—devoted his attention to the differences between Egyptians, Greeks, and Persians—differences that often led to mistrust and war. Voltaire, a great French Enlightenment thinker, devoted an entire work to reflecting on the differences between English Protestants and French Catholics. Sociology, like the work of these thinkers, began with important comparisons. A prime example is the set of books Max Weber wrote, analyzing Protestantism, Catholicism, Judaism, Confucianism, Hinduism, and other religions, to understand why capitalism arose in northwestern Europe, but not elsewhere.

Also, sociology has always been oriented to solving problems—to finding better ways of living together. Throughout the nineteenth and twentieth centuries, sociologists struggled to develop a language that could describe the new problems of living in an industrial society, and to make theories about the nature of these problems.

One of the first steps was to move social theorizing away from moral philosophy—away from ideas of blame, guilt, sin, and wrong-doing. To blame is not to understand. In everyday life, we are still inclined to blame people without thinking through what happened and why. An example might be blaming your city's transit workers for rising bus and subway fares. But maybe they aren't to blame, and maybe blame is not a useful approach if our goal is explanation and understanding. Often, the best we can do is to reduce the harm done, without eliminating the causes. Social life is innately contradictory and paradoxical. Many good intentions produce bad results; many social institutions yield both good and bad outcomes; many groups are laudable in one respect but reprehensible in another. Faced with these paradoxes, people often resort to the easy solution of blaming someone or something, but this rarely helps.

This book, therefore, is not about finding fault. Although everyone has agency and free will, everyone is also constrained and manipulated. Taking it further, everyone is, more or less, to blame for *something*. Consider, for example, that everyone living in the economically developed nations of the northern hemisphere benefits from the oppression—low wages and poverty—of workers in the southern hemisphere's less-developed nations. And everyone who enjoys a high level of material consumerism benefits at the expense of future generations, whose natural non-renewable resources we are using up.

Unlike the general population, sociologists find that using 'common sense' to understand the world is usually not enough. 'Common-sense knowledge' is that uninspected package of beliefs, understandings, and propositions that people (merely) assume to be prudent and sound. This blind assumption often leads to incomplete and inaccurate explanations. That's why, instead, sociologists use study and research to seek scientifically sound explanations. They avoid using psychological and psychiatric theories to explain apparently widespread social problems. To look for psychological explanations is, often, to ignore the root social causes and, in this way, to miss finding a solution.

For example, have you ever noticed that wrongdoers—schoolyard bullies, say—usually act the way they do because they themselves are victims? Many come from troubled homes and neighbourhoods where they have been pushed around by parents and peers. This has taught them to push others around as they try to find ways to control their world.

sociology

The systematic study of social behaviour, or the study of society.

society

The largest-scale human group, whose members interact with one another, share a common geographic territory, and share common institutions.

Seeing bullies in this way—as victims as well as victimizers—is sociological, because it looks at the broader social factors that influence how individuals act within society. Many psychological problems—even varieties of mental illness—have social origins. This social understanding is important, since it helps us understand the social contagion of violence: for example, the problem that bullies often grow up to hurt their own children, whether physically or mentally. The only way to end this vicious cycle of violence is to get to the interpersonal root of the problem. So blaming, obviously, is not enough. Blaming is not explaining, and without explanation and understanding, there is no remedy.

Likewise, sociologists ask us to consider the unequal distribution of social rewards. The average person probably thinks that people get what they deserve in life, and thus people who lead good lives deserve them because they start out with good ideas, attitudes, and values. But do *you* think people who lead bad lives deserve what they've gotten? Most sociologists note that what people get in life is largely the result of circumstances beyond their control—for example, patterns associated with unequal opportunities. Such patterns perpetuate from one generation to the next, shaping the ways people can lead their lives. Those born in higher social classes tend to stay there, and so too do people in humbler circumstances. The difference in life experiences from one person to the next is rarely a simple result of higher intelligence, more hard work, or other personal characteristics.

In short, the common sense of ordinary people—untested, traditional, based on blind belief about the justice of the universe—is likely to misinform us. It leads to explanations about the way society works that are more often wrong than right. The central goal of sociologists is to replace such faulty common-sense reasoning with scientific explanation. Each sociologist does this through unbiased research of his or her own, and through the knowledge of other sociologists' research.

Sociologists always ask: What does the field of sociology—that body of published work that by now comprises hundreds of thousands of articles and books—tell us about the sources of human health, wealth, and happiness? Fortunately, there is much agreement about the findings reported in this book; where these findings converge, we feel confident that our conclusions are valid. In this chapter, we introduce the approaches to sociology that have led to these findings, and discuss how these approaches are applied in sociological research.

Ways of Looking at . . . SOCIOLOGY

The two main macroanalytical approaches that have emerged in sociology are the *structural functional* (or simply, *functional*) *theory* and *critical theory*, while the major microanalytical approach is *symbolic interactionism*. *Feminist theory* and *postmodern theory* are important additions to and variants of these major forms. We will spend more time on the two latter approaches in later chapters, so we can focus on functional theory, critical theory, and symbolic interactionism in this chapter.

Functional Theory

Functional theory views society as a set of interconnected parts that work together to preserve the overall stability and efficiency of the whole. Individual social institutions we will discuss in this book—families, the economy, government, education, and others—each contribute to the continued functioning of society. Families, for instance, reproduce and nurture members of society, while the economy regulates the production, distribution, and consumption of goods and services.

macrosociology

The study of social institutions (for example, the Roman Catholic Church or marriage) and large social groups (for example, ethnic minorities or college students).

Robert Merton, a key figure in developing this perspective, argued in his classic work *Social Theory and Social Structure* (1957) that **social institutions** perform both manifest and latent functions. *Manifest functions* are those that are intended and easily recognized; *latent functions* are unintended and often hidden. Education, for example, is intended to provide students with the knowledge, skills, and cultural values that will help them to work effectively in society. Both the school and its participants—students, teachers, parents, and others—formally recognize these **roles**. At a latent level, however, education also works as a regular 'babysitter' for young children and teenagers not yet ready to take full-time jobs; it also works as a 'matchmaker', a place where older high school and university students can meet and mingle with potential lovers or marriage partners.

Or consider another example—one of the classic ideas in sociology introduced by French sociologist Émile Durkheim. The manifest function of crime—law-breaking—is usually to benefit the lawbreaker: a robber, thief, embezzler, or the like. But Durkheim notes that crime is universal (found everywhere, at all times), so perhaps it serves a latent function for society as well: by mobilizing popular sentiment, it helps clarify the social boundaries for proper behaviour. In this way, it strengthens social solidarity, which every society needs.

Latent functions, as important to society as manifest ones, are considered latent because they are not the intended results (e.g., of educators or criminals), nor are they typically admitted to be such. When did you last hear school administrators, students, or parents admit that public school is a daycare service?

This distinction is important because it helps us understand, from the functionalist standpoint, how every social institution has a 'purpose'. The emphasis on the interconnection of society's parts, and how these parts support one another, usefully highlights how they also influence one another. This approach helps us understand why changes in one part of society bring about changes in other parts—for example, why changes in family life, such as increasing divorce and single-parenthood, have important, usually unconscious and unintended consequences for work and education.

Functionalists also characteristically explain social problems by focusing on the failure of institutions to fulfill their roles during times of rapid change. This view of social problems holds that sudden cultural shifts disrupt traditional values and common ways of doing things. By this reckoning, industrialization and urbanization in North America a century ago caused a sharp increase in social disorganization, leading to an upsurge of crime, mental illness, poverty, unsanitary living conditions, and environmental pollution. As we will see, there are other sociological explanations of the same phenomena.

French sociologist Émile Durkheim (see, e.g., 1964 [1893], 1964 [1897], 1965 [1912]) introduced the term *anomie*, or 'normlessness', to reflect the condition

This image of police restraining a protester during a riot illustrates what can happen when social control and norms break down, a condition Durkheim termed '*anomie*'.

microsociology

The study of the processes and patterns of personal interaction that take place among people within groups.

sociological imagination

An approach to sociology that situates the personal experiences of individuals within the societal context in which these experiences occur.

social institution

One kind of social structure, made up of a number of relationships (i.e., stable patterns of meaningful orientations to one another). People use institutions to achieve their intended goals, as students use schools, or patients use hospitals.

role

The expected pattern of interaction with others.

Children must be socialized to obey rules. Rule-breakers may have been improperly trained to follow social norms as children.

typical in times of rapid social change, in which social norms are weak or in conflict with one another. From the functionalist perspective, the best way to deal with social problems is to strengthen social norms and slow the pace of social change.

Critical Theory

Critical theory, a second major approach, arises out of the basic division between society's 'haves' and the 'have-nots'. Critical theories—whether they focus on class, gender, race, or something else—are always about the unequal distribution of power—about domination of one group by another. Critical theorists reject the functional explanations of social problems, criticizing their limited attention to power struggles and special interests. Critical theory instead views society as a collection of varied groups—especially, social classes—that constantly struggle with each other to dominate society and its institutions.

Critical theory originates in the works of German economic-political philosopher Karl Marx (see, e.g., 1970 [1843], 1965 [1867]). Marx, unlike functionalists, attributed the social problems of the modern age not to industrialization and urbanization, but to capitalism, an exploitive economic system. In any capitalist society, two broad groups will emerge: the *bourgeoisie*, elite owners of the means of production, and the *proletariat* or working class, who sell their labour in exchange for a liveable wage. As the social class that controls the economic system, the bourgeoisie use their great economic power and political influence to ensure that they remain dominant.

Proponents of Marxist critical theory argue that social problems stem from the economic inequality of these two groups. To uphold its wealthy, privileged status, the capitalist class works to prevent the proletariat from encroaching on bourgeois power. Because of their powerlessness, members of the proletariat feel alienated from the processes and products of their work. They feel unable to control or change the conditions of their work, or improve their wages and conditions of employment.

Given its emphasis on economic inequality, the Marxist solution to social problems requires abolishing the bourgeoisie—indeed, abolishing class differences and even private ownership of the means of production. It proposes that workers gain more control of their workplaces and receive wages that reflect the true value of their work. As we will see, Max Weber—another founder of sociology—later shifted the focus of critical theory away from a strict focus on classes to a more inclusive focus on contending *status groups*. This enabled critical theory also to address other struggles for domination: for example, conflicts between men and women, and between people of different racial or ethnic groups.

Symbolic Interactionism

Functional theory and critical theory focus on large elements of society, such as social institutions and major demographic groups. By contrast, *symbolic interactionism* focuses on small-group interactions. Symbolic **interactionists** focus on the 'glue' that holds people together in social relationships: the shared meanings, definitions, and interpretations of interacting individuals. In studying social problems, they analyze how certain behaviours come to be defined or framed, and how people learn to engage in everyday activities.

interaction

The processes by which, and manner in which, social actors—people trying to meet each other's **expectations**—relate to each other, especially in face-to-face encounters.

expectation

A shared idea about how people should carry out the duties attached to a particular status.

Labelling theory, a major theory in the symbolic interactionist tradition, rests on the premise that any given social problem is viewed as such simply because an influential group of people defines it so. Howard Becker (1963), for example, argues that marijuana smoking is a social problem only because influential 'moral entrepreneurs'—people who make a point of changing other people's thoughts and actions—make it one. There is nothing intrinsically harmful about marijuana in itself, says Becker—at least, nothing more harmful than, say, alcohol or cigarettes, which are both legal. The questions of interest, then, are 'How do societies come to share such a perception of reality?'—e.g., 'Marijuana smoking is bad and should be against the law'—and 'How do they promote and defend this perception?'

Symbolic interactionist Herbert Blumer (1971) proposes that social problems develop in stages that include *social recognition*, *social legitimating*, *mobilization for action*, and finally the *development and implementation of an official plan*, such as a government-sanctioned 'war on drugs'. We will have more to say about this and related processes in the course of this book.

Symbolic interactionists are also interested in the consequences of people being labelled or branded as deviants, criminals, or rule-breakers. For example, we will discuss classic studies on the roles of 'stigma' and 'stigmatization' as forms of social control. In short, symbolic interactionists are interested in the processes of interaction by which people make and use symbols to construct a society, every single day.

Feminist Theories

Many consider feminist theory to be a branch of critical theory, since it also focuses on relations of inequality—in this case, relations of dominance and subordination between men and women. As the name implies, the feminist approach focuses on gendering and gender inequality—and especially, on how gender-based inequality makes women's lives different from men's.

To be a woman in our society is often to act out a role that others—men—have defined. This fact shapes all of women's most important social activities, at home, at work, and in the public domain. It forces women to acquiesce in their own domination and to risk exclusion and even violence. Thus, acceptance of the female role is far more costly—and even dangerous—to women than is men's acceptance of the male role.

The feminist approach is not new. The first wave of the feminist movement occurred between the mid nineteenth century and the early twentieth century, culminating in women gaining the right to vote in many Western countries. Up to the late 1960s, feminism was concerned with understanding the oppression that some believed all women experience. Recent feminist scholarship, however, has stressed the diversity of women's experience as members of different nations, classes, and racial and ethnic groups. As a result, in recent decades we have seen the growth of various 'feminisms' that focus on different female experiences.

The common theme in the many types of feminism is the view that domination of women is not a result of biological determinism but is a result of socio-economic and ideological factors—of what Weber called *closure* and *usurpation*. Though feminists differ in thinking about how they might achieve change, they are all committed to erasing women's continued social inequality. Feminism's general goal is equality between the sexes; they hope to promote political, social, and psychological change by calling attention to often-neglected facts and issues.

In practice, most feminist research is a mixture of symbolic interactionist and critical theory. A unique set of assumptions informs feminist research:

- all personal life has a political dimension;
- both the public and private spheres of life are gendered (that is, unequal for men and women);

- women's social experience routinely differs from men's;
- patriarchy—or male control—structures the way most societies work; and
- because of routinely different experiences and differences in power, women and men view the world differently.

So, for example, men and women typically have different views about divorce, since each experiences divorce very differently. For men, divorce usually means a brief drop in the standard of living, if any decline at all, and a huge drop in parenting responsibilities. For women, it usually means a dramatic, long-term loss in income and standard of living. Poverty is common among single mothers and their children. Divorce also means an increase in women's parental responsibilities, since mothers usually keep custody of the children.

Several features that come through in the literature on deviance and control, as we will see, characterize feminist research. First, feminist research pays the greatest attention to gendered influences on social life, or *the gendering of experiences*. Some experiences are specifically female or male, and cannot be automatically generalized to both sexes. Here, certain topics receive a great deal of attention, including violence against women, women's economic vulnerability through job insecurity and divorce, and women's vulnerability to male-dominated standards of attractiveness and social worth.

A second interest is in the *problem of victimization*. Since women are often victimized, feminists are especially interested in women's victimization and the experiences of other victimized groups (for example, the poor, racial minorities, and people of alternative sexual orientations). Following from this, feminists are especially interested in *intersectionality*— the interaction of gender with other victimizing social characteristics such as class and race, to produce particular combinations of disadvantage (e.g., the particular problems of black men, lesbians, or Muslim immigrant women).

Given these starting points, feminists—not surprisingly—stress the gendered nature of both deviance and control. For example, they call our attention to the relationship between events in the private sphere (e.g., domestic violence) and events in the public sphere (e.g., the cultural and legal tolerance of domestic violence). They note the gendering of law enforcement practices (for example, how the police treat prostitutes compared with how they treat prostitutes' customers). They note the survival of patriarchal values in the legal system—for example, the centuries of failure to concede that a husband might be guilty of raping his wife—and in the established religious denominations we will discuss later. Here, as in other areas of sociology, the feminist approach combines macro- and microsociological perspectives—fitting for an approach that stresses that personal lives and political issues are intertwined.

Postmodern Theories

Postmodernism too may be considered a form of critical theory, though it is more than that. Proponents of postmodernism are especially interested in unmasking ideologies that protect the dominant social order. Various definitions and interpretations of postmodernism abound, but in all cases they can be traced to an attack on modernism—a nineteenth- and twentieth-century approach to studying social phenomena.

Modernism holds the view that through science we can discover 'the truth' about reality, and there is only one 'truth' per situation. If so, it should be possible to change and improve society through social engineering, using discovered 'truths' or natural laws about the social order. It follows from this that social 'progress' is possible and, perhaps, inevitable if we take a scientific (or as the 'first sociologist', Auguste Comte, called it, a *positivist*) approach to social life. Then, social life will continuously improve through the application of science; societies will become more highly evolved socially, culturally, and perhaps morally; and life will be better for all.

Postmodernism, however, denies all of these assumptions and conclusions. Postmodernists, opposing modernist and Enlightenment rhetoric, argue that rationality is neither sure nor clear, and that our knowledge is situation-specific—always limited to particular times, places, and social positions. These and other factors shape the way people *construct* their unique views of knowledge. To escape from knowledge constructed and imposed by others, then, one needs to critique and deconstruct it.

Central to this debate between modernism and postmodernism is the concept of *objectivity*. The postmodern position hinges on the denial of objectivity and the rejection of claims based on purported objectivity. At the same time, this underlying hostility toward the notion of objectivity is a common point of attack for critics of postmodernism—whether functionalists or critical theorists. From their standpoint, the rejection of objectivity undermines postmodernism's epistemological stance: for if objectivity is impossible, how can the blanket claim that 'objectivity is impossible' be true, or even judged? Clearly, logicians would say, this is a nonsensical claim.

Ignoring this, postmodernists assert that reality is fragmentary; all we have are disjointed, often conflicting accounts of reality. Any claim that there is a single knowable and known truth, or that any one account is 'the truth', is false and illusory. Efforts to find and promote universal or essential truths are self-deluding or, even worse, are forms of propaganda designed to confuse and dominate the population. It is the job of the postmodern sociologist, then, to analyze these universalizing 'accounts' and expose their flaws. At best, postmodernists hold that we can discover only particular explanations for particular situations, not universal, timeless laws of social life.

The postmodern movement, by denying universal knowledge and highlighting the value of local or particular insights, has an obvious attraction for counter-cultural movements and parties. Its rebellious, anti-hegemonic insights appear to support, and gain support from, movements for gender equality, racial equality, gay rights, anti-globalization, environmentalism, and other popular movements. However, none of these movements embraces all aspects of postmodernism; they mainly just borrow from its various ideas.

Postmodernism is fascinated by the mass media and cultural production in general. From the postmodern, anti-hegemonic perspective, the 'modernity project' depends on a propaganda machine that, in turn, rests on widespread, unquestioned beliefs about 'science', 'universalism', and 'normality'. Many modernists and social engineers, for example, believe it is the job of science is to find out what is normal, then work at propagating normality. The job of applied science is to establish norms that, through surveillance and control, turn abnormal people into normal people. From a postmodern perspective, this raises several questions: Is there any such thing as normality, and if there is, what makes it so good? Within our current context, is deviance abnormal or normal? In either event, should we use social control to wipe out abnormality and enforce normality?

The mass media are important in this context because they are largely responsible for framing and transmitting conventional ideas about normality, gender, class, and even science. They are, in large part, the propaganda machine that postmodernists are bound to attack.

An especially influential example of postmodern research, as we will see, is Michel Foucault's analysis of prisons and imprisonment. For Foucault, all of modern society is a prison—indeed, a panopticon, as Jeremy Bentham named the design for a prison in which unseen guards could constantly watch their prisoners. Foucault's work *Discipline and Punish* (1975) thus aims at uncovering a new type of domination in modern society: domination afforded by 'technologies of power'.

Foucault links the birth of the modern prison in the nineteenth century to a long history of institutions. Out of this institutional evolution comes a disciplinary society, with new means of enforcing power. In this new society, power is diffuse and internalized—controlling people far more completely than any despot could do before. At the core of Foucault's picture of a modern 'disciplinary' society are three primary techniques of control: hierarchical observation, normalizing judgment, and continual examination. As he shows, control (power) over people can be largely achieved merely by watching and examining them.

In *Discipline and Punish*, the prison provides maximum surveillance, so it is an institution powerfully charged with negative meaning. However, Foucauldian analysis is applicable to any space—including schools, factories, and offices—characterized by power differentials. We will discuss other postmodern insights into hidden sources of social control over behaviour—even over the body—in the chapters that follow.

Classic Studies
Suicide

Émile Durkheim was born to a Jewish family in Épinal, France. Originally studying to become a rabbi, Durkheim eventually took another path, leading to an academic career in Paris. He was passionate about the social sciences, especially about learning the keys to the organization of society and its effects on individual members. In 1902, the highly regarded Durkheim became a sociology professor—the first Jew ever to hold a university professorship in all of (then) anti-Semitic France. Throughout his life, he wrote on many sociological topics of importance to his society. One of his most famous works is *Suicide* (1897), which laid the foundation for quantitative methods in modern sociology, and established sociology as a distinct, recognized discipline in academia.

Sociology, Durkheim asserts, 'must try to become more than a new sort of philosophical literature' (Durkheim, 1970: 36). Durkheim's approach in *Suicide* is based on what he calls 'the sociological method', which involves a systematic analysis of suicide statistics—specifically, of the rates of suicide in different localities and groups. The principle of this sociological method is that 'social facts must be studied as things, as realities external to the individual' (ibid: 37–8). That is, group suicide rates not only reflect individual behaviours; they reflect something that is compelling individuals to certain behaviours.

Durkheim begins by ruling out the plausibility of strictly psychological explanations of suicide. Listing four types of suicide due to insanity—maniacal, melancholic, obsessional, and impulsive suicide—Durkheim uses the example of the Jewish community to illustrate the inadequacy of a purely psychological explanation. This community, with the highest rate of recorded neuropathy (or neurosis), had the lowest rate of suicide. Further, Durkheim argues that if suicide were strictly psychological, the sign of a person's insanity, then it would show no social patterns. However, Durkheim notes that social patterns *are* visible in the suicide rates; so insanity and other purely individualistic explanations are insufficient. There are indeed factors outside the individual that influence his or her highly personal decision to commit suicide. In Book II, Durkheim discusses these 'social causes and sociological types of suicide' (ibid: 179). Following his examination of the statistical evidence, Durkheim groups suicides into three main types, which he terms egoistic, altruistic, and anomic.

According to Durkheim, egoistic suicide is likely to occur when people fall out of the social groups they belong to, or when the groups' bonds are weakened by excessive individualism. Here, Durkheim discusses in detail the social value of churches, schools, and families in building social bonds, noting that the dissolution of these social bonds leads to an increased likelihood of suicide. On this point, he examines statistics comparing Protestants and Catholics. Noting that the Protestant faith is more individualistic than the Catholic, Durkheim predicts that Protestants will feel less tied to their religious institutions and communities, and will therefore be more likely to kill themselves than Catholics. The data support this prediction.

In this analysis, social institutions such as families are central to social integration (and therefore to personal survival). Durkheim, again examining the statistics, finds that married people have lower rates of suicide because of their higher integration and obligations. An interesting finding here is that women benefit significantly less from marriage than men, except when children are present. Single or divorced women without children are no more suicide prone than married women, and much less suicide prone than divorced or separated men. Women with children are much less likely to commit suicide, likely because of the responsibility they feel for their dependants.

By altruistic suicide, Durkheim means suicide that is motivated by a sense of societal duty. Durkheim claims that this type of suicide explains why the rate of suicide is higher among soldiers than among civilians. Today, we might cite the examples of Japanese kamikaze pilots (in World War II) or suicide bombers (in the Middle East). Unlike the people who kill themselves because of a lack of social integration, the people who kill themselves 'altruistically' reflect too much social integration: they are motivated by self-abnegation in the interest of the greater good (though also by a desire for glory in serving the community).

Finally, by anomic suicide, Durkheim means suicide resulting from an absence of social regulation and norms, as sometimes happens after a sudden social shock or disturbance such as a financial crisis. (A more up-to-date example might include the recent natural disasters in New Orleans and Haiti as possible causes of anomie and social disorder.) In this case, people commit suicide because they suddenly confront the confusion and distress of social uncertainty, requiring rapid readjustment. They kill themselves because they are in pain, and they are in pain because society isn't telling them how to live.

Durkheim's general conclusion is that rates of suicide in any society correlate inversely with a person's degree of integration into domestic, religious, and political society. Highly integrated people are least likely to kill themselves; highly isolated and undirected people are most likely to do so. Later researchers have found that the same explanation applies to other kinds of deviant behaviour, such as juvenile delinquency. For people to keep well mentally, they need a 'stake in conformity', as one researcher has called it.

Despite criticisms, Durkheim's work continues to be widely read and highly important in sociology today. *Suicide* is still considered a starting point for anyone trying to understand the social causes of suicide. This remains one of the most important, if not the most important, studies in sociology, not only for its findings, but also for the ways it helped Durkheim to establish sociology as a field of scientific research.

One World, Many Societies

BOX 1.1

Swiss to Tighten Assisted Suicide Rules to Stop 'Death Tourism'

Always a controversial issue, suicide is not illegal in Canada. However, euthanasia—physician-assisted suicide—is illegal under the Health Care Consent Act. Switzerland is one of the few places in the world where assisted suicide is legal, but that may soon change. The Swiss government wants to ensure that assisted suicide is only a last resort for the terminally ill. It also wants to limit so-called 'death tourism'—people travelling to Switzerland to end their lives, often with the help of organizations promoting assisted suicide. The Swiss government is expected to either tighten regulations or ban the involvement of organizations in assisted suicide.

Source: Adapted from Thomasson and Cage (2009).

Business leaders such as Bill Gates may exercise legitimate power because of their wealth and economic influence.

Modern Functionalism

The modern *functionalist* perspective on sociology emerged out of Durkheim's work, building on his macrosociological view of social trends. By the mid-twentieth century, functionalism was particularly important in North American sociology, under the leadership of such theorists as Robert Merton and Talcott Parsons. Their rendering of the perspective presents society as a set of interconnected elements that operate together to maintain the overall stability and efficiency of the society. In other words, each part of society contributes to the whole and keeps it in equilibrium.

For example, individual social institutions—families, the economy, the state, the schools, and so on—are said to each make a vital contribution to the functioning of the larger society. Families operate to reproduce and nurture members of society; the economy regulates the production, distribution, and consumption of goods and services; the state controls conflict and contributes to the sharing of values and norms; and schools socialize young people.

Functionalists note that social institutions often fail to fulfill their manifest (intended) functions, especially during times of rapid change. Sudden, major changes sometimes disrupt traditional values and common ways of doing things. As noted, Durkheim named this condition *anomie*. As traditional forms of guidance break down, social control declines and people bond less with one another; they become more likely to commit deviant acts (crime, drug abuse, and the like). The general solution to this problem, according to functionalists, is to strengthen social norms and slow the pace of social change.

As Durkheim argued, insufficient social control sometimes results in suicide. In families, it more often results in conflict and even domestic violence. Here we see plainly the value of functionalist thinking. The functionalist emphasis on the interconnectedness of society usefully highlights the problems associated with disorder. It also helps us understand how one part of the society influences other parts. For example, it helps explain why recent trends in family life, such as the rise in rates of cohabitation, divorce, and single parenting, have important consequences for work (and vice versa); and why recent trends in the workplace translate into increased work–family conflict.

Functions of Deviance and Conformity

As Foucault suggests, social institutions and groups are continuously imposing rules on us. Life sometimes seems like an endless procession of rules and commandments at home, at school, at work, and elsewhere. But why do we 'choose' to obey them? Is it because, as Durkheim suggests, without rules we would perish? And, since we sometimes fail to follow all of society's rules, we should ask: Under what conditions are people *likely* to obey society's rules, and under what conditions are people likely to break them?

These are broad, general questions, and people have been trying to answer them for centuries. But disciplines differ in the ways they go about this. Criminologists tend to focus on the reasons that people break laws and the ways police, judges, lawmakers, and jailers try to reduce the likelihood of crime. Political sociologists focus on political movements, rebellions, and revolutions, and study the factors influencing the breakdown and reestablishment of political order. Medical sociologists study the conditions under which people judged to be 'ill' play the patient role, one that releases them from the duty to conform to normal rules of social activity. What, then, is the role of sociologists in answering this question?

Sociologists note that all societies allow a margin of tolerable or invisible deviance—deviance that will go unseen, or if seen, unpunished. We have all taken advantage of this margin of safe nonconformity at one time or another. Conformity is easier when we know there are occasional opportunities to break the rules.

Since sociologists—especially functionalists—are mainly interested in the persistence of social order, they study deviance differently than do other researchers, especially psychologists, and draw different conclusions. Psychologists typically focus on individuals and the factors that influence them in a social context. In particular, clinical psychologists take the position that deviance is the usual behaviour of abnormal people. Crimes and other anti-social acts, by this reasoning, are due to a personality defect: a 'nut on the loose'.

However, just as in Durkheim's *Suicide*, sociologists look for answers to deviance *outside* the individual. They look for social reasons for people breaking the social rules, and in doing so, they turn the question around. They ask: Why do people conform? Of course, there are many theories and many approaches about conformity. But most simply, people learn to behave in conforming ways and most of them feel rewarded for continuing to do so. So we should ask ourselves what is more remarkable: that people conform most of the time, or that people sometimes deviate and break the rules? Both conformity and deviance are normal, universal, and continuously present; we need theories to cover both.

Here, sociologists in the functionalist tradition often follow either the 'social control theory' or the 'rational choice theory' of deviance. Social control theory posits that even normal people have deviant impulses; the question is why they don't act on these impulses and break the rules. In answer to this question, social control theorists believe that people conform to the rules when they develop a 'stake in conformity', thinking they will benefit, or at least avoid punishment, by doing so. Children learn to follow rules under the supervision of their parents. As people get older, enmeshed in long-term social relationships with friends, spouses, neighbours, and workmates, they find themselves locked into networks of reciprocal obligation. Their friends and acquaintances reward conformity and punish deviance with exclusion, shame, or contempt. Then, people continue to conform because they want (and need) the rewards conformity brings, and fear the punishments for deviance. Feeling secure and socially connected, they are unmotivated to deviate.

Of course, some people conform to the rules of groups that value deviance, even criminality; and by upholding one set of (deviant) rules, they are breaking another set of (convention) rules. Then, just as some people get locked into conventional conformity, so other people get locked into deviance, in so-called deviant or criminal 'careers'. Sampson and Laub (2003) show that an early involvement in crime weakens the social bonds to significant others and conventional institutions. The failure, early in life, to build social networks outside crime can trap people in a criminal lifestyle, for example. Some people are able to escape this lifestyle by undergoing a key life event, such as marriage, parenthood, buying a home, or taking on a valued job. These events can lead to new social bonds that impose controls on behaviour and reduce the risk of further criminal behaviour.

Rational choice theory, a second approach that is arguably part of functionalism, is concerned with the reasons that normal people might purposely set out to commit criminal acts. Proponents of this theory assume that most people are competing for desired social and economic resources, because they value the dominant goals of society: success, wealth, power, respect, fame, and so on. Under some circumstances—for example, if they believe they will not get caught, or if caught, will not be punished—people are motivated to maximize their own welfare even if they have to break some rules.

From the rational choice standpoint, illegal work (crime) and legal work are merely points on the same continuum of income-generating activities: just ways of making money. The links between crime and legal work involve trade-offs among crime returns, punishment costs, legal work opportunity costs, and tastes and preferences about both types of work. Often, ordinary people engage in illegal work because of the low wages and harsh conditions they experience in legal work. Some would rather rob a house than dig a ditch, for example. Many criminal offenders engage in *both* legal work and crime, either at the same time or sequentially, moving between the two as opportunities arise.

Businesses as well as individuals behave rationally where crime is concerned, weighing the benefits and costs of criminal activity. In that sense, corporate crime—crime by seemingly upstanding people—is similar to street crime. Although street crime is a primary concern of most people (and criminologists), in recent years, crime committed by corporations has increased greatly and gained a great deal more public attention. The factors encouraging corporate crime include the failure of government regulation, lack of corporate self-regulation, and a lack of public awareness about corporate crime, among other things.

Thus, sociologists since Durkheim have shown that people break social rules all the time, when the norms are weak or the controls over deviance are weakened. Beyond that, many rule-breakers may have been improperly trained in childhood to obey the rules. The rules themselves may conflict with one another, creating what sociologist Robert Merton (confusingly) called *anomie*. Finally, the rules themselves may be in doubt because of a rapidly changing culture, or because of conflicts between the main culture and competing subcultures. We will say more about all of these matters in the chapters to come.

Ironically, as Durkheim pointed out a century ago, not only are deviance and crime common, they are universal—found in all societies at all times. This leads Durkheim to the

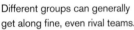

Different groups can generally get along fine, even rival teams.

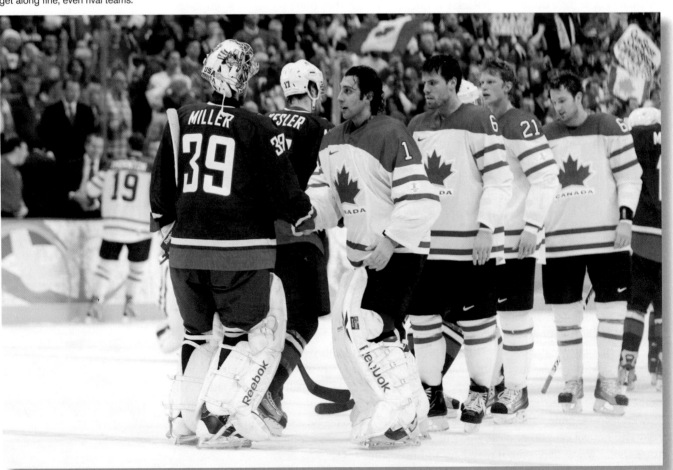

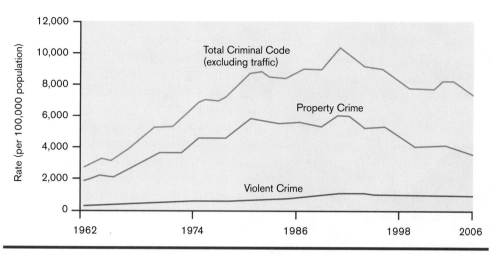

Figure 1.1 Crime Rates, Canada, 1962–2006

Source: Statistics Canada (2007).

interesting speculation that perhaps deviance and crime are *necessary* and societies could not survive without them. If so, perhaps it would be useful to think of crime and deviance as analogous to forest fires, which, while damaging to particular ecosystems, also serve an essential purpose. While destructive and dangerous, forest fires nevertheless complete the carbon cycle, promote new growth, and enable species' diversification. In this way, destruction promotes renewal and healthy growth.

The Functions of Conflict

Another irony of social life, from the functionalist viewpoint, is that not only can deviance be constructive, but so can conflict. Usually, we think of conflict as irritating, stressful, and unhealthy. After all, conflict sets people against one other. However, let's consider the possibility that conflict—like crime—is not only normal and universal, it is also healthy for society.

Like crime, which clarifies the social boundaries between right and wrong, conflict clarifies the boundaries between people who take opposing positions. And like punishment, which (according to Durkheim) strengthens social cohesion among the law-abiding members of society, intense conflict strengthens social cohesion, co-operation, and unity among people who share the same point of view. It does this by dramatizing the difference between the opposing groups.

All societies face the enduring problem that both conflict and order are necessary. Every effort to draw people together—whether peaceful or violent—runs the risk of dividing people along new or existing boundaries. Émile Durkheim, in his classic work *The Division of Labor in Society* (1893), discussed later, argues that, very gradually, societies develop new forms of cohesion based on mutual interdependency. In modern societies, we all depend economically—if not socially and psychologically—on one another's efforts, Durkheim says. For example, teachers rely on car mechanics to fix their cars, shopkeepers and factory workers rely on customers to buy merchandise, and textbook writers rely on students to read their books. Thus, conflict is unavoidable, but social order requires finding ways to limit and channel this conflict.

Critical Theory

Critical theorists do not consider conflict a destructive force in society. Instead, they believe it focuses attention on social problems and brings people together in efforts to solve them. Sociologists working within this perspective emphasize that conflict has been central to

According to Goffman, any distinguishing features that separate the individual from the norm may open the individual to stigma.

status

A socially defined position that delineates people's rights and responsibilities.

the progress of many social movements—the women's movement, LGBT (lesbian/gay/bisexual/transgendered) movements, civil rights movements, and trade unionism, among others. So, conflict can serve as the vehicle for positive social change.

The critical approach also focuses attention away from supposedly shared values and toward manipulative ideologies. Ideologies are beliefs that guide people's interpretations of and reactions to external events. The ideology of the dominant social class, known as the *dominant ideology*, justifies that class's power and wealth. If we ask why society doesn't rebel against class inequality (or gender inequality, or racial inequality), often the answer is that society has been programmed to believe in values promoted by the dominant ideology. We teach young people this dominant ideology in schools and religious institutions, and through the media; we hear it repeated throughout our lives. We learn to think inequality and domination are normal, even natural.

As we will see, the work of Max Weber, following Karl Marx, inspired sociologists to develop critical theory. Weber, in what he described as a debate with Marx, expanded the approach to include conflicts arising over cultural values, social **status**, and issues of personal honour. Weber was as interested in what he called 'status groups' and 'political parties' as in what he and Marx called 'social classes'. From Weber's point of view, even a modern corporation, with multiple owners and managers, experiences economic conflict with its employees. Further, Weberian theorists argue, we will see conflict in any large society with status groups, classes, or political parties. Conflict isn't restricted to classes, or to capitalism. It even applies to the international Communist Party which, under Stalin, Mao, and Pol Pot, oversaw the murder of many party dissidents.

Out of the works of Marx and Weber comes modern critical theory, transformed and nourished by the so-called Frankfurt School of sociology. This school arose at the Institute for Social Research, affiliated with the University of Frankfurt, in 1923. Marxist scholars there considered that Marxism had come to be tied too closely to the workings of Communist parties, so they tried to develop a brand of Marxist theory that was distinct from the practice of political parties. Prominent sociologists associated with the Institute have included Max Horkheimer, Karl Wittfogel, Leo Lowenthal, Herbert Marcuse, Theodor Adorno, Walter Benjamin, and Jürgen Habermas. Many of these figures fled Germany during the Nazi era and made major contributions to American sociology. The current critical theorists include women such as Nancy Fraser, Seyla Benhabib, and Agnes Heller.

Horkheimer has contrasted modern critical theory with earlier forms of the theory by pointing to some important differences. The more traditional version, steeped in nineteenth-century positivism, used scientific methods to formulate general 'laws' about society. By contrast, the twentieth-century version (and beyond) has taken a more subjective, less dogmatic approach to shed light on society and thus bring about change.

This less scientific approach, Horkheimer has argued, is necessary, because he, like Weber, sees a distinction between social science and natural science. He claims that rarely can an observation about society be truly objective, a point we discussed earlier this chapter. The researcher inevitably shapes the observation according to his or her own perspective and ideology. As a result, the researcher's 'conclusion' is likely to confirm what he or she already believes to be true. The only apparent way out of this dilemma is to acknowledge one's goals and biases at the outset.

Conflicts over Power and Authority

Central to Max Weber's traditional version of critical theory and its concern with power and conformity is the phenomenon of compliance: Why do a few people get to make society's rules while other people have to follow them? Why are certain people seemingly more in command than others?

The answer has to do with *power*, the ability to get your own way or to force another person to do what you want. Sociologists have spent a lot of time studying power, as have political scientists, anthropologists, and psychologists. They have found that people use many varied techniques, tools, and strategies to get their own way. Some use roundabout methods: trickery, seduction, and deceit, for example. Others use methods that are more direct: a raised voice, a loaded gun, a threat of violence, and so on. Some people specialize in using naked power or brute force—mainly, gangsters, schoolyard bullies, and political dictators—but this is not always needed. Let's not forget economic power—the influence of wealth and poverty. However, more often than by any other means, compliance is gained through the exercise of *authority*.

Authority is what we might call 'legitimate power': power that is exercised in what seems to be a justifiable way, by people whom we think have the 'right' to exercise it. For example, police authority confers the right to carry and use a firearm (or taser!). The elected government has the authority to demand that we pay taxes. These facts (about the social monopoly on death and taxes) lead us to ask important questions about the source of authority: How and why do societies come to grant authority to particular people or institutions, and under what conditions?

Weber identified three main sources of authority in history, calling them traditional, rational–legal, and charismatic. He pointed out that the large social change we call *modernization* was associated historically with a massive cultural shift from traditional to rational–legal bases of authority. In modern societies, no longer would people claim legitimacy for actions or ideas on the traditional grounds that 'this is what we have always done'. Now, new and better reasons were needed to gain compliance. This meant placing new importance on scientific (empirical) investigation, the rule of law, and democratic decision-making.

Major social upheavals are also associated with a shift from traditional to charismatic authority—authority associated with the leadership and teachings of so-called charismatic figures like Jesus and Mohammed, and more recently Gandhi and Hitler. These emotional and moral upheavals always give way (in time) to a stabilizing process that Weber called the 'routinization of charisma'. (We will talk in more detail about these upheavals in Chapter 13.) Thus, even social upheavals have a regular, predictable pattern; but the shifts from tradition to charisma, and charisma to routinization can be shattering.

Weber's conflict analysis is more powerful than that of Marx, because it generalizes from class conflict to all kinds of intergroup conflict. Some might even argue that Marxian class analysis can be viewed as a special case of Weberian group analysis. In Weber's framework, the capitalist class—like other dominating groups—is set on social closure—forming a 'power elite'—and seizing wealth through exploitative labour practices. What's more, Weberian conflict analysis can be used to analyze conflict between nations and empires; it can even be used to analyze conflict between peer groups—for example, bullying by cliques in high school. And, as we will see, it is useful in studying conflict between different ethnic groups within Canadian society.

Classic Studies
The Vertical Mosaic

As mentioned earlier, critical theorists focus on the power relations between different members of society: between people of different social classes, races, genders, age groups, and so on. As also mentioned, Karl Marx is the theorist best known for looking at society from a critical theory perspective, although Max Weber runs a close second.

The most eminent Canadian sociologist in this critical tradition, obviously influenced by founding sociologist Max Weber, was John Porter. Porter contributed many works to the sociological canon, but he is best known for his book *The Vertical Mosaic* (1965), which examines the inequalities faced by different ethnic groups in the Canadian labour market.

The Vertical Mosaic is considered a landmark study because it puts to rest many common misconceptions about Canada as a classless society. Like the United States, and contrary to popular myth, Canadian society is a class-based society: a *vertical* social hierarchy of wealth and power. However, unlike the US, to which it is often compared, Canada is also a cultural *mosaic* of unassimilated ethnic groups who hold different positions in this hierarchy.

To write this book, Porter collected and examined the best available statistical information on power and class in Canadian society. He used these data to show who is on top, who is on the bottom, and to explain the reasons for this inequality, employing a sociological theory that draws on several different theorists, including Marx and Weber.

Porter reports that Canada is socially stratified, with economic power in the hands of a small elite group that promotes and protects one another's interests. Porter also finds 'status inequalities' in the patterns of ethnic division and ethnic loyalty that separate immigrants from non-immigrants, and WASPs (white Anglo-Saxon Protestants) from non-WASPs. Elites are mainly people with a WASP background, though a few have a French background. Native American and Inuit people, reportedly the most disadvantaged in Canada, have the least power and influence.

Thus, in Canada ethnic differences reproduce class differences in social inequality and set limits to social mobility. Low-status groups seemingly and voicelessly accept their inferior economic position, while 'charter groups' (that is, English and French Canadians) aggressively preserve their historical advantage. They do so in part by monopolizing higher educational opportunities, according to Porter.

For this reason, Porter calls for a transformation of the educational system, to open it up so the most able people from every background can advance occupationally and economically. Porter also calls for cultural assimilation. This has worked well in the US, he argues. There, immigrants are encouraged to shed their ethnic traditions and adopt an American identity, while in Canada they are allowed—even encouraged—to preserve their traditions. This lack of assimilation fosters a multi-ethnic, mosaic effect in Canada, Porter notes, and because of this, a lack of immigrant access to higher education. This in turn deprives ethnic minorities of upward social mobility and economic assimilation.

The Vertical Mosaic was widely influential in its day. After its publication in 1965, a great many other books and papers focused on elites in Canada, including Wallace Clements's *The Canadian Corporate Elite: An Analysis of Economic Power* (1975) and Dennis Olsen's *The State and Power* (1980). Many of these later works showed that elites were gaining increased power in society, and using this power to promote the success of those within their social group. In other words, the problem Porter diagnosed was getting worse, not better.

However, in the years since Porter's book was published, we have had ample opportunity to evaluate the work. Today, some critics say the findings of *The Vertical Mosaic* are dated (since Porter's data is from the 1950s) or inaccurate (Ogmundson, 1990). Many agree that today, *ethnic* origins pose little obstacle to educational and occupational advancement, though *racial* minorities continue to suffer a disadvantage (Darden, 2005). Many argue that opportunities for upward social mobility are beside the point: what matters for Canada is the persistence of a small, ruling elite of capitalists, whatever its ethnic or racial composition. Finally, others note that Porter had nothing to say about women or racial minorities, nor did he say much about social movements or open conflict between the English and French 'charter groups' in the Canadian mosaic.

Today, this book remains significant in Canadian sociology. When first published, it was instantly popular and set off twenty years of sociological research on power, mobility, ethnicity, and immigration in Canada. By challenging previous misconceptions, Porter led sociologists and policy makers to develop new ideas about Canadian society (Helmes-Hayes and Curtis, 1998). Additionally, Porter's support for a more open, more accessible educational system influenced a huge expansion of post-secondary education in Canada. The reader of this book has, probably, benefitted from Porter's call for educational expansion, and so have millions of other Canadians.

Modern Critical Theories

In recent decades, critical theory has developed dramatically, in new and interesting ways as we will see below, but it is important to always remember its starting points. From Marx, critical theorists took the idea that conflict arose from hierarchical relations of dominance and subordination—from a class structure in which capitalists control the means of production and workers must sell their labour to survive. The ruling class also uses the legal system to dominate the workers; and the workers, in turn, develop strategies and practices of resistance. No wonder workers and unemployed people often lack a deep commitment to the prevailing social order, given its exploitive organization.

From Weber, critical theorists took the idea that conflict arises also out of horizontal relations of difference and distrust—from status structures in which groups compete to seize (i.e., usurp) and protect their resources. Such status groups may include ethnic, religious, linguistic, regional, gender, or even age groups. To 'protect their turf' and ensure their survival, they practise closure, by setting up group boundaries and promoting social cohesion within the group. To achieve and keep dominance, they practise usurpation, capturing new resources for the group. In this battle of status groups, crime and deviance may arise out of intergroup conflict (for example, gang fights over turf), with the less powerful group resisting and trying to undermine the more powerful one.

In short, critical theorists understand that conflict develops between any groups with differing or (especially) opposing goals—for example, the rich and the poor, men and women, workers and management. For a conflict theorist, there is one basic sociological question: Who benefits from the existing social order and who suffers?

Both Marx and Weber see ideas—whether as ideology, propaganda, or religion—as important in justifying domination. The so-called 'dominant ideology' in any society serves to justify prevailing inequalities, explaining, for example, why the rich are rich and the poor are poor. Take the role of the media, which are complicit in this spread of ideological ideas. The media often distort people's understanding of the causes of conflict in our society. They are likely to single out young people, poor people, and racial minorities as particularly given to conflict, deviance, crime, and even violence. However, as the story in Box 1.2 shows, conflict is present in all areas of society, among people of all ages and types.

In recent decades, a key modern proponent of critical theory has been Jürgen Habermas. In *The Theory of Communicative Action* (1984) a critical analysis of Western institutions and rationality, Habermas stresses the humanist side of Marx's work and examines tensions between philosophical theory and practice. At the same time, he has linked scientific methods to social analysis and argued for social improvement, not revolution. Habermas, then, represents a prime example of the fusion approach we have been discussing.

Media Distortion

BOX **1.2**

Mean Girls, but with Walkers

In her examination of retirement home culture, *Globe & Mail* reporter Rebecca Dube explains how difficult it can be for newcomers to gain acceptance within the community of residents, which is typically 'fraught with the same jealousies . . . as any close social environment', and where 'cliques abound':

> There are the cliques everyone respects, such as the Holocaust survivors who gather to share stories. . . . And there are the cliques that stir envy. . . . Jean Goldstein, 86, and her husband, Milton, 87, share a lunch table with two other couples . . . . The male halves of all three couples can still drive, which is a huge deal. Much like in high school, a driver's licence is a membership card to the cool kids' club, conferring freedom at a time when it's in short supply. And in a world of widows, having a live husband who drives is the equivalent of dating the varsity quarterback with a sweet Mustang . . . . Cliques are such a problem that some long-term care facilities have hired outside consultants to work with residents on busting up the exclusive groups.

Source: Adapted from Dube (2008).

Classic Studies
Stigma

We come now to the third major sociological approach—symbolic interactionism—and its classic figures; and begin with a brief discussion of sociologist Erving Goffman. Like other symbolic interactionists, Goffman was interested in studying people's face-to-face interactions, not large impersonal societal structures. His insights had a major impact on the content and methodology of world sociology, by means of a significant body of interesting books and articles. Here, we will focus on only one of these books, *Stigma*.

In the classic study *Stigma* (1963), Goffman examined people who are stigmatized—condemned, ostracized, or in other ways viewed negatively—by the people around them. Second, he considered how this stigmatization affects their social interactions and sense of self. The reasons for social stigma are many and varied, from physical or mental defects, to ethnicity and religion—anything that distinguishes a person from the norm and, in this respect, 'discredits' them. When Goffman was writing, the norm in America, according to Lemert and Branaman was 'a young, white, urban, northern, heterosexual Protestant father of college education, fully employed, of good complexion, weight and height, and a recent record in sports' (1997:78). Yet, many, if not most, people did not fit this norm and, therefore, were discreditable, if not actually discredited.

Goffman assumes, rightly, that people usually don't want to make waves—to attract unwanted attention or be treated with ridicule. So, in their social interactions, people usually try to present themselves *and* others involved as 'normal'. This allows them to follow the shared, widely understood scripts for the given situation (whether in school, on a date, at work, or elsewhere.) But this means they need to hide both their own discreditable features and those of others. Goffman argued that discreditable individuals are especially anxious to protect their identity against discredit and this motivates them to hide stigmatizing features through processes he called *passing* and *covering* (Goffman, 1963).

Passing is the effort to hide discreditable facts about one's identity. Here, the stigmatized individual tries to appear as normal as possible by making up stories about his or her past, or denying discreditable stories that others may have heard. However, certain stigmatizing features, such as race or physical disability, are harder to conceal than others, so passing is not always a choice. Where possible, people will devise strategies of information management to prevent discredit. Goffman uses the example of ex-mental patients to illustrate this process of information management. Often, ex-mental patients (or even ex-convicts) are able to hide their history in social interactions, because their stigma is not readily visible. Visually-impaired people may make a point of looking toward a speaking voice, just as a seeing person would do. Hearing-impaired people may assume a joking or offhand manner, to suggest that they prefer not to hear precisely what is being said.

On the other hand, people already discredited by a visible stigma may attempt to use the strategy of 'covering'. This technique does not manage information so much as it manages tension in an interaction. The aim is to deflect attention from the stigma so the interaction proceeds smoothly—at least as smoothly as contact between people considered 'normal'. Covering, then, may mean removing the disability from sight in an effort to appear 'normal'.

So, for example, a blind man with a disfigurement around the eyes may wear large dark glasses, and a woman with a missing leg may wear a carefully dressed artificial limb. Covering may also mean taking on a new identity, or at least, a new identifier, as when a member of an ethnic minority changes his or her name to fit into the majority (for example, Goldstein becomes Golden and Rosenberg becomes Robinson). Along these lines, a recent news item from the US noted that, recently, in applying for jobs, black people are hiding or playing down African-American given names and affiliations, so they don't seem 'too black' for potential employers.

Often, however, these strategies don't work as intended so people devise strategies for dealing with the pains of stigma by associating only with people who are similarly stigmatized—to spend time only with people like themselves. This helps to explain the high degree of residential segregation of ethnic and racial minorities in cities, and the institutional completeness of their communities.

The techniques Goffman discussed are extreme versions of what everyone does in everyday interaction; they are simply more visible when we look at the strongly stigmatized.

Goffman's work, which came as a flash of blinding insight to many, was criticized by others for its methodological approach. First, Goffman did not use interview data or other forms of primary sources to any significant extent (Lemert and Branaman, 1997). The book was based on qualitative data, yet Goffman had had little contact with the stigmatized people about whom he wrote. This meant the quality and credibility of his data were suspect. For this and other reasons, some questioned whether the book was 'scientific', since Goffman's theoretical analysis was unsupported by rigorous factual evidence (ibid).

To most, however, these criticisms seemed largely irrelevant. Goffman's work was exploratory and theory-forming, rather than theory-testing. It gave sociologists a set of provocative ideas and useful concepts with which to do hundreds, if not thousands, of later studies. In this respect, Goffman's *Stigma* was just like Durkheim's *Suicide* and Porter's *Vertical Mosaic* —what scholars like to call a 'seminal work'.

Key Ideas of Symbolic Interactionism

Symbolic interactionism, as its name suggests, sees society as a product of face-to-face interaction between people using symbols. To repeat, Erving Goffman was a key figure in the development of this approach, and to help place Goffman's work on stigma in its context, we should consider the theoretical underpinning of the approach. To do so, let's consider another classic work in this tradition: *The Social Construction of Reality*. The authors, Peter Berger and Thomas Luckmann (1966), claim that the purpose of sociology is to understand 'the reality of everyday life'—how it is experienced, coordinated, and organized. They point out the everyday world is intersubjective, meaning that we must all find communicative meeting places for common or shared understanding. Berger and

Luckmann also stress that the everyday world is 'taken for granted'. It is the job of the sociologist to make us all aware of the socially constructed nature of the world—to shine a light on what is 'taken for granted'.

Symbolic interactionism studies how **social structures**, as patterns of behaviour, arise out of processes by which people interpret and respond to each other. In naming the approach *symbolic interactionism*, Herbert Blumer described the basic elements of the model with three propositions: (1) 'human beings act toward things on the basis of the meanings that things have for them'; (2) these meanings 'arise out of social interaction'; and (3) social action results from a 'fitting together of individual lines of action' (1969 [1937]: 172). This perspective, strongly promoted by Blumer, has its roots in the work of scholars centred at the University of Chicago in the early twentieth century, including George Herbert Mead, W.I. Thomas, and Robert Park.

One forerunner of the interactionist approach was German sociologist Georg Simmel, who studied the effects of urbanization on people's lives in cities (1950b). He sees the urban lifestyle to be markedly different from rural or small-town life: as relentlessly, supremely alienating, with inhabitants numbing their emotions to cope with the excessive stimulation that city life offers.

As noted, symbolic interactionists consider society to be the product of interaction between people in their everyday social relationships. In these relationships, people adapt the culture of the society to everyday life, and they may even develop new ways of doing things. Culture in modern societies, therefore, is fluid rather than static; it is always open to revision. Culture does not sit unchanging on a pedestal, to be memorized and mechanically enacted; it is situated in specific relationships and enacted, often creatively through face-to-face interaction. Thus, society and its social relationships are dynamic, always changing, and always under renovation by living people (Blumer, 1969 [1937]).

One type of shared meaning highlighted in the symbolic interactionist approach is the 'definition of the situation'. This is a shared understanding of the norms and meanings that govern a social situation, whether in a classroom, a bedroom, or a football stadium. These shared situational norms guide the course of interaction, suggesting the social rules suitable for people's participation in the situation and the goals one could properly pursue within it. (For example, don't practise sex in a classroom or conjugate French irregular verbs in your friend's bedroom.) It spells out how specific social goals may properly be achieved and regulates the relationships among the various participants. Because these definitions of the situation are shared, they allow people to coordinate their actions in pursuing their own personal goals.

Definitions of the situation typically emerge out of interpersonal **negotiations**. These negotiations may be formal and direct (for example, a contract drafted between a union and an employer). However, most negotiated agreements are less tangible, the result of people informally and tacitly communicating with each other about the situations they share. Their communication may be verbal, or consist of gestures, body language, and even material symbols like clothing.

The impressions we give one another—whether intentionally or unintentionally—have consequences for how people interact with us. Even first impressions foster understandings: about the meanings people attach to their relationships, their goals, and what actions are deemed acceptable and unacceptable. People have many motives that govern how they present themselves and the kinds of interpretations they invite. (If you doubt this, try going to church in a bathing suit or meeting your new girlfriend's parents in a ratty pair of jeans and paint-splattered T-shirt.)

Further, although interactionists argue that society is dynamic, they recognize that situations physically and socially constrain what people can reasonably do and therefore limit the kinds of definitions that are available. This means that although a 'definition of the situation' constrains interaction, it is not rigid. (There may be some defined circumstances

social structure

Any enduring, predictable pattern of social relations among people in society; the subject matter of sociology. All social structures *control us*, so that we act in a certain way in a given situation, despite personal differences; they *change us*, so we behave differently in different situations, despite our more or less fixed 'personalities'; and although they *resist* the efforts of individuals to bring about social change, they also *produce social change*.

negotiation

The ways in which people try to make sense of one another, and make sense to one another; for example, by conferring, bargaining, making arrangements, compromising, and reaching agreements.

under which you *may* wear a bathing suit to church or a ratty pair of jeans to your girl-friend's house.) Symbolic interactionists are therefore interested in the tactics people use to redefine definitions, relationships and situations.

Social Constructionism

The most important thinking to emerge from symbolic interactionism in recent decades is the social constructionist approach to social issues.

The goal of *social constructionism* as a sociological enterprise is to examine how people interact to create a shared social reality. Berger and Luckmann (1966), cited earlier, claim that *all* knowledge—including the most taken-for-granted knowledge of everyday life—is created, preserved, and spread by social interaction. That is, our understanding of the world is socially constructed. According to this social constructionist approach, any idea, however natural or obvious it may seem to the people who accept it, is just an invention of a particular culture or society. So, we need to understand how some ideas become widely accepted as 'true' and compelling, while many others do not.

It is easy to see that this approach grows out of symbolic interactionism and the early twentieth century work of George Herbert Mead. Mead (1934) writes that children learn to interact with others by acquiring a shared system of symbols, including language, which allows them to share and negotiate meanings. With shared meanings, they can play together, perform complementary roles, and relate to the social group as a 'generalized other'. For Mead, this ability is the basis of all social order. Shared meanings (including shared symbols) make social interaction possible, and interaction allows people to co-oper-ate and influence one another. Social life, for Mead, is thus the sharing of meanings—that is, the co-operative (social) construction of reality.

A generation later, Erving Goffman (1959), proposed that we can usefully think of society as a theatre in which people compose and perform social scripts together. We come to believe in the truth of the roles we play; often, we even become the person we pretend to be. In the end, social life is little more than a set of scripted, directed performances. It is inside our social roles that we find and express (or hide and protect) our true identity.

In the eyes of social constructionists, human beings react not to physical objects and events themselves, but to the shared meanings of these objects and events. The shared mean-ings are not essential features of the objects and events, but socially imposed or constructed meanings. In our society, for example, a red rose is considered beautiful and romantic, while a daisy is simple and a cabbage, ugly. These are social constructions, but they are powerful

Point/Counterpoint

BOX **1.3**

'Head-of-State Debate Makes for Bizarre Spectacle'

After Governor-General Michaëlle Jean used the phrase 'head of state'—a term many people believe applies to Canada's monarch and not her viceroy—Canadians are discussing the role of the head of state, who should fill that role, and where the constitutional centre of power should lie. Monarchists are eager to re-assert the primacy of the Queen as Canada's ruler. Others feel it is time for Canada to detach itself from the British monarchy, either with a Governor General–style ceremonial head of state, or with the elected prime minister being both head of government and head of state.

Source: Adapted from Boswell (2009).

nonetheless. (If you doubt the social power of such a construction, give your loved one a dozen cabbages on Valentine's Day.) Thus, the meaning of anything, including a social problem, is the product of the dominant cultural and symbolic practices in a group or society.

People Are Talking About . . .
ANTHONY GIDDENS

Born in 1938, Anthony Giddens grew up in a lower-middle-class family in London. He studied sociology and psychology at the University of Hull in 1959, and later received a Master's degree from the London School of Economics, and a Ph.D. from King's College, Cambridge. In 1985, Giddens was appointed a professor of sociology at Cambridge, where he lectured for 12 years. Since 1997, he has served as director of the London School of Economics. For a period, he served as a policy advisor to British prime minister Tony Blair.

Giddens established himself as an interpreter of the ideas of classical social theorists like Émile Durkheim, Max Weber, and Karl Marx. He turned his attention to structuration theory in the 1970s and 1980s. In *New Rules of Sociological Method* (1976), he sets out the principles that serve as guidelines for the fusion approach we follow in this book:

- Sociology is not about an existing or given universe of objects; people are always producing it through their actions.
- Therefore, sociologists should view the production and reproduction of society as a skilled performance by members of the society.
- Humans are limited in what they can produce, and act as historically located actors, under conditions not of their own choosing.
- We must think of social structures as constraints upon human agency, but also as enablers of human action; thus society both constrains and frees us.
- The processes of structuration by which people create society involve an interaction of meanings, norms, and power.
- The sociological observer cannot stand outside the society he or she studies, but instead constantly draws on his or her knowledge of it as a resource even while framing society as a 'topic for investigation'.
- Ironically, only by immersing oneself in life can one watch and study it, to create an understanding of the social rules.
- Therefore, all sociological theories obey a double hermeneutic; they reveal both the organization of society and the organization of the viewer.
- Therefore, the tasks of sociological analysis are to reveal the structures of society in the conceptual language of social science; and specifically, to explain how human actors manage to produce and reproduce society, under constraints.

Steven Loyal (in Scott, 2006: 108) writes that Giddens 'has been criticized for his eclecticism, inconsistency, and lack of empirical utility . . . [and] for placing an excessive emphasis on individual agency'. In Giddens' view, the modernist self is almost constantly re-inventing and re-interpreting itself, having shaken off the bonds of tradition. When applied to politics, this notion makes the left/right political dichotomy obsolete, thus blurring the distinction between previously opposed ideologies, and reducing the value of traditional class analysis for sociologists studying the present day.

Source: Adapted from *Fifty Key Sociologists: The Contemporary Theorists* (edited by John Scott, London: Routledge, 2006) and other sources.

Anthony Giddens has, among other things, revived and refined the sociological goal of *positivism*—a goal enunciated by sociology's first proponent, Auguste Comte. Positivism, simply, is the scientific study of social life conducted in hope of discovering and stating general principles that apply across a wide variety of times, places, and settings. A product of the European Enlightenment, positivism is—as we have noted—the polar opposite of postmodernism, which rejects the notion of finding 'general narratives'.

Yet, unlike earlier positivists, Giddens recognizes the contingency and conditionality of social life. This comes through clearly in his celebrated and widely cited theory of structuration. In this theory, social structure is not a visible, concrete thing, but the result of ongoing performances. Like language or music, society has rules, but the regularities sociologists study can be understood only within the framework of 'free' human choices and constrained opportunities. Thus, the daily reproduction of 'social structure' is like a long-running theatrical production: always there, microscopically changing over time, yet always at risk of closing down. Within this framework, the ideas of 'risk', 'blame', and 'responsibility' have (suitably) complex meanings. Nothing is ever a certain cause or certain effect of anything else. All humans have agency, however constrained. For this reason and others, as we said earlier, the so-called 'culture of blame' reflects political, not sociological, understandings. (cf. Lau, 2009).

Though one might imagine a diametric opposition between Giddens-the-neo-positivist and the postmodernists, no such simple opposition is possible. Giddens' notion of social structure as performance makes ample room for the notion of cultural discourse—a means of social communication and accountability that is central to postmodern understandings of reality (cf. Cooky, 2009).

Still, Giddens is criticized for providing 'grand narratives' of late modernity that are hard for some to accept. For example, Mulinari and Sandell (2009) examine how Giddens' theories of late modernity (as well as those of Ulrich Beck) view issues related to women and gender. They claim this 'late-modern story' is possible only through 'the reinvention of the heterosexual matrix, the private sphere as the location of women/gender, reproduction coupled to biology, and gender as an intimate relation between women and men'. Allegedly absent from Giddens' account is an analysis of 'reproductive and productive labour, of the role of the state, and of gender as a social relation created through and within other social inequalities'.

Attacking from another direction, Elchardus (2009) notes that Giddens' analysis leads to a view of modernity as a highly individualized social order. However, Elchardus rejects this view on empirical grounds, and proposes instead to view modernity (which he calls 'post-tradition') as a change in how social control operates, and not as an individualized and reflexive movement away from control. Although religion, ideology, tradition, and authority are diminishing as forms of social control, it does not necessarily follow that individual autonomy predominates. Elchardus claims that social control is emerging in new forms, which, although centred on the self, are influenced by education, media, consumption, and therapy. Here, the theoretical influence of Michel Foucault is obvious, as we will see again later.

Thus, a review of recent writings finds a heady debate about Giddens and his writings—at least 200 journal articles disputing Giddens in the last five years alone. Clearly, sociologists are talking about Anthony Giddens. Like Habermas, Giddens, as we have seen, is key to a comprehensive, fusion approach to sociology. His recognition of reflexivity and multiple narratives, and macro- and micro-perspectives, is key in any attempt to provide a systematic account of life in the present-day world.

New Insights

You will find, as you continue through the book and into the vast published literature, that sociologists everywhere are struggling with the traditional notions—the starting points—in the face of attacks by postmodernism, critical theory, and everyday life. Certainly, the scientific (or positivistic) model of sociology is under attack. As evidence of current debates, consider a brief pot-pourri of new insights aimed at extending the classic tradition.

For example, Erdmans (2007) notes that 'the art of life-story telling' has begun to supplant traditional scientific methods in studies of feminism, culture, history of ethnic groups and minorities, and postmodernism. This narrative method of research, incorporates 'oral histories, life stories, personal narratives and auto-ethnographies'. Erdmans points out how story-telling allows the people or groups being studied to speak for themselves—their voices are not drowned out by the academic voice of the researcher, and they are not so much objects of study as partners with the researcher in exploring the research interest.

Such narrative methods are useful in studying issues like civil liberties and universal rights, where it is important to hear the voices of participants, in their own words, making sense of their lived reality.

Another recurring theme in the new sociology is the debate over relations between inequalities—including determining which inequalities are dominant or central. In earlier decades, feminists argued that women's issues represent a unique form of experience that could only be addressed through women's studies and feminist theories. Today, some make similar arguments for race, showing the need for a so-called critical race theory (CRT).

Mills (2009), a proponent of critical race theory, likens CRT to feminism. Like feminist theory, CRT has many types and subtypes, meaning sociologists will vary in the ways they analyze social situations and prescribe political remedies. For this reason, there may even be a Marxist version of CRT, though Marx himself had nothing to say about race relations. In seeing the problem, Mills calls attention to 'white Marxism', a version of Marxism that fails to grant the importance of race and says it is incompatible with CRT.

An example of this critical race theory is provided in new work by Preston (2008) on the connection between civil defence concerns and whiteness. Preston writes that what he calls 'civil defence pedagogies', spread through schools and community organizations, focus mainly on the protection of white people, especially white middle-class families. He suggests that, in this way, middle-class white people are the main beneficiaries of a state-centred civil defence policy, and also are its main supporters. Examples of this situation can be seen in the United States during the 1950s, and in the UK in the 1980s, highlighting the higher status of white over racialized people.

Some have already asserted the value of intersectionality—the interaction of equally significant forms of inequality, especially, race, class, and gender—as a way around separate theories. However, others—mainly Marxists—continue to assert the dominant role of class in any study of inequality. Thus, Cole (2009) defends the continued vitality and relevance of Marxism today and clarifies how Marxist analyses also show an awareness of race and gender. With this in mind, Cole claims that a Marxist version of CRT is possible because there is enough common ground between the two schools of thought to 'unite around an anti-racist socialist project for the 21st century'.

However, Cole outlines four problems he sees with the CRT's term 'white supremacy': (1) it diverts attention away from modes of production; (2) it 'homogenizes' all white people; (3) it fails to consider 'non-colour coded racism'; and (4) it is 'counter-productive as a political unifier and rallying point against racism'. Cole, while admitting the racialized and gendered nature of social class, defends social class as the primary variable affecting society today. Indeed, he admits that modern capitalism depends on racialism and gender inequality, a point we will hear echoed later in work by Canadian sociologists Pat Armstrong and Hugh Armstrong.

Identity issues continue to interest current sociologists, and many of them—following Giddens—view identity as a performance, not a fixed trait. This is displayed, for example, in research by Brown (2009) on what the performance of karaoke might reveal about the construction of identity. While critical theorists have dealt widely with identity and its construction, there has been little attention to how this process actually takes place. Brown uses karaoke as a 'microscopic analysis' of how identity is constructed through performance in everyday life. (Of course, karaoke is a public performance in front of an audience, in which the performer plays a chosen musical role.)

The mass media continue to interest sociologists of all types, both as an influence on people's values and identities, and a reflection of dominant thinking about various social roles, categories, and identities. Some current work focuses on the symbolic meanings of social life and their implications for class, gender, or other inequality. So, for example, Slattery (2008) notes that a new tram system in Dublin, Ireland links both a working-class and a middle-class neighbourhood to the centre of the city, but does not link these neighbourhoods to each other. Slattery suggests that the gap in the tram lines is due not to inept planning 'but to a form of resistance by the city itself'. However, he says, 'The idea that we actually know what we are doing strikes me as manifestly absurd. Psychology helps us to preserve such mythologies especially when it comes to building cities.'

Finally, the postmodern interest in showing an intersection of various types of inequality is nowhere more obvious than in Sangster's (2007) analysis of the Canadian fur industry. Sangster shows how gender, race, and labour intersect in the creation of a fur coat, by studying the Aboriginal women who supply the furs, the eastern European Jewish immigrant women who sew the coats, and the often-female retail clerks who sell the coats. She examines the role of protest and organized labour in this industry. Sangster takes a feminist perspective in critiquing the race and gender hierarchies of the fur industry, and a materialist, rather than a 'dematerialized' view of the role of the labouring body, as well as of social class.

Chapter Summary

As we have seen in this first chapter, there are different ways to approach key sociological questions. We organized this chapter around three founding theoretical approaches—functional theory, critical theory, and symbolic interactionism—but we also note that these approaches can (and do) coexist with each other.

The three approaches do not contradict each other in their macrosociological or microsociological viewpoints, their focus on conflict versus social order, or on the role of individuals in shaping the social structure they live in. In practice, they complement each other. Any sociologist who has ever done 'applied sociology' for a client, seeking the answer to a problem of social policy or social organization, knows there are no real boundaries. Some theories, some ideas, some concepts are useful in the particular situation, and others are not.

All the established sociological approaches, and others, are important for our discipline because they all provide explanations of how society works. They may lead us to look at different dimensions of the problem under study, but their answers are often complementary. Therefore, the best course in sociological research is to keep an open mind and consider the insights and evidence provided by each approach. Remember, a perspective is just that—a 'perspective', meaning it only offers one way of looking at a social topic. A holistic understanding of the topic is always best—one that makes up for the failings of each view and builds on their respective strengths.

In the end, our personal beliefs shape where we begin as sociologists: what questions we ask and what personal biases we may have at the start of a research project. However, these biases should affect neither the ways in which we carry out research nor our willingness to recognize the story our data are telling.

We sociologists must take humans as we find them and study how they create and preserve social relationships, and how they act as members of society. As sociologists, let's look for the truth and describe it to one another. Then, as citizens, let's seek a better society together, understanding that we may not all agree on what might characterize this 'better society'. With that in mind, reasoned debate—using empirical evidence—is the best place to start.

Critical Thinking Questions

1. Using the microsociological approach, consider your experiences as an undergraduate university student. Then, through the macrosociological approach, consider the implications of the common undergraduate experience at university. Using the sociological imagination, discuss how the two perspectives are interrelated and explain the significance of making connections between personal and societal issues.

2. Recall that social structures both *resist* and *produce* social change. Provide an example of this notion in practice.

3. Consider the social roles that you fulfill in your life. How have some of these roles—perhaps 'student', 'young adult', or 'friend'—become part of your identity?

4. In *The Communist Manifesto* (1848), Marx and Engels wrote, 'The history of all hitherto existing society is the history of class struggle.' Do you agree with this claim? What is the significance of class conflict in sociology?

5. Choose an important sociological topic, such as the division of labour in society, and briefly note how it can be considered from the three different theoretical approaches. What is the value of using several approaches when considering a single topic?

Recommended Readings

Michael S. Kimmel, *Classical Sociological Theory* (New York: Oxford University Press, 2007). Kimmel's main purpose is to expand the sociological 'canon'; that is, to describe the life and works of more than just the typically included practitioners of sociology. He discusses the work of early feminist sociological theorists and also the work of individuals with ethnic backgrounds other than European, which predominates among the scholars of the nineteenth and twentieth centuries.

Kenneth Allan, *The Social Lens: An Invitation to Social and Sociological Theory* (Thousand Oaks, CA: Pine Forge Press, 2007). The goal of this book is to provide a comprehensive discussion of both classical and contemporary social theory, outlining different approaches to sociology and describing the scholars who put these forth. However, Allan does not present these perspectives as competing with each other, as do some other books. Instead, each perspective is intended as a starting point for students, an introduction to its ideas and a base for future exploration.

David Cheal, *Dimensions of Sociological Theory* (New York: Palgrave Macmillan, 2005). This is a clear and reader-friendly discussion of five key debates in relation to sociological perspectives. The organization is innovative, taking a thematic mode of introducing the paradigms, rather than a conventionally historical one.

Jonathan H. Turner (ed.), *Handbook of Sociological Theory* (New York: Kluwer Academic/ Plenum Publishers, 2001). This is a compilation of essays written by prominent scholars on sociological theory. It is centred on five main themes that highlight the diversity of theoretical perspectives in modern sociology.

Paul Blackledge, *Reflections on the Marxist Theory of History* (Manchester, UK: Manchester University Press, 2006). Blackledge takes the reader on a journey of the Marxist tradition in social theory. Each chapter outlines the theory's transition, from Europe in the nineteenth century, to the Soviet Union in the twentieth, to its relevance in modern sociology.

Vikki Bell, *Culture and Performance: The Challenges of Ethics, Politics, and Feminist Theory* (Oxford and New York: Berg, 2007). Bell places feminist theory within the context of ethics, politics, and the concept of 'performativity'. She considers both this latter concept and feminist theory with reference to other philosophers and presents a new approach to considering contemporary feminist ideas.

Websites

Statistics Canada
www.statcan.gc.ca/start-debut-eng.html

E-STAT for Education
www.statcan.gc.ca/estat/estat-eng.htm

SocioSite
www.sociosite.net

Socioweb
www.socioweb.com

Marxist Internet Archive (MIA)
www.marxists.org

Verstehen: The Sociology of Max Weber
www.faculty.rsu.edu/~felwell/Theorists/Weber/Whome.htm

Émile Durkheim Archive
http://durkheim.itgo.com/main.html

Sociology Undergraduate Network (SUN)
www.sociundergradnetwork.org

2 Material Settings

Learning Objectives

In this chapter, you will:

> Learn the effects of population size and type on life experiences
> Consider the interrelationship between the natural and built environments we live in
> Recognize the problematic relationship between population and environment

Chapter Outline

In this chapter, you will learn how population, cities, and natural environment continue to affect us as human beings living in societies. We will look at patterns in population size and population growth in both developed and developing countries and consider the many pressures endured by both the built and natural environment in accommodating the billions of people on Earth. We will then reflect on the importance of technology in our lives—our humanly created environment. In doing so, we will establish the material settings that serve as a background to social life, creating a foundation for the chapters to follow.

The single most important, least debatable fact about societies is that they are made up of people: they are collections of human beings. Thus, almost inevitably, social organization will affect people's health and happiness. Human beings are flesh and blood, they need food, and they occupy space. Since in every important sense people possess materiality—they are embodied in ways we can perceive with our senses—we need to say something about ourselves

as material beings. Different disciplines—evolutionary history, biochemistry, neuroscience, and so on—would do so from different angles.

Many of the issues discussed in this chapter are especially urgent. After all, societies exist in time and space, within a material environment that is always changing. In the past 50 years, Canada's population has more than doubled. This trend toward population increase has occurred not only in our country but also in many other parts of the world. In fact, the world's population has been rising exponentially over the past two centuries, leading to great concern about overpopulation and its effects on the environment.

Today, it is hard to ignore the environmental destruction that our world's growing population has caused. Climate change has become an important social and political issue, especially in the last few decades. It has forced us to think more critically about our impact on the environment, as well as the effects we will have to endure if we continue to destroy the natural resources we depend on for survival.

Everyday Observations

Population size matters, so consider this example: Emily took her first subway ride while visiting her sister in the city. Coming from a small town, she was not used to the crowds of people and the noise (not to mention the smell) of the subway station. While she and her sister were waiting for the subway to arrive, Emily admired the interesting artwork along the wall. However, while doing so she noticed something scurrying in the dark corners of the tracks. Suddenly, the train came roaring into the station, blowing cold, stale air onto her face. Emily stood back a little, startled by the speed of the subway and intensity of the wind. When the doors of the subway opened, people quickly pushed and shoved past her, fighting for a place inside. By the time she was able to wrestle her way through, Emily was pressed tightly against other passengers. She looked at her sister anxiously, who smiled back and simply said: 'It's always busy at rush hour'.

If you grew up in a rural area, you likely know that urban life is different from rural life. Many factors play into these differences. First, the populations of cities are much larger and denser than those of small towns or villages. Second, the technologies that are central to city life, such as subways or other forms of rapid transit, are unlikely to be found in a rural area or a small town, since they were developed to deal with large populations,

The subway has enabled people to travel across the city in large numbers at inexpensive prices.

transporting people from one place to the next as efficiently as possible. Third, the built environment of a city conflicts with the natural environment in many harmful ways, unlike the built environment of smaller communities.

Sociologists address many different questions about cities and their built environment: How long have people been living in cities? How many people live in cities today compared to a century ago? How does this larger urban population affect the social and economic circumstances of people in cities—for example, their job opportunities?

Throughout this chapter, we will try to answer some of the key questions about population, environment, technology, and material life, always bearing in mind that space to do so is limited. Note however, that population, built and natural environment, and technology are interconnected and are all important in people's lives.

Ways of Looking at . . .
POPULATION

In the realm of population and environmental analysis, the two main approaches are macroanalytical: namely, the functional and critical theories. As we will see, each approach weighs differently the factors that cause population and environmental problems, though they might agree that all of these factors play a part.

Functionalism

The idea that population issues—including impacts on the environment, food supply, and population health—might pose a serious problem for humanity was first put forward in 1798, by one of the founders of **demography**, Thomas Malthus (1766–1834). Malthus was the first to take seriously the possibility that Earth would eventually become 'over-populated'. Further, in every important sense, this was arguably the world's first piece of functional analysis—even pre-dating the work of Durkheim.

Malthus argued that, while the Earth's available food increases *additively* (or arithmetically), population increases *exponentially* (or geometrically). A population increasing exponentially at a constant rate is adding more people every year than it did the year before, while an arithmetical increase in food supply means that it grows by the same amount each year. In the end, arithmetic growth is slower. The growth in food supplies is slow, limited as it is by the amount of land available, the soil quality, and the level of technology a society has attained. So Malthus believed that there is a real risk a population will grow faster than its food supply will increase. As a result, the food per capita would inevitably decline and people would starve, posing a threat to the survival of the human race.

Therefore, Malthus proposed that 'checks' (or limits) would keep population growth in line with the food supply. *Positive checks* prevent overpopulation by increasing the death rate. They include war, famine, pestilence, and disease. *Preventive checks* prevent overpopulation by limiting the number of live births. They include abortion, infanticide, sexual abstinence, delayed marriage, and the use of contraceptives. Malthus urged people to use preventive checks so that they would not have to suffer the horrible consequences of positive checks.

This argument was a recognizable piece of functional analysis. Like other functional analysis, it is concerned with the conditions that maintain social equilibrium and the dangers associated with losing equilibrium (e.g., war, famine, and epidemic). It asserts that Nature, through positive checks, will re-assert societal equilibrium in its own way unless humans, through preventive checks, take the initiative. There is no arguing with Nature, or with natural laws of social life. Trying to ignore them—for example, by redistributing the wealth—will merely delay the inevitable. As the poor procreate more heavily, the problem will re-assert itself—naturally.

demography

The study of human populations—their growth and decline through births, deaths and migration.

But was Malthus right? It is hard to put meaningful numbers on the world's *carrying capacity*—that is, the number of people who can be supported by the available resources at a given level of technology. And, as the technology improves—for example, the technology associated with food production—a society's carrying capacity increases, so more people can be fed.

Today, in central Africa, women still bear an average of four, five, or six children, and in some communities, even more. Even a more modest four children per mother is common in southeast Asia, the Islamic world, parts of Africa, and Latin America. In short, hundreds of millions of mothers are still producing children at this rate; with four children per mother, a population doubles every 25 years or so.

Will the world be able to feed 50 per cent more people, let alone 100 per cent more, in 25 to 30 years? Here, expert estimates vary. However, in the event of widespread crop failures, the world's store of available food may last only a short time. Futurist Lester Brown notes

> World food production continues to increase, yet the rate at which it is increasing has slowed. From 1970 to 1990, world grain production grew by 64 percent. From 1990 to 2009, it increased by only 24 percent. Past growth in agricultural production was fueled in part by expanding irrigation: world irrigated area tripled from 1950 to 2000. However, expansion of irrigated area has since slowed significantly as land and water availability has declined, showing almost no growth in the past decade. When growing global population is taken into account, this trend becomes even more concerning. The world irrigated area per thousand people has declined from a high of over 47 hectares (116 acres) in the late 1970s to only 43 hectares (106 acres) per thousand people in 2007. Growing populations and pressures on agricultural production have meant increasing food insecurity around the globe. The number of hungry people in the world declined from 878 million in 1970 to 825 million in the mid-1990s, but it has been rising ever since. In 2009, for the first time, the world's hungry numbered more than 1 billion. (Brown, 2010)

Other ecologists conclude that by 2100, the number of people on Earth will have to drop to one-third the current level (or less) for the population to survive in relative prosperity. Although some claim an optimum population is between 1 and 2 billion people, the world's current population is already 6.9 billion and growing. Demographers currently estimate that world population will peak around 2070 at 9 billion people, and then slowly decrease to 8.4 billion by 2100.

Critical Theory's Approach to Malthus

Sociologists who take a critical theory approach always deny that a social equilibrium is attainable, or that any social arrangement will benefit everyone equally. On the contrary, they say, people in power take actions that benefit themselves the most and support theories that justify their actions. For critical theorists, arguments about 'overpopulation' are a case in point. They would claim that the problems poor countries face today result not from overpopulation but from an unfair and harmful distribution of the world's wealth.

By this reasoning, recent famines that have plagued various less-developed parts of the world—such as Africa, Central and South America, and South Asia—are not a result of overpopulation. Rather, they are a result of improper land use, civil wars, and other social and political factors, such as protectionist tariffs established by more-developed countries to keep out goods and agricultural products from the Third World. Less-developed countries accordingly have trouble producing the food they need to eat or gaining the capital they need to industrialize.

So we cannot take famine, in itself, as proof of overpopulation. Indeed, in order to keep food prices in balance, many developed nations pay their farmers *not* to grow crops, even if this causes shortages elsewhere in the world. Furthermore, historical records and computer simulations used to study the effects of famine on human history suggest that, contrary to what Malthus argued, famine has *not* historically been a significant 'positive check' on population size. Nor can we assume plagues or epidemics are positive checks that result from overpopulation. In fact, they may indicate economic development is taking place (albeit perhaps unevenly).

Poverty and inequality often cause problems that are similar to those caused by overpopulation and may also contribute to overpopulation. For example, peasants often produce large numbers of children to do the farm work and care for them in their old age. They can see little benefit in having fewer children and they are wary about 'modern' farming techniques and 'modern lifestyles'. Eventually, for a variety of reasons, they are dragged or lured into modernity, and with economic development, the population explodes, at least in the short term. Only gradually does population growth slow down, especially in the cities. Then, a society enters a 'demographic transition' towards lower death and birth rates, leading eventually toward zero growth and less common starvation.

So, history shows that poor people have much to gain by reducing their fertility and much to lose by failing to do so. With lower death rates, they have less need for many children, especially once old-age security benefits become available. A large family—a benefit in farm work—is a liability in urban industrial societies, especially where children are expected to attend school for an extended period. In poorer nations, then, the problem is not merely too many people; it is also a shortage of capital for industrialization, and a lack of markets for their agricultural products. In this context, a large, rapidly growing population merely compounds the problems of poverty, dependency, plague, and famine.

So, faced with a rapidly growing population, many have come to advocate *zero population growth* (ZPG) as a temporary solution. Zero population growth occurs when births are exactly balanced by deaths. Under conditions of ZPG, births and deaths are equal. Then the size of the population remains constant over time—in the state of equilibrium Malthus was urging. From this standpoint, ZPG is a global strategy of survival, and not merely a national one.

Ways of Looking at . . . URBAN LIFE

How should we think about cities—those huge communities where a majority of people try to work out their lives in the company of strangers? The answer is not simple, and in the study of cities and urban built environments, we find a debate between functionalist and critical theories that is both fruitful and provocative.

Functionalism

Some functionalists would view social problems in the city as resulting naturally from growth and specialization. For example, more wealth in the city means more theft and robbery, higher density means more intense competition for local resources (like housing), and more privacy translates into more private vice, such as drug use.

Other functionalists focus on those tendencies of the city—its size, variety, and fluidity in particular—that promote social disorganization, weak social controls, and consequent deviance and distress. From this perspective, social problems such as crime, addiction, and mental illness are foreseeable consequences of urbanization. They are the price to be paid for the positive aspects of city life. While they hardly contribute to the quality and survival of city life, they illustrate the functional problem of finding a new social equilibrium in the context of rapid social change. (That said, sociologist Robert Merton famously argues that even crime, addiction, and mental illness are functional 'adaptations to anomie'.)

City life is profoundly different from rural and small town life. Pre-industrial communities were mainly small, rural settlements in which members shared the same experiences and developed similar values, norms, and identity. Émile Durkheim (1964 [1893]) called this *common conscience*. Moreover, the lives of these people were often interconnected in a tight, homogeneous social order, which Durkheim called *mechanical solidarity*. By contrast, the new urban-industrial society was based on interdependent, though not necessarily intimate, relationships. Linked together by *organic solidarity*, members of this new society were no longer self-sufficient; all were dependent on one another for survival and prosperity.

The main point to note about functionalist approaches is that they look for universal laws of social development and, especially, for the ways that particular institutions or arrangements—like cities—help society move to a new equilibrium, with a higher level of functioning.

Critical Theory

Unlike functionalists, critical theorists always ask whose interests are served by the actions of the dominant groups in society and their ideologies. These theorists attribute urban problems such as homelessness and poverty not to the effects of size, variety, and fluidity, but to the workings of capitalism. By their reckoning, cities suffer urban problems because no powerful group is interested in preventing this from happening. And unlike functionalists, critical theorists believe that solving urban problems requires more than housing—as important as this may be.

The problem of cities is, ultimately, a problem of economic inequality—an unequal distribution of urban wealth and poverty. This distribution of wealth determines whether city-dwellers will live or die, stay or leave. In many cities (especially in the US), well-off residents have fled the inner city to distant suburbs, suggesting a lack of interest in solving the urban problems facing poor people. In other cities of the world, well-off residents remain in the inner-cities in gated compounds or homes protected by walls and electronic security. This segregation also signifies a satisfaction with the prevailing degree of economic inequality.

Symbolic Interactionism

Symbolic interactionists study how people experience city life on an everyday basis. Georg Simmel (1950) was one of the earliest writers to take this approach. As noted in Chapter 1, Simmel argues that cities are so inherently stimulating and quick-paced that to prevent sensory overload, inhabitants need to reduce their sensitivity to events and people around them.

However, symbolic interactionists tend to doubt that everyone in the same structural setting—for example, in a city—has the same experience. Herbert Gans (1982), among others, focuses on how the meaning of city life varies among groups and subcultures. A *subculture* is a group of people who share some cultural traits of the larger society but who, as a group, also have their own distinctive values, beliefs, norms, style of dress, and behaviour. Urban subcultures allow individuals who are otherwise isolated within an impersonal city to form connections with others—often, their neighbours. An ethnic urban community is one common example of a subculture; skinheads and youth gangs are another kind of example. By this definition, the corporate elites, who determine the future of urban areas, are also an urban subculture.

Ways of Looking at . . .
THE ENVIRONMENT

Functionalism

Functionalists recognize that everyone is implicated in the pollution of the environment, some more than others perhaps. In a consumer society like ours, we seem willing to do almost anything to increase our current pleasure. So, functionalists are not surprised that modern people's activities have contributed to the pollution of their natural surroundings and the overharvesting of resources. Several types of cultural ideologies help support these ecologically harmful practices.

One example is the *cornucopia view of nature*. This way of thinking views nature as a storehouse of resources that exists only for the use of humans—especially, those humans currently living. Another environmentally unfriendly belief is the *growth ethic*, especially popular in North America. This view, linked closely with *materialism*, celebrates the (imagined) ability of technology to easily solve all the problems in the world, including those that technology itself has caused. It promotes the belief that things will always get better and therefore encourages us to discard just about everything in favour of the production and consumption of new items.

Finally, the Western notion of *individualism*, which privileges personal goals and desires over collective interests, is the driving force behind the so-called 'tragedy of the commons'. This term, coined by environmentalist Garrett Hardin in 1968, refers to the unwelcome result of actions by many self-interested individuals, acting independently, that taken together deplete a shared limited resource, even though none intended to have this effect.

Critical Theory

A critical theorist will emphasize that when environmental problems arise, they hurt the poor more often and more severely than they do the rich.

Over 90 per cent of disaster-related deaths, for instance, occur among the poor populations of developing countries. By contrast, developed nations experience 75 per cent of disaster-related economic damage, since there is more property to lose in developed societies. So, for example, in Pakistan, Indonesia, or Ethiopia, a drought can lead to catastrophic famine and thousands of deaths. An agricultural drought in Canada's prairies, by contrast, would result in reduced crops and even farm bankruptcies but almost no deaths. Note, further, that of the 25 per cent of the world's population currently living in regions prone to natural disaster, most live in less-developed countries (Smith, 2001).

Sociological research shows that disasters result more often from 'the spread of capitalism and the marginalization of the poor than from the effects of geophysical events' and offers possible solutions that involve 'the redistribution of wealth and power in society to provide access to resources [rather] than . . . the application of science and technology to control nature' (Smith, 2001). The destruction caused by the South Asian tsunami of December 2004, for example, would have been greatly lessened had the region's protective coastal mangrove forests not been significantly destroyed earlier to make room for aquaculture farms and upscale tourist resorts, and had the coral reefs not been slowly decimated by years of unsustainable fishing methods.

Symbolic Interactionism

The symbolic interactionist perspective studies how the meanings and thought patterns learned in social interaction affect environmental problems, with a particular focus on how they influence people's perception of these problems.

environmental geography
The systematic study of the interaction between humans and the surrounding natural world, focusing on the human impact on the environment and vice versa.

Here, the social constructionist framework is especially relevant. Sociologists who approach environmental problems from this perspective ask why and how certain environmental problems enter the public consciousness: What kinds of 'claims' make the greatest impact, and under what circumstances? For instance, sociologists Clay Schoenfeld, Robert Meier, and Robert Griffin (1979) have looked at how environmental issues have become a 'problem' in the public's eye. How and why, for example, does the greenhouse effect become a widespread public concern one year, and AIDS or women's rights or child labour in India become a concern another year?

The symbolic interactionist perspective also offers insights into how environmental polluters manipulate symbols to protect themselves from criticism. Many companies and businesses, increasingly sensitive to greater public awareness over their impact on the environment, have attempted to boost their image and profits by using a public relations strategy known as 'greenwashing'. This technique involves redesigning and repackaging their products as 'environmentally friendly' or 'green', playing to (some) consumers' wish to help solve the environmental problem by purchasing ecologically friendly items.

Feminist Theory

The feminist perspective questions the prevailing capitalist celebration of increasing growth, unlimited resources, and unregulated commerce. Ecofeminism emerged as a social movement that linked the exploitation of marginalized groups with the degradation of nature in Western cultural values.

Ecofeminists, for example, unite around a central belief in the convergence between women and nature. Françoise d'Eaubonne coined the term *ecofeminism* 'to identify theoretical work on the potential for women to bring about an ecological revolution and to ensure the survival of the planet' (Humphrey et al, 2002). Ecofeminism, then, is a value system, a social movement, and a practice. It encourages political analysis that explores the links between androcentrism and environmental destruction (Rynbrandt and Deegan, 2002). Ecofeminists adopt a 'feminine' way of engaging with environmental social problems that is said to be nurturing, co-operative, and communal.

A central argument for ecofeminists is that the domination over women, leading to gender inequality, is analogous to domination over nature that leads to environmental destruction. Some ecofeminists explicitly link the exploitation of women and the 'rape of the wild' (Plant, 1990; Rynbrant and Deegan, 2002). In short, according to Gaard (1993) the environment as a social problem 'is a feminist issue'.

Where, then, is the natural world headed, and how will humanity resolve some of its problems around population, ecology, and resource depletion? This was the concern of a landmark study carried out nearly 40 years ago under the sponsorship of the Club of Rome.

Classic Studies
The Limits to Growth

As the world population rapidly approached 4 billion people around the third quarter of the twentieth century—it currently exceeds 6 billion—researchers Donella H. Meadows, Dennis L. Meadows, Jørgen Randers, and William W. Behrens III published *The Limits to Growth* (1972), a book that examines the consequences of human population growth for human survival. This classic study addresses many of the key issues and concerns of all sociologists, as we will see.

These four authors, international experts who assembled at the MIT Sloan School of Management, had been commissioned to write this book by the Club of Rome. The so-called 'Club' had been founded a few years earlier as a global think tank (or policy institute) focusing on pressing international issues. To carry out their commission, the authors created the 'World3 model', a computerized method for studying the future of the world by simulating interlinked changes over a 100-year-long imaginary history. The goal of this computer simulation was to track how complex human systems have changed, and will change, over time. They built the model to investigate five major trends of global concern: accelerating industrialization, rapid population growth, widespread malnutrition, depletion of non-renewable resources, and a deteriorating environment.

The researchers assumed that each of these variables increases exponentially while the capability of technology to increase availability of resources grows linearly—an assumption as old as the first demographer, Thomas Malthus. The results of the simulation shocked the world and provoked debate about 'global overshoot'. Most of all, the research focused attention on humanity's tendency to demand too much of Nature—much more than the biosphere can readily supply or replace.

The Limits to Growth was not planned to make specific predictions about the future, so much as to examine how exponential growth affects finite resources. The book analyzed 12 different scenarios, which all showed that, should then-current economic growth and population trends continue, within 100 years the world's natural resources would be either almost exhausted or too expensive to buy. Hugely influential at the time, the report was translated into dozens of languages and read by millions. It came to two key conclusions: First, if population, industrialization, pollution, food production, and resource depletion continue to grow at the current rate, humanity will reach 'the limit to growth' on this planet at some time in the next 100 years. The result will be an immediate and uncorrectable decline in both world population and industrial capacity.

Second, however, it is still possible to change these current growth patterns, to bring about a state of environmental and economic stability. Slowing growth would ideally mean achieving a state of global equilibrium, so that all human basic material needs are fulfilled and every person can reach his or her individual human potential. However, it may not be possible to achieve this equilibrium at the highest current levels of human consumption. Cutbacks in spending, buying, and consuming would be needed. Said another way, it would be impossible to achieve world equilibrium at North American standards of living, though it would be possible to achieve equilibrium at standards far higher than those currently enjoyed by most of humanity.

The authors conclude that the sooner people begin to strive for global equilibrium, the sooner it will be attained, and doing this would eliminate the dire risks of worldwide system collapse spelled out in their computer model. However, these conclusions were widely criticized and, in the end, ignored. Clearly, people—especially in the wealthy West—were unwilling to hear this message, much less take steps to lower their own standard of living in the interests of humanity.

Yet, nothing in the past 40 years has invalidated the book's central warning that humanity is in trouble, living beyond its means. If anything, that fact is even clearer today than it was when our population was a third smaller, and before we understood the dangers of climate change. Continuing interest in the topic gave rise, in 2004, to an update of the classic work, simply called *Limits to Growth: The 30-Year Update* by Meadows, Meadows, and Randers. Here, the authors tried again to gain public attention with their message.

In the updated version, the authors stress that humanity is coming seriously close to 'global overshoot'. The new book asserts that in the next 70 years or so, the system-collapse will no longer be preventable, as environmental decline is almost inevitable. Instead, the challenge will be containing and limiting damage to the Earth and to humanity (Meadows et al, 2004). The authors conclude that it is too late for sustainable development. Now we must choose between unrestrained collapse and what we might call 'harm reduction'—a conscious reduction (to supportable levels) of the energy and materials we consume. In this updated version, World3 is used to provide 10 new scenarios, in which the gap between the rich and poor expands, the industrial production in developed nations declines, and essential non-renewable resources become harder to obtain and more expensive to use.

Still, the book remains largely unread, the message largely ignored.

Why Demography?

Why begin a book about sociology with a long discussion of demography—the study of population? Well, we might begin by noting that all people live in populations. In early human history, community populations were small—sometimes numbering no more than a few dozen, at most a few hundred. Even today, hunter-gatherer communities remain small. By contrast, modern cities are large, containing millions or even tens of millions of people. Clearly, people can adapt to living in communities of widely varying sizes.

Demographers are trained to ask a variety of important questions about population. First, does it matter socially whether a human population is large or small? Second, does it matter socially whether a population is densely concentrated in space—that is, if the population is crowded? Third, does the makeup or composition of a population, such as the number of young people versus old, females versus males, or the mixture of occupational skills, matter? Fourth, does it matter whether the population is mainly healthy or unhealthy, and whether the lifespan is short or long? And fifth (related to the fourth), does it matter whether people pass through the population quickly or slowly? That is, do they migrate a lot or a little? Do they live a long time or a short time?

The answer to all these questions is yes—it matters. So, we need to consider the significance of these population features: how and why they serve as important material conditions of social life. We also need to ask whether changes in the population lead to, or can result from, changes in other societal processes. We will find out that they do, and that population processes and social processes are closely intertwined. Rapid population shifts can change societies. Our purpose is to find out how, why, and to what extent; understanding this will give us important insights into the evolution of social life.

Population size is important for several reasons. First, a large population puts more pressure on the natural environment than a small population does. Second, a large population is more likely to innovate—to invent new technologies and develop new ways of producing food and wealth—or else break into smaller populations. Large populations (and this is especially true of large, rapidly growing populations) need the systematic production of food—that is, agriculture. There are no hunter-gatherer societies with large populations.

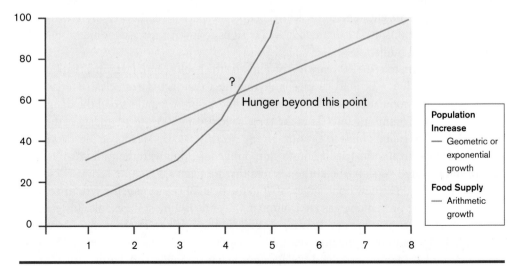

Figure 2.1   Malthus's Theory of Population and Resource Growth

Source: Feed Others at www.feedothers.org.

Conversely, industrial, mainly post-agricultural, societies don't really need large populations to the same degree. Population quality is more important than population quantity; so the growth rate typically slows down dramatically there, until populations actually start to shrink.

Large populations are usually dense or crowded, and often they live in cities. So, when the human population became very large in the last few hundred years, it also became mainly urban. Urban communities, housed not merely horizontally but also vertically in tall buildings, can hold many more people than rural communities, and this vertical increase results in more crowding. Urban life is clearly a very different experience than rural life, and this will be examined later in this chapter. The important point to remember is that as humanity grew in number, people changed from transient hunter-gatherers, to settled agriculturalists, then to urban industrialists and post-industrialists. Population growth was both a cause and consequence of these economic and geographic changes.

Third, large, dense populations tend to invent new social and economic roles, or as Durkheim said, they divide the labour of society in specialized ways. Productive tasks are broken into smaller, detailed tasks that require training. Increasingly, social roles are distinguished not only by age and sex but also by characteristics associated with skill, aptitude, and interest.

Moreover, within any set of social roles, the population composition makes a difference. For example, it makes a difference whether a population of 20,000 people is composed of 95 per cent men and only 5 per cent women—that is, 19 men for every woman—or 50 per cent men and 50 per cent women. A predominantly male population is typical of a frontier town—say, a mining or mill town—with many single, transient, young men who often behave in disorderly ways. A population evenly split between males and females is typical of a settled family community that includes children and old people. Here, disorder poses much less of a problem.

Many Canadian cities are densely populated and largely diverse.

Just as sex ratio clearly makes a difference, so does the age composition. It makes a difference whether the population is 'young', where half the population is under the age of 15; or 'old', where half the population is over the age of 45. A young population demands a good deal of spending on education, whereas an old population needs spending on pensions and health care.

The health and longevity of a population also affect how a society works. A healthy, long-lived population is likely to contain a higher level of **human capital**. Other things being equal, this human capital—based on the health, education, and training of the population—contributes to higher productivity and increased prosperity. As well, leaving aside immigration, a healthier, longer-living society has a lower rate of population turnover. As a result, people develop stronger loyalties to the community. And with population stability, the social networks on which people rely for information and support remain intact longer.

At the same time, an older, longer-living society relies more on immigration to provide needed population renewal through new skills and human capital, which the older community is unable to provide for itself. So, population turnover has both a negative and a positive effect. On the negative side, it continuously undermines traditional culture and existing social networks. On the positive side, however, it continuously re-invigorates the culture and introduces new social elements that may enrich existing social networks through diversity. In Canada, demographically an aged and aging society, this is especially important, since many immigrants are young parents of young families.

Note, finally, that such changes—for example, a sudden rejuvenation of the population through increased childbearing, such as occurred during the so-called 'baby boom' after World War II in North America—have a huge effect on culture, politics, and social institutions. Moreover, as Canada and other Western countries are finding, a dramatic aging of the population (through less and less childbearing) also has a huge effect. Such changes in the age structure lead to dramatic shifts in the relations between generations.

Population Trends Reveal a Society's History

We can learn a lot about societies and their histories by examining population trends. By noting patterns in **population composition**—differences and similarities in age and gender—we can make good guesses about what a society has gone through, whether a baby boom, an epidemic, a war, or another circumstance that has significantly affected the population.

Often, demographers use a model called a **population pyramid** to study such trends. A baby boom substantially, and usually unexpectedly, increases the number of children born in a given **cohort**, and thus shows as a bulge on the bottom of the pyramid. If a population pyramid reveals a decrease in both males and females of all ages, this most likely indicates an epidemic, such as the plague, known as the Black Death, during the Middle Ages in Europe. A war manifests on the pyramid as a sudden disproportion of men to women, the result of a sudden loss of thousands or even millions of young men in a few years.

Sometimes, a dent in the number of men or women in a given cohort can also indicate gendercide, an unfortunate reality in some parts of the world. The term *gendercide*, introduced in Mary Anne Warren's book *Gendercide: The Implications of Sex Selection* (1985), is often perceived as synonymous with *femicide*. This is because members of some cultures in Asia and Africa who value sons over daughters may sometimes kill their female infants, who are seen as economic liabilities. We know about this, often, through an inspection of the population pyramid, since such murders significantly lower the female-to-male ratio.

Ironically, when the many men born into such cultures reach maturity, they encounter a shortage of available brides (Plambech, 2005). They may use different methods to solve

human capital

A skill or skill set, usually including educational attainment or job-related experiences, that enhances a worker's value on the job; the result of foregone income and a long-term investment in personal improvement.

population composition

The makeup or mix of different social types in a population; for example, the different numbers of men and women, old and young people.

population pyramid

A graphic depiction of the age–sex composition of a population.

cohort

A set of people with a common origin or starting point; *birth cohort*—a set of people born in the same year or set of years.

this problem that sometimes include bride kidnapping and trafficking of women, to meet the demand for young women (Handrahan, 2004; Grant, 2005; Harris, 2006). More often, perhaps, the men import 'mail-order' brides from poorer countries: for example, some Taiwanese men import brides from mainland China, Vietnam, or the Philippines.

However, not only women are targeted for gendercide. Men too can be targets of gendercide—especially men of 'battle-age'. In some war-torn parts of the world, each conflicting side systematically kills able-bodied civilian men on the other side to dispose of potential future threats (Jones, 2000 and 2006; Lindner, 2002; Buchanan, 2002; Holter, 2002).

In short, the inspection of population pyramids can give us an insight into historical events we might never have imagined. And, if we put two population pyramids of the same country side by side, we may be able to draw interesting conclusions about the way the population has been changing. For example, note the population pyramids in Figure 2.2, created from statistics in Finland.

The 1917 pyramid is typical of a country with a high fertility rate. In this case, children aged 0 to 14 make up the largest percentage of the population: 35 per cent on this graph. As we can see, by 2006 the ratio of young people has drastically fallen, hovering somewhere around 17 per cent. The second graph illustrates the typical age-sex pyramid for a Western, developed nation: with a birth rate hovering around zero, the graph no longer even resembles a pyramid. It is nearly rectangular, meaning that population growth is at a replacement level. Each year, nearly the same number die as are born that year; and nearly as many people are 67 years old as are 7 years old.

World Population

The increase of world population in the last three centuries has been phenomenal, when considered in the context of world population change over the whole of human history. As

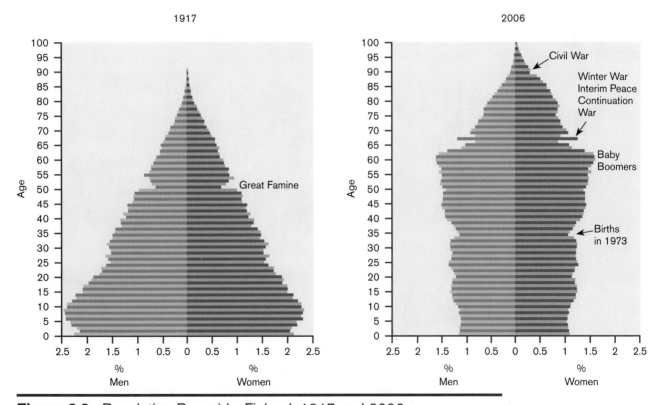

Figure 2.2 Population Pyramids, Finland, 1917 and 2006

Source: Adapted from Statistics Finland (2007).

Figure 2.3 shows, world population was relatively unchanging for most of human history until the eighteenth century. It began to increase slightly as the quality of life improved through better sanitation and more access to food. In 1750, the world's population was only 800 million people; today, it is just under 7 billion, and most of this increase has occurred in the last two centuries (UN Population Division, 2009).

In studying the population history of humanity, American demographer Ansley Coale (1974) divided human history into two parts. The first part covers the beginning of human-ity's existence over a million years ago (the Stone Age) to around 1750 CE. As mentioned already, this period was characterized by slow population growth—almost no growth at all—with the number of people being born more or less staying consistently equal to the number dying. From 1750 to the present, however, the population grew exponentially, meaning a larger number of people has been added each year for the last 260 years.

Thus, the human population reached its first billion in 1804, and each successive billion has arrived more quickly than the previous one: the second billion occurred in 1927, the third in 1961, the fourth in 1974, the fifth in 1987, and the sixth in 1999 (UN Population Division, 2009). Maybe it would help to think of it this way: humanity's second billion people arrived just before your grandmother was born, the third billion just before your mother was born, the fourth billion around the time your older sister was born, the fifth billion just before you were born, and the sixth billion around the time your baby brother was born. That's billions of births to pack into your own short family history!

Note, however, that the world population is not growing as quickly today as it was during the last century. This is due to a worldwide fertility decline that took hold in the past few decades. If worldwide fertility levels continue to fall in the economically developing, as well as the developed, countries, the United Nations predicts world population will reach about 9 billion in 2050, then soon start to level off (UN Population Division, 2009).

The key mechanism here is childbearing: women around the world are having fewer babies. Globally, total fertility is projected by the United Nations to decrease from roughly 2.56 children per woman to only 2.02 children per woman 40 years from now (UN Population Division, 2009). The decline of one-half child over 40 years may not sound

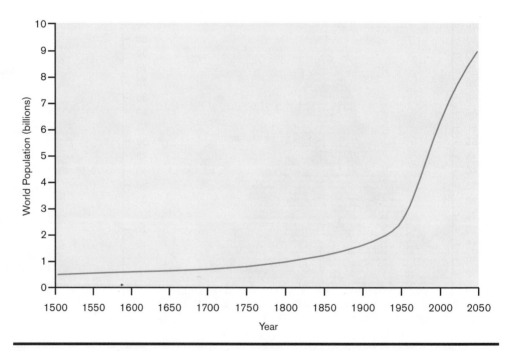

Figure 2.3 World Population, Recorded and Projected 1500–2050

Source: Adapted from Mongabay.com (2008).

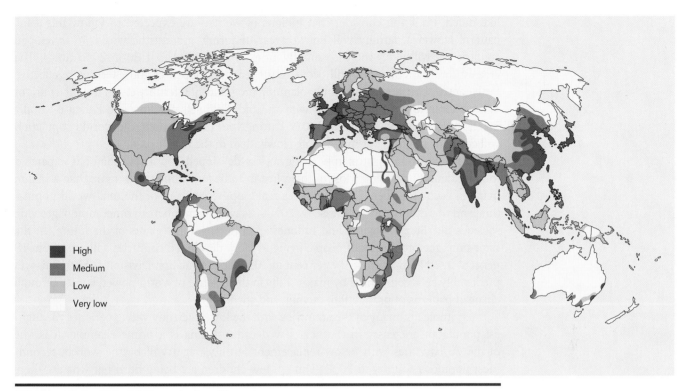

Figure 2.4   World Population Density

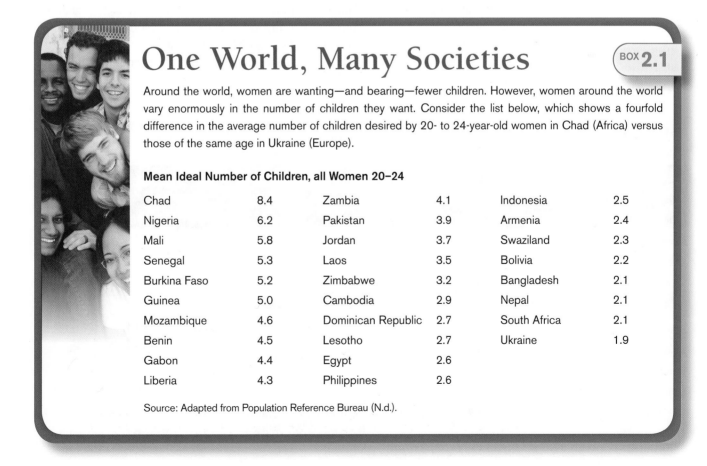

One World, Many Societies

BOX **2.1**

Around the world, women are wanting—and bearing—fewer children. However, women around the world vary enormously in the number of children they want. Consider the list below, which shows a fourfold difference in the average number of children desired by 20- to 24-year-old women in Chad (Africa) versus those of the same age in Ukraine (Europe).

Mean Ideal Number of Children, all Women 20–24

Chad	8.4	Zambia	4.1	Indonesia	2.5
Nigeria	6.2	Pakistan	3.9	Armenia	2.4
Mali	5.8	Jordan	3.7	Swaziland	2.3
Senegal	5.3	Laos	3.5	Bolivia	2.2
Burkina Faso	5.2	Zimbabwe	3.2	Bangladesh	2.1
Guinea	5.0	Cambodia	2.9	Nepal	2.1
Mozambique	4.6	Dominican Republic	2.7	South Africa	2.1
Benin	4.5	Lesotho	2.7	Ukraine	1.9
Gabon	4.4	Egypt	2.6		
Liberia	4.3	Philippines	2.6		

Source: Adapted from Population Reference Bureau (N.d.).

like much, until you consider that billions of women are expected to follow this same pattern. However, fertility will not decrease uniformly around the world. In developed countries, it will likely increase slightly, from 1.64 in 2008 to 1.80 in 2050 (ibid). The greatest fertility reductions will occur in the least developed countries, as more effective birth control, education, and family planning programs pull fertility down from the current 4.39 children to 2.41 children per woman (ibid; Caldwell, Phillips, and Barkat-e-Khuda, 2002; Morgan, 2003; Campbell, 2007). During your lifetime, then, the world's population will continue to grow, but much more slowly than in the recent past.

The proportion of humanity living in less-developed countries today has expanded to more than 80 per cent. Most of them live in India and China, with more than a billion living in each. Together, these countries make up 37 per cent of the total world population, and this number will increase by 2050—as will the numbers in other rapidly growing societies like Brazil, Nigeria, and Indonesia, all demographic giants of the future. At the same time, the proportion of people living in more-developed countries will drop from 18 per cent in 2008 to less than 14 per cent in 2050 (UN Population Division, 2009). This will predictably be accompanied by major shifts in the balance of world power, largely through changed patterns of production, buying, and spending.

Yet, ironically, many of the countries with the lowest fertility will experience the highest population increases in the next few decades. China is a prime example. It is one of the 76 countries with below-replacement fertility, yet it will be the world's second-most populous country in 2050. Though few children are being born per woman, there is already a huge Chinese population. Thus, even though China's population growth is expected to slow down over the twenty-first century, it will continue rising in the first half (UN Population Division, 2009).

In Canada, a continued decline in fertility and continued aging of the baby boomers means that a large part of the Canadian population will soon be elderly. In fact, Canada and many other industrialized countries (especially in Scandinavia and Northern Europe) will have the largest, oldest population of elderly people in all of human history. We will discuss the implications of this scenario, including its impact on health care, economy, politics, and other aspects of society, in more detail in Chapter 8, which is about age groups.

Table 2.1 Distribution of the World Population by Development Groups and Major Areas, Estimates and Projections According to Different Variants, 1950–2050

Major Area	World Population (%)						
	1950	1975	2009	2050			
				Low	Medium	High	Constant
More-developed regions	32.1	25.8	18.1	14.2	13.9	13.8	11.4
Less-developed regions	67.9	74.2	81.9	85.8	86.1	86.2	88.6
Least-developed countries	7.9	8.8	12.2	18.4	18.3	18.1	22.4
Other less-developed countries	60.0	65.4	69.7	67.5	67.8	68.1	66.2
Africa	9.0	10.3	14.8	22.0	21.8	21.7	27.2
Asia	55.5	58.6	60.3	57.0	57.2	57.4	54.5
Europe	21.6	16.6	10.7	7.6	7.6	7.5	6.0
Latin America and the Caribbean	6.6	8.0	8.5	7.9	8.0	8.1	7.6
Northern America	6.8	6.0	5.1	5.0	4.9	4.8	4.2
Oceania	0.5	0.5	0.5	0.6	0.6	0.6	0.5

Source: UN Population Division (2009), Table I.2.

Table 2.2 Total Fertility for the World by Development Groups and Major Areas, Estimates and Projections According to Different Variants, 1970–1975, 2005–2010, and 2045–2050

| Major Area | Total Fertility (average number of children per woman) | | | | | |
| | 1970–1975 | 2005–2010 | 2045–2050 | | | |
			Low	Medium	High	Constant
World	4.32	2.56	1.54	2.02	2.51	3.24
More-developed regions	2.17	1.64	1.31	1.80	2.30	1.73
Less-developed regions	5.18	2.73	1.56	2.05	2.53	3.40
Least-developed countries	6.74	4.39	1.93	2.41	2.90	5.04
Other less-developed countries	4.97	2.46	1.44	1.93	2.42	2.84
Africa	6.69	4.61	1.91	2.40	2.90	5.06
Asia	4.76	2.35	1.41	1.90	2.40	2.68
Europe	2.19	1.50	1.30	1.80	2.29	1.52
Latin America and the Caribbean	5.01	2.26	1.32	1.82	2.32	2.41
Northern America	2.07	2.04	1.35	1.85	2.35	2.05
Oceania	3.29	2.44	1.49	1.98	2.48	2.79

Source: UN Population Division (2009), Table II.1.

The characteristics of populations—their age composition, sex composition, and size, among others—are important for understanding societal, environmental, and economic problems, and for developing solutions. One significant concern related to population growth is that of the environment, since an increasing population means more consumption and intensified pressure on the natural surroundings. These implications are discussed in the next section.

Classic Studies
Risk Society: Towards a New Modernity

In pre-modern societies, people tended to see natural dangers as God-made or supernatural in origin. When disasters occurred—plagues, wars, droughts, or earthquakes—people deemed these events to be the uncontrollable results of fate and destiny. Today, we generally no longer hold these views. Most of us understand human-produced risks such as wars and pollution—even plagues and droughts—to be results of modernity itself. So, in principle, they should be under our control. However, in practice, they remain largely uncontrollable, unexpected, and unintended consequences of modern humanity trying to control nature. Sociologist Ulrich Beck was the first to understand the origin and significance of these risks, so he labelled contemporary society a 'risk society'.

In 1986, Beck published his most famous work, *Risk Society: Towards a New Modernity*, a book that has become one of the most influential sociological works of the late twentieth century.

There, Beck emphasizes that in this era of advanced modernity, societies are dominated by the presence of manmade risks. Essential to understanding modern risk is the concept of 'reflexive modernization' (Beck, 1992 [1986]: 1–2). Beck uses this term to describe the shift in thought between the modern and postmodern eras on the social role of technology.

In the modern era, people had almost unlimited confidence in the social and economic benefits of technology and assumed that technology would forever improve. Eventually, however, they began to doubt the benefits derived from technology, due largely to many catastrophes that resulted from technology gone wrong: oil spills, nuclear power melt-downs, toxic wastes leaching into the ground water, and so on. The BP oil spill in the Gulf of Mexico in 2010, the greatest oil spill in human history, exemplifies the problem. People knew how to dig a hole to release the oil they wanted, but not how to plug the hole when the pipes exploded. The result: billions of dollars of damage to property and untold damage to wildlife and the world ecosystem.

Today, in so-called postmodern society, we are more aware of the dangers associated with technological advancements. We know that no technological benefits come without risks and even harms; so by its nature, our high-technology society is a highly risky society. Our new 'reflexive modernization' not only re-defines risk but also begins to imagine ways to manage it. According to Beck, risk is 'a systematic way of dealing with hazards and insecurities induced and introduced by modernization' (ibid: 21).

In the last half of the twentieth century, we increasingly looked to science and rational expertise to manage risk, by learning more about nature and society and by rationally calculating the costs of what we don't yet understand (ibid). International conferences, like the one on climate change in Copenhagen in 2009, exemplify this process of knowledge-sharing. However, the new reflexive modernization has also called into doubt the previously unchallenged authority of science in human affairs. Today, many purposely ignore the findings of science, criticize their imperfections, or call them into question based on traditional beliefs (e.g., biblical scripture). The Enlightenment notion that science could do no harm, only good (through progress), no longer enjoys universal assent.

Many past and recent events support Beck's ideas of a risk society, a classic example being the Chernobyl accident of 26 April 1986. At the Chernobyl nuclear power plant, located in Ukraine, an explosion in one of the plant's reactors released deadly amounts of radioactivity. Over the next decades, thousands died or contracted radiation sickness. The full toll of this disaster is yet unknown, for nuclear radiation dissipates very slowly. This, and other technological accidents, caused people to pay closer attention to Beck's questioning of the advancement of technology in a social context. Humanity may continue to pay for the Chernobyl accident—through cancers and genetic mutations—for generations to come.

Beck asserts that such risks are inevitable. 'Risk is not the same as catastrophe, but the anticipation of the future catastrophe in the present. As a result, risk leads a dubious, insidious, would-be, fictitious, allusive existence: it is existent *and* non-existent, present *and* absent, doubtful *and* real' (ibid: 3). As such, the 'risk society' must be a cautious, careful, and even fearful society. Moreover, Beck states that risk is both an individual and social responsibility: 'Accordingly, two concepts of responsibility can be distinguished: an *individual* responsibility that the decision maker accepts for the consequences of his or her decision, which must be distinguished from responsibility for others, *social* responsibility' (ibid).

Critics of the *Risk Society* hypothesis contend that natural risks and social risks have always been interconnected. If so, these critiques weaken Beck's claim that Western society has transformed from a safe and organized industrial society to a uniquely chaotic and dangerous society. Nonetheless, Ulrich Beck's *Risk Society* offers us a significant insight into the effects of global risk on social and political development. Beck's ideas have become increasingly relevant in analyzing the troubled interaction between humanity and the natural environment, giving us crucial insights in an era troubled by globalization and ecological destruction.

The Natural Environment

Today, compared to a generation or two ago, we are all much more aware of the natural environment. This is due in large part to the rise of the environmental movement as expressed in the important work of environmental and climate scientists, as well as campaigning scientists, such as Rachel Carson, David Suzuki, and Ulrich Beck. Equally, organizations like Greenpeace have raised our awareness of deeply problematic issues, from Alberta's tar sands projects to the accumulation of plastic in our oceans. In particular, former US vice-president Al Gore's award-winning film *An Inconvenient Truth* drew needed international attention to climate change.

Further, consider the success of International Earth Day, held every April 22 since 1990. According to Earth Day's website, in 2009 more than 6 million Canadians joined 1 billion people around the world in organizing events to promote environmental awareness and responsibility. Also, recall the success of the World Wildlife Fund's Earth Hour, held every year on March 28. A poll by the WWF shows that more than half of Canada's adult population (52 per cent) participated in the 2009 event (World Wildlife Fund, 2009). Nearly 4,000 cities took part, and this number is likely to grow, showing that people today are concerned about improving our threatened natural environment.

By natural environment, we mean all of those natural processes that affect us as animals having survival needs similar to those of other animals. Take for example the processes that affect the fertility of the land: the availability of soil nutrients, water, sunlight, and so on. All humans need food and water; concerns about the food supply and clean water are essential. This is why Thomas Malthus was interested in the relationship between food supply and population growth.

Humans compete with other species for survival. For the most part, we have developed tools and strategies that give us an advantage over these species. For example, we have invented weapons to hunt some animals for food and keep predators at bay. We have learned how to domesticate and harvest animals for food—chickens, cows, pigs—and constantly improve our efficiency at doing so. We are still struggling to keep up with the rapid and sometimes fatal mutation of viruses and bacteria, but millions are being spent to win this war.

To this end, we have learned to understand and control many biochemical interactions, through the creation of pesticides, herbicides, fungicides, and antibiotics and other medicines. We are increasingly able to manage our relationships with problematic species—from bacteria to protozoa, mosquitoes to cockroaches, invasive plants to cereal rusts. Currently, the war with our natural competitors is at a standstill: it is unlikely we could ever fully destroy our smaller competitors (and, given the complexity of the biosphere, it would be unwise to try). So, we usually keep them under control; but now and then, an epidemic like SARS, swine or avian flu, or HIV/AIDS reminds us that even our best efforts can fail.

To survive in the natural environment—to produce enough food and shelter, for example—and develop the tools we need for protection against other species, we need to harvest and process natural resources. Modern medicine depends on modern pharmaceuticals, but these rely, in turn, on natural minerals and plants. The same is true of modern agriculture, which relies on mineral fertilizers. To heat our homes and transport our food we still depend on petroleum-based fuels. The plastics we use for food transport and storage also rely on petroleum. To build our homes we need wood from trees; granite, limestone, and sand for concrete and bricks; iron ore and bauxite for steel; and other materials. Clearly, to fulfill our most basic needs, we depend on natural resources: water, minerals, plants, and petroleum. And of course, we crave luxuries too, from televisions to CD players to cars to home furnishings. These too are all derived from natural resources, all requiring energy to manufacture. Finally, the manufacturing processes themselves almost always take large amounts of water.

For all these reasons, today water is an especially valuable resource, and its rapid depletion by (mainly) developed nations will increasingly make water conservation even more important. As we know, humans depend on water for drinking, washing, and cleaning, but also for economic survival. Water is used in manufacturing, mining, agriculture,

After the Chernobyl disaster of 1986, people began to doubt the benefits derived from technology. Society became more aware of the risks involved in highly developed technology.

and energy production, as well as for other purposes. According to a 2008 report by the Population Reference Bureau, 'modern society's demands on water grew rapidly during the last century [and] . . . global water consumption grew six-fold—twice the rate of population growth in the same period' (PRB, 2009). This consumption has been made possible by the building of dams and reservoirs, which affect over 50 per cent of the river basins in the world. However, the water available to humanity is not equally distributed. Currently, 2.3 billion people live in areas that lack an adequate water supply, and by 2050, 3.5 billion people will be in this situation (ibid).

Media Distortion

BOX **2.2**

Another Fight Over Global Warming

According to a film aired in the UK on 8 March 2007, global warming is a lie. *The Great Global Warming Swindle* claims that climate change observed in the twentieth century was caused not by carbon dioxide emissions, but by sunspot activity, and that climate-change scientists are perpetrating a hoax by misrepresenting and distorting data.

However, an investigation by the British newspaper *The Independent* showed that the film's makers have themselves used faulty or misused data, or have failed to locate readily available data that would refute its claims. The film, *The Independent* claims, appears to be guilty of the very practices that it purports to expose in the science of climate change.

Source: Adapted from Connor (2007) and other sources.

Like water, most of the natural resources we need are non-renewable: there is only so much petroleum, aluminum, iron, and wood on (or in) the Earth. Once we have used it all . . . well, no one knows how to finish that sentence yet. One preventative strategy is recycling. Another is to invent alternatives (for example, nuclear energy) or find natural alternatives (for example, wind or solar power). A third strategy is to find another planet to inhabit, or perhaps to look for new resources in currently inaccessible places (for instance, under the sea or at the centre of the Earth). A fourth is to reduce the rate at which we use these resources; however, this is only a short-term answer—it only slows down the inevitable disappearance of these vital finite resources.

Location, Location, Location

When thinking about the natural environment, we also need to think about location. Where people live influences the location of environmental problems and costs of importing needed resources. This fact gives rise to the study of **human geography**, which is also important to sociological analysis.

Where do people live, and why? In addition, how does location affect people's social lives? A preliminary answer is that historically, people have lived near bodies of water. Besides the immediate biological necessity, water is also essential for traditional communication and transport networks, sanitation, and irrigation. Mountains have also long provided homes, with their own advantages and limitations. Often there is enough water available in streams or glacial runoff, and food can be produced from grazing animals and light agriculture. Minerals are often found in mountains (coal, for example), as well as timber and stone for housing. And importantly, mountain settlements are easy to defend from attack. Often, they are hard to travel through and thus they discourage visitors, but this difficulty can be an advantage for mountain-dwellers who want their privacy.

There are many other kinds of natural environments—plains and prairies, forests and jungles, deserts, and rain forests, for example—and they all provide opportunities and challenges for people to secure food, shelter, transport, and communication. Climatic variations are also factors affecting the human lifestyle: living in a hot climate (near the equator) is different from living in a cold climate (far from the equator). The diverse combinations of location, climate, and terrain provide a wide variety of human experiences, natural resources, and inter-species competitions. In this way, they influence the kinds of social and cultural life that develop within a region.

Consider the following example: Because people who live near water—whether on the Atlantic coast or the Mississippi River, say—have more encounters with travellers and strangers, they are more likely to develop a tolerant, cosmopolitan, and

human geography
The systematic study of the location of human enterprises and characteristics; for example, health, education, commerce and trade; closely linked to other social sciences like sociology.

One alternative to using non-renewable resources is to develop ways to use natural alternatives such as wind power.

changing culture. In the early twentieth century, New Orleans, a port city located where the mighty Mississippi River empties into the Gulf of Mexico, was populated by traders and sailors who spoke French, Spanish, and English, and by the descendants of black slaves from Africa. It's no wonder, then, that New Orleans was the birthplace of jazz music, with both African and European roots, and of Creole food, which is a fusion of many different cuisines.

By contrast, people who live in mountains—for example, in the Ozarks of the United States, or some regions of the Middle East and Eastern Europe—have few contacts with outsiders and are thus much more likely to preserve a traditional, insular culture. They are also more likely to be warlike and suspicious—to be fierce and cunning fighters, a skill noted even by the early Romans in their battles with the Basque tribes of Andorra and the Samnite tribes of central Italy. However, these tendencies do not apply to all peoples who live in mountainous regions. For instance, people who live in the shadow of the Alps in Europe are not typically described as insular, so clearly other factors are at work as well. As sociologists, we cannot be geographic determinists—imagining that geography has uniform, inevitable effects on human societies—any more than we can afford to be technological determinists. That said, we cannot underestimate the role of geography.

Buildings and Cityscapes

Buildings and cityscapes provide a human-made environment that interacts with, and intervenes in, the relation between humans and the natural environment. In this sense, we can think of houses as tools for protecting us from harsh weather, roads as constructed 'rivers', and cities as planned human ecosystems, not unlike beehives or anthills.

Throughout history, cities have always been centres of commerce and administration, locations of trade and government. Therefore, the historical rise of cities coincided with the rise of markets and states. Generally, cities have relied on other regions for the supply of food, importing most of it from rural areas. The growth of cities, then, was only possible when surplus food was available in rural areas. This means that cities could not come into being until the development of settled agriculture and systematic farming techniques: plowing, irrigation, and crop rotation, for example.

That said, from time to time most cities have troubled and even conflictual relations with their rural and semi-rural neighbours. Cities have always provided markets for the neighbouring rural communities, and the surrounding areas have provided commuting workers as well as food. But this division of roles has also meant a differentiation of activities, morals, and wealth. Cities have usually been the richer, more powerful neighbours of farming areas, a fact that has often caused envy, irritation, and hostility. Cities typically have also developed more varied, cosmopolitan, and 'civilized' social practices, for which they have been chided by their more parochial rural neighbours.

The friction between culturally tolerant city people and more traditional—some would say, narrow-minded—rural (and small-town) people has proven a constant source of political creativity in North America, spawning the Social Credit movement in Alberta during the 1930s, the Moral Majority in the United States in the 1980s, and the so-called 'culture wars' in the 1980s onward. The recurring political conflicts over immigration, abortion, capital punishment, decriminalization of marijuana, and gay marriage have all largely centred on this urban–rural dividing line.

Urbanization

Because of the advantages urban centres provide, many more people now live in cities than ever before. In fact, according to the Population Reference Bureau, 2008 was a landmark year. It marked the first time ever that the world's population was divided more or less equally between urban and rural areas (PRB, 2009). This fact is significant, considering that in 1950, less than 30 per cent of the world's people lived in urban areas. Developing countries such as Nigeria and India had the fewest urban dwellers then, but today these countries are urbanizing rapidly.

Another surprising feature of modern life is the continued distinctiveness of rural and urban life, especially in developing nations. While most developed nations have urban centres spread all around the country, a developing nation tends to have only a few, massively populated urban areas that act as magnets for the rest of the national population. Consider India for instance, which is widely known for its **megacities**, including Mumbai (earlier known as Bombay), Kolkata (earlier known as Calcutta), and Delhi (PRB, 2009; UN Population Division, 2009). Even though these megacities are huge by Canadian standards, their populations taken together make up only 30 per cent of all the people living in India (UN Population Division, 2009). Even today, a majority of Indians continue to live in rural villages or small towns.

No end of this urbanizing trend is in sight, and by 2050, the percentage in urban areas is expected to rise to about 70 per cent. Of course, estimates and predictions are uncertain. Around the world, people use somewhat different definitions of *urban* and *rural*. In Peru, for example, an urban area may contain only 100 people, while in Japan, an urban area will always contain over 50,000 people. Clearly, other factors besides size enter into these varying definitions, including population density, the presence of governmental authority and policies, and economic activity (ibid).

Paradoxically, although half the world's population currently lives in urban areas, most of today's urban growth is occurring in towns, villages, and cities with 500,000 citizens or fewer, not in megacities of 10 million or more (PRB, 2009). Indeed, only 37 per cent of all the world's urban dwellers live in cities with more than a million people, and only 8 per cent live in megacities (ibid). In the next few decades, most of the world's population will live in these smaller cities, especially in developing nations where the rate of urbanization is accelerating, as in Latin America, Asia, and Africa (ibid; UN Population Division, 2009; Vlahov et al., 2005). The UN predicts that, of an estimated 2 billion people who will join the world's population by 2050, as many as 1.9 billion will live in smaller-sized cities in developing nations (Vlahov et al., 2005; UN Population Division, 2009). By 2050, Africa's

megacity

A geographic locale with a large concentrated population, sometimes defined as exceeding 5 million people (also, *megalopolis* or *megapolis*).

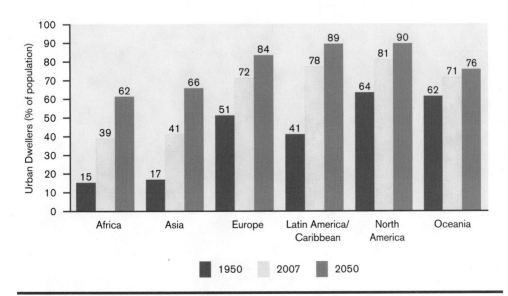

Figure 2.5 Urban Dwellers, 1950, 2007, and 2050

Source: Adapted from Population Reference Bureau (2009).

urban population alone is expected to triple, and in North America, 90 per cent of the population is expected to live in or near cities (PRB, 2009).

Real-estate agents sometimes say that three things affect the price of a home: location, location, location; so we need to talk about location. The entire reach or catchment area of a city is usually called the Greater Metropolitan Area—the urban, semi-urban, and suburban areas within an hour's drive of downtown. In Canada and other developed nations, many GMA residents live in surrounding communities—some call them **bedroom suburbs**—and commute downtown to work every day. The term *bedroom suburb* implies that adult family members use their home mainly as a place to sleep, with little time between working and the long commute downtown to do much else. The rise of bedroom suburbs, and the commuter revolution of the past century, was made possible by the building of high-speed roads for automobiles, and of tracks for trains and subways. Thus, over the last few centuries, the conquest of distance implied in suburban development has relied on innovations in transportation technology and construction.

Built Environments

Cities today continue to develop, and not only through the spread of commerce and rapid transit. They also continue to rely on varied forms of new technology, for cities are humanly constructed ways of living together and separating ourselves from the natural environment. In our human efforts to improve and enlarge the built environment, innovations of many kinds have been critical.

Take tall buildings as an example. The use of any tall building demands elevators as well as stairs, reliable heating and cooling systems, complex electrical wiring, and developed communication technology—telephones, computers, fax machines, and so on—so people on the thirtieth floor of one building can contact people on the fiftieth floor of a building

bedroom suburb

A residential area near a large city that provides housing and services for people who commute each day into the downtown urban area.

The built environment of cities is in direct conflict with the natural environment.

10 or more kilometres away. (This seems obvious, but we need to say it because—except for the occasional times when a city's electrical system goes down and most human activity is paralyzed—we all tend to take it for granted.) Therefore, technological innovation in the past few centuries has largely been driven by the needs associated with living and working in a vertical urban environment.

The built environment, and our reliance on it, has put a huge pressure on the natural environment, well beyond what one might expect from the number of humans alone. North Americans use a disproportionate share of the entire world's energy and mineral resources, much more than would be predicted based on the size of its population. This imbalance comes about because our quality of life—or standard of living—relies on the built environment we have created through technological ingenuity.

People Are Talking About . . .
MANUEL CASTELLS

Manuel Castells is Professor of Sociology, and Director of the Internet Interdisciplinary Institute at the Open University of Catalonia, in Barcelona. He is also University Professor and the Wallis Annenberg Chair Professor of Communication Technology and Society at the Annenberg School of Communication, University of Southern California, Los Angeles. Born in Albacete, Spain, in 1942, he lived in Barcelona during his youth. At the age of 16, he began to study law and economics at the University of Barcelona, and there was caught up in leftist politics and the anti-Franco student movement, despite the fact that his conservative father worked in Franco's government. In 1962 he fled to France to continue his studies. After completing a degree at the Sorbonne, he earned a doctorate in sociology from the University of Paris, where he then was a professor from 1967 to 1979. He accepted a position at the University of California at Berkeley in 1979, as professor of sociology and of city and regional planning, where he worked for many years.

Castells's work encompasses a broad range of fields, including urban sociology, organization studies, internet studies, social movements, sociology of culture, and political economy. In his biography of Castells, Frank Webster (in Scott, 2006: 52) notes, 'Castells calls himself an empirical sociologist. A striking feature of his work is its saturation in empirical detail and evidence . . . . He advocates 'disposable theory', to emphasize his antipathy towards the abstract theorizing that periodically enters social sciences'.

During the 1970s, Castell focused on urban social movements and the changing post-industrial urban life. In the 1980s, he turned his attention to the relationship between information and communications technology and economics, and the role of information networks in the emergence of a global economy. His trilogy, *The Information Age: Economy, Society and Culture*, encompassing *The Rise of the Network Society* (1996), *The Power of Identity* (1997), and *End of Millennium* (1998), synthesizes his thinking on the social and economic transitions inherent in the information society. In *The Information Age*, he argues that social movements and other means by which people create meaning for themselves are distinct from the dominant economic and social organizations or networks.

Source: Adapted from *Fifty Key Sociologists: The Contemporary Theorists* (edited by John Scott, London: Routledge, 2006) and other sources.

Castells's Marxist urban sociology shows how, in the post-industrial city, social movements can bring about radical transformation, especially in areas where political entities control such matters as public transportation and housing, which can be termed areas of 'collective consumption'. So, for example, Arantes (2009) notes that political circumstances led Brazilian sociologists in the 1970s to critically examine the notion of the city, following

Castells's structuralist blueprint. In their view, city life combined collective consumption and collective production, making it central to the working class experience of capitalism. To change the city was, therefore, to change capitalist class relations and (potentially) to limit the expansion of capitalist power.

Sociologists' views of urban social movements were significantly changed by Castells's theory that to be considered effective, local activism must produce *profound, class-related* social change. So, for example, Serbulo (2009) describes how urban protesters in Portland, Oregon, and Seattle, Washington, set out to change the social fabric of their cities in the 1990s by challenging 'existing social relations in neighbourhoods, at work, in public services, in the construction and use of urban space, and in the imagination of the city'. By changing city life, they effectively changed the daily lives of billions—the very texture of class relations.

Early in his career, Castells questioned what urban sociology was really about, and whether the term *urban* had become obsolete (Gans, 2009). In this prescient question, he was hinting at the need for a synthesis of research on human settlements of varying size (cities, greater urban areas, suburbs, and smaller settlements, for example) and—perhaps—non-locational communities in cyberspace. In his current work, Castells stresses that the organization of the economy, of state institutions, and of the ways that people create meaning in their lives through collective action, must be understood as both discrete and inter-related entities. This has resulted in various research projects on different types of social change.

For example, Johnson (2009), uses Castells's typology of identities to examine racial dynamics within labour unions, and how the 'identity practices' of different factions within a union, perhaps based on class, religion, or age, might bring about racially inclusive strategies. Equally important, he considers how more complex and dispersed social networks affect worker's experiences and identities.

One might say that Castells is concerned mainly with 'people in places' but he is just as concerned with their movement between places. Knox et al. (2009) draw upon Castells's notion of a 'space of flows' to study the movement of people, baggage, and airplanes through an airport.

We noted earlier that one social phenomenon of interest to demographers is the turnover or flow of people through social structures. In the era of what Baumann (2000) has called 'liquid' modernity, airports are particularly distinctive institutions, constituting what Castells calls a 'space of flows'. By promoting flow, they help to extend and integrate a global economy and 'glocal'—that is, globally-influenced local—culture. As sociologists, we might wonder how it is possible to achieve this monumental task; Knox et al., using empirical research at Fulchester International Airport, undertake it by studying the movement of passengers, bags, and airplanes. The researchers show how these flow processes are controlled by 'modes of ordering' to simplify global exchange and interaction. Who would have imagined baggage-handling could be so consequential!

Castells posits that horizontal organizational networks—networks across distance—began to emerge before the widespread use of electronic networks such as the Internet. Equally important, through the Internet and other technologies, the development of horizontal networks has challenged the traditional vertical hierarchies that used to predominate in commercial, state, military, academic, and social organizations. Take, as an example, the actions of a single Australian computer whiz who set up a website that, in summer 2010, was used to display internationally thousands of classified defence documents from the US and elsewhere. Transmitting this information around the world broke the secrecy of powerful governments, thus undermining global hierarchies of power, by exposing a history of lies and deception in decision-making around the wars in Iraq and Afghanistan.

As well, the global transformation of information flow has led to new questions about schools, curriculum, and teaching strategies in a globalized network society (Tjeldvoll, 2009). Further, Pregowski (2009) notes the new media have resulted in a need for 'netiquettes': varied systems of good manners and ethical conduct in cyberspace. Netiquettes are an example of self-regulation of the first virtual societies, in particular—as per Manuel Castells—of techno-elites and hackers. To discover the guiding principles, shared values, and undesirable attitudes of Internet propriety, Pregowski conducts content analysis on rules of netiquette culled from various sources.

Globalization, urbanization, and advanced communication technology tend to detach us from a sense of belonging in a local setting. Thus, paradoxically, as we are attached to ever more people around the globe, more and more of us feel rootless. Caldarovic and Sarinic (2009), armed with Castells's concept of the 'flow of spaces' and other new notions of globalization, cosmopolitism, localism, and localization, consider how rootlessness might be alleviated. Clearly, there will be no return to the small town or even urban village; the question is how to root us in (near and far) human relationships while maintaining the benefits of globalization, such as the enjoyment of other cultures.

Many people continue to think about globalization in terms of mobility, openness, and fluidity. Thus, notions of network, flows, and transnationalism are often used to characterize and depict globalization as the seamless flow across national borders, of goods, services, capital, culture, technologies, and so on. Devadas (2008) recognizes that present-day flows and networks contrast with 'borders, differentiated zones and spaces, and immobility'. And, as Castells himself noted, there is still 'The Fourth World', comprising those 'sub-populations socially excluded from the global society—including the nomadic, pastoral, and hunter-gatherer ways of life beyond the present-day industrial society norm'. One question for the future, then, is how to pull this Fourth World into conversation with the rest of the world, and how to ensure that no portions of humanity are disadvantaged by distance or segregation from the global network.

Thus, a review of recent writings finds plenty of interest in Castells and his writings—at least 150 journal articles citing or disputing Castells since 2002. Clearly, sociologists are talking about Manuel Castells. Castells contributes to our comprehensive, fusion sociology by providing a sense of the hugeness of social analysis: its historical scope, its need to grapple with new technology and new virtual spaces where social life takes place, and the continuing role of power in the face of almost chaotic change.

New Insights

In the area of demography, urbanization and environment, lots of new research is taking off from tradition concerns. For example, current research is examining the ways birth, death, and migration differ today from the earlier 'modern' or even premodern era. Consider the matter of death. Malthus viewed high death rates as reflecting a failure to apply preventive checks: a result of nature striking back at humanity. However, death can also have political causes and may happen despite the availability of food.

For example, Gazdar (2002) notes that in August 1990, international trade with Iraq virtually disappeared due to economic sanctions enacted by the UN Security Council after Iraq's invasion of Kuwait. Most of Iraq's food had been imported, and most of its GDP had been derived from exports. It is estimated that between 200,000 and 1 million deaths in Iraq since 1990 can be directly attributed to the famine resulting from these sanctions.

But the Iraqi famine cannot be entirely blamed on failures in food availability or entitlement. It is a 'postmodern famine': excess mortality that occurs in spite of protected food claims, because of non-food crises—notably, shocks to the health and social-welfare systems of Iraq. Indeed, Iraq illustrates what we might consider the famine of the future. Here, intentional, policy-induced macroeconomic shocks in a globally integrated economy can lead to dramatic long-term increases in mortality. (However, contrary to Gazdar's assertion that this was a uniquely postmodern famine, the Ukraine was subjected to a similar famine by Russia in the 1930s, resulting in millions of deaths. Some might even say that Ireland was subjected to a similar (potato) famine by England in the 1840s, resulting in millions of deaths and migrations. So, not every form of mass murder is necessarily postmodern.)

Another interesting development is the research on ways less-developed societies are being affected by population issues that are well advanced in Western developed societies: aging, migration, lower fertility rates, lower marriage and higher cohabitation rates, more single people, and so on. An example is the research by Erol (2008), which shows that people in Turkey are living much longer than they did a century ago, and that older people make up a much larger percentage of the population. Erol also found that Turkish people are consuming more, with leisure activities constituting a large part of that increase. Increased consumption of services is a sign of the postmodern age, in contrast to the rise in consumption of goods that followed the Industrial Revolution. Erol draws on Veblen's notion of 'conspicuous consumption', and Bourdieu's idea that social classes can be distinguished by their consumption patterns, in showing that retired, well-off Turkish city dwellers increasingly tend to purchase leisure commodities such as travel and sports club memberships. In short, Turkey—a relatively new participant in the modern, globalized world—is quickly taking on foreign notions of leisure and recreation.

Similarly, people in less-developed nations are coming to deal differently with childbearing and its meaning in a postmodern society. Miranda and de Oliveira Moreira (2006) note the current widespread concern with 'correcting' infertility and its relationship to a woman's body and identity. The authors wonder whether the yearning to have children in newly developed countries is rooted in traditional notions of family life or in more up-to-date notions about the fulfillment of personal desire in a consumerist culture.

Or consider the contemporary problem of immigration and exile. Many sociologists today write about the immigrant experience in more-developed societies. Increasing numbers of people today are migrants: whether voluntary or involuntarily displaced, economic migrants or refugees, temporary sojourners or exiles. According to Marin (2002), the stories of exile tell us about the struggle between cultural identity and adjustment. Through their discourse, exiles weave distinct elements of culture, migration conditions, or social positions into constructions of personal identity. This research, ultimately, addresses the question of what (or who) will be the typical world citizen in fifty or a hundred years: likely, a person with many diverse ancestors and experiences, able to live almost anywhere. (Perhaps US President Barack Obama is an example of this cosmopolitan, postmodern human.)

In the past, concerns about identity framed the condition of exile as problematic, caught in the conflict among otherwise meaningful roles. Through a new, postmodern lens, we can examine the discourse of exile as offering useful accounts of identity. Consider the discourse of Joseph Brodsky, a famous Soviet exile and author who has lived in exile, in difficult conditions, often forced to make sense of his many experiences in his work and in himself as an expatriate. According to Brodsky, exile is a central postmodern condition in which social, political, and cultural constructions of reality can be interpreted in different ways. Brodsky equates the condition of exile to postmodernity itself, characterized as it is by factors that multiply experiences of estrangement and change in multiple settings.

Some believe that only a postmodern analysis can grasp this multiple identity. So, for example, Rosewarne (2004) argues the radical leftist critique of globalization has transformed migrants into disembodied subjects and removed their human agency. To change this, we need to see migrants as subjects and active agents in finding their own place in the world. This postmodernist reorientation has emerged in migration studies, which understands the centrality of flow and rootlessness in the contemporary world.

New populations and new communities call for new research methods. Antweiler (2004), for one, calls for new, anthropological approaches to the study of cities. He notes that in a city we find dense populations of diverse people in constructed environments and fixed public spaces. Beyond that, the city is also a nexus in the movement of goods, information, and people. City people, as we know, have much interaction, but their relationships are often superficial and based on social categories rather than personal knowledge. Traditional ethnographic research—based on the notion of spatially static rural populations—is not the best tool for studying cities, therefore. Modern anthropology needs to approach the study of internal urban microstructure with more complex tools, such as network analysis.

Increasingly obvious too is the role of public policy in specifically creating excellent 'global' cities. This intentionality marks a change from traditional approaches to urban planning. In the 1970s and 1980s, planners in Singapore (for example) focused on the swift development of urban infrastructure. Their policies made affordable housing readily available to much of Singapore's population and preserved racial harmony. But in the 1990s, housing policy was revised with the goal of turning Singapore into a 'global city'. Such a plan would necessarily affect many areas of the built environment to include the introduction of postmodern architecture and new types of public housing. In the end, this new goal was to re-shape traditional patterns of governance, class structure, social mobility, and community values (Goh, 2001).

In short, recent decades have created new demographic, urban, and environmental concerns, and sociology has changed dramatically in its attempts to study and understand these issues.

Chapter Summary

As we have seen in this chapter, a study of human societies might sensibly begin with the study of human populations, since their size, density, composition, sex ratio, health, longevity, and migration patterns have significant implications for people's lives.

We can see this significance especially when comparing urban populations to rural populations. City life is different from rural life, and ever more people are living in cities today, around the world. It is now healthier for people to live in cities, since the city's large population provides better access to health care—not the case a little over a century ago. On the same note, geography has historically shaped the way people live in societies. For instance, we learned that there are large cultural differences between societies located along bodies of water compared with those isolated in mountainous terrain.

We are now also aware that the world population has been increasing exponentially for over a hundred years. This has caused much concern about the human impact on our natural environment and the growing scarcity of natural resources. However, the world's population is currently increasing more slowly than it did during the twentieth century, mainly because of a worldwide fertility decline. Some countries, such as China, have even created strong incentives for families to limit their numbers of children. This shows us that it is possible consciously to solve the issues we face in respect to rapid population growth.

The environment we live in today—mainly, a built environment—is intended to accommodate our large numbers, especially if we live in cities. Yet, we know that the effects of our built environment on the natural environment are staggering, and they have resulted in what we know today as climate change. In response to these concerns, many people have begun to mobilize collectively to reduce these effects.

Finally, we noted the role of technology in shaping our built and natural environment. This expression of human creativity is important sociologically, because technology influences how societies are organized and how people within them relate to one another.

Later chapters will show that many of the social problems we experience are affected by the characteristics of our populations, our built and natural environments, and the technology we create to sustain ourselves. In this chapter, we have therefore discussed the material settings of social life; this discussion will serve as a backdrop to the sociological analyses we tackle in later chapters.

Critical Thinking Questions

1. The global population is increasing steadily and will soon include the largest number of elderly people in the history of humanity. Canada, as a developed country, will experience this phenomenon first-hand. What are the sociological implications of this aging process and how will it affect Canadian society—its social policies, health care, government funding, entertainment, etc.?

2. Do you think Malthus's theory of population has merit? Support your opinion by doing some preliminary research on the topic. Propose an alternative prediction about the future of humanity.

3. Governments around the world are experiencing significant pressure to find solutions to environmental problems; meanwhile, the world population is still rising, further intensifying this problem. In your opinion, in what key ways will the worldwide population in 2050 affect the environment? What should humanity do to handle this predicted situation?

4. How do humans adapt to cities—the densely built environments that separate them from nature? Do you think this is a healthy and sensible way of living? Discuss.

Recommended Readings

Riley Dunlap, Frederick Buttel, Peter Dickens, and August Gijswijt (eds), *Sociological Theory and the Environment: Classical Foundations, Contemporary Insights* (Lanham, MD: Rowaman and Littlefield, 2002). This is an overview of sociological theories of the environment, both classic and modern. It discusses the major themes significant in environmental sociology today, including globalization, urbanization, the rising world population, resource consumption, and more.

Michael N. Dobkowski and Isidor Wallmann (eds), *On the Edge of Scarcity: Environment, Resources, Population, Sustainability, and Conflict* (New York: Syracuse University Press, 2002). This collection of essays deals with an important topic in the study of population since its formulation by Thomas Malthus in the nineteenth century: vital resource shortage. This topic is unsettling yet realistic, as the world population continues to grow and habits of consumption have not changed. The problems of rising population and resource depletion are considered with reference to the social conflicts they will cause.

Everett C. Hughes, *French Canada in Transition* (New York: Oxford University Press: 2009 [1943]). During the Depression, Hughes, of the Chicago School, did a study of the rapid industrialization of a small French-Canadian community. His ethnographic analysis uncovered trends and underlying conflicts that would later escalate in the events of the 'Quiet Revolution' of the 1960s. It provides a valuable insight into the development of Canada and remains one of the most important founding works in Canadian sociology.

Tim Dyson, Robert Cassen, and Leela Visaria (eds), *Twenty-first Century India: Population, Economy, Human Development and the Environment* (Oxford: Oxford University Press, 2004). This book outlines the population and development of India with recent data. Population in India is growing at an unprecedented rate, and the authors undertake the complicated task of analyzing data and applying it to society to determine how the large increase in people will impact urbanization, education, health care, employment, poverty, economy, and the environment.

Gayl D. Ness and Michael M. Low (eds), *Five Cities: Modelling Asian Urban Population: Environment Dynamics* (Singapore: Oxford University Press, 2002). This book examines the dynamic relationship between population growth and ensuing change in the urban environment. As the title suggests, it focuses on five small-scale cities in Asia. Each is described and analyzed in a case study that outlines its urban development. The focus on smaller cities is useful, since most of the future population will live in such cities and therefore this is also where most urban development will take place.

Stefan Goodwin, *Africa's Legacies of Urbanization: Unfolding Saga of a Continent* (Lanham, MD: Lexington Books, 2006). This book is a modern consideration of the rapidly urbanizing African continent. Avoiding Eurocentric assumptions about urban development in African countries, it examines the complex history, ecology, anthropology, and geography of this diverse area.

Websites

United Nations Population Division
www.un.org/esa/population/unpop.htm

Population Reference Bureau
www.prb.org

The Life and Legacy of Rachel Carson
www.rachelcarson.org

The David Suzuki Foundation
www.davidsuzuki.org

Earth Day Canada
http://pub.earthday.ca/pub/index.php

Environment Canada
www.ec.gc.ca

The Sustainability Report
www.sustreport.org

Population Action International (PAI)
www.populationaction.org

3 Social Structures

Learning Objectives

In this chapter, you will:

> Learn how social structures, roles, and identities influence our behaviour
> Find out how the size of a group affects the way people behave within it
> Differentiate between the functions of gangs, teams, and bands, while recognizing how each group is similar in their goals
> Consider the characteristics of cliques
> Understand the processes that occur within bureaucracies

Chapter Outline

In the last chapter, we discussed the material backdrop for our social relations: all those non-human factors that influence how we get along with one another. In this chapter, we will discuss some of the human factors that influence our social relations. In particular, we will discuss what sociologists call *social scripts* and *social forms*.

Social scripts are those culturally constructed, socially enforced practices that we are all expected to follow when we interact in social situations. Each situation has its own script in a given community or society, and most adult members of society are aware of that script. They have learned it through many years of observation and practice.

Within a given situation, certain scripted deviations are allowed. For example, women are often allowed—even expected—to act differently from men, and adults are allowed and expected to act differently from children. People who deviate too far

from their proper script—adults who act like children, for example—are criticized and sometimes even punished. At the least, they often lose respect and credibility within the community.

Social forms are those social arrangements that arise out of interaction often below the cultural radar—that is, below people's consciousness. We might define social forms as social objects—symbols, roles, or relationships—that help people achieve their individual and collective goals co-operatively. Fashions are social forms, and so are newly coined words like 'tweet' and new practices like tweeting. Social forms can be as informal as Facebook posting styles or as formal as prenuptial agreements. One thing they can't be is idiosyncratic: unique to one individual. People may not always know about social forms, and they are not socially enforced, but they appear everywhere and influence our behaviour nevertheless. The sociologist whose name is most associated with social forms is Georg Simmel. He theorized about them a century ago in Germany; since then, many sociologists have developed and extended his insights.

As we will see, both social scripts and social forms constrain the ways people relate to one another in social situations. They are the human, social factors that influence how social life proceeds—for example, how conflicts arise and co-operation is negotiated. Unlike other chapters, where we consider the contending points of view of different sociological approaches, this chapter focuses almost exclusively on the symbolic interactionist point of view, which provides the richest insight into microsociological processes like interaction, negotiation, and co-operation.

Everyday Observations

Here's a fact that may hit home if you have ever felt edgy making a public presentation: many people would rather be dead than talk in front of their classmates or business associates. In one survey, respondents ranked public speaking as their greatest fear — ahead of death. And even adults who report making presentations to large audiences as part of their work often consider it to be one of their biggest fears. Far fewer admit to being afraid of spiders or being afraid of heights for example. That's because humans are social animals; we seek the approval of others, and fear exclusion and ridicule. And because of that fear, we can control one another through unspoken threats of rejection.

When you see a police officer, how do you react? Even if you are not doing anything illegal, do you feel nervous and act cautiously? From a young age, our parents teach us to respect—even fear—the police and act 'good' when they are around. We are told to treat them with respect and are warned that if we don't, we will be punished. Therefore, our primary socialization—our earliest childhood training—initially causes us to view police officers in this way, and throughout our lives, this view is reinforced. In short, we follow particular social scripts when we are around authority figures, and play our roles very properly. But even among other people not in authority, we are still careful to avoid blame, shame, guilt, or humiliation. We do this by following **social scripts**.

You yourself follow a number of scripts—mostly unconsciously—because you play a variety of roles. Reading this, you are probably a student, but you are also probably a child, a friend, a sibling, and perhaps someone's 'significant other'. To what extent do these roles conflict with each other? For instance, have you ever wanted to hang out with a friend on the weekend, but were not able to do so because, as a student, you had to study for a test? How do you decide which roles are more important? Often, our scripts tell us the answer, though sometimes they do not.

Although our roles and identities play an important part in shaping our behaviour, the groups we belong to also have a large influence. What role do you play in a group? For instance, if you were part of a clique in high school, were you a leader or a follower? Perhaps you did not belong to a particular clique, and instead, people viewed you as an outsider. How did this 'outside role' influence your actions and the way you thought about yourself?

Consider the other groups you have been a part of during your teen years. Have you ever been a member of a sports team, a band, or a gang? If you were, what position did you occupy? For instance, if you played on a team, were you the 'star' of the team or just an

social script

Guidelines that people follow to carry out interactions and fulfill role expectations as seamlessly as possible.

average player? A goal scorer or an enforcer? As you will have learned, all of these roles are important for the team to function, since leaders are needed to unify the team and average players (and enforcers) are needed to carry out the commands of the leader to achieve the group's goals.

Likely, the first group you belonged to is your family. Is your family large or small? How did the size of your family influence your role within it? Often, the experience of a child differs depending on whether he or she is an only child or a first, middle, or last child. If your family is large, you likely learned the values of sharing and co-operation; but an only child may not have learned these same types of values. Are your parents married or separated? If your parents have separated, you are already aware of how easily groups can break down, and what consequences members experience when this happens.

We are often socialized from childhood to act a certain way around a police officer.

Now let's stop thinking small and think big instead. Consider the importance of vast bureaucracies in our lives today. Do either of your parents work in an organization structured according to written bureaucratic rules, with a long chain of command and many named positions? If so, you are well aware of how the impersonal functioning of a large bureaucracy affects people's lives. How do your parents, and others who work in a bureaucracy, feel about it? Are they content or do they feel alienated and estranged from their jobs? As we will see, people in large organizations often feel estranged from their jobs, since both the size of a bureaucracy and the ways bureaucracies achieve their goals can be largely impersonal. (Remember from the last chapter: size matters!)

Let us begin this chapter on roles, rules and expectations by walking around the boundaries of the topic and discussing rule-breakers—clearly, the mirror image of conformists and enforcers.

Classic Studies
Outsiders

Many sociological studies have looked at the roles people play and the statuses they occupy, but up until the early 1960s, there were few in-depth studies that focused primarily on deviant roles. This changed with the work of a sociologist named Howard Becker.

A student of the Chicago School of sociology, Becker was especially influenced by the work of his professor, Everett C. Hughes. Becker was also a professional jazz musician, and this role led to his involvement with the subjects of his research in the classic work *Outsiders* (1963). In *Outsiders*, Becker sets the groundwork for *labelling theory*, as it is known today. In explaining this approach, Becker notes that 'social groups create deviance by making rules whose infraction constitutes deviance and by applying these rules to particular people and labelling them as outsiders' (ibid: 9). Thus deviance is a result of a group expelling an individual or subgroup.

Becker's analysis of deviance, as noted, is largely based on his observations of jazz musicians, as well as marijuana users. In *Outsiders*, Becker shows how members of these two groups are labelled deviant because of their actions. However, he turns the tables on this analysis, emphasizing that their outsider status is really due not to any failing on their part, but merely to their actions and the way others respond to these actions. He argues that people learn to smoke marijuana, just as they learn anything else—for example, how to drive a car. They are normal people learning deviant things, in a normal way. However, once labelled deviant by others or themselves, people tend to set themselves apart and develop their own language and patterns of behaviour. This formation of an outsider community is especially evident among jazz musicians. Often, they take great pains to distance themselves from their listeners, who are perceived as unhip and square.

Becker stresses a sequential rather than a simultaneous model of deviance. Because learning and group formation are involved, Becker analyzes deviance as a *process* of becoming someone outside the community's accepted rules. Different factors in people's lives become relevant at different stages during this period when people become outsiders. For example, there may be different factors affecting the reasons people take up marijuana smoking or jazz, compared to factors affecting their persistence 'in the life'.

Over time, the deviant learns socially provided reasons for both starting an activity and for continuing it. Initiation—first becoming a deviant—for example, requires a progressively greater commitment to norms and institutions that endow the deviant action with meaning and value. In this process, the new deviant acquires both a community and community identity within the marijuana-smoking or jazz-playing subgroup, and not solely from the larger, 'straight' community. Being labelled as deviant—part of 'being a deviant'—thus requires interaction with, and commitment to, an outsider group, and the rejection of views held by the larger society.

One of the main points Becker makes in *Outsiders* is that the study of deviance must pay as much attention to rule *enforcers* as it does to rule *violators*. Instead of always asking 'Why are they deviant?' we should be asking ourselves 'Why do we label a particular behaviour as deviant?' From Becker's perspective, we can never simply assume fault on the part of the deviant, or attribute the deviance to a dysfunction or mental illness. Becker underscores this in his later writings, paying closest attention to questions like: 'Who accuses who? What do they accuse them of doing? Under what circumstances are these accusations successful, in the sense of being accepted by others (at least by some others)?' (Becker 2005).

This approach is not without critics. The strongest criticism of Becker's theory of deviance is that it ignores personal motivation for deviant actions, focusing on the effects and not the causes of this behaviour. However, this focus is intentional. Becker admits that in his model, 'instead of the deviant motives leading to the deviant behaviour, it is the other way around; the deviant behaviour in time produced the deviant motivation' (Becker 1963:42).

Common sense seems to tell us it is difficult to understand deviance without some reference to the actors' motives, and many question this labelling approach. Yet Becker's *Outsiders* was, and remains, one of sociology's most influential studies of deviant individuals and their position in 'normal' society. And despite the criticism, Becker's work on outsiders emphasizes that social rules make deviance. In the face of other people's social norms, people find themselves labelled as 'deviant', experiencing stigma and social exclusion as a result. This important fact applies not only at a societal level but within groups of all sizes and compositions.

Identity, Roles, and Role-Sets

Social scripts are most closely associated with the *dramaturgical approach* of symbolic interactionism, an approach systematized and popularized by sociologist Erving Goffman. Goffman, in his earliest book *The Presentation of Self in Everyday Life* (1959), showed that we can understand and think about social life much more fruitfully in terms of a theatrical production, complete with costumes, scripts, audiences, and roles. In fact, the term *social role* is borrowed from theatre, and the word *role* originated from *roll*, on which scripts for theatrical plays were originally written.

The dramaturgical approach helps to account for why we dress and act a particular way on prom night.

Of course, we all know that social life is *not* a scripted play. For one thing, we all have some freedom to act as we choose in society. For another, the 'scripts' we do have are often incomplete and confusing. No social script completely covers any social situation, so improvisation is always needed. Gaffes and errors are always possible. Situations and the people in them are too diverse to allow for complete scripting, even if we wished it. So, Goffman's approach is, at best, a useful metaphor about social life. Yet it is a powerful metaphor, allowing us to predict how situations may unfold.

This approach also helps us explain the sheer fact of social structure: that predictable, enduring feature of social life that is the subject matter of sociology. The dramaturgical approach helps to account for other features of the situation that are play-like: for example, the fact that we use costumes and makeup to prepare ourselves for performances in particular situations. We dress differently for church, say, than for Sociology 101 or for a romantic occasion, because it is important for everyone involved to set and maintain the mood.

But even more convincing is the observable fact that in socially scripted situations, we behave like actors in plays when someone fails to perform as expected—in effect, when he or she steps out of character or forgets some lines. An immediate result is that we feel embarrassed by this flubbed interaction. We do not know what to say next or what to do to get the interaction back on track. We will do almost anything to ignore the blunder and keep the interaction moving along. At best, we are confused and upset until someone figures out a way to fix the interactional glitch (or as commentators after a famous Super Bowl performance called it, a 'costume malfunction').

The social scripts we follow are usually imperfect. They give us the general outlines of what to say and do, but not the details. We need social skills and insight to deduce what behaviour is suitable on a date, for example. Most of us know generally how to communicate a romantic or sexual interest in someone, how to act when other people are around, and how to act when in public rather than in private. With all these clues, we should be able to compose, or recall, a workable script for a dating situation. Yet, who hasn't run into interactional problems on that first date?

role

The expected behaviour of an individual in a social position and the duties associated with that position.

identity

All the ways in which we view and describe ourselves (female/male, friend, student, attractive, unusual, etc.) and in which others perceive us.

The clues to success are contained in the role itself. In theatrical scripts, there are characters, each playing a particular **role**. The roles we play provide us with social scripts: guidelines for what to do and say. Fulfillment of these expectations promotes effective interaction—a smooth sequence from one person to another, back to the first, and so on. Yet a breach of these expectations can lead to embarrassment, bewilderment, regret, and other unpleasant feelings.

The roles we play and social scripts we follow are related to another important concept in this theatrical perspective: **identity**. According to the dramaturgical perspective, the social roles we play are the source—not necessarily the expression—of our identities. We tend to think that our identities are unique, and that they evolve from our personalities, experiences, desires, and wishes. In contrast, symbolic interactionists argue that the social roles we play are the main origin of our identities, so roles and identities are interrelated. Roles shape our identities and, perhaps, interact with and even conflict with our personalities and basic inclinations.

In thinking about roles and identities, it is useful to start with the related concepts 'category' and 'community'; roles and identities are embedded in categories and communities. Indeed, nowhere is the production and reproduction of social structure more obvious than in communities.

A community, defined sociologically, is a group of people who interact and communicate often with one another and share common interests, values, and goals. Often, these people live in close proximity. Most importantly, they identify themselves as members of a community—often their community even has a name—and identify one another as members. Membership in the community is important to these people. In many communities, people will do almost anything, conform to almost any rules, to stay in good community standing. People in communities dread exclusion or expulsion, and feel shamed by gossip and guilt.

So, a community is made up of individuals who have immersed their personal identities in the community enterprise. They conform to community standards, despite their individual differences—for these individuals do have individual characteristics. And, as individuals, they belong to demographic categories: some are men, some women; some are young, some old; some are rich, some poor; and so on. However, demographic categories are different from social communities. People belonging to the same category do not communicate or interact with each other merely based on their shared membership in that category. What's more, people are less likely to identify with the demographic categories to which they belong than with the social communities to which they belong. So, demographic categories are of less interest to sociologists than are communities, at least until a category mobilizes and becomes a community.

Category mobilization, of course, is what social movements are about—the women's movement, the gay rights movement, the black power movement. In each instance, by interaction, communication, raising awareness, and taking political action, a demographic category—woman, homosexual, black—became a political movement and then a social community—with an identity, a membership, a belief, and a fierce commitment.

Of central concern to sociologists is the question: What is the connection between roles and identities? This is related to the important question: Where does social conformity originate—inside or outside the conforming person? That is, do we experience conformity as imposed servitude or as voluntary subordination to a set of rules we largely agree with?

In fact, the answer is 'both'. Sometimes there is nothing we would like better than to leave a situation or voice our disapproval of what is going on, but we continue to obey the social rules all the same. Most of us have suffered from boring teachers or irritating bosses. We keep our mouths shut and do what we have to, because we fear the punishment of doing otherwise or wish for the reward for conforming: the gold star, the high grade, the pay raise, the retirement package. At the same time, few of us are *constantly* irritated, frustrated, and disappointed about the social rules we obey. Somehow, we come to tolerate them and take them for granted. More than that, we often come to embrace them, as though we had chosen them.

Before the dramaturgical approach, many sociologists explained identity formation with *labelling theory*, which, as you know from Becker's work, states that we gain knowledge or understanding of who we are by seeing how other people view or treat us. This theory has its foundation in the work of Charles Horton Cooley (1902) who formed the concept of the **looking-glass self** to illustrate how we form our identities.

Related to labelling theory is the notion that the way others treat you influences how you treat (and view) yourself. Thus, if you have loving parents who encourage and support you, you look at yourself differently than if you have parents who doubt your abilities and achievements. Clearly, this theory has some validity, but there are limits to its applicability. Undoubtedly, our identities are based *in part* on how others regard and respond to us, but to what extent do we absorb other people's opinions, and under what conditions? Obviously, we do not absorb into our identities *all* the traits and descriptions that *everyone* labels us with. Therefore, something else must also influence our identity formation.

Goffman (1963) notes that roles and identities are so closely intertwined that the two almost overlap, as suggested by the concepts *role embracement, role distance, and role exit*. In role embracement, a person willingly accepts both the social role and the identity associated with it. For example, a woman who becomes a nun implicitly agrees to assume the identity (as well as role) of a deeply religious, upright person. In role distance, a person may take on a role but keep separate their behaviour from the identity associated with that role. If you have ever asked your parents to drop you off a few blocks from your school rather than right in front of it, then you have introduced role distance. Although you probably embrace your role as a son or daughter, when you asked them to do this you probably wanted to put some distance between your role obligations as affectionate child and those as dependent child.

Finally, *role exit* is the process a person undergoes when leaving a role. This process includes not only the rejection and loss of certain activities, rights, and responsibilities, but also the loss of an identity associated with the role. For instance, now you may be a 'student', with the rights and duties that implies; but after you earn your diploma or degree and find a job, you will likely not describe yourself as 'a student' any longer. You will pay more attention to exploring the rights and duties associated with being an economically independent wage earner.

Thus, the interactionist perspective argues that identities are socially determined, based on the social roles we play. They are not inborn, like 'personality'. According to this theory, we internalize the roles we play so that they become an integral part of our identities. But how does this happen? Imagine yourself as a first-time mother or father; you will likely feel that you do not know what this role entails. In fact, the experience may be nothing like what you expected; and you may even feel like an impostor. Such feelings are common when we embrace new roles for the first time, especially roles as consequential as 'parent'. Gradually however, most people take on the responsibilities associated with their new roles and begin to identify with them.

Further, your new identity, as 'parent', for example, begins to structure your life, and you now take on other new roles associated with it—whether as soccer coach, swimming teacher, or even moral guide. All these other roles are part of the original role of 'parent'; sociologists call this collection of roles a **role-set**. Sometimes, a gap opens up between your original identity and the most important new identity, or identities, you are obliged to take on. This is a common experience in professional socialization—people's preparation to practise a professional occupation.

Some roles are clearly defined, especially when they are paired with other particular roles: for example, husband–wife, parent–child, or teacher–student. They are well defined

looking-glass self

A process in which people come to see (and value) themselves as others see them.

role-set

The collection of roles any individual plays.

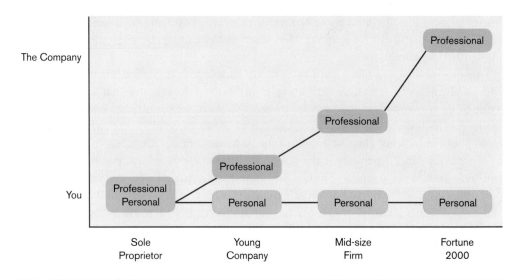

Figure 3.1 The Gap between Personal Identities during Professionalization

Source: Adapted from Carpenter (2008).

in the sense that we know how people in these roles are *supposed* to act towards one another. A classic pairing discussed by the American sociologist Talcott Parsons is the doctor and patient pair. Doctors and patients are interdependent: one cannot play his or her particular role without the other. For the doctor, the patient is an opportunity to display expertise and exert control. For the patient, the doctor is a source of socially approved deviance. By declaring you 'sick', the doctor releases you from social duty and responsibility.

The point sketched by this example is that our culture accepts the 'sick role' and the procedure associated with it as an excuse for rule-breaking. That is why you can bring a doctor's note to your teacher or boss and miss class or work without penalty.

As you can see, the interconnection of social roles is a rich area for further discussion, and sociologists have theorized extensively about this connection. One question we haven't discussed is: How do roles change over time? According to the interactionist approach, social roles are unlike theatrical roles in that they are not predetermined. They are not literally written down sets of words, and you will not get fired from the play if you flub your lines. Moreover, individuals—not societies—can exercise control over the roles they play. That is, they can choose certain roles and avoid others.

George Herbert Mead, an early twentieth-century sociologist, studied roles extensively. He argued that people adopt roles throughout their lifetime in a process he called **role-taking**. They do so by learning from the people around them, as well as from 'society' at large (1934). To take on a role, such as becoming a doctor, is to take on a prearranged set of expectations. To do so, one must first enter and fulfill several other roles, playing the role of the student and then the intern, for example. Thus, for symbolic interactionists, role adoption is a dynamic process—a sequence—that is under the control of our own motivations, the motivations of others around us, the groups we are seeking to enter, and the culture and society.

Central to this process is the learning and use of symbols. In Mead's (1934) view, the interaction of roles depends mainly on **symbol** systems, especially language. Interaction is possible only because we humans understand the meaning of certain symbols expressed as language. Without language, social life would be impossible, because communication, interaction, and negotiation would be impossible. Our understanding of other people's communication depends on us interpreting their message correctly.

role-taking

The process in which we take on existing defined roles.

symbol

A thing that stands for or represents something else, and provides a means of communication (e.g., through spoken words, written words, facial expressions, or body language).

In elaborating Mead's theory of social roles and identities, Ralph Turner (1962) introduced another concept of role change called **role-making**. Like role-taking, role-making is a social process that works through social interaction. People invent new social roles with the assistance and co-operation of others. However, this concept helps us identify a major flaw in the interactionist approach, and a major difference between it and functionalism.

Here's the problem: a pair of people may agree to 'make' a new role, but this agreement may not bind the rest of society. Consider a role relationship, *grokking*, described in the classic science fiction book, *Stranger in a Strange Land* by Robert Heinlein (1961). Heinlein tells us 'Grok means to understand so thoroughly that the observer becomes a part of the observed—to merge, blend, intermarry, lose identity in group experience. It means almost everything that we mean by religion, philosophy, and science—and it means as little to us (because of our Earthly assumptions) as color means to a blind man'.

So, just because two people make a new role, or even import a new role from another culture (or galaxy), the role may not play well in our culture. It may not work, because all social relations and social conflicts have a scripted aspect. To work, the script must be widely known and generally accepted in the population. Unless it forms part of a stable subculture, it might as well not exist.

Part of the problem is that a newly invented role may not have an accompanying **status**, which provides needed resources for role-play. Statuses are social positions usually associated with roles, and stable statuses are components of a complex social system. We can't just introduce a new activity (like grokking) or role (like groksters) without establishing how these fit into society as a whole. Otherwise, they are deviant roles, subject to exclusion, stigma, and attack. The roles we play are dependent on the statuses we occupy in society; they exist outside of us, yet nevertheless regulate our behaviour.

Statuses and roles are closely related but not the same things. As explained by anthropologist Ralph Linton, people play roles but occupy statuses. Statuses are characterized by certain qualities, duties, and privileges—the responsibilities and rights associated with particular statuses in society. Statuses stand in a hierarchical relationship to other statuses, and the hierarchy itself is determined by the structure of society. It is easiest to understand a status system in the context of a formal organization. Consider the army: the bottom status or rank is the private or ensign, and above private, the ranks in ascending order are corporal, lieutenant, captain, major, colonel, and general. Each of these ranks dominates all of the ranks below it; each has a set of duties and obligations, and a corresponding set of rights.

It is easy to see why, in this functionalist image of society, order is all-important. Without an orderly agreed-on hierarchy of statuses, there are no stable roles, and without stable roles, no stable interactions. For this reason, Parsons (1949) views statuses as central ingredients of social order, and asks us to imagine that the obligations and privileges associated with each status are well known and widely accepted, because of socialization. When socialization is incomplete or faulty, or people refuse to accept the rights and duties associated with hierarchical statuses, there is a breakdown of social interaction and disorder follows. Society resists breakdown by using methods like embarrassment and shame to restore the social equilibrium.

role-making

The process of creating new social roles in and through interaction.

status

A person's social position, which is associated with a role and its associated scripts.

status sequence

The array of statuses we occupy over a lifetime, through which we pass in a socially recognizable order.

Both teachers and students are expected to play certain 'roles', as part of their identities.

One World, Many Societies

BOX 3.1

Non-verbal Communication

The most commonly used language is non-verbal communication, defined by anything consisting of eye contact, facial expressions, patterns of touch, gestures, spatial arrangements, tones of voice, or expressive movement. Both visual and verbal communications are defined by the culture in which they are created, so they vary from one culture to another. Consider how non-verbal gestures of greeting differ among different countries:

- In Canada, men greet each other with a firm handshake.
- In the US, women may briefly hug other women and men may quickly kiss the cheek of a woman; men greet each other with handshakes.
- In most of South and Central America, women and men greet with a warm and soft handshake; men greet friends with the 'abrazo', a slight hug with a few pats on the back, while women lightly hug friends and kiss them on the cheek.
- In the Middle East, greetings are exchanged with the nod of a head or a handshake.
- In Africa, the handshake is the most common form of greeting, sometimes followed by a touch on the elbow (e.g., in Egypt); women often curtsey when greeting others.
- In China, greeting usually requires just a slight nod and bow.
- In India, when greeting someone, say, 'Namaste', and press palms together with the fingers pointing upward.
- In the Philippines, greetings are done with a quick flash of the eyebrows.
- In most of Europe, warm hugs and kisses on the cheek are common. This varies slightly from one country to another.

Source: Adapted from Wu (2005).

As mentioned, we learn how to live in society through *socialization*. In other words, we learn from others—our parents, teachers, friends, and the mass media. Contrary to popular belief, socialization does not end when we become adults; we experience socialization throughout our lives. So, as we experience and pass through new and ever-changing roles, we continue to learn how to be effective members of society.

Role Conflicts and Role Strains

Sociologists theorize about roles, especially the way people manage the various roles they play, as well as the statuses they occupy. But because people play multiple roles, they sometimes have trouble fulfilling all of their role requirements. When the roles a person plays conflict with each other, the individual experiences **role strain**, which reveals itself as stress.

We have all experienced role strain at some time or another. As a student, you are likely familiar with one form of this strain called *role conflict*. This occurs when a person has to satisfy the demands of two or more incompatible or contradictory roles, such that playing one role necessarily undermines the other. Imagine you need to study for an upcoming mid-term test, despite competing obligations: your mother is depressed, your boyfriend has the flu, your boss needs you to take an extra shift at work, your sports team is practising for an important game next week. So, you may want to play the role of 'good student' whose main priority is to prepare for the upcoming test. But you also want to be a 'good daughter', 'good girlfriend', 'good employee', or 'good team member'. You are bound to fail at one of these and, sometimes, you will fail at all of them.

role strain

A result of role conflict, when the demands of some roles conflict with the demands of others.

Despite these strains, society continues to work amazingly smoothly and social order is maintained. Somehow, people find ways of managing the stress associated with role strain. They do so in various ways, by using sometimes-ingenious social mechanisms.

One such mechanism is *prioritizing* social roles, which allows a person to resolve role strain quickly and efficiently when it arises. Say that, as a student, you decide that your grade has to take the highest priority. Your rule is: No matter what conflicts arise, always protect your grade-point average. So, during the school year, you will run the risk of (occasionally) being a lousy daughter, girlfriend, employee, or team member. As a second mechanism, at the extreme, assigning priorities is like adopting what is known as a *master status*: making one role more important than all the others. Such a role—whether based on sex, race, social class, occupation, even illness or disability—is one that most distinctly characterizes an individual, in his or her own eyes. By comparison, all other roles hold a secondary importance.

A third mechanism for reducing role strain is by *compartmentalization*, or the division of activities into categories or sections. This often involves keeping your groups separate—for example, keeping your parents separate from your friends, or your work-friends separate from your school-friends. By keeping these groups separate, it is easier to keep the roles associated with each group separate too—many young people do not act in the same manner with their parents as they do with their friends. In this way, you minimize the risk of humiliation when one group discloses something embarrassing to the other group, like when your parents show your baby photos to your friends.

This long train of concepts—roles, identities, and so on—is necessary because it provides the building materials for a more complex picture of social life. Let us now proceed to an interesting insight that we may, perhaps, view as a fourth mechanism for reducing role strain—though it is more than that. This is the skilful use of secrecy.

Classic Studies
'The Sociology of Secrecy and of Secret Societies'

As noted, people do all sorts of things to make their adherence to society's rules—and its social scripts—easier and more tolerable. We may, in principle, accept society's rules about marriage, work, or friendship, for example, but we don't always feel fully attached to these rules. Everyone feels the need to deviate, or break the rules, from time to time; the question is, how do people do this with impunity? The answer is, through the use of secrecy. The first sociologist to study secrecy, and secret societies, was Georg Simmel (1906).

Simmel's insights into the social construction of deviance and deviant communities help us to understand the importance of secrecy, secret worlds, and secret societies. He showed how our 'second' or constructed (often, secret) worlds build on our 'real' world of daily life. Indirectly, Simmel asserted the normality of deviance and the universality of secret strategies for performing deviance.

Our 'first world' is the recognized world of socially acceptable activities. Our second world includes (usually) hidden deviant activities—such as sexual affairs, drug addictions, treacherous plots, violent acts, and dishonourable schemes— that most people cannot see most of the time. According to Simmel, everyone uses secrets to create and occupy these second worlds.

Social life, then, is a like a game of hide-and-seek. One person intentionally hides something and another person tries to find out what is hidden. By Simmel's reckoning, secrecy is a normal part of social relations. It is functionally necessary in complex societies; and cities are especially useful in this respect, since they allow much more secrecy than small communities do. Strangers in cities capitalize on secrecy even more than other people, gaining social freedom at the expense of inclusion. These arguments fit well with Erving Goffman's treatment of 'impression management' in his classic book *Stigma*, discussed earlier.

In Simmel's view, both secrecy and a lack of secrecy can be harmful. Lies are especially dangerous in modern societies, Simmel asserts, because individuals base important decisions on assumptions they cannot easily confirm. (Lies and secrets are not the same thing, but they are often related by the suppression of needed information.) Yet, he says, we all need some concealment. Sometimes, as with *white lies*, our relationships benefit more from concealment than from openness. ('No, your butt doesn't look huge in those pants'.) In practice, every relationship has its own notions—stated and unstated—about secrecy and discretion. Every relationship has its own tolerable limit of deviation and secrecy. Today, we cannot understand the operation of social institutions—especially small ones like families—unless we understand their secrets and the processes by which people disclose and deal with secrets (about lawbreaking, addiction, infidelity, homosexuality, and so on.)

Within this general context, *secret societies* hold a particular importance for religion and politics. Members of a secret society (e.g., al Qaeda) are necessarily concerned with protecting their most important ideas, sentiments, and information. They do so by controlling the flow of public information. A secret society is 'an interactional unit characterized in its totality by the fact that reciprocal relations among its members are governed by the protective functions of secrecy' (Simmel, 1906: 324).

There are two main components to this definition. First, there is a concern by the members of a group to protect the ideas, activities, and 'sentiments to which they attach positive value' (ibid). Second, members defend the secrecy and privacy of their community by 'controlling the distribution of information about the valued elements' (ibid). For Simmel, secret societies develop in one of two frames dependent upon 'the extensity of secrecy' within the group. Where there is a high level of security and protection of the group and its higher members, 'the secrecy incorporates information about all aspects of the interactional unit including its very existence' (ibid). At a lower level of concealment, 'only some aspects such as membership regulations or goals remain secret' (ibid).

So, communication and concealment are central to our performance of social life; and through social scripts, we all have some understanding of what society requires. Far more remarkable, since less obvious, are *social forms*: they control our behaviour even though we may be quite unaware of how or why this is happening.

Dyads, Triads, and Small Groups

Social scripts direct our behaviour. Social forms, by contrast, are not prescriptive but descriptive. Social forms emerge without people's intention—and often even awareness—in a social situation. In his 1908 essay 'Individuality and Social Forms', Georg Simmel defines sociology as comprising two elements, which are distinguishable only analytically. One element is *content*, the purpose or motive of an action or interaction. The other is *form*, the mode of interaction among individuals through which the specific content achieves social reality.

Consider an example of social forms that involves two scenarios. In the first scenario, two friends are deciding what movie to see on Saturday night. In the second scenario, three friends are deciding the same thing. Largely, the situations are identical. Certainly, the motivations are identical—to see a movie with friends. However, the two interactions are likely to differ because dyads (two-person groups) rarely work the same as triads (three-person groups).

Speaking broadly, binary groups—two-person groups or multiples of two—tend to either agree easily or fall into a hard-to-resolve conflict. By contrast, odd-numbered groups (of three people, for example) may take a long time agreeing, but they do not usually fall into polarized, hard-to-resolve conflicts. Odd-numbered groups are characterized by compromise and shifting alliances. One person of a triad is likely to serve as peacemaker or intermediary between the other two. No such intermediary is available in a dyad. Any decision-process, indeed, any interaction process, is different in a group of three than in a group of two, even when the goal is the same. (Larger-sized groups tend to follow similar patterns, depending on whether they have an even or odd number of members; however, the analysis is far more complex, since more people are available to serve as intermediaries and peace-makers.)

As expressed by this example, the idea of social forms is fundamental to sociological thinking, and it opposes what has been called the *voluntarist* position. Voluntarism, a social psychological approach, argues that our social behaviour is a clear reflection of our goals, values, and intentions, and that our identities shape our interactions. But contrary to this view, sociologists believe that our social behaviours often have little to do with our true goals, values, and intentions. People do what they have to do to gain social acceptance. Further, their interactions shape their identities, not the other way around. So, we strive to fit into the social form confronting us, and tailor our actions to its requirements.

That is, we develop our social purposes or motives after being thrust into social roles. The most interesting claim of this sort was made by American sociologist Robert Bales, who in the 1950s studied 'training groups' at Harvard University. These groups of undergraduates were recruited to meet once a week over the course of a year and discuss assigned topics or solve problems together while being watched through a one-way mirror. Bales' study revealed that in each of his groups, three social forms emerged: a task leader, an emotional leader, and a joker. The task leader helped the group organize itself to solve the problem that had been posed; he or she helped to set goals and organize the work. The emotional leader helped the group cope with frustration and conflict, so strong feelings did not deflect the group from its task. In effect, the emotional leader was the peacemaker. Finally, the joker was—as the name suggests—the person who helped release tensions in the group by joking and fooling around. This seemingly slack time-waster was fully as important as the task leader and emotional leader. Without the periodic tension release afforded by joking, the group might not have performed successfully, or even survived (Bales, 1950).

The take-home message: since groups are collections of individuals linked together by regular interaction, in order to survive they need some of their members to perform special kinds of roles. Eventually, in every group, people step forward to fill these roles—otherwise the group breaks up. This fulfillment of roles happens without planning or even a conscious awareness of group needs. If the group survives, the process just happens, and vice versa. This, then, is a small-scale version of the functionalist model of social systems as put forth by Parsons and his students, including Robert Bales. The functionalists argued that all social systems—groups, communities, organizations, societies, and empires—have these systemic, self-maintaining features that enable them to survive, to move forward, and to achieve their goals.

This highlights an interesting difference between functionalists and symbolic interactionists in the sociological approach to social relations. Though there are many overlaps and convergences between the two approaches, at their extremes, they lead in somewhat different directions. At the extreme, symbolic interactionism argues that we are all, everyday, creating and invigorating 'the social structure' which would not exist without our intentional, co-operative efforts. At the extreme, functionalism argues that 'social systems' persist outside the efforts and intentions of individuals; they force us to conform whether we are aware or unaware, willing or not. From this perspective, functionalists far more easily explain social forms than symbolic interactionists.

Teams, Bands, and Gangs

Small groups are perfect places to watch social scripts and social forms in action. They are small and informal enough to be creative, but large enough to need a division of labour and some kind of rules and leadership. And, though there are many types of small group— families, work groups, and friendship cliques among them—teams, bands, and gangs are particularly useful in illustrating key theoretical points about social organization. For reasons that will become evident, we will lump together teams, bands, and gangs and even give them a group label, TBGs.

TBGs—as social forms—operate very similarly, despite their very different goals and activities. In a way, this is a central fact about sociology as a discipline: it looks for deep structures—for important operating similarities—in social units of every size and type. Often, it finds them, leading to the conclusion that all 'social systems'—whether families, groups, communities, or total societies—have important features in common that help the unit continue to function.

People typically join TBGs because they want to be members, not merely as the means to another end, such as to earn a course credit or receive a paycheque. They are not born into TBGs as they are into families; rather, joining them is a matter of choice. Usually, people join because they want to identify with, and be identified with, the particular team, band, or gang. Accordingly, each TBG has a defined membership—a clear idea of who belongs and who does not. It also has a clear set of goals and main activities. Moreover, TBGs have hierarchies, with leaders whose job it is to set specific goals, mobilize resources to achieve these goals, and motivate other members to participate, according to set rules and directives. In these respects, TBGs are like families, with the leaders acting as parents.

Like teams and gangs, musical bands tend to operate according to many unwritten rules. For example, band members are expected to avoid openly criticizing one another. If they have issues about another member's performance, they are supposed to direct these concerns to the leader; the leader then deals with the problem, if deemed appropriate. Some leaders convey their criticisms in gentle or roundabout ways, suggesting, for instance, that there is a general problem in the band, or in a particular section of the band, but usually without pointing a finger of blame at the particular offender.

Although the above observations apply generally to teams, bands, and gangs, there are clearly differences among individual TBGs. For example, some TBG leaders are more inclined than others to micromanage their members, whether because they want the group to achieve their stated goals or because they have personal needs to feel they are 'in control'. Some leaders may even pit group members against one another as rivals, in an attempt to motivate greater efforts. Or instead of rewards to motivate their members, they may use punishments, such as ridicule, shame, and threats. Sometimes these methods work, but sometimes they backfire. When they backfire, some members leave the group, overthrow the abusive leader, or simply give up.

In sports teams, we may be able to distinguish between those who play offence and those who play defence; between starting pitchers and closers; between guards and running backs or quarterbacks; between high scorers and enforcers; and between 'stars' and average players. Thus, all teams—like bands, gangs, and other secondary groups—have a stable division of labour.

All teams, bands, and gangs must also address problems of leadership, recruitment, communication, and control. Most especially, they must master the basics of group communication and co-operation that we commonly associate with 'teamwork': for example, building links, solving problems, managing conflict, and giving and receiving feedback.

The members of this rowing team were not born into it, they chose to join the team and probably wanted to be identified with being on the team.

In other words, even in social organizations as small as teams, bands, and gangs, we find important task specialization, associated with differences of personality and social identity. All the members are expected to work together to achieve group goals, but they do so by carrying out different tasks, under the general supervision of a leader. It matters little whether the group's goal is to sound like The Rolling Stones or win a football championship. In either case, forming and maintaining a group demands good leadership and social cohesion.

Consider now a very different social form—the social network—that, unlike TBGs, has no membership list, no sense of group identity, and no shared goal. Yet, social networks, like TBGs, also help people to achieve their individual goals.

Cliques, Networks, and Small Worlds

The social network is another social form that is of increasing interest to sociologists. To help you understand a network, imagine 20 people connected, either directly or indirectly, to one another. A *direct connection* is a link of kinship, friendship, or acquaintance. Within this set of n=20 people, there can be 190 different paired direct connections—mathematically expressed as $[n(n-1)/2]$. As you will quickly note from this formula, if the network size merely doubles to 40 people, the number of direct connections explodes, rising to nearly 800 direct connections.

Indirect connections are as interesting as are direct connections to sociologists. In fact, some sociologists such as Mark Granovetter (1974) argue that *weakly tied networks*, based mainly on indirect links, may be even more useful than *strongly tied networks*, based mainly on direct links. A great deal of information, social support, and other valuable resources flows through incompletely connected, or weakly tied, networks. Other things flow as well: rumours, diseases, innovations, and job information, for example. All these spread most rapidly through networks of weak ties, because weakly tied networks have a vast outreach, connecting large numbers of people at a few removes.

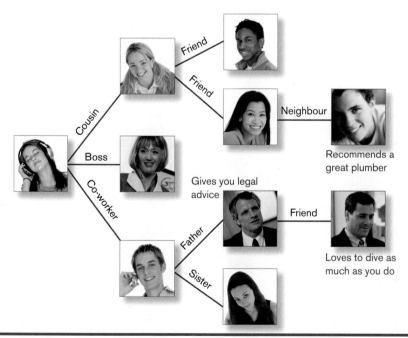

Figure 3.2 Social Networks

Source: Adapted from 'The Social Networking Imperative' (2007).

The reason for this is purely mathematical, as psychologist and mathematician Anatol Rapoport (1953) showed in classic papers on the topic, using computer simulation. Stated simply, information that is permitted to pass only through strong links—what Rapoport called 'biased nets' (e.g., brothers, sisters, first cousins, or best friends)—will cycle repeatedly through the same set of people, since they will tend to be strongly linked to one another, as well as to the (original) reference person. However, information permitted to pass only through weak links—what Rapoport called 'random nets' (e.g., third cousins or tenth-best friends)—will rapidly spread to new nodes. This fact underlies the important differences observed between (for example) international epidemics (random nets) and diseases associated with genetic inbreeding (biased nets).

At the same time, a social network is only as strong and stable as the pairwise connections—called *dyadic relationships*—that make it up. In stable dyadic relationships, based on social exchange, people give each other things they want and need. So long as these relations satisfy their needs, people remain in the network. This means that people are forever entering and leaving their social networks, though many also stay. As people enter and leave their dyadic relationships, the networks change in their size and composition; and this, in turn, affects the type of resources flowing throughout the network.

Each figure in a network is called a *node*. In most social networks of interest to sociologists, nodes are individual people; but nodes can also be groups, institutions, cities, or even countries. Cities themselves constitute vast political, economic, and social networks and establish connections around the world, especially with the globalization of recent decades. Of course, some cities are dominant in the world network of cities—they are the key nodes in the relations between cities worldwide.

Increasingly, in cyberspace people are setting up *virtual* networks of relationships, as well as *real* ones. In recent years, Internet-based social networking services such as LinkedIn, Friendster, and Facebook have rapidly increased in popularity, and are continuing to do so. Among younger generations in North America, about 75 to 85 per cent say they have a profile on at least one social networking site (Pew Internet, 2008; Delvinia Interactive, 2009).

These services collect information from an individual's profile and list of social contacts to create a display of his or her personal social network—or at least, the first-order links in this network. No one knows the precise size and composition of any person's network; likely, it comprises hundreds or even thousands of indirectly linked individuals. These popular online services are often provided free to users, although individuals must disclose personal information to register and use the site. Such services build on the premise that individuals may be merely a few 'links' removed from desirable business or social partners and may discover these links only when they use the service. In large part, such 'discoveries' are mainly a result of chance events within the network structure.

An interesting feature of social networks is their 'small world' property. That is, most people are indirectly tied to everyone else at a few removes (the so-called 'six degrees of separation'). However, people within the network differ in their number of linkages. Some are 'sociometric stars' or 'connectors', people who link an especially large number of network members directly and indirectly. Because of their network positions, a disproportionate share of information and influence flows through these people.

Consider the result of a small study by Canadian sociologist Sasha Stark (2009) to reveal the links between five leading researchers in the area of problem gambling. Stark coded all the publications of these five researchers to identify the direct collaborations between them, their collaborations with others, and the interlinkages of these collaborators. Then, a specially designed computer program identified and graphed the network of connections. The resulting diagram shows clearly the 'small world' character of a research network; many and likely all social networks have a similar structure.

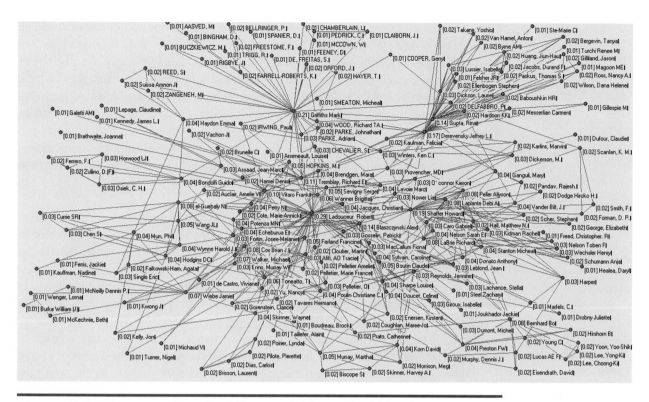

Figure 3.3 Computer-Graphed Research Network of Five Important Gambling Researchers

Source: Stark (2009).

The most highly interlinked members of the network—the 'stars' may also serve as 'brokers' or 'entrepreneurs', meaning they have the ability to link two or more separate networks, so each can benefit from the others. Sometimes they even represent members of one network to members of another. In this sense, then, leadership involves integrating people from the top down—through linkages between leaders, brokers, or entrepreneurs.

Point/Counterpoint

BOX **3.2**

The Debate on Social Networking Sites

Does social networking foster valuable relationships? A 1974 study of people looking for work showed that 56 per cent found good jobs through 'weak ties', indirect connections such as friends of friends. Websites such as Facebook or MySpace make it easier to connect with people you don't know directly. And people doing the hiring are likely to look for you online before they call you in for an interview.

But some believe nothing beats a face-to-face meeting. It can be hard to get a sense of the real person behind the online profile, and separating likely prospects from 'spam' can be more trouble than it's worth. For many, social-networking sites prove more of a distraction than a tool. 'A good old-fashioned handshake or happy-hour cocktail will do more to seal the deal than any MySpace profile'.

Source: Adapted from Goudreau and Pelzak (2008).

In practice, this is far easier to achieve than integration at the bottom, by interweaving all the members of a single social network.

The integrative role of leaders is especially important because many of us belong to inward-looking *cliques*: group nodes nested within social networks. Sociologists define a *clique* as a group of tightly interconnected people—a friendship circle whose members are all connected to one another, and to the outside world, in similar ways. Usually, clique members feel strong positive sentiments or liking for one another and contempt for outsiders. They spend more time with one another than with non-clique members, share their knowledge with one another, and think and behave similarly. They also try to ignore or exclude outsiders—people who are not like themselves, and are not friends of their friends.

In short, cliques are groups characterized by friendship, similarity, interaction, exclusion, and the flow of valuable resources, such as information, support, and opinions. In these respects, cliques are mini-communities, almost mini-states. Like states, they amass power and resources. They receive, censor, and direct information flow. Also like states, cliques remain distinct. Resources flow readily within the clique and less readily outside its borders. Cliques gather and redirect information. They also produce information, distort it, and send it out as gossip.

Cliques have no obvious reason to exist, given that they have no practical goals. In this respect, they are very different from the teams, bands, and gangs we discussed earlier. But, although they are seemingly without goals, cliques nevertheless have an unstated 'mission' or purpose: to raise the status of clique members at the expense of non-members. Though lacking an organizational chart or stated division of labour, cliques usually have a clear hierarchy of influence and popularity, with the leader on top surrounded by his or her favourites. In this sense, then, a clique is a group of people working together, coordinated by communication and leadership to achieve a common goal or goals.

Cliques form in every area of life, even within bureaucracies and other formal organizations. However, cliques are most familiar to us from our childhood school experiences. In school settings, cliques usually have a well-defined membership. Clique members are typically similar to one another in background and behaviour. Members often have rituals that exclude outsiders and integrate insiders. A leader, usually the most popular member, dominates the other members. Usually, the leader defines the group boundaries, invents group rituals, and controls membership.

Cliques, though supportive to insiders, can be cruel to outsiders. Although the cruelty of cliques is often exaggerated in mass media (for example, in popular teenage movies), there is some truth to these depictions. In addition, cliques do not form only within high school settings. They can form and do just as much damage among younger children as well. Some elementary schools implement specific rules or organize educational friendship workshops to break down the barriers between identified cliques (Batiuk, Boland, and Wilcox, 2004).

Some wrongly believe that cliques mainly exist within school settings. On the contrary, research shows that cliques exist in all areas of social life, wherever people interact, no matter their age, ethnicity, culture, or sex. They are found in workplaces, cyberspace—even in seniors' homes (recall the news story about seniors' cliques in Box 1.2).

In recent years, social networking websites have proliferated, giving rise to online relationship networks. Some say that online communities are changing the way we look at the physical communities in which we live.

The cohesion of a clique is based mainly on loyalty to the leader and the group. This loyalty, in turn, is based as much on exclusion as it is on inclusion. Group members begin by separating themselves from non-members. Lack of contact with these 'outsiders' encourages members to believe that non-members are different and less socially desirable than themselves. Then, clique members use gossip to reinforce their ignorance of outsiders, and to ridicule and spread nasty rumours about them. Finally, they may even pick on or harass outsiders. Doing so instills fear, forcing outsiders to accept their inferior status and discouraging them from rallying together to challenge the clique's social power.

Cliques control their members by defining the behaviours that are proper and acceptable. Leaders are in charge of this, and usually skilled in exercising control. Often, they build members up and then cut them down, pushing the other members to try harder. Cliques, and the rituals of inclusion and exclusion on which they rely, are more than mere children's games. They are small-scale models of how organizations teach and enforce rules; in this way, they provide a lesson in severe social control. Cliques remind us that every inclusive action is, at the same time, exclusive. Organizations such as cliques have shared goals that are unstated but real. Their norms are unwritten but compelling, their hierarchies undocumented but powerful, and though their division of labour may be unplanned, it is usually effective.

Now it is time to extend these ideas to an understanding of social control in larger social structures; and no recent sociologist has been more gifted, or more celebrated, for this than Michel Foucault. Foucault is most important for showing how experts and people in power introduce notions of 'normality' into social scripts about mental health, criminality, and sexuality to consolidate their own power. He is also notable for his discussion of surveillance structures which, in a variety of larger organizations, try to regiment people according to prevailing ideas of normality.

People Are Talking About . . .
MICHEL FOUCAULT

Michel Foucault was born in 1926 in Poitiers, France, the second of three children in a middle-class family. He received his license in philosophy in 1948, in psychology in 1950, and a diploma in psychopathology in 1952. After graduating, Foucault held teaching positions from 1954 to 1958, teaching French at the universities of Uppsala, Warsaw, and Hamburg. He received his *doctorat d'état* in 1959, based on a doctoral thesis published two years later titled *Madness and Unreason: A History of Madness in the Classical Age.* He held positions in various universities and involved himself in political causes in Europe and Iran. Foucault died in Paris from an AIDS-related illness in 1984.

Foucault focused on 'the critical history of the present'. He began with an 'archaeological' approach, looking at the history of disciplines such as science, philosophy, art, and literature, and how the paradigms of knowledge in each discipline changed over time. He later adopted a 'genealogical' approach, in which he examined the complex relationship of power to knowledge. Most important, he claimed that together, knowledge and power control people by creating and enforcing social norms for human behaviour. In Foucault's view, these norms are not derived from evidence or rational argument, but are rather produced by historical circumstance. This genealogical view informed his understanding of deviations from these norms within psychiatry, medicine, and criminology. For example, it gave Foucault a new understanding of madness and its social meaning.

In 1975, Foucault published *Discipline and Punish: The Origin of the Prison,* which is widely considered his most influential work. It examines how the power–knowledge relationship uses coercion and surveillance to exert direct, physical control in enforcing standards of behaviour, as found in modern prisons (beginning in the nineteenth century), following patterns developed in the military and in factories and schools.

Foucault also published several works on sexuality, in which he described 'bio-power'—a form of power that falls outside of traditional notions of political and social authority. Where discipline exerts control over an individual, bio-power exerts control over a population, through government policies that influence reproduction, health, and mortality. His goal was to show that individuals, by recognizing this form of power, could free themselves from its influence.

Source: Adapted from *Fifty Key Sociologists: The Contemporary Theorists* (edited by John Scott, London: Routledge, 2006) and other sources.

To understand Foucault is to understand how our conceptions of social life—including our social forms and social scripts—are historically specific, arbitrary yet compelling. All of these are nested in notions of 'normality' and enjoy much of their hold over us because they are all visible—that is, subject to surveillance by others. No source of surveillance, and no source of social rules, is as compelling as the state and its institutions. Thus, the social order, at bottom, is a structure of power relations underwritten by the state but watched by all of us, as state minions.

At the centre of Foucault's work is the notion of 'governmentality', by which he is usually understood to mean the regulation of people's behaviour—whether regulated by themselves or by others, especially the state. Of this, Lemke (2001) remarks, 'All in all, in his history of governmentality Foucault endeavors to show how the modern sovereign state and the modern autonomous individual co-determine each other's emergence.' Thus, paradoxically, the growth of individualism as we understand it today is part of the same process that produces monstrously large and powerful institutions for control and repression: the state, the school, the military, the civil bureaucracy, and so on. The question, then, is by what means is governmentality achieved in different historical periods—especially our own—and why? Further, how do individuals make a space for their 'selves' amid this totalitarian surveillance? Finally, how do states preserve control even when surveillance is, necessarily, limited and imperfect?

On these matters, Debrix and Barder (2009) note the decentralization of fear and power in a governmentalized modern society encourages the use of danger, threat, insecurity, or hostility to control behaviour. This 'mobilization of fear' in a population depends on widespread terrifying mechanisms to generate anxiety about losing a 'normal' way of life.

Usually, however, the mechanisms of control are less obviously terrifying. Consider the widespread fear of aging and its effect on people's behaviour. Castle (2009) notes, for example, following Foucault, that professional power in gerontology makes seniors dependent on the governing system through assessment and surveillance. According to McDaniel (2009), power and bodies are both concepts that are relevant to aging and the care of older people, whether they are the people cared for or their caregivers. Many of those who care for the elderly are themselves disadvantaged: women of a visible ethnic minority, who often have not obtained citizenship or landed immigrant status.

Svihula (2009) notes that through Foucault's analysis we can identify relations of power and state governmentality at the local level within the field of gerontology. However, she claims that 'power at the macro level'—specifically, the 'market ethos' that leads to local deregulation of assessment and surveillance—in the care of the elderly needs to be examined. As well, Svihula considers how older people can become 'agents of resistance' in the system in which they are also subjects.

We can apply similar Foucauldian notions to understanding the issues around cosmetic surgery among younger people. Here, issues around 'normality'—a topic of continuing interest to Foucault—become relevant. For example, someone diagnosed with Body

Dysmorphic Disorder (BDD), which causes a pathological aversion to some part of his or her appearance, will usually not be considered a good candidate for cosmetic surgery, since the disorder is not cured by surgery and the patient will continue to be dissatisfied. Heyes (2009) follows Foucault in arguing that the surgical profession exercises disciplinary power in attempting to drawing a line between normal and abnormal concern with appearance. Heyes suggests that this distinction between normal and abnormal helps 'legitimize' the 'ethically suspect' field of cosmetic surgery, by making it appear that its practitioners exercise professional restraint in selecting patients on whom to perform cosmetic surgery. He contends that, instead, these surgeons merely ensure the profitability of their practice by claiming that negative results must be caused by a patients' disorder.

Evans and Colls (2009) call similar attention to the current debates about obesity, examining the justifications and implications of the Body Mass Index (BMI) as a tool in public health policy on obesity, and specifically its use in the UK in diagnosing obesity among schoolchildren. They use Foucault's notions of bio-power and governmentality to suggest that BMI measurement does not take into account the whole body and experiences of the people being measured, and contributes to a false image of health and illness. More important, the measurement provides a way of drawing lines between 'normal' and 'abnormal', between virtuous and blameworthy people, for purposes of control.

Similar reasoning can be used to understand how many (if not all) discourses serve to normalize and control people. Hay (2009) provides the example of employee conversations between manager and employee focused around employee development, which are widespread in the Danish labour market. Such conversations, required by many labour market agreements, aim at continually adjusting personal competences to corporate visions, missions, and goals. Toward this goal, employees are invited to participate in the conversations once every year. Hay argues, following Foucault, that these conversations are the hidden technologies of power and, in this way, like early Christian rituals of confession (but without the relief and release of absolution).

Such rituals of self-examination, identification of inner impurities, disclosure of the self, and renunciation of the self are basic elements of Foucault's 'technologies of the self'. Through time, these rituals undergo change and transformation, only to resurface in our time as a widespread way of changing the self. In a framework of freedom and choice—the modern rationale of control—technologies of the self, combined with formal relations of domination, form a specific type of governmentality. This regulation needs the voluntary participation of the employee to confess faults that keep him or her from achieving corporate goals. Ideally (from the organization's standpoint), the soul is transformed in an endless striving for perfection as an employee. In this instance, it is particularly clear how people, through norms and rules, are implication in their own self-criticism and institutional subjection.

Foucault, originally a Marxist, developed his own theories about power and control that Marxists continue to contest today. Consider the nature of 'neo-liberalism': a political philosophy that, under the guise of liberation, undermines collective efforts to redistribute wealth and power, and in this way help the vulnerable. Lazzarato (2009) draws on Foucault and argues that, by emphasizing the importance of the individual, and market competition, this ideology has transformed society into an ever less equal 'enterprise society'. The institutional effect of this emphasis on individuals in markets is to create social insecurity and to weaken the role of the state—to depoliticize social issues. In this way, they undermine the co-operative practices of planning and redistribution the welfare state had, for decades, promoted.

From this standpoint, the aim of neo-liberal politics is the restoration of capitalist power over the distribution of wealth. From the Foucauldian stance, then, the new, neo-liberal state provides conditions for the triumph of rampant market capitalism and the new type of individual suitable for it.

Finally, Blain (2009) examines the American 'war on terrorism', following both Foucault's genealogical approach to the relationship of power and knowledge and his theory of governmentality. Here, Blain traces the origins of the notion of 'terrorism', from the English response to the French Revolution. For the last two centuries or so, following that Revolution, governments in liberal democratic societies have labelled some acts of political violence illegitimate while continuing to consider other acts legitimate. Thus, it is the government's perception of the violent act, rather than the nature of the act itself, that determines whether it is considered terrorism—a practice that remains intact today in all reporting on the Middle East and other foreign conflicts.

Thus, a review of recent writings finds heated debate about Foucault and his writings—at least 200 journal articles disputing Foucault since 2008. Clearly, sociologists are talking about Michel Foucault. More than any other modern theorist, Foucault has helped us understand the nature of power in present-day societies, and the ways power is exercised often without our awareness, by obliging us to conform to notions of 'normality'. These notions and practices are nested in the social scripts we perform and the social forms we inhabit, however unwittingly. The powerful, he shows us, always use modern methods and modern institutions—even professional experts to 'theorize' the dominant views—to their own advantage, to control the rest of us.

New Insights

Earlier in the chapter, we discussed sociological notions of community, and much current writing is concerned with reconceiving the traditional notions of 'community'. For example, Adler and Adler (2008) look at people who injure themselves. From a psychological perspective, one might investigate the reasons people injure themselves: their motives and psychopathologies. But from a sociological perspective, we are inclined to ask about self-injury as a social (not antisocial), communal (not isolated) activity. Previously loners, many self-injurers have formed Internet communities. Adler and Adler analyzed the subculture that these people have formed on the Internet, through participating in these communities and their various forms of online communication, and speaking directly to self-injurers. This social constructionist research sheds new light on the creation of virtual communities made possible by computerized technology, and the ways deviant groups avoid isolation, stigma, and exclusion.

Increasingly, researchers realize that communities can take various forms and serve a variety of purposes. So, for example, Purcell (2009) criticizes Old Left theories of protest: not every social movement needs to be class-based, nor does it have to follow a particular recipe. He argues that one fruitful way to think of present-day political movements is to imagine them as different in form but similar in their intent, resulting in a formation he calls 'networks of equivalence'. Using an example of political movements in Seattle creating such networks, his point is that different organizations with related purposes can take a wide variety of different forms to achieve their common goals. Not all communities need be the same in form to pursue the same result.

There are political ramifications to the use of the term *community*, which implies a degree of organization, identification, and commitment that demands our attention. Consider, along with Merrill Singer (2006), the difficulty in assessing the application of 'community' to deviant groups such as drug addicts. Singer reviews the literature on 'the drug user community', and suggests that the increasing use of *community* applied to drug users may have unknown future implications for public health policy. He notes that the idea of community, a central concept in public health for 30 years, is hard to define in a way that suits the various contexts in which it is used. This discussion reminds us of the

Total institutions such as prisons exercise total control over their 'clients'.

importance of distinguishing correctly between different kinds of social units: between communities, groups and categories, for example.

The same problem is inevitably associated with studies of consumerism and mass culture. Everywhere, communities of consumers—or are they categories of consumers?—are forming around particular activities or commodities. In Poland, for example, Antonowicz and Wrzesinski (2009) relate Thomas Luckmann's notion of *invisible religion* to sports fans' devotion to their teams as a form of community, with shared tradition, team colours, and emblems. This postmodern devotion encompasses a range of degrees of participation and 'faith', just as traditional religions do, and is made more complex by the increasing commercialization of sports. But does this represent a true community—or for that matter, a true religion? Or is it symptomatic of brief, manic bursts of consumer enthusiasm that dot the cultural landscape in postmodern societies?

Consumerism as an organizing principle of community sentiment is evident in an article by Thompson and Coskuner-Balli (2007), who examine community supported agriculture (CSA)—a system in which consumers buy 'shares' in local farms, and are supplied with fresh produce throughout the growing season. People are usually drawn to join CSAs by a desire to eat local organic produce, which is often an ideological stance for them, and an expression of idealized romanticism around farming. Getting produce from CSAs usually means little choice and some inconvenience, but CSA supporters see these as 'moral virtues'. The authors remind us that, in what Weber called a 'disenchanted' modern age, people continue to seek transcendent meanings and moral guidance—even in their market relations. How else can we explain the investment of 'green' (i.e., pro-environmental) shopping with the degree of moral righteousness evident in our supermarkets and on our television screens? From mere local market relations grow large ideological meanings, the authors say.

These writings about sport fandom and consumer fetishism suggest that modern community life is little more than fantasy and the imaginary. However, Rabot (2007) reminds us that even shared fantasies have social value. What others might see as the product of alienation, he sees as a 'vector of socialities'. It is through the broadcasting of images—however fanciful—that human communion is created and heightened. Thus, in the images around us (iconic, advertising, television, virtual, etc.) we see the signs of a committed tribal membership in an otherwise fragmented, disenchanted, and rootless society. We rely on new technologies to 're-mythologize' and re-enchant our postmodern lives.

Moreover, if fantasy and imagination have social value, so does anxiety, according to some. On this, Conroy (2007) writes 'anxiety, and particularly that of a social nature concerning the ability to relate to others is a prominent feature of my generation'. Conroy shows how postmodern understandings of uncertainty are linked to the social causes of anxiety. He concludes that globalization contributes to the social anxieties and attachment disorders that are common in the younger generation, for example by creating chronic job insecurity that results from the export of good jobs overseas. Rather than seeing this as pathological, we can more usefully see anxiety as normal and the basis for generational unity.

In the new postmodern world view, perspectives have changed towards social structure, culture, lecture, sociology, psychology, and the economy. According to Yeygel (2006), postmodernism caused social class to lose its importance for people, replaced by a postmodern tribal concept instead. Alongside this has been a shift in consumerism from the mere exploitation of a mass public to something far more individualized, yet still communal. While modern marketing is built on mass culture, mass production, and mass consumption, postmodern marketing is built on one-to-one communication with consumers, with their similar yet seemingly unique styles and desires.

In the face of continued attacks by postmodernists on their reductiveness and oversimplification, some Marxists are striking back. For example, Rehmann (2007) claims to see two main flaws in postmodernism. One is that it 'de-materializes social relations', focusing mainly on signs and symbols, thoughts, fantasies, and images. The other is that postmodernism doesn't try hard enough to decipher the contradictions and antagonisms in our social relations—for example, in our class relations.

Faced with these defects, Marxist theory has a double task, the author says. On the one hand, it must continue to critique the social fragments and fetishes that are promoted by neo-liberalism and dominant (capitalist-oriented) ideology. However stylish, hilarious, or entertaining it may be, a consumerist culture is an exploitive culture. At the same time, Marxism should re-interpret the valid insights of postmodernism in the framework of a historical materialist theory of domination. For example, it has to reinsert the concrete labouring bodies into a social and cultural analysis of present-day capitalism, on the ground and in cyberspace.

Salerno (2006), too, argues for a radical re-imagining of community. He notes that the 'American ambivalence' toward community—the tension between social engagement and individual hedonism—reflects an alienation in modern capitalistic economies that prevents any real communal life. Romantic dreams of utopia, coupled with social paranoia, have led to barred windows and gated communities. A sense of community remains unattainable in capitalist societies, where market forces alienate and isolate the residents.

Modern neighbourhoods are less communities than commodities that are rooted in private property but owned mostly by financial institutions, not the residents. In this respect, people have about as much real connection with their community as they do with their local Walmart superstore: it is there, they use it, and it belongs to someone else. The locus of control and planning lies elsewhere. Integrated as they are into the same system of production and consumption as workplaces, residential communities are extensions of workplaces. A result of this ambivalence and alienation is the superficiality of place—that is, community—in people's lives.

Chapter Summary

As we have seen, social structures, especially social scripts and social forms, provide a backdrop to our social relations, as do population and environment, discussed in the previous chapter.

Our identities and roles are a central part of the way social structure controls us through our interactions with others. And, our group relations are shaped by the demands and characteristics of social groups which, as we have seen, have system 'needs' of their own. Pressures for loyalty and conformity, for example, influence group members to relate to other people in ways that are useful to the group, community, or organization, even if not directly beneficial to the individuals involved.

In large organizations, people are often nested within smaller structures—in roles, cliques, and small groups. In these large organizations, people are under constant strain to withstand the varying cross-pressures of their different roles and relationships, all at the same time. In turn, these large organizations are nested in, and dominated by governmentality, market relations, global trends, and the fantasy world of media and advertising.

As we will see throughout this book, people's relations are further complicated by the social inequalities that shape and constrain their roles and group memberships. These inequalities, resulting from characteristics such as gender, age, social class, race or ethnicity, and region or nationality, work both separately and in combination to push individuals apart. They create feelings of distance and distrust that keep people from communicating openly and effectively. They make social interactions more difficult, social scripts more uncertain, social cohesion more unlikely; they undermine the social scripts and social forms we have discussed in this chapter.

But before we explore the effects of these inequalities—how they evolved, why they persist, and how people adjust to them—we will examine the idea of 'culture'. Second in importance only to 'social structure', culture is a key sociological concept, conveying various meanings. As we will see, no concept is more significant than 'culture' for understanding ideology, media, hyperreality, religion, and symbolic interaction.

Critical Thinking Questions

1. Recall an experience when someone violated a socially scripted norm. Describe the situation and the reactions of the people involved. What do you conclude about the significance of underlying social scripts in human interaction?

2. Take a moment to think about who you believe you are. How do you think this self-concept has shown itself? What is the importance in your identity of the roles you play in your life? How is your identity intertwined with the social roles you play?

3. Think about an example other than the ones in this book to show *role embracement*, *role distance*, and *role exit*. How does an individual's identity change throughout this process? (For example, consider the history of a love affair you may know about: its elated beginning, complicated middle, and sorry ending.)

4. What is the importance of status in our society? What kinds of advantages do people who occupy higher statuses gain? Are there any disadvantages? How do you think social position matches to income, education, health, longevity, and satisfaction?

5. Do you have a personal profile on at least one online social networking site? If so, do you believe this service is a good way to preserve and expand your social network? What do you think are the advantages and disadvantages with having such a profile?

6. Try to remember a social situation in which you participated, where many or most of the people present were strangers. How did you identify and learn the norms of the situation? How did you contribute to emerging group culture? By what stages did the key players—the task leader, emotional leader, and joker—emerge?

Recommended Readings

Max Travers, *The New Bureaucracy: Quality Assurance and Its Critics* (Bristol, UK: The Policy Press, 2007). This analysis of British bureaucratic organizations is written from a symbolic interactionist viewpoint. It also overviews the classic works on this topic, including material by Weber, Merton, Durkheim, Marx, Parsons, Goffman, and others.

Paul Du Gay, *The Values of Bureaucracy* (Oxford: Oxford University Press, 2005). This book explores why bureaucracies are such successful, and therefore persistent, organizational structures. The book outlines the characteristics that make bureaucracies efficient in various settings.

Linton C. Freeman, *The Development of Social Network Analysis: A Study in the Sociology of Science* (Vancouver, CA: Empirical Press, 2004). Humans have an inherent need to be social; therefore, social networks and social structure have existed for centuries. This book considers the development of sociological research on these topics over the course of the twentieth century. It also discusses the characteristics of social network composition as vast webs of connections between nodes.

John Mirowsky and Catherine E. Ross, *Education, Social Status and Health* (New York, Aldine De Gruyter, 2003). This book examines the connection between social status and health and well-being. It is well-known that higher social status—including high income, high educational background, occupational success, and prestige—is associated with better health and vitality. The book also provides useful historical information, outlines of previous research, and statistical analyses.

Michel Crozier, *The Bureaucratic Phenomenon* (Chicago: University of Chicago Press, 1964). Crozier, a French sociologist, explores whether and why bureaucracies work differently in different societies and cultures, despite their common organization as described by Max Weber. With reference to societies' varying histories and circumstances, Crozier argues that the ways in which bureaucracies function vary according their societal context—for example, according to cultural conceptions of inequality and freedom.

Websites

Society for Study of Symbolic Interaction (SSSI)
www.espach.salford.ac.uk/sssi/index.php

Sociology of Organizations
www.sociosite.net/topics/organization.php

Correctional Services Canada
www.csc-scc.gc.ca

4 Culture

Learning Objectives

In this chapter, you will:

> Interpret culture as a symbolic environment in which humans live

> Connect micro and macro aspects of culture in several ways

> Consider the significance of cultural differences in our society and around the world

Chapter Outline

As human beings, we live in a world that differs dramatically from the world other species inhabit. For the most part, animals live in a natural environment to which they must adapt. Humans, however, also live in a social environment that is gradually coming to dominate the natural environment. For the most part, we adapt the environment to ourselves. This human-created environment in which we live is culture.

Our social environment is 'symbolic' as well as material, in the sense that every human group produces 'meanings' that remain in a society's memory. From this standpoint, what we often call 'culture'—concretized in a society's literature, arts, and sciences—is the group's memory. As memory, it supports the identity of that group or society. Thus, culture is a shared and remembered symbolic environment, and the people who share a culture are bound to experience the world similarly in certain ways. Culture structures a person's perception of the world and shapes his or her behaviour. A common culture helps to hold a society together. On the other hand, people brought up in a different culture perceive the world in a different way. They have different memories, traditions, values, attitudes, and beliefs. They may seem to be outsiders, strangers, even aliens, from the perspective of the culture to which they do *not* belong.

If we are to understand a society and the people who live in it, understanding its culture is essential. That is why sociologists and anthropologists focus on culture to get a sense of the whole society, whether they are looking at small-scale societies or large and complex ones. Sociologists are particularly interested in the kinds of social differences that are found within a society—differences of class, gender, ethnicity, and so on. We analyze the role of culture in creating or preserving these differences. And we examine the implications of the fact that these differences, and not others, are considered worth noticing.

Everyday Observations

When Kaori entered her third year of university she had the option of travelling to a foreign country to do some volunteer work, helping some of the people there and gaining experience in preparation for graduate school. She was excited by this possibility, but also anxious about what the experience would entail. Would she be able to get past the inevitable culture shock, learning the ways of life of the people and the hardships they face every day? The first few weeks were the most challenging—Kaori experienced many difficulties trying to understand the culture and mentality of the people she was trying to help. They just seemed so different from anyone she had ever met at home. Yet over time, Kaori found that after she became accustomed to those initially striking differences, she began to see many similarities between their culture and her own. She began to identify traits that made them all humans— humans living in a distinctive symbolic environment.

culture

Our uniquely human environment. It includes all of the objects, artifacts, institutions, organizations, ideas, and beliefs that make up the social environment of human life.

organizational culture

The way an organization has learned to deal with its environment; it includes norms and values that are subculturally distinct to the organization.

Just how significant are **cultural** differences in our daily lives? Undoubtedly, cultural differences do matter. They underlie many of the of the misunderstandings that arise in the interactions between people and are behind many of the challenges societies face in reconciling how some groups of humans live versus others. Especially living in Canada, we constantly hear about what cultural differences mean for our country and our national identity. As in other countries that accept immigrants in large numbers, cultural differences are the focus of debates on how best to integrate people from increasingly diverse cultural backgrounds. And at the microsociological level, think about the role of culture in shaping the lives of individuals. Perhaps you knew two people who were in love but who decided against marrying because they found it difficult to reconcile the influences of their different cultural upbringings.

Yet if we dig a little deeper, we will find that most other cultures are quite similar to our own. Despite variations in speech and dress, the people you meet on the streets of Canada are a lot like one another. Even in the cities of Europe, Asia, Africa, and Latin America, you meet people leading lives you can recognize, because in telltale ways their lives are like your own. You will see music videos on television in Paris, inline skates on the streets of Rio de Janeiro, and skyscrapers in Delhi, Hong Kong, and Lagos.

Outside giant international cities, we are likely to see more cultural variation from one country to the next. Cultural differences between people are especially striking once we set foot in the rural regions of Asia, Africa, and Latin America. There, we see poorer versions of our own society mixed with remnants of older, less familiar cultures. But even this degree of difference from our own culture does not capture the full range of human possibility. Only the study of history and anthropology makes us aware of how widely cultures have varied over space and time—of how very strange other people can seem to be. This variation tells us that people are able to create a huge variety of social relationships and forms of social **organization**.

So why the focus on differences? We tend to take culture for granted because often we assume that our behaviour is a result of human nature or common sense. We like to think that our own ways of seeing the world and behaving in it are natural: that we just do things because it is 'only natural', 'obvious', and 'unquestionable' that we should. Sometimes we even think that our goals, motives, attitudes, and beliefs are the only sensible ones. Everyone else would share them with us if their cultures did not get in the way, making them behave irrationally.

Yet nothing could be further from the truth. We are born with few predispositions to any particular forms of social behaviour or organization. We can see this, in part, by studying animals.

Like people, most animal species co-operate and communicate. Animal groups even have a division of labour and a ranking system, among other things. However, among most animals, both the small interactional processes and larger social arrangements, for the most part, are genetically programmed. Neither is open to a great deal of choice or voluntary change.

Because animal behaviour is largely genetic or inborn, it does not vary much within the species. Nor does it change within a generation, or even scores of generations. And so far, researchers have found little ability among higher animals to learn what people can learn. In contrast, few of our human ways of thinking and acting are either 'natural' or genetic. We humans change our environment, learn from our experiences, and pass on what we have learned to our children, so they can live differently than in the past. Our human abilities to think, plan, remember, and communicate give us a decided edge in creating complex social structures. Among people, both the micro and macro structures of society are open to change. Indeed, the human ability to change micro structures—to imagine, plan, and set about creating new futures—is precisely what allows us to change our larger social structures.

Is there anything that limits how widely human cultures can vary; if so, what is it? The search for an answer to this question has led generations of sociologists and anthropologists to look for cultural universals, or those practices found in every known human culture. Anthropologist George Murdock (1945: 124) listed many cultural universals, including the following general attributes: athletic sports (arranging exercise and harmless competition), bodily adornment (indicating status and selfhood), cooking (preparing food and eating sociably), dancing (expressing feeling through movement), funeral ceremonies (handling death and corpses), gift giving (showing gratitude and fondness), and language (giving commands and communicating views). Each one of these universals deals with a fundamental and general social issue. Other researchers have identified additional universals, such as the human ability to use fire. This ability to use fire serves as a good example of how people have historically sought to control nature—in effect, to transform nature into culture.

If certain cultural concerns are universal, we must allow for the possibility that they meet universal human needs, whether physical, emotional, intellectual, or spiritual. Yet, however 'natural' or original these needs might be, people meet them in a great variety of cultural ways. To say that all human cultures contain sport, religion, or marriage is to point to something that unites human beings. Yet you are well aware that cultural customs in relation to sport, religion, or marriage vary enormously. The processes people use to meet a common need differ widely among cultures.

The only real universal is culture itself: the central role culture plays in tying people to their society through its connections with both social structure and private experience. At the macro level, the dominant **values** of a culture—the socially shared conceptions of what

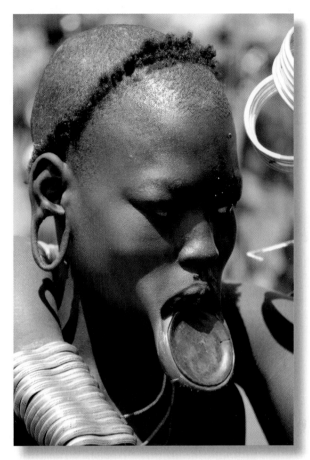

While some cultures resemble our own, others are very different, and the differences can often lead to 'culture shock'. A young woman with a plate lip from the Mursi tribe near Jinki, Ethiopia, displays a common cultural practice that would seem shocking to other cultures seeing it for the first time.

values
Socially shared conceptions of what a group or society considers good, right, and desirable.

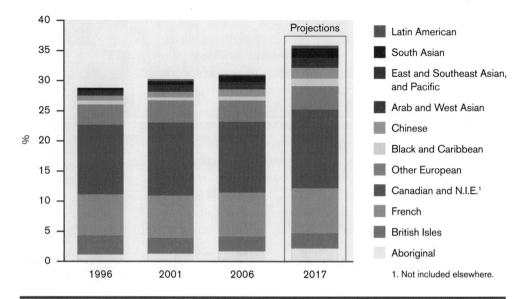

Figure 4.1 Diversity in Canada, 1996, 2001, 2006, and 2017

Source: Citizenship and Immigration Canada (2009), Figure 1.

a group or society considers good, right, and desirable—are expressed in its social institutions. And at the micro level, culture works to shape personalities through socialization, a process that we will discuss later on in the book. So, the concept of culture is an important link between the macro and micro perspectives on society. For this reason, and because culture is universal, the topic is important for sociologists.

However, as usual, sociologists vary somewhat in the ways they approach this complex topic.

Functionalism

Functionalists view culture as having an integrative role in society. Because culture organizes behaviour, these sociologists—who emphasize order—typically look to culture to explain consensus and stability. For example, they note that in societies where people hold 'modern' values, people tend to express trust in others and confidence in social institutions, with the result that they have more stable democratic governments than do other societies. These sociologists conclude that a 'civic culture'—a culture of participation in everyday social and political life by ordinary citizens—is functional to the survival of democracy. 'The police officer is your best friend' is a sentiment typically invoked in the cultural materials of 'civic culture'.

The functional approach, as we mentioned before, emerged from the work of Émile Durkheim. Instead of looking at the role of culture in creating social tensions, the functional perspective identifies ways in which culture creates social solidarity, provides stability and assurance, and unites the members of a social group or society. And, instead of seeing culture as the mere reflection of economic interests, functionalists see cultural elements, such as shared **norms**, values, and beliefs, as arising out of the social structure and influencing economic life. The implication is that these cultural elements signify consensus and mutual approval in society. Thus as sociologists we can look at these elements

norms

The rules or expectations that serve as common guidelines for behaviour in daily life, telling us what kinds of behaviour are appropriate or inappropriate in specific social situations.

as evidence of what is important for a society, not what the capitalistic enterprise seeks to promote for its own gain.

For instance, functionalists would say that the importance of education in our modern culture has emerged in response to a modernizing society that, to function properly, requires more highly educated individuals. Thus, culture itself serves the essential purposes of ensuring that through shared values and beliefs, society remains coherent, and that each constituent part of the society can carry out its respective functions. We will touch on this perspective again later in this chapter, when we look specifically at Durkheim's work on religion as a motivating force in society.

Critical Theory

Unlike structural functionalists, critical theorists focus on group differences in power and belief. For example, they point out that strongly stated values—which suggest value consensus—often indicate a conflict between two groups within the society. One approves of a given action and the other strongly opposes it; each states its preferred values forcefully and unequivocally. The ongoing public debate over legalizing recreational drug use is a good illustration of this. Remember that cultural values, norms, and **taboos** do not always tell us what is really going on. Often, formal disapproval of an action, such as laws prohibiting drug use, prove that the behaviour is far more common than people would like to admit and that groups are in conflict over the issue. Critical theorists might also show how overtly stated 'general' values often work to benefit some people at the expense of others.

The critical perspective is based in part on the insights of Karl Marx. Writing in the mid nineteenth century, Marx was responding to philosophical arguments that focused on the role of culturally based ideas in shaping society, such as the ideas of German philosopher Georg W.F. Hegel and his followers. Marx critiqued these arguments for ignoring the role of material, chiefly economic relations in shaping people's thoughts and actions. Marx focused his attention not on ideas and the culture within which they are situated, but on the *mode of production* that characterizes a historical period and shapes the ideas that develop in a society of that time.

In this way, Marx argued that it is not culture and ideas that shape society and the beliefs and decisions of its members, but rather that it is the material relationships between members of society—especially, between social classes—that shape culture, including beliefs, values, art, and religion. From this perspective then, the culture and its constituent elements are rooted in the economic relations of industrial, and increasingly global, capitalism. Capitalism gives rise to a *dominant ideology*, a system of thoughts and beliefs that justify capitalism and perpetuate it by limiting criticism and encouraging support of a neo-liberal consumer culture.

Since Marx, the critical perspective has less rigidly focused on economic relations as the foundation for culture and its elements and focused on other sources of domination. Although theorists in this newer perspective still believe that the culture of modern industrial societies perpetuates capitalism, they recognize the role of other factors as well—especially, the role of the state. They have also led for an increased recognition of the importance of ideology and the political role of intellectuals. For instance, Antonio Gramsci (1992) argues that during the 1920s and 1930s, intellectuals provided knowledge and advice to the general public, which worked to subdue revolutionary movements in an increasingly harsh economic environment. Many today still consider this to be the chief role of academics and 'public intellectuals'.

Another example is provided by the Frankfurt School of theorists who wrote during the same time period. These theorists, including Max Horkheimer, Theodor Adorno, Herbert Marcuse, and Walter Benjamin, focused on analyzing capitalist ideology, mass consumerism,

folkways

Norms based on popular habits and traditions, and ordinary usages and conventions of everyday life.

mores

Norms that carry moral significance. People believe that mores contribute to the general welfare and continuity of the group.

taboos

Powerful social beliefs that a particular act, food, place, etc. is totally repulsive and dangerous. Violation of the taboo is supposed to result in immediate punishment.

and especially popular entertainment, which they claimed promoted capitalist ideals. They emphasized a critical viewpoint and independent thinking on the part of social actors, despite the homogenizing tendencies of a consumerist mass culture. Nevertheless, although there are differences within the critical perspective on the root and role of culture in society, collectively these theorists view culture as part of the generally conflictual nature of society, and view it as helping powerful social groups to maintain their dominance.

Symbolic Interactionism

In contrast to the conflict and functional perspectives and their macrosociological view of society, symbolic interactionists, often working in the dramaturgical perspective, see culture through a microsociological lens. For symbolic interactionists, culture arises out of the individual face-to-face interactions of social actors and the symbols they communicate through the exchange of meaning.

Culture, for them, shows itself in the creative use of values and norms in the course of everyday interaction. Two people may share the same cultural values and norms about, say, conversing, but they still have to work out the details of their conversation. This can be a thrilling process or a painful one—often it is both—but is never the same twice. Human beings are complex and creative, so symbolic interactionists caution us against thinking of values or norms as commands that people are programmed to follow always in the same ways. To simplify, then, think of a culture as a dictionary of words, actions, and symbols from which we build our conversations. The 'sentences' and 'paragraphs' we build together, using these materials, will be intelligible to one another, but they are not predetermined, nor are they precisely the same.

Culture also shows itself in the decisions we make in choosing to communicate in the first place, or to avoid doing so: in what we say and what we don't say, what we reveal and what we keep secret. In interacting every day with others, we learn new ways of using culture and, through interaction, add to our culture. So, symbolic interactionists allow more room for social actors in shaping and impacting their culture than either functional or critical theorists. While the latter two tend to see culture as being imposed on the individuals within it, regulating their behaviour, symbolic interactionists point out the significant role that social actors play in managing and changing their own cultures by participating within them.

Cultural Studies Perspective

Cultural studies arose in the 1970s out of the work of theorists at the Centre for Contemporary Cultural Studies at the University of Birmingham, who merged sociology with literary scholarship. These theorists looked at how subcultural groups at the margins of society lay claim to elements of the dominant culture, redefine them through alternative meanings or ideas, and thus shape their own cultures outside the dominant environment.

The Birmingham theorists borrowed some of their ideas from the critical perspective, especially the notion that dominant groups in society use ideas to justify and perpetuate their domination over less powerful groups. Applying this to culture, the cultural studies perspective argues that culture is shaped by dominant economic groups to maintain their advantage—that is, the status quo. Moreover, economic (i.e., class) relations are only one of the many sites where this domination occurs. Thus, although culture maintains class divisions, it also (similarly) maintains divisions of many other kinds, including those based on gender, race, ethnicity, sexual orientation, and geography.

Moreover, cultural studies, in some ways like symbolic interactionism, focuses on the role of meaning in culture. Here the theorist Stuart Hall is particularly important, with his influential idea that all communication requires *encoding* and *decoding* (1980). For example, dominant groups encode information about a society in cultural products such as televisions shows; only by decoding can we fully interpret and understand their hidden content. Both encoding and decoding are subtle, often unconscious processes, involving, for example, the way in which a television show depicts patriarchal gender roles or the advantage of one ethnic group over another. Encoded in these depictions are, usually, assumptions about normality and social values.

Hall points out that while the dominant group encodes this material, other people decode it—interpret it—based on their own social and cultural position. Thus, for cultural studies theorists, culture originates in the ideological actions of dominant individuals, but its effects depend on the characteristics of individuals. In this way, culture is both unifying and fragmenting.

The Production of Culture Perspective

Despite the insights it provides, the cultural studies perspective has little to say about the origin of culture, except to assert it serves the interests of the dominant class or classes. This is mostly because of its Marxist and critical roots, meaning it sees culture as arising out of economic (i.e., class) relations and other divisions that create tensions in society. Instead, the *production of culture* perspective sees the origin of culture in **material culture**—including the mass media, technology, art, and other material domains that produce symbols—and in social action around this material culture (Peterson, 1994).

This perspective looks more closely at the concrete ways in which culture is produced, rather than simply accepting that it somehow arises out of the underlying social structure. True, culture may somehow reflect the social structure—even, the class relations—on which it is founded; but someone has to create it. Plays, symphonies, and even advertisements for female hygiene products all come from somewhere. Production-of-culture theorists consider the cultural studies approach too vague and dismissive about the actual, and tangible, sources of culture.

For instance, while most cultural theorists would see modern art as the product of its specific time period, the values of the societies in which this art movement arose, and the role of the political and social atmosphere of the time, the cultural production perspective would look at the labour processes by which these cultural elements were communicated and perpetuated (ibid). These concrete considerations, which take into account the day-to-day production of cultural elements, provide a better understanding of cultural content—especially, where it comes from and how it changes.

A good example of this approach is found in the book *Canvases and Careers*, by Harrison White and Cynthia White (1965). Their study of the rise of Impressionism as a new art style in nineteenth-century France highlights the role of 'the artist' and his or her need to make a living—that is, to have a career, not merely show and sell a few canvases. In this context, the breakdown of the traditional Royal Academy system for training and promoting artists who followed the classical style left room for the growth of a new system. This new system, organized by dealers and critics, ensured that new canvases—small paintings featuring everyday themes—would find their ways on to the walls of new, middle-class art buyers, thus assuring a market for new, less grandiose, and even experimental styles of painting.

Today, as indicated in Table 4.1, fine arts continue to find their support through federal and provincial granting councils like the Canada Council for the Arts, which provide a smaller amount of direct support for artists and a slightly larger amount of support for gallery acquisitions and upkeep. With these funds in hand, plus gifts donated, the galleries can buy new Canadian art works, and keep the artists at work. Visual artists in Canada, then, support themselves through a combination of sales, commissions, fellowships, teaching, and day jobs not necessarily related to artistic production. In this way, they eke out careers in art, just as the Impressionists did.

material culture

The physical and technological aspects of people's lives, including all the physical objects that members of a culture create and use.

non-material culture

People's values, beliefs, philosophies, conventions, and ideologies: in short, all the aspects of a culture that do not have a physical existence.

In one sense, fine art is a very particular aspect of culture, because it requires highly specialized culture producers who, in turn, require a market for their wares—thus, dealers and critics (or, at least, Canada Council grants). On the other hand, language is a more general form of culture, since everyone uses it and in principle, anyone can create it; but even language requires interaction and exchange—therefore, a market.

Table 4.1 Canada Council for the Arts Visual Arts Grants, Fiscal Year 2008 (1 April 2008–31 March 2009): Acquisition Assistance for Art Museums and Public Galleries

Recipient	City	Province	Riding	Grant ($)
Art Gallery of Greater Victoria	Victoria	BC	Victoria	13,000
Art Gallery of Ontario	Toronto	ON	Trinity–Spadina	25,400
Art Gallery of Peel Association	Brampton	ON	Brampton West / Brampton-Ouest	1,600
Beaverbrook Art Gallery	Fredericton	NB	Fredericton	11,550
Canadian Clay and Glass Gallery	Waterloo	ON	Kitchener–Waterloo	1,750
Carleton University Art Gallery	Ottawa	ON	Ottawa Centre / Ottawa-Centre	20,500
Confederation Centre Art Gallery	Charlottetown	PE	Charlottetown	4,400
Dunlop Art Gallery	Regina	SK	Wascana	4,300
George Gardiner Museum of Ceramic Art	Toronto	ON	York South–Weston / York-Sud–Weston	3,300
Glenbow–Alberta Institute	Calgary	AB	Calgary Centre / Calgary-Centre	30,000
Hart House—The Justina M. Barnicke Gallery	Toronto	ON	Trinity–Spadina	9,800
Kamloops Art Gallery	Kamloops	BC	Kamloops–Thompson–Cariboo	11,850
Kelowna Art Gallery Association	Kelowna	BC	Kelowna–Lake Country	28,475
Kitchener-Waterloo Art Gallery	Kitchener	ON	Kitchener Centre / Kitchener-Centre	2,500
Macdonald Stewart Art Centre	Guelph	ON	Guelph	11,500
MacKenzie Art Gallery	Regina	SK	Wascana	24,500
Mendel Art Gallery	Saskatoon	SK	Saskatoon–Wanuskewin	14,800
Morris and Helen Belkin Art Gallery, University of British Columbia	Vancouver	BC	Vancouver Quadra	30,000
Musée d'art contemporain de Montréal	Montreal	QC	Westmount–Ville-Marie	30,000
Musée des beaux-arts de Montréal	Montreal	QC	Westmount–Ville-Marie	24,700
Musée national des beaux-arts du Québec	Quebec	QC	Québec	30,000
Museum London	London	ON	London North Centre / London-Centre-Nord	30,000
New Brunswick Museum	Saint John	NB	Saint John	9,700
Oakville Galleries	Oakville	ON	Oakville	29,200
Robert McLaughlin Gallery	Oshawa	ON	Oshawa	30,000
The Ottawa Art Gallery	Ottawa	ON	Ottawa–Vanier	16,900
Thunder Bay Art Gallery	Thunder Bay	ON	Thunder Bay–Rainy River	7,500
Tom Thomson Memorial Art Gallery	Owen Sound	ON	Bruce–Grey–Owen Sound	5,875
University of Lethbridge Art Gallery	Lethbridge	AB	Lethbridge	1,300
Vancouver Art Gallery	Vancouver	BC	Vancouver Centre / Vancouver-Centre	30,000
Winnipeg Art Gallery	Winnipeg	MB	Winnipeg Centre / Winnipeg-Centre	9,100

Source: Canada Council for the Arts (2009b).

Language: A Key Cultural Realm

How people use language is a topic of interest to many sociologists, especially symbolic interactionists and feminists. As we have noted, symbolic interactionists are interested in how people work out patterns of action—including conversation—often making tactical alignments or hammering out agreements in order to do so. Other theorists are also interested in language as a cultural element. For example, structural functionalists are interested in the ways different subgroups, such as prisoners, develop their own language to express unique concerns and maintain the cohesion of their social group. Critical theorists may be interested in how language is used to subordinate disadvantaged groups in society.

In this latter respect and stemming in part from the critical perspective, feminist sociologists draw our attention to the way in which culture, through language, shapes our perception of reality: for example, our perception of men and women. For feminist sociologists, *androcentric* or *sexist language* not only illustrates gender inequality in our society, but also helps to perpetuate the problem. Most of the assumptions embodied in language are encoded or hidden—known but implicit, or even unrecognized. These tacit assumptions lurk everywhere in our language, including the use of androcentric language in English. We are all accustomed to using the words *mankind*, *policeman*, *chairman*, and other words that include the word *man*. Historically, many of these words have aptly described the role in question; in the past, most police personnel and holders of chairs really were men, not women.

The view that people should switch to gender-neutral terms such as *police officer* and *chairperson* is more than a quibble. Our continued use of the masculine words implies that women are still absent from these roles, and perhaps even that they should be. If we continue to see women who fill these roles as deviant, we end up discouraging women from seeking to do so. When we use masculine terms, we affirm the traditional exclusion and subordination of women. The changeover from masculine to gender-neutral words has taken several decades already, and it is well-advanced. Yet, it has only occurred through interactive processes,

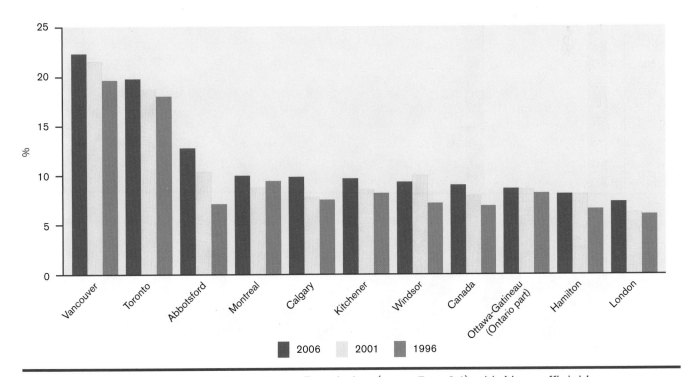

Figure 4.2 Proportion of the School-age Population (ages 5 to 24) with Non–official Languages Spoken at Home, Selected Census Metropolitan Areas, 1996, 2001, and 2006

Source: Based on Statistics Canada, *Education Matters: Insights on Education, Learning and Training in Canada* 81-004-XIE, vol. 5, March 4, 2009. www.statcan.gc.ca/pub/81-004-x/2008005/quickf-clindoeil-eng.htm

Physical gestures mean different things in different cultures. This gesture, the prayer sign or 'namaste', as it is called in India, signifies thankfulness.

signs

Gestures, artifacts, or words that express or meaningfully represent something other than themselves.

symbol

A sign whose relationship with something else also expresses a value or evokes an emotion.

with each 'offer' of a masculinist word rejected and reproached—in effect, turned down—in the conversational marketplace.

However, the language issue goes far beyond issues of gender neutrality, for language structures all of the ways we perceive reality. At the most basic level, language is an abstract system of sounds (speech), **signs** (written characters), and gestures (non-verbal communication) by which members of a society express their thoughts, feelings, ideas, plans, and desires. This means that language, whether spoken or written, verbal or non-verbal, is the means by which the achievements of one generation are passed on to the next. Words and symbols are, therefore, the tools of memory.

But words are ambiguous, sometimes confusing tools. Like other signs and **symbols**, words carry both intended and unintended meanings. We learn both kinds of meanings as active members of a culture, as much through observation and through trial and error as by formal instruction. According to anthropologists Edward Sapir and Benjamin Whorf (Sapir, 1929), language expresses our thoughts but also structures them. Therefore, the way in which a language is structured has immense significance for the way we experience the world. Different languages provide people with different conceptual tools to organize and interpret reality, making cultural assimilation difficult, especially for adults socialized in a different language.

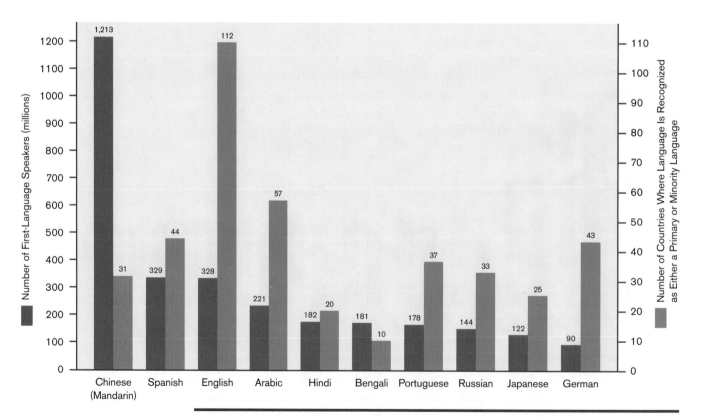

Figure 4.3   World's 10 Most Common Languages, 2009

Source: Based on data from M. Paul Lewis (ed.), 2009. *Ethnologue: Languages of the World*, 16th edn (Dallas, TX: SIL International), available online at www.ethnologue.com.

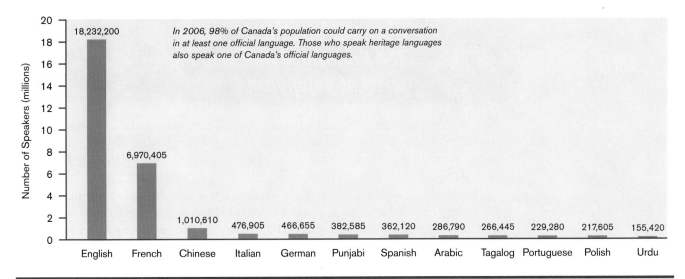

In 2006, 98% of Canada's population could carry on a conversation in at least one official language. Those who speak heritage languages also speak one of Canada's official languages.

Figure 4.4 Top 12 Mother Tongue Groups, Canada, 2006

Source: Citizenship and Immigration Canada, 2010.

One World, Many Societies

BOX **4.1**

The Do's and Taboos of Body Language around the World

Planning to travel? Need to do business with people from other countries and other cultures? Roger Axtell, the author of *Gestures: Do's and Taboos of Body Language around the World*, tells us that a 'seemingly casual, innocent gesture in one society can actually be crude and insulting in another'. So watch your step. In another culture, an inappropriate gesture might be humorous, or it might get you into serious trouble.

You're probably pretty safe with what anthropologists call 'instinctive' gestures—these, such as a raised eyebrow, tend to mean the same thing everywhere. Caution is needed, though with 'coded' and 'acquired' gestures, which are both developed within specific social contexts, and are prone to misinterpretation in other cultures, when even a slight variation from the socially acceptable form turns a 'nonchalant gesture' into an offensive sign.

Source: Adapted from Matthews (2002).

When children learn to speak the language of their culture, they learn to make the assumptions that pervade that language. Cultures provide words to describe, and thereby teach members of a society to see what the society cares about. For example the Slave, a native group of the Northwest Territories and Alberta, have a culture that traditionally involved travelling and fishing on ice. Accordingly, they developed a complex vocabulary related to describing ice conditions, one that included separate terms for ice that is thin, thick, brittle, muddy, wet, hollow, slippery, blue, black, white, seamed, cracked, or floating.

Thus, people create the language they need to transact their cultural business and make social life possible. It is unclear whether, with globalization, there will be a continued loss of indigenous languages and cultures, to create one shared, universal culture (perhaps in the English language), or whether diversity will continue to prevail socially, and therefore culturally.

Classic Studies
The Protestant Ethic and the Spirit of Capitalism

We have seen that cultural values influence people's behaviour and that values from one area of life influence behaviours in other areas. Max Weber studied this phenomenon in one of the most important classical works in sociology, called *The Protestant Ethic and the Spirit of Capitalism* (1905).

The Protestant Ethic and the Spirit of Capitalism was written by Max Weber in 1904 and 1905, beginning as a series of essays in German. Today it is considered a founding text in sociology, especially economic sociology. First translated into English by American sociologist Talcott Parsons, it appeared in English in 1930. Parsons used the book in his classic work *The Structure of Social Action* (1937) to document the growing importance of 'the nonrational' in sociological thinking.

The book is concerned with the way religion can create material progress and not merely justify the rule of a dominant class, as Marx had claimed. Weber wrote that capitalism in northern Europe evolved when the Protestant (especially, Calvinist) ethic influenced large numbers of people to engage in work in 'this world'. By downplaying other-worldliness, Protestantism encouraged people to develop their enterprises and engage in trade, accumulating wealth for capital investment. Thus, the Protestant ethic was a force behind an unplanned, uncoordinated mass action that supported the development of capitalism in the West.

However, Weber's theory was not deterministic; this idea, also known as 'the Weber thesis', is not a rigid law, since Weber rejected deterministic approaches. Instead, Weber presented the Protestant ethic as one element of several leading toward capitalist modernity. In this sense, Protestantism had an 'elective affinity' with capitalism.

In this work, Weber develops a previously identified link between Protestant Christianity and its cultural milieu, and the capitalistic economic system of the time. Weber begins by demonstrating a correlation between Protestantism and involvement in business. Not all Protestants became capitalists, but to Weber's mind, it is no accident capitalism arose in the same place, and around the same time, as Protestantism: that is, in sixteenth- and seventeenth-century northwestern Europe. He then explores the possibility that religion is a cause of the modern economic situation, accounting for the non-emergence of capitalism in other locales where Hinduism, Confucianism, and ancient Judaism prevailed (for example).

To do this, he first looks at the nature of capitalism and claims it is characterized by a view of profit as an end in itself, and of the pursuit of profit as righteous. Capitalism is profit-oriented; it embraces the investment of capital in risky commercial enterprises; to this end, it requires diligence, thrift, and sobriety. Most important, it emphasizes the importance of this-worldly life, not merely concerns about the other-world of Heaven that may (or may not) follow death.

Weber tries to find the source of this belief system, and concludes that Protestantism is concerned with questions of ultimate importance: Am I saved or damned? What does God have in store for me, and how can I know? What is the best, most moral way to live? As a cultural or philosophical system that confers meaning and interprets reality, religion can have a wide variety of consequences. As Weber shows, these include political and economic consequences (Schumpeter, 1991).

Weber links the rise of capitalism—a new style of economic thinking from the seventeenth century onward—with the rise of Protestant beliefs and new interpretations of Christianity. For Weber, the economic behaviour we associate with modern life in Western

Hannah Montana? Remember, as sociologists, we try to take nothing at face value). Why do people spend so much money on NFL team shirts? On *Star Trek* memorabilia? On crucifixes and trips to the Holy Land? And why is the name of Jesus invoked so much by Christians, or the name of Gene Roddenberry by Trekkies, or that of Brett Favre by football fans?

Whether they are important or trivial, we know that religious-style artifacts and rituals exercise a powerful hold over us. We behave differently when we are in a sacred setting, surrounded by ritual objects and directed by an expert in ritual behaviours. A sacred object or event is one that excites strong sentiment and awe. This is the difference between something that seems ultimately important to us and something that seems trivial.

Cultural Integration, Ethnocentricism, and the Mass Media

Durkheim argued that religious values—and cultural values more generally—serve to forge strong social bonds between the members of a society. Yet Durkheim's theory was based on the study of a small-scale, tightly knit, and interrelated community living a traditional way of life. Compared to modern societies, those like the ones Durkheim studied were more culturally integrated than our own, since most people's lives had little variety and held out few possibilities. As a result, there was little difference between what people expected and what they experienced. People's lives and thoughts were similar. Changes in any element of the culture, though rare, brought changes in all the other elements of culture.

In these respects, modern societies are different. The specialization of activities, isolation of social groups, and rapid pace of change prevent a high level of integration. Technology and the marketplace are always changing North American culture. New goods and services are continually entering and changing people's lives, even if they do not square with the **ideal culture** that old goods and services supported.

The result is a wide variation in people's real lives (by region, ethnic group, social class, and so on), as well as vast differences between what people claim they want—their stated values—and what they really want. On the other hand, several social processes and institutions are important for increasing **cultural integration**. They include **ethnocentrism** and cultural comparison, and an increasingly globalized mass media.

Though one language may fit a given situation better than another, most people would agree that no one language is necessarily better than any other. Yet we would have a hard time persuading people that some particular values—especially, the values of other people—are better than their own. People are so emotionally involved with their own culture that often they do not see that their own values, like other cultural traits, are merely one approach to human life. Their ethnocentrism leads them to view everything from the point of view of their own culture. Often, they simply fail to take note of other ways of thinking. Yet paradoxically, it is often by comparing their own culture to another that people are able to clarify and integrate their own values and behaviours.

Accepting cultural variation as a fact and avoiding ethnocentrism are not easy matters. After all, ethnocentrism is not merely cultural short-sightedness; it is rooted in people's upbringing and is (in that sense) therefore normal. Consider, for example, a stereotype of Asian students as passive and overly methodical, one held by some North Americans. Teachers may see these students as poor communicators, but the difference is mainly cultural—the result of a different style of communicating. More often than not, the problem lies with the teacher, not the student. Put another way, Asian and non-Asian students have the same desire to excel but express it in different, culturally specific ways.

Of course, some would argue that cultural relativism can be taken too far. Take a different example: some might say that cultures that promote racism, sexism, violence, or genocide cannot possibly be condoned, and that they are self-evidently inferior to cultures that reject these things. Some might imagine they could root this critique in first principles about human rights, but others would base their conclusion on a particular reading of Western cultural values, meaning just another version of ethnocentrism.

ideal culture

That aspect of culture that lives only in people's minds. It is the set of values people claim to believe in, profess openly, hold up for worship and adoration, and in day-to-day life pay 'lip service' to.

cultural integration

The process whereby parts of a culture (for example, ideal culture and real culture) come to fit together and complement one another.

ethnocentrism

The tendency to use one's own culture as a basis for evaluating other cultures.

There is no easy way to solve this problem, but we must be continually vigilant. As travellers, we continually bump up against other people's ideas of proper behaviour. When this happens, we are forced to re-examine our own rules and ask whether there is any good reason for obeying them. Often there is. And often we realize that other societies have a more engaging—more sociable, leisurely, or healthy—lifestyle than our own. Whatever our conclusion, comparing our own culture with another one is likely to lead us to think more clearly about what we value or expect, and why we do so.

The mass media, which we will discuss at length in a later chapter, are an important source of cultural integration in the modern world—a way around ethnocentrism. Mass media are forms of communication that pass information to, and influence the opinions of, large audiences, without any personal contact between the senders and receivers of the information. The mass media include television, movies, newspapers, and radio. We consume mass media to a degree that no one would have imagined a century ago.

The invention of printing is important, for it set off the cultural explosion we associate with mass communication and the mass media. Johannes Gutenberg's invention of the printing press in the 1430s had many social effects. By making possible the mass distribution of printed books, it started a revolution in communications. One long-term effect was the spread of literacy, a growth in the number of people who could read and interpret information for themselves. People no longer needed to rely on the village priest to teach them what the Bible said; they could do it for themselves, particularly after it was translated into languages other than Latin, which people could understand. This change undermined the power of priests and supported the breakaway of Protestants from the Catholic Church in sixteenth-century Europe.

The spread of printed information through newspapers, handbills, and manifestos also helped people to mobilize for political action. Information, and the sense of power it gave people, helped to support the French and American revolutions of the eighteenth century, and other revolutions ever since. The press also made it possible for writers to convey

Media Distortion

BOX 4.2

The Representation of Aboriginal Peoples and Culture in the Media

The images of Aboriginal people of North America in popular children's media—films, television, and books—give a 'skewed vision' of Aboriginal life. They are largely portrayed in stereotypical fashion, and it is these images that formed the hard-to-dispel first impressions of Aboriginals for many Canadians and Americans. Children form lasting attitudes and values up to the age of 15 or so; the false, negative images of Aboriginals presented to them in childhood will carry over into adult attitudes. These impressions will lead them 'to think of Aboriginal people as inferior (passive, aggressive or drunk) or simply as non-entities, obliterated by omission'.

Movies such as *Peter Pan* show one-dimensional, primitive, cruel characterizations of Aboriginals; even more positive depictions of Aboriginal life in the film *Pocahontas* perpetuate some stereotypes, such as the 'sexual savage'. And the face of the character Pocahontas was based on several real-life models—curiously, none of these were Aboriginal.

But Canadians are starting to see more positive, realistic portrayals of Aboriginal people in film and on TV, including programming aimed at children. As well, the increasing presence of Aboriginal artists in the mainstream performance media, and Aboriginal television and radio networks, contribute to a balanced, realistic view of Aboriginal culture.

Source: Adapted from Media Awareness Network (2010).

meaning to people who weren't in the same place—people they didn't know and couldn't fully imagine—just as we are now conveying meaning to you.

In the twenty-first century, we have technologies—the camera, radio, telephone, and television, not to mention computers—that convey information through sound and image. These technologies inform us about problems and opportunities, conflicts and peace settlements around the globe. By listening to a simple transistor radio, even people who are illiterate and live in remote parts of the world know what is going on.

This explosion of information technology has made cultural integration and political rebellion equally possible. People have even claimed that the dramatic changes that swept through Eastern Europe in 1989—resulting in the so-called 'fall of communism'—were a result of information technology freely crossing national borders. We have yet to see all of the impact that the computer-driven Internet—a new generation of information technology—will have, a topic we will discuss in a later chapter.

Classic Studies
Theory of the Leisure Class

The shift from a society based on raw materials to one centred on information and its development is evidence of cultural change. Thorstein Veblen was one of the first social theorists to address this issue of cultural change, as well as the cultural variation that distinguishes between upper and lower social classes.

Veblen's book *Theory of the Leisure Class* (1899) is a critique of modern Western society, especially the 'conspicuous consumption' of the upper-class bourgeoisie, whom Veblen described as living a life of ease and leisure as though every day were a holiday. Veblen argued that the symbolic nature of social prestige—its emphasis on fads and fashions, for example—encouraged a wasteful, even barbaric consumption of time and goods.

Sports team fans are in many ways similar to religious followers, practising what sociologists call a 'civil religion'. For many sports fans in Canada, hockey is more than a sport, it is a kind of religion.

Nevertheless, Veblen shows that this wasteful consumption does serve a purpose: it reaffirms the status and power of those groups that can afford to live in such a manner. In this way, the groups ensure their own stability and purposely distinguish themselves from people even slightly less wealthy than themselves. So, for example, a lawn is trimmed because it provides evidence of surplus financial security and labour power, and a butler is hired to manage all the other domestic service (Stabile, 2002). Elaborate costume parties are given, to which people must wear expensive rented costumes, coming perhaps as Cardinal Richelieu or Marie Antoinette. In addition, the host might hire guest celebrities to appear at great cost, so that this party will indeed be the party of the year.

Veblen's book is important because, although published in 1899, it foreshadowed the growing culture of consumption that would characterize the twentieth century, from the display of status-enhancing goods in the 1920s to the furious (shop-'til-you-drop) consumption characteristic of present-day North American society. Veblen's work was one of the first to consider this topic in detail. As such, it provides the foundation for many of the other works concerned with consumerism, such as those by the critical theorists working in the 1930s (Wood, 1993). Thus, Veblen's work underpins a critical analysis of topics like the advertising industry and the mass media, both of which are primarily interested in fostering conspicuous consumption.

In *Theory of the Leisure Class*, Veblen analyzes the root and nature of consumption, focusing on its wastefulness and, usually, utter needlessness (Dorfman, 1961). He especially points his critique at those at the very top of the social ladder, who have the means to lead such a life. Moreover, as Veblen shows, they do so precisely because it allows them to separate themselves from those below them. In contrast, Veblen recommends a simpler and more austere lifestyle oriented toward civic mindedness and conservation culture (Stabile, 2002). In this and other works, he praises the contemporary German society for its dedication to science, industry, and 'the instinct of craftsmanship'.

However, maverick that he was, Veblen failed to locate his analysis in any kind of recognizable paradigm: for example, in neither the Marxist analysis of class relations nor the Weberian analysis of status groups. This is no flaw in itself, but it helps to account for the book's failure to attract readers and followers, or to generate follow-up research. As well, this lack of systematic grounding meant that Veblen failed to take advantage of Marx's insights into capitalist class relations, nor Weber's insights into status group practices of exclusion and inclusion, discussed earlier. Had he done so, his work would have been even better.

Despite this critique, we can still view Veblen as an important sociologist, economist, and social critic who shed light on the developing tensions and contradictions of modern society, especially its tendency to over-consumption. Evidently, this is still a significant issue in our consumption-driven contemporary society (Edgell, 2001). Veblen remains an important theoretical figure, and his ideas are still relevant, informing diverse academic fields like economics, feminist economics, and sociological theories of **high culture**, **popular culture**, and **cultural capital**. The modern embodiment of Veblen's concerns can be found in the work of French sociologist Pierre Bourdieu.

high culture

The set of preferences, tastes, and norms that are characteristic of, or supported by, high-status groups, including fine arts, classical music, ballet, and other 'highbrow' concerns.

popular (or mass) culture

The culture of ordinary people. It includes those objects, preferences, and tastes that are widespread in a society.

cultural capital

A body of knowledge and interpersonal skills that helps people to get ahead socially, which often includes learning about and participating in high culture.

People Are Talking About . . .
PIERRE BOURDIEU

Pierre Bourdieu was born in 1930 in southwestern France. He studied at the École normale supérieure, where philosopher Jacques Derrida was a classmate. After serving in the army in Algeria, Bourdieu lectured at the University of Algiers, University of Paris, and the École pratique des Hautes Etudes. In 1968, he became the director of the Centre de Sociologie Européenne.

And in 1981, he was appointed as chair of sociology at the prestigious Collège de France. In 2002, Bourdieu passed away from cancer in Paris.

Bourdieu's early research examined the ways the dominant culture maintains its power and privilege. In *Reproduction of Education, Society, and Culture* (1970), he argued the French educational system acts to reproduce the cultural divisions in society. Bourdieu's interest in the 'learning of class' continued throughout his life. His central claim was that learned expertise and competent practices are the means by which social domination is transmitted or reproduced from one generation to the next. As David Swartz (in Scott, 2006: 42) writes in his biography, Bourdieu 'advanced the bold claim that all cultural symbols and practices, from artistic tastes, style in dress and eating habits to religion, science and philosophy—even language itself—embody interests and function to enhance social distinctions'.

Bourdieu notes that social class is 'most marked in the ordinary choices of everyday existence, such as furniture, clothing, or cooking, which are particularly revealing of deep-rooted and long-standing dispositions because, lying outside the scope of the educational system, they have to be confronted, as it were, by naked taste', and that 'the strongest and most indelible mark of infant learning' would probably be in the tastes of food (Bourdieu, 1984 [1979]: 77). As novelist Marcel Proust has reminded us, the remembered taste of food—food enjoyed in childhood, for example—is one of the strongest, most primitive and longest-lasting of our memories. This powerful stimulus, Bourdieu claims, is at the root of social class: its learning and enactment.

Bourdieu showed that members of the ruling class teach their children aesthetic preferences in order to pass along class-based *cultural capital*, a resource that transfers class position across generations. Cultural capital includes 'symbolic goods, especially those regarded as the attributes of excellence, . . . [as] the ideal weapon in strategies of distinction' (Bourdieu, 1984 [1979]: 66). And naturally, as Veblen had shown earlier, the dominant class defines which attributes and tastes are to be deemed excellent: whether a taste for champagne or Sugar Pops, escargots or Egg McMuffins.

In short, Bourdieu writes, 'differences in cultural capital mark the differences between the classes . . . . [Taste] functions as a sort of social orientation, a "sense of one's place", guiding the occupants of a given . . . social space towards the social positions adjusted to their properties, and towards the practices or goods which befit the occupants of that position' (Bourdieu, 1984 [1979]: 65).

Bourdieu criticized Marx for giving primacy to economic factors in class analysis; instead, he stressed the ability of social actors to use cultural and symbolic systems to police class boundaries. To be sure, Bourdieu does not neglect the role of social and economic capital as influences on cultural capital. However, unlike Marx, he claims that social capital and economic capital are won and increased by the use of cultural capital—specifically, learned skills, tastes and distinctions.

Source: Adapted from *Fifty Key Sociologists: The Contemporary Theorists* (edited by John Scott, London: Routledge, 2006) and other sources.

Bourdieu's central theme, as we have seen, is the process by which cultural and social values are reproduced across generations, and the influence of socio-cultural capital on human behaviour. Within this approach, several of Bourdieu's key concepts have gained importance in sociology. Among these are *habitus* and *social field*, as well as cultural capital, which we have already discussed.

Habitus refers to a habituation gained through a prolonged, usually lifelong, process of learning and socialization within a particular context. A habitus can be seen as a 'cultural competency'—an ability to live properly and effectively within a given culture. Simply, habitus is something that within a specific culture 'goes without saying'—it does not need to be explained because it is understood by most people in the group. So, for example, a properly socialized member of the upper class will know when to wear a tuxedo, which yachting club to join, and where to vacation in France or South America.

Social field, or simply *field*, is the social setting, domain, or institution within which the habitus is to be exercised. Examples of fields in society are politics, education, and economics, each of which comprises a particular set of cultural relations. A field is also flexible, interacting with the social agents within it and being shaped by these interactions. As well, fields are the sites for competition. Within fields, social agents are constantly competing for material and symbolic resources and acting out power relationships. A social agent's chance of success is determined by cultural competence (or cultural capital), defined earlier in the chapter.

All three of these concepts—habitus, field and agent—have gained importance in sociology since Bourdieu began to use them in his work. For example, Glastra and Vedder (2010) use the concept of field to explain the experiences of asylum seekers and refugees in The Netherlands. Likewise, Catlaw and Hu (2009) use this concept to 'analyze the construction of the bureaucratic or public administrative field' in the United States (ibid: 458). And for Wright (2009), cricket becomes a restricted field unavailable to those lacking the necessary cultural capital and social class.

Likewise, the concept of habitus is widely used in much contemporary sociological work. For example, Gruner (2010) uses the concept of habitus to inform the analysis of neighbourhoods in Germany segregated by race. Ignatow (2009), for his part, uses a slightly modified version of Bourdieu's habitus to look at 'moral culture and the ways people use culture to make changes in their lives' (ibid: 643). Many more authors use the concept of cultural capital in their work, like Zarycki (2009) in a study of its importance in Central and Eastern Europe following the fall of the Soviet Union.

Finally, a number of recent studies combine several of these ideas. For instance, Kerr and Robinson (2009) use both cultural capital and habitus in looking at the reproduction of domination in a British corporation situated in Ukraine. And Pollmann (2009) draws on Bourdieu's habitus, as well as cultural capital, to understand how people's attachment to their country will influence the creation of programs to build 'intercultural capital'.

Bourdieu's theory of the reproduction of cultural and social values has been criticized on many fronts. Some say he focuses his analysis too much on so-called high culture (opera, ballet, and the like), and thus his analysis is incomplete. Others question his claim of an existence of a class-based differences in knowledge about fine art (Rossel and Bromberger, 2009). Still others point out that although Bourdieu mentions the importance of social capital, defined as the extent and quality of social networks and relationships, he considers it to a much more limited extent than cultural or economic capital (Bottero, 2009).

Norval Morrisseau was an aboriginal Canadian artist who was integral in promoting the cultures and traditions of native peoples through art.

Nevertheless, a majority find Bourdieu's work useful and provocative. Kim (2009) defends his field theory from those who claim that it is theoretically unsound and empirically untestable. Instead, Kim shows that in fact the theory is unique and well-developed, and can be tested through observation. Ignatow (2009) counters the critique that Bourdieu's theory ignores the moral significance of social judgments, and uses Bourdieu's concept of habitus to develop a theory of morality.

As is clear from the growth of sociological work employing his ideas, Bourdieu remains a prominent figure in the field today. In the last two years alone, over two hundred journal articles have applied his work on cultural capital. Clearly, sociologists are talking about Pierre Bourdieu and he deserves a place in our comprehensive, fusion approach to sociology. His work has ignited new debates about the connection between culture and power that resonates among all postmodern and critical theorists today (though they study the relationship in different ways.) And notably, his book *Distinction* was named one of the twentieth century's most important sociological works by the International Sociological Association.

Cultural Variation

Unlike high culture—the stuff of cultural capital—popular culture is fragmented along age, sex, and social-class lines. We see this fragmentation in market surveys that identify the viewers of different kinds of television programs: for example, educational television versus soap operas versus sports. We find just as much fragmentation in people's tastes for leisure, dress, eating, and even living-room decoration. Market research shows us there are many lifestyle types (at least 40, by one count—on this, see Weiss [1988]) in North American society.

At the same time, popular culture reflects the influence of high culture. We see this influence even in mass advertising, which panders to the lowest common denominator in our culture. Advertising has borrowed many images from classical painting, for example, including poses that represent stereotypes of women: serene mother, freewheeling secretary, perfect hostess, and sex object. There are also physical stances that are used to suggest the wealth and power of men (Berger, 1972).

The mass media and modern popular culture have developed together. They both reflect the rise of enormous new audiences with money to spend and a ready responsiveness to mass sales messages. But trends in high culture reflect the growth of new audiences too. The fine arts began to change as early as the nineteenth century with the rise of middle classes who were eager to prove their social worth by buying pictures. But as the middle classes adopt the cultural tastes and practices of the upper classes, the upper classes seek out new practices in an effort to preserve their cultural distance. Eventually, the middle classes catch on to the new practices and the process repeats itself. This is one of the dynamics of cultural change, and it has been going on at least since Veblen wrote *The Theory of the Leisure Class* a century ago.

As we saw in the discussion of Bourdieu, culture reflects and supports the stratification system in a society. It allows powerful people to use culture—especially, high culture—to

The opera is an example of what has come to be known as 'high culture', and knowledge of opera is considered to be part of cultural capital.

glorify themselves, set themselves apart from others, and interact meaningfully within their restricted domain. It follows that learning the 'cultural code' of the powerful would help other people establish relations with them.

Familiarity with high culture is one form of cultural capital. Research by DiMaggio shows that young people with more cultural capital—more familiarity with good books, opera, and art, and a tendency to identify themselves as 'cultured'—do better in life than otherwise similar young people with less cultural capital. Cultural capital affects their educational attainment—college or university attendance and completion, graduate-school attendance—even their choice of marriage partners.

Cultural capital includes a wide variety of skills that improve social relations. These include knowing how to speak interestingly, what topics to discuss, how to order food and eat graciously, what beverages to drink, how to dress stylishly but tastefully, how to play a variety of games and sports common in high social circles (for example, tennis, sailing, bridge, chess, polo), how to appraise scotches, wines, racehorses, European hotels, and so on. In Canada and elsewhere, cultural capital also includes the ability to speak confidently and persuasively about the business world.

Few people learn these skills in public school (though some learn them in private schools). To learn them best, one needs a wide variety of personal experiences, indulgent and knowledgeable parents, devoted teachers, and time and money to spare. In short, like other capital, cultural capital is unequally distributed throughout the population. Cultural capital helps people get ahead because it marks them out from the rest of the field. They end up with more advantages because they start out with more.

Middle-class parents often try to provide their children with enriched and enriching experiences that will give them cultural capital: ballet lessons, private schooling, trips abroad, instructional summer camps, and so on. Working-class parents, however, are rarely able to do the same. As a result, working-class children are less likely to get ahead socially than middle-class children.

Without the benefits of this cultural enrichment, people in the middle class, not those in the upper class, stand to gain most by conforming to the conventional rules of a culture. If they conform, they are eligible to move up the social ladder; if they do not, they risk sliding down it. People at the bottom of the social scale stand to gain the least of anyone from conformity. They also have the least to lose from nonconformity: thus they can risk forming **countercultures**. No wonder, then, that the poorest people often have the weakest attachment to the existing cultural order.

As for people at the top of the social scale, they run little risk of losing their power, wealth, and position, and they stand to gain nothing by conforming to ordinary standards of behaviour. So, many members of the upper class engage in a **subculture** that is just as outlandish as a delinquent or punk counterculture. They love doing what the French call *épater les bourgeois*, enraging the middle-class by their outlandish behaviour. This accounts for the lavish, often grotesque 'lifestyles of the rich and famous'. People like Paris Hilton are merely the latest in a long line of rich people to seek our attention by flouting the mainstream lifestyle.

Yet among the poorer members of society, gaining **cultural literacy**, not cultural capital, is often the critical issue. Unlike cultural capital, which is a luxury, cultural literacy is an absolute necessity. Historian E.D. Hirsch (1988) argues that schools ought to provide their students with a store of cultural knowledge, instead of abstract thinking skills. Hirsch cites research to show that effective learning does not depend on general intelligence, creativity, or an ability to solve problems. It depends on an ability to understand words and concepts and quickly recognize common patterns of meaning.

This means that knowledge is more important than creativity, experience more important than 'ability'. A chess grandmaster, Hirsch claims, is much better than anyone

counterculture

A subculture that rejects conventional norms and values and adopts alternative ones.

subculture

A group that shares the cultural elements of the larger society but which also has its own distinctive values, beliefs, norms, style of dress, and behaviour patterns.

cultural literacy

A solid knowledge of the traditional culture, which contains the building blocks of all communication and learning.

else at identifying traditional game strategies and responding to them; this is what 'playing chess' is. But outside a chess game—say, in fixing a car, filling out an income-tax form, or preparing a meal—the grandmaster is no more capable than you or I. Similarly, the experienced chef is extraordinarily creative in the kitchen, but no more creative than anyone else outside it. In addition, that creativity consists of a knowledge of edible foods and the traditions of preparing them. So, creativity and problem-solving abilities depend on concrete knowledge.

This suggests that, before people can learn anything else, they need to master a body of information. What is more, the body of information they need for everyday life is easy to identify. In North America, it is a storehouse of common knowledge—a few thousand names, dates, concepts, and expressions to which most people refer in their thinking and communication. Most items in this storehouse date back 50 years or more.

The storehouse of common knowledge is not only useful and slow to change; it is also widely known. Literate people from every ethnic and racial group, region, and social class use cultural items in this storehouse. All of us know (or ought to know) what is meant by an 'Achilles heel', for example, an expression that refers to a hero in a Greek myth which dates back well over 3,000 years. But it is now similarly important to be able to identify Madonna, Quentin Tarantino, Jonas Salk, Bill Gates, 'Brangelina', Hannah Montana, and Justin Bieber.

Cultural Change

All cultures change. Both external and internal dynamics cause them to constantly morph, reshape, progress, dissolve, and evolve. Consider the example of fashion. Fashion changes for the sake of change, forever introducing new 'looks' for the latest season. But fashion does not refer only to clothes or hairstyles. Fashion is present in every aspect of social life.

One clear example of fashion is the vocabulary we use. While a few decades ago people said *swell*, *groovy*, and *mod* to express approval, today no one would use these words, since they would seem outmoded (or square, uncool, unhip, freaky, or weird) if they did. Or, consider the change in the popularity of first names. In *A Matter of Taste: How Names, Fashions, and Culture Change*, Lieberson (2000) argues that the practice of naming itself does not change. Every baby gets a name, sooner or later. However, the aesthetics of the names chosen is constantly changing, seemingly without the influence of economic or political forces. Though powerful companies and corporations may have commercial interests in influencing other areas of cultural taste, they have no vested interest in the names chosen for children, but only the products that are purchased for them.

Although Lieberson recognizes the effect of some outside forces, such as the emergence of a popular public figure like a movie star, on naming practices, he stresses the existence of 'internal taste mechanisms' that change over time despite these influences. He applies this insight to the study of the naming practices of different social groups. These include Mexican name choices, African-American choices from the time of slavery onward, the adoption of anglicized names by Asian immigrants, and the meaning behind the recent popularity of Biblical names (such as Noah, Zach, Leah) in the Western world. He also discusses how names become dated and go out of style. For example, while girls' names like Ethel, Mildred, and Betty were popular only a few decades ago, today they have almost entirely been replaced by names like Emily, Jennifer, and Madison.

Yet culture changing for its own sake is cultural change at a subtle level. Usually, major cultural change means important social, economic, and political changes too. Below, we discuss two examples of major cultural change. One has to do with the struggle to synthesize a distinct Canadian culture out of many competing regional cultures. The other addresses whether national cultures will survive in the future or be replaced by a single global culture—a question we raised a little earlier.

Canadian Culture

Despite many similarities, Canadian cities are unlike the cities of other countries: for example, they are less racially segregated and less dangerous than same-sized American cities. This reminds us that Canadian society is, in some respects, different or even unique. But unique how?

Francophone Quebecers feel they have a distinctive culture. But what about Canada as a whole? Do Canadians have a culture that distinguishes us from, for example, Americans? Sociologist Seymour Martin Lipset (1990) has argued that we do. His work presents an image of Canadian culture as elitist, traditional, and collectivistic—focused on the group instead of the individual. This difference, he claims, results largely from the birth of the US nation in revolution, and the birth of the Canadian nation in counter-revolution (the arrival of Loyalists from the Thirteen Colonies) and compromise.

Some survey data questions the validity of Lipset's argument. On many dimensions, Canadians and Americans are nearly indistinguishable. Where researchers *do* find cultural differences between Canadians and Americans, they find Canadians being *less* traditional and less elitist than American. Both in our social policies, such as medicare, and in our attitudes towards the disadvantaged, Canadians are much more egalitarian. If any difference exists, it is probably a difference in preferences between liberty (Americans prefer more) and order (Canadians prefer more). As is evident in their taxation and social policies, Canadians are much more committed to social equality than Americans.

However, other observers argue that Canadian culture does not exist at all, or if it does, it is little than a collection of regional cultures: such as a Newfoundland culture, a Quebec culture, or a British Columbia culture. Some believe that Canadian culture is precisely the cultural mosaic provided us by Canada's different regions and ethnic and linguistic groups: no more and no less!

Hippie culture began as a youth movement in the 1960s. This movement grew to embody a set of ideologies and values that were counter to the established norm. Common issues the movement embodied were protesting of the Vietnam War, advocating for women's rights, and promoting sexual liberation.

Persuasive evidence on this question is provided by an analysis of the ways North Americans in all the regions of Canada and the United States answered several dozen survey questions. The findings (Baer, Grabb, and Johnston, 1993; developed further in the book by Grabb and Curtis, 2005, *Regions Apart: The Four Societies of Canada and the United States*) gave just about everyone some ammunition. First, they provided (slight) evidence of Canadian–American differences (on this, see also Sniderman, Russell, Fletcher et al, 1996). Second, they provided (slight) evidence of geographic or regional differences. Most of all, they found evidence of four distinctive 'culture areas' in Canada and the United States: Quebec, Dixie (the southeastern US), English Canada, and the rest of the United States.

On various topics, respondents in Quebec consistently showed the most progressive or liberal attitudes. Respondents in the American South consistently showed the most conservative attitudes. The remaining North American respondents were often nearly indistinguishable, whether they lived in Toronto or Toledo, Winnipeg or Washington, Vancouver or Vermont, although (as noted earlier), English Canadians tend to be more egalitarian, more collectivistic, and less religious than Americans, wherever they live. More research is needed to confirm this finding with an even wider variety of questions.

So, it seems Canada is culturally distinguishable from the United States, and likely from other countries—England, Scotland, Australia, France, and so on. Whether a *unified* Canadian culture exists, and indeed, whether there should be one, are also important questions. Nationalists argue that without a unified Canadian culture it will be impossible to escape economic, cultural, and political assimilation by the United States. Others say that Canadian culture is already strong enough to resist that possibility. Regionalists, like the Quebec nationalists, would argue that cultural unification can only come at the expense of lively ethnic and regional cultures that people care about. Multiculturalists would assert that as much would be lost as gained if we tried seriously to create a unified Canadian culture.

Therefore, it would seem that nearly 150 years of nationhood has not provided Canada with an unambiguously distinct national culture. What is more, it seems unlikely the future will increase Canada's cultural integration.

Point/Counterpoint

BOX **4.3**

Does Canadian Culture Exist?

Canadian culture—what is it? It's hard to find a clear definition. But Canadians of different ethnic backgrounds, living in different parts of the country, seem to agree that the diversity of Canada's population means that there is no one definable Canadian culture. But is this diversity itself, and the way that the Quebecois culture, for example, has persisted for several hundred years, the distinctive Canadian culture?

Gisele Beaulieu, whose family has lived in Quebec since the 1600s, appears to think so. Quoted in an article by *Globe & Mail* reporter Sean Phipps, she declares: 'It exists! A Québécois is very different from someone living in Ontario or British Columbia. . . . [But] we are multicultural now. Regional cultures still exist but now we have different people living here too, with their own heritages. . . . Canadian culture is Multi-Cultural'.

Phipps, after interviewing Canadians across the country, concludes: 'Canadian culture: it doesn't exist, it's regional, and it's multicultural or any combination of the three. In many ways it's all of those things. It is a complex culture, shaped by all the cultures that form it. Maybe it's this complexity that causes it to defy definition'.

Source: Adapted from Phipps (2009).

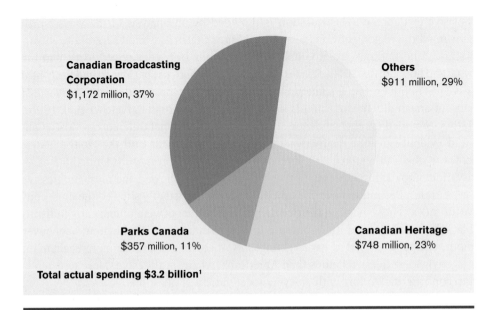

Figure 4.5 Distribution of Actual Spending by Federal Organization in a Vibrant Canadian Culture and Heritage, 2008–2009

1. Due to rounding, numbers may not sum exactly to totals.

Source: Treasury Board of Canada (2009), Figure 3.5.

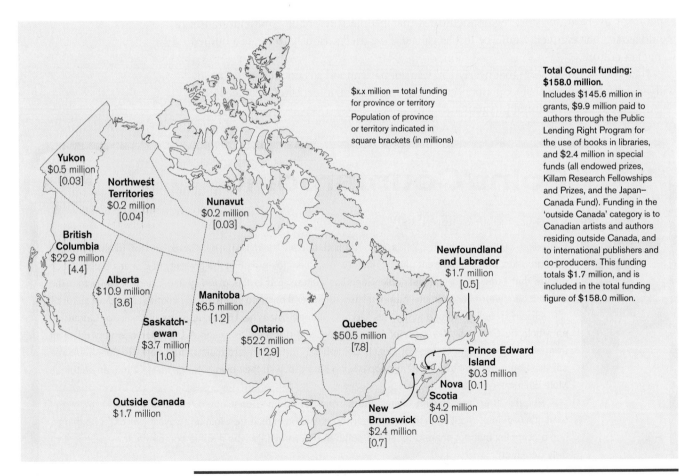

Figure 4.6 Canada Council for the Arts: Total Funding 2008–2009

Source: Based on Canada Council for the Arts (2009a).

A Global Culture?

As we look around the world today, we see ethnic fragmentation, the increasing import-ance of culturally based political movements and a lack of faith in such nineteenth-century cultural ideals as 'progress' or 'civilization'. All this suggests a global struggle between trad-itional national (or subnational) cultures and present-day transnational cultures.

A world culture, if it is ever to form, will have to overcome two obstacles. One is the idea that 'development' means the gradual elimination of differences for mass participation in one, and only one, culture. The other is the idea that participation in one particular culture, or nation, should limit communication with others. Neither idea is plausible and neither will survive. The trick is to find a kind of global organization that encourages both *intra*cultural development and *inter*cultural communication.

 **New Insights**

Over the last few decades, culture and its elements have proven to be a key concern for cur-rent sociologists, especially those whose approach to the field is informed by postmodern theory. Like other postmodern writers, Agger (2001) argues that cultural 'texts', or cultural products, must be viewed with the author's social context and personal subjectivity in mind. In this sense, authors are in themselves 'authored', meaning they are in themselves a product of the 'culture industry and its literary political economies' (ibid: 183). Agger stresses that this consideration is especially important in the age of the Internet, where the production of culture is increasingly attainable for its countless users.

Many scholars have applied a postmodern approach to their research on culture. Arvidsson (2001) analyzes the roots of present-day postmodern consumer culture, espe-cially the notions of identity and lifestyle choice. Focusing on a case study of an Italian producer of motor scooters (including the Vespa) called Piaggio, the article analyzes the marketing strategies employed by the company to attract consumers. Arvidsson argues that the company used the popularity of its vehicles in 1960s and 1970s subcultures to produce a lifestyle image attached to the scooters, popularly called the 'mod subculture', from the word *modern*. The company thus employed countercultural elements to create a consumer culture for their products.

Another example is Bishop's (2001) analysis of the 'changing nature of professional sports logos, using semiotics and the work of postmodern writers' (ibid: 23). Bishop argues that wearing or displaying a professional sports team's logo was once a sign of loyalty and commitment to the sport and particular team. Today, logos are more likely to show social rapport and social power than devotion. In essence, sentiment has turned into material consumption.

Some scholars have studied groups or organizations that have themselves been inspired by postmodernism in their efforts to reach some goal. For example, Till (2006) examines the link between popular culture and religion in his study of club music. He argues that although club (or rave) music and its associated counterculture are often depicted as in opposition to, and in conflict with, the mainstream culture, it incorporates many elements of mainstream Christian religion and spirituality. Therefore, Till studies the postmodern-inspired action taken by a church in England in creating an innovative alternative service called The Nine O'clock Service (NOS) that adopted elements of popular culture to appeal to younger worshippers.

Although the NOS movement faced challenges, they managed to adopt several key principles that helped them to manage their program. For example, they came to believe the real purpose of music and the arts was worship and communal celebration. So, they

Corporate advertising reaching all the corners of the world has led to debates about whether a global culture is emerging.

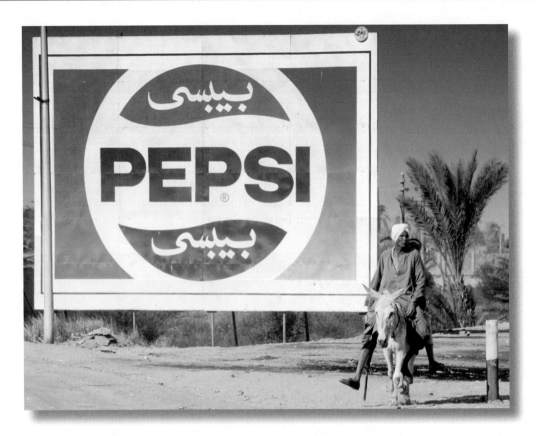

criticized the mainstream arts industry for turning these cultural elements into a bid for profit. Thus, NOS chose to support club culture, which they considered an opposition to the mainstream.

Other scholars have explored postmodernism itself, as revealed in the cultural arena. For example, Boggs and Pollard (2001) focus on postmodern cinema, which arose during the 1980s and 1990s. According to these authors, its main themes include 'class polarization, social atomization, urban chaos and violence, ecological crisis, mass depoliticization', and other topics which are in themselves the subject of sociology (ibid: 159). Its cinematographic elements include 'disjointed narratives, a dark view of the human condition, images of chaos and random violence, death of the hero, emphasis on technique over content, and dystopic view of the future' (ibid: 159). The authors argue that although such themes may seem like a departure from the mainstream, they are popular in today's society.

Like postmodernism, critical theory also has much to say on the topic of culture. The early critical theorists, like Max Horkheimer, Theodor Adorno, and Walter Benjamin from the Frankfurt School of the 1930s focused their work on a critique of modern popular culture and mass consumption. Critical theory, as Horkheimer (1937) noted, assumes that both reality and science, including sociology, are socially created (Castro-Gomez, 2001). For this reason, the key goal of critical theory is to 'reflect upon the structures from which social reality and the theories that explain it [including critical theory] . . . are constructed' (ibid: 139). Today, Castro-Gomez argues that critical theory, unlike traditional theory, is a useful tool for understanding culture as a socially created, dynamic, and constantly changing subject for sociology (ibid).

Modern critical theory, as informed by feminist approaches, sees culture as a 'complex combination of critical cultural elements . . . that are forged, reproduced, and contested within asymmetrical relations of power that primarily constrain one's self' (Qin, 2004: 297). These cultural elements include gender, race, ethnicity, class, and sexuality. Not only are these concepts socially constructed, they are culturally bound and must be considered within their cultural, as well as other contexts—social, political, historical, and so on. If so, universalistic assumptions about the self and identity are impossible, since even self and identity are manifested in the cultural environment.

Kirkpatrick (2007) uses a critical theory orientation, as well as insights from early critical thinkers, to analyze the modern cultural product of computer games. Intriguingly, he argues that 'computer games can occupy an oppositional or critical role within contemporary aesthetics and culture' (ibid: 74). As artistic products, computer game images are infinitely reproducible, losing their uniqueness; and used as recreational or sporting equipment, losing their purely expressive value. These and other features suggest the decline of artwork as a purely cultural phenomenon, as argued by Adorno and Benjamin in their own time.

Meanwhile, Rief (2008) would likely see computer games viewed as another form of consumption in modern society. Nevertheless, Rief believes we can understand consumption as a cultural and social practice, not as evidence of social decay. Consumption, however preoccupying, is not a societal disease or some other psychopathology. Instead, it is connected to 'spheres of work, politics, families, and communities', each existing within a social and cultural context (ibid: 561). For this reason, we must study consumption in light of the way it is viewed by the individuals engaging in it, and their understanding of it.

Despite this work, Goldfarb (2005) claims the modern sociology of culture is not yet developed enough from a critical theory perspective, and needs a more specific understanding of its subject, concerns, and ideas. Therefore, he urges us to make several distinctions in the field: between culture and ideology, high culture and autonomous culture, and power and knowledge (ibid: 281). He also calls for a consideration of the links between the arts and sciences and everyday life, and all of these with politics (ibid: 281). Such analysis will lead to a better understanding of culture and, beyond that, to the better use of sociological imagination in considering society's constituent elements.

Chapter Summary

The sociological study of culture offers a prime example of the connection between macro- and microsociological perspectives. On the one hand, culture is a macro phenomenon. It exists outside and 'above' individual people, in their language, institutions, and material artifacts. In this sense, culture is all encompassing and slow changing—like a huge glacier. The main elements of a culture outlast individuals and even generations of individuals. On the other hand, culture is inside all of us and, as the symbolic interactionists remind us, is something we all change or reproduce every day. Culturally accepted patterns change over time because dozens, then thousands, then millions of us change our way of doing things.

Likewise, the study of culture—especially, the visible gap between ideal and **real culture**—recalls the importance we have placed on the connection between 'private troubles' and 'public issues'. Few people manage to live up to the supposed goals and values of their society; as a result, almost everyone has something to hide, something to feel ashamed of. For many, this blameworthiness—real and imagined—may contribute as much to the maintenance of conformity as people's actual commitment to leading 'worthy' lives.

At the beginning of this chapter, we said that culture can best be understood as a symbolic environment within which we live. As we looked more closely at this environment, however, we discovered that it differs radically from one group to another. The cultural world of poor people is very different from that of rich people. The cultural world of the atheist is different from that of the religious adherent. The cultural world of the Italian Canadian is, in many important ways, different from that of the Inuit. All of us, living together in the same country, are to some degree living in different cultures. Understanding these cultures, and how and why they are different, is an important task for sociologists, especially in a rapidly changing world.

real culture
The ways people dress, talk, act, relate, and think in everyday life, as distinct from their idealized or proclaimed culture.

Critical Thinking Questions

1. How does culture relate to the social structure of society?
2. What does language tell us about culture?
3. How do the mass media shape culture? What were some sources of cultural change before the mass media?
4. Why do people consider art to be part of culture?
5. What does cultural change suggest? How is it related to economic, political, and social forces?
6. Do you think that a global culture is developing? If so, what are its implications on the cultures and societies of the world?

Recommended Readings

Victoria D. Alexander, *Sociology of the Arts: Exploring Fine and Popular Forms* (Oxford: Blackwell, 2003). This is a comprehensive and sophisticated overview of the sociology of art, outlining the theoretical perspectives and both classic and current research on art, music, literature, and popular culture.

Angela McRobbie, *The Aftermath of Feminism: Gender, Culture, and Social Change* (Los Angeles: Sage, 2009). This book provides an intersection of feminism and culture, laying out a theory of gender power used to analyze social and cultural phenomena in women's lives today.

James Burke, *The Day the Universe Changed* (Boston: Little, Brown, 1995). This account of the key changes in the cultural history of the world is based on a PBS television series and focuses on the issue of a global culture.

Lyn Spillman (ed.), *Cultural Sociology* (Malden, MA: Blackwell, 2002). This is an engaging overview of several empirical studies and theoretical works in the sociology of culture. It is a good foundation for someone interested in exploring and learning about the field in greater depth.

Stanley Lieberson, *A Matter of Taste: How Names, Fashions, and Culture Change* (New Haven, CT; London: Yale University Press, 2000). This is a highly interesting study of how cultural taste and fashion change over time. Presented in a clear and scholarly manner, it explores how cultural patterns shape the names chosen by parents for their children for the past two centuries.

John Berger, *Ways of Seeing: Based on the BBC Television Series* (London: British Broadcasting Corporation and Penguin Books, 1980). As the subtitle suggests, this book is based on a 1970s BBC television series about how we view paintings. Although some do not approve of Berger's arguments, the work was seminal in shaping the view of postmodern art.

Websites

Canadian Heritage
www.canadianheritage.gc.ca

Culture Web
www.ibiblio.org/culture

National Film Board of Canada (NFB)
www.nfb.ca

Canadian Broadcasting Corporation (CBC)
www.cbc.ca

United Nations Educational, Scientific and Cultural Organization (UNESCO)
www.unesco.org

Ontario Ministry of Culture
www.culture.gov.on.ca/english/index.html

Canadian Culture
www.canadianculture.com

Baby Name Wizard
www.babynamewizard.com

5 Gender Relations

Learning Objectives

In this chapter, you will:

> Distinguish between sex and gender, and discuss how these concepts affect the lives of men and women

> Distinguish between types of feminism and the ways each proposes to change society

> Describe several ways in which gender socialization occurs, and in what settings

> Understand which aspects of women's lives are most affected by socially constructed gender roles, and how this experience is different for men

> Find out how socially constructed gender roles and gender socialization have changed over time, and how they are likely to continue to change in the future

Chapter Outline

Sex is a universal and ancient basis of social differentiation. We know of no human society today or in the past without a division of roles and statuses according to sex. Likely, this distinction has some biological basis, given that females—human or otherwise—can bear offspring while males cannot. Females are also, on average, physically smaller and weaker than males and therefore less suited for combat and hunting. Further, childbearing makes females vulnerable and dependent for extended periods. These biological realities have likely led to the widespread social roles of men acting as protectors and breadwinners while women serve as procreators and caregivers.

However, these simple distinctions between roles fulfilled by men and women vary from one society to another. History and anthropology show us that women have also been breadwinners and protectors, and even in the animal world (for instance, among lions), it is often the female that hunts. Men, on the other hand, though unable to bear children, are able to serve as caregivers, and many do so. More important, as fertility rates around the world decline, women are spending less time pregnant and caring for small children; and they are less expected to shoulder the entire burden of child care. Therefore, they are able to engage more in public life. In this way, women are leading lives that are increasingly similar to those of men. In this chapter, we will look at how these gendered social roles have changed over time, and why.

Everyday Observations

A familiar brainteaser, perhaps: A man and his son are in a car accident. The man is killed instantly. The boy is badly injured and unconscious. He is rushed to hospital, and taken into the operating room for surgery. The doctor enters the room, looks at the boy, and says: 'I can't operate on this boy, he is my son.' How is this possible?

sexism

The perceived superiority of one sex (most often men) over the other (usually women).

gender

The expectations of behaviour or appearance that we describe as *masculine* or *feminine*; a set of social expectations.

The sexual double standard may be on the decline as traditional gender stereotypes are being challenged with new ways of doing things.

Have you ever witnessed an instance of gender inequality? Many young Canadians grew up in a society that outwardly discourages, and even prohibits, **sexism** and **gender** inequality, and this may lead them to think that these issues do not concern them as they did their parents. However, if you think carefully about some everyday occurrences, you might be surprised to see some subtle (and some not-so-subtle) signs that this is not always so. Some types of gender inequality have disappeared with feminist movements and societal change, but others have not.

Unlike the women of a century ago, many women today work and even have long, fulfilling careers. Did your grandmother or your mother have a full-time career? If you are a woman, do you expect to work full-time in the future? Perhaps you already have a career in mind, and you are working toward the needed credentials. If you are a man, do you expect your women colleagues, sisters, and future spouse to complete their education and have careers? Do you expect them to quit their jobs once they have children, to care for them at home? If not, do you expect men to stay home with the children, and do the cooking, cleaning, and child care? Or do you imagine these tasks will be shared equally between men and women in heterosexual relationships?

More generally, what do Canadian men and women want today? Are women willing to rely on men as breadwinners, or do they want to be financially independent? Are men intent on dividing the work in this way, especially if it means depriving their partner of a desired career?

Research shows that many young women today are finding themselves at a fork in the road. Should they work hard to develop a career or opt for motherhood, with its biologically limited window of opportunity? Some hope to have the best of both worlds. Others feel that forgoing or leaving a career to raise children is like stepping back into the past. Women have worked hard to be eligible for higher education and good jobs, so why give that up? Perhaps you know some women who are grappling with this choice, or who have already made a decision.

Young Canadians today believe they have complete freedom in choosing their careers, and the options for study and work seem endless and ever-changing. Perhaps, however, you have noticed a gendered trend in certain job markets. How many female school principals have you had in your lifetime, and how many male primary-school teachers? How many women politicians can you name, versus men politicians? Look at the photos of CEOs of the top North American corporations—do you see more images of men or women? How can we explain these observations? Is it that, inherently, men and women gravitate towards different types of careers? Or is this distribution a result of social prejudices that allow males and females different opportunities, whatever their original goals?

Clearly, we see much evidence that men and women receive different kinds of encouragement. In today's mass media, we see gendered information continuously being produced, sold, and consumed. Why is it that so many images of men and women in the media perpetuate gender stereotypes—such as the dashing, strong, capable man and the pretty, weak, simple woman? Why are men supposed—and in fact, encouraged—to have sex on their minds all the time, while women are criticized if they are 'too sexual'? (Or has all this changed with *Sex and the City*?) At the same time, we see sexualized images of women everywhere in the media, even of pre-adolescent girls. How should we reconcile these opposing attitudes? What does it mean to say 'Boys don't cry', 'Toughen up and be a man', or 'Act like a lady'? How do we learn these gender stereotypes, and why are they so hard to change?

Ways of Looking at . . . GENDER

Functionalism

We will briefly review competing approaches to the study of gender, starting with the functionalist approach. Remember that functionalists ask of every social arrangement: *What function* does it perform for society as a whole? In this case, how does gender inequality contribute to the well-being of society as a whole? Functionalist theorists starting with Talcott Parsons (1955) would say that a gendered division of labour is the most effective and efficient way to carry out society's tasks of reproduction and socialization. It may even have evolutionary survival value for the human race. A mother, by her early attachment to her child (via pregnancy and breastfeeding, for example), is well suited to raising the family's children. Since she is at home with the children anyway, the mother is also well suited to caring for the household while the husband is at work outside the home. This, at least, is the skeleton of the argument.

Critical Theories

Critical theorists, by contrast, always ask the question: *Who holds power and benefits* from a particular social arrangement? In this case, who is best served by gender inequality? Marxists would tend to answer this question by referring to class relations: capitalism requires the low-cost social reproduction of a workforce from one generation to the next. Families are the best and cheapest way to raise new workers, and women (as mothers) provide the cheapest family labour. Mothers have the job of keeping all the family earners and earners-to-be healthy—well fed, housed, and cared for emotionally. They do this at no cost to capitalists, who will benefit from the surplus value workers produce.

   The Marxist approach assumes that working-class men and women are on the same side, both equally victims of the capitalist class. By contrast, the feminist approach assumes that women have a different experience from men and may be exploited by men of their own class, as well as by capitalists. Therefore, they see gender inequality as mainly serving the interests of men who, by lording it over their girlfriends, wives, and daughters, at least have someone as subservient to them as they are to their own bosses. The theory of patriarchy—that men are the main and universal cause of women's oppression—is compatible with Marxist analyses that view working-class women as being the victims of both class and gender oppression (Knudson-Martin and Mahoney, 2009). But the two theories place slightly different emphases on the role of class.

Symbolic Interactionism

Symbolic interactionists ask: *How* is a social arrangement *symbolized*? For example, how is gender inequality negotiated, symbolized, and communicated in our society? The presumption is that inequalities arise where social differences have been symbolized, communicated, and negotiated—that is, made into something that is 'taken for granted' by the population at large. From this standpoint, people are always trying to understand and normalize social interaction through shared meanings. Thus, symbolic interactionists are concerned with the ways that gender differences become stable gender inequalities—for example, the ways that young women become 'objectified' and turned into sex 'objects'. They also want to understand how the **sexual double standard**, which has allowed men more sexual freedom than women, has been 'negotiated' so that many women go along with an agenda that, it would seem to many people, benefits males more than females—for example, to define 'sexual freedom' as men's free access to women.

sexual double standard

The expectation that women will feel or behave differently from men in sexual matters.

Social Constructionist Approaches

Social constructionists always ask: *When* and *how* did the arrangement *emerge*? When, for example, did gender inequality emerge in a particular society, what events preceded this emergence, and what individuals or groups were especially instrumental in this process of 'moral entrepreneurship'? And by what steps has gender equality begun to emerge? This approach is much more historically oriented than the related symbolic interactionist approach. So, for example, a social constructionist would note that gender inequality began to decline (for a second time) in the 1960s and 1970s, largely because of the actions of the women's movement.

The women's movement was especially successful then because social protest (against the rich, against imperialists, and against racists, for example) was in the air throughout the Western world. Besides, the baby boom had already ended; and because of an economic downturn, there was now a need for two family incomes, and therefore a need for women with fewer children and more education. This new agenda—getting women out of the home and into the workplace—was aided significantly by the development of reliable birth control that made it possible for people to have sex without having babies. Cutting the links between gender, sexuality, and childbearing was central to the emergence of women as full-fledged members of society. It also helped gay and lesbian people stake a claim to full social inclusion, for similar reasons.

Notably, all these explanations are compatible with one another. Each focuses on a different aspect of the rise, maintenance, and decline of gender inequality. However, by far the most influential approach to studying gender issues has been the feminist approach, which has shaped this chapter.

Types of Feminist Sociology

Usefully viewed as a branch of critical theory, feminist theory postulates that most gender differences are socially constructed. For moral reasons, they should be abolished, since gender-based discrimination and segregation pose important problems for society and for individual women. However, not all feminists agree about the causes of gender inequality. So, various forms of feminism have emerged, a few of which are briefly outlined in Table 5.1. Feminist theories also try to describe social life and its aspects (for example, in social institutions) from a gendered perspective. More recently, feminist theory (specifically anti-racist/postmodern feminism) argues for the elimination of prejudice and domination over other deprived groups, including racial and ethnic minorities and LGBT groups.

One of the most important contributions of feminist sociology has been to forefront the importance of taken-for-granted everyday life as a window on important social facts about the distribution of power.

Table 5.1 A Comparison of Types of Feminism

	Liberal	Marxist	Radical	Socialist	Anti-racist/ Postmodern
General	Believes men and women are essentially the same Concerned primarily with equal rights	Believes women are the first exploited class Subordination of women comes with the advent of private property	Believes men and women are different Patriarchy is not specific to capitalism; rather, it is universal	Combines Marxist and radical feminisms	Criticizes essentialism in other feminisms (not all women are the same, no single source of inequality) Some men and women share oppression in complex ways
Why does gender inequality exist?	Discriminatory legislation bars women from entering public life	Capitalism and private ownership	Patriarchy	Capitalism and patriarchy	Multiple inequalities: race, class, gender, sexuality, ability, etc. These inequalities overlap in unique ways for different women
Key issues	Right to vote, access to education and paid employment, pay equity		Male control of female sexuality Women's reproductive capacity	Inequality as a result of the intersection of race, class, and gender Inequality in paid and unpaid work, in the home and outside	Post-colonial exploitation of women of colour
How are we to fix inequalities?	Do not change the structure of society, just remove legislation barring women from public life The 'best women' like 'the best men' will rise to the top	Need to change the social structure: for example, abolish capitalism	Need direct action, political opposition, radical social change	Attack both patriarchy and capitalism	No single solution for all women Need to address differences among women in a non-universalizing, non-essentialist way

Classic Studies
The Sociology of Housework

Not until the early 1970s did any sociologist seem to notice that housework, traditionally a woman's responsibility, was work, not just a casual outpouring of family affection. This is mainly because until the mid twentieth century, most sociologists were men, and many of them viewed housework as unskilled labour, worthy of little attention.

It was in 1974 that British sociologist Ann Oakley published her seminal book, *The Sociology of Housework*, which addressed these misconceptions. As a result, housework began to emerge as a type of legitimate, difficult, and worthwhile work, not just the 'labour of love'. This classic work drew needed attention to domestic inequality and its relation to other forms of gender inequality. Since men rarely did housework, early sociologists and economists (almost exclusively male) had failed to consider it an important topic and given its unpaid status, ignored its contribution to the economy. Oakley changed all that.

Oakley based her housework research on a small sample of working- and middle-class homemakers. Social class, in her sample, made little difference: both classes of women reported similar (negative) attitudes about housework and a similar (high degree of) identification with their homemaker role. All the women in Oakley's sample viewed housework as unpleasant. Despite this dislike, many of the informants viewed the role of homemaker as central to their identity; they felt mainly responsible for tending to the home and children. For this reason, most of these women swallowed their dissatisfaction with the monotony, isolation, and low social status that it provided them. They took it for granted as unavoidable.

Recent research shows that these findings still hold true to some extent today. Johnson and Johnson found that 'in spite of large-scale social and political changes, women still bear the primary responsibility for housework' (2008: 487). When Oakley was writing, many (like Parsons, mentioned earlier) viewed marriage, family values, and societal stability as inseparable from contemporary suburban life—this was the idea of the 'golden nuclear family'. Messages like these fostered in women the identity of the loving mother and home-maker (Baxter and Western, 1998). Today, research shows that such views remain more prevalent among the baby boom generation than in later generations, highlighting the fact that human values like these change over time, as the products of societal context (Lyons, Duxbury, and Higgins, 2005).

Oakley concluded that women are disempowered and imprisoned by their beliefs about the proper role of women, especially, of mothers, in a modern society. Despite their unhappiness, many housewives feel obliged by their culture to play a basically alienating and frustrating role. They have been socialized by a patriarchal gender ideology into accepting slavery in marriage and motherhood. Housework is the visible symbol of this submission.

Oakley had strong views on this topic. Consider a few of her thoughts about families, women, and housework:

- 'Society has a tremendous stake in insisting on a woman's natural fitness for the career of mother: the alternatives are all too expensive.'
- 'Families are nothing other than the idolatry of duty.'
- 'Housework is work directly opposed to the possibility of human self-actualization.'
- 'There are always women who will take men on their own terms. If I were a man, I wouldn't bother to change while there are women like that around.' (http://www.brainyquote.com/quotes/quotes/a/annoakley159403.html)

Some empirical evidence has contradicted Oakley's findings. For example, Bonney and Reinach (1993) used data from the UK Economic and Social Research Council's Social Change and Economic Life and Initiative's surveys to analyze the attitudes and experiences of 300 full-time homemakers. This sample contained a wider variety of women than Oakley had studied. Moreover, only a minority of these women had preschool children or had left work to care for their children. These researchers conclude that if we allow for a wide variety of female domestic and employment roles, we find a broader variety of views about housework than Oakley has reported. Moreover, people do not evaluate their current lives only in relation to past and present goals; they also look toward the future. Women tending children at home view their lives differently if they are eager to return to an attractive paid job than if they are largely indifferent to paid work. Likewise, in a review, Judith Hammond (1977: 1104) writes that Oakley 'narrowed and distorted the picture of housewifery into that of a thankless joyless task'.

Perhaps this is so; however, Oakley forthrightly called our attention to the neglected topic of housework. It is because of her insight that we are now aware of housework's relation to gender inequality and the need for sensitive qualitative research to explore this problem.

Gendered Socialization

Most of us first learn about the opposite **sex** from our families. Children learn about what being a girl or boy entails through their families, largely by a process called *socialization*. Parents tend to treat their daughters and sons differently from an early age, choosing specific colours for their rooms, buying different kinds of toys, dressing them in gender-specific clothes and so on. Often, parents discourage girls from playing roughly and boys from crying too often. Such practices occur because the parents themselves have been socialized to believe that girls and boys are different and thus should be treated accordingly.

Children are further socialized into their respective gender roles by learning to co-operate with family members of the opposite sex. These cross-sex forms of interaction—between brothers and sisters, mothers and sons, or fathers and daughters—may be emotionally charged in ways that are different from same-sex interactions (for example, those between fathers and sons). If so, this may happen because most cultures expect same-sex family members to pass along gender-specific knowledge to one another. For instance, there is an expectation that fathers will socialize sons to 'become men', and older brothers will socialize younger brothers by introducing them to the 'secrets'—pleasures or demands—of manhood. Similarly, there is an expectation that mothers will socialize daughters, and older sisters their younger sisters in the skills, rules, and etiquettes of womanhood. Of course, Freud would say that there is also a latent sexual charge in cross-sex relations, even within families, even in childhood.

From early childhood, through their elementary and high school years, children are also socialized as males or females through various school practices. Because they are social institutions, schools are an integral part of the socialization process; and in schools, children develop a wide range of relations with peers from very different backgrounds and those of the other gender. In elementary schools in particular, gender is often used to classify and organize people. You likely remember a time when your elementary school teacher divided the class into boys and girls for an activity. In this case, gender is emphasized—perhaps for the first and certainly not the last time—as a basis for distinction among people.

In daycare centres in early childhood, and later in school settings, many children join peer groups and cliques that influence their understanding of, and interaction with, people of the opposite sex. Though many peer groups and cliques are same-sex, many

sex

The biological characteristics that make a person male or female; a biological fact at birth.

Early gender socialization starts at birth, with boys and girls being treated differently by the members of their own environment, and are taught the differences between boys and girls, women and men.

are not. Besides, peer groups include both actual and notional groups—called *reference groups*—from whom we gain ideas about proper behaviour. (Thus, for example, young girls may compare themselves to the fictional Hannah Montana, in thinking about how girls should dress, talk, and behave, and discuss these ideas with their friends.) These groups may be large and loose or small and compact. What is important is that all peer groups provide access to peer culture and ideas about age- and sex-appropriate norms of behaviour.

Some research shows that gender differences are further underlined in schools when boys are encouraged to be bolder and take more part in class discussion, whereas girls are discouraged from doing so (Smith, 2000). Further, schools both directly and indirectly influence boys and girls to take certain courses and follow certain fields of study—with boys being steered to more technical domains and girls to more commercial, artistic, or domestic ones (Arnot, 2002).

Educational sociologists call this a *hidden curriculum* (Ronholt, 2002). Hidden curricula often define gender roles as well as encourage gender stereotypes; for example, guidance counsellors may fail to advise a boy to go into nursing, for example. In this way, schools develop *gender regimes* which produce masculinity and femininity and attach certain practices to these labels (Connell et al., 1982: 353). As well, these practices vary for children from different social classes, leading to different relations between boys and girls (also, men and women) from different economic backgrounds (ibid).

There is evidence that the hidden curriculum is less prevalent today than it was even a few decades ago, with both men and women increasingly entering fields traditionally out of line with their biological sex. That said, important gendered differences remain in the occupational choices of men and women. Based on findings of the 2006 Canadian Census, Statistics Canada reports that

> Women now account for the majority of university graduates; the gender gap in labour market participation in 2009 narrowed to a small fraction of its size in 1976; and increasingly, women are found in non-traditional occupations and fields of study. That being said, there still are many occupations that reflect historical gender roles . . . . In 2009, for example, over half of women were found in two occupational groups: sales and services and business, finance and administration. Women were also more likely than men to work in occupations in social services, education, government services and religion, and in health. In contrast, men continued to predominate in occupations in trades, transport and equipment operators and, to a lesser extent, in occupations in the natural and applied sciences; management; and occupations unique to manufacturing, processing and utilities. (McMullen et al., 2010).

Mass Media

Similarly, the mass media play a role in preserving the traditional occupational activities of women as 'people workers' and 'caregivers'. Through the mass media, young people gain additional vicarious (or indirect) experience with people of the opposite sex. By watching cross-sex relations being modelled, they see how men and women are supposed to act toward one another, and what supposedly happens when they break the rules. The mass media dramatize differences between men and women in advertising, music videos, movies, beauty pageants, situation comedies, pornography—in fact, in almost every aspect of popular culture.

The changes that have occurred in gender equality—and those that have not—are obvious in various ways. For example, there have always been jokes about the opposite sex and about marriage. Such jokes, especially by male comedians about their wives, were a

Media Distortion

BOX 5.1

Women, News, and Politics

Researchers have found that in the mainstream media, women are rarely called upon to give expert opinions on business, politics, and economics. According to Quebec political analyst Denis Monière, women are likely to be asked to give opinions as 'average citizens' rather than as experts. Monière also found that profiles of successful politicians or businesspeople were almost always about men. One study, by Canadian journalist Jenn Goddu, found that in reporting interviews with representatives of women's lobby groups, journalists would focus not on the lobbyists' positions on the political issues, but rather on aspects of their appearance and personal lives—including 'details about the high heels stashed in her bag, her habit of napping in the early evening, and her lack of concern about whether or not she is considered ladylike.'

A similar bias is seen in the US media. A study of the popular Sunday morning TV news shows by the White House Project reveals that about 90 per cent of the guests are men, and that even when a woman is on a show, the men do 90 per cent of the talking.

Source: Adapted from Media Awareness Network (N.d.).

staple of the professional 'humour industry' for a long time. Today, we still see male comedians on television making these jokes. However, sometimes the tables are turned, with both male and female comedians, as well as situation comedies, depicting women (both wives and daughters) as savvy and competent, while men are dreamers and goofs. (Some would say that this is not really new: consider Alice and Ralph Kramden in *The Honeymooners*—a classic comedy series from the 1950s that made the women appear smart and effective, the men dopey blowhards.)

However, the mass media continue to objectify women—that is, to portray them as sex objects on display and seemingly for purchase. This is evident in advertising (especially for cars and alcohol), in pornography, at televised sporting events, and in other entertainments aimed at young male viewers. True, there has been some decline in the depiction of women as brainless beauties: some women are now depicted as intelligent, while others do not necessarily fit into the mould of perfection that has characterized women in the mass media for decades. But there is still a long way to go, and none of this is lost on children, who grow up thinking males and females really (naturally) are different in these ways.

Men, for their part, also face problems of meeting the ideal standards for their gender. If women are expected to be sexy and passive, men are expected to be economically successful, the family's primary breadwinner for many decades. Men, unlike women, are permitted to age: they even, some say, become more attractive as they take on greying temples. However, society expects men to work from graduation until retirement or even later in a well-paying occupation without any interruption (Malenfant, Larue and Vézina, 2007). Men who are unemployed or underemployed often face stigmatization and are seen as less desirable dating and marriage partners. And none of this is lost on children, either.

Another type of ideal male definition has emerged, however, and it may supplant the traditional one. Analyses of advertising in the 1980s revealed that the ideal male image was becoming smaller-bodied, had a less pronounced jaw, smiled more often, and was often represented like a woman—that is, partly undressed or in the act of changing clothes (Judith Posner, 1984a). Such depictions suggest that people were beginning to view seemingly vulnerable men as more socially acceptable and even desirable. Some researchers have argued that this trend did not represent a move toward gender equality but only the commercialization of male sexuality, as with women (Wernick, 1987). Whatever the reason, this trend persists today, encouraging men to spend as much as women on fashion and personal products—for example, on sprays and perfumes that supposedly make them irresistible sexual partners.

With these exceptions in mind, the more traditional stereotypes of femininity and masculinity have not died out.

The Beauty Standard

Our society, and every society, has appearance norms—shared notions about beauty that literally attract us to some people and not to others, whether as friends, mates, or merely media idols. Violation of these norms leads us to apply sanctions like ridicule, exclusion, or disapproval to people who fail to meet our culture's standards of beauty and attractiveness. Further, these appearance norms are felt most keenly by women, since historically women have been valued most (by men) for their beauty, youth, and supposed fertility. Appearance issues, then, interest sociologists because they shed so much light on the boundaries between deviant and conforming behaviour and the measures people take to control and shame other people. In this respect, they call attention to the ideal versions of male and female that prevail in our society.

No wonder then that women fear aging more than men do; aging brings with it a natural reduction of what our culture considers attractive. That is, aging pushes women most dramatically across the normative boundaries from attractiveness to unattractiveness, if youthful standards are applied. For that reason, our culture forces women to take a position on aging, or 'natural aging'—and thus on our society's most important appearance norms (Hurd Clarke and Griffin, 2007). While some women argue for acceptance of the physical realities of growing older, others claim that an aged appearance should be resisted using any cosmetic interventions possible, including (for example) cosmetic surgery. In short, aging women—like all of us—know our society's appearance norms and the importance of obeying them.

The traditional stereotypes of femininity have not died out with mass media portrayals of women still emphasizing their sexuality and beauty.

Like it or not, people *do* judge books by their covers and strangers by their appearances. In judging appearance, people often look for points of likeness and familiarity that make them feel secure. Beyond that, they look for evidence of the cultural ideal. People admire others who look especially prosperous, healthy, and attractive according to society's standards. Thus, appearance features that approximate the ideal—not merely the familiar—are important, because individuals want to be admired and accepted. Such ideal features frame what we consider *appearance norms*. Most people prefer others who meet their appearance expectations; they criticize those who seem unconcerned about the appearance norms of their own subculture.

Appearance norms are often measurable, in body size and shape, dress, and other adornment. And since these norms are specific and quantifiable, it is easy to see deviations. We look at deviations from appearance norms as signs of rebellion, carelessness, or ignorance. Violations of the appearance norms may lead to mistrust, stigmatization, and exclusion.

Consider, for example, the norms we hold about suitable clothing. How a person dresses influences the first impression he or she makes. It will affect our opinion of the individual, and in this way, may affect that person's ability to get a needed job, make friends, or receive respect. How a person dresses affects employers' views of, expectations for, and responses to job applicants. To their disadvantage, many poor people can't afford to dress well (much less get cosmetic surgery) and as a result, they may look needy and unsuccessful. There are programs to help poor women get job-appropriate clothing, but these are limited in scope.

Society's attention to social norms—even appearance norms—teaches us about deeper cultural ideals of beauty, decency, and worth—especially where women are concerned. Some physical attributes—for example, perfect facial features or flawless white teeth— are valued because they are scarce, but this is far from the whole story. Abundant images glorify ideal men and women in the mass media; the interesting variations in these images show us various ways to meet the culture's appearance norms. By judging attractiveness based on images of 'beautiful people', our culture idealizes youth, a slender toned body, and symmetrical delicate facial features. Departures from these norms suggest poor genes, poor grooming, or a lack of self-discipline and self-worth. But many people—especially younger people—are able to approximate the cultural requirements.

Although gender stereotypes still exist, there is some blurring of the lines between behaviours that were once viewed as typically male or female.

However, few can meet the cultural ideals. Spitzer et al. (1999) compared the body standards of North Americans aged 18 to 24 years, looking for changes and inconsistencies. Using data from 11 national health surveys in Canada and the US, the researchers compared these data to *Playboy* centrefold models, Miss America pageant winners, and *Playgirl* models, and found a growing inconsistency between real and ideal bodies in North America.

They found that, since the 1950s, the body sizes of Miss America winners have *decreased* noticeably and those of *Playboy* centrefold models have remained below normal body weight: ideal women have become lighter and thinner. Over the same period, the body sizes of average young North American women and men—that is, of real people— have *increased* considerably, mainly because of an increase in body fat and growing obesity in the general population. Maybe slenderness has become an ideal precisely because of the obesity epidemic—because slenderness is rare.

The conclusion: since the 1950s, the body sizes and shapes of average North American women increasingly deviated from the ideal. Further, male and female body images have changed in opposite ways over this period. As ideal *women* became smaller, more toned, and physically fit, ideal *men* bulked up, mainly through increased muscularity. The difference between real men and women in the general population remained small, since both men and women took on more body fat. The difference between ideal men and women increased, playing to a (very old) stereotype that men ideally should be the muscular protectors and property of petite women.

There are two take-away messages here. First, the mass media, and especially advertising, do not show us reality; they show us fantasy but use it to generate sales. Second, and more relevant to the topic of gender, fantasies about the ideal male and female are different fantasies—not unisex. They tell us to expect very different things of men and women, many of them virtually unattainable by either.

Conflict between the Sexes

Living in Canada, we are all aware of the high rates of relationship dissolution (for example, divorce) between intimate partners. These rates of dissolution are especially high in dating relationships, where an estimated 60 per cent of couples break up at least once, often reuniting to ultimately break up again. The rates are somewhat lower for couples who cohabit, though these are often difficult to calculate with consistent accuracy. Nevertheless, the rate is still high. Finally, the rates are lower still (though again, still high), for married couples. In Canada and throughout the Western world, rates of legal divorce are much higher today than they were a century ago, or even 50 years ago. The risk of divorce is somewhere between one-quarter to one-third over the life of a relationship, depending on various social characteristics.

Since the liberalization of divorce laws in the late 1960s, the chances of divorce have risen to somewhere around 35–40 per cent in many countries. As noted, these rates vary demographically. For example, wealthier, more educated people are less likely to divorce than less educated people, especially if they marry late. This is also true for religious people (Bumpass, Martin, and Sweet 1991). Nonetheless, the high rate of marital dissolution argues that mating, attraction, romance, and love are no guarantee of long-term co-operation or attachment between the sexes. Often, people rebound from divorce with a new cross-sex effort to bond intimately; but these new relationships also carry high risks of failure—some would say, even higher risks.

Divorce aside, all families are fertile grounds for conflict between parents and children, and among siblings. Not all of this conflict is based on gender differences. What is clear, however, is that the institution called 'family' provides no more guarantee of stable bonding across the sexes than it does of bonding between husbands and wives. The differences and inequalities between boys and girls, men and women are evident, and poisonous even in families.

Some would say this situation is improving and people—especially young people—are more gender-blind today than they once were. For example, many young people date in groups, allowing them to enjoy the benefits and pleasures of opposite-sex interaction while protected by the nearness of same-sex friends. That said, we continue to see—in cliques, teams, fraternities, sororities, and elsewhere—ample evidence of same-sex mobilization. We see the same in gendered entertainment (for example, in 'chick flicks' like *Sex and the City*, which celebrate shopping, lunching, and gossiping as common forms of female bonding, and 'homosociality', in which, for example, young men go around slapping each other with towels and loudly drinking beer together). Young people, though perhaps less inclined toward stereotyping than their parents, have not lost sight of culturally defined differences between men and women.

In workplaces, for the most part, the more blatant forms of sex discrimination have been outlawed and eliminated. For example, anti-discrimination human rights legislation makes it illegal for bosses to promote men over more competent women, or to pay women less than men for the same work. However, suspicions of a continuing **glass ceiling** at work are still present for women. Moreover, in various circumstances, a wage gap remains between men and women, certain types of work remain segregated by gender, and child care remains a significant concern for working women, though not usually for their husbands or male colleagues.

glass ceiling
Any sex-based barrier to equal opportunity for hiring and promotion.

The Gendering of Crime

Families, schools, and workplaces are not the only places we see gendered behaviour. Even crime, generally less subject to conventional rules than workplace and families, is heavily gendered. Men, especially young men, are far more likely than anyone else to commit crimes. In general, they are far more likely to take dangerous risks: to drink to excess, drive wildly, or demand unsafe sex, for example. They are also far more likely to get into fights—either giving a beating or taking one. And they are more likely than women to commit every kind of crime.

This observation is interesting in light of Robert Merton's strain theory of 'adaptations to anomie': men are far more likely than women to behave like many of the people Merton described in this theory. In particular, men are more likely to behave as so-called 'innovators': people who seek new anti-social ways of gaining success in our culture's goals. They are also more likely to take on the role of 'rebel', a role that rejects both the culture's goals and the accepted means for gaining them. Women, by contrast, are more likely to choose other, non-criminal 'adaptations' like ritualism and retreatism. That is, they are less likely to break society's rules in an obvious way, and more likely internalize their disappointment and frustration in a variety of forms: especially depression, physical illness, or addiction (Merton, 1957).

It will be interesting to see, as childbearing continues to decline in our society and women have increasing access to education and better jobs—in effect becoming more like men—whether women also take on more male 'adaptations' to anomie, becoming more violent and rebellious in their criminality. Currently, male murderers widely outnumber female murderers, largely because murder is the most brutal form of externalized aggression. Women, historically, have been socialized to be gentle, not brutal, and to internalize their aggression, as noted. Ironically, a rise in the proportion of female murderers may be a positive sign that women are finally gaining gender equality.

Classic Studies
Men and Women of the Corporation

A continuing problem is the minority-group status that women often hold when they enter occupations previously restricted to men. This issue was explored in a landmark study by the American sociologist Rosabeth Kanter.

Kanter argued that the barriers women meet, and roles women play, in large corporations today are mainly a result of their numerical minority, not their sex. Her classic work, *Men and Women of the Corporation* (1993 [1977]), challenged many assumptions about the traditional system of merit and reward within large organizations. Most important, perhaps, Kanter showed that women behave in 'womanly ways' in organizations when they are denied authority; in authority, they behave in 'manly ways'. This says something important about socially structured, versus supposedly natural differences between the sexes.

Thus, in true sociological fashion, Kanter argued that structural and situational aspects—not individual characteristics—limit people's careers. Contrary to the belief that women's opportunities are limited because they act differently from men (that is, they are too 'feminine'), her study shows that women have less *opportunity* for promotion, and *this forces them* to act 'like women'—subservient, devious, seemingly unambitious. But men do the same when they have limited opportunity for promotion. In short, when men and women have the same opportunities (or lack of opportunities), they act in generally the same way. Weak, unproductive behaviour is a result of holding a weak position, not a natural difference of sexes. People who suffer from blocked opportunity, powerlessness, and tokenism, regardless of sex, act in similar ways, for example, displaying less ambition.

In Kanter's view, a woman's sense of self reflects her real opportunities. Change her opportunities and you change her identity and ambition. If our goal were to make women (or any minority) bolder, more willing to take risks, and more adventurous, we would give them more opportunity—more scope to show their abilities. Submissiveness, by this reckoning, is a social structural requirement, not a personality trait (as psychologists might assert).

Kanter got some of her data from a mail survey of the sales managers of Industrial Supply Corporation (a fictional name). She also interviewed 20 female sales support staff (secretaries), watched and recorded group discussions and group meetings, and analyzed various documents. She focused her attention on three key roles: (male) managers, (female) secretaries, and (female) wives of managers. She wanted to understand each role—its constraints, power, and opportunities—and to find out how the female experience of corporate life differs from the male experience, and for what reasons.

She found that women in large business organizations are often severely disadvantaged. Secretaries, however ambitious and talented they may be, are tied to the fortunes of their male bosses. Their earnings rise and fall directly with those of the boss, regardless of the women's own efforts. Similarly, the wives of executives, also often ambitious and talented, are tied to their spouses' fortunes. Both secretaries and wives are powerless, yet heavily dependent upon men; because of this, they behave in 'typical' female fashion. Regrettably, this behaviour supports the male view that women, by nature, are too submissive, coy, or round-about—not good executive material.

Kanter also hypothesized that group members who are in a numerical minority will feel restricted in what they can do. Kanter's 'tokenism theory' predicts that members of a social group who are outnumbered by members of another group will suffer adverse effects, including greater stress at work. The more outnumbered the token individual, the more pressure he or she will experience. However, this all changes as minority and majority social types within a group approach equal numbers. Then, isolation between the two groups lessens; and interaction and communication across group boundaries increases. This may call for a major transformation of the organization, however. Merely adding a few 'token women' to the group or organization will not be enough to increase interactions, improve the choices available to women, or encourage women to flourish in their new-found freedom.

Some research has failed to support Kanter's 'tokenism' argument. For example, Sonnert and Holton (1995, 1996) carried out wide-ranging research to find out why even brilliant women are more reluctant than men to make a career in science, and why they do less well in scientific careers. As Kanter might have predicted, in all but biology, women in any given cohort were almost one full (university) rank behind men of equal productivity. Discrimination, perhaps; however, this may also have been the women's own doing, in part. For example, the female scientists were reportedly more likely than men to leave promising jobs or to turn down career opportunities because of family responsibilities, or to locate their post-doctoral work where they could be with their spouses. Women who made these decisions—decisions men would be much less likely to make—were less successful in their careers. The female scientists also report less self-confidence, ambition, and self-perceived ability than their male counterparts. These findings suggest that some women scientists—even brilliant, highly celebrated young Ph.D.s—are bedevilled by gender scripts, not a lack of opportunities.

In an extensive review article, Blum and Smith (1988) report that researchers continue to debate the merits of both the gender script approach and Kanter's structural approach. Still, Kanter's tokenism theory can be applied to any organizational setting that contains different 'kinds' of people: men and women, visible minorities and whites, anglophones and francophones, immigrants and native-borns, and so on. We can apply the general principle—that tokenism prevents us from seeing how people could adapt and grow into their roles—in a wide variety of situations. This makes Kanter's work fertile and valuable, even beyond the study of gender. Kanter's research on women in the workplace was extraordinarily influential in understanding the social mechanisms that underlie gender inequality in the workplace. And, there are *many* ways that gender affects women in the workplace, as we will see next.

Gender Influences in the Workplace

In the workplace even more than in the home, school, or playground, gender visibly influences the distribution of authority, status, income, and power. Besides learning what it means to be a boss, subordinate, and colleague, workers also witness and perform gender-play within the context of work roles. In general, people learn workplace etiquette—the unwritten rules of behaviour across occupational status—in combination with gender etiquette. Cross-sex relations in the workplace expose us to the opposite sex in ways that allow us to co-operate, compete, and compare our own skills and merits. As in school, in the workplace we learn that both males and females can be competent, ambitious, meritorious, lazy, double-dealing, or backstabbing. This discovery is an important basis for future cross-sex alliances.

Because the number of women educated at higher levels has increased, the number of women in the labour market has also increased in recent decades. Today, both continue to increase, even in fields chiefly occupied by men (Fortin and Huberman, 2002). As a result, earnings by men and women are coming closer to equality (Chaykowski and Powell, 1999). A shift is undoubtedly occurring and the balance of power between men and women is changing too.

However, in these respects Canada is behind some other developed countries, like Denmark and Sweden. In Canada, only about 60 per cent of women are in the labour force (compared to 73 per cent of men), while in Scandinavia it is about 10 per cent higher. (Andres and Adamuti-Trache, 2007). Moreover, in Canada, women are still less likely than men to hold positions of authority. Kay and Brockman (2003) note that women have been historically excluded from the legal profession in Canada, for example. In recent years, although women have made gains in law school enrolment and in representation in the profession, women 'remain on the margins of power and privilege in law practice' (ibid). Further, they show that women are under-represented in private practice and are less likely to be promoted to positions of authority and prestige than their male counterparts.

Nor are women treated the same as men in the workplace. Mills (2002), for example, shows that women working for Air Canada are often treated as idealized and sexualized objects. This objectification of women in the airline industry has narrowed the definition of women's roles and trivialized their contributions. Other recent literature notes that 'women's work' often involves emotional labour—maintaining an atmosphere of warmth and comfort, or providing customer satisfaction and service. Though important, anything associated with emotion (versus reason) in our society tends to be undervalued.

Is the situation improving? Bradley (2000) studied the changes in 29 countries between 1960 and 1990, and found a significant increase in the number of women continuing their postgraduate education worldwide. However, gender differences remained in all of these societies, and were especially obvious where women were entering traditionally female-dominated disciplines in large numbers.

The Earnings Gap

Even though more Canadian women are gaining a higher education, they are still being educated largely for female-oriented disciplines and will likely work in domains that traditionally pay lower wages (Bradley 2000). Thus, it seems likely that gender differences in wage and status will remain largely unchanged in the near future, in Canada and elsewhere. For, as Andres and Adamuti-Trache explain, 'fields of study mirror the power relations between associated occupations in the labour market' (2007: 95).

According to Clark (2001), in 1998 only 49 per cent of female university graduates in Canada were working in high-level jobs, compared to 64 per cent of male graduates. Although the proportion of women in professional occupations has increased from 5 to 27 per cent in the last quarter of a century, and that of women in clerical positions has declined by 16 per cent, the *wage gap* between men and women still remains (Fortin and Huberman, 2002).

The gender gap in education is narrowing, with more women than men enrolled in graduate education.

The implications of a gendered wage gap become even more consequential when we realize that women, on average, live longer than men do, and in our society they are also the main caregivers for children, relatives, and other dependants. Both these factors mean that women have to support themselves and others for longer and with less money.

Women reportedly accumulate less wealth throughout their lives because they typically have less ability to build secure savings for the future (Denton and Boos, 2007). Some research shows this happens because women tend to invest their earnings in their children, rather than in stocks, bonds, or savings accounts (Phipps and Woolley, 2008). Consider also that most women have only recently begun to earn independent incomes, and many elderly women in our society have spent their entire adult lives as homemakers, without payment for their work. They are now forced to live on public pensions or welfare, unable to support themselves independently.

For these reasons, women (on average) amass only two-thirds of what men do throughout their lives (Denton and Boos, 2007). Specific groups of women, especially divorced or separated women, are at an even higher risk of poverty, since they are often unable to save money and must struggle to get by. After a relationship breakup, women are more likely than men to enter poverty, especially if they have custody of children, as most divorced women do (Gadalla, 2008). In fact, one in five women in Canada have low incomes the year they break up with their partner, compared to only one in 13 men (ibid). As well, 25 per cent of women continue to have a low income in the year after the breakup, while only 9 per cent of men do (ibid).

Because they are the most likely to have dependent children with them, women under 40 years of age are at the highest risk of falling into poverty, and once they do, there is considerable risk they will remain poor for a prolonged period—sometimes indefinitely (Denton and Boos, 2007). Women are also much less likely than men to remarry after a divorce or separation (ibid; Simon, 2002; Williams, 2003), and this further lessens their ability to get by financially.

Despite these remaining problems, the gendered wage gap has narrowed in recent years. According to Fortin and Huberman (2002), this has happened mainly because larger numbers of women have entered fields of work traditionally dominated by men, therefore gaining higher income. At the end of the twentieth century, women were still over-represented in 'women's' fields like social work, household science, and nursing, and under-represented in 'men's' fields like mathematics, engineering, computer science, and physics, among others (Breslauer and Gordon, 1989). Two decades later, much of this has changed. Today, both women and men are crossing over traditionally gendered occupational boundaries. Table 5.2 shows the progressive entry of women into traditionally male-dominated fields.

Some research predicts that even though the wage gap is narrowing, it will never likely be eliminated completely (Shannon and Kidd, 2001). Another unsettling trend is that any profession traditionally dominated by men that women enter in large numbers—pharmacy and law are two examples—see a rapid decline in the profession's prestige and income. Conversely, when large numbers of men enter a profession traditionally dominated by women—social work, for instance—an opposite trend is evident. This tells us something important about the survival of gender inequality, and gender prejudice, in our society.

| **Table 5.2** | Median Earnings of Full-time, Full-year Employees Aged 25 to 29 by Sex, Canada, 1980–2005 | | |

Year	Median Earnings (2005 constant dollars)		Female–Male Earnings Ratio
	Males	Females	
1980	43,767	32,813	0.75
1990	40,588	32,068	0.79
2000	38,110	32,579	0.85
2005	37,680	32,104	0.85

Note: Full-time full-year employees worked 49 to 52 weeks during the year preceding the census, mainly full-time (that is 30 hours or more per week). Individuals with self-employment income and those living in institutions excluded.

Source: Statistics Canada (2008).

Gender and Immigration

Recently, sociologists have tried to understand the effects of Canada's immigration policy on gender relations. Specifically, researchers have begun to study the unique meaning of migration for women (Boyd and Grieco, 2003), signalling a shift away from the more male-focused studies of migration that ignored women's motives and deemed their experiences the same as those of men. Previously, when women's motives for immigration were taken into account at all, they were viewed as based primarily on family responsibilities, not as independent choices (ibid).

Today, scholars are more likely to examine female migration as a complex and gender-specific experience based on several factors, including the gendered restrictions that often exist in a woman's home country. Canadian immigration policies may also assume a 'dependent' status for women and an 'independent' status for men, meaning that women are more

Point/Counterpoint

BOX **5.2**

The Hijab—Symbol of Freedom or Oppression?

In a *Globe & Mail* Facts & Arguments feature, Naheed Mustafa, whose hijab attracts the 'gamut of strange looks, stares, and covert glances', wonders whether non-Muslims see her as 'a radical, fundamentalist Muslim terrorist' or 'the poster girl for oppressed womanhood everywhere'. Then again, her decision to wear the hijab is really none of their business, as she explains:

> I [wear the hijab] because I am a Muslim woman who believes her body is her own private concern. . . . The Qur'an teaches us that men and women are equal, that individuals should not be judged according to gender, beauty, wealth, or privilege. The only thing that makes one person better than another is her or his character. Nonetheless, people have a difficult time relating to me. After all, I'm young, Canadian born and raised, university-educated. Why would I do this to myself? they ask. . . . Because it gives me freedom . . . from constant attention to my physical self. Because my appearance is not subjected to public scrutiny, [it] has been removed from the realm of what can legitimately be discussed.

Source: Adapted from Mustafa (1993).

likely to be classified in relation to their family and husbands, rather than independently. Such differences in status automatically place a woman within a family role and men in a market role, reinforcing traditional patriarchal relations between the spouses. So, even if immigration policy is intended to be 'gender neutral', such gendered differences in entry status may have important implications for new immigrants to Canada.

Classic Studies
The Double Ghetto

As we have shown, women's lives are complex (as are men's), and are becoming even more so as more opportunities are made available to them. Along with this complexity, however, comes conflict. How do families, organizations, and communities reconcile modern views of a woman's life with traditional ones? *The Double Ghetto* (1994) is an influential book by Canadian sociologists Pat Armstrong and Hugh Armstrong that addresses this disconnect.

The title implies that modern Canadian women lead lives that are in some way like those of medieval Venetian Jews: captive, segregated, ghettoized lives. What is more, it suggests that women do not live in only one ghetto; they live in two ghettos at once—a double ghetto. When they go out to paid work, they occupy a women's ghetto for paid workers—perhaps this is the so-called 'pink-collar' work force, or the precarious labour market we discuss later. In offices, factories, and shops, they experience job segregation at low pay. Then, when they come home at night, they occupy a women's ghetto for unpaid workers, becoming the houseworkers described at length by Ann Oakley.

The Double Ghetto documents first the fact that average Canadian women are segregated in paid jobs that are less secure and less well-paid than those of average Canadian men, and this gender difference is narrowing only slowly. Second, it seeks to explain gendered segregation theoretically by comparing three explanatory models: biological determinism, idealism, and materialism. The authors explain why gender segregation is socially constructed, and not due to biological differences between the sexes. They also argue that we cannot explain the segregation with reference only to ideas—for example, gender scripts. Ideas have sources, and from a Marxist perspective (which Armstrong and Armstrong embrace), these are material sources rooted in the relations of economic production. So, they argue that capitalist relations of production must account for the gendered segregation in paid work.

The authors assert that, by its nature, capitalism needs insecure, poorly paid workers and a reserve army of unemployed people. (This much Karl Marx told us a century earlier.) Women play a valuable role in this system, for several reasons noted earlier. First, women physically reproduce and nurture the next generation of workers. Second, they provide unpaid care and support for the paid workforce in the form of housework, preserving a healthy, profit-making workforce at no cost to the capitalist. Third, women move in and out of the workforce as opportunities and needs change. With significant family duties to perform, women always have a foot in two camps: one at home, one at the paid workplace.

Of course, many aspects of the sexual division of labour predate capitalism. Recall that, even in the smallest, earliest human communities, men were hunters and women were gatherers. This reflects the fact that women can produce babies and men cannot. Yet, there is a sexual division of labour particular to capitalist society, according to Armstrong and Armstrong. Moreover, domestic and paid servitude are related in capitalist societies. This is an important connection because it implies that breaking down ghetto walls in paid work may also mean breaking them down in unpaid work. Women cannot free themselves from segregation, discrimination, and servitude unless they do so both at home and in the paid workplace. A double ghetto means a double change is needed.

Some critics have viewed *The Double Ghetto* as one-sided, theoretically confused, and methodologically naïve. What, then, makes Armstrong and Armstrong's work important?

First, it builds on Oakley's observations about the gendered nature of housework. Second, it relates this domestic issue to larger social class issues that grow out of capitalism and conceivably could be resolved with an end to capitalism. Third, the book is important because it is a Canadian work, by Canadian sociologists, about Canadian women. In it, the researchers present Canada to the rest of the world and develop ways of understanding gender inequality that may be widely applicable across economically developed nations. Further, it highlights the importance of *standpoint*, or understanding the oppression of particular women in relation to the unique location or context of each (see the discussion of Dorothy Smith, below).

As even the critics agreed, *The Double Ghetto* calls our attention to the continued existence of a gendered division of labour at home and in the workforce, using the best statistics available. It argues that we cannot understand or change our private lives without addressing the public issues of social and economic organization. As Armstrong and Armstrong have pointed out, women lead doubly disadvantaged lives, as compared to men. In this section, we discuss the evidence of these disadvantages, how research has led to a better understanding of these issues, and their implications for the future.

Women continue to be responsible for balancing multiple tasks such as full-time employment, child care, and housework.

At Home: Women's Second Shift

Today, the problem of balancing work and family life is a key issue, for both men and women. As more and more women have entered the labour force, the question of achieving this balance has greatly concerned working women, especially mothers. In 1990, Arlie Hochschild (with assistant Anne Machung) wrote *The Second Shift: Working Families and the Revolution at Home* about the difficulties women face when entering the workforce. With increased gender equality, more women have succeeded in entering the workforce. Yet, as Armstrong and Armstrong point out, husbands and children have continue to expect mothers to be mainly responsible for the household domain.

In recent years, women have been doing less housework than in the past (Bianchi et al., 2000). This is mainly attributed to women having less time to do housework due to their paid work, since household responsibilities are not being divided equally between the sexes. According to Canadian researchers Gazso-Windle and McMullin (2003), the men's share of domestic labour has increased in recent years; but women are still primarily responsible for the 'second shift' at home, despite income gains and other changes in gender roles (on this, see also Sullivan, 2000; Johnson and Johnson, 2008). Men are doing more, it's true, but women are doing the most important work, and they are responsible for ensuring all the work gets done.

Typically, the average wife does roughly 70 per cent of household work and the average husband, the other 30 per cent (Baxter, 2000; Greenstein, 2000). Moreover, the household chores men do are usually conventional male-oriented chores, like yard work, minor repairs, or auto maintenance (Lennon and Rosenfield, 1994). Though these are kinds of 'work', they are usually more enjoyable and discretionary in their scheduling than the repetitive cooking and cleaning that women usually do. The 'men's work' is also less important than the work done by women—feeding the family is necessary every day; mowing the lawn or changing the auto oil can be left for weeks, if necessary. And when husbands have to spend more time on paid work, wives have to spend more time on housework, taking over their husbands' responsibilities as well. But such sharing is rarely reciprocal. When wives have to spend more time doing paid work, husbands generally spend no more time than before on housework (McFarlane, Beaujot, and Haddad, 2000).

On the weekend, a typical wife will clean the floors and windows, mind the baby, do the laundry, and prepare meals for the coming week, while her husband relaxes. Though this wife may also work outside the home throughout the week, she remains responsible for balancing multiple tasks: driving children to team practices and music lessons, taking them to doctor's appointments, preparing meals, doing dishes, cleaning the house, and the countless other things a household requires regularly. When the husband comes home, traditionally he is not responsible for anything else; his shift has ended. When the wife comes home, her second shift begins.

The arrival of children noticeably affects domestic roles; and many couples put away their progressive, gender-neutral ideas (at least temporarily). Wives take on a heavy child-care responsibility, because in Canada child-care services outside the home are, for many families, not readily available or affordable. Quebec is exceptional, with more progressive child and family policies (Bureau de l'actuaire en chef, 2008). Lone parents, most of whom are mothers, need social support the most, especially in cases where the other parent is unwilling to provide financial aid (Beaujot and Ravanera, 2009). But outside Quebec, they are often unable to get child-care support and, as a result, cannot take paid work either.

In these ways, the household division of labour is structured not only by time demands and availability (McFarlane, Beaujot, and Haddad, 2000), but also by societal ideologies about gender, embedded within the social structure (Gazso-Windle and McMullin, 2003).

Gender Influences on Health

Everything has consequences and this is especially true of social inequalities. As we know, certain health problems are more prevalent in men and others in women. There is evidence that in some cases, there are biological differences to account for this. However, men and women continue to lead quite different lives, and their particular social circumstances affect their health differently (Denton, Prus, and Walters, 2004). For example, women are more likely than men to experience anxiety, depression, migraines, and arthritis/rheumatism in Canada and other developed countries.

Intriguingly, according to Walters, McDonough, and Strohschein (2002), social circumstances—socio-economic status, social support, and domestic organization for example—are also more consequential for women's health than for men's. Men's health seems to depend more on individual lifestyle choices—whether they smoke and eat an unhealthy diet, for instance (Denton, Prus, and Walters, 2004).

Muhajarine and Janzen (2006) note there are few innate differences between men and women, but specific features of their social environment affect them differently. For example, important factors that influence a woman's well-being include satisfaction with her intimate partner and financial security, meaning basic family needs are being met. On the other hand, important factors that influence a man's well-being are more likely to include the community and physical environment.

Moreover, the many roles and responsibilities that people fulfill, including paid and unpaid work, also affect well-being. Since women typically do more (paid and unpaid) work than men in total, their health is also affected in various ways. Paid

Women today occupy several social roles at once, often resulting in considerable role strain and leading to greater likelihood of unhappiness, depression, and anxiety.

work has the greatest negative effect on women if it is excessively demanding, pays poorly, and lacks autonomy. Unpaid domestic work—including child care, eldercare, household chores, and other such household chores—has a negative impact on women's well-being that increases linearly with the amount of time spent on these activities (MacDonald, Phipps, and Lethbridge 2005). Even though the unpaid work women do is ultimately motivated by love and family attachment, it is still *work*—it needs both physical and emotional effort, just as paid work does (ibid).

Many women occupy several work-like roles at once, often resulting in great role strain. The more roles women juggle, the more vulnerable they are to poor health, since they have little time to eat well, exercise, and sleep (Janzen and Muhajarine, 2003).

In addition, more women are working **double shifts**, for more years than they used to. In earlier generations, women who had infants took extended time off work or else quit altogether to concentrate on caregiving. Today, women are going back to work much sooner after giving birth, because of various pressures at home and work. For example, they worry they may be fired for taking off too much time, or fear their families will be unable to survive without two incomes. Women who are single parents are likely to experience the most pronounced health problems, because of greater-than-average strains at home and work (Ibrahim et al., 2001; Strohschein et al., 2005).

Researchers have also found a greater likelihood of unhappiness, depression, and anxiety among women than men (Kessler, 2003; Mirowsky and Ross, 1995). And since measures of depression are quite reliable today, we can assert confidently that, other things being equal, women are far more likely to be depressed than men. Among young adults, like the readers of this book, for example, the prevalence of depression in Canada is 5 per cent for men and nearly twice that for women (Endler, Rutherford, and Denisoff, 1999; Patten, 2000).

We have seen that women and men lead different and unequal lives, with women (on average) experiencing more stress. So, it may be that women are more depressed than men because (on average) they lead more depressing lives; and some evidence supports this premise. For instance, Haines III et al. (2008) found that both men and women are more susceptible to depression if they do shift work. We might hypothesize that women, who are much more likely than men to be employed precariously, do more shift work, and so they are depressed by this and not by some biological predisposition.

However, the available data do not fully support this theory. Consider shift work, a kind of work that is known to increase stress and, therefore, would likely increase depression. Canadian data show that in 2005, the latest year for which statistics are available, women accounted for only 37 per cent of full-time shift workers. Women with full-time jobs are *less* likely than men to work shifts (though women with part-time jobs are *more* likely than men to do so [Carex Canada, 2009]). So, it is impossible to claim that women monopolize the stressful jobs in society and, in that sense, lead the more depressing lives.

Perhaps the answer is that another, still unidentified, difference between men and women accounts for the difference in stress and depression levels; or perhaps it is the combination of negative factors that does so. If the circumstances were the other way around—that is, if men experienced the same prejudice, discrimination, underpayment, objectification, exclusion, and abuse that women do currently—would men then be just as depressed? At present, we cannot answer this question. Obviously, Rosabeth Kanter would think so.

Further, we see no proof that women are becoming less depressed as their lives equalize with men's, although there is some evidence that suggests that women are less depressed when they are treated equally. For example, even women who are time-crunched—as long as they are in challenging careers they love, with responsibilities to families they love—tend to be happier than women *without* career and family demands (Barnett, 1994; Barnett and Hyde, 2001). (Of course, this is true for men too.) Despite some evident obstacles, the double day of work and home responsibilities does not necessarily result in depression if the woman has chosen and continues to want this life for herself.

double shift
Heavy daily workloads, both at the workplace and at home, that women are far more likely than men to experience.

Conflict between the Sexes

One important concern in gender relations is abuse or violence against women by men. This abuse, the most telling evidence of continued conflict and dissension between the sexes, occurs in various forms—physical, mental, sexual, and financial. As well, it takes place in every type of cross-sex relationship: dating, cohabitation, marriage, separation, and sometimes even after divorce (Spiwak and Brownridge, 2005).

Women who leave their partners are at particular risk of violence, especially if they are obliged on occasion to meet the former partners—for example, when sharing care of the children. Then, they must face the difficult challenge of sharing custody while protecting themselves and their children from abuse (Varcoe and Irwin, 2004). However, on occasion, even total strangers attack, molest, and sexually assault women, using dangerous weapons to do so.

By contrast, women rarely abuse men in these ways, and rarely as severely as men do. Of course, there are issues around reporting here: men are less likely than women to report domestic abuse, since it is 'unmanly' to do so. However, in the survey data researchers have collected, women appear far more likely to resort to verbal, emotional, or mild physical abuse. And women's and men's motives are usually different. For example, men are far more likely to murder their wives and girlfriends than the other way around, and men usually do so to secure and preserve control over their partner. In contrast, women who murder their spouse typically do so in self-defence or to free themselves from continued control and abuse.

Dangers of abuse and violence against women are greater in some societies and communities than in others. According to international research by sociologist Rosemary Gartner, the risks of femicide—the murder of women—are highest in societies that are transitioning to equality from male dominance—often, societies that are deeply religious and patriarchal. It seems likely that the transition from stable male dominance to gender equality unleashes especially harmful male violence, given the uncertainty associated with the loss of their status.

In Canada, the same dynamics lead to greater risks of abuse and violence in some ethnocultural communities than in others. In Korean and Vietnamese immigrant communities for example, men with little formal education are most likely to use violence toward

One World, Many Societies

BOX 5.3

Violence against Women—Female Genital Mutilation

'Tahereh vividly remembers the day in her native town of Marivan in Iran when she was circumcised with a razor, leaving her with physical and psychological pain that endures nearly forty-five years later. "We were five sisters—we didn't really understand what was happening. My mother just said that someone was coming to our house."'

Tahereh (not her real name) and her sisters are among the estimated 100 million women and girls around the world who have suffered female genital mutilation (FGM), or the deliberate alteration or injury of genital organs, usually the clitoris, without medical cause. The practice may be a rite of passage to show that a woman or girl is available for marriage, be meant to reduce sexual desire, or be performed due to mistaken beliefs about its health benefits. FGM, besides being painful in itself, can cause infection, lifelong psychological trauma, painful sexual intercourse, and infertility.

FGM is most common in northern Africa, as well as parts of Asia and the Middle East, including the Kurdish areas of Iraq and Iran. Some immigrants have continued the practice in Western countries. While the reasons given for FGM are associated with religion and culture, it is not required by any religious practice.

Source: Esfandiari (2009).

non-compliant wives and daughters (Kim-Goh and Baello 2008). According to various studies of immigrant communities in Canada, the risk factors for abusive relationships include patriarchal authority, strict gender roles, lack of education, and women's financial dependence on partners, and dependency related to immigration status (Ayyub, 2000; Jaaber and Dasgupta, 2003; Morash et al., 2007; Ammar, 2007; Hadas, Markovitzky, and Sarid, 2008; Yick and Oomen-Early, 2008).

Bui and Morash (2007) note that social networks within immigrant communities can help protect these abused women. Family and friends can also help to alleviate the distress associated with abuse. However, for various reasons related to traditional gender roles and responsibilities, family and friends often discourage abused women from seeking legal services. Also, closed, tight-knit social networks limit women's opportunities to learn about other sources of help. So, there is a need for government to inform immigrant women about such alternatives. With assimilation and education, along with continued vigilance and law enforcement, these group differences will begin to disappear and more women will be able to live safely.

People Are Talking About . . .
DOROTHY SMITH

Born in 1926 in Yorkshire, England, Dorothy Smith earned a B.Sc. in sociology with a Major in social anthropology from the London School of Economics (LSE) in 1955. She and her husband, William Reid Smith, then studied at the University of California (Berkeley), where she received her Ph.D. in Sociology in 1963.

After her divorce, Smith began to teach in the Women's Studies program, which she helped found, at the University of British Columbia in 1967. From 1977 until her retirement, she taught at the Ontario Institute for Studies in Education, associated with the University of Toronto. Her books include *Everyday World as Problematic: A Feminist Sociology* (1987) and *The Conceptual Practices of Power: A Feminist Sociology of Knowledge* (1990).

In teaching women's studies, Smith rediscovered Marx, whom she had first studied at LSE, and applied her ethnomethodological insights to developing so-called 'standpoint theory'. Joan Busfield (in Scott, 2006: 2003), in her biography, notes that Smith offered 'a critique of the discipline that was written from the standpoint of men located in what she called the 'relations of ruling': a complex of organized practices, including government, law, business, and financial management, professional organization, and educational institutions, as well as the discourses in texts that interpenetrate the multiple sources of power'.

Smith developed *institutional ethnography*, which is a sociological method of studying how people and power interact in day-to-day life. Using this method, she has developed a 'sociology for women', based on studies of women in their everyday domestic role, and how social structures influenced that role.

Learning and practising feminism was crucial to her critique of sociology. Smith found that it was the domestic work of women that freed men from having to provide for their own bodily comfort and allowed them more intellectual pursuits. Men work as they do because women are there to provide for them. Women's knowledge, on the other hand, is more 'embodied'—derived from experience.

Smith suggested that it is abstract knowledge, which men are able to pursue unhindered, that forms the basis of social power structures, rather than the embodied knowledge of women and others who find themselves subordinated in society. The 'ruling practices' are mediated through text, Smith argued, and thus are able to make the perspective of the powerful widely dominant. Institutional ethnography begins with the 'local', embodied knowledge, rather than the ruling discourse, to discover the perspective of those who are subordinated.

Source: Adapted from *Fifty Key Sociologists: The Contemporary Theorists* (edited by John Scott, London: Routledge, 2006) and other sources.

One of the most often-cited contributions by Dorothy Smith is *institutional ethnography*: any sociological inquiry that studies people's experiences in the everyday world. However, this also means querying how things actually happen, not how they are supposed to happen or might be wished to happen. In general, the goal of this kind of sociology is to make the invisible visible, question what is taken for granted, and promote the overlooked people to be the central characters in the social drama. Doing so means bringing to the fore the people who are most knowledgeable and most affected.

Along these lines, Luken and Vaughan (2008) write that conventional sociological theory can sometimes get in the way of understanding how people perceive their own lives. Worse, standard research practices often substitute sociological frameworks, concepts, and categories for the realities of people's everyday worlds and the social organization in which their actions are embedded. They note that Dorothy Smith has developed both a thorough critique of these practices and the institutional ethnography method, which is not governed by any particular theory of sociology, and which focuses on those everyday experiences.

Sociologists using institutional ethnography look at life stories to discover where people's experiences diverge from the dominant sociological discourses and to describe the local social context of those experiences, and the wider, less visible relations that influence that local context. In an earlier piece, Luken and Vaughan (2007) also note that Smith's institutional ethnography relies heavily on first-hand life stories and accounts of people's experiences. Starting with these accounts, the researcher looks at the outside social relations that coordinate and shape them. Exploring these social relations as they are textually mediated uncovers points of disjuncture (or fault lines) between the subjects' narratives and the professional ruling practices. Often, such investigations show that the subject's experiential (i.e., firsthand) knowledge is subordinated to that of the professional (who provides second-hand knowledge). This is often consequential for people, as a society's ruling practices are embedded in administrative, bureaucratic apparatuses and the political economy.

Consider, for example, the everyday problems older people may face—for example moving house and storing their belongings, and their experiences of these unglamorous events. Luken and Vaughan (2007) explore women's experiences of moving and the social organization of the 'work of moving', noting that extra-local, material, and ideological contexts give that work its distinctive shape. Using the oral histories of older women and historical archival materials, they describe how women coordinate the work with others when moving. They also describe present-day American moving and housing industries. They find that moving and its related industries are indeed gendered and classed through the coordinating efforts of families, employers, and agents.

Sprague and Laub (2009) have used Smith's ethnographic method to study the discipline of sociology itself. They note that public sociology has become more prominent in sociological circles. In other words, professional sociologists are coming to realize they have a social responsibility to bring their knowledge and expertise directly to ordinary people—to engage with their various publics and sometimes, even the people they have studied. But doing so is not always easy. Individual interviews with 50 academic feminists and group interviews with 15 feminists engaged in some form of public sociology identify two related institutional barriers to doing this: the culture of professional sociology and the standards used for evaluating scholarship. In short, the discipline itself places a low value on such 'public sociology' and gives it little recognition or reward.

Comber and Nixon (2009) note that schoolteachers face similar institutional pressures. The researchers find that educational policy-makers assume that teachers will accept and welcome whatever changes are implemented in schools—or even that a teacher's purpose is merely to implement policy. But teachers often feel they have other responsibilities beyond those to their bosses—principals, school boards, and provincial ministries of education, for example. They feel a responsibility as well to their students and the students' parents, and to the community in which they teach. So, as in universities, in public schools a clash may develop between bureaucratic demands and social responsibilities.

As Sprague and Laub above, have hinted, Stone-Mediatore (2007) finds that the use of 'engaged', passionate, and creative 'marginal-voice texts' is often viewed as unprofessional in traditional sociology. Those who teach these texts, generally in courses on feminist and multicultural issues, may be called on to justify their 'unorthodox' approach. Stone-Mediatore references Dorothy Smith, as well as others, in defending the use of such texts to study the problems of marginalized people, while distinguishing the use of these texts in academic study from 'politicized teaching'.

Olofsson (2006) argues that Smith's work is also useful in making the link between self and social structure. Gerth and Mills, with the help of the sociological concept of role, define the concept of the person thus: 'For man as a person . . . is composed of the specific roles which he enacts and of the effects of enacting these roles upon his self' (1974). This is true, but role-incumbents, besides following rules, communicate as embodied persons. On the one hand, this offers the possibility to use this communication to change the rules of the game. On the other hand, it often puts ordinary people in a position of conflict, between the demands of their role and their own personal goals and values.

In this sense, as Olofsson says, the 'person' is an embodied and personal meeting place or battleground between actual and past role-performances, with emotionally anchored human beings called upon to enact the dictates of an institution with its own, impersonal agenda. This embodied social realism—developed by Dorothy Smith, among others—helps us to understand the difference between structure and personal reflexivity. It also helps us see this difference—this inherent conflict between personality and social structure, or conflicting value systems—as a central conflict of late modernity, nested particularly in bureaucratic settings.

Thus, a review of recent writings finds great appreciation of Smith and her writings—nearly 70 journal articles applying Smith's work in the last 20 years. Clearly, sociologists are talking about Dorothy Smith. Dorothy Smith has a secure place in a comprehensive, fusion approach to sociology by reminding us of the two-sided character of all social organization: on the one side, it is structural and symbolic (disembodied); on the other side, it is performed by real people in real settings (embodied.) Further, we can learn about this embodied setting, and especially about the real meanings of power, community, and conformity there, only by hearing the accounts of all the participants, for they are all key informants.

New Insights

Nowhere has this approach proved its success more dramatically than in the study of *intersectionality*—the convergence and interaction of multiple identities and experiences of exclusion and subordination. Kathy Davis (2008) writes that since its beginning, the concept of intersectionality has been recognized as one of the most important contributions to feminist scholarship. The reason is that, through intersectionality, we come to recognize the contingency and particularity of instances of domination. To give an example, there is not one kind of 'women's experience'—there are many kinds, based on the intersection between gender and age, or gender and class, or gender and immigrant status. To say someone is a woman, not a man, is to say something sociologically important; but to say someone is a young, immigrant woman—not a middle-aged, native-born woman—is to say something much more informative and powerful: it situates the woman and her likely problems in an imaginable setting. Still, Davis argues that the ambiguity and open-endedness of intersectionality are what makes it a successful feminist theory.

Women's writing about gender continues to be strongly antipatriarchal, whether it is about young or old, immigrant or native-born women. This means that traditional problems, such as discrimination and harassment are still being studied, but in more sophisticated ways. So, for example, Markert (2009) notes that globalized business can create cultural conflict. When women work abroad, in highly traditional societies, problems such as sexual harassment may result when the two cultures meet. Within our own society, people continue to grapple with workplace sexuality issues. For example, Emerson (2009) interviewed people about flirting in the workplace, and analyzes these narratives in terms of the motivations for flirting and also of sexual harassment. She finds that people use cues to communicate their flirtatious intent but that men and women often interpret both the flirting cues and the motivations behind them differently.

Advertising continues to pose a problem for gender relations and the objectification of woman. A study by Howkins (2009) shows that advertising images often subtly communicate social divisions and power relations among classes, races, genders, and so on. So, for example, white, blonde models remain the favourite photographic models to advertise clothing. While the ads appeal to people of all races, the hierarchical message is there: white, blonde women set the beauty standard for all women. They remain the pacesetters for appearance norms.

In the domain of gender studies, as elsewhere, researchers are debating the advantages of a postmodern approach. Hamlin (2008) observes an 'elective affinity', or shared thinking, that has emerged between feminist theory and postmodern constructivism, such as doubts of the existence of objective, universal truth.

For example, Einstein and Shildrick (2009) propose that women's health is a powerful arena in which to challenge the modernist 'scientific' underpinnings of current biomedical paradigms. These paradigms, it is claimed, limit our understanding both of 'health' and 'illness' and of the impact of current health care treatments on the body. They argue that women's health can be improved if we recognize the contribution of humanistic as well as scientific notions of health, and recognize that the human self comes in a variety forms, with a variety of uncertainties and instabilities. Underlying this discourse is the notion that male 'experts', and their masculine, 'scientific' approach have dominated all health discourse at the expense of alternative feminine discourses and, worse still, at the expense of female patients. (Views vary as to whether this approach yields verifiable health improvements, as compared with traditional 'scientific' methods.)

The reluctance to accept 'universal objective truth', while attractive from some perspectives, will make it harder to draw firm conclusions too. So, for example, some researchers link gender and sexuality concerns to argue in favour of pornography. Here Sabo (2009) writes that pornography is a victim of prejudice against popular culture, although it is also vigorously opposed by some conservatives and feminists on the grounds that it exploits women and may promote abuse and rape. Sociologists and psychologists began to study pornography in the 1960s, in the context of the sexual revolution. In contradiction of its critics, Sabo points out that pornography, in the view of some feminists, can help women, as well as LGBT minorities, explore their sexuality and understand its relationship to power.

In particular, the reluctance to accept 'universal objective truth' will make it hard to take strong ethical stances that are fundamental to feminism. For example, Edwards and Jones (2009) examine the effect of postmodernism and queer theory on sports feminism (Edwards and Jones, 2009). On the plus side, postmodernists look at women in sport in terms of intersecting identity concepts: sex, gender, sexuality, race, and ethnicity. On the minus side, postmodernism often implies ethical relativism, and this relativism can impair criticism and remedies for injustices. People inclined to social criticism, or critical sociology, may have a hard time using postmodern approaches for this purpose.

What is evident in the current literature is a continued stress on the dangers of essentialism and overgeneralization: for example, a continued reluctance to suppose that 'male' and 'female' have any universal, unchanging meanings or characteristics. This being so, discussions continue about the possible meaning of 'emancipation' or 'empowerment'—traditional goals of the feminist movement. With this in mind, Tong (2007) issues a challenge to this movement, noting that from 1960 to 1980 second-wave feminism was liberal and radical, and drew upon Marxist socialism. Since the 1980s, however, the third wave of feminism has developed toward particularism and individualism, which leads Tong to question whether the term *feminism* has a useful meaning outside of the category of gender.

In these respects, Tong seems to agree with critical theorist Seyla Benhabib's claim that 'postmodernism has produced a "retreat from utopia" within feminism' (2005: 29). Tong also seems to agree with second-wave feminist Catharine MacKinnon's claim that 'if it is to contribute to feminism's future', postmodernism must put forward a distinctive political project (2000: 75). Rushing (2007), however, disagrees, arguing that postmodern theorists like Judith Butler come far closer than MacKinnon does in voicing a genuinely future-oriented feminist politics and in expressing a distinctly utopian impulse. Without a plan, agenda, detailed prescription, or 'closure', the postmodernists (allegedly) give us reason for hopefulness by opening us up toward others and toward the future.

Chapter Summary

As we have seen in this chapter, the most significant difference between men and women, sociologically speaking, is the difference in their power in society, whether at work, at home, or in a variety of public roles. This includes, most importantly, economic power.

The job of the sociologist is to understand why women are forced to occupy separated, largely invisible workspaces both at home and in paid work. Moreover, it is to uncover the connection between these two kinds of segregation. We must especially consider the link between the household and the economy, between private and public spheres. Gender segregation cannot be explained without considering material sources of inequality that are rooted in the relations of economic production, both at home and in the paid workforce.

Often, women with children are forced to remain with their husbands—they cannot afford to leave—even under degrading, abusive conditions. The reason, as we have seen, is that single-parent, female-led families are likely to live in poverty. True, today more women work outside the home and are gradually gaining more education and therefore earning more income. However, for most working-class women, work outside the home means just an increased workload—balancing work and family demands. Since most cultures have historically been, and still tend to be, patriarchal, the husband/father has always been 'the boss' in this societal structure. Largely, most men still have significant advantage over women, due to larger incomes and lesser child-care burdens, both in marriage and divorce (since women typically have child custody).

Of course, middle-class, better-educated women have more choices. We know from intersectionality theory that the gender experience in our society depends on a variety of other factors, especially education and social class. Among more-educated, privileged, middle-class women, most choose only to have one or two children. Many, when possible, have a career as well, usually thanks to the help of a nanny. These women have the best opportunities to live independently, if need be. But that is only one kind of women's experience among many.

Though this chapter focuses in detail on how gender affects men's and women's lives, it will not be the last time we discuss gender in this book. You will see that issues of gender affect almost every social issue and social institution. So, the power relations between women and men will come up again in other, less obviously gendered aspects of social life.

Critical Thinking Questions

1. Why were women in the past thought to belong to the subordinate gender while men were considered dominant? To what extent does this belief persist today, and why?
2. What is the 'second shift'? What is its impact on the lives of women? Does it have any impact on the lives of men?
3. Do you think men and women are, or should be, equal? In what ways can people increase gender equality in their relationships? Discuss the significance of unpaid work for equality—especially child care and housework.
4. Though sociologists tend to oppose essentialist and universalizing statements about women and men, are there any differences that are inescapably and permanently due to their different biology—i.e., women can bear babies, men cannot? If so, could this all change in a society where all babies were produced in test tubes and raised in communal homes?
5. Do you think the sexual double standard still applies in modern society?

Recommended Readings

Janet Siltanen and Andrea Doucet, *Gender Relations in Canada: Intersectionality and Beyond* (Toronto: Oxford University Press, 2008). This book discusses the implications of gender throughout life. Some of the examples are personal reflections or insights provided by graduate students and the authors themselves on life experiences in regard to gender. These additions underscore the important connection between micro- and macrosociological phenomena.

Michael Kimmel (ed.), *The Sexual Self: The Construction of Sexual Scripts* (Nashville, TN: Vanderbilt University Press, 2007). Although sex and sexuality are not the focus of this chapter, understandably the two are closely related to gender. This book examines this interconnection with reference to 'sexual scripts', a concept developed by sociologists John Gagnon and William Simon. As such, the authors treat sexuality as a social phenomenon that is subject to social and cultural context.

Antonella Pinnelli, Filomena Racioppi, and Rosella Rettaroli (eds), *Genders in the Life Course: Demographic Issues* (Dordrecht, The Netherlands: Springer, 2007). This book offers a comprehensive approach to gender and its relation to demographic behaviour through a life-course perspective, including an overview of topics such as intimate union formation and dissolution, fertility, migration, aging, and gender inequality. It is geared toward an academic audience of social scientists and other scholars but is also useful as a taste of the field for undergraduates.

Judith Kegan Gardiner (ed.), *Masculinity Studies and Feminist Theory: New Directions* (New York: Columbia University Press, 2002). Most academic research and literature on gender relations focuses on women; however, in recent years the field has embraced issues of masculinity as well. This book reflects this flurry of interest. Here, masculinity is considered from a feminist perspective, and according to Michael Kimmel, 'the wisdom of this collection . . . is its portrayal of feminist theory and masculinities studies as partners'.

Michael Kaufmann (ed.), *Beyond Patriarchy: Essays by Men on Pleasure, Power, and Change* (Toronto: Oxford University Press, 1987). Although this book is not recent, it is worth reading because it marks the beginning of an interest in sociology on the topic of masculinity. The authors of the various essays are sympathetic to the feminist cause, and integrate several of its principles into their considerations of the various topics covered. From undermining patriarchy to changing legislation, the authors support the move toward gender equality in our society

Pat Armstrong and Hugh Armstrong, *Double Ghetto: Canadian Women and Their Segregated Work*, 3rd edn (Toronto: McClelland and Stewart, 1994). This work was first published in 1978, and described the demeaning condition of Canadian women in the workplace and at home, living as they were in what the authors called a 'double ghetto'. Since then there have been two new editions. In the most recent (1994), the authors note that this condition has not changed much, and that Canadian society is still organized and divided according to sex.

Websites

Equality Between Women and Men
www.acdi-cida.gc.ca/CIDAWEB/acdicida.nsf/En/JUD-31192610-JXF

Milestones in Canadian Women's History
www.unb.ca/par-l/milestones.htm

Gender and Work Database
http://wds.genderwork.ca

Status of Women Canada (SWC)
www.swc-cfc.gc.ca

The Third WWWave
www.3rdwwwave.com

Global Database of Quotas for Women
www.quotaproject.org/about.cfm

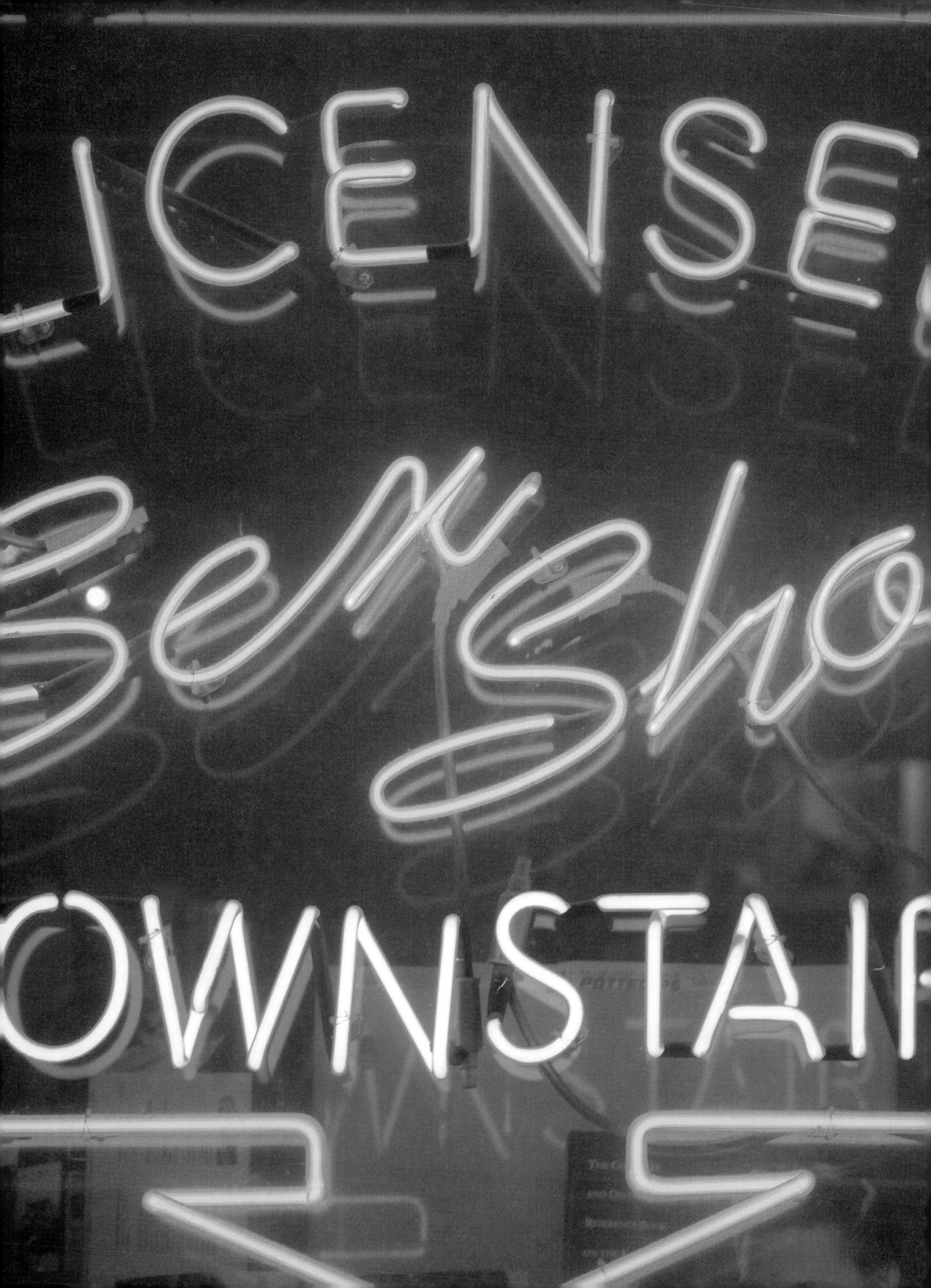
ICENSE
OWNSTAI

6 Sexuality

Learning Objectives

In this chapter, you will:

> Learn that sexuality is socially constructed
> Consider why some forms of sexual behaviour are considered deviant, and how these views change over time
> Gain perspective on the sexualization of our culture

Chapter Outline

We will see in this chapter that sexuality is socially constructed, meaning that sexuality is not innate or given in our biology, but is rather a product of our social context—the result of a complex interaction between biological, chemical, psychological, cultural, and social factors.

Undoubtedly, biology does play a role in the experience of sexual arousal, but society will usually define the way in which our sexuality is expressed. In this respect and others, biology exists within a social environment; social structure, sometimes so liberating, can also be enormously confining where sexuality is concerned. Nevertheless, in our society commonsensical arguments about sexuality persist in popular speech. We imagine that our sexual desires and actions are the unmediated expression of uncontrollable urges; but nothing could be further from the truth. Such arguments overshadow the significant role of the social context in shaping human sexuality.

This fact is evident in many ways, but consider one: the pressure that society puts on people to mate in traditional ways with people of the opposite sex, of roughly the same age and similar social background. How differently would we behave in a society that assumed the purpose of sexual activity is pleasure, where different people take pleasure from different kinds of sexual activities and sexual partners? Then, there would be no more reason for the idea of 'sexual deviation'; various sexual preferences would be on a par with diverse sandwich preferences: not a matter for social comment.

Many societies—our own included—label heterosexuality the norm and homosexuality the deviation, married monogamy the norm and multiple partners the deviation, procreative sexual intercourse the norm and other types of sexual behaviour the deviations, and so on. There are many varieties of sexual expression and, at one time or another, someone has condemned or labelled nearly all of them as deviant. Perhaps because of the strong feelings sex produces, people want to regulate sexual behaviour more than most other actions.

Against this human tendency to label, regulate and disapprove, there is the equal—sometimes greater—torrent of sexual desire. People, especially young people, will commonly experience their sexuality in thoughts, fantasies, wishes, beliefs, attitudes, values, roles, and relationships, as well as in behaviour. Sexuality reveals itself at the intersection of many factors—biological, psychological, economic, political, cultural, ethical, legal, historical, religious, spiritual, and social, meaning that it shapes and is shaped by a variety of social activities and institutions. There is a sociology of sex because sex is a part—an important part—of social reality.

Everyday Observations

When Juliette moved to the city from her small town for university, she was surprised by the contradiction between the conservative views of sexuality back home in her family and community, and the liberal views of her roommates. She soon realized that here sex was an expectation early on in intimate relationships, and even casual sex with 'no strings attached' wasn't seen as a huge deal. Although she knew of people back home who had experienced sex early on, there this was seen as something much more consequential. On one hand, Juliette felt liberated from the sexual constraints her family and community imposed on her. On the other hand, she felt uneasy about the fleeting nature of casual 'one-night stands'. She had to learn to negotiate her wants and desires with her boyfriend, Rhys, a city boy, and that this wasn't always a straightforward matter. She had to find a balance between the expectations of those around her and with what she felt comfortable.

In the past 30 years, Canadian public opinion on sexual matters has become much more liberal. People today are much more willing to view nudity in the media and to accept the marketing of magazines and films with pornographic content—a testament to the sexualization of our culture. Besides, sexual education is a standard part of the high school curriculum, since our society believes that educating young people about sex is more useful than trying, and likely failing, to encourage complete abstinence.

Generally, people view **sex** as a normal and healthy part of human relations. So, today people are much more open about discussing sex and debating its implications. And, with this increasing openness, the norms surrounding **sexuality** are changing. People are having sex younger, more often, and with more partners, outside of marriage. The sexual double standard, which judges women much more harshly than men if they engage in sexual behaviour, is on the decline. And the stigma of premarital sex is largely absent. Of course there are still many people who decide, for various reasons, to postpone sexual intercourse until marriage. However, most believe that premarital sex is acceptable and useful in gaining some experience and perspective, especially if the sexual behaviour takes place in a loving intimate relationship.

New liberal views of sexuality have also meant that people are more accepting of sexual practices that deviate from the dominant norm. People today are even more individualistic than earlier generations, and the upside of this reality is that you are also likely more accepting of difference than people of previous generations, and value upholding individual rights (Baute, 2010). Most people feel that they should not be concerned about other people's sexual activity unless it is harmful.

sex

Both the biological characteristics that define a person as male or female and the act of sexual intercourse.

sexuality

Feelings of sexual attraction and any behaviours related to them.

The rights of gays and lesbians are slowly spreading around the world. The 13th annual Gay Pride Parade in Tel Aviv, Israel drew crowds numbering in the thousands.

This idea has come up in debates about homosexuality and other forms of sexual behaviour. Thirty years ago homosexuality was seen as a medical or psychiatric problem, and homosexual acts were punishable under law. Since 2005, gay and lesbian couples in Canada have the right to marry. This is an achievement to be celebrated, since it represents the end to a form of social discrimination; and it serves as evidence that perceptions of what is normal or deviant sexual behaviour change over time. These definitions and labels are not static, and they vary from one society to another.

Sometimes, new liberal views about sexuality have questionable implications, however. Pornography and prostitution remain two central issues in debates about sexuality, especially because both phenomena are prevalent in our society. Is pornography degrading to women? Does it promote unrealistic views of sexual possibilities, and thus contribute to widespread sexual unfulfillment? Or does it serve as an outlet for people to release sexual urges and fantasize about unattainable sexual experiences? Should cities in our country recognize prostitution or 'sex work' as the reality that it is and designate 'red light districts' where this service can be easily found? Should conditions of sex work be regulated, so that prostitution is safer for its workers? Why are there more female prostitutes than male? Why is human trafficking for the purposes of prostitution increasing all over the world?

These are only some of the questions being debated. However, the topic of sexuality also invites us to ask about apparent contradictions in our society. For example, if popular norms remain strongly opposed to extramarital sex, why does this practice appear to be so common? Consider the popularity of online services that promote infidelity within marriage—such as the company Ashley Madison, with the slogan 'Life is short; have an affair'. People can even add such services as applications on their mobile phones. What does the existence of this service say about our society, and about hypocrisy?

Our take on sexuality is also the product of social interaction at the micro level, such as sex talks between partners and friends, all the while influenced by broader macro factors that determine how our sexuality will finally be experienced. Like Juliette, you've probably had to negotiate issues around sex and sexuality in your own intimate relationships (Langlois, 2009, in Fox, 2009). Sometimes, power, persuasion, and even violence may enter such negotiations. Since our discipline is about human interaction, sexuality is an important topic for sociologists. Above all, when studying sexuality, sociologists are not studying an internal psychological process but a social one—a process of interaction, communication, negotiation, within the wider social context that frames reality.

Ways of Looking at . . .
SEXUALITY

Functionalism

Functionalists argue that although people may claim to view them negatively, some sexual deviations—for example, prostitution and pornography—play a valuable role in our society. At the least, all deviations test the boundaries of socially acceptable behaviour, and in this way help society to celebrate and promote social cohesion.

Like other deviant sexual behaviours, **prostitution** fixes the boundaries of acceptable morality within our society. By calling prostitution immoral and stigmatizing people who practise it, our society clarifies the boundaries between acceptable and unacceptable behaviour. This increases social cohesion, which from a functional standpoint is valuable and desirable.

Also, sexual deviance provides people with varied sexual outlets. Many people fantasize about sexual variety and yearn to fulfill these desires. Prostitution gives them the opportunity to fulfill some of these desires without putting undue pressure on spouses or other partners to engage in sex that they may consider distasteful or immoral. Without such an outlet for their fantasies, they might indulge in other, more socially disruptive activities, such as marital infidelity and affairs that can cause divorce. Therefore, prostitution may help to keep families together and the family institution intact. By upholding individual families and the institution of marriage and family, prostitution serves society as a whole.

As long as sexual conformity and sexual deviance are isolated from one another, they do not interfere or create tension. Secrecy and compartmentalization allow each to survive and even thrive. So, for example, in societies where the family is strong, a well-defined system of sexual deviation is marked off from family life. Deviants can be members of a separate social grouping and there is little movement between the family and deviant group. This segregation enables the two opposite types of institutions to work side by side. They include different people and follow different paths.

Critical Theory

Critical theorists ask the basic question: Who benefits from the existing social order and who suffers? Many types of sexual deviance—for example, prostitution—reflect social inequality and differential access to money and power. Dominant groups in our society have the greatest influence over defining what kinds of sexual activities are to be considered normal and control whether they will be legal or illegal. As we have seen, prostitution reflects gender inequality, because it permits men to gain income or pleasure, or both, by exploiting women. Whether the men are the owners and managers of an escort service, for example, or the purchasers of the sexual services it provides, they are the main

prostitution

The provision of sexual services for reward, usually money.

beneficiaries of this sex industry. Though some men serve as paid gigolos—that is, male prostitutes—they are a minority we will ignore here, since the vast majority of prostitutes are women who provide sex for men.

In the end, prostitution is often just about poverty. Typically, women (and occasionally men) who resort to prostitution lack access to legitimate means of earning the money they need. This is obvious in the enormous numbers of prostitutes in the developing countries. There, poverty marginalizes many women and forces them to earn money by selling their bodies, often to affluent tourists. In our own society, prostitution recruits less-educated and socially disadvantaged women.

Symbolic Interactionism

Sexual norms and values change over time for a variety of reasons, especially through the social (and sexual) interaction between individuals. This change occurs with a rewriting of rules and restrictions on sexual behaviour, which take the form of **sexual scripts**. One of the dominant sexual scripts of our society is that of the sexually assertive man and the passive or resistant woman who is expected to desire sex much less than her sexual partner, or at least to be less forthcoming in expressing these desires. In practice, many couples rewrite these scripts to reflect their own personal tastes and needs.

As more people come to know and accept varieties in the sexual behaviour of others, they come to admit the acceptability and 'normality' of behaviours formerly considered abnormal, thus supporting new 'rules' of sexual behaviour. In this way, some kinds of sexual deviance—including homosexuality, sex changes, cross-dressing, and fetishism—have become increasingly accepted sexual practices in the general population.

Interaction with members of minority groups—including minority sexual groups— also makes members of the majority more accepting of deviance. Thus, people who live in communities where they are likely to meet many homosexuals are more accepting of homosexuality. Large cities and large, heterogeneous social networks both broaden a person's sexual understanding in this way. Familiarity breeds understanding, so friendship or contact with known homosexuals is important to mitigating homophobia.

Further, the symbolic interactionist approach is useful in studying the socialization of prostitutes, their entry into this line of work, and how they develop strategies to deal with 'johns' (customers) and 'pimps' (managers). Prostitution has its own language, professional ethics, ways of exercising control and working around formal authority, and so on.

Finally, the interactionist approach is useful in studying the social construction of social problems around sexual activity. So, for example, sociologists in this tradition would be interested in tracking public discourse around changes in prostitution or pornography, including increased public demands for policing and prosecution. Equally, they would be interested in studying public views about changes in the age of initiation into sexuality. So, for example, there was a recent public outcry in Ontario against the government's stated plan to introduce more specific knowledge about sexual behaviour to elementary school children. Some critics argued that doing so would encourage earlier initiation into sexual activity, leading to risk-taking that was immature and premature. But would such public education create a problem or solve a problem? And how do such matters of public debate get resolved? These are both interesting questions for social constructionists.

> **sexual scripts**
> The guidelines that describe socially acceptable ways of behaving when engaging in sexual activities.

Sex trafficking occurs all around the world, but it is most common in countries such as Thailand where large numbers of women and children live in poverty. Seen here, Mukta is a child prostitute who was sold into slavery by her father, a common and desparate solution for poverty-stricken families.

Feminism

Feminist theories argue that Canadian society is patriarchal: male-dominated, unfair, and exploitive of women and their bodies. Sexual behaviour expresses or indicates this inequality in the roles of men and women.

A given sexual encounter between a man and a woman may mean different things to the two participants, may have different consequences, or may be interpreted in different ways by other members of the society. As we have seen, people typically condemn a sexually active teenage girl, for example, more strongly than they do a teenage boy. Many people regard the problems of teenage sex, pregnancy, and out-of-wedlock births as problems almost exclusively resulting from the behaviour of girls, thus gendering the blame around sexual behaviour.

Boritch (1997) refers to the 'fallen woman' as one who as has violated her gender role, losing her culturally required purity through sexual looseness. The 'fallen woman' trope serves as an example of what can happen to a woman, or in this case a teenage girl, who does not display the supposedly normal feminine purity. As another example of this sexual inequality, we commonly view female sex workers as deviant women, while viewing their customers as essentially normal men out for some fun. Thus, the criminal justice system targets the prostitute and not the 'john'. Prostitutes are more likely to be charged and convicted than are their customers, a prime example of what sociologists sometime call 'blaming the victim'.

Sex work—and prostitution in particular—has long divided feminist thinking. Much feminist thought condemns prostitution as a practice and wants to help individual prostitute women to leave their way of life. However, feminists are also aware of the financial imperatives that lead many women into prostitution. Should feminists, therefore, support legalizing prostitution and the immigration of foreign prostitutes? Under the current exploitive conditions, feminists have good reasons to criticize the sex industry. However, this stance should not prevent them from supporting more social rights and protections for sex workers, whether immigrants or locally born. They understand that people concerned with prostitution as a form of work need to look beyond liberal discourse for new ways of thinking about the rights and wrongs of sex work.

Media Distortion

BOX **6.1**

Women and Sex in the Media

Has women's sexuality really been set free? The answer, judging by how it is treated in the media, seems to be 'not really'. Women's magazines, according to *Elle* executive editor Laurie Abraham, 'lie about sex'. Nicole Krassas finds in a review of magazines—*Cosmopolitan* for women, and *Playboy* for men—that sex is still thought of as primarily for men's pleasure, and that the notion persists that women are to devote themselves to satisfying men. According to media activist Jean Kilbourne, women are treated as sexual objects rather than human beings, particularly when only parts such as breasts or legs are shown. Countering the argument that explicit sexual imagery in the media is morally wrong and encourages promiscuity, Kilbourne says that sex in the media 'has far more to do with trivializing sex than with promoting it. The problem is not that it is sinful but that it is synthetic and cynical. We are offered a pseudo-sexuality that makes it far more difficult to discover our own unique and authentic sexuality.'

Source: Adapted from Media Awareness Network (N.d.).

The sexualization of our culture is evident everywhere—especially in the mass media.

Feminists also remind us of the sexualization of our culture and the depiction of women as sexual objects in advertising; also, that women remain more likely than men to be victims of sexual crime. Girls and young women are much more likely than boys and young men to be sexually abused within their Canadian homes—by parents, stepparents, or siblings. As we noted in the previous chapter, violence (like crime) is gendered in Canadian society, with girls and women typically at the receiving end.

Postmodernism

As we have noted, sexual scripts are based on what people—members of a particular society at a particular time—consider 'normal' or natural. The postmodern sociological approach questions our thinking about 'normality'—what we think is normal, and how we came to think that. A key figure in the early development of this approach is the sociologist Michel Foucault.

During the 1970s and 1980s, Michel Foucault wrote three volumes of *The History of Sexuality*, a project he would never finish. His history of sexuality was intended as a straightforward extension of the genealogical approach taken to sexuality in *Discipline and Punish* (1979). As well, Foucault was gay, and his experiences in a stigmatized sexual minority may have motivated him to undertake such a work.

Foucault's goal is to compare ancient pagan and Christian ethics on sexuality and trace the development of Christian ideas about sex to the present day. Foucault believes that modern thinking about sexuality is intimately associated with the power structures of modern society. The Western understanding of ourselves as sexual beings, and the relation of this understanding to our moral and ethical lives, evolved over a long period. In early Christianity, sexual pleasure became linked to unlawful conduct and rule breaking. In the Christian view, non-procreative sexual acts were evil in themselves. Unlike the morality of ancient Greeks, who stressed the proper pursuit of pleasures, including a full range of sexual activities, the Christian moral code forbade or restricted most forms of sexual activity, even within marriage.

Foucault agrees that pleasure comes from regulation and self-discipline, not wild or excessive behaviour. However, unlike the Church, he argues that it is everyone's right and duty to seek pleasure in this way, without impediment by the state. Yet, the state intervenes nonetheless. In Foucault's mind, the modern state control of sexuality parallels modern control of criminality by making sex—like crime—an object of allegedly scientific analyses that offer both knowledge and domination of their objects. Today, science (in place of religion) will render judgments about what is normal or abnormal, therefore right or wrong, producing a new set of repressive controls.

The supposed sciences of sexuality exercise control via their claimed knowledge of individuals. Not content to merely control behaviour, they even try to tell people what to think about themselves as sexual beings. By internalizing the norms laid down by the sciences of sexuality, people try to conform to these norms. In doing so, they become objects of external discipline and self-monitoring, self-forming subjects. About homosexuals, Foucault argues that their strategically placed marginal position in society gives them special insight into how others interpret and act out their sexuality. Even heterosexuals, like homosexuals, are at the mercy of the dictates of science about proper and improper behaviour, it seems.

Underlying this line of argument is Foucault's assumption that the 'truth' as we know it is not necessarily true. Discourse—how we talk about sex, for example—constrains us because it teaches us to look at sex in a certain way. However, it is only one of many ways—a way privileged by current scientific belief and, often, by the state. By this reasoning, any official change in sexual thinking, even including the increased acceptance of gay sexuality, is just another form of constraint—not liberation. This realization brought Foucault to a dead end, as least as far as escape from domination was concerned.

For Foucault as for Marcuse (1955), an early critical theorist from the Frankfurt School of sociology, our goal should be the liberation of bodies and pleasures from their imprisonment in conventional sexuality. We need to escape from conventions, not receive new lists of conventions from people in authority. Liberation may not demand the rejection of civilization as a whole, but will require us to resist convention through a new awareness and re-evaluation of sexuality.

Sexuality, as a lifestyle choice and means of seeking pleasure, can be related to consumption of many kinds, especially the consumption of commodities. Today, commodity consumption or consumerism—for example, the purchase of fashionable clothing and accessories, interesting experiences, and fancy vacations—is central to the survival of capitalism. With such consumption often preoccupying us, expressing our sexual tastes and desires means paying more attention to sex-related commodity consumption and cultivating more consciously erotic appetites. For example, it means attaching erotic levels of pleasure and desire to the consumption of material goods: eroticizing our materialism.

This postmodern approach strongly supports the study of alternative sexualities, including homosexuality and its practices. Such research, in turn, has led to a growing recognition that multiple homosexual subcultures already coexist. To differing degrees, conventional masculinity norms are being both subverted and reproduced in the larger queer community. There, people continue to innovate and reform their identities within sexually tolerant communities. Traditional notions of macho masculinity are celebrated by some, satirized by others, and ignored outright by still others in the pot-pourri of sexual rethinking.

Nowhere is this rethinking more important than in the realm of physical disability. Erotic pleasure continues to extend far beyond the conventional notion of an able-bodied, two-gender, two-sex society. Traditional conceptions leave the bodily impaired, for example, out of the sexual picture. People who deviate from the conventional physical norm—for example, people who lack fully functional arms and legs or even conventional sex organs—must re-invent sexuality for themselves and negotiate their inventions with one another. In this respect, they are like Merton's (1957 [1938]) 'adapters to anomie': unwilling to give up sex altogether and unable fully to conform, they have to innovate. Physically handicapped people have gained a particular advantage from developing new forms of cybersex that, in effect, level the playing field. They make sexual seduction and sexual pleasure much less dependent on physical location or mobility, and enable all people to interact sexually at a distance.

We will talk more about postmodern approaches later in the chapter, when we discuss the work of Judith Butler and more recent postmodern theorists.

Classic Studies
The Social Organization of Sexuality

The most comprehensive, scientifically accurate study to date on sexual behaviour and practices in the general adult population is *The Social Organization of Sexuality* (1994), by Edward Laumann, John Gagnon, Robert Michael, and Stuart Michaels. The authors bring to the job an invaluable medley of skills: Laumann is a sociologist trained in the 'classics'. Gagnon is a sociologist and sexologist known for developing the concept of 'sexual script', Michael is an economist, and Michaels an expert survey methodologist. The study represented a breakthrough in our systematic knowledge about sexual behaviour in the United States.

The study began as a grand project to broaden existing knowledge on the sexual behaviour associated with acquiring the AIDS virus, as AIDS was spreading quickly during the 1980s. Originally, the study was to be funded by the federal government, with a sample size of between 10,000 to 20,000 respondents (Schmidt, 1997). However, the government backed out of publicly funding the study, perhaps wishing to ignore the then-growing AIDS epidemic that held little interest for the then-Republican (Reaganite) government. In the end, the researchers found financial support from private funders, though they had to significantly reduce their sample size. In 1992, they carried out a nationwide, representative survey of 3,432 American men and women between the ages of 18 and 59. They reported the findings in two books: the more scientific report intended for an academic audience that we discuss here, and a book intended more for a general audience, called *Sex in America*, published in 1994 (Moss, 1996).

The scientific report is organized into four parts. The first discusses the study's theoretical framework and design (the theoretical approaches used were script theory, choice theory, and network theory, the latter of which was Laumann's area of expertise [Chancer, 1995]). Next follows a series of chapters on sexual experience and preferences (e.g., number of partners, sexual networks, forced sex, homosexuality). Later chapters discuss sexual satisfaction, sexual dysfunction, sexually transmitted diseases, fertility, cohabitation, and marriage. A final section features technical appendices, including the questionnaire that was administered to respondents in the study.

Contrary to expectations, the findings showed a sexually conservative nation (Wellings, 1995). First, they revealed that Americans favour monogamy both in principle and in practice (Moss, 1996). The norm is to have more than one sexual partner in a lifetime. However, most Americans surveyed gained their sexual experience early in life, then got married and settled down with just one mate. In this sense, American marriage 'regulates sexual behaviour with remarkable efficiency' (ibid: 540). The study found few examples of adultery within marriage and few people visiting prostitutes (16 per cent), of whom most are men (Pellauer, 1995).

The study did show people engaging in more sexual diversity than in the past. However, there was little evidence of unconventional sexuality. For example, only about one in 20 men report having experienced some form of homosexual activity. This is far fewer than the one in 10 estimate Kinsey's research reported decades earlier, based on data collected in the 1940s and 1950s using a non-probability (i.e., non-random) sample (Wellings, 1995: 540). (We will discuss the Kinsey reports in more detail below.)

Further, Laumann's study showed that people are most likely to have sex with others who are like themselves in many ways (Wellings, 1995: 540). Ninety per cent of couples are of the same race, religion, social class, and similar in age, for example. Finally, the study found that overall sexual activity is not as frequent as many had thought. Only a third of American adults have sex as often as twice a week or more. Another third have sex a few times per month, and the last third have sex only a few times per year, or do not have sex at all (Pellauer, 1995). Likely, this reflects variations in sexual activity by age; so with an aging population, there will be lower rates of sexual activity overall, and (perhaps) lower rates of unconventional sexuality.

Most criticisms of this research focus on the size of the sample, rather than its structure, which was praised as carefully constructed and representative of the population (Wellings, 1995). Critics agree that the sample was not large enough to provide reliable detailed information about minority groups, including homosexuals and Jews (Pellauer, 1995). On this matter, the researchers were purposely cautious, deciding not to report data for categories containing fewer than 50 people, which was often the case for both these groups (ibid). They recognize that since these groups are statistically under-represented, they cannot yield reliable findings about sexual behaviour. Others question the validity of the findings, since they are based on self-reports of respondents on a sensitive subject (Moss, 1996). Conceivably, people would lie or bend the truth on such matters. Moreover, some thought the study lacked a deeper understanding of the meaning and context of sexual behaviour, or the lived experiences of sexual activity (ibid).

Nevertheless, the study sample is larger and more reliable than that of any other study on this topic, and its scientific rigour and quality are exemplary—even better for providing accurate and comprehensive data on sexuality than the well-known Kinsey reports (Adam, 1996). Finally, and contrary to what many had expected, the study provided a sense of relief to Americans. Many feared what a picture of the hidden sexuality of America might reveal, just like those who feared the Kinsey report findings in their day (Wellings, 1995).

The study sociologically challenges many common assumptions about the nature of sexuality in modern society and shows that it is a socially constructed behaviour, not something innate in our biology (Chancer, 1995). As well, by disputing many sexual myths, the study provides facts that could inform our understanding of other sociologically relevant topics, such as adolescent pregnancy, contraceptive use, family formation, and divorce (Moss, 1996). It helps us to begin to answer questions like: Why do some people have many sexual partners at the same time? Why do some people practise risky sex? How do people choose their sexual partners? Why do people begin or end their sexual lives when they do? Insights into facts like these are crucial for useful policy debates about sex education, harm or risk reduction strategies, and—in the end—what we mean by 'normal' sexuality, if we mean anything non-ideological at all.

The Sexual Double Standard and (Other) Changing Trends in Sexual Behaviour

double standard

The notion that women are supposed to feel or behave differently from men where sexual matters are concerned.

In general, Canada—like the rest of the Western world—is becoming more permissive about sexual attitudes and behaviours; and this permissiveness expresses itself in a variety of trends we will discuss briefly. Of these, none is more important than the gradual decline of the sexual double standard.

As studies like Laumann's show persuasively, the sexual **double standard** is shifting dramatically as patterns of behaviour of males and females converge. So far as we can tell from the data available, women and men are approaching sexuality in more similar, more equal ways. However, sexuality is still seen differently by women than by men, perhaps because women (still) run the risk of pregnancy and men don't. No wonder, then, that some of these gender differences are obvious in views about contraception.

Both partners need to take contraception seriously. That's why a woman-centred approach to family planning services and research is slowly being augmented by one that encourages male responsibility and participation (Hansen et al., 2004). Russell-Brown (2000) determined that, given the strong influence of the husband's beliefs on the couple's sexual activity, male co-operation might increase contraceptive use. Of course, female participation continues to be necessary. A 2000 study that investigated sexual activity in Uganda found that women's ability to negotiate the timing and conditions of sex with their partners is central to their control of reproductive health outcomes. Though men there still have more influence over the timing and frequency of sex, women (especially city dwellers and more educated women) are now more likely to refuse sex under a variety of circumstances (Wolff, Blanc, and Gage, 2000).

Besides contraception, a willingness to practise safe sex also depends on cultural and social factors. Belgrave, Van Oss Marin, and Chambers (2000) found that among African-American girls aged 10 to 13, some are less likely to engage in risky sex than others. Those who were most careful were characterized by more interest in school, more family cohesion and religiosity, and higher self-esteem. Espiritu (2001) also found moral convictions to be important for Filipino-American girls, who considered themselves morally superior to Anglo-Americans in respect to sexuality. Though concerns about purity—also, racial

Table 6.1 Number and Percentage of 15- to 19-year-olds Who Had Sexual Intercourse at Least Once, by Gender, Age Group, and Province, Canada (excluding territories), 1996/1997, 2003, and 2005

	1996/1997		2003		2005	
	(thousands)	(%)	(thousands)	(%)	(thousands)	(%)
Total	920	47*	862	45	868	43
Gender						
Males[†]	434	43	437	46	432	43
Females	486	51[**]	425	45	435	43
Age group						
15 to 17[†]	380	32	348	30	362	29
18 to 19	540	70[‡]	514	68[‡]	506	65[‡]
Province						
Newfoundland and Labrador	23	46	19	54[‡]	17	49
Prince Edward Island	4[E]	37[E]	5	52*	3	35
Nova Scotia	16[E]	31[**E]	29	49	29	49
New Brunswick	28[E]	43[E]	24	52[**‡]	19	43
Quebec	297	59[‡]	252	62[‡]	263	58[‡]
Ontario	269	41[**‡]	302	40[‡]	302	37[‡]
Manitoba	30	39[‡]	31	43	27	39
Saskatchewan	38[E]	54	27	39[‡]	28	43
Alberta	82	44	80	39[‡]	77	39
British Columbia	133	47	93	37[‡]	103	40[‡]

[†] reference category
* significantly different from corresponding estimate for 2005 (p < 0.05)
[‡] significantly different from estimate for reference category or within year rest of Canada (p < 0.05)
[E] use with caution (coefficient of variation 16.6 to 33.3%)
Note: Because of rounding, counts may not add to total.

Source: Statistics Canada (2003).

discrimination—in immigrant communities create generational conflict, they reduce the incidence of risky sex.

Age of initiation into sexual activity also seems to depend on family influences. In black and Hispanic families, variables such as maternal monitoring, mother–adolescent communication on general and sexual matters, and maternal attitudes about adolescent sexual behaviour have a great influence (Miller, Forehand, and Kotchick, 1999). Fingerson (2000) also discovered that a good parent–child relationship lowers the likelihood that a teenager will have sex, or have many different partners if he or she does have sex.

Social and cultural factors even influence the long-lived double standard, which proves to be at odds with another valued tradition: romantic love. Cross-cultural comparative research suggests that sexual equality is a necessary ingredient for romantic sexual intimacy. Drawing on data from 75 societies, De Munck and Korotayev (1999) find that some societies treat male and female sexuality similarly, allowing both men and women to enjoy guilt-free sex before marriage, for example. These societies rate romantic love much more highly than do societies with a double standard. These findings suggest that, if a society wants romantic intimacy between men and women, the starting point is a single standard for men and women, even gender equality—or something close to it.

Cross-cultural analyses also find that the absence of a double standard toward sex outside marriage—premarital and extramarital sex—is correlated with other variables suggesting gender equality. For example, in societies where women are considered equal to men, women are as sexually free as men, they are as likely as men to take leadership roles in family and business, a high value is placed on female life, and husbands are prevented from physically disciplining their wives (Artemova and Korotayev, 2003).

Marital Infidelity

sexual infidelity
Sexual relations between a married (or cohabiting) person and someone other than his or her spouse.

What some view as sexual liberation in Western societies, others view as promiscuity—whether sex before marriage, sex outside marriage, or non-traditional types of sexual activity. That said, **sexual infidelity** continues to receive widespread public disapproval and is thus considered a form of sexual deviance. Perhaps because it is disapproved of and stigmatized, the frequency of sexual infidelity is hard to discover.

Not surprisingly, such infidelity poses problems for married couples. Meldrim (2005) notes that a large fraction of the couples who seek help from marriage and family therapists report problems related to infidelity. Almost invariably, the offended spouse feels abandoned as well as cheated; and women with children living at home see the infidelity as an abandonment of their children as well. Still, little research has been done on the severity and duration of infidelity's impact on a couple.

The increase in cyberspace relationships has increased the likelihood of marital infidelity at a distance. In research on Internet infidelity, Whitty (2005) discovered that not all respondents saw such infidelity as a real act of betrayal. However, most did see it as real infidelity, with as serious an impact on the couple as a traditional (offline) affair. Equally interesting, the respondents attached as much importance to *emotional* infidelity as to *sexual* infidelity. This supports the evolutionary theory that men will be more concerned about women's sexual infidelity while women are equally or more concerned about their husband's emotional infidelity (see e.g., Cramer et al., 2000; Michalski et al., 2007; Schützwohl, 2008). According to this theory, husbands are concerned about raising children who are not their own, while wives are concerned about abandonment for another woman.

Marital infidelity tends to be a sign of marital conflict, and when discovered, it contributes significantly to the extent of that conflict. From this standpoint, prostitution may be a safer sexual outlet for married people than having affairs. At least, this would be the argument by sociologist Kingsley Davis.

Classic Studies
The Sociology of Prostitution

Kingsley Davis (1908–1997) was one of the outstanding social scientists of the twentieth century, an internationally recognized sociologist and demographer. Davis is credited with coining the term 'population explosion' and was central in developing a series of major sociological theories, including the 'demographic transition theory' and the 'functional theory of stratification'. In recognition of his eminence, Davis was elected president of both the American Sociological Association and the Population Association of America.

As a structural functionalist, Davis asks, What does the social phenomenon of prostitution contribute to society that would account for its survival and universality? He also explores the paradox that prostitution flourishes in our society, yet is despised as a social evil. Prostitution, he argues, fills the need for sexual satisfaction without imposing the socioeconomic ties of relationship and marriage. When other intimate arrangements fail or are unavailable, prostitution fills a biological need. For example, it is the most convenient sexual outlet for an army, for unattached people, or for married people without a sex life. At the same time, it threatens marriage by fulfilling one of the same functions as marriage—sexual intimacy—and for this reason, prostitution is widely viewed as a social evil. A result of this perception is that prostitutes hold a low social status in our own society, and most others.

Compared to 1937, when Davis published *The Sociology of Prostitution*, more people today get sex outside of marriage without paying for it. This fact—free access to sex—would seem to threaten the profitability of prostitution, even drive it out of business. In addition, the increase in number of alternative work opportunities for women might be expected to reduce their willingness to enter prostitution. However, fewer women entering prostitution would lower the supply and increase the price of prostitutes, which would once again bring more women into this 'profession'.

Space does not permit a lengthy discussion of the study's shortcomings, but clearly there are some. The first and most obvious flaw is that, in his functional analysis, Davis pays far too little attention to the human side of prostitution: for example, to the reasons why women become prostitutes, what they think about this line of work, and why they continue. Davis admits there are many reasons women enter prostitution, but he focuses mainly on the economic incentive, as though prostitution were part of a rational strategy. By doing so, Davis may pay too little attention to other reasons many people enter prostitution today, which typically include sexual abuse, drug addiction, and low self-esteem.

That said, the study is provocative because it calls attention to an obvious sociological paradox: everywhere prostitution is decried and everywhere it is practised. This fact calls out for a sociological analysis, but perhaps a better, newer one is needed now.

Pornography

In some respects, extramarital sex is like **pornography**. Both violate traditional norms, yet neither is uncommon. There is much debate over whether pornography is healthy or not, and if unhealthy, how it should be controlled. Particularly pressing are the concerns about pornography's effects on children. Many fear that children will develop twisted ideas or practices from watching pornography. On the other hand, many resist the imposition of controls on pornography, since a lot of money is changing hands. Many people buy pornography and many profit from its sale.

Today, pornography is a multibillion-dollar worldwide business with alleged links to organized crime. So-called soft-porn magazines are available at every newsstand and convenience store, with harder-core material widely available at adult-entertainment outlets.

pornography

The explicit description or exhibition of sexual activity in literature, films, or elsewhere, intended to stimulate erotic, rather than aesthetic, feelings.

Sex workers await customers in the Netherlands.

Pornography's popularity is seemingly exploding as the legal restrictions on the depiction of sex (in movies, television, and magazines) continue to weaken.

The essence of pornography is *easy sex*: sex without limits or commitments. Heterosexual pornography creates utopias of sexual abundance—especially, an abundance of attractive, naked, sexually obedient women for men who might in real life have trouble getting a date with one such woman, let alone several. The chief theme of pornography is abundance and gluttony—an unending, unquenchable desire for sex, and an unending supply of it. With the growth of photography, movies, and television, the visual media have played a key role in 'sexualizing' modern life through pornography. As a result, since the late nineteenth century, pornography has relocated from elite society to mass culture and increasingly, pornographic material can be accessed on the Internet.

Are the media to blame for this explosion of sexuality, including pornography? Some argue that the media merely reflect a society's sexual and behavioural norms. However, others note that the media also shape these norms: people learn at least some of their sexual roles and responsibilities through media outlets. So, the media are partly responsible for teaching understandings of sexuality, as well as reflecting them. That said, pornography is not, as a rule, either educational or transformative. For some men, pornography merely reinforces pre-existing sexist beliefs. For sexist men, porn merely solidifies their misogyny. Mostly, porn supports patriarchal views by promoting the idea of women as commodities and playthings.

The role of pornography is of particular interest to feminist sociologists, since women are the 'sex objects' or commodities portrayed in most pornographic media. As a result, feminist scholars were among the first to see the naked body as a legitimate area of sociological inquiry (Sabo, 2009). In response, they have produced a vast literature that examines the link between the mass-media commodification of women's bodies and various personal troubles such as low self-esteem, eating disorders, and the increasing use of cosmetic surgery.

An area of great continuing concern is the display and consumption of pornography depicting children. Many view this pornography to be a form of child abuse. However, Ost (2002) fears an over-reaction, asking whether there has been a *moral panic* about

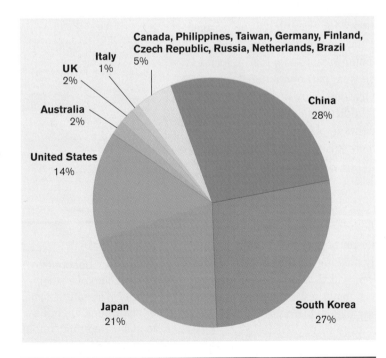

Figure 6.1 Worldwide Pornography Revenues, 2006

Source: Adapted from Family Safe Media (N.d.).

child pornography and the possession of such material. More research is needed to establish a causal link between the possession of child pornography and the commission of child sexual abuse. As yet, we have no proof that criminalizing the possession of child pornography reduces the market for such material.

Pornography may be only one point on a continuum of sexually abusive acts against children that include incest, pedophilia, and prostitution. To single out pornography is to neglect the crossover of victims and perpetrators and the overlap of child sexual abuse both within and outside families. Even normal, ordinary, heterosexual family men have been known to sexually abuse their own and other people's children, making them not so

Many artists painted and sketched in brothels in the nineteenth century.

different from pedophiles and child pornographers. As always, we have trouble knowing where to draw the line, and how to name different types of deviants in the sexual domain.

Classic Studies
American Gay

As **homosexuality** has become more accepted in our society, it has become more visible. Before its decriminalization, little was known about the people who engaged in homosexual behaviour, and how they did so. Laud Humphreys's *Tearoom Trade* (1970), a scandalous study in its time, revealed the secret world of publicly straight men who engaged in homosexual acts in public washrooms. The study contributed some knowledge about the gay culture. However, it is mainly remembered today as an example of covert research with questionable ethics.

More recently, a key researcher on homosexuality has been Stephen Murray (b. 1950), a gay sociologist and anthropologist who works mostly out of San Francisco, California. Murray has produced several provocative and controversial books and many papers about homosexuality. His better-known writings include *Latin American Male Homosexualities* (1995), *Homosexualities* (2000), and the work we discuss here, *American Gay* (1996).

American Gay is especially valuable because it discusses the formation of gay communities and subcultures. For example, Murray discusses the role of gay bars and bathhouses in providing safe meeting places for homosexuals. He also discusses the particular cultural issues that arise in this subculture, such as the problems of 'gay promiscuity', multiple versions of sexuality (such as bisexuality, transgendering, and sadomasochism, or S&M), and cross-class or cross-racial relationships within the gay community. And, most fundamentally, Murray is concerned with the problem of setting up stable roles and relationships—for example, intimate partner or couple relationships—among people who have long had to hide their relations and now have to invent norms for them.

American Gay delves deeply into the topic of homosexuality from a sociological standpoint. As Murray describes, being gay is often sensationalized and stereotyped in the media, which typically associates it with leading a single life and dying alone. Instead, Murray

homosexuality

A sexual or romantic attraction to people of the same sex; in males, called 'homosexuality' and in females, 'lesbianism'.

affirms that gay men can care for each other just as deeply as heterosexual partners do. He regards gay peoples' efforts to be included in 'straight' institutions (such as marriage and the military) as forms of resistance, not assimilation to a heterosexual lifestyle.

Not all homosexual Americans (or Canadians) belong to a gay community, since many prefer to keep their sexuality hidden or to share it at most with a few chosen others. Thus, the rise of gay communities in many of the world's large cities is an important new social development. And the increased willingness of homosexuals to take part in the local gay community reflects a conscious, often cautious, acceptance of a particular lifestyle and identity. In making this choice, gays cut themselves off from the mainstream to some degree. And for members of particular ethnic groups that are homophobic, the costs are even higher. For this reason, many Latino or African-American and African-Canadian homosexuals present two faces to the world: in public or in their home community, they are heterosexual, even having steady opposite-sex partners, while in private they are otherwise. In the Caribbean and African-American cultures, this practice is called a 'down-low' lifestyle. Likewise, Asian gays are particularly likely to keep a space between their original community and their gay lifestyle, to avoid conflict with their family.

At one time, sociologists who wanted to study homosexuality were questioned or even ostracized. Murray reports having faced great difficulty during his master's program in Arizona over his desire to study this topic. Faculty as well as students expressed their dislike for his 'gay lifestyle'. In one instance, Murray's research proposal was rejected by his professor who wrongly asserted, 'No one is interested in your lifestyle.' Overcoming this barrier, *American Gay* proved that studying homosexuality from a sociological standpoint is not only possible, but interesting and provocative as well. The lesson here is that sociologists need to pursue research questions that seem important to them; in time, they will seem important to others too.

Homosexuality and Heteronormativity

heterosexuality

A sexual or romantic attraction to people of the opposite sex.

Our society has defined **heterosexuality** as normal and natural, to discourage homosexuality. Of course, if this were the case, no discouragement (or encouragement) would be needed: everyone would just naturally gravitate to heterosexuality. But this is not what happens, because homosexuality is also natural and normal.

Valverde (1985, in Fox, 2009: 212 et passim) suggests that arguments normalizing heterosexuality are really arguments that favour procreation, monogamy, and a traditional family life. They are stereotypical in seeing 'Mother Nature' as a 'manipulative mother-in-law', men as predators concerned only with sex, and women as weak and sexually passive (ibid: 213). The social definition of heterosexuality as normal and natural is further reinforced by the seemingly inevitable compatibility of male and female reproductive organs. In this context, the physiological differences between men and women are eroticized and their similarities played down.

heteronormativity

The social institutions, practices, and norms that support an automatic assumption that other people are or should be heterosexual.

What's more, in socially defining sexual intercourse between a man and a woman as the privileged form of sexuality and intimacy—the only natural form of sexuality—our society undermines the potential for humans to engage in a wider variety of sexual experiences and to embrace these practices as equally reasonable. This preoccupation with sexuality between a man and a woman has eclipsed and in some ways stigmatized other forms of intimate expression. As a result, the sexual definition of heterosexuality as normal, natural, and the only valid choice for fulfilling sexual desire has constructed its own prominence in modern society.

heterosexism

A belief in the moral superiority of heterosexual institutions and practices.

How are these narrow ideas about sexuality taught and learned? Martin (2009) argues that mothers of young children play an important part by framing heterosexuality as normal for their children through the process of **heteronormativity**. By privileging and taking for granted heterosexuality, mothers thus construct children's sexual attitudes and experiences.

Martin stresses, however, that mothers are not to be blamed for this behaviour. Many are unaware of the assumptions they promote. Others are understandably reluctant to parent in unconventional ways, since mothers are themselves constrained by the social expectations that surround mothering.

Martin describes two sets of practices through which mothers manage heteronormativity. This first set assumes children's heterosexuality: here, many mothers consciously or unconsciously create a world where only heterosexuals exist for their children. For example, they may interpret their children's behaviour as signalling heterosexual interest, thus projecting their own expectations about 'proper' sexual interaction onto gender-neutral interactions between young children. This has the effect of sexualizing—indeed, heterosexualizing—what most other people would consider asexual behaviour. One example is labelling their children's friends as 'girlfriends' or 'boyfriends' if they are of the other gender, and only as 'friends' if of the same gender. This makes little sense at ages below puberty.

Mothers engage in a second set of practices for managing heteronormativity when they have to consider the possibility that their children may one day be gay or lesbian. In this situation, some mothers prepare for this possibility, a few more hope their children will still 'turn out' heterosexual, while the largest group deliberately tries to 'prevent' homosexuality in their children. Thus, in their different ways mothers try to construct a heteronormative context for their children's upbringing. Undoubtedly, this has some impact on how these young individuals will come to see their sexuality in the future. Within this context, children will do their best to interpret, ignore, resist, or alter the messages they receive in this way. However, messages received in this way will make it more difficult for homosexual children to reveal their true selves and will create an abiding sense that homosexuality is, in some respect, wrong or unnatural.

Certain key figures in social and sexual thought have helped to change Western thinking about sex—including homosexuality and heteronormativity. English author and scientist Henry Havelock Ellis (1859–1939), in his classic work *Psychopathia Sexualis* (1886), challenged accepted sexual norms in Victorian England (famous for its sexually repressive norms and abundance of secret erotic literature). Among other things, he assured his readers that masturbation does not lead to illness, and homosexuality is not a disease, vice, or amoral choice but an innate variation from the norm.

Even more influential and recent was American zoologist Alfred Kinsey, who carried out a statistical study of American sexuality in the mid twentieth century. Kinsey (1894–1956) was critical of biologists and psychologists who assumed that heterosexual responses are part of an animal's innate or instinctive equipment, and was especially critical of views that saw non-reproductive sexual activity as perverse or abnormal. In effect, Kinsey was the first scientific opponent of heteronormativity.

In 1947, Kinsey founded a research lab now known as the Kinsey Institute. During the 1940s, he surveyed about 18,000 Americans on their sexual practices. The survey's findings showed significant differences in sexual behaviour among men of different social classes in terms of various forms of sexual behaviour, including masturbation, homosexuality, oral sex, sex with prostitutes, and premarital and extramarital sex. On the other hand, sexual variations in women were much more likely to be influenced by their age or views about gender equality than by their social class. The latter suggests, as we discussed earlier, that gender equality may be a necessary feature of deep intimacy.

Some would say that Kinsey's most important contribution was the discovery that Americans have more varied sexual desires and behaviours than people had previously recognized. Others would say his biggest contribution was the Heterosexual–Homosexual Rating Scale, a seven-point continuum depicting a wide range of sexual inclinations. Kinsey refused to consider people themselves 'heterosexual' or 'homosexual', but rather attached this label to their *life histories*, lifestyles, or sexual experiences. This nuance introduced a sense of flexibility into his approach, in various ways. First, it acknowledged that sexuality

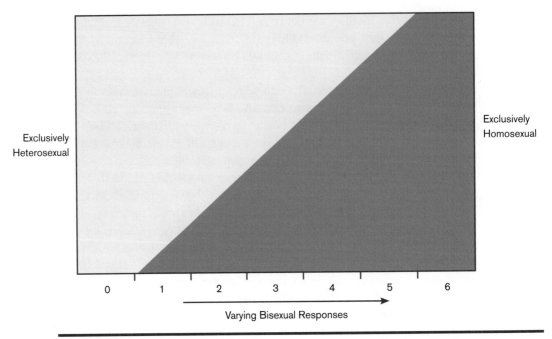

Figure 6.2   Kinsey's Heterosexual–Homosexual Rating Scale

Source: Kinsey, Alfred C. 1948. *Sexual Behaviour in the Human Male.* The Kinsey Institute. Reprinted by permission of The Kinsey Institute for Research in Sex, Gender, and Reproduction, Inc.

is not an either–or matter for many: some have both homosexual and heterosexual tendencies. Second, it recognized that people's preferences and behaviours may change over time: for example, to be somewhere in the middle of the scale when they are younger and then gradually move to one side or the other, or the other way around.

Third and finally, Kinsey argued that no position on the continuum is intrinsically normal or abnormal. As a zoologist, he recognized that what people are and what they do—not some lofty morality—defines what is normal. Or as the Greek philosopher Protagoras is remembered for saying, 'Man is the measure of all things.'

Another important contribution to the field of sexuality is Anna Koedt's book *Myth of the Female Orgasm.* First published in 1968, the book quickly became a feminist classic because it deals with basic issues of female sexuality, including sexual freedom, the political meanings of sexual pleasure, and the psychological roots of male domination. Koedt's celebration of clitoral sexuality as a form of sexual expression—neither purely homosexual nor heterosexual—was a breakthrough for feminist sexual theories and American sexual thought. Most important, it affirms that the goal of sex is pleasure, not reproduction. This was a key step in developing varied and tolerant attitudes to sexuality.

Recent surveys have collected more reliable information about the prevalence of homosexuality in Canada, but we still await a comprehensive survey on this topic. The Canadian Community Health Survey, Cycle 2.1 (Statistics Canada, 2003) was the first—and to date, the only—Statistics Canada survey to include a question on sexual orientation. Among Canadians aged 18 to 59, 1.0 per cent reported that they consider themselves to be homosexual and 0.7 per cent considered themselves bisexual. About 1.3 per cent of men considered themselves homosexual, about twice the proportion of 0.7 per cent among women (Statistics Canada, 2004). These figures are far lower than other estimates of homosexuality, particularly those by representatives of the LGBT community.

Over time, social and legal policies toward homosexuality have changed (as shown by the legalization of same-sex marriage in Canada in 2005) and so have public attitudes. Canadians are rapidly becoming less tolerant of exclusionary and discriminatory treatment at work, in school, and in the community. Many people believe there is no excuse for letting ignorance and intolerance damage the self-esteem of gay, lesbian, bisexual, transgender, and questioning people. Gradually, homophobes—not homosexuals—are becoming the sexual deviants in our society. With the passage of time and with secularization—the dwindling importance of institutional religion—homosexuality is increasingly accepted in Canada and elsewhere.

Nevertheless, our culture and society continue to display a preference for traditional cultural norms about love and sex which aim to promote childbearing, and are therefore intrinsically heterosexual. In short, a pronatalist culture will remain heterosexist, so any further gains in the acceptance of homosexuality will require further declines in fertility.

In response, homosexuals have developed a subcultural world or community of people who support and befriend each other—the so-called gay community we discussed earlier. This subcultural world has its own words (or language) to help distinguish its members from others. It has subcultural norms that define proper homosexual relations. It has special meeting places where homosexuals can gather, at certain coffee shops, cafés, bathhouses, and clubs. The homosexual community provides its newest members with socialization in the norms and values associated with a gay lifestyle, in a setting where people may live safely and receive informative social support.

Like many minority groups, homosexuals and lesbians have worked hard to educate, organize, protest, and build self-protective communities, all in order to shed their caste-like status. D'Emilio (1983) dates the beginning of the homosexual subculture, as we see it today, to World War II. Unintentionally, that war separated the sexes and gave homosexuals more access to other homosexuals. After the war, cities like San Francisco and New York began to attract homosexuals to 'the gay life'. The growth of gay communities also coincided with scientific studies like Kinsey's that challenged the accepted definitions of sexuality.

With the open emergence of a gay subculture in the 1960s, some groups were particularly militant. The Mattachine Society, for example, was a left-leaning group that called for the recognition of homosexuals as an oppressed minority. They sought to promote a homosexual culture whose members would be positive about and proud of their sexuality. The group helped to bring frightened men and women together and provide them with an organizational network in which they could form their own distinctive culture.

Today, as a result, sizeable gay and lesbian communities exist in various North American cities, including Toronto. Not only are these communities and their members increasingly visible—they are increasingly celebrated. Geographer and policy researcher Richard Florida, for example, has argued that cities with large homosexual populations typically have high levels of artistic and intellectual creativity, skills that are central to the development of new knowledge-based economies. This creativity results in much innovation and economic growth in the service sector, as well as a high quality of life for city residents. So, in this case as in many others, we see that human diversity pays off economically, as well as socially and culturally.

Michael Stark and Michael Leshner were the first two people to enter into a legal, same-sex marriage in Canada in 2003, making history both nationally and across the globe, and paving the way for same-sex marriages in Canada.

Homophobia

In Canada, gay men and lesbians are finally receiving the legal rights and

One World, Many Societies

BOX **6.2**

Gay and Lesbian Rights Increase around the World

- In 2001, the Netherlands was the first country in the world to legalize gay marriage.
- In 2003, Belgium also legalized gay marriage, followed by Spain in 2005.
- In 2004, Massachusetts was the first state in the United States to legalize gay marriage.
- Mexico City began to recognize gay marriages in 2006.
- In 2002, Buenos Aires, Argentina, permitted gay civil unions.
- Four states in Brazil have legalized gay civil unions.
- South Africa was the first developing nation to legalize gay marriage, in 2006.
- In India, where homosexuality is still illegal, activists marched in 2009 in New Delhi and Bangalore to protest this ban. India's gay rights movement is just beginning to gain acceptance.
- Thailand is becoming more tolerant of homosexuality, while much of Asia has not yet addressed gay rights.
- China is becoming less strict about homosexuality, but activities such as a 2009 gay rights march in Shanghai attract official attention.

Source: Adapted from Youngren (2010).

homophobia

An overt or covert hostility toward gay and lesbian people, sometimes stemming from an irrational fear or hatred of homosexuals.

social acceptance they deserve as citizens. Yet, despite increased visibility and acceptance, some people remain **homophobic**, even in Canada.

There is a voluminous literature on the causes and correlations of homophobia, and we can only summarize it briefly here. In large part, people remain homophobic because they are still unfamiliar with homosexuality or don't know any homosexuals (or perhaps don't know that they do). With sexuality, as with most other things in life, familiarity through first-hand experience reduces fearfulness. It is easy to hate and fear abstract categories of people, but harder when they have particular names and faces. In the case of homosexuality, more sexual experience of any kind reduces fearfulness about sexuality of many kinds, including homosexuality. For example, childhood sex play predicts earlier non-marital sexual activity in adolescence and young adulthood. In turn, premarital experiences reduce marital fearfulness about sex. More generally, people with first- or second-hand knowledge of premarital sex, extramarital sex, or homosexuality are less homophobic than people with more limited sexual knowledge and experience.

As well, familiarity breeds acceptance. People who know homosexuals personally are less often homophobic than people who do not. Research shows that personal contact with homosexual friends and relatives has more influence on attitudes toward gay men than any other social or demographic variable.

Additionally, we know that class and education correlate with homophobia. People with more education and higher incomes tend to be less homophobic. In part, these factors may work through the principle of familiarity: people from larger, more varied, and prosperous cities, with more education and higher incomes, and therefore, larger, more varied social networks, are more likely to know homosexual people. Also, higher class and education may reduce homophobia by increasing a personal sense of self-worth. People with less self-worth and a less secure position in society have more reason to attack and oppose vulnerable groups like homosexuals. These factors provide at least a working hypothesis based on the available evidence.

Another social factor characterizing homophobes is their place of residence. Rural areas are typically more homophobic since they have no gay communities. This seriously restricts opportunities for seeking and giving help. In contrast to rural people, urban people are more tolerant of homosexuals, and this tolerance includes a willingness to protect the civil liberties of homosexuals.

The research literature consistently shows that homophobia is more often found among men than among women, with study after study confirming this gender difference. In particular, men usually hold more negative attitudes than women toward homosexuals of either sex. And typically, heterosexual men are more hostile to gay men than to lesbians. Gender-specific homophobia appears to be connected to male bonding. That is, men tend to learn and express homophobic views in male-only environments.

The best single predictor of anti-gay sentiment is *sex-role rigidity*: a learned belief that men and women's roles are clearly defined, and there should be no confusion or blending between the two. By this standard, men have to be 'real men', and women have to be 'real women'. Some have suggested that homophobia is fed by *sex-role confusion*, or people's uncertainty about their own sexuality. This may explain why men are more prejudiced against gays than are women, why gay men elicit more negative reactions among men than do lesbians, and why effeminate gay men are less threatening to heterosexual men than are their 'macho' counterparts.

Along similar lines, the research literature shows that people committed to traditional sex roles show both high levels of homophobia and low levels of openness to (heterosexual) intimacy. These traits, in turn, are related to a preference for traditional sex roles, an opposition to emotional self-disclosure to female (though not to male) friends—suggesting a distrust of women—and a resistance to treating (female) intimate partners as equals.

Moreover, as we mentioned earlier, homophobia is evidently correlated with **homosociality**. Since male homosocial groups exclude both women and gays, homophobia and anti-femininity—though distinct—are correlated. Both are also correlated with the inability to form intimate non-sexual relationships.

Finally, the literature continues to report that religiosity and social conservatism, variously measured, contribute to homophobia. This pattern may be rooted in a larger syndrome of traits that Adorno et al. (1950) refer to as the 'authoritarian personality'. In this study, people who were homophobic tended also to be conservative, anti-democratic, racist, superstitious, and opposed to the inspection of their own or other people's feelings and emotions. In short, the classic 1950 study of authoritarianism found almost everything that later studies would find about homophobia.

Paraphilia

Although homosexuality is no longer considered a form of sexual deviance by most people, other types of sexuality grouped under the term **paraphilia** do continue to be viewed as such. Many of these forms of sexuality are considered extreme or, at the least, strange and

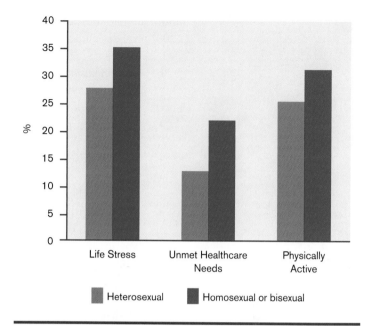

Figure 6.3 Differences in Health-Related Measures for Heterosexuals, Homosexuals, and Bisexuals

Source: Statistics Canada (2004).

homosociality
A social preference for members of one's own gender.

paraphilia
Any sexual deviation or departure from the norm.

abnormal. The fourth edition of the *Diagnostic and Statistical Manual of Mental Disorders* (2000) provides clinical criteria for these paraphilias and defines them as follows:

- '*Exhibitionism*: recurrent urge to expose one's genitals to an unsuspecting person, or this behaviour; or, the recurrent urge to perform sexual acts in a public place, or in view of unsuspecting persons
- '*Frotteurism*: recurrent urges or behaviour of touching or rubbing against a non-consenting person
- '*Pedophilia*: sexual attraction to prepubescent or peripubescent children
- '*Sexual Masochism*: recurrent urge to be humiliated, beaten, bound, or otherwise made to suffer for sexual pleasure, or this behaviour
- '*Sexual Sadism*: recurrent urge or behaviour involving acts in which the pain or humiliation of a person is sexually exciting
- '*Voyeurism*: recurrent urge to observe an unsuspecting person who is naked, disrobing, or engaging in sexual activities, or this behaviour; the activity might not be sexual at all
- '*Fetishism*: use of inanimate objects to gain sexual excitement; *partialism* refers to fetishes specifically involving nonsexual parts of the body.
- '*Transvestic fetishism*: sexual attraction towards the clothing of the opposite gender'

Psychoanalyst Sigmund Freud was among the first to describe sexual *fetishism* (1927). It is a form of sexual deviance where the object of affection is a specific object or body part. Fetishism, like other forms of sexuality, can be varied and affect almost any aspect of human behaviour. Almost anything can become a fetish, a compulsion, an obsession, or an addiction. Like other compulsions, obsessions, and addictions, sexual fetishism is considered a problem when it begins to interfere with normal sexual or social functioning.

Voyeurism is another type of sexual deviance that is non-criminal if it is a consensual act. Voyeurs seek sexual pleasure by watching other people either in states of undress or having sex. Considered a deviant sexual act in most cultures, voyeurism is most often practised by males. Likely, male voyeurism is related to a male desire for dominance, the objectification of women in our society, and to the sexual gaze that puts women under male scrutiny at all times.

Sadism is taking sexual pleasure by inflicting (physical) pain and suffering on another person. It takes its name from the Marquis de Sade, a philosopher who wrote voluminously on sexual experimentation, pain, and pleasure in eighteenth-century France (his most important work, *The 120 Days of Sodom*, was published around 1785). In cataloguing sexual violence during his time, Sade noted that many people engaged in non-consenting practices. Today, sadomasochism is different: consent is a principle of the behaviour. The counterpart of sadism is *masochism*, named after the nineteenth-century Count von Masoch, an Austrian writer (1836–1895). Masochists take sexual pleasure from being beaten, humiliated, bound, tortured, or otherwise made to suffer.

Together, sadomasochism (S&M) describes the dominant (sadist) elements and the submissive (masochist) elements. Often, role-playing is involved and takes the form of master–slave or teacher–student. Sadomasochism typically has an underlying element of sexual meaning. To gain the greatest pleasure in any sadomasochist behaviour, the partners share a common definition of the activity. Ideally, sadists find their corresponding masochists, and vice versa—all for mutually consenting pleasure. There are no reliable numbers to show how common or rare these paraphilias —or others—may be.

Paraphilia that is consensual is not considered criminal. However, some paraphilia *is* both criminal and/or non-consensual. For example, *exhibitionism*—the display of one's genitalia in a setting where this display is socially inappropriate or legally banned—if done without consent and in a public place—is deemed a criminal activity. Other types of criminal paraphilia include necrophilia (a sexual attraction to corpses), pedophilia (a sexual attraction to young children who have not yet reached puberty), bestiality (or zoophilia: a sexual attraction to animals), and lust murder (taking sexual pleasure from the commission of a murder).

Pedophilia is probably one of the most common criminal paraphilias in our society today. Two-thirds of molested children are girls, usually between the ages of 8 and 11, giving the lie to a common prejudice that pedophilia is a feature of male homosexuality. Most pedophiles are men, it is true, but their victims are usually female, and there are also cases of women having unwanted sexual contact with young boys. Note, then, that pedophiles are rarely people who commonly practise homosexuality with other consenting adults. Pedophiles, whether homosexual or heterosexual, are people who gain their sexual pleasure from people who are below the age of consent. Pedophilia is a form of violent domination, while homosexuality is not. While many pedophiles seduce and abuse strangers, far more commonly they seduce and abuse the children of family and friends.

As is evident, the world of sexualities is complex and in need of theorizing. That is the role that Judith Butler has, for many people, come to play.

People Are Talking About . . .
JUDITH BUTLER

Judith Butler was born in Cleveland in 1956. She studied philosophy at Yale University, where she received her bachelor's degree in 1978 and completed a doctoral dissertation in 1984, called *Subjects of Desire: Hegelian Reflections in Twentieth-Century France*. She lectured at various universities before becoming a professor of comparative literature at the University of California, Berkeley, and is a leader in the field of sexuality and gender.

Her most famous works are *Gender Trouble: Feminism and the Subversion of Identity* (1990); *Bodies That Matter: On the Discursive Limits of 'Sex'* (1993), *The Psychic Life of Power: Theories of Subjection* (1997), and *Undoing Gender* (2004). Butler's work centres around the idea that gender is not innate, but is derived from a narrative based on patriarchal culture. Thus gender consists in signs imposed via the psyche and internalized.

Gender Trouble is considered the most influential of Butler's works. In it, she tries to separate identity from the notion that human gender is binary—that one is either male or female. Feminists uncritically accept this notion, and thus mistakenly view women as a homogenous group having traits and interests in common. Through an account of patriarchal culture that assumes clear-cut masculine and feminine genders built on 'male' and 'female' bodies, sex-as-destiny seems inescapable. By erecting a 'natural' binary for sex, binaries for gender and heterosexuality are likewise constructed as natural. In this way, heterosexuality becomes 'essential' and normal, providing a basis for sexually limiting heteronormativity.

In her biography, Janet Borgerson (in Scott, 2006: 50) notes that, for Butler, 'Identities form over time [via iteration] and through repeated performances of socially constructed characteristics and appropriate gestures and signs . . . but if typical iterations elide, alter and shift, then the previously recognized definitive category—the apparent ideal—may be altered . . . opening up possibility for diverse gestures and characteristics, demonstrating contingency and allowing change over time.'

Thus Butler tries to deconstruct the 'grand narratives', found in psychoanalysis and other fields, which together promote the notion that genders are unitary categories. To overcome this and other essentialisms, Butler suggests that genders be multiplied in what she calls subversive 'gender trouble', and that gender and identity be 'free-floating'—linked not to inherent characteristics but to performance. In this way, gender does not cause performance, but performance defines gender—an important aspect of so-called queer theory.

However, the performance of gender, sex, and sexuality is not a voluntary choice for Butler, since only some structured possibilities of sex, gender, and sexuality are socially allowed to appear as coherent or 'natural'. What Foucault has called *regulative discourse* includes within it disciplinary techniques which force subjects to perform specific stylized actions. In this way, they preserve the appearance in those subjects of the 'core' gender, sex and sexuality the discourse itself produces.

Source: Adapted from *Fifty Key Sociologists: The Contemporary Theorists* (edited by John Scott, London: Routledge, 2006) and other sources.

Gender Trouble is Butler's most influential work on gender and sexuality. In it, she argues that feminism made a crucial mistake in asserting that 'women' are a clearly-defined group that shares common interests and concerns (Gauntlett, 1998). In doing so, feminism established a dichotomous view of gender that divided human beings into two groups: women and men (Gil Rodriguez, 2002). Feminists reject the idea that biology controls sexuality. However, they did contribute to an understanding that society is characterized by femininity and masculinity that is essentially based on female and male, or gendered, bodies (Nayak and Kehily, 2006).

Butler further argues that this distinction acts socially to create desire toward the other gender, thus fashioning heterosexuality (Komiya, 2009). In turn, the distinction curbs individuals' choice or potential for sexual difference and innovation (Hey, 2006). Drawing from Foucault's work, which we discussed earlier in the chapter, Butler tries to separate the link between gender and sexual desire, arguing that they are both flexible and creative. The term 'gender trouble' refers to the 'the mobilization, subversive confusion, and proliferation of genders, and therefore identities' (The European Graduate School, 2010).

Butler uses the idea of *performativity* to explain gender identity, which she develops further in later work, including *Undoing Gender*. Through this concept, it is argued that a person's gender is continually performed, not given as a fact, and that this performance shapes an individual's sexuality (Baldick, 2008). This idea has been central to the development of *queer theory*, which emerged out of Butler's work. Queer theory states that people's identities are *not* fixed and do *not* determine who they are (Stormhoj, 2003). And regarding sexuality, queer theorists argue that sexuality and sex itself are socially constructed. As well, cultural and historical factors affect our judgments concerning what constitutes normal sexuality and what constitutes sexual deviance (Cordoba Garcia, 2003). This applies to issues of heterosexuality, homosexuality, bisexuality, and transgendering; yet queer theory does not support the conceptions that arise out of these identity categories and instead encompasses a wide range of sexual orientations and subcultures.

Several current sociologists have used the idea of identity performavity in their work, more than any other concept or orientation proposed by Butler. Some apply this concept to the field of sexuality. For example, Rooke (2007) examines how sexual and gendered identities are played out, or performed, in physical space, specifically the urban city. And for Grindstaff (2003), the concept informs a study of same-sex marriage and its social and cultural implications, focusing especially on heteronormative relations of power.

Others have taken the idea of performavity into other theoretical fields. For example, Baril (2007) draws on the concept of performativity to describe the behaviours of resistance by social workers within welfare-imposing institutions. Powell and Carey (2007) also apply this concept to social work, examining the balance between social workers' personal sentiments in their occupation and its increasing, confining professionalization. Many more have applied this concept to modern cultural texts, such as movies, television shows, and other media productions (see, e.g., Tyler and Cohen, 2008; Emig, 2006; Tillotson, 2007).

Butler's work has been criticized from various angles. Brickell (2005: 24) believes that her 'formulations of performativity and subversion express a lack of clarity and cause problems with respect to agency, action, interaction, and social change'. Schwartzman (2002) believes that Butler's analysis ignores the significance of socially structured power relations. Further, Reiche (2004: 11) criticizes the way Butler uses psychoanalytical theory in her work, and claims that her work is not as radical or innovative as is often claimed, even though Butler does provide 'an attractive alternative for those who cannot or do not want to pin down their sexuality'. And Calder (2004), applying Butler's framework to the study of forced sex, finds that it is inadequate to fully understand this phenomenon. Similarly, many conclude that the idea of gender or sexuality as a performance is too abstract and ignores the physical (flesh-and-blood) reality of the body. Finally, many reviewers agree that Butler's writing is complex and unclear.

Despite these criticisms, Butler's theories are undoubtedly current and her ideas a valuable contribution to the field of sexuality, as well as others. In *Gender Trouble*, *Bodies That Matter*, and *Deconstructing Gender*, Butler creatively examines the paradox of identity as fixed yet continually changing, shedding light on the social and cultural forces that shape masculinity and femininity (Hey, 2006). In addition, her notion of performativity takes the discussion of sexuality beyond the physical to the realm of identity and perception—important aspects of the way people experience sexual behaviour (Nayak and Kehily, 2006). Even if other theorists disagree with her approach, her ideas are nonetheless provocative and inspire further work and debate.

Thus, a review of recent writings finds continued application of the work by Judith Butler—over 200 journal articles applying Butler's work on sexuality in the last eight years. Clearly, sociologists are talking about Judith Butler. She deserves a place in our comprehensive, fusion approach to sociology because her work has emphasized the performative, evanescent character of all human identity—including sexual identity. This fact has allowed us to look in new, non-judgmental ways at sexuality and such barriers to free expression as the double standard and heteronormativity.

New Insights

During the 1980s and 1990s, sociologists were developing the orientations, research methods, and scientific validity that support postmodernism. Today postmodernism is a well-established theoretical orientation in sociology, and sociologists are now beginning to carry this perspective into practice, empirically studying the social world, all the while keeping in mind its subjective nature, and therefore the uncertainty of their conclusions (Mirchandani, 2005). This has especially been so in the field of sexuality, where postmodernism has taken significant strides.

As many theorists point out, sexuality is paradoxical: it is both the most intimate and personal part of our private lives, and one of the most pressing issues fuelling debates in the public arena (Johnson, 2001). Sexuality has also been studied by various theoretical perspectives and with several different assumptions in mind. With the work of Foucault, whom we discussed earlier, and later that of Butler, the field of sexuality has experienced no less than a paradigm shift: a new way of considering this topic (Green, 2002).

Undoubtedly, the modern world is, as Attwood (2006: 77) describes, 'sexed up'. Everywhere we turn, the products of our culture are sexualized. This means we must pay special attention to the topic of sexuality and how it influences our society. With this in mind, postmodern researchers have been looking at sexuality from all sides, studying factors that affect it, such as democratization, taste formation, sexual citizenship, and the spread of pornography (ibid).

On the latter, Sabo (2009), discusses the debate among researchers, especially postmodernists and feminists, on the nature and effects of pornography, already discussed in

Chapter 5. Pornography first became a subject of interest in the academic realm during the 'sexual revolution' of the 1960s and 1970s. Then, most conservatives and many feminists—perhaps for different reasons—strongly opposed pornography, seeing it as degrading to women and as contributing to violence against women. In feminist theory, pornography was then viewed as the epitome of female subordination under patriarchy, which we have mentioned throughout this chapter, especially because of its gendered nature.

But Sabo and many other feminists, most working from the postmodern perspective, as well as supporters of the LGBT movement, came to see pornography as liberating for the sexuality of women and minorities. For them, pornography provides the means to satisfy sexual desires, increase sexual equality, help to lessen sexual inhibition, allow for an exploration of sexual differences, and fulfill sexual fantasies (ibid). Many postmodern feminists today support the increasing diversification of sexuality seen in pornography, some of which has been created specifically for a woman-centred audience.

Similarly, views about prostitution have come in for a re-assessment. After a review of both sides of the debate, Scoular (2004) concludes that seen from various theoretical perspectives, prostitution is more complex than most make it out to be. Because it shows itself under many different conditions and in different circumstances, prostitution must be understood in the context of its complex meanings and implications.

Other researchers have taken postmodernism into the field of sexual education. For instance, Allen (2008) looks for divergence between young women's and men's preferences for the issues covered in their 'sex ed' in school, and finds that there are no significant gender differences in sex-related content preference among young adults. Taking a different approach, Nathanson (2009) uses her own experience as a bisexual teacher to discuss how sexual orientation affects teaching style. She argues that her sexual orientation, more so than that of lesbian or gay teachers, has contributed to a 'bisexual pedagogy', making her more sensitive to other 'blended identity categories' (ibid: 71), such as in gender, race, or religion.

Many other postmodern researchers have contributed extensively to the queer theory proposed by Judith Butler and others. Some of these queer theorists are also informed by other theoretical orientations. For example, Plummer (2003) highlights the usefulness of symbolic interactionist insights into understanding the meanings people attach to sexual behaviour, as well as the role of social interaction in sexual exchange. Others have gone beyond queer theory, fashioning a new 'post-queer' study of sexuality that targets the undeveloped areas of the original queer theory. Green (2002) argues there are two undeveloped strains of queer theory: radical deconstructionism and radical subversion, and both need focus and analysis. These approaches, when fully developed, will inform a more detailed consideration of sexual possibilities from the queer perspective.

Moreover, researchers are also layering their queer study analysis with further considerations of the nuances of sexual experience. Hines (2006) argues that the concept of 'difference' is not developed enough where it concerns transgender and its meanings. More exploration of transgendered experiences, complete with personal narratives, would give us much more insight into its complexity. On the same topic, Broad (2002) uses ethnographic, interview, and observational data to study transgendered social movements and argues that the 'identity politics' surrounding transgendered people are not well understood, needing further research and attention.

So, postmodernism has proven a useful theoretical perspective in sexuality. It rejects grand explanations and the universal principles sought by positivists, stressing instead the need to consider the diversity that surrounds sexuality and the myriad factors that affect how it is experienced by social actors (Edwards and Jones, 2009).

Meanwhile, other researchers have taken a more critical perspective on sexuality, informed by the tradition of critically examining the culture and products of society. We already mentioned the sexualization of modern culture; many critical theorists focus on this phenomenon in developing their new insights. For example, Johnson (2001) presents several writings by authors who see postmodernism and its approaches as inadequate for fully explaining sexuality and its implications in modern society. Some argue that sexuality is still regarded as something too abstract, rooted in identity and self-perception rather than the realities of modern society, such as its economic (or class) situation.

Many remain silent on these issues around sexuality, afraid to venture their own views and theories in a field that has, until recently, been ignored in the academic community. As a result, even considering all of these new insights, sociology and the social sciences are still behind in understanding sexuality from an experiential standpoint (Hurley, 2002). More qualitative research on the lived experiences of sexuality is needed, which would help develop directions for new research.

Chapter Summary

Over the last few decades, our society has become much more liberal when it comes to issues surrounding sexuality. Partly, this has to do with the feminist movement, changing economic conditions, the widespread availability of contraception, and individualistic attitudes that stress a person's right to choose their lifestyle, including their sexuality. All of these changes are evidence that sexuality is socially constructed, and that it exists (and changes) within a social context. Sexuality is not what we feel or do, but the beliefs, values, roles, relationships, desires, and other such elements that form a part of our culture and our society.

Only thirty years ago homosexuality was considered a deviant behaviour that was punishable under law. Today homophobia—not homosexuality—is the more criticized deviation, as people come to tolerate and accept those who identify themselves as homosexual. We saw that homosexuality has been stigmatized because we live in a heteronormative society, where many still assume that men are sexually attracted only to women and women only to men—an assumption that permeates many of our interactions. And perhaps without even knowing it, we privilege this sexual orientation. This heteronormativity is a social issue that needs to be addressed and tackled.

Besides homosexuality, there are many varieties of sexual expression—we mentioned some of these in the chapter—all of which have been condemned at one point or another and in one society or another. This fact reminds us that sexuality is both an important and complex phenomenon, and that sexual norms change over time.

In this chapter we also discussed the issue of pornography, which has raised a distinctly two-sided debate. Some argue zealously that pornography degrades women and sexualizes our culture, while others argue that it liberates our sexual desires. Likewise, debates surround the issue of prostitution. Most of these focus on whether prostitution should be regulated and whether steps should be taken to make it safer for sex workers. Finally, as we move into a global culture, we are witnessing more international trafficking in sex, and the impact of this practice all around the world. These and other issues are the future concerns of sociologists of sexuality.

Critical Thinking Questions

1. What does it mean to say that sexuality is socially constructed?
2. Do you think the sexual double standard has been on the decline in the last few decades? Why?
3. Where do you stand in the debate on pornography—what does it represent and what does it mean for our society?
4. How is homosexuality related to heteronormavity?
5. What does sociology tell us about sexual deviance and sexual normality?
6. What do you think is the best way to handle problems associated with prostitution around the world?

Recommended Readings

Edward O. Laumann, Stephen Ellingson, Jenna Mahay, Anthony Palk, and Yoosik Youm (eds), *The Sexual Organization of the City* (Chicago: University of Chicago Press, 2004). The findings in this study are based on results from the Chicago Health and Social Life Survey, which was designed to assess how people meet their sexual partners. The authors propose the existence of a 'sex market', a spatial and cultural arena in which individuals search for sex partners. According to their theory, sex markets constrain people's choices in expressing their sexuality.

Lauren Gail Berlant (ed.), *Intimacy* (Chicago: University of Chicago Press, 2000). This collection shows the ways in which intimate lives are connected with the institutions and ideologies that organize people's worlds. Showing how intimacy has entered the public spheres of culture, politics, and capitalism, the book challenges traditional notions of private life.

Thomas W. Laqueur, *Solitary Sex: A Cultural History of Masturbation* (New York: Zone Books, 2003). In this book, the author addresses the changing nature of Western culture's continuing obsession with masturbation. Masturbation's history is filled with anxiety, since it was often thought to irreversibly harm its practitioners. This long-lasting belief seemingly no longer persists. The author outlines how this turnaround occurred and why.

Claudia Nelson and Michelle H. Martin (eds), *Sexual Pedagogies: Sex Education in Britain, Australia, and America, 1879–2000* (New York and Basingstoke: Palgrave Macmillan, 2004). This thought-provoking volume looks at over a century of efforts, in Britain, the United States, and Australia, to shape citizens' understandings of their own sexual needs. The anthology of essays examines the interplay of radical and conservative ideologies of sex, noting the influence of market forces, cultural beliefs about childhood and gender, and sometimes geopolitics. Understandings of sexuality and sex education have changed dramatically, yet in many ways the link between what is taught and what is practised is as little understood as ever.

Mary Louise Adams, *The Trouble with Normal: Post-War Youth and the Making of Heterosexuality* (Toronto: University of Toronto Press, 1999). This is an excellent discussion of the social construction of sexuality after World War II, showing how the view of heterosexuality as normal was tied in with both politics and the larger social context.

Steven Seidman, *Beyond the Closet: The Transformation of Gay and Lesbian Life* (New York: Routledge, 2004). This book is based on interviews with gay and lesbian individuals, exploring the experience of living 'in the closet' and of 'coming out' of it. The findings show differences in experiences from gay and lesbians of different generations, races, and classes. They also show changes in the 'closet' along with the social changes occurring in history.

Websites

Sieccan: The Sex Information and Education Council of Canada
www.sieccan.org

The Sex Atlas
www2.hu-berlin.de/sexology/ATLAS_EN

Sexuality and U
www.sexualityandu.ca/home_e.aspx

Sexpressions
www.sexpressions.ca

Federal Initiative to Address HIV/AIDS in Canada
www.phac-aspc.gc.ca/aids-sida/hiv_aids

Prostitute Research and Education
www.prostitutionresearch.com

Queer Theory
www.theory.org.uk/ctr-quee.htm

Judith Butler at Theory.org.uk
www.theory.org.uk/ctr-butl.htm

7 Racial and Ethnic Groups

Learning Objectives

In this chapter, you will:

> Learn that racial and ethnic classifications are historically specific and socially constructed
> Consider the influence of past and present immigration trends on Canadian society, as well as on social policies, including multiculturalism
> Discover that the 'social distance' between different racial and ethnic groups has shrunk over the last century, pointing to a brighter future in human interaction

Chapter Outline

Over the past 100 years, more than 13 million immigrants have arrived in Canada. They now make up over 200 different racial and ethnic groups, speaking over 100 different languages (Statistics Canada, 2007). But when you think about it, every Canadian is an immigrant or the descendant of one. (Aboriginals too are descendants of immigrants, though their ancestors immigrated 10,000 years ago.) Partly as a result of this vast immigration, in Canada's major cities—Toronto, Montreal, and Vancouver—multiculturalism is the norm, not the exception.

Why study this topic? Because today, we spend much of our lives in contact with people who may not resemble us physically and may live differently than we do. Although people from different cultures have interacted and mixed for thousands of years, these processes are even more common today. And because of massive migrations around the world and people's increased interaction with others unlike themselves, issues of race and ethnicity are discussed in societies everywhere, and in sociology too.

Sociologists studying this topic are concerned with questions surrounding the effect of race or ethnicity on educational attainment, employment opportunities, and health and well-being. What are the causes and effects of strained relations between racial and ethnic groups, and what are some of the possible solutions to these social problems? We will consider all of these questions in this chapter. In considering these questions, and others, we will situate racial and ethnic relations within a historical context, noting that the large number of immigrants who entered Canada in the last two decades differ from those that came before, in many ways. Their arrival has consequently changed our society as the new immigrants seek a better life for themselves and their families.

Everyday Observations

Loving across boundaries: Neda and Julian met at university, and what initially seemed like just a friendship soon developed into an intimate relationship. Despite caring deeply for each other, the two were uneasy about their feelings, and knew they faced a problem. Coming from different racial and cultural backgrounds, their parents questioned their union, constantly reminding them about the challenges they would face if they decided to marry. They would have to reconcile their different cultural traditions, religious practices, and beliefs about the preferred ways to rear children, among other potential difficulties. However, to Neda and Julian, it seemed strange to think they would have to trouble about such things. While embracing their own heritages, they both considered themselves Canadians, and therefore tolerant of differences. Surely here of all places, people of different racial and ethnic backgrounds could manage to preserve loving relationships across cultural boundaries.

race

A set of people commonly defined as belonging to the same group by virtue of common visible features, such as skin colour or facial characteristics.

ethnic group

A set of people commonly defined as belonging to the same group by virtue of a common birthplace, ancestry, or culture.

racial variations

Differences in behaviour which some people attribute to differences in race.

Consider Neda and Julian's dilemma: Do you have close friends that are of different **races** or **ethnic groups**? Have you ever dated someone of a different race or ancestry, or thought about doing so? If so, why do you think this relationship worked or did not work out? How about your parents—do they have close friends of different races, or ethnic or cultural heritages, and if not, why not (in your view)? How do you think your parents would react if you told them you were getting serious about someone of a different race or ethnic background? What it is about getting close to someone from a different 'background' that sometimes causes problems in families and communities?

Only a few decades ago, interracial marriage was illegal in some parts of North America. It reflected the last vestiges of racism and even of slavery through the Western world—a shameful record of violence and mistreatment aimed at people who were seen as 'different' and 'lower'—less human, even—than the dominant European white group.

Think about the ways you see people deal with race and ethnicity in our society every day. Are these patterns characterized by co-operation and mutual respect, or by violence and abuse? Sometimes, it is the latter, for historical reasons. While some of the conflict among different racial and ethnic groups is a result of the competition for jobs or housing, some is the result of continued, culturally formed anxieties about social and sexual intimacy, as represented by inter-racial or inter-ethnic dating and mating—the residue of traditional distrust and ignorance.

Ways of Looking at . . .
RACIAL AND ETHNIC GROUPS

Functionalism

According to functionalists, even the inequality between racial or ethnic groups has a social purpose. As we noted in earlier chapters, functionalists stress that social inequality provides incentives in the form of status and material rewards that prompt people to take on the most important social roles. Also, functionalists see exclusion, prejudice, and discrimination as providing benefits for society as a whole, and for particular groups within it. In any society, ethnic solidarity increases social cohesion. In a multicultural society like Canada, ethnic solidarity also gives newly arrived groups a landing pad and strategies for assimilating.

Ethnic identity provides people with roots and social connectedness in an otherwise individualistic, fragmented society, in this way serving like a religious identity. For many people, their ethnic heritage serves as a link both to a rich cultural past and to current members of their ethnic group. The complete dissolution of ethnic boundaries might reduce inter-group conflict, but it would also mean the end of ethnic group identity and cohesion. As well, ethnoracial diversity benefits society as a whole, functionalists argue, since it allows for the discussion of more widely varying opinions and perspectives than might be available in a homogeneous society. In this respect, one might argue that ethnic diversity has an evolutionary survival value for the country—even for the human race. And even social conflict has value (see, e.g., Coser, 1965). By drawing and enforcing boundaries, conflict intensifies people's sense of identity and belonging and gives groups more cohesion and a heightened sense of purpose.

Critical Theory

Unlike functionalists, critical theorists focus on how one group—the more powerful group—benefits more than another from differentiation, exclusion, and institutional racism. They explore, for instance, how economic competition may promote the creation and preservation of racial stereotypes. Critical theory proposes that majority groups seek to dominate minorities, to gain an economic advantage and because domination makes them feel superior.

Consider the case of the Chinese in Canada. Chinese workers were first brought to Canada in the nineteenth century as cheap labourers, to help build the transcontinental railway. Once the railroad was built, however, many Euro-Canadians, especially in British Columbia, came to see these Asian workers—originally recognized and admired for their hard work and discipline—as a threat to their own economic well-being. To limit and control their competitiveness, a federal head tax was put in place, preventing further immigrant flow from China. In 1923, the Chinese Exclusion Act was passed, effectively reducing the number of Chinese immigrants entering Canada to a handful. This law remained in place until 1947, and large-scale Chinese immigration did not really resume until 40 years after that.

Such exclusionary regulation is a form of racism, which (in turn) is the outcome of a process called racialization, the tendency to introduce racial distinctions into situations that can be managed without such distinctions (Abu-Laban and Bakan, 2008). In a racist society, race becomes a substitute for distinctions (in immigration, hiring, or promotion, for example) that otherwise would be based on education or job experience, for example. And in a racist society, even decisions about buying, renting, befriending, and marrying may be affected. All these practices can easily be racialized unless people take pains to ensure this doesn't happen.

Preventing racialization means staying on the lookout for stereotypical descriptions and explanations. For example, sports commentators who praise a black athlete for his 'natural athletic ability' and praise a white athlete, under similar circumstances, for his 'intelligence' or 'extra effort', may be falling prey to racialized stereotypes. Though both statements convey positive sentiments, the praise of 'natural ability' plays to a traditional stereotype of blacks as physically strong but mentally weak, and not industrious or dedicated. In this way, racialized sports commentary, however unconscious, reveals deep and persistent racial prejudices.

Similarly, in police forces and judicial systems, racial profiling—a tendency to expect individuals to act differently, and to interpret their actions differently based on their race—can easily replace fair treatment. When police pull over cars driven by young black or Aboriginal men, but not by young white men, because they expect to find alcohol, drugs, weapons, or stolen property, they are racializing law enforcement (Parmar, 2007).

Symbolic Interactionism

Symbolic interactionists focus on microsociological aspects of race and discrimination, such as the ways people construct ethnic differences and racial labels to subordinate minority groups.

Nigger, dago, wop, chink, kike, jap, gook, and *spic* are just a few of the many slang terms used for race, sometimes casually, sometimes with cruel intent. Even when they are used without cruel intent, such behaviour is troubling. Not only do such terms imply condescension and the intention to humiliate, they can also create a self-fulfilling prophecy. If people come to believe the slurs against their ethnic or national group—coming to think themselves stupid, lazy, cheap, underhanded, and so on—they may come to hate themselves, reject their own group, or give in to impulses to live up to others' worst expectations.

Interactionists also point to **racial socialization** as another factor that contributes to ongoing racial conflicts in society. Racial socialization is a social process that, through interaction, exposes people to the beliefs, values, history, language, and social realities of their own and other people's racial or ethnic identities. In other words, it is the process of learning 'what it means' socially and culturally to be Jewish, Chinese, Ukrainian, and so on. Of course, such racial socialization may not accurately depict the particular groups and their beliefs, values, and so on. The point is, this information is transmitted and learned socially—often in family or peer groups, and sometimes in the media.

Racialization of reality—creating a constant awareness of race (or ethnicity) in daily social interaction—is likely to increase the likelihood of racial conflict. In racialized situations, whenever a conflict arises —particularly where there is a troubled and volatile history (such as between Aboriginal and non-Aboriginal people in Canada)—questions of race and racism are never far from people's minds. Moreover, if people are exposed to other groups and cultures only through stereotyped images, they are likely to act on distorted perceptions of ethnic minorities.

Structural Theory

Another perspective, structural theory, helps us understand the economic experiences of racial and ethnic minorities. Generally, people who are most similar—racially, culturally, and educationally—to members of the host society will enjoy the easiest, most rapid assimilation into the labour market. They will be able to compete most successfully for the best jobs and get them fastest, particularly during times of economic growth. In short, people's lives depend on their economic opportunities, and economic opportunities are often structured on ethnic or racial grounds. In this context, some groups are far more advantaged than others.

In Canada, the sorting of people into jobs usually begins in schools. Through the deliberate application of subtle and complex procedures like tracking and grade-weighting, some students are encouraged while others are discouraged, reducing the opportunities of the latter group following high-school graduation. Once out of school and in the workforce, people of 'different kinds' are streamed toward some types of jobs and away from others. For example, far more women and visible minorities are streamed into the secondary labour market, and far more white men into the primary labour market, than could occur by chance. However, even within these different markets, there are important

racial (or ethnic) socialization

The process by which we learn to perceive and evaluate people (including ourselves) according to presumed racial or ethnic differences.

differences among jobs. For example, although both teachers and doctors are in the primary labour market, teachers have fewer benefits and advantages than doctors do. So, it is of interest to sociologists to know according to what criteria people become teachers or doctors, and prior to that, professionals or salespeople (for example).

Some job markets still exclude or discourage people on the grounds of race, ethnicity, or gender, though these exclusions are becoming less common and less obvious. For better or worse, immigration status tends to level the playing field. Many immigrants from all backgrounds complain of problems arising from the non-acceptance of their foreign credentials and foreign work experience. Many highly qualified immigrants are forced to re-qualify through lengthy, often costly training in Canada.

So, whatever the immigrant's race or ethnicity, credentials, or job experience, in Canada, new immigrants routinely hold similar positions in the labour market; usually, the lowest entrance statuses. In big cities especially, even immigrants with advanced degrees—such as doctors, dentists, architects, engineers, professors, social workers, and nurses—can be found driving taxis, serving hamburgers, selling computers, and providing low-paid personal services. And even when they earn good wages, recent immigrants earn less than native-born Canadians with equivalent education and job experience.

To compensate for these (hidden) structural barriers, many immigrants become 'middlemen'—that is, entrepreneurs, agents, or brokers. Research on 'middleman minorities' finds the following typical pattern: a culturally or racially distinct group immigrates and suffers discrimination. Members of the group come to see themselves as 'strangers' in the country and, to protect themselves, settle in the larger towns and cities among others from the same birthplace. There, they set themselves up as wholesalers, small merchants (e.g., shopkeepers), or even professionals. In doing so, they come into competition with members of the dominant ethnic group. To survive in their marginal role, they have to work harder than anyone else: their economic survival depends on thrift, co-operation, time management, and the strategic use of family and community ties. By these means, the group achieves a middle-class standard of living. No wonder, then, family and community remain so important in the lives of these immigrants to Canada.

Classic Studies
Social Distance

How 'far' are immigrants from native-born Canadians? How much 'distance' separates white people from visible minorities? Are Canadians coming together or are they still isolated in distinct ethnic or racial communities? These and related questions have been usefully addressed in classic research which aimed at measuring what is meant by 'social distance'.

Social distance is a concept devised by the psychologist Emory S. Bogardus in the early twentieth century to measure the extent of intergroup segregation and, conversely, the willingness of group members to mix with other groups (Bogardus, 1959). To measure the distance between groups, Bogardus's scale measures the extent to which participants would accept members of a certain racial or ethnic (or other) group into closer or more distant social relationships, as follows (listed from the closest to the most distant):

1. Close relative by marriage
2. Close personal friend
3. Neighbour on same street
4. Co-worker in same occupation
5. Citizen in own country
6. Temporary visitor in own country
7. Someone excluded from own country

So, for example, a Quebec French Canadian might be asked to indicate whether he would be willing to have an Pakistani person as a close relative—say, to marry his daughter. And would he be willing to have a Pakistani person as a close friend? How about as a neighbour on the same street? As a co-worker at the same workplace? And so on.

For each selection, the respondent gets a certain number of points, which correspond to the number of the question. So, if the respondent wants to exclude Pakistanis from Canada, they get the highest social distance score; permitting them in the country only temporarily would yield a slightly lower score; and so on. Conversely, the respondent who is open to having a Pakistani person in the family, as a son- or daughter-in-law, is showing the lowest social distance and presumably would also be fine with Pakistani friends, neighbours, and co-workers. In effect, social distance is like a ladder: a group that is accepted at a certain level is also accepted at all the levels below it, from both their own perspective and that of the host society.

Each respondent is asked the same set of questions about a variety of different ethnic groups. This yields an average social distance measure for each respondent and each respondent group: for Quebec French Canadians, Quebec English Canadians, and so on. As well, by asking a variety of respondents the same questions, we can calculate an average social distance measure for each 'target group'—for Pakistanis, West Indians, Aboriginals, and so on. In consequence, we can determine what 'types of people' are most open to minorities and which are most closed or distant, and which 'types of minorities' are most accepted and rejected by the majority.

This measurement method was, and remains, innovative for its simple effectiveness in measuring intergroup sentiments. It is highly useful in providing a single, easily calculated measure of the willingness of one group of people to accept or reject another group. It is also a measure that can be used repeatedly across time and place, to measure change and other variation. The method has been used many times, with interesting results. Over the last century, Bogardus' original study (1925) was several times replicated and adjusted, by the researcher himself (as reviewed in his work *A Forty-Year Social Distance Study* [1967]) and by other researchers (Katz and Foley, 1974; Byrnes and Kiger, 1988).

The repeated use of this Bogardus method has yielded three key findings. First, some groups are commonly less tolerated than others; for example, Gypsies are widely disliked and excluded, and research is needed on the sociological factors that produce this widespread, almost universal prejudice against the group. Second, some groups are less tolerant than others; for example, small, isolated communities—especially those that hold to traditional religious and cultural beliefs—are particularly intolerant. Finally, tolerance in a society tends to increase over time: Canada in 2010 is more tolerant of ethnic minorities than it was in 1910, and the same is true of every economically developed society. This also calls for sociological explanation, which we will explore here and elsewhere in the book.

Of course, the Bogardus measure is not the only way to assess the distance between groups. Another simple way is to look at rates of intergroup marriage: marriage between Quebec French Canadians and Pakistanis, for example. (Following Bogardus's reasoning, we could hypothesize that, if these rates of intermarriage were increasing, all types of social distance were likely decreasing.) Recently, Statistics Canada reported the 2006 Census finding that, of the roughly 2 million Canadians who belong to visible minorities and are in a couple relationship, roughly 15 per cent are in a mixed-race union—that is, have married into another racial and/or ethnic group. Reportedly, interracial mixing is much more common in large cities like Vancouver and Toronto than in smaller centres. Some groups—for example, Japanese Canadians, three-quarters of whom are in mixed-race couples—are more likely to 'marry out' than other groups; for example, among

One World, Many Societies

BOX **7.1**

It's a Wonderful, Mixed-up World

Racism is slow to disappear from some ways of thinking. In October 2009, a Louisiana justice of the peace denied a marriage license to a mixed-race couple, claiming that their children would suffer from rejection by both parents' communities. And in Britain, the British National Party opposes mixed marriages as well. Its leader, Nick Griffin, calls the mixing of races 'essentially unnatural and destructive', and mixed-race children 'the most tragic victims of enforced multi-racism'.

But Griffin appears to be mistaken in calling genetic diversity destructive, and the children of mixed couples seem to be anything but victims. It has long been known that inbreeding contributes to disease and deformity. In contrast, we see throughout Nature that genetic diversity helps species adapt to changing environments and resist disease. And studies, statistics, and anecdotal evidence overwhelmingly suggest that people with parents of diverse origin are stronger, healthier, more attractive, more creative, and better able to deal with stress.

Source: Adapted from Prasad (2009).

Chinese or South Asian Canadians, roughly 15 per cent are in mixed-race couples. Finally, and least surprisingly, the tendency to form mixed-race couples is strongest among the descendants of immigrants, not among immigrants themselves. While only 12 per cent of visible-minority Canadians born outside the country form mixed-race couples, 69 per cent of their grandchildren do so (Statistics Canada, 2006a).

This fact could be stated in any of several ways, depending on the point you want to make. One could say that, with the passage of two generations, seven in ten descendants of visible-minority immigrants assimilate maritally. Or, that it takes two generations for a visible-minority family to gain full acceptance in Canadian society. Or, finally, that grandchildren are nearly six times as likely as immigrant newcomers to reject their ancestral community.

The History of Racial and Ethnic Relations

From the sixteenth to the twentieth centuries, (and some might say, even into the twentieth century), the members of powerful nations claimed they were morally and culturally superior to the members of other nations—especially, colonized nations. Sometimes, they even used this alleged superiority as an excuse or justification for conquest, colonization, and economic exploitation.

The logic of moral and cultural superiority has a long and complex history in religion and politics. Colonialism didn't begin with Christianity; certainly, the Egyptians and Persians were just as imperialistic as Christian Europeans, several millennia earlier. However, much of the modern world was created by Christian imperialism two, three, four, or more centuries ago. First, Christianity—as the supposed 'true faith' —traditionally justified the European conquest of all unbelievers. From the eleventh-century Crusades onward, imperialistic European rulers claimed that it was the right, if not the duty, of Christians everywhere to defeat the heathens and convert them to Christianity. In a later version, this forcible conversion was even proclaimed the 'white man's burden'—a moral responsibility of white Christians everywhere.

Consider, for example, Rudyard Kipling's famous 1899 poem, *The White Man's Burden*, celebrating the American takeover of the Philippines after the Spanish-American war. The poem begins:

> Take up the White Man's burden—
> Send forth the best ye breed—
> Go bind your sons to exile
> To serve your captives' need;
> To wait in heavy harness,
> On fluttered folk and wild—
> Your new-caught, sullen peoples,
> Half-devil and half-child.

Though some critics have proposed alternative, and even ironic readings, of this internationally known poem, there is little doubt that a majority of people read it as a straight-up celebration of white (American and British) Christian superiority. Many Americans today might hold similar views about the war in Afghanistan, though the British are generally more cautious about such matters than they were a century ago.

Second, cultural parochialism (narrow-mindedness) and a commitment to nation-building—as well as advantages in technology, weaponry, and other material achievements—allowed European countries to conquer less powerful and 'less advanced' civilizations in the European national interests. Great economic and military (strategic) benefits were gained by doing so. Finally, and perhaps most importantly, a (misunderstood) version of Darwinism maintained that European imperial successes proved the natural superiority of Western European societies and cultures over 'primitive' societies.

These beliefs spread to every part of the world as part of the colonial enterprise. Even colonized people sometimes came to believe in these 'natural' distinctions, leading, for example, to lighter-skinned people within an overall dark-skinned group enjoying higher status and more power in many former colonies (as can still be seen in Haiti and Colombia, for example). Similar dynamics continue today in many parts of the world. For example, in India today, as well other countries, women use products with names like 'Fair and

This 1917 photo shows some of the thousands of Chinese labourers who were brought to Canada to build the Canadian Pacific Railway.

Lovely' to lighten their skin, in the belief that such alterations—if they work—will make them more attractive and desirable. The same is true in the mating patterns of American black people today; lighter-skinned blacks are considered more attractive and desirable—for some commentators, evidence of learned self-hatred. And of course, many West Indian Canadians straighten their hair to seem less African and more white.

Such beliefs about the cultural, religious, and racial superiority of white European groups and the corresponding inferiority of others have influenced relations among all groups in North America, to some degree. In Canada, for example, well into the twentieth century there was a tendency to portray white Anglo-Saxon Protestants ('WASPs') as being somehow ethnically superior to white francophone Catholics, white allophone northern Europeans (for example, German immigrants), white allophone eastern Europeans (for example, Ukrainian immigrants), and white allophone southern Europeans (usually Catholics, particularly Italian immigrants).

All of these, in turn, were preferred to non-Caucasian peoples: Asians from India or China, Africans or West Indians, or Latin Americans. Within this hierarchy, Jewish and Aboriginal groups have traditionally held a peculiar, often undulating, position. We know about these historical preferences because people spoke about them and wrote about them. Most important, Canada's immigration laws—with their more or less obvious ethnic and racial preferences—were based on such beliefs.

The History of Immigration Policy

If we go back to the beginnings of Canada in the mid nineteenth century, we can see that groups from northern Europe were favoured by Canadian immigration policies, allegedly because northern Europeans were considered more likely to survive—even thrive—in the cold climate. Supposedly, a northern climate prepared immigrants for hard work and sobriety in Canada. Whether this view was merely a mask for prejudice against other, less-familiar Europeans—against southern European Catholics, including Spanish, French, and Italian 'Papists' who were supposedly lascivious and lacked Northern hardiness and virtue—cannot be easily determined.

Whatever the reason, the immigration procedures discriminated in favour of white British and northern European Protestants and against other ethnic groups, especially people of other 'races' who were non-Christian. Yet that didn't keep the country from importing non-Christians and non-whites for heavy labour. Near the end of the nineteenth century, as we mentioned earlier, Chinese labourers were brought to Canada to build the Canadian Pacific Railway. They were not encouraged to stay afterwards, nor to bring their families. Many Euro-Canadians, especially in British Columbia, saw the Asian immigrants as a threat to the economic welfare of the dominant white majority. As noted earlier, the federal government imposed a racially discriminatory head tax between 1885 and 1923 to discourage further immigrant from Asia. After that, the Chinese Exclusion Act, in place from 1923 to 1947, strictly forbade Chinese workers from bringing in their wives or families, to discourage settlement and prevent an increase in the Asian-Canadian population.

As the example of Chinese male labourers suggests, Canada historically used immigration as a means to satisfy its various economic and social needs, not to help the world's disadvantaged (Green and Green, 2004). As noted, some labourers admitted into Canada at the turn of the twentieth century were here specifically to build the Canadian Pacific Railway (Comeau and Allahar, 2001). Then, in the 1920s and again in the 1950s to 1970s, immigration was used to meet demands for other labour skills—for example, to build the roads, office towers, and houses of Canada's rapidly growing cities. Since the 1980s, Canada has needed immigrants to compensate for the low fertility of aging baby-boomers in the native-born population (Green and Green, 2004: 133), as mentioned in an earlier chapter. In every instance, the large immigrant inflows were aimed at satisfying particular

New immigrants receive ESL training in order to familiarize themselves with the language of their adopted country and to help assimilate into the unfamiliar culture.

social and economic needs. Today, Canada gets a large fraction of its most highly educated and ambitious working-age population from less-developed countries—a fact that does not always please the countries losing these people.

At other times, when jobs were scarce, immigration into Canada was significantly reduced; entry restrictions ensured that groups that were not needed (and not liked) were turned away (McLean, 2004). As Green and Green (2004: 135) note, Canada accepted only 'the number of immigrants that the Canadian economy [could] easily absorb'. In the last 20 years, this short-term focus on demand and fulfillment has, however, shifted to a longer-term strategy that considers immigration an essential contributor to economic growth and prosperity. This newer policy allows for immigration inflow even during periods of economic hardship, an openness that has helped many immigrant families to start new lives in Canada.

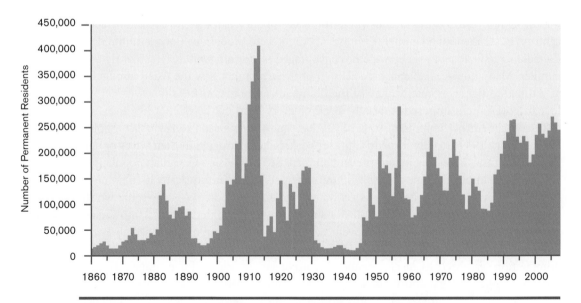

Figure 7.1 Permanent Residents, Canada, 1860–2007

Source: Adapted from Citizenship and Immigration Canada (2008a).

Immigration in the Twenty-first Century

Along with changes in policy, in recent decades we have seen evidence that the 'colour' of Canada's cultural mosaic is changing, as increasingly more immigrants from traditionally less-favoured countries have entered and started new lives in our country. The source countries of Canada's immigrants have changed. Table 7.1 shows that in 1950–5, the United Kingdom and Europe accounted for 88 per cent of all immigrants to Canada (Statistics Canada, 2006a). The next highest percentage came from the United States, at a mere 6.3 per cent of immigrants (ibid).

By the beginning of the twenty-first century, the number of immigrants coming from Europe had decreased substantially, down to just 19.7 per cent by 2000–4. And in 2006, this percentage was even lower, a mere 15.1 per cent. This huge shift toward immigration from Asia and Africa has occurred largely because the standard of living in Europe has improved, especially with the formation of the European Union. People born in Europe today are more likely to stay there, rather than immigrate to Canada. However, it also reflects a growing willingness in Canada to admit large numbers of non-Europeans.

So, the number of immigrants coming from other, generally less developed countries has shot upward in recent decades. Every year, Canada admits about 260,000 new immigrants, 55 per cent of them from the ten main source countries listed in Table 7.2 (Statistics Canada, 2007). Currently, the two main source countries for new immigrants to Canada are India and China (see Walton-Roberts, 2003 and Ahmad et al., 2004). As Table 7.2 shows, people from China accounted for 11.4 per cent of all immigrants in 2007 and those from India for 11.0 per cent (Citizenship and Immigration Canada, 2009). Both groups are growing rapidly in the Canadian population, and because of higher fertility, the south Asian group is growing faster. Despite a slightly higher rate of immigration from China, for the first time in 2006 South Asian Canadians surpassed Chinese Canadians as the largest visible-minority group in the country (Statistics Canada, 2006a).

Since 1967, immigrants to Canada have been rated on a *point system* that determines each applicant's eligibility with respect to specific criteria, for which points are awarded. For example, the applicant's age, educational credentials, work experience, and English and/or French language ability are all considered relevant to the application, but the applicant's country of origin no longer is considered relevant. This has helped to eliminate racialist and racist concerns from the immigrant selection process, a change that began only in 1962 (Citizenship and Immigration Canada, 2009).

Table 7.1 Permanent Residents Admitted, by Country of Origin, Canada, 1950–1955, 2000–2004, and 2006

Region	1950–1955 (%)	2000–2004 (%)	2006 (%)
Africa and the Middle East	0.4	19.1	20.6
Asia and Pacific	3.6	50.3	50.2
South and Central America	1.5	8.3	9.7
United States	6.3	2.6	4.4
Europe and the United Kingdom	88.0	19.7	15.1
Source area not stated	0.2	0.0	–

Source: Figures for 1950–5 compiled from Canada, Department of Manpower and Immigration, *Immigration Statistics*; figures for 2000–4 compiled from Citizenship and Immigration Canada, *Facts and Figures 2004: Immigration Overview*, at: www.cic.gc.ca/english/pub/facts2004/permanent/12.html; figures for 2006 from Citizenship and Immigration Canada, *Facts and Figures 2006*.

Table 7.2 Permanent Residents Admitted by Top 10 Source Countries, Canada, 2007

Country	Number	%	Rank
China, People's Republic of	27,014	11.41	1
India	26,054	11.00	2
Philippines	19,064	8.05	3
United States	10,450	4.41	4
Pakistan	9,547	4.03	5
United Kingdom	8,128	3.43	6
Iran	6,663	2.81	7
Korea, Republic of	5,864	2.48	8
France	5,526	2.33	9
Colombia	4,833	2.04	10
Total—top ten	123,143	52.01	
All other source countries	113,615	47.99	
Total	236,758	100.00	

Source: Citizenship and Immigration Canada (2008b), Table 5-A.

Applicants today are divided into four major categories: *skilled workers, business immigrants, family class,* and *refugees.* The largest immigrant class admitted each year, skilled workers, usually makes up about half of all immigrants admitted (51.1 per cent in 2007). These are applicants admitted solely on the results of the point system. Family members being reunited with earlier immigrants make up the second-largest category, and they are not assessed by the point system. Refugees, the third-largest category—11.8 per cent of all immigrants in 2007—are escaping countries known for their human rights violations.

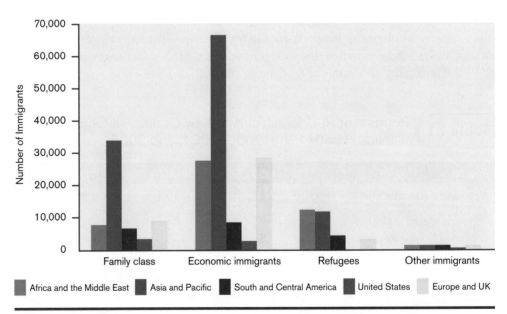

Figure 7.2 Immigrant Landings, by Category and Source Area, Canada, 2004

Source: Citizenship and Immigration Canada (2006: 23). Reproduced with the permission of the Minister of Public Works and Government Services Canada, 2010.

Canada, along with some other countries, has signed an international treaty that obliges them by international law to provide asylum for such refugees (UN Refugee Agency, 2009).

Immigrants, though they rarely know one another and come from a variety of places, tend to behave in patterned and predictable ways. For example, after entering Canada, most immigrants settle in Ontario, British Columbia, or Quebec—(together, nearly 85 per cent in 2006) (Citizenship and Immigration Canada, 2007). In fact, in 2006, half settled in Ontario. Some also settled in Alberta and Manitoba, but very few settled in Saskatchewan or the Maritimes, and virtually none settled in the three territories. As a result, Canada's provinces and regions differ significantly in their makeup of immigrants and native-borns. In general, immigrants go where they know or believe jobs are available, where they have friends or relatives, and where institutionally complete ethnic communities can be found.

Like other Canadians, immigrants tend to head for the cities. Increasingly, as local communities form, they migrate to smaller cities—for example, to Calgary, Ottawa, Edmonton, Victoria, and St. John's—in short, wherever there is economic growth taking place. No longer are all the immigrants headed for Toronto, Montreal, and Vancouver.

On arrival in their destinations, the immigrants then begin another set of patterned and predictable experiences. Whether they come from Damascus or Denmark, Hong Kong or Honduras, their family lives start to change in ways described nearly a century ago. At that time, the group of interest was Polish immigrants—in fact, Polish peasants in America.

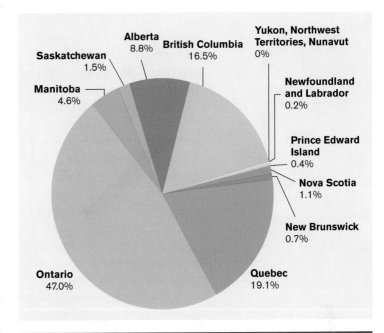

Figure 7.3 Permanent Residents, by Province or Territory, Canada, 2007

Source: Citizenship and Immigration Canada (2008a: 43). Reproduced with the permission of the Minister of Public Works and Government Services Canada, 2010.

Classic Studies
The Polish Peasant in Europe and America

Already by the beginning of the twentieth century, ethnic differences in North America were of great interest and social importance, because by then Canada and the United States were already nations of immigrants.

One of the first major studies of immigration in North America was William I. Thomas and Florian Znaniecki's multi-volume *The Polish Peasant in Europe and America* (1918–1920). It examined the social and family lives of Polish immigrants—specifically why they often struggled, and failed, to overcome the challenges of assimilating into a new culture.

The Polish Peasant in Europe and America is now considered a classic study in sociological theory and immigrant history. In it, the authors begin by describing the social life of Polish peasants at home, and the processes of disorganization that served as background for their immigration to America. We cannot, the authors say, understand the problems of adjustment that peasants face as immigrants to America unless we understand the society in which they grew up and were forced to leave.

Ultimately, the authors want to explain how and why immigrants to America often fail to meet new opportunities and challenges while trying to assimilate into a new culture. They begin their work with an analysis of the cultural tradition of Poland and its growing social disorganization. Partly due to macrosocial changes associated with urbanization and industrialization, not to mention the Russian Revolution and the First World War, many peasants came to America with expectations of success. In hindsight, we can see these expectations were unrealistically high. Of course, they came with the desire for new experience, recognition, security, and fulfillment. However, problems were quick to surface. Many immigrants had trouble altering their social customs—a necessity if they were to assimilate into American culture and achieve economic success.

Yet, neither could they maintain the traditional system of life. Limits on travel and communication meant that, for most, after they came to America they had little chance of seeing their families again; and sometimes, even communication broke down. However, emotionally and culturally, these immigrants were neither entirely disengaged from their native land, nor fully integrated into American culture; they could not wholly identify as Polish or as American. Robert Park, another prominent University of Chicago sociologist who studied immigrants, called them 'marginal men' (Park, 1928).

The results of this marginality included poverty, delinquency, mental illness, marital conflict, and social isolation. Thomas and Znaniecki were quick to note that that immigration demands prodigious change and adaptability from the immigrant, yet society provides none of the means needed to help bring this about. The stresses and difficulties—especially the conflicts between spouses, and between parents and children—that Thomas and Znaniecki describe are still common among new immigrants to Canada and the US today. In short, this study has stood the test of time.

In part, that is because of the study's remarkable methodology. In fact, many feel that the data collection procedure overshadows the conclusions of the study. In their analysis, Thomas and Znaniecki applied a new qualitative, empirical approach to their investigation of Polish peasants in Europe and America. They did so by using primary documents as a main source of information to combine social facts with theoretical interpretations. Included in the published volumes are numerous court documents, newspaper articles, archives of charitable societies and church parishes, hundreds of letters exchanged between immigrants and their families in Poland, and the lengthy autobiography of a Polish worker. Through these lenses, Thomas and Znaniecki examine every aspect of the immigrant life, including family relations, work experiences, personal aspirations, and deeply held concerns.

Inter-Ethnic Interaction

Given the huge mass of different 'kinds of people' that make up the Canadian population, how do we meet, get to know, work with, and even marry people of different ethnocultural and racial backgrounds? For some, the mechanism is love and marriage. As we saw earlier, the numbers of intercultural and interracial marriages are increasing, but they are still relatively rare; so, few children are growing up in ethnically, and racially, mixed families today.

Table 7.3   Proportion of Canadians Who Socialized with People from Other Cultures, Rural and Urban, 2007

	Proportion That Agreed It Is Important to Learn from Other Cultures (%)	Proportion That Socialized with Other Cultures on a Regular Basis (%)
Canada	93.0	71.5
Large cities	94.2	82.3
Rural communities	92.6	61.4

Source: Canadian Council on Learning (2007), Table 1.

For many others, schools, universities, neighbourhoods, and workplaces provide the best opportunities to meet and associate with others. Though some workplaces are socially homogeneous, the vast majority of large ones comprise people of many ethnic and racial backgrounds. The same is true—even more so—of schools, universities, and large-city neighbourhoods. We spoke in an earlier chapter about the historical importance of sociologist John Porter's classic 1965 work *The Vertical Mosaic*. It called attention to the historical link between ethnic immigrant origins and current class location. Porter favoured the growth of Canadian colleges and universities for many reasons, not least to provide minorities with opportunity for upward mobility through higher education. And as expected, institutions of higher education *have* served to bring different ethnic and racial groups into more contact with one another.

Any large urban university has huge numbers of ethnic and racial minorities—both because of the presence of immigrants in cities and the arrival of many foreign students. Cities themselves are melting pots—places where people readily meet others from very different backgrounds. Ethnic concentration, or segregation, is less marked in Canadian cities than it is in American cities, so even with 'ethnic neighbourhoods' there is some inter-ethnic mixing.

That said, ethnic self-segregation is common in Canada's cities, with the result that we can find a Chinatown, a Little Italy, a Greektown, and so on in many of the largest ones. In Canada's three major urban gateways—Toronto, Montreal, and Vancouver—ethnic groups settle together largely for economic and linguistic reasons. For example, recent Portuguese immigrants live near other recent Portuguese immigrants so they can speak Portuguese together; the same is true for most other immigrant groups. However, ethnic communities do more than let people continue to speak their ancestral language: in fact, they play a key role in preserving the cultural heritage against **assimilation**. They are, in this respect, an impediment to social mixing though they have many other benefits for their members.

Ethnic communities are made up of individuals who consider themselves (and are usually considered by others) to share common characteristics that distinguish them from other people in society. For example, they have a shared history and seemingly common fate. Moreover, they usually have a common origin (a shared ancestry) and distinct cultural behaviours and beliefs, and they choose to remember these shared characteristics (*je me souviens*—'I will remember'—on Quebec licence plates reminds us of the French Canadian determination to preserve the French cultural tradition, no matter what!).

Benedict Anderson (1983) coined the term **imagined communities** to highlight the socially constructed aspect of all ethnic group life. Anderson says that ethnic groups are 'imagined' because the borders they draw around themselves are socially constructed—that is, imagined by the group, a group vision. In imagined communities, people live and work with others they perceive as 'like themselves'. However, the survival of imagined communities also depends to some degree, like the survival of racial differences, on the behaviour of outsiders. People belong to a race because other people say they do. Likewise, ethnic membership and identity tend to maintain themselves best when people feel endangered by outsiders. In that way, ethnic communities are like cliques (recall Chapter 3), in which membership requires adopting shared criteria of evaluation, communication with non-members is often restricted to areas of assumed common understanding, and symbolic markers are used to designate a group and people's membership in it.

Imagined communities often take the form of **ethnic enclaves**. The largest cities have many ethnic enclaves, often including a Little India, Little Jamaica, Little Portugal, Little Italy, Little Vietnam, Greektown, Koreatown, and usually multiple Chinatowns. No wonder the United Nations identified Toronto, of all cities, as home to the world's second-largest immigrant citizenry, behind only Miami, Florida (UN Development Program, 2004: 99); but Montreal and Vancouver are also home to large and diverse ethnic populations. In 2002, 14 per cent of all new immigrants chose to live in Montreal, while 13 per cent chose Vancouver (Statistics Canada, 2006a).

assimilation

The process by which an outsider or immigrant group becomes indistinguishably integrated into the dominant host society; similar to *acculturation*.

imagined communities

Social groupings, like races or ethnic groups, that are treated as real because they are widely believed (or imagined) to be real.

ethnic enclave

A neighbourhood that is mainly or exclusively populated by people who belong to the same ethnic group.

institutional completeness

The degree to which a community or enclave has established services aimed at a particular ethnic community, often in their traditional language.

diaspora

A dispersion of people through migration, resulting in the establishment and spread of same-ethnicity communities throughout the world.

diasporic group

Any ethnic group that has established multiple centres of immigrant life throughout the world.

On arriving in Canada, many immigrants choose to live in ethnic enclaves. As they become more assimilated culturally and economically, they tend to move to more prosperous and, often, more culturally mixed areas outside the city core. Within the ethnic enclaves, many groups develop **institutional completeness**: a full set of services (even including schools, churches, and mass media) that cater solely to the needs of that ethnic group, often in their own language. Raymond Breton (1964) has shown that such institutional completeness plays an important role in preserving ethnic identities and ethnic communities against disappearance.

Recently, the number of ethnic enclaves in Canada has been rising, and some see this as evidence that Canada supports people choosing their own way of life. However, others see this as an indicator that people are increasingly segregating themselves, and avoiding active engagement with Canadian society as a whole. There is some merit to this view; and if true, Canada is not a unified society made up of diverse cultures, but merely a collection segregated communities. However, over time, ethnic identities tend to weaken, and immigrants (and their descendants) increasingly identify with the Canadian society. Though some continue to live in ethnic enclaves, many explore the world outside their ethnic communities. This occurs especially among youth, who are most exposed to people of different backgrounds through mass media and interaction at school.

Working to delay or prevent integration—along with institutional completeness, and residential segregation—is the persistence of **diasporic** networks. These are complex links between the homeland and immigrant minorities in other countries. Often, these **diasporic groups** of dispersed immigrants form links with one another, creating a worldwide network of connected immigrant communities: a global Hong Kong, Jewish, or Pakistani community, for example. One effect is to preserve the emotional, social, and even financial ties of immigrants to their original homeland and its problems. Often, these diasporic immigrants both welcome new immigrants from the homeland and send home funds to promote economic development or even military activities.

Interaction between ethnic groups in Canada takes place at school and work, and also during ethnic food and culture festivals, when people of different cultures come together to sample each other's specialties. Of course, it takes more than eating baklava together to bridge the gap between Greeks and Turks; but it's a beginning. This kind of everyday, unremarkable mixing of peoples from different ethnicities will eventually lay to rest the ethnic memories of mistreatment, and exclusion that maintain ethnocultural segregation among many of Canada's immigrants.

In the past, interracial marriage was very rare. Today, interracial marriages—including such high-profile unions as the one between former Canadian governor general Michaëlle Jean and filmmaker Jean-Daniel Lafond—have become much more common in North America and don't carry the social stigma they once did.

Multiculturalism

In Canada, ethnic enclaves also are the product of **multiculturalism**, a belief that all citizens and their respective cultures and backgrounds are equal and have a right—indeed, should be encouraged—to preserve their own interests and ways of life (Department of Canadian Heritage, 2009). Multiculturalism is an official policy in Canada, and 'ensures that all citizens can keep their identities, take pride in their ancestry, and have a sense of belonging' (Citizenship and Immigration Canada, 2008c). The policy also promotes tolerance and acceptance of cultures among all Canadians and 'encourages racial and ethnic harmony and cross-cultural understanding' (ibid).

multiculturalism
A Canadian political and social policy aimed at promoting ethnic tolerance and ethnic community survival.

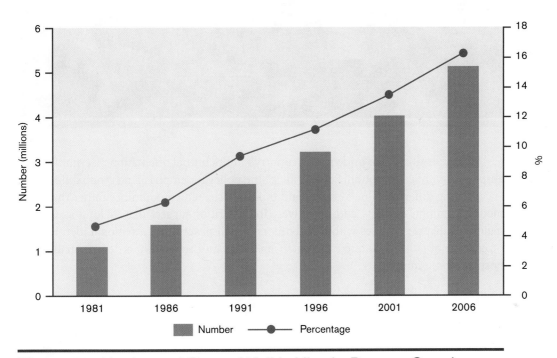

Figure 7.4 Number and Share of Visible-Minority Persons, Canada, 1981–2006

Source: Statistics Canada (2006a).

Inter-ethnic interaction is becoming more common in Canada as immigrants from different countries form friendships with one another.

Toronto's Chinatown displays a multitude of signs in both Chinese and English.

Most Canadians take pride in this country's multicultural orientation. Yet multiculturalism is a complicated notion. Some criticize the policy for emphasizing group differences, encouraging different value systems, and building isolated communities rather than promoting common interests and objectives (ibid). Critics suggest that as long as Canada maintains diverse cultures within its borders, it will never build a national identity. The promotion of cultural differences splits Canadians into separate (and occasionally even hostile) ethnic camps.

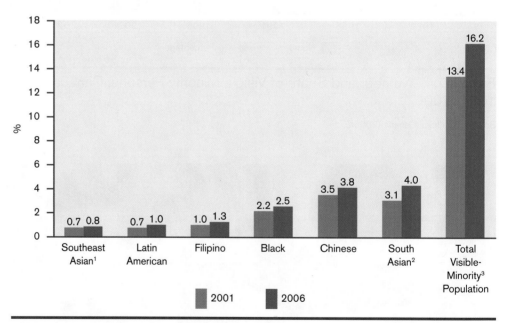

Figure 7.5 Proportion of Visible-Minority Groups, Canada, 2001 and 2006

1. For example, Vietnamese, Cambodian, Malaysian, Laotian, etc.
2. For example, East Indian, Pakistani, Sri Lankan, etc.
3. The Employment Equity Act defines visible minorities as 'persons, other than Aboriginal peoples, who are non-Caucasian in race or non-white in colour.'

Source: Adapted from Canadian Council on Learning (2007).

For some, treating minority groups in a different, special way violates the former Canadian norm of equal treatment. Moreover, it may unwittingly increase the chance of exclusion, prejudice, and discrimination, by highlighting group differences rather than commonalities. Nowhere is this more evident than in relation to Aboriginal groups and French Canadians, as we will see next.

Multiculturalism and Aboriginal Peoples

Aboriginal communities, for several reasons, do not favour the notion of multiculturalism. First, an official policy of multiculturalism turns Aboriginals into just another minority group among hundreds of others, and fails to recognize their distinctive status as the original settlers of the country. As well, they feel that their own collective concerns warrant more attention, and many Canadians seem to agree that some degree of political autonomy for Aboriginal peoples may even be in order (Warburton, 1997). Time and money spent celebrating other ethnic minorities is time and money taken away from the Aboriginals, then.

Will Kymlicka (1995) believes we should view Canadian Aboriginal peoples as 'national minorities'. Their rights should include both individual equality and collective self-determination within the framework of liberal democratic principles (see also Spaulding, 1997). So far, however, movement in that direction has been slow. In particular, the two principles Kymlicka calls us to honour—individual equality and collective self-determination—may not be compatible.

Aboriginal efforts to achieve self-government have not been entirely without effect, however. Consider Canada's alternative Native justice systems, which stress collective, as opposed to individual, rights and give special priorities to Native principles and practices of justice. Participation in these systems is voluntary and limited to minor offences (Clairmont, 1996). In general, they uphold traditional Aboriginal principles and practices. Such power-sharing between judges and Native communities seems to satisfy the federal government, at least more than the application of Aboriginal values to jury selection, trial location, and criminal liability (Melancon, 1997).

Land claim settlements, though slow in coming, have also provided individual First Nations and peoples with the opportunity and the resources to govern themselves as nations within the nation of Canada. The territory of Nunavut, where Inuit of the eastern Arctic make up 85 per cent of the population, is a prime example (Statistics Canada, 2006a). So, there is some, gradual recognition of the special minority status of Aboriginal people; but the Canadian government's commitment to multiculturalism is far stronger.

Multiculturalism and French Canadians

French Canadians express the same kinds of concerns about multiculturalism as do Aboriginal peoples, but even more forcefully. Under multiculturalism, French Canadian nationalists claim they are treated as merely a national minority, not one of the two 'founding groups' that established Canada.

In Quebec, some have viewed multiculturalism as an attempt by the federal government to undermine legitimate Quebec aspirations for 'nationhood'. As such, Quebec governments over the last few decades have promoted a different policy in Quebec called *interculturalism,* a practice also followed in Europe (Gorrotxategi Azurmendi, 2005). Although similar to multiculturalism, interculturalism differs in a few ways. Interculturalism encourages tolerance for different cultures, but demands their forceful acceptance and incorporation into Quebec society. For example, it assimilates immigrants by requiring them to learn French (Nugent, 2006). By doing so, French language use becomes the 'common ground' among all Quebecers and the basis for Quebec cohesion, as promoted through the province's educational system. Interculturalism, then, integrates all cultures under a common

A crowd waves their provincial flag to celebrate Quebec's national day, St Jean Baptiste day, a clear display of Quebec nationalism.

language. Not surprisingly, it discourages the formation of ethnic enclaves, since it undermines the linguistic segregation that hinders intergroup relations.

By comparison, the federal policy of multiculturalism is more tolerant, encouraging each culture to use and enjoy its own unique language, religion, and way of life. The differences between interculturalism and multiculturalism illustrate the conflict between French Canada—especially, Quebec—and the rest of Canada.

Point/Counterpoint

BOX **7.2**

Is Multiculturalism on Its Deathbed?

Following the terrorist attacks on the London subway in July 2005, questions were raised in the UK, as well as in Canada, about how immigrants integrate into mainstream society. Canada has long maintained a policy of multiculturalism, meaning that newcomers are encouraged to adhere to many of their cultural customs and beliefs. But almost three-quarters of Canadians feel that 'immigrants should be encouraged to integrate into broader Canadian society rather than maintaining their ethnic identity', according to a survey by the Strategic Council in 2005.

Yet multiculturalism, its defenders say, gives ethnocultural groups a sense that 'the larger political society respects them and regards them as equals'. Rather than being a problem, they claim, multiculturalism is the best way to accommodate ethnocultural diversity. As well, 'this debate about whether multiculturalism should stay or go, however, is a false debate. Ethnocultural diversity is a fact of democratic political life that will not change anytime soon and ignoring it is not an option.'

Source: Adapted from Munro (2005).

Classic Studies
An American Dilemma:
The Negro Problem and Modern Democracy

In Canada, race relations have become visible and problematic only in the last few decades, with the large-scale arrival of immigrants from Asia, Africa, South America, and the West Indies. However, race relations have been visible and problematic throughout the history of the United States and, therefore, throughout the development of North American sociology.

In the US, racial conflict—rooted in a history of slavery and oppression—has always been part of the American cultural psyche. An important work on this topic was *The Souls of Black Folk* by sociologist W.E.B. Du Bois (an African-American), who stated that the 'problem of the twentieth century is the problem of the colour line' (1995 [1903]). As well, many white sociologists, both inside and outside the US, have focused on this problem, including the author of the classic work profiled here—Swedish economist, professor, and politician (as well as later Nobel prize winner for Economics) Karl Gunnar Myrdal.

In 1937, the Carnegie Corporation in New York commissioned Myrdal to examine the condition of African-Americans in the United States, specifically analyzing American black–white relations. Myrdal's goal was to provide guidelines for government policy makers. The resulting report was Myrdal's two-volume work, *An American Dilemma: The Negro Problem and Modern Democracy*.

Myrdal's study tries to trace racial discrimination from the beginnings of American history up to 1938, to show how racist attitudes had damaged an entire society by limiting the opportunities and actions of African-Americans. Although the 'American Creed' preached equality, the white majority, applying a 'white moral standard', felt equality did not apply to African-Americans. Thus, from their arrival in the US as slaves, black Americans were treated differently from whites. Even after the legislated ending of slavery, African-Americans continued to lead more limited, less healthy, and less prosperous lives. This continued restriction of African-Americans was rooted in an assumption of black inferiority, and ultimately in the historical slave–master relationship that existed until the American Civil War. In short, Myrdal suggests, present-day discrimination grows out of earlier discrimination: psychologically, it is as though the slaves were never freed.

Myrdal proposes several solutions to America's racist dilemma. First, he suggests expanding the role of the federal government in education, housing, and income security. In all of these areas, if the government adopted and *enacted* policies of racial equality, racial minorities would have the same opportunities for healthy, prosperous lives as white people. Second, Myrdal suggests encouraging the migration of African-Americans from the rural south to the industrial north, where high-paying jobs were more plentiful. Finally, Myrdal urges Americans to apply the intentions of the American Creed wholeheartedly; however, he believes that federal legislation would be needed to achieve equality.

Myrdal's recommendations foresaw some of twentieth-century America's most important changes. For example, the American Civil Rights Act of 1964 and voting rights legislation in 1965 gave African-Americans new legal, political, and social rights. As recommended, vast numbers of African-Americans migrated northward in the 1950s and 1960s, to the large industrial cities where they could get decent jobs and incomes. Yet, racism and racial segregation continued in the US, even in the north. African-Americans—especially, African-American men—were far more likely than white men to be unemployed, underemployed, poorly housed and educated, and, worst of all, thrown into jail. This suggests Americans had failed to apply the intentions of the American Creed wholeheartedly; and better federal legislation would still be needed—for example, in the realm of education—to achieve equality.

In part, the problem continued because of a larger-scale problem in American society: the loss of stable, well-paying, unionized jobs in northern cities. Only a few decades after the African-Americans arrived in large numbers, good jobs began to migrate—first to the non-unionized southern United States, then to even lower-paying, less developed countries in Asia and Latin America. With each successive national crisis—the rise in oil prices that began in the 1970s and the financial crisis of 2008 and afterward—African-Americans were the first and most likely to suffer.

What should sociologists learn from this story? Myrdal, also foreseeing the difficulties of major social change, challenges American social science to do better for society's most vulnerable members. He criticized sociology for failing to try to improve humanity, for avoiding controversial research and failing to study significant problems that would result in real change. Like today's postmodernists, Myrdal rejects the notion that research can be entirely unbiased. Sociologists cannot fully remove their personal bias and experience from their analysis, he says. If this bias is not recognized, the result will be misleading conclusions. However, he does not encourage sociologists to drain their research of biases; on the contrary, they should work for valuable social goals, to help society's underdogs.

Racialization

Today, in keeping with the advice of Du Bois and Myrdal, many academic sociologists are attuned to the human significance of race and racism, and to the importance of doing rigorous research with policy implications.

Ironically, one of the biggest advances in the sociological study of race has come from outside sociology—namely, from the study of genetics. A better understanding of the genetic makeup of humanity has redoubled the sociologist's conviction that race is merely a social construct, not a genetic reality. This has moved the discussion from race and racism to racialization. The term *racialization,* means, first, to differentiate or categorize people according to race—often, an unnecessary and suspicious activity. Second, it means to impose a racial character or context on a situation that can be interpreted in other terms (for example, in class terms). Finally, it means to perceive or experience the world in racial terms. Thus, for historically oppressed people, it means to be always on the lookout for evidence or threats of racial mistreatment.

As we know, human beings are a migratory species; so, after a long history of contact between different human groups through trade and international migration, we now find virtually every racial feature in almost every part of the world. And increasingly, we find mixtures of people with different racial features. This is clear from the genetic evidence mentioned earlier. As a result, some people have begun to hope that intermixing will lead to the decline of humanity's long and shameful history of racialization and possibly even the end of *racism*, the mistreatment of some people based on apparent physical differences.

This mistreatment has often occurred because some people believe that others belong to a different race—they racialize them as 'others;' and see members of this perceived different 'race' as essentially different from themselves. Such people—call them racists or racialists—have tremendous difficulty accepting that race has little biological basis. Instead, they see each 'race' as possessing unique physiological characteristics, based in genetic differences that are absent in other races. Moreover, they often believe that cultural or personality dispositions are genetically based as well. For these reasons, they are often on the lookout for racial differences.

Increasingly, however, scientists reject this view of race in light of growing genetic evidence showing that so-called human races are significantly more alike than different. The Human Genome Project has shown, for example, that only a tiny fraction of our genetic makeup as human beings varies by characteristics historically associated with 'race'. Indeed, 85 per cent of the genetic variability that exists within the entire human species can be found within a single local population (Barbujani et al., 1997). That is to say, there could be more genetic difference between two randomly selected Cambodians than between a Cambodian and a Norwegian. Besides, the physical attributes commonly associated with race are not genetically associated with each other; for example, the pieces of DNA that determine a person's skin colour are inherited separately from the pieces that determine if that person's hair is curly or straight.

Typically, the physical features supposedly shared by members of one race are a result of collective evolutionary adaptation to specific environmental influences (for example, the darkening of skin colour where strong sunlight shines most of the time, as it does near the equator). What's more, race and ethnicity are not necessarily connected. People who look different may share the same cultural values, whereas people who look the same may think in strikingly different ways.

Prejudice and Discrimination

Many of the conflicts that arise between racial groups stem from intergroup prejudice and discrimination, and there are various explanations why people are prejudiced and discriminatory. Some explanations are more sociological, others more psychological. However, they all have some empirical support and all seem credible, to some degree.

One explanation of prejudice and discrimination is racial socialization. As we mentioned at the beginning of the chapter, this is the process by which we learn 'what it means' socially and culturally to be a Jew, a Ukrainian, a Sikh, and so on. A constant awareness of race or ethnicity in daily social interaction—one possible result of racial socialization—increases the chance we will perceive (or at least imagine) differences and racial or ethnic conflict will result. So, racialization is liable to increase people's attention to supposed racial differences, with potentially harmful results. Consider the socialized perception of inter-caste differences in India: this way of thinking, rooted in culture and religion, has often been used to justify harshly unequal relations of superiority and inferiority.

Another explanation of prejudice and discrimination is that they confer economic or social advantages on the discriminating group. When we discriminate, we usually discriminate in favour of people 'like us' and against people we consider very different. This makes discrimination a form of self-love, and a sign of ignorance about people unlike us. So, when we hire people 'like us', perhaps we are merely practising nepotism, the desire to hire only friends and relatives. This becomes a form of ethnic self-protection or self-advancement: protecting and advancing one's ethnocultural group at the expense of other groups.

Protection or advancement of one's own ethnic group is more about discrimination than about prejudice. When discrimination is (or seems) economically rational, we do not need to import the concept of prejudice—essentially, a form of irrationality (whether as ignorance or error). People are behaving rationally, however unjustly, when they try to limit or undermine their competitors. However, some discrimination *is* based on prejudice, and here we have to turn to the troubled concept of *racial profiling*: the practice of taking into account a person's race to predict their engagement in criminal activities (Rice, Reitzel, and Piquero, 2005).

A common example of racial profiling involves driver spot checks. Some assert that police, for example, tend to pull over black drivers more often than white drivers, merely because they are black. If so, racial profiling by the police is a form of harassment against blacks, especially blacks who look prosperous and drive nice cars. As some say, it is a punishment for 'driving while black'. One interpretation is that the police force is staffed by bigots who hate black people and enjoy giving them a hard time. Maybe they even want to goad the black drivers into stepping out of line so they can be arrested or beaten. Perhaps this explanation applies to some police officers at some times and in some places. If so, we are looking at blind, irrational prejudice as the basis for racial profiling.

Media Distortion

BOX 7.3

The Invisible Visible Minorities

Lionel Lumb, of Carleton University's School of Journalism, wonders 'why are the millions of minorities that are so visible on our streets and in shopping malls, our offices and health care centres, so invisible on our television screens?' This observation contrasts with a 2002 survey that indicates that over 80 per cent of Canadians favour multiculturalism. Almost three-quarters of the drama and sitcom programming on Canadian TV originates in the US. Researcher Shane Halasz notes that these shows rarely feature major characters 'of colour', and there seems to be an element of tokenism, where a minority character might be included in a neutral setting such as a workplace, but wouldn't be shown in the context of their own culture or home life.

Source: Adapted from Media Awareness Network (N.d.).

Another interpretation, however, is that the police force is staffed by people who have studied the statistics on, say, illicit drug or weapon possession. Suppose the statistics show that one out of every 20 vehicle inspections will uncover a drug or weapon, but the yield is twice as high for black drivers as for white. If this is a valid statistic, all else being equal, the police officer whose job is to search suspicious vehicles would make a rational choice to concentrate on vehicles with black drivers. Here, as once before, we do not need to import the concept of prejudice to understand this behaviour, which is rational but unjust.

Psychologist Gordon Allport (1947) proposed a third and much less obvious theory about prejudice and discrimination, stressing its irrational side. Adapting a variant of Freudian thought, Allport argued that racial and ethnic minorities sometimes become a kind of blank screen onto which we project our fears and fantasies. We all have fears, from time to time, about being cheated or deceived, and may come to focus those fears on particular racial or ethnocultural groups that are identifiably different from us. Doing so simplifies the process of finding a scapegoat to blame in the future.

For instance, stereotypes of 'the Jew' have often fulfilled this role in European history. In many societies where they were reviled and excluded, the Jews were blamed for usury (lending money at interest) and also for communism, for clannishness, and for cosmopolitanism. Interestingly, such images have not been restricted to Jews, however. In fact, any group that has historically served as a minority merchant or money-lending class has been envied, hated, and feared—also, characterized—in the same ways. Depending on the society, Scots, Arabs, Turks, Armenians, Asian Indians, Chinese, and Koreans—as well as Jews—have all historically played this middle-man role and been hated for it. This imaginary characterization of these groups corresponds to a version of Freud's *superego*: all brain and cunning.

Where groups are singled out for prejudice and discrimination, often violence is not far behind.

Abuse and Violence

In some parts of the world, inter-ethnic strife is characterized by extreme violence. Certainly, this has been true in the US since the days of slavery; it continues today in the disproportionate imprisonment and execution of African-Americans, especially in formerly (mainly southern) Confederate states. Some scholars believe that violent racism may have simply changed form, and the continued practice of capital punishment in the United States is a holdover from the days of slavery and lynching (illegal hanging). American states that

Many see immigrants as a threat to national economic and social wellbeing. This has given rise to various racist and neo-Nazi groups.

today make the greatest use of capital punishment are those that held slaves and practised lynching in the nineteenth century. So, violence against black people in the US has certainly not ended; it has arguably taken a more legitimate, legal form.

In other parts of the world too, we see ethnic violence flaring up in the recurrence of historical hatreds. Consider the mass murder of Kosovo Muslims under the Serbian (Orthodox) leadership of Slobodan Milošević in the 1990s, or the 1994 genocidal warfare in Rwanda where one tribe, the Hutu, tried to exterminate another, the Tutsi. While the Hutus did not succeed, they may have killed as many as 800,000 in one short, explosive period. Currently, the mass murder of hundreds of thousands continues in Darfur in southern Sudan, loosely based on regional, ethnic, and religious differences.

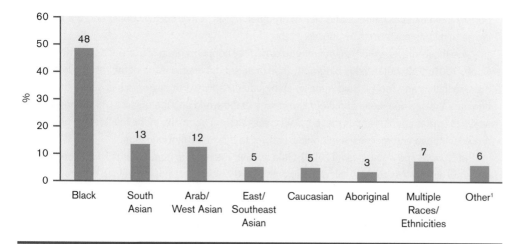

Figure 7.6 Percentage of Race/Ethnicity Motivated Hate Crimes, Police-Reported, Canada, 2006

1. Includes all other hate crimes where the type of race/ethnicity is not otherwise stated (e.g. Latin American, South American).

Source: Adapted from Statistics Canada (2006b), Chart 2.

These events are real and the hatreds that give rise to violence all have a history; the fears of future violence are not entirely imaginary. A history of violent relations between groups is likely to engender fear in at least one of the groups—fears of revenge and retribution, for example. In Rwanda's neighbouring country Burundi, the Tutsi had wiped out an estimated 100,000 Hutu in 1972. Similar intergroup strife between Sunni and Shi'ite Arabs has characterized the history of Iraq. Moreover, the Poles have a long history of conflict with the Russians, Germans, and Ukrainians. Typically, the group that has been most victimized most fears further victimization; but sometimes the victimizers also fear reprisal.

Today, there is a seeming cycle of violence between the Israelis and Palestinians, with each justifying its violent actions by referring to earlier outrages by the other party. Some have claimed there is a historical clash or misunderstanding between the West and East, and between the Judeo-Christian and Islamic faiths. Whatever the reasons for this continued violence, there was a need to open up the discussion about Western perceptions of non-Western peoples, and Edward Said made a start.

People Are Talking About . . .
EDWARD SAID

Edward Said was born in Jerusalem in 1935, when the city was part of British-occupied Palestine. His father was an American citizen of Palestinian descent; his mother was half Lebanese. The language of their home was English, rather than Arabic, and they belonged to the Anglican church. The family spent much time in Cairo during Said's youth, moving there permanently in 1947, and maintained ties with family in Jerusalem. Said's father ran a small business in Cairo, and Edward attended a British preparatory school there.

Said began to study at an elite Massachusetts preparatory school at the age of 15. He graduated from Princeton University in 1957, and did graduate studies at Harvard, earning his doctorate in 1964. He began teaching at New York's Columbia University in 1963, eventually becoming a professor of English and comparative literature in 1970, where he remained for the rest of his career.

His best-known and most influential work, *Orientalism*, was published in 1978. In it, Said contends that the Western view of the Middle East, which is perpetuated in scholarship and journalism, as well as fiction, has imposed upon the cultures of the Middle East stereotypes that portray them as superstitious and violent. In other words, it has socially constructed a harmful image of middle easterners, especially Arabs.

Are these images wholly manufactured or do they contain a grain of truth? David Howarth (in Scott, 2006: 198) notes in his biography that, on this most crucial issue of the relation between representation and reality, Said remains ambiguous. As Howarth says, 'This is a vital question because it raises questions about our knowledge of the world and the objects which knowledge seeks to apprehend.' In various places, Said gives different accounts of the relationship between representations and realities, and no final answer to this important question.

In *Culture and Imperialism* (1992), Said applied the notions from *Orientalism* to look more generally at how Westerners, through hegemony and colonialism, have imagined other cultures, and how those cultures now respond in the post-colonial age.

Said's work, however was not only theoretical; like Gunnar Myrdal, he also took a practical interest in the politics and policies of inter-ethnic conflict. In particular, he began to write and speak about political and social justice for Palestinians in the 1980s. He supported the 'two-state solution' for allowing Israel and Palestine to co-exist in the same territory, while protesting Israel's oppression of the Palestinians.

As his health deteriorated in the early years of this century—he had long been ill with chronic leukemia—Said worked to finish several more books, including *On Late Style, From*

Oslo to Iraq and the Road Map, and *Humanism and Democratic Criticism*. These all appeared after his death in 2003 in New York City.

Source: Adapted from *Fifty Key Sociologists: The Contemporary Theorists* (edited by John Scott, London: Routledge, 2006) and other sources.

Jung (2009) reports that Edward Said's *Orientalism* theory was widely viewed as an application—a special case—of Michel Foucault's discourse theory. (We will discuss Foucault again in a later chapter.) It is easy to see the merit in this view; for in analyzing the Western, essentialist image of Islam as a core feature in Orientalist scholarship, Said claimed to be inspired by the work of Foucault, in particular by his books *Archaeology of Knowledge* and *Discipline and Punish*.

And as with the work of Foucault, so too with Said's work it was difficult to disentangle images from realities, and causes from effects. For example, Jung notes that Said may have been unaware that both Islamist and Arab nationalist thinkers applied to themselves Orientalist concepts in constructing their ideologies. If so, Jung argues, Said should have been aware of the reciprocal power of discourses in shaping an essentialist image of Islam; it was through the dialogs of Orientalists and Islamists that the essentialist image of Islam emerged.

Taking a slightly different course, Hevia (2009) asks whether the Western view of the Orient was truly distorted, using the example of 'kowtowing' to do so. Hevia's essay in *The Politics of Gesture: Historical Perspectives* examines the gesture of respect known as kowtowing (kneeling and bowing the head to the ground), a practice that caused much controversy in relations between imperial China and the West, especially among British and US diplomats and scholars there. The full kowtow (also *kotow*, *ketou*) involved three kneelings and nine prostrations as a 'ritual of abject servitude'. Like other Asians, the Chinese were abject subjects of despotic rulers, but the Westerners were not. If despotism and servitude were indeed more characteristic of Eastern than Western cultures, surely we cannot claim that perceptions of the 'Oriental difference' are wholly constructed, as Said might do.

On the other hand, there is no doubt that Westerners—scholars and diplomats alike—have been inclined to imagine that despotism and servitude—even passivity—are what mark people as deeply different from European cultures. Figueroa (2009) examines some of the fiction associated with Latin America—especially, the influential fiction of Garcia Marquez—and notes that one can find in it descriptions of patriarchal power, traditional peasant beliefs (even mysticism), and a confining moral economy that some liberal intellectuals might think explains rural backwardness, even colonialism. Yet, in the 1970s, Latin American peasants threw off these image of themselves when they began to protest for land reform and political change.

In many parts of the world, nineteenth-century Orientalist (and similar) scholarship reinforced colonialism. Edward Said himself believed the project that created modern Israel in Palestine was an extension of such imperialist undertaking. More generally, the enterprise of orientalism is like the enterprise of 'imagining a community' described by Benedict Anderson, with the difference that, in 'orientalizing' a population, one attributes to a group supposedly essential features that are undesirable, even shameful, and worthy of repudiation. In this respect, the viewer is imagining a community that deserves dominating. But once again, one wonders where the imagined traits come from; are they irrational fantasies, like what psychologist Gordon Allport described, or do they build on some real differences, however trivial in other people's eyes?

Given the importance of this question, and the failure of scholars to answer it (so far), we should not be surprised that a review of recent writings finds continued application of the work by Edward Said—at least 150 journal articles applying Said's work since 2001. Clearly, sociologists are talking about Edward Said. Said is important in our effort to create a comprehensive, fusion approach to sociology. His work reminds us of the relativity of perceptions in the social world. He also reminds us that insiders and outsiders will, invariably, have different views of themselves and others, especially when they compete or conflict with one another.

New Insights

Even in our dealings with other species—with non-human animals, for example—we reproduce some of the same differences we show in dealing with one another. As usual, race, class and gender enter the equation. Pedersen (2007) examines how humans interact with animals in schools, both in programs that teach animal care, and in laboratory settings where animals are used in experiments. Specifically, the study explores how social practices (both inside and outside the classroom) grant certain animals standing and credibility as actors, while denying the same standing to other animals. The more we stress the differences between animals and humans, the more likely we are to mistreat animals, this author argues. It is our view of animals as essentially 'other' than human that permits us to do so. That is why, in the end, human–animal relations are contradictory. Often, human contact with animals in schools can help improve how animals are treated in our culture. However, schools also perpetuate the notion that it is acceptable to use animals for human purposes. From this, we can generalize to other kinds of relations—for example, colonial relations—with beings that are also perceived and treated as 'others'. In this sense, human–animal (inter-species) relations can be considered a paradigm for the study of inter-ethnic and inter-racial relations.

Extending this interest, Kay Anderson (2008) examines the unstable, often nasty history of essentialist ('us' versus 'them') thought. Looking at nineteenth-century racial discourse, she finds that Europeans encountering indigenous Australians, whom they expected to be 'savages', had to rethink what it means to be human. Like explorers meeting other non-Western peoples, early explorers and settlers in Australia had their notions about culture and humanity challenged by the indigenous people they met there. Indeed, the whole array of people, animals, and plants there would have forced them to re-think their understanding of the non-European world, and to re-think their attempts to dominate it.

Critical race theory (CRT) is helpful in unpacking some of these themes around domination. For example, Romero (2008) discusses how critical race theory can usefully be applied to the field of immigration studies. He finds that sociological research on immigration in the United States is still very similar to what it was almost a century ago, as developed in the Chicago School of sociology. Researchers continue to use theoretical categories such as race, ethnicity, and immigration to investigate assimilation, acculturation, conflict between generations, and social mobility. These categories and questions contrast with more global studies of immigration that, instead, focus on racialization, social exclusion, and social inequality. He suggests that CRT could help in understanding current issues in the United States, such as racial profiling and anti-immigration sentiment, which has caused an increasing military presence, and more deaths of immigrants, at the US–Mexico border. Along similar lines, Brown (2008) argues that critical race theory is helpful in studying the effect of racism on mental health, and how racial inequality can contribute to mental illness.

According to Campbell and Kumari (2008), CRT can even be used to examine how disabled people cope with 'ableism', which, like racism, can be used to discriminate against a certain group, influencing their lifestyles and limiting their life chances. In both instances, racism and ableism, people are sorted into two categories: like us (or normal) and not like us (abnormal or 'Other'). People considered 'Other' may be excluded, ridiculed, re-imagined (as with 'Orientalization') or even viewed as animals, less than human.

In all these social constructions of imagined communities (that is, of insiders and outsiders), racial distinctions are preserved through symbolic discourse. Consider, in this connection, the role of the Confederate flag in the US. It connotes southern pre–Civil War society in which slavery was an accepted practice; and today the flag is often seen as a symbol of racist thinking. Using focus groups in a chiefly white southern university in the United States, Holyfield, Moltz, and Bradley (2009) try to understand whether the Confederate flag symbolizes racism to them, and how it relates to southern white identity. They find that young southerners consider whiteness normal, implying 'normal' behaviour and values, and view the Confederate flag as nothing more than a neutral historical emblem. This highlights the taken-for-grantedness of insider thoughts and actions that may have heavy implications for outsiders.

Analyses of race, and their relation to colonialism, continue to be useful in understanding the mass media and popular culture. So, for example, Ozkisi (2007) notes the term 'world music' started to be used to describe 'all the music of world people' by some ethnomusicologists towards the end of the 1970s. However, since the 1980s it has been used only to describe the music that belongs to non-Western societies. This reminds us, again, of the tendency to take the West as 'normal' and to take non-Western things as needing a special, non-equivalent recognition.

Chapter Summary

In this chapter, we have seen that it is only in the last few centuries that race and ethnicity have emerged as significant sources of difference in our society. We have also seen that the history of immigration to Canada is less praiseworthy than we sometimes like to think. You have learned about the impact of early immigration policies on the history of racial and ethnic relations in Canada, as well as on immigration trends in the twenty-first century. So, we elaborated on multiculturalism, both as a social policy and a characteristic of modern Canadian society.

The ideas of 'race' and 'ethnicity' are socially constructed and historically specific. In the past, people have used many different physical, religious, economic, and other kinds of markers to distinguish some human groups from others. In the future, people may make other distinctions, or none at all.

We looked at the relationship of race and ethnicity to other social factors—especially, class issues such as educational attainment and employment opportunities—and to health and crime. We considered the social interactions between different racial and ethnic groups and noted that sometimes this interaction is unquestionably negative, spurred by prejudice and discrimination, and resulting in conflict—even violence.

On the other hand, over the last few decades, the intergroup relations between minorities and the majority have grown increasingly positive in North America and around the world. In North America, at least, the social distance between racial and ethnic groups is decreasing, and in effect, people are learning to better understand and appreciate those they see as 'different' from themselves. As we suggested in the beginning of the chapter, the future of racial and ethnic relations is rooted in the friendships and relationships that students like you are creating today.

Critical Thinking Questions

1. What is the distinction between race and ethnicity? How does this distinction compare with the distinction between sex and gender?
2. How has the study of race and ethnic relations evolved over time?
3. How did discriminatory immigration policies prevent immigrants from entering Canada throughout the twentieth century? Do you think the point system is an effective method for selecting immigrants? Can you suggest a more effective way?
4. Do you think ethnic enclaves are useful or harmful? Consider this issue from the point of view of recent immigrants versus that of mainstream Canadian society.
5. Consider the differences between multiculturalism and interculturalism. Why do you think most of Canada supports the former while Quebec prefers the latter? Which do you think is a better approach? Can you suggest a third alternative?
6. How do you think race and/or ethnicity affects such things as income, health, and well-being?

Recommended Readings

Vic Satzewich and Nikolaos Liodakis, *'Race' and Ethnicity in Canada: A Critical Introduction* (Toronto: Oxford University Press, 2007). This book is an excellent and thorough introduction to concepts such as immigration, aboriginal/non-aboriginal relations, French-English relations, notions of racial and ethnic identity, sociological explanations for racism, and other race- and/or ethnicity-related issues in Canada. It encourages critical thinking when examining these topics.

Peter Wade (ed.), *Race, Ethnicity, and Nation: Perspectives from Kinship and Genetics* (New York: Berghahn Books, 2007). This book links the ideas of race and ethnicity with those of family and genetics, in the context of an ever-diversifying society.

Jorge J.E. Gracia (ed.), *Race or Ethnicity? On Black and Latino Identity* (Ithaca, N.Y.: Cornell University Press, 2007). This collection of essays explores the relation between race and ethnicity and their connection to social identity.

Frances Henry and Carol Tator, *The Colour of Democracy: Racism in Canadian Society*, 3rd edn (Toronto: Thomson Nelson, 2005). This critique of racism in Canadian policies and institutions examines the contradictions of multiculturalism and democratic racism in contemporary Canadian society.

Benedict Anderson, *Imagined Communities: Reflections on the Origin and Spread of Nationalism* (London: Verso, 1983). This classic work discusses the spread of nationalism by means of European colonialism in Latin America and Asia. A key issue examined is what social factors make people nationalistic, willing to risk everything in the name of their nations.

John Porter, *The Vertical Mosaic: An Analysis of Social Class and Power in Canada* (Toronto: University of Toronto Press, 1965). This is the first truly Canadian study on race and ethnicity in Canada, and remains influential to this day. It asks how and why ethnicity is related to a group's position in the economic structure, and examines the role of education in fostering social mobility.

Websites

Multicultural Canada
www.multiculturalcanada.ca

Citizenship and Immigration Canada
www.cic.gc.ca

Canadian Heritage
www.pch.gc.ca

First People's Heritage Language and Cultural Council
www.fphlcc.ca

Multicultural History Society of Ontario (MHSO)
www.mhso.ca

Global Gathering Place
www.mhso.ca/ggp

Toronto's Mosaic: A Reality Check
www.cbc.ca/toronto/features/diversity/index.html

Race: The Power of an Illusion
www.pbs.org/race/000_General/000_00-Home.htm

8 Age Groups

Learning Objectives

In this chapter, you will:

> Learn how population age is measured and the ways in which it is influenced by fertility, mortality, and immigration

> Recognize that Canada's population is aging more quickly than that of many other countries

> Identify the ways in which aging and age groups change in response to changes in demography and society

> Recognize the concerns of an aging society

Chapter Outline

Today, people are leading longer, more varied, and more complex lives than ever before. Within this extended lifespan, there is almost enough time now for people to lead several lives—they could have several careers, several mates, and several families, if they wanted. In the past, one career and one family were usually enough (and all you could manage in the available time). This new opportunity holds great importance for social organization.

The ideas of age and aging usually hold the most interest for older people, since they have aged the most. And because our society has recently aged rapidly and will continue to do so, there has been a surge in the study of aging and age groups. At the same time, there is also a great popular interest in the study of young people, since they are, and will become, increasingly important as consumers and citizens. This chapter looks at how the ideas of age and aging have changed over time, how sociological researchers have tackled them, and what types of challenges different subgroups (the elderly, young people) will face as they grow older.

Everyday Observations

One candle for Grandpa: Peter is at Uncle Joe's house, celebrating Grandpa Ted's eighty-fifth birthday. His large family has all turned out: aunts, uncles, cousins, second cousins, great-aunts, and great-uncles. The smaller children are all running around playing tag—largely ignoring (and being ignored) by the adults. The adults are mingling with each other, and sharing funny stories with Peter's grandfather and the great-aunts and great-uncles. Peter, in his late teens, is sitting awkwardly at the table with his cousins who are roughly his age—none of them are quite sure how to relate to their grandfather, and they sure don't want to play tag with the little ones. Finally, Peter's mom brings out the birthday cake, and they all start singing 'Happy Birthday' to his grandfather. Peter stares at the single lit candle atop the cake and wonders what it would look like with 85 candles instead.

Think about your last birthday. How many candles were on your cake? As you passed through childhood and adolescence, every year meant another candle. However, there usually comes a time when the cake holds just one candle, symbolically recognizing that too many candles are now needed to represent your age. What does this change mean to you?

Do you remember having any particular feelings about turning 10? Or about turning 17? Maybe turning 10—the first two-digit number in your life—was more momentous. When you are young, each year is important and brings many new changes and experiences. That's because each day, month, or year adds proportionally more to your lived experience than the same time does in the life of an 85-year-old.

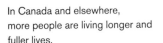

In Canada and elsewhere, more people are living longer and fuller lives.

So aging is important, but it also takes place within a historical context. It means something different to be a young adult today compared to three decades ago. The lives of young Canadians today likely include MP3 players, high-speed Internet, Harry Potter, and little spandex. Of course, some things never change, like having fights with parents, feeling insecure about the future, and wanting to change the world (or at least, your corner of it). As a university student, you may feel like you're just skirting the upper acceptable limit for not having a life plan. And almost certainly, you feel like you've heard too many stories begin with the phrase 'When I was your age . . .'. Maybe things are different because when your parents were your age, they likely had a *plan*. Maybe a few centuries ago, most fifteen-year-olds had a *plan*. Most of them would have had jobs and some may even have had children.

The fact is, different generations grow up in different times, and more often than not, finding agreement between generations is a challenge. Cultural meanings are specific to times and places, which, as you might have noticed, make it all the more difficult for different generations to understand one another. Each age group has its own concerns and worries—while the middle-aged are concentrating on being good parents, for example, the elderly are more worried about staying healthy. While the young look *forward* to better days, many of the elders look *backward* to better days.

Age distinctions become less relevant as individuals age—case in point: Celine Dion and her manager/husband René Angélil, happily married in spite of the 26-year difference in their ages.

Some things get simpler. For example, age differences concern us less as we grow older, especially when it comes to dating and marriage. What would you think about a romantic relationship between a 13-year-old and a 23-year-old? Now what would you think about a relationship between a 43-year-old and a 53-year-old? Although in both scenarios there is a 10-year difference in age, the former is more likely to raise eyebrows. For obvious reasons, the law tries to protect people thought to be vulnerable (the young and the elderly), but between the less 'vulnerable' ages—say, 20 and 70—less social protection is needed. Moreover, the law has no upper-age limit for marriage, only a marriage age floor.

Consider the legal drinking age. In Canada, it is either 18 or 19 depending on the province. In the US, it is 21. The difference in rules appears arbitrary—it does not make much sense. And what about the legal age of sexual consent? Can governments protect minors without being too intrusive and restrictive? The meanings of age and aging are always in flux, so our age-related policies need to keep changing to reflect these changes in attitudes and behaviours.

Another problem with age is that it leads to prejudice and stereotyping. Classifying people by age—even for well-intentioned purposes—can lead to discrimination: for example, the perception that teens are outrageously irrational and headstrong while elders are sickly and technologically illiterate. Or consider the 2008 US federal election. What do you think about the disapproval that Republican presidential candidate John McCain faced for being in his 70s? Was he a victim of **ageism** in his campaign against the much younger Barack Obama? Was the public warranted in its concern about McCain's age, especially given his pre-existing health conditions (cancer, heart disease), or was it just discrimination?

What does age mean to you? How does it affect your decisions? What does it mean to be 20, 40, 60, or 80? And do you think aging means the same thing it used to mean? After all, with increased life expectancy, we are gaining more time to do the things we want. So, '40 is the new 30', right?

ageism

All types of prejudice or discrimination against members of society based on an individual's age, whether old or young.

Ways of Looking at . . .
AGE GROUPS

Functionalism

As we have seen throughout this book, functionalists think that society is like a well-oiled machine, made up of supporting parts that together work as an efficient, productive whole. This perspective also views society as being only as strong as its weakest members.

One functionalist theory of aging, first promoted by Elaine Cumming and William Henry (1961), is *disengagement theory*. This theory holds that elderly people are among the weakest members of the population and that society has, therefore, devised a means of displacing them from central positions of power and influence. As people age, they undergo physical and mental decline, Cumming and Henry note. Muscles weaken, bones become fragile, most perceptual abilities decline, and cognitive faculties become slower and diminished. Elderly people are also more prone to illness and disability. At work, elderly individuals are often less efficient than their younger, stronger, and more energetic counterparts. For the good of society and for themselves, disengagement theory argues, elderly people finally give up their positions and withdraw to the edges of society, where they begin to prepare for their eventual death.

Retirement from work serves several functions for society as a whole. Each retirement empties a work position, allowing someone from the next generation to move up the social hierarchy. It also allows the retiree a moment of recognition—for example, a retirement party—for his or her contribution; and it also ensures that society replaces outdated skills and ideas with (supposedly) more useful ones. Though it may sound cold and cynical, functionalists stress that such change is both natural and crucial to society's effectiveness. Without such turnover, the economy would be less efficient and less equipped to compete globally.

Critical Theory

Many disagree with the assumptions of functionalism, especially with the assumption that the exclusion of older people from financially rewarding and socially important roles is good for society. Nor is age-related discrimination against the young necessarily useful to society, either. Critical theorists believe that ageism does not serve society as a whole but is merely a form of inequality exercised by people in the middle ages (say, 20–60) to further its own interests.

Many scholars have criticized disengagement theory as too simplistic. They say it depicts humans as robots who contribute to the financial institution for many years before voluntarily delivering themselves to the dustbin of later life, waiting listlessly for death to overtake them in retirement communities. This view is wrong, the critics say. Contrary to what disengagement theory predicts, many elderly individuals remain active and refuse to retire. Only some elderly people withdraw from society of their own will. In other cases, employers rules push them out of the workforce into retirement. Without these pushes, many elderly people would remain active for as long as possible, for many reasons. For example, active people are healthier, therefore people value being active, and retirement limits this activity. Even after retirement, many stay active as long as opportunities in the family and the wider community will allow. When elderly people disengage, then, it is often because of other people's wishes, not their own. This is the perspective taken by most critical theorists.

Critical theorists also recognize that age groups hold different interests, and each group competes against the others to enlarge its share of society's resources. A problem with this arrangement is that the young and the old are less able to prevail, since they lack the organization and the power to influence public policy that the middle-aged have. As a result, the interests and needs of elderly people and children are often ignored (or set aside) by middle-aged decision-makers.

Finally, many assumptions about aging lead directly to the financial dependence of elderly people on the rest of society. These incorrect assumptions view age itself as the cause of dependence. However, only aged people with physical and mental problems are likely to need financial help; the rest remain able to support themselves, through earnings and savings.

Symbolic Interactionism

Symbolic interactionists focus their attention on how we symbolize elderly people and enact aging in our society. They study how socially constructed definitions of age and aging affect a person's experience of growing old. The symbolic interactionists stress that age is a state of mind shaped by the labels society applies. For example, they might note that remaining happy and satisfied in the later stages of life depends largely on adopting a positive attitude toward aging. Therefore, interactionists stress that satisfaction with aging means rejecting the definition of old age as disabling.

Proponents of *activity theory* (Havighurst and Albrecht, 1953) argue that, contrary to disengagement theory (which holds that people readily give up their social roles as they age), people in fact take on new roles as they age. Such continued activity preserves a sense of continuity, helps people preserve their self-concept, and contributes to greater life

Many elderly women are living below the poverty line, on average living longer than men on less income.

satisfaction. People who keep up a high level of activity age more 'successfully' than people who do not. This can be considered a symbolic interactionist theory, because it relates role-play to self-identity and psychological well-being.

Other symbolic interactionists have examined how society, and its media in particular, portrays elderly people. These portrayals reflect society's stereotypes about older people and help reinforce those images. As a result, women tend to disappear from the media as they age more than men do. Male lead actors continue to make Hollywood movies, but same-aged women actors lose their marketability. Since the largest group of ticket-buying moviegoers is people in their teens and twenties, older women are no longer allowed to serve as compelling love interests. As well, in our society, while younger women might be paired with older men, it is rare for a younger man to be romantically involved with a significantly older woman. Here, we again see a double standard around sex and romance that disadvantages women.

Feminist Theories

The experience of aging is different for men and women, largely because, for women, aging is associated with a culturally defined loss of youth and glamour—a less critical concern for men. Women and men age differently owing to different biological constitutions. Research on medical interventions that affect the aging process—vitamin supplements and estrogen replacement therapy, for example—is still in its early stages, however. Women and men also bring different resources to old age. Moreover, they are subject to different expectations as young, middle-aged, and elderly humans (Ginn and Arber, 1995). Women in our culture dread getting older in a way that most men do not.

Today, women and men lead similar lives, in the sense that both may aim for careers. However, their careers are likely to be in different sectors of the workforce. While in the workforce, most women earn less pay than men and are less likely to qualify for a private pension during the years in which they are working. Because of this, and because their spouses or partners usually die before them, women are at particular risk of finding themselves living alone on a meagre income in their senior years. As well, a reduced income and exhausted savings may mean that elderly women are forced to sell their family homes and move to rental or institutional homes. Besides their heavier weight of disadvantage in aging, older women have more domestic duties and social responsibilities than older men.

Women also have a different role in the family division of labour. For example, unlike men, they play a vital role in kin-keeping through social networks and caregiving. These social responsibilities over the entire life course carry important results in old age. The family caregiving roles women take on at younger ages often remove women from the labour force, again limiting their pension benefits (Moody, 2000). This limits their lifetime earnings and may result in poverty after retirement. At the societal level, this contributes to a 'feminization of poverty'.

Classic Studies
Centuries of Childhood

You may imagine that childhood simply happens, like rain or the coming of winter. But 'childhood' didn't always exist as we understand it today. It was invented at a particular time, for particular reasons, as revealed in a classic study by French social historian Philippe Aries. His book, *L'Enfant et la vie familiale sous l'Ancien Regime*, which first appeared in 1960 and was later translated into *Centuries of Childhood*, is arguably one of the most influential works in the sociological study of childhood. Using historical materials that include paintings, literature, diaries, and other sources, Aries argues that 'childhood' as we know it is a cultural invention—or as we might say, a social construction. In fact, it was invented in late medieval Europe and perfected in industrial times.

Specifically, the idea of childhood came to apply first to some children, not all. Children whose families could not afford to send them to vocational schools continued to learn how to earn a living by working as apprentices to adults. These 'children' lived in an adult world with adult concerns, so their transition to adulthood was smooth though, by current standards, early. They learned very early to behave like adults and were almost immediately integrated into the adult world. Even in the upper classes, very few European children were educated at schools before the sixteenth century. Some served in the military, where they too learned to mature early and take on adult roles. And even in schools, for the few who attended, children were not divided by age. In short, age was relatively unimportant before industrial times, and childhood was almost non-existent.

It was not until the sixteenth century that people started to view children as strikingly different from adults: as pets, toys, or sources of amusement for parents. It is only then that we begin to see the growth of schooling and the introduction of child-labour and child-protection laws. But these changes had profound, unexpected effects. The emergence of childhood as a distinct stage in life had the effect of segregating children from adults. No longer were young people, say under age 10, to be viewed as proto-adults with adult-like tasks to perform in the home and workplace. Now people came to view them as different kinds of beings, with pre-adult developmental needs to fulfill before they could enter adult life.

Increasingly, children were ever more segregated from adult society by ever-increasing periods of formal education, and this process has never ended. Today, people stay in school for as long as 15 to 25 years. In schools, children form age-based communities of their own. These closed communities, with their own norms, expectations, and practices, isolate children almost completely from the world of adults—a topic we will return to in the chapter on schools and education. Unfortunately, this segregation has the effect, in some respects, of preparing children poorly for adult life. Certainly, the first few years after leaving formal education are usually difficult, as people struggle to adapt to a new way of life.

With the rise of mandatory public education in the nineteenth century, all families were forced to give up their children for at least some part of their youth to this developmental, educational task. Since then, as the paid workforce has required ever more literate and better-educated workers, formal education has continued to increase in length and complexity. In effect, this growth of education has extended the period of 'cultural childhood'—a period of non-adulthood characterized by social marginality, behavioural irresponsibility, and economic dependence. In the late nineteenth and early twentieth centuries, it became necessary to invent a cultural label to cover the new life stage between 'childhood' and 'adulthood' marked by prolonged education: this term was 'adolescence'.

Although, like 'childhood', the idea of 'adolescence' was socially invented, it also corresponds with certain important, visible changes that distinguish older children from younger ones: notably, hormonal changes (including menstruation for girls and increased sexual attraction for both sexes) and the emergence of secondary sexual characteristics (e.g., breasts on girls, facial hair on boys). Some believe that adolescence also brings with it a greater emotional volatility than is normally witnessed in young children. Such volatility may be a secondary result of rapid physical growth, hormonal change, new sexual interest, issues of sexual embarrassment and confusion, and prolonged economic dependency.

Some have questioned this strictly sociological analysis of aging, with its focus on the social invention of 'childhood' and 'adolescence'. For even childhood was seen differently before the seventeenth century, and many scholars believe that children have always constituted a separate age group. Small children have always had special needs for food, shelter, affection, and protection, and their relative physical vulnerability makes them distinct from larger, self-sufficient adults. Aries has also been criticized for using unrepresentative data, relying too heavily on the writings of moralists and educationalists (Hendrick, 1992).

Perhaps what most troubles us is that we know very little about the ways children them-selves experience and perceive childhood, as adults—not children—publish studies on the topic. Imagine how much less we know about the thoughts and perceptions of children who lived four centuries ago!

Still, Aries' analysis of the ways age groups become more distinct over time, in response to emerging social concerns, is crucial to understanding age-group relations in the past and today. As we begin to live longer and as the population becomes increasingly older, there may be even more differentiations made between age groups. History suggests that we shall have to 'invent' more age groups. In fact, we have already started to do so, referring to returned-home young adults as 'the boomerang generation'.

Youth: A Time of Risk-taking

The single most decisive difference between young people, middle-aged people, and elders—at least in our society—is the willingness of youth to take risks. Old people are the most cautious and risk-averse. Youth are the most reckless. The recklessness of young people has a variety of consequences for parents, educators, law-enforcement officials, and health-care providers.

Risky behaviours include dangerous driving and unsafe sex. For adults, these behav-iours are deviant—that is, they break rules and violate expectations. Some risky behav-iours even break laws. The first thing to note is that teenage risk-taking is commonplace and ordinary. Second, perpetrators and victims are often the same people. Third, risky behaviours tend to be largely defined by age and sex. Old youth get into more trouble than younger ones, and boys get into more trouble than girls.

Youthful risk-taking, then—even to the point of *delinquency*—is commonplace; a great many youth reading this book will have, at one time or other, been either victims or perpe-trators of delinquent acts, or both. As sociologist David Matza (1964) wrote in his classic work *Delinquency and Drift*, a great many young people 'drift' into delinquency without a strong motivation to do harm, armed with little more than 'techniques of neutralization'. These so-called techniques provide varied excuses or justifications for the rule-breaking and make the drift into delinquency morally easier.

Matza believes that delinquents share the same values and attitudes as non-delinquents, and need only the help of 'neutralizing' excuses to break rules. The drift into delinquency is common, and so is the tendency for young delinquents to leave delinquency as they become young adults with adult responsibilities.

Sociologist Travis Hirschi (1969) has developed a comprehensive theory to explain why individuals choose to conform to conventional norms and, by implication, why they break them. He assumes that everyone has the potential to become delinquent and that social controls, not moral values, preserve law and order. Without controls, he argues, people are more likely to commit delinquent or criminal acts. According to this theory, delinquents defy moral codes because their attachment to social convention is weak.

Four social bonds that routinely promote conformity are attachment, commitment, involvement, and belief. The first bond, attachment, is a person's interest in or attach-ment to others—especially parents and peers. The second bond is commitment. Time, energy, and effort spent in conventional activities—school, homework, and paid work, for example—tie an individual to the moral code of society. People who invest their time building a good reputation and acquiring property are less likely to engage in criminal acts that endanger their achievements. The third bond is involvement in activities that support the conventional interests of society—in sports, music, or community service—since such activities don't leave time to engage in delinquent or criminal acts. Finally, the fourth bond promoting conformity is a belief in the laws of society—and in the people and institutions that enforce such laws.

According to this theory, adolescents take risks and break the rules if their bonds to conventional society are weak and they feel they have less to lose than other people do. They do have only a weak 'stake in conformity'—no reputation, career, mortgage, or credit rating to endanger. Often, they have nothing they are working toward that would keep them busy and, therefore, keep them out of trouble.

Age Group Relations

As we have seen, each age group—whether young, middle-aged, or old—occupies its own social and cultural sphere, and is largely preoccupied with its own immediate concerns. Old people often focus on health and finding a new purpose in life after retirement from paid work. Middle-aged people are often concerned with marriage, career, paying the bills, and providing care for children and aging parents. Young people are usually concerned with finding their personal identity, deciding on life goals, developing relationships with intimate partners and friends, enduring a lengthy period of education and economic dependency, and weathering conflict with their parents and peers.

The conflict between generations sometimes leads to surprising alliances. Sociologists have noted that age groups sometimes ally themselves against a common generational enemy. For example, grandparents and grandchildren may form stronger bonds than parents and children, precisely because they share a common enemy—the middle-aged parents. This means that the social distance between two age groups is not always linear, a simple function of the number of years separating one group (or individual) from another. It also reflects the alliances and coalitions that cross generations.

Within this context, the aging of a population changes a society. As children become fewer and seniors more numerous, the balance of power in society changes. As one example, the flow of resources between age groups changes. In most societies throughout human history, social resources—wealth, respect, obedience—flowed upward from the young to the old. The implicit social contract used to read as follows: young people will serve the old; when they survive to old age, the next crop of young will serve them in turn. Today, the social contract reads something more like this: parents will serve their children; when they become parents themselves, these children will return the favour, paying forward wealth, respect, and obedience to their own children.

Of course, this oversimplifies the age-related changes that have occurred. Some parents are far less willing than others to endorse this agenda. Some ethnocultural groups

One World, Many Societies

BOX 8.1

Rethinking China's One-Child Policy

China's one-child policy is 30 years old. Intended to control China's fast-growing population, this policy has changed the demographic makeup of China, especially in its cities—perhaps in ways that its creators didn't foresee. In China as a whole, one in ten people are over the age of 60, but in Shanghai, for example, where the birthrate is the lowest in the country, that figure is one in five. Shanghai's population is 'getting too old, too fast'. This could change, however, if enough people take advantage of an often overlooked regulation. The one-child policy permits couples to have two children if husband and wife are each an only child. But many young couples, burdened with the care of aging parents, and without siblings to share the load, are considering whether they would be able to support even one child.

Source: Adapted from Germain (2009).

resist the child-centred transformation, remaining stubbornly 'traditional' in their views. Even so, the evidence of this transformation can be seen everywhere. First, it is amply evident that young people are no longer a source of benefits for their parents and grandparents. Prolonged formal education makes this impossible, not merely unlikely. On the other hand, many young people are no longer as dependent on their parents, or their extended families, for job opportunities or even school financing, so parents have lost much of their power to demand compliance.

Second, the age-related changes have led to, and reflected, a 'flight from parenthood'. One good reason for the worldwide reduction in fertility is that today, financially speaking, parenthood is a net cost, not a net benefit. It costs a great deal to raise children today and the benefits of parenthood are mainly psychological. There are also few economies of scale in childbearing today: when everyone needs a university education to succeed, childbearing is not 'cheaper by the dozen'. Therefore, middle-aged people have less reason to put their hard-earned time, effort, and money into raising children and more reason to put it into other economic investments and psychosocial pleasures (e.g., relaxing and vacationing).

Changing Age Relations

We noted earlier that the age structure of Western societies has been changing for well over a century. This orderly movement toward more old people and fewer young ones has been interrupted in only two ways. First, the so-called baby boom (roughly between 1947 and 1967) unleashed a surge of childbearing that had previously been held in check by the great Depression and World War II. Second, continuing high rates of immigration have slowed and masked the movement toward an older society. Most immigrants to Canada are of childbearing age and typically come from countries with higher fertility norms.

On balance then, Canada has remained young for longer than most of Europe, which didn't have a significant baby boom and hasn't had as much immigration; but this difference is about to disappear. With the rapid assimilation of immigrants and evidence that many will face economic hardship, there has been a general decline in the birthrate, sometimes called the 'baby bust'. The proportion of old people is also rising rapidly in parts of Canada with low rates of foreign immigration and high rates of youthful emigration; this is seen, for example, in small towns and rural areas, especially in the Maritimes, Manitoba, and Saskatchewan, the last having the oldest population in Canada (15.4 per cent over the age of 65[Statistics Canada, 2007e]). And, the aging population is rising wherever we find retirement communities specifically aimed at attracting seniors.

Other areas of Canada continue to draw high numbers of young people, and therefore have lower proportions of old people. Alberta was Canada's 'youngest province' in 2006, largely because of its high number of youth—the result of higher-than-average in-migration of young people looking for well-paid work (Statistics Canada, 2006c). For similar reasons, Calgary is the youngest city in Canada, with a **median age** of 35.7 years (Statistics Canada, 2007a). Younger still are the so-called frontier areas of northern Alberta, which draw many young adults, mostly male, in search of work. For the same reason, Alberta is the only place in all of Canada where men outnumber women (Statistics Canada, 2007c; Statistics Canada, 2007e).

Thus, the west of Canada is younger than the east, which has proportionally more people aged 65 and above than any other region in Canada (Statistics Canada, 2006b). Quebec also has a high proportion of old people, above the national average at 14.3 per cent—mainly the result of rapidly decreased fertility since 1960. By comparison, Ontario is a slightly younger province with about 13.6 per cent of the population 65 years and older.

To some degree, the Maritimes and Prairies (excluding Alberta) are aging because, like Saskatchewan, they are losing much of their young population to other provinces like Alberta, British Columbia, or Ontario, which offer more work opportunities.

median age

The point that divides a population into two groups of equal size based on age, with half the population above that age and half below it.

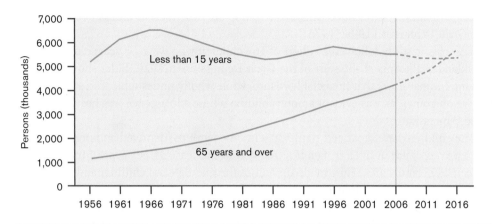

Figure 8.1 Number of Persons Aged 65 Years and Over and Number of Children Aged Less than 15, Canada, 1966–2017

Source: Adapted from Statistics Canada (2007b).

The three Canadian territories, Yukon, Northwest Territories, and Nunavut, enjoy both high rates of fertility (mainly Aboriginal, especially among the Inuit) and high rates of youthful immigration for resource-related jobs. However, the life expectancy is also lower here, which contributes to the low proportion of older adults (Statistics Canada, 2007e). For example, in Nunavut only 2.7 per cent of the population is 65 or older (ibid.). Mostly, this reflects the hardship of life in this terrain, whether in rural areas or on reserves, where many people live below the poverty line in crowded and inadequate housing.

Recently, life expectancy has been increasing among the Aboriginal population across Canada, so that by 2017, 6.5 per cent of that population is expected to be 65 or older, compared to only 4 per cent in 2001 (Statistics Canada 2007c; Statistics Canada, 2007e). Aboriginal elders remain important members of their communities, providing the children with a link to their past traditions, including language and cultural customs.

As the number of youthful dependants (infants and children) has decreased, there has been an explosion in the number of aged dependants. As the number of people over 65 steadily rises, reaching unprecedented proportions within the next few decades, the age **dependency ratio** will also increase. This increase is a source of worry for researchers and policy makers, many of whom fear that an enlarged elderly population will set off a medical and economic crisis and intergenerational conflict. Some use terms like 'agequake' to illustrate the significance of this, in their opinion, imminent problem.

dependency ratio

The proportion of people who are considered 'dependants' (under 15 or over 65 years old) compared to people 15 to 64 years, who are considered of working age.

Classic Studies
Children of the Great Depression

We have seen, broadly, how changes in population composition can affect age relations. Here we take a more microsociological look at the ways age and aging can affect individuals.

Because we age within a social context, changes to society will affect our experiences of age and aging. Glen H. Elder's life course perspective on aging describes the ways that historical and biographic forces act together—and on one another—to influence life decisions within specific contexts. From this perspective, aging is an accumulation of experiences and influences, so that what happens in early life has consequences for later outcomes. Elder used this life course perspective to study the effect of financial hardship during adolescence on adult outcomes, to find out the factors that mediate (or soften) such experiences. The results of this investigation are described in Elder's book, *Children of the Great Depression* (1999 [1974]).

This classic study followed a cohort of 167 children who were 11 years old and living in Oakland, California at the start of the Great Depression in 1929. Elder shows through this longitudinal study that financial hardship, while wholly undesirable, can still produce positive outcomes, as was evident among children whose adolescence was heavily affected by the Depression.

The children were separated statistically into two groups, deprived and non-deprived. The deprived children lived in families that had lost at least 35 per cent of their income between 1929 and 1933. They made up half of the middle-class children and two-thirds of the working-class children Elder studied. Their sudden financial loss altered, among many things, the dynamics of family relationships. One notable consequence was a shift in power from the father to the mother, who assumed the role of decision maker and provided emotional support. However, the Depression not only changed the role of the parents, it also changed the children's roles.

To compensate for their fathers' lost income, many teenaged sons had to work for pay, and this gave them more independence, as well as a sense of importance. It also gave them the opportunity to mingle with adults and extend their social networks. As a result, these deprived children became more likely to seek advice from a strong social network of friends and acquaintances. Exposed earlier to the adult world, these deprived children also matured sooner than their non-deprived counterparts. While assuming adult economic roles earlier, they also dated earlier and went out more often on school nights. Daughters, in addition, were expected to take over some of the household chores their mothers had previously done. This helped to scramble household roles, and a generational redistribution of work helped create a more equal sharing of power in the family.

Thus, the Depression affected some children—the deprived—more than others. And deprivation affected boys and girls differently too. Further, how children experienced the Great Depression also depended on personal qualities and family relationships. Favourable personal traits—intelligence for boys, physical attractiveness for girls, and an easy temperament for both—somewhat lessened the effects of financial hardship for these deprived adolescents. Strong positive mother–child relationships helped to buffer the effects of fathers' often-negative behaviour. However, these experiences had long-term effects too. Deprived girls, after experiencing a distant relationship with their father and stronger socialization into the homemaker role, were likely to marry and have children earlier than other girls, during or just after World War II.

On balance, Elder argues the shortened childhood and earlier entry into adulthood caused by the Great Depression did not harm deprived children in the long run. On the contrary, many children who were deprived during the Depression grew up to be useful and successful members of society. As adults, they even reported higher life satisfaction than their non-deprived counterparts. However, the outcomes were different for girls and boys: the early deprivation was more likely to damage girls' self-concepts than boys'.

As we see from this work, a longitudinal study may be needed if we are to learn the outcome of early childhood experiences. However, the results of such a study may be limited to that cohort and not always generalizable. Some reviewers criticized Elder's study on this basis, saying the study's 'sample consist[ed] of one birth cohort who . . . passed through the depression at an "optimum age" for minimizing its detrimental effects' (Mechling 1976: 419). Perhaps the results were different for children who were slightly younger or slightly older when the Depression struck; another study will be needed to find this out.

In spite of its limitations, this study shows how individual experiences are connected to socio-historical contexts. Aging occurs in families and societies; therefore social context influences the experience of a particular age—say, adolescence—and the personal history after that stage of life. Where and when we 'come of age'—have our formative early adult experiences—can make all the difference to how we age later on.

Relations between Young and Old

We gain our first experience with cross-age relations as children in the family home. There, we learn about older people by observing our older siblings and cousins, our parents, aunts, and uncles. We learn about 'old people' from our grandparents, our great-uncles, and great-aunts. And, as we age, we learn about younger people from younger brothers and sisters.

We may all have difficulty remembering the first time we actively thought about what it meant to be young or old, younger or older. Being small is probably the first kind of thing we learn about age: when you are young, you are small, and when you are small, there are advantages and disadvantages. With small size comes powerlessness—perhaps the single most important fact about infancy, childhood, and youth. Because of their size, which symbolizes their dependence and vulnerability, infants do not make the household rules they must obey. As infants, we enter a world that is not of our creation—a world that we can scarcely understand.

This is not to say that children have no influence over their parents and other older people. Children have *enormous* influence over their parents, and vice versa. But parents have the benefit of larger size and greater power. Children, like other disadvantaged groups, have great powers of resistance, however. For one thing, they have less to lose; and for another, they have time to waste. Without other important duties (the need to hold a job, clean the house, or pay the mortgage, for example) little children have a clear opportunity to employ 'terrorist tactics', using chaos, noise, and subversion to their advantage. This is the way of all disempowered groups in society. A lack of obvious power (ironically) leads to agency, and often the tactics that spring from this agency are effective. These tactics are often successful in forcing the larger, savvier parents to make treaties—to give in to children's wishes in return for temporary peace and tranquility.

As well, parents are terrified by the prospects of failure, blame, and guilt. Besides loving their children, parents usually feel a responsibility to raise them well and prepare them for life. They feel obliged to ensure their children do well at school, are healthy, make friends, and stay out of trouble with the law. They do not want to fail at these tasks—either to feel like failures or to stand publicly accused of failure. So they make strategic deals that, while keeping the peace, will raise the likelihood that a child develops as well as the experts say they should expect.

In every household then, there is the basis for an implicit deal between parents and young children. To some degree, the same even applies to grown children and their aged parents. Besides love, grown children feel a responsibility to help and care for their increasingly dependent and infirm parents. Like children, elderly parents sometimes capitalize on guilt and shame to encourage greater efforts by their children (for example, more frequent visits and telephone calls). However, elderly parents are less likely to use terror tactics with their grown children than are young children with their parents. As dependants, elderly parents are more obedient than young children, for several reasons.

First, elderly parents often have their own independent lives and do not want to abandon them. Second, they often have their own resources and do not need or expect resources, including service or money, from their grown children. In fact, some elder generations, such as the generation that came through the Depression, may even be a source of resources for their grown (baby boom) children. Third, and perhaps most importantly, elderly parents—unlike young children—have already experienced what it means to be a middle-aged parent, squeezed by young children at one end and elderly parents at the other. As a result, they are more capable of empathy and self-restraint than young children, who have (so far) experienced little of life.

Age in School and the Workplace

Other opportunities for cross-age co-operation are presented at school and, later, in the workplace. At school, children are introduced to other children, both older and younger than themselves. They experience bullying, for example, as both victim and perpetrator, often across age lines. More importantly, the age distinction is linked (once again) with authority: teachers are old, and pupils are young. Old people (the teachers) give out the homework and dole out the rewards and punishments. Young people (the pupils) must do the homework, gain the rewards, and avoid the punishments.

In workplaces, we find some of the same dynamic as in schools. In most workplaces, seniority and rank are closely linked. This means that age and rank (and authority and power) are closely related. In turn, this means that younger workers often have to take orders and punishments from older ones, on the unstated assumption that when they are more senior, they will dole out orders and punishments to new younger workers.

Of course, the fit between age and rank is looser in workplaces than in families, or even in schools. In workplaces, some people fall behind, failing to advance with seniority for various reasons (incompetence, discrimination, or the hatred of superiors, for example). More importantly, some classes of workers are younger at every stage than other classes of workers. For example, an organization may have a relatively stable and therefore old secretarial or administrative staff but a constantly turning over professional (for example, engineering or legal) staff. As a result, young engineers or lawyers will often be interacting with, and even giving orders to, older secretaries and administrators.

This poses a classic problem in social organization: the problem of respect for age (also, seniority and presumed experience) versus the respect for expertise. How should the respectful young lawyer or engineer relate to the supposedly less powerful, but older, more experienced, and knowledgeable secretary or administrator? Everyone with experience in organizations knows the wisdom of cultivating workmates with inside information, even if they hold positions of nominally low authority in the organization. People who foolishly

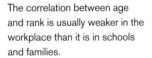

The correlation between age and rank is usually weaker in the workplace than it is in schools and families.

ignore this rule of thumb often find themselves organizationally blindsided by misinformation or false information, rumours, or gossip. A failure to learn from older subordinates may derail or at least slow down their careers.

Francis Ianni's classic book, *A Family Business* (1972), the ethnographic study of an American crime family, provides another interesting example of the age-versus-experience problem. In organized crime, success means millions of dollars in revenue and failure can mean death or imprisonment, so members of the 'crime family' are keenly aware of organizational problems related to authority and succession. Here's the kind of problem they need to consider: Should they take advice from nephew Donny, the bright young whippersnapper with an economics degree from MIT but little experience or standing in the 'family'? Or should they take advice from Uncle Vito, the high-ranking 'capo', not too bright but a tough, responsible, and reliable leader in times past? True, it's Vito's 'time' to rule, but Donny has more up-to-date ideas about marketing, competition, and legitimate business. Remember, a wrong decision can be costly—even, fatal.

Classic Studies
Mean Streets: Youth Crime and Homelessness

Not only the elderly experience problems of deprivation. Consider the problems that young people face when they live on the streets, as revealed in a classic study by John Hagan and Bill McCarthy.

The primary goal of Hagan and McCarthy's study *Mean Streets: Youth Crime and Homelessness* (1997) was to examine how and why youths leave home for life on the street. The study sheds light on the daily toils and survival strategies of nearly 500 street kids in Toronto and Vancouver. In *Mean Streets*, the authors go against most current criminological research on youth crime which 'has been almost exclusively based on the work of 'school criminologists', academics whose work is based on the self-reports of young people living at home' (Piliavin, 1998: 414). Thus, the authors are focusing on a particularly deprived, crime-ridden group of young people.

The study first identifies the risks facing youth who come to live on the street. Street kids' problems have often begun at home with parental abuse and neglect, often in impoverished neighbourhoods where their parents may suffer unemployment. Many of the youth, especially boys, have suffered from violent outbursts by parents depressed or angered by a low or insecure income. Eventually, their schoolwork starts to slip, and a combination of poor grades and conflict with parents and school administration leads many of the youth to drop out of school. But too little social capital and poor skills limit the choices of these youth after leaving home and school, so the street is all that's left.

Why do youth subsequently turn to criminal behaviour after leaving home? The authors say it is because they cannot meet their basic daily needs like food, shelter, and clothing, so for them crime is a survival strategy. The authors note that hunger leads to

Despite Canada's relative economic prosperity, approximately one third of the homeless population in Canada is comprised of adolescents.

theft of food; hunger and lack of shelter lead to serious theft; and unemployment may lead to prostitution. Lacking social and economic capital, street youth develop 'criminal capital' to survive—'knowledge and technical skills that promote criminal activity, as well as beliefs or definitions that legitimize offending' (Piliavin, 1998: 138). Their social embeddedness in a network of other street kids helps them pick up information and necessary skills for criminal activity—in short, it provides 'criminal capital'.

This study shows the effects of faulty parenting, 'anomie' (Merton), and 'differential association' (Sutherland) on the development of criminality among young people. It also addresses issues of social policy. For example, Hagan and McCarthy note that Toronto and Vancouver approach their street youth differently. While Toronto adopts a social welfare approach, with organizations like youth hostels that provide shelter, Vancouver adopts a crime control approach, with the police picking up homeless adolescents and either jailing them or returning them to an abusive home environment.

Neither of the latter strategies offers a successful solution 'to the problems that cause youth to leave home in the first place' (ibid, 1997: 108). In fact, recent research on the homeless shows a large proportion are caught in a 'revolving door' of movement between jail and the streets. However, the policy differences result in different youth crime rates in the two cities. Where street youth receive social assistance to meet their daily needs, crime rates are lower. Otherwise, the problem continues unabated. The study concludes that 'fundamental social problems of family unemployment and underemployment, lack of flexible education and training opportunities and crime control responses to the by-products of socio-economic marginalization increase the probability of these youth turning to crime' (Benjamin, 1999: 423).

Like Glen Elder, whom we discussed earlier, Hagan and McCarthy employ both quantitative and qualitative methods to 'build a complex longitudinal picture out of class, family, school, parenting and other issues that significantly contributed to adolescent homelessness' (Flesher, 2001: 1586). Their findings pose a major challenge to social welfare legislation and crime control strategies. However, despite recognizing the greater effectiveness of Toronto's approach to street youth, compared to Vancouver's, the study fails to recommend policy changes. This is particularly unfortunate since, likely, the problem has worsened since the book was written. Research for this study was carried out in the late 1980s and early 1990s, and the book was published in 1997. Since then, cuts to social spending have continued, especially in Ontario. We need more research to assess how, and how much, homeless adolescents have been affected by these changes. Then, we need legislation to solve the problems this population faces.

Hagan and McCarthy's study sheds light on the harsh realities that a specific age group—adolescents—sometimes has to face. Teenagers, however irrational, reckless, and brash, do not run away—or at least remain away—from home just to spite their parents. It takes a strong determination to stay on the street. What is happening at home must be bad enough to make living on the street a better alternative. So the findings of this study also provide a strong indictment of family life in many Canadian homes.

Note the difference between this study and the classic study by Elder, mentioned earlier. Contrary to Elder's seeming claim, children do not always benefit from adversity; it does not always make them stronger or wiser. Conceivably, many children were strengthened by—or at least not permanently harmed by—the Great Depression because they understood the causes lay outside their families' control. Even parental abuse could be understood as the result of a massive economic dislocation in the society. However, many of the children who take to the streets today are unable to accept this explanation for their parents' neglect or abuse; and for them, the loss of childhood may have longer-term, and far from beneficial, effects.

Bad parenting and its negative consequences, including abuse, are often reasons enough for a child to leave home. However, different types of problems arise at different points in the lifespan—so older and younger age groups face their own unique challenges. Here we will outline the ways in which age creates adverse conditions (crime, poor mental and physical health, abuse) for younger and older age groups.

Age and Crime

One of the best-understood facts about delinquency is that few of the young people who commit delinquent acts graduate to serious, adult criminality. Likewise, few of the young people who experiment with nicotine, alcohol, and recreational drugs graduate to adult drug addiction. From this, we learn that an important transition takes place between youth and adulthood that turns most people away from addiction and crime, whatever tendencies they may have shown to that point.

A theory proposed by Jackson Toby (1957) is that tendencies toward crime and addiction weaken as people develop a 'stake in conformity'. This happens as they pursue educational and occupational plans, form strong love relationships, and otherwise develop a sense of purpose in their lives. A more general version, *social control theory*, asserts that we are all inclined to break the rules (whether these are criminal laws or rules about drug use), but we are less likely to break these rules if we accept the legitimacy of social control. Typically, this social control regulates our relations with significant others, for example, including the rules our mates lay down. However, it can also mean *internalized* values that grow out of relations with significant others in childhood or adolescence.

The crimes and misdemeanours of young people, including their abuse of drugs, may indeed be a response to conflicts with parents, teachers, and other adults in authority: a form of acting out or youthful protest. They may also be ways that young people ingratiate themselves into their peer group, demonstrating rebelliousness and, therefore, worthiness of respect and love. In only the rarest, most extreme cases—cases illustrated by the street youth we discussed above—do these tendencies persist and flourish, for obvious reasons.

Age and Mental Health

One of the great paradoxes about aging is that, for mainly chemical reasons, many old people often develop depression; yet the majority do not and they tend to be happier and more contented than young and middle-aged people. If asked, they are more likely than, for example, adolescents, to say they are satisfied with life (Henchoz, et al., 2008).

One might wonder then, what do old people have to be so happy about? Or to put the question differently, how can they possibly be happy, given the evidence of prejudice, ridicule, abuse, and loss of social importance that they experience? Likewise, what are young people so miserable about? How can they be so unhappy, given their physical health and all their sexual, educational, and career opportunities, as well as the many new experiences that await them? The answer is so simple as to be (almost) overlooked: how happy you are depends on how high you set your expectations. With low enough expectations, you can be happy with almost anything. In addition, a long life gives people plenty of time to lower their expectations, and ample experience in doing so.

Perhaps equally important, seniors today are, as a group, far more economically secure than seniors were in the past. If they compare their own lives with those of their parents and grandparents, they are likely to feel happy, even blessed. This may be particularly true of people who grew up with memories of the Great Depression, as discussed by Glen Elder.

Thus, unhappiness, anxiety, and depression may not be good indicators of an age-related problem for old people in our society. However, these same indicators—and even suicide—are likely to call our attention to the many pressures young people face in our society. These pressures are certainly age-related, reflecting the difficulty of transitioning from dependence to independence, and childhood to adulthood. They also reflect the challenges young people face in meeting the huge pressures on them to succeed and to make their parents proud. These problems are not issues of ageism or age-related mistreatment by parents and other elders. Instead, they are a result of societal and cultural pressures that surface when society begins to view someone as a responsible, soon-to-be citizen.

Age and Physical Health

Some have judged that poor physical health may provide a better indicator of faulty age relations than poor mental health; and certainly, we see evidence that both young and old people suffer distinctive health problems. For example, young and old family members both suffer elevated risks of domestic violence. They also suffer elevated risks of domestic neglect, including poor nutrition, poor supervision, poor preventive health care, and poor compliance with medical advice. These forms of health negligence often translate into poor health for young and old family members, though they sometimes also affect other members of the family who are old (or young) enough to know better.

Accidents are another source of poor health for both young and old people. To some degree, this reflects family characteristics, as some families are much more accident-prone than others. Childhood accidents in some families result from a lack of adequate parental supervision, which in turn may reflect too many competing time demands—an especially common problem in single-parent families. Faulty supervision may also reflect other familial problems, such as parental addiction or depression. Finally, higher rates of accidents may reflect residence in a particularly dangerous household, neighbourhood, or community; and this in turn tends to reflect income and class disadvantages.

So, like unhappiness and depression, poor physical health is a poor indicator of faulty age-relations, or ageism. Young and old people may suffer worse-than-average health, but

On average, older adults are more likely to experience chronic diseases and have poor health than younger adults. However, older adults are much healthier today than in the past.

not because of prejudice and discrimination. These may play a part in producing poor health, but so do many other important factors.

Due to better lifestyles and health care, today's seniors are actually healthier than previous generations, so they are living longer. However, this comes at a cost. According to the Canadian Community Health Survey (CCHS), seniors are more likely to see family doctors on a daily basis than are younger people (Statistics Canada, 2003). Moreover, 92 per cent of seniors take at least one type of medication, 14 per cent have been hospitalized in the past year (three times the rate of people under 65), and 15 per cent receive home care.

Though healthier than their parents and grandparents were, older adults are less healthy (on average) than their children and grandchildren—for example, they are much more likely than younger people to have poor health or experience chronic conditions (Statistics Canada, 2006a). According to the CCHS (Statistics Canada, 2003), 81 per cent of older adults suffer from at least one chronic disease and 33 per cent have three or more such conditions.

The conditions listed in Table 8.1 are the top ten most prevalent in Canada, and the percentages are shown both for older and younger adults. Arthritis/rheumatism and high blood pressure are especially significant problems, and higher among elderly women than elderly men, partly because women live longer, but also for other reasons such as generally higher distress and anxiety among women. Senior women are also more likely to receive home care and take a wide variety of medication more frequently (ibid).

A higher prevalence of health problems in seniors taxes the health-care system, and will increasingly become a major economic issue as Canada's population, and the world's, increasingly ages. Already, adults 65 years and older (and children less than a year old) take up most of the funding and services provided by Canada's health-care system. Seniors account for one-third of all hospitalizations and more than one-half of hospital days (Statistics Canada, 2006a). In 2006, seniors alone consumed about 44 per cent of all health-care spending. So, the use of health care by seniors is not only higher than that of any other age group, but three times higher than their share of the population.

With universal health care in Canada, the use of health care by seniors does not vary much by social class. In 2003, Statistics Canada found that poorer and less educated seniors were no more likely to use Canada's health-care services than were wealthier, more educated seniors (Statistics Canada, 2006a). Only their number of chronic conditions

Table 8.1 Prevalence of Chronic Conditions, by Age Group, Canada, 2003

	25–34	55–64	65–74	75 and over	65 and over
Arthritis or rheumatism	11.1	31.8	44.2	51.5	47.3
High blood pressure	8.5	29.2	41.0	45.2	42.8
Back problems excluding arthritis	21.1	25.5	24.0	24.3	24.1
Other allergies	28.3	26.2	23.2	21.1	22.3
Cataracts	0.7	4.6	15.7	27.6	20.7
Heart disease	1.9	8.8	15.7	25.3	19.8
Diabetes	2.6	9.9	14.1	12.7	13.5
Thyroid condition	4.5	9.3	11.9	14.2	12.9
Urinary incontinence	1.5	4.2	8.2	14.0	10.7
Asthma	7.5	7.8	7.5	7.7	7.6

Source: Statistics Canada (2003).

predicted the frequency with which seniors saw a physician and took medication. Stated simply, in Canada, people with many health problems see the doctor more and take more medicine, whether they are rich or poor. This differs markedly from the findings of US studies that income and educational attainment have an impact on health, with poor people at higher risk for poor health and less health care. Likely, this reflects a central difference between Canada and the US: the effect of universal health care in Canada and its absence in the US.

In the past, we thought of old people as disabled, because aging was indeed disabling for many. However, this link between disability and age is weak today, if not non-existent. Many seniors are not physically disabled until quite advanced ages, while many younger people live for decades despite a physical disability. Statistics Canada shows that incidence of disability has been rising in recent years across the age span, for both young and old (Statistics Canada, 2007d; Statistics Canada, 2008). An increase in disability rates at all ages likely indicates a true change in disability profiles and reporting practices. It means that, thanks to modern health care and social services, people are able to lead long, often active lives despite physical disabilities that, in the past, might have significantly limited and shortened their lives.

Abuse and Violence

In recent years, just as we have become more aware of domestic violence against women, we have also become more aware of domestic violence against children and elders (World Health Organization, 2002b; Deshaw, 2006).

In general, any vulnerable individual or group is at risk of violence and abuse, whether physical, verbal, emotional, sexual, or otherwise. What is especially pernicious about *domestic* violence is that it takes place within the family setting, which is supposedly committed to loving and protecting its members. Child abuse and elder abuse are therefore not only dangerous and hurtful; they are deeply hypocritical.

Evidently, children are at greatest risk of violence in the households where women (that is, wives and mothers) are at risk. Seen from this angle, child abuse is part of a package of domestic abuse associated with patriarchal values: the notion that an all-powerful father has the right to punish family members at any time, and in any way, he thinks proper. This generalization about patriarchy likely covers many cases, but it does not cover them all. First, in many families women—mothers—are the family disciplinarians, the source of at least some child abuse. Related to this, violence is often intergenerational. People, whether male or female, who experienced violence and abuse as children are more likely to dole it out as adults.

Second, the patriarchal theory also fails to explain elder abuse, whether by the husband or wife and administered to an elderly male or female. Sometimes, grown children (or grandchildren) abuse their elders as revenge for the abuse they suffered in their own childhood. As some people say, 'What goes around comes around'. No doubt, many grown people harbour continued resentment towards their parents, owing to abuses, neglects, and other hurts they suffered at the parental hand as children. The stewardship of these now-infirm parents provides an opportunity for payback.

A third, more general explanation has to do with caregiver burden. Even in countries like Canada, with universal health-insurance programs, many informal caregivers (made up mostly of family members) are needed to support dependent children and older adults with health-care problems. For older adults, support networks provide 75–85 per cent of the care received in total (Statistics Canada, 2007d). This means that many people in our society are caregivers; and caregivers are heavily burdened—often burnt-out—by the responsibility. Caring for sick children or other vulnerable and infirm dependants can be taxing physically, mentally, psychologically, financially, and socially. Long-term caregiving can result in depression and illness in the caregiver, among other problems (Goldner and Drentea, 2009). Abuse may be a result of long-term effects on the caregiver.

Much of the research on aging and elders is non-theoretical, aimed at solving the many practical problems facing children, older people, and their caregivers. An exception to this seeming rule is the work by German sociologist Karl Mannheim who was, perhaps, the first to generate theories about age relations as a sociological, rather than social, problem.

People Are Talking About . . .
KARL MANNHEIM

Karl Mannheim was born in 1893, in Budapest. In addition to the social sciences, he studied philosophy and languages at several universities in Hungary, France, and Germany. He taught sociology for a few years at the University of Heidelburg, and then headed the department of sociology at the University of Frankfurt until 1933, when he, a Jew, was forced to leave by the Nazi government. Mannheim then taught sociology at the London School of Economics until 1945, and died in London in 1947.

In his early work, Mannheim promoted the idea that the intellectual elite should lead the way in championing freedom. *Ideology and Utopia* (1929, translated into English in 1936) pioneered the field of the sociology of knowledge. Later, he began to write about the struggle for democracy and freedom, and the moral, social, and political aspects of these concepts.

In their biography, David Kettler and Volker Meja (in Scott, 2007: 83) note that 'In explaining the linkages between social locations and ideologies, Mannheim expressly avoided the notion that groups only talk about the world in a certain way because this promotes their economic interests. He . . . did not consider it to be the ultimate account of ideology. He explores instead the metaphorical language of "perspective" and "standpoint". Things simply look different from different locations.'

This holds true for his understanding of generation as a social influence. Mannheim was the author of roughly 50 major essays and treatises, and one of those essays founded generational research. 'On the Problem of Generations', published in German in 1928, outlined Mannheim's analysis of the impact of generational experience on groups of people across class and geographical lines. Mannheim portrayed generations as 'sources of opposition, challenging existing societal norms and values and bringing social change through collective generational organization'.

The three building blocks of Mannheim's theory of generation are identified by Bryan Turner and June Edmunds in their book *Generations, Culture and Society* (2005):

Generational Site or Location: Mannheim taught that a generation could be defined by the shared experience of a traumatic event or catastrophe—for example, the experience of war loss suffered by German youth in 1918—that unites a particular cohort of individuals into a self-conscious age stratum.

Generation as Actuality: Mannheim critiqued the Marxist tradition of class analysis, a too-narrow approach to understanding knowledge and identity. Age groups, he observed, are able to act as agents of social change and become carriers of intellectual and organizational alternatives to the status quo. In this respect, they may just as important as social classes.

Generational Units: Mannheim wrote about 'articulate structures of knowledge or consciousness that express particular location'. Even though each generation may include within itself 'differentiated, antagonistic generation-units', they belong together because of their orientation toward each other. Here Mannheim foreshadows the work of people like Dorothy Smith and others who promote a 'standpoint' theory of social knowledge.

Source: Adapted from *Fifty Key Sociologists: The Formative Theorists* (edited by John Scott, London: Routledge, 2007) and other sources.

Mannheim played a central role in the twentieth century development of a new concept of 'generation' (Kuljic, 2007). Related to this is his understanding of the link between class and generation, and how ideas about the formation of generations help us to understand social dynamics over time. Mannheim's essay on this topic stems from the generational experience of Hungarian intellectuals during the collapse of the old order of the Dual Monarchy and the Revolution of 1918–19. The Budapest intellectual life in the 1910s was important for Mannheim's 'On the Problem of Generations', although it has implications far beyond that. It is for that reason the generations concept has migrated from one culture (Germany) to others (Canada and the United States, for example), and from one discipline (sociology) to many others.

Feixa and Leccardi (2008) note that since August Comte and Karl Mannheim, the concept of generation has been a relevant topic in social sciences and humanities. 'Generation' has influenced both academic and public debate; in the latter, especially those about youth. Like Weber's debate with Marx about the importance of status groups, Mannheim's debate with Marx about the importance of generations reflects an attempt to re-conceive politics and power in an age of upheaval. No wonder the concepts also became important in the ideological and political debates of other regions like Latin America, Africa and Asia, wherever youth have played a central part in revolution-making.

Merico (2008) agrees that Mannheim's works on generation offer a useful framework for the analysis of youth's role in significant social change. In 'On the Problem of Generations', Mannheim himself connected the concept of generation with social change, arguing that individuals, social groups, and the socio-historical context all affect one another. Throughout the 1930s and 1940s (the 'English period'), while looking at different aspects of social reality, Mannheim continued to pay attention to young people and their role in social change. For this reason, he paid particular attention to the importance of 'social education' as a means of forming, mobilizing, and focusing generations of young people around important political issues.

Weller and Pfaff (2008) agree on this point, pointing out that this may be why much of youth research today is concerned with the links between education, political change, and social change.

Laaksonen and Oinonen (2008) attempt to apply Mannheim's theory on generation to the youth of today, noting that individuals of the same age make up a generation with distinctive characteristics if they experience a forceful social, cultural, economic, or political event during their formative years. So, for example, today's young Europeans were in their teens and early twenties when the Berlin Wall came down in 1989, beginning a chain of significant political, social, and economic changes in Central and Eastern Europe. They entered their adulthood in the enlarging European Union. So, during their formative years, these young adults have lived in a different world than their parents did at the same age. This fact shows up in different attitudes toward working life and family formation in three Catholic European countries: France, Poland, and Spain. Young adults in all three countries bring higher expectations of freedom and fulfillment to both intimate relations and the workplace in these countries, reflecting the possibility that such expectations are more attainable today.

Mannheim suggested that one's view of an event depends on one's location, and that different perspectives provide different insights. Schwartz (2005) examines whether different perspectives can produce distortions as well, by looking at how interpretations of Lincoln's Gettysburg Address have changed over the years. Lincoln made this speech in 1863, during the American Civil War. At that time, and for some generations following, people understood the address to urge them to continue the fight for freedom and the preservation of the American Union. Today, however, many historians understand the speech to be about emancipation of slaves and racial justice. Schwartz suggests that people today read into a text such as the Gettysburg address more modern struggles, such as those for minority rights.

De Sousa (2006), however, notes the difficulties and complexities involved in studying generational change. These include the lack of homogeneity within generations and the different ways generational changes play out in different countries. Here, it seems evident, an intersectionality approach is needed: the effect of generation, like the effect of gender or race, is often filtered through a set of interacting influences.

At the same time, generational influences are globalizing. Edmunds and Turner (2005) note that generations are often discussed within national boundaries. However, since communications technology can now bring people together around the world as traumatic events unfold, 'global generations' have come into being. The authors trace the beginning of 'international generations' in the late nineteenth and early twentieth centuries, showing how people are linked by books, magazines, and newspapers. In the mid twentieth century they find the 'transnational generations', linked by radio and television. And in the late twentieth century, the 'global generation' emerged, linked by the electronic media.

Thus, a review of recent writings finds continued application of the work by Karl Mannheim—over 60 journal articles applying Mannheim's work on generations in the last 20 years. Clearly, sociologists are talking about Karl Mannheim. He deserves a place in our comprehensive, fusion approach to sociology because his sociology of knowledge approach reminds us that every social location—whether defined by class, gender, race, age, or generation—gives the social actor a unique vision of society. The problem, then, is to understand how people create or negotiate a shared vision, for purposes of collective action.

New Insights

As noted, these 'local perspectives' on aging are made even more complex by cross-national differences. Yet, often, it helps us to rethink our understandings of aging and generations through the eyes of sociologists who live outside North America and Western Europe. So, for example, Ondrejkovic and Majercikova (2006)—Slovakian sociologists—write that, like those around the world, families in Slovakia are changing in every way—in education, work, standards of living, liberalization, and women's self-image. Young Slovakians are adopting postmodern attitudes that survive alongside more traditional notions. For example, in an increasing number of marriages, young people no longer appear to see marriage in a patriarchal context, and imagine in it new possibilities. This may be familiar to Canadians but new to Slovakians, an indication that people are coming to lead more similar lives throughout the world.

Phillipson and Biggs (1998) note that developments in social **gerontology** have brought an increased confusion about social identity in later life. Central to this has been a growing interest in lifestyle choice as evident in a change from modern to postmodern forms of aging. A key part of this process has been the erosion of a predictable framework for an aging identity, previously supplied by the welfare state. Today, we tend to rely on state policies to define who is old—e.g., has a right to old-age pension—and those who are not. However, these policies are starting to fray, with a departure of many states from the social welfare arena. So, the emergence of 'no-care zones' in health and welfare, alongside postmodern ideas on consumerism and the body, have undermined identity in old age. Blank spots—'no-identity zones'—have emerged that fail to sustain an authentic framework for supporting experiences in old age.

The study of aging, naturally, is related to the study of time and how we view time. D'Agostino (1998) argues that the very concept of identity and its evolution through stages of the life cycle toward adulthood are intertwined with the symbolic representation of time. Whether considered in prehistoric, historical, or transhistorical terms, time is always related to the idea and reality of death, though related to each in different ways. In the

gerontology
The scientific study of aging and old age.

postmodern world, where accounts of the past are hotly debated and accounts of the future are distrusted, conceptions of time tend to focus on the present—a present that incorporates the past and the future. As a result, many feel ambivalent about death because it is clearly an event in a 'future' they cannot contextualize. This keeps their identity trapped in a time warp that is deeply individualized, even isolated.

However, for more traditional thinkers, the study of aging is also the study of flow over time. Johnson (2003) claims that though life is essentially transient, we are wrong to focus on death to find the significance of time, and that we should give our attention to 'lived time'.

Biggs (1999) argues that, given the social norms that surround aging, it may be difficult to determine what lies behind the mask and whether it is possible to outline what an authentic existence in later life might be like. Contemporary trends, through stereotyping, decontextualize old age, separating it from the life course as it has been lived. To surmount this problem, we must examine memory and the life course to find the authentic foundations of aging. This means recognizing the importance of multiple identity choices, a unique personal past, and social possibilities that promoted the expression of some selves and not others. In short, Biggs adopts the Elder life course approach as postmodern.

We also need to rethink how we theorize later life, by introducing the insights of Foucault and drawing out social issues largely ignored in applied gerontology (Powell, 2009). Powell uses 'Foucauldian gerontology', to show how the discourse of health care providers creates a social construction of aging and constrains older people.

These problems of inauthenticity are compounded in groups that are already stereotyped and stigmatized. Consider the visibility and identity problems faced by older lesbians.

With more generations co-existing, there are more opportunities for both cooperation and conflict.

Fullmer, Shenk, and Eastland (1999) note that lesbians tend to form their identity around their sexuality, as this is how society defines them. But for older lesbians, this important aspect of identity, with its associated empowerment, is often missing, as society does not characterize older women as sexual beings.

Hockey and James (2002) explore how such identity-making across the life course might best be theorized. Despite debates around this, the body remains central to such a theoretical project. Human embodiment is central to any understanding of aging and the life course, because we are all embodied beings passing through time. While medical science has pushed back the material limits of bodily aging in ways that promise delivery of the authentic, idiosyncratic 'life course', traditional, chronological notions of aging persist. In this context, media debates that privilege a naturalist discourse are presenting a regulatory framework to preserve age-based sexual and reproductive identities. Such regulatory structures—that is, such notions about 'normal aging'—impinge on the body's materiality, but they are also resisted by the agency of individuals.

Blakeborough (2008) agrees the media can have complex, regulatory meanings for the viewer, but they can also be subversive. Consider the images of aging in *The Simpsons*. Although these can be understood as stereotypical depictions of ageism, this cartoon series also uses parodic irony to invert meaning and undermine stereotypes, thus achieving a postmodern, culturally subversive goal.

Continuing this line of argument, Powell and Longino (2002) claim that postmodern gerontology looks at how aging is culturally depicted, and attempts to see aging in a positive light. They believe that by focusing on the 'aging body' as a primary form of analysis, scholars can generate new theoretical understanding into cultural representations of the body.

For her part, Torres (2000) argues that postmodernism's interest in erasing traditional conceptions of majority and minority populations threatens an understanding of ethnic conditions that affect aging processes. By contrast, a more explicit ethno-gerontology supports a solution-oriented approach. That said, a postmodern approach to critically assessing ethno-gerontological knowledge would also benefit future research and theorizing.

Chapter Summary

In this chapter, we looked at aging and the ways in which the trend toward living longer, more complex lives affects individuals, families, and societies. With longer life expectancies, populations are getting older and more generations are co-existing. Sociologists attribute this increase in population age to decreased fertility (and only secondarily, to decreased mortality). Sometimes this pattern may not be readily recognizable, as immigration can conceal the dramatic and continuing drop in fertility. An aged and aging population raises many concerns, including the cost of health care, the provision of care at old age, and elderly poverty.

We have seen that the concept of distinct age groups is socially constructed. Nevertheless, because this concept is socially important, it is real. Different roles are ascribed to members of different age groups, resulting in distinct groups with sometimes opposing outlooks. The friction between age groups can be partly explained by Glen Elder's life course theory, which posits that aging is always situated in a socio-historical context. Different generations, socialized into different social contexts, have different expectations. If left unresolved, these intergenerational disagreements can produce terrible outcomes that may include violence, depression, and abuse.

However, it may be possible to overcome these conflicts. With increased awareness and policy changes that reflect the changing demographics of society, multiple generations may be able to co-exist more happily in relative peace.

Critical Thinking Questions

1. What main factor has contributed to the significant rise in the proportion of older people worldwide? How do we know?
2. Keeping in mind the current phase of economic recession, how do you think the large population of old people in the future will affect your own role as a citizen of this society?
3. How are the experiences of aging likely different for Aboriginal seniors, immigrant seniors, and other Canadian seniors?
4. How are the experiences of aging likely to be different for women and men?
5. As mentioned earlier, a Statistics Canada survey found that poorer or less educated seniors are no more likely to seek health-care services than their wealthier, generally more educated counterparts. Why do you suppose this is? And why is this finding surprising?
6. Why were the concepts of 'childhood' and 'adolescence' socially constructed? That is, how did society, or any social groups, benefit from this construction?

Recommended Readings

Philippe Aries, *Centuries of Childhood: A Social History of Family Life*, trans. Robert Baldick (New York: Knopf, 1962 [1960]). This is a classic work about the social construction of age periods, such as childhood. It examines the history of how Western society 'invented' the concept of childhood with the advent of education and other social changes.

V.L. Bengston, N.M. Putney, and D. Gans (eds), *Handbook of Theories of Aging*, 2nd edn (New York: Springer, 2009). This is a highly useful book for students, covering differences among aging theories. The authors promote cross-disciplinary theorizing in the field of gerontology, with an aim to inform public policy and contribute to positive social changes for older adults.

Neena Chappell, Lynn McDonald, and Michael Stones, *Aging in Contemporary Canada*, 2nd edn (Toronto: Pearson Prentice Hall, 2008). This is a useful introduction to social gerontology in Canada, with demographic, theoretical, and research information on aging in relation to women, ethnic groups, health and well-being, health care, families, retirement, and so on. All the information is comprehensive and current.

Sara Carmel, Carol A. Morse, and Fernando M. Torres-Gil (eds), *Lessons on Aging from Three Nations* (Amityville, NY: Baywood, 2007). In this two-part volume about research on the 'art of aging well', the authors examine aging populations in three countries: Australia, Israel, and the United States. Among the topics examined are how people cope with aging and especially how they deal with health problems in reference to each country's health-care system.

Jennifer Cole and Deborah Durham (eds), *Generations and Globalization: Youth, Age, and Family in the New World Economy* (Bloomington, IN: Indiana University Press, 2007). This collection of studies argues that societal conceptions of childhood, youth, adulthood, and old age will shift as the world continues to globalize, transitioning to a global economy and an international flow of information.

Ingrid Arnet Connidis, *Family Ties and Aging* (Thousand Oaks, CA: Sage, 2001). This book by a Canadian sociologist of aging examines issues of intergenerational family ties with a microsociological focus. From specific examples, the book draws out the significance and macrosociological implications of these relationships in reference to aging.

Websites

Canadian Association on Gerontology (CAG/ACG)
www.cagacg.ca/whoweare/200_e.php

International Association of Gerontology and Geriatrics (IAGG)
www.iagg.com.br/webforms/index.aspx

The Gerontological Society of America (GSA)
www.geron.org

Zoomer Magazine Canada
www.zoomermag.com

Canadian Association for Adolescent Health (CAAH)
www.youngandhealthy.ca/caah

9 Classes and Workplace

Learning Objectives

In this chapter, you will:

> Learn about the theories of class relations that various sociological thinkers have proposed
> Observe how the organization of work has changed over time and recognize the factors that have influenced these changes
> Identify the kinds of class inequality that exist today and their effects on health and crime

Chapter Outline

The study of social class is one of the oldest, most central topics in sociology. The importance and influence of class relations is reflected in the many terms people use every day to refer to social class, such as *powerful* and *powerless*, or *wealthy* and *poor*. Historically, the best-known, most influential sociologists were concerned with studying and understanding social classes, so this topic has a long pedigree.

Any discussion of class also concerns class conflict. This conflict, as we will see, usually results from conflicting economic interests. For example, wealthy business owners will likely want to pay their workers the lowest possible wages and spend very little on their working conditions. For their part, the employees will likely want to secure the highest possible pay and best possible working conditions. These kinds of tensions between employers and employees may have always existed, but their expression has undoubtedly changed over time, with changes in the organization of work.

The organization of work has indeed changed over human history. In this chapter, we will explore some historical changes in the workplace, and then examine the organization of work today. For example, the shift from a rural, agricultural to urban, industrial society, and from simple to complex tools, had a profound effect on human work and class relations. This chapter will review what sociologists have had to say about social classes and labour, and the trends that support or contest their ideas. Finally, we will discuss the outcomes of class relations, in terms of how they affect other aspects of people's lives.

Everyday Observations

Gaining a foothold: Getting his first job was a challenge for Daniel. Few of the resumes he sent out led to call-backs, and even fewer led to interviews. Every potential employer wanted prior experience in the field—but how could he get this experience if he wasn't hired anywhere in the first place? After weeks of trying, Daniel finally had some offers. But choosing between these was also difficult, since none were ideal. Some jobs paid less, others required long hours; still others were only part-time. Where were all the careers? Daniel's father had entered his career in his mid-twenties and stayed there securely until retirement. For Daniel, it seemed like all he could find—at best—were jobs, jobs, jobs.

Consider a job you held at one time or another. How did you get that job and why did you leave it? Did you ever feel deeply dissatisfied with that job—the work you had to do, the pay you received, or the way your employer treated you? Well, people have various experiences when they try to earn an income, and some of their experiences are unpleasant. Some feel they should be receiving a higher wage and better working conditions. Many leave to look for better jobs, even better careers; and college advertisements fan this flame, urging people to advance their careers through more education, thus becoming happier in their work.

Of course, the satisfaction people feel depends largely on what they want out of work and what they have come to expect. When considering your own future work life, do you want a stable and fulfilling career, or a series of jobs that don't demand too much effort? Some people look for creative challenges in their work. Other people are more concerned about stability and financial security. They may even take a boring job that gives them stability instead of a job in a domain that is continuously evolving, adapting, and generating new sources of conflicts. For an interesting discussion of that difficult choice, read hockey-great Ken Dryden's book, *The Moved and The Shaken* (1993).

The three founders of sociology—Marx, Weber, and Durkheim— all were concerned with the workplace conflicts arising out of **class** relations. They all were writing a century or more ago, in a period when the power of early capitalists was virtually uncontrolled. This privileged capitalist class exploited the working class to gain high profits and social dominance. Note, however, that Marx, Weber, and Durkheim all offered somewhat different analyses of this situation and suggested different solutions. For example, Marx saw this conflict as a problem inherent in capitalism, while Durkheim saw it as one inherent in industrialism.

Today, this debate and others continue, but the questions are now slightly more complex, because the modern workplace is more complex. Equally complex is the modern economy, characterized by global competition. As a result, modern legislation about the relations between workers, managers, and owners is also more complex than it was a century ago. So, our job as sociologists is more complicated today than in the days of Marx, Weber, and Durkheim. Yet we continue to be fascinated by the same questions: How does economic and social exploitation affect the 'have-nots' in our society? How do the powerful 'haves' maintain their dominance? How does the working class struggle to improve its situation? Are high rates of unemployment or underemployment necessary? And there is a new question: Are class relations better today than they were a hundred years ago, and are they improving or getting worse?

class

According to Marx, a group of people who share the same relationship to the means of production, or to capital; according to Weber, a group of people who share a common economic situation, based on (among other things) income, property, and authority.

The organization of work today is much different than it was in previous decades, let alone in previous centuries. Though still highly influential, in our age of late capitalism the theories of Marx, Weber, and Durkheim are a little too simple. For example, these days, mainly managers and directors, not 'owners', control capital. This means 'relations of production' and 'class relations' are far more complicated than they once were. Moreover, state institutions, not private interests, exercise much of the power in our society, and state institutions can be as oppressive as capitalists, even if they don't own the means of production. Most important, the exercise of economic and political power today is global and multinational, so we must ask: How should we re-conceive class conflict in global terms?

Yet, amid these huge questions, we continue to wonder about smaller, more micro-sociological questions: for example, about the 'work experience' and how it can be improved. Like Marx, we ask about the social, economic, and psychological consequences of being exploited at work. Marx warned that capitalism alienates workers—isolating and estranging them from their work, the products of their work, their fellow workers, and even from themselves. Under some conditions, workers may become aware of their exploitation, and surmounting their alienation, take action to resist the oppression. Under other conditions, they do not, channelling their frustration and rage in other directions (for example, against women, children, and minority groups).

If they mobilize for action, workers may form unions, demanding that working conditions improve; in doing so, they may even take the concerns of the workplace into the streets. This leads us to ask questions about unions and unionization: What are the advantages of unions for the working class? Are there any disadvantages? How have unions changed over the decades? What are the factors that cause union membership to vary over time, from one country to another, and one industry or occupation to another? Why has union strength declined in the West over the past 30 years?

Above all, we need to understand that work is fundamentally important in our lives. Few people do not work, or can afford not to. Yet, for most people, work is not only about money. Work is what most of us do, most of the days in our lives, so it is a major source of our social and personal identity. When adults meet for the first time, they often ask each other 'So, what do you do?', hoping to find out something *important* about the other person. This shows that work—the way we fill our days and earn our income—is highly significant to us and other people. Like sex and age, work status is a defining feature of all social life.

Ways of Looking at . . .
CLASS AND WORK

Functionalism

As we have noted, workplace inequalities translate into broader social and economic inequalities; and sociologists often debate the significance of these inequalities. A functionalist, for example, may argue that poverty and inequality serve important purposes in society. Under capitalism, inequality comes to be defined as a graded ladder of people with different occupational roles and income levels. In this context, poverty motivates people to work harder to move up the ladder. The jobs at the top of this ladder require much more investment in education and effort, and they therefore carry greater rewards. They are also, according to this theory, the most socially useful and valued jobs. So, inequality is good because it brings out excellence and productivity.

Consider, as an example, the job of physician. Doctoring requires a great deal of skill and expertise. A physician needs many years of education to develop his or her skills. After obtaining a medical degree, the physician then faces a highly stressful career filled with long shifts and hard, challenging work. By contrast, consider the job of serving coffee and doughnuts at Tim Horton's. The training required to do this job is minimal; likewise, the job complexity and associated stress and responsibility are perceived to be minimal.

When investments in skill and effort are consistent with compensation, as with doctors and doughnut servers, the functional theory of inequality works well. However, investments and compensations are not always in balance. Consider the inflated salaries received by professional athletes, entertainers, and criminals, or the much lower salaries of nurses, teachers, and child-care workers. In these cases, the compensations do not obviously suit the social importance of the jobs and the study and sacrifice required to do them. Of course, the athletes, entertainers, and criminals may have invested thousands—even tens of thousands—of hours perfecting their 'skills', but how valuable are these skills to society? Could we survive without them? Of course we could.

Functionalists also believe that everyone needs work—also, love and hope. Work is especially important because it gives people a way to acquire the material necessities of life—food, water, shelter, and clothing—for themselves and their families. However, not only does paid work let workers satisfy their physical needs, it also allows them to satisfy their emotional needs. These include the needs to be productive and valued members of society, to gain recognition and praise, and to interact and co-operate with others. Thus, work has social as well as economic purposes. It provides a basis for social interaction, social solidarity and cohesion, and the sharing of lifestyles and meanings. The workplace, ideally, lets people exercise all of their social and creative impulses while earning a living and producing national wealth.

Critical Theory

A critical theory of poverty and inequality will typically rely on ideas first developed by Karl Marx and Max Weber. This sociological approach, focused on class conflict in industrial economies, has always been popular outside North America and enjoyed a surge of popularity everywhere in the late twentieth century. Whether as followers of Marx, Weber, or later synthesizers (like Rolf Dahrendorf, C. Wright Mills, Gerhard Lenski, Erik O. Wright, and Anthony Giddens), critical theorists always look for power inequalities and exploitation. In relation to class, they ask, *Who benefits* from the way power is organized in society, especially in the workplace?

In functionalist analysis, unemployment is the sign of a personal failure—perhaps, a lack of skill or ambition. In critical theory, unemployment is a structural condition manipulated by the ruling capitalist class to boost profits. According to Marx, capitalism inevitably creates cyclic (or repetitive) unemployment. Bursts of high productivity, under profitable conditions, lead to overproduction, which in turn drives down prices. With the fall in prices, capitalists stop investing and the economy slows down, creating the conditions for a recession and loss of jobs. This alternation between boom and bust leads to periodic cycles in the economy that repeatedly leave workers unemployed. The trick, for capitalists, is to get into a market while the profits are rising and get out before they start falling. However, workers—reliant on a wage for their survival—do not have the same flexibility; so they inevitably suffer most when markets collapse and gain least when markets expand.

The threat of unemployment also lets capitalists threaten workers who demand too much. Repeatedly, the cycle of employment and unemployment empties and fills a **reserve army of labour**. Workers who protest too hard in times of high unemployment find themselves replaced by people from the great pool of the unemployed. In this way, capitalists use the unemployed to prevent or quash labour unrest. Workers are less likely to demand higher wages if they fear they will be replaced by even cheaper labour; and lower wages means higher profits for the capitalists.

reserve army of labour

People who, because they are impoverished and often unemployed, form an easily mobilized, easily disposable workforce at the mercy of employers.

Marx claimed that class relations under capitalism cause all the conflict within and between societies. Given their opposed interests, the two classes are locked in a conflict that plays itself out largely in the workplace. In this 'contested terrain' (to use economist Richard Edwards's term), there can never be peace and co-operation because the interests of workers and capitalists are opposed. From this point of view, the workplace is not a place for sociability and creativity; it is a place for repression and mistreatment, in which some groups of workers are even more vulnerable than others. Here, low-end workers—the most vulnerable workers, those most in need of a stable income—are often the first to lose their jobs when the economy periodically goes into a slump.

Feminist Theories

While feminist theorists tend to subscribe to a critical analysis of the workplace, they note that women and men, even within the same class, may have very different experiences. For example, they note that Canadian women—whatever their class—are still disproportionately engaged in work that provides little or no pay—that is, they engage in social reproduction. As a result, capitalists profit from the hard work of women even more than they profit from the hard work of men; and men, who usually occupy higher-paid jobs than women, often profit at the expense of women who work for them. The result among women is job dissatisfaction, a lack of job control, and a rising prevalence of depression and other psychosomatic illnesses.

Symbolic Interactionism

For their part, symbolic interactionists focus on the ways that meanings are attached to social inequality: for example, how the labels 'wealthy' and 'poor' are constructed through social interaction. The typical though unspoken stereotype of a poor person in North American society runs as follows: a lazy, irresponsible, undeserving, freeloading ethnic minority member (probably black, Latino, or Aboriginal) who relies on welfare and social assistance rather than finding a steady job to support him- or herself; a person who probably dabbles in petty crime and spends much of his or her money on alcohol and drugs; possibly a violent and dangerous threat; and a nuisance to society. On the other hand, the stereotypical depiction of a rich person is this: a person who is greedy, shallow, snobbish, egotistical, callous, wasteful, and probably white, with no qualms about stepping on others for personal gain; someone born into a well-off family and accustomed to living a life of sheltered privilege; someone who has inherited the already sizable wealth of mommy or daddy, and therefore has not had to expend any personal effort to build the family fortune.

Symbolic interactionists also focus on the meanings of work and unemployment for the individual. Work, especially in a modern, individualistic culture, provides a major part of our identity. Because a person's line of work is so central to his or her identity, others often use it as a source of information. 'So what do you do for a living?' is the second-most common question asked whenever two strangers strike up a conversation (behind only 'Hi, what's your name?'). Many people also treat occupational titles as status symbols, basing their assessment of an individual largely on the prestige and income associated with the work that he or she does.

Social Constructionism

Social constructionists always ask, *How* did the arrangement *emerge*? We know from *Contested Terrain: The Transformation Of The Workplace In The Twentieth Century* (1979) by Richard Edwards that historically, management practices evolved from simple (or direct) control, to technological control, to what he calls bureaucratic control. Accompanying this was an evolution of management strategies and ideologies that reflected changes in the work done and technology used in the workplace. As well, they responded to changing worker strategies to thwart managerial practices of control. As one means of control no longer worked, another would be invented and taught to new generations of managers; and with each change of strategy, there was a new ideology of control.

Social constructionists are interested in charting the changes in ideologies about work and worker control. Similarly, social constructionists are interested in the evolution of popular thinking about work. In the 1950s and 1960s, many people expressed concern about alienating work—how work in large organizations turns people into robots. In the 1970s and 1980s, the main concerns changed to the exploitation of workers here and abroad, the possibility of computers replacing humans in the workplace, and the need to secure more leisure. Since then, with the rise of globalism, the main concerns have been job insecurity, job loss (that is, the export of jobs to low-wage countries), and the spillover effects of bad work lives into people's family lives and health.

Some of these concerns are evident in the classic work of sociologist Harry Braverman.

Classic Studies
Labor and Monopoly Capital

Harry Braverman began his working life as a coppersmith and laboured for years in related trades. As a skilled craftsperson, he saw first-hand how capitalism transformed craftwork —a transformation that shaped his later union activism and writing career.

His major work, *Labor and Monopoly Capital* (1974), influenced by the writing of Marx and Engels, explores the evolution of capitalist production over the last two centuries. Braverman argues that work, while demanding ever higher levels of education and expertise, is becoming ever more mindless, bureaucratic, and alienating. It is being 'degraded' as capitalists seek to increase their control over the labour process by separating execution from design, or 'hand-work' from 'head-work'. Despite occasional claims to the contrary, the goal of management under capitalism is not to humanize work but to lower labour costs and increase efficiency, to improve the firm's ability to compete internationally.

In this study, Braverman recognizes that not only does the separation of skill and knowledge degrade the meaning of work, it also separates jobs into those requiring (1) a small number of highly skilled, highly trained individuals whose time is seen as valuable, and (2) a mass of simple labourers whose time is considered worth next to nothing. In the twentieth century, white-collar work (including clerical work) came to enjoy higher status than blue-collar or manual work. However, in recent decades, even white-collar work has lost its cachet, due largely to its growth and depersonalization. Braverman argues that in the nineteenth century, the few clerical workers were considered to be '. . . highly skilled, trusted assistants to an owner'; but with the '. . . growth in banking, intermediary stages in the movement of goods, distrust built into accounting systems within and between firms, and the rise of the independent audit', clerical labour expanded (Coleman, 1975: 647). In doing so, office work also 'proletarianized'—that is, became more regimented and controlled, like factory work.

The proliferation of clerical workers led to the application of *scientific management* techniques, the standardization of operations, subdivision of skills, and eventually the freezing of pay levels into a hierarchy. In time, this pattern of proliferation has led to degradation even in the new, more highly skilled occupations of the modern workplace. Even highly regimented professional careers, such as law practised in large law offices, is becoming degraded, through a loss of professional discretion and job security. Braverman highlights this spread of job degradation in society by quoting efficiency theorist Frank Gilbreth (1914) who said, 'Training a worker means merely enabling him to carry out the directions of his work schedule. Once he can do this, his training is over, whatever his age', of which Braverman (1974) writes, 'Is this not a perfect description of the mass of jobs in modern industry, trade, and offices?' In other words, work, and our mental image of work, is being degraded slowly but surely whether we recognize it or not.

Despite its limitations and criticisms, Braverman's book highlights an important and worrisome trend in modern work, which degrades the well-being and satisfaction of workers and reduces society's ability to profit from the creativity of these workers.

Labour and Classes

As we have seen, 'social class' in Marxian terms is defined by the way people earn a living (whether as owners of the means of production, or as wage-workers); and in Weberian terms, defined by how much money and status people gain from their occupation. Therefore, classes and the work people do for a living are fundamentally linked. However, there is more to 'social class' than the work people do. To fully capture the significance of the concept, we also need to relate it to power, as well as to earnings and status.

Marx was the first theorist to place class at the forefront of sociological thinking, so it is useful to return to his ideas of class. As mentioned earlier, in Marx's logic there are two main classes: the **bourgeoisie** and the **proletariat** (2008 [1848]). This binary—the 'haves' and 'have-nots' of society—is fundamental to all social relations and all class conflict, since these two classes have different interests and are therefore permanently locked in conflict. At the same time, the two groups are interdependent, since each gains at the expense of the other. This link between bourgeoisie and proletariat is, therefore, a paradoxical relationship.

Because they do not have the capital needed to own the means of production, the proletariat must sell to the bourgeoisie the only thing they *do* have—their time or labour power. They do so to earn wages that allow them to survive. The bourgeoisie, in turn, buy the workers' time and labour power and gain profits from the goods and services that workers produce. The profit depends mainly on the price of the manufactured product minus the cost of labour and materials. As a result, making a profit depends on keeping prices high and wages (and other costs of production) as low as possible.

But high prices, low wages, and poor working conditions harm the health and well-being of workers. Accordingly, they struggle using every possible means—unions, co-operatives, legislation, and other avenues—to improve their wages, working conditions, and job security, and to moderate the prices they have to pay for food, shelter, and health care. This, in essence, is the class struggle under capitalism—a struggle that is inevitable and never-ending, according to Marx.

It is clear that people in the same relation to the means of production *ought to* have an interest in banding together. Proletarians do so to protect their wages and working conditions, and capitalists do so to protect their profit, authority, and control. But such co-operative action is far from inevitable: it takes planning and coordination. For united action to happen, people must develop **class consciousness**. However, as Marx recognized, this development, especially for the proletariat, is harder to attain than it may sound. Many factors stand in the way.

For example, employers often take steps to prevent unionization or even the discussion of worker concerns. Legislators sympathetic to the interests of owners may make laws that give employers more power (or workers less power) in these conflicts. To achieve this, corporations with a vested interest in the legislation may lobby (or pay off) the legislators. Police or military forces may be called in to break strikes.

As well, workers themselves may be reluctant to co-operate with people of different racial or ethnic groups within the proletariat. Or, the workers' representatives in unions may not agree on how best to promote workers' interests. However, much subtler factors may also prevent workers from mobilizing. For example, workers may be under the

bourgeoisie

According to Marx, the controlling class, which owns the means of production.

proletariat

According to Marx, the subordinate class, who work for wages from the bourgeoisie.

class consciousness

A group's awareness of their common class interest and their commitment to work together to attain collective goals.

false consciousness

A willingness to believe in ideologies that support the ruling class but that are false and disadvantageous to working class interests.

influence of **false consciousness**, a state reinforced by the *dominant ideology* of society, perpetuated by capitalists to keep workers in line. The workers may believe they are powerless to organize against the capitalists, that they are to blame for their economic condition, or that they have no right to demand higher wages and more job security, for example.

Often, for ideological reasons, workers are unable to understand that they are being exploited. *Exploitation* by the bourgeoisie includes three necessary criteria, as outlined by Eric O. Wright (1997:10) in the form of three principles. First, according to the *inverse interdependence principle*, the economic well-being of capitalists requires the economic deprivation and exploitation of workers, since profits are shared between them. Second, according to the *exclusion principle*, capitalists must keep up the pressure on workers by excluding them from access to productive resources—for example, making it difficult for them to get capital set up their own businesses. It may even mean limiting their access to jobs, housing, and other fundamental needs. Third, according to the *appropriation principle*, capitalists take advantage of the workers, appropriating (that is, taking) their labour for a fraction of its real value.

This focus on 'exclusion' in the formation of a social class marks the introduction of Max Weber's thinking on this topic. Weber spent much of his life in a one-sided debate with Marx (who died when Weber was only 19 years old) about the nature and significance of social class in society. Marx and Weber held many similar views about social class and its relation to work and workplaces; for example, they shared a belief in the importance of power in class relations. However, Weber understood power somewhat differently than did Marx, and focused on its distribution among the classes, rather than its significance in the exploitation of one class by another. Where Marx had viewed classes as mainly economic groups, Weber viewed classes as mainly power groups.

As well, in Weber's view, there are more social classes than simply the bourgeoisie and proletariat. Consider the **petit bourgeoisie**, who may own the means to production, though its ownership is small scale. An example is the dentist you visit once or twice a year: this self-employed holder of a professional degree is (typically) also the employer of a secretary and dental hygienist. So, a petit bourgeoisie owner may hire employees, but only a few compared to the hundreds or thousands hired to work in a large factory, for instance. Obviously, members of the petit bourgeoisie do not belong to the working class, neither do they belong to the capitalist class Marx described.

petit bourgeoisie

The lower middle class; a group of people who own the means of production on a small scale, such as owners of small shops.

Point/Counterpoint

BOX **9.1**

The Debate over Call Centre Outsourcing

When you call a customer support line, chances are good that you're talking to someone on the other side of the world. Many multinational companies take advantage of plentiful, lower-cost labour (one-tenth to one-fifth the cost of North American labour) and outsource their call centres in countries such as India. The savings from outsourcing can be huge—it is estimated that General Electric, for example, saved $340 million (US) in 2002. Many companies say that the savings on call centres lets them spend more on research and development, which may, in the long term, benefit the North American economy.

It is expected that by 2015, 3.3 million jobs will have disappeared in North America due to call centre outsourcing. There is concern that savings will go to increasing shareholder profits, and not to creating new jobs to replace the ones lost. Critics of the practice urge government and business to act to protect jobs here, particularly in view of the rising North American unemployment rate.

Source: Adapted from Prodialing.com (N.d.).

What makes dentists different from business tycoons on the one hand, and clerical staff on the other? Clearly, the answer has something to do with differences in education and social status, which may also translate into differences of power. That's why Weber distinguished economic class from two other sources of power: *parties* and *status groups*. According to Weber, *parties* are associations and organizations that give people non-economic power and influence. These include the familiar political parties of our own day, but they may include other (larger and vaguer) political formations, such as political lobbies. By *status groups*, Weber means sets of people who share a social position in society, with a common degree of prestige, esteem, and honour. These status groups may be organized around any one of many shared features, including religion, ethnicity, region, or even race. Their chief defining feature is that they practise exclusion to maintain the boundaries between their own group and others.

To elaborate our earlier example, we can think of dentists as an economic *class* if we focus on their comfortable income and relation to the means of production; as a *party*, if they organize to lobby for (or against) publicly funded dental care; or as a *status group*, in their capacity as a regulated profession with the authority to train, certify and de-certify practitioners.

Weber's parties and status groups, in short, are related to social class but they are clearly different from class. Like social class, they all provide members with access to power but do so in different ways. While Marx believed that people could gain power only by owning the means of production, Weber asserted people could gain power by entering influential parties and high-status groups. In this way, they could gain power through their social position, regardless of whether they also wielded economic control. People in such positions of power would be capable of dominating others, just like the capitalists Marx described.

To summarize, Marx provided the foundations of class analysis, and Weber built on them. However, the modern sociological conception of social class is based more on Weber's theorizing than on Marx's, because Weber's is more inclusive. In a present-day **post-industrial** society, Marx's portrayal is far too simple, for several reasons. First, it is no longer necessary to own a business to control the means of production; it is only necessary to manage the organization and/or serve on its board of directors. The effective control of productive capital began to pass from owners to managers nearly a century ago, in a process James Burnham influentially called 'the managerial revolution' (1941). Second, the working class today is international, because of multinational ownership and global competition. This 'globalization' of work—an advanced version of economic imperialism heralded by Marx and Lenin in their writings on capitalism—has introduced even more difficulty into the mass mobilization of workers in any given country; for jobs can always be shipped overseas if the workers demand higher wages or more job security.

Mass production has become the most efficient method of production for many large-scale operations all over the world.

post-industrialism

An economic system based more on services and information than on manufactured goods or primary production.

The Organization of Work Today

Today, much of our work is done using computerized technology. This has led some to imagine that work will become—is becoming—less arduous, more satisfying, and more humane. For in principle, mechanization might lead workers to expect more opportunity, leisure time, and job autonomy; fewer boring repetitive tasks; more opportunity to spend time on interesting work; and generally, a more satisfying work experience.

That said, computer technology has had negative as well as positive effects. For one, it has increased, rather than decreased, workplace inequality. Computers have replaced people at the bottom of the work hierarchy, or rendered their skills redundant. For example, surveillance is now chiefly done by technology and requires only one or two employees to supervise video footage. Likewise, fewer secretaries are needed in offices to type and file documents. Increasingly, organizations have reduced the number of full-time and permanent jobs, to increase their profitability and flexibility. Though technology has not caused this trend, it has made many people more readily replaceable.

No wonder some have feared that technology, by replacing human workers, could lead to an unprecedented rise in unemployment. To some extent, this fear has been justified. However, people are still needed to invent, use, maintain, and fix technology in the workplace. Today, we understand that what is needed is a better match between the skills that people acquire and the skills that jobs require. Some workers without the necessary job skills—whether computer-based or otherwise—have had to accept **non-standard work arrangements**—sometimes called 'McJobs'—a growing type of employment in Canada. These arrangements usually do not guarantee a career, as most jobs did in the past. Such arrangements have made work less predictable and more variable.

Non-standard work typically gives employers full control over the labour process. They are able to hire and fire employees with great ease and frequency, since the kind of work they typically do—work requiring little skill and quickly learned—makes them readily replaceable. These jobs are the 'degraded' work that Harry Braverman warned against. Though profitable for employers, these jobs are often harmful for workers, who suffer stress and health problems as a result. Non-standard workers tend disproportionately to be women, immigrants, and young people, since these are typically the most economically vulnerable members of society.

Non-standard work is the fastest-growing type of employment in developed countries today. Take Canada as an example: according to Statistics Canada, non-standard work represents about one-third of all jobs (Statistics Canada, 2004). In many developed countries, there are as many people working part-time as those working full-time (Jackson and Robinson, 2000). To increase their autonomy and control, many people have become 'self-employed'. However, this self-employment does not end all problems, as people sometimes imagine. Self-employed workers must struggle to make a living in a competitive world. They have no job security and receive no pension or health benefits, unlike the employees of large organizations. Few can afford to hire others to work for them, and many work excessively long hours to build and keep a clientele.

The rise in non-standard work arrangements, such as part-time work, has even affected full-time workers. With fewer full-time jobs, more is expected of full-time workers. Many are forced to work longer hours, often unpaid, to compensate for the shortage of workers on site (Jackson and Robinson, 2000). So, while some workers today are unemployed or fear unemployment, others are under-employed—working well below their skill and training level—while others still are over-employed. This development means greater differentiation in the workforce, which leads to less solidarity and more inequality among workers.

Another change Marx would not have expected is the submergence of class politics. In many countries, class politics—the politicized version of class conflict—has been replaced by identity politics. Today, many more people express concerns about racism, sexism, ageism, or religious discrimination than about achieving economic equality or reducing class-based poverty. Concerns about economic equality are often filtered through these 'identity' issues that appeal to particular portions of the working-class or middle class: to women, visible minorities, gays and lesbians, or the elderly, for example. As a result, there is much

non-standard work arrangements
Dead-end, low-paying, insecure jobs, also known as *precarious employment*.

less concern expressed today than in the past about the economic plight of white, working-class men and their families.

This shift from twentieth-century class-based politics to twenty-first century status group–based politics illustrates more clearly than anything else the importance of Max Weber's contribution to our understanding of social inequality. However, we cannot neglect the contribution of Émile Durkheim, the third founder of sociology, who saw modern inequalities as arising from industrialization and the shift to a more differentiated, complex society.

Classic Studies
The Division of Labor in Society

In his book, *The Division of Labor in Society* (1933 [1893]), Émile Durkheim argues that modern industrial societies have different moral codes—including different laws and beliefs—than pre-modern, pre-industrial societies. This moral evolution has resulted from society's adjustment to a larger size and economic complexity, and to increased capacities for communication. Modern societies, he says, are marked by a 'moral density' that increases with the growth in division of labour. Durkheim believed two factors associated with industrialization were responsible for this growth in moral density: 'social volume' and 'material density'. A society's 'social volume' is simply the total number of its members. A society's material density is its frequency of social connections, which increases when the spatial distance between individuals is reduced (as in cities) or through advances in communication and transportation.

To see these changes, Durkheim invites us to compare societies without a significant division of labour, and those with it. In pre-industrial (older) societies, the division of labour is slight, so people lead similar lives and are bound together by their similarity. In industrial societies, with a high division of labour and specialization, people must depend on others to complete their work and achieve their goals. From this mutual interdependence in modern societies springs *organic solidarity*—with its greater individualism, variation, and the general recognition that diversity is necessary.

In turn, these changes in social experience and social communication lead to changes in law and social tolerance. In pre-industrial (older) societies, which depend on homogeneity, repressive law is the norm, and individualism is considered harmful to the functioning of society. Everyone is expected to think and act the same ways. In modern society, people are permitted to be different. Since society depends on the co-operation of all, the law becomes more flexible, practical, and open to differences. Increasingly, the legal system is based on contract, not tradition.

These changes do not run smoothly, however. They tend to weaken the moral fabric that binds people to one another and to the norms of society. One result is often *anomie* or normlessness, which Durkheim discusses at length in his book *Suicide*. Another result is the greater reliance on non-traditional units of organization (e.g., occupational groups, rather than tribe or kin). Durkheim recognizes we have yet to complete this transition. Even today, a century after Durkheim wrote his influential works, we are still searching for supportive yet flexible sources of social cohesion.

Durkheim's concern about the apparent loss of social cohesion, and the seemingly rampant individualism, has led some to criticize Durkheim for favouring society over the individual. As well, some have criticized Durkheim's assumptions about the homogeneity and simplicity of earlier societies. Misconceptions about the simplicity of so-called 'primitive' societies were common at the end of the nineteenth century, but they have been increasingly questioned since then. For example, we understand that earlier societies often had a more detailed division of labour than was previously recognized. Despite these criticisms, however, Durkheim's work was the first piece of functionalist analysis in sociology, and as such it showed how much we individuals all need society. Without social cohesion and social support, we are less productive, less secure, less fulfilled. These ideas have been enormously influential in sociology (and anthropology too), and we can see Durkheim's influence in the work of leading twentieth century sociologists, including Robert Merton, Kingsley Davis, George Homans, and Talcott Parsons, to name a few.

Though different in many respects, Marx and Durkheim both understood the importance of social solidarity, as a source of personal meaning and a basis for community mobilization.

Alienation and Collective Action

Marx, like Durkheim, noticed a sense of dislocation among the new industrial workers—dissatisfaction with and detachment from their lives. However, Marx saw this as a result of the exploitation workers were suffering under capitalism, a result he called *alienation*. Marx claimed that, under capitalism, workers experience four types of alienation. First, the worker feels alienated from the product of his or her work; once the product is finished, it is appropriated by the capitalist, meaning the worker has no connection to his or her creation. Second, and as a result, the worker feels alienated from the act of production. Since the products of his or her labour are taken away, work itself becomes a meaningless activity over which the worker has no control and no autonomy. Third, the worker feels alienated from his or her own essence as a human being—feeling like a robot, simply 'going through the motions' to carry out the labour. Finally, the worker feels alienated from other workers. Since capitalism reduces workers to replaceable commodities, workers begin to see themselves and others as less than human. This makes it hard for them to have a meaningful, authentic relationship with others and may even induce self-hate.

After its introduction by Marx, the concept of 'alienation' disappeared from sociology briefly, then resurfaced in the 1950s. American Melvin Seeman revived the concept of alienation in 1959, when he brought together the ideas of Marx and Durkheim to show how they could be used in empirical research. Seeman identified five distinct dimensions of alienation: (1) powerlessness; (2) meaninglessness; (3) normlessness; (4) isolation; and (5) self-estrangement (Seeman, 1959). Powerlessness and self-estrangement are easily related to Marxian analysis, normlessness and isolation to Durkheimian analysis, and meaninglessness to both. Throughout the 1960s, more work on alienation followed Seeman's, testimony to the fruitfulness of this concept.

Today, alienation is less often studied, but it retains its conceptual importance. Alienation remains part of the reason that many working-class people do not develop a collective sense of their class position and try to overcome their disadvantage. Many workers are alienated from politics and from one another. They find it hard to put their faith and trust in the collective enterprise of unionization and class warfare. However, when workers do manage to recognize their disadvantage, they mobilize together and often form *unions*.

Unions

Unions are for the working class what professional associations are for professors, doctors, lawyers, and others in professional fields. For example, both regulate entry into paid jobs. However unions are more concerned with improving pay, job security, and working conditions. Professional associations are more concerned with upholding the reputation and independence of the profession.

Traditionally, union membership has been higher in Canada than in the United States and Japan, but lower than in the United Kingdom and Western Europe. Historically, union formation has always been highly correlated with class consciousness. It has also been highly correlated with class awareness—the significance people attach to class in a

Workers have used their ability to strike in order to secure better working conditions for decades.

country's politics: for example, whether people are interested in and concerned about the conditions of working-class people.

Unions give working people strength in numbers: they negotiate wage settlements, set standards for working conditions, and argue for job security, among other measures. As such, unions are important to their members, the working class as a whole, and the economy. And since work is socially structured, it is always negotiable; unions ensure that such negotiations get underway.

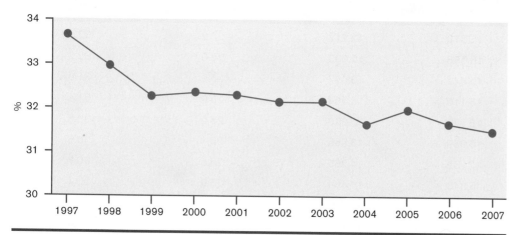

Figure 9.1 Unionization Rate, Canada, 1997–2007 (percentage of employed workers)

Source: Human Resources and Skills Development Canada (2008). HRSDC calculations based on Statistics Canada. *Labour Force Historical Review 2009* (Table 078). Ottawa: Statistics Canada, 2010 (Cat. No. 71F0004XVB)

For these reasons, it is significant that in recent decades, union membership in Canada has declined. It has been declining since the mid twentieth century, and in the last decade the percentage of the civilian labour force in unions decreased from 26.2 in 1999 to 25.2 in 2009 (Human Resources and Skills Development Canada, 2009). The decline is more marked if we focus attention on the non-agricultural (industrial) sector, where the percentage of membership in unions dropped from 32.8 in 1999 to 29.9 in 2009. This latter drop, in particular, reflects dramatic changes in Canada's labour movement, workforce demographics, labour laws, and the economic structure. Unionization has decreased among technical health workers (medical, dental, and veterinary technologists), but the statistics also reflect a loss of manufacturing jobs that have moved overseas.

Because most of the employees in manufacturing are male, this drop in union participation has been most evident among men (ibid; Jackson and Robinson, 2000). However, in recent decades, the unionization of traditionally female-dominated sectors (for example, public schools and hospitals) has actually increased slightly, marking an important difference between the experiences of working men and women. Today, the largest union (with 570,000 members) is CUPE—the Canadian Union of Public Employees, a union with a much higher percentage of women members than, say, the Teamsters Union (with 108,516 members). The emergence of vast unions of public employees, once again, illustrates the importance of taking a Weberian approach to understanding power outside traditional class boundaries.

Union membership varies according to several factors besides sex. First, unionization is more common among full-time, permanent workers than among workers in non-standard work arrangements. It also varies by region, with the highest rates of unionization in Quebec, Newfoundland and Labrador, and Manitoba and the lowest rates in Alberta, New Brunswick, and Ontario (Statistics Canada, 2007; Human Resources and Skills Development Canada, 2007). Further, union membership varies by age. A greater number of employees in

Table 9.1 Union Membership, Canada, 1999–2009

Year	Union Membership (000s)	Civilian Labour Force* (000s)	Non-agricultural Paid Workers* (000s)	Union Membership as a Percentage of Civilian Labour Force (%)	Union Membership as a Percentage of Non-agricultural Paid Workers (%)
1999	4,010	15,316	12,212	26.2	32.8
2000	4,058	15,588	12,603	26.0	32.2
2001	4,111	15,847	13,027	25.9	31.6
2002	4,174	16,110	13,304	25.9	31.4
2003	4,178	16,579	13,650	25.2	30.6
2004	4,261	16,959	13,965	25.1	30.5
2005	4,381	17,182	14,265	25.5	30.7
2006	4,441	17,343	14,464	25.6	30.7
2007	4,480	17,593	14,782	25.5	30.3
2008	4,592	17,945	15,111	25.6	30.4
2009	4,605	18,245	15,383	25.2	29.9

* Statistics Canada, The Labour Force Survey, Labour Statistics Division.
Note: Civilian labour force and non-agricultural paid employment data shown for each year are annual averages of the preceding year; data shown for union membership are as of January of the years shown and as reported by labour organizations.

Source: Human Resources and Skills Development Canada (2009).

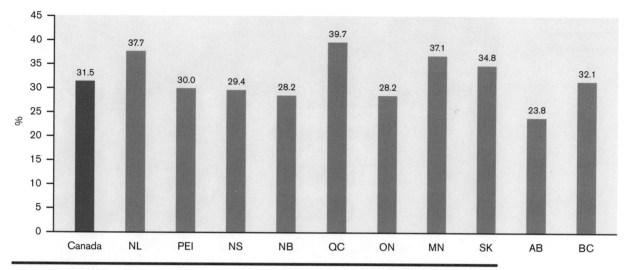

Figure 9.2 Unionization Rate, by Region, Canada, 2007 (percentage of employed workers)

Source: Adapted from Human Resources and Skills Development Canada (2008). HRSDC calculations based on Statistics Canada. *Labour Force Historical Review 2009* (Table 078). Ottawa: Statistics Canada, 2010 (Cat. No. 71F0004XVB).

unions are older (for ages 45 to 54, 41.6 per cent) than younger (for ages 15 to 24, 13.3 per cent), perhaps reflecting their long-term membership in older industrial unions.

As suggested, there are advantages to being in unions. For one, union members usually enjoy higher pay than their non-unionized counterparts do. They also gain other benefits, such as job security and extended health-care plans. These advantages are especially important for people who work in traditionally low-paid jobs. According to Statistics Canada, in 2003 the average hourly wage of full-time unionized workers was $21.01, while for non-unionized workers it was $16.65 (Statistics Canada, 2006). Part-time workers also gain from unionization, earning more and getting more paid hours of work than their non-unionized counterparts.

However, union membership in Canada and around the world has been on a steady decline over the last few decades. This decline is even more striking when we consider how strong unions were just half a century ago. What has changed in this period is the social and economic organization of Canadian society, related in large part to the rise in global capitalism, the liberalization of international currency markets, the developments in technology, the huge growth of labour participation by women, and the decline of stable working-class jobs in sectors such as manufacturing (Hyman, 2002).

The Culture of Poverty

Many people in Canadian society are poor, and many of these are unemployed or under-employed; but many others are members of the 'working poor'—people who earn the minimum wage. In a society as economically unequal as ours, poverty is particularly harmful, because, to some, it suggests a personal failure. While sociologists are inclined to look to economic or class dimensions for explanations of poverty, and the ways they interact with other issues such as racism, sexism, and imperialism, non-sociologists often wonder about the influence of cultural values. Those who are inclined to 'blame the victim' are often inclined to embrace the so-called urban culture of poverty explanation.

Anthropologist Oscar Lewis first studied this so-called 'culture of poverty' in the slums of Mexico, Puerto Rico, and the United States, noting that urban poor people are unduly likely to embrace a particular world view. A poignant version of this is found in Lewis's book *The Children of Sanchez* (1961), told from the biographical standpoint of sons and daughters of the impoverished Sanchez family, who live 'from hand to mouth'

At a protest in Vancouver, a man tries to combat perceptions of people who struggle with poverty.

in a Mexico City slum. The values and norms of this culture include a short-sighted view of the future, an impulsive or hedonistic attitude that lacks self-discipline, a failure to participate in mainstream culture, and a tendency to accept marginalized status—to hang back in the shadows.

Lewis found that many of these urban poor, like the Sanchez family, come from rural backgrounds that provided little in the way of coping skills. Without kin or social supports, let alone a social welfare net, in the city they struggle to understand an otherwise chaotic social world. Most lack the skills to attain better lives in better communities. So, they

Media Distortion

BOX **9.2**

Media Representations of the Working Classes

Think of the working-class characters you see on television—do they seem stereotyped? Social researchers such as Richard Butsch, in his article 'Ralph, Fred, Archie and Homer: Why Television Keeps Recreating the White Male Working-Class Buffoon', find that working-class men and women are under-represented in television series. When working-class men do appear, they are portrayed as unintelligent, irresponsible 'clowns'. The wives of these male characters rarely work outside the home, unlike the middle-class women seen on TV, who have not only jobs but careers.

Barbara Ehrenreich, in her article 'The Silenced Majority', finds that working-class issues are largely ignored in news and current affairs programming, and that when they are covered, it is middle-class white professionals who give 'expert' opinion on the topic. A study by the City University of New York showed that over two years, the US Public Broadcasting System devoted almost ten times as much prime-time programming to middle- and upper-class issues as it did to issues affecting the working class. And in mainstream news coverage, according to the Institute for Alternative Journalism, and Fairness and Accuracy in Reporting, union and labour issues, such as strikes, which are primarily working-class actions, either go unreported or are covered in a negative way.

Source: Adapted from Media Awareness Network (N.d.).

remain isolated, unemployed, and poor. The boys are lured into violence and crime. The girls are plunged into early pregnancy and violent marriages. Early hopes and aspirations are dashed by a cruel, unyielding reality.

This description, though too brief to capture the richness of Lewis's original analysis, is full enough to suggest why the culture of poverty theory has polarized scholarly opinion. Some say it portrays the poor as deserving their poverty because they do not make enough effort to escape it. It appears to support stereotypical characterizations of poor people as 'naturally' lazy or incapable—an idea that has long since fallen out of favour with most sociologists and anthropologists. However, the idea that certain values and ways of thinking hinder people's efforts to improve their lives and therefore keep them in poverty is still valid in current sociological thinking. And it is as old as Marx's own writings on false consciousness and the problem of class awareness.

However, in case we find ourselves thinking that poor people are morally inferior and rich people are morally superior, it helps to remember that even rich people have moral lapses: they even commit crimes. The first work on this topic was done by sociologist Edwin Sutherland.

Classic Studies
White-Collar Crime

Edwin Sutherland was another of the many eminent graduates of the sociology department at the University of Chicago, where he completed his Ph.D. Sutherland's primary area of interest was deviance, especially crime, and his book *Principles of Criminology* (1924) quickly became a standard textbook in the field, going through many editions over the next two decades. In his classic book *White-Collar Crime* (1961 [1949]) Sutherland makes an original and thorough exploration of the largely neglected illegal activities of US corporations. He even coins the term 'white-collar crime', which we understand today as corporate crime committed by individuals of high socio-economic standing.

In his research, Sutherland examined court records of 70 corporations covering a span of 45 years. Here, he found crime was widespread: in total, the 70 corporations were convicted of 779 offences, 158 of which were criminal convictions. Most offending corporations (60 per cent) had at least four convictions each, as well as many other offences. Sutherland notes that were they individuals, these corporations would likely be considered 'habitual criminals' in most states. Their crimes were deliberate and consistent, like the criminality of professional thieves. What's more, the executives of law-breaking corporations often expressed contempt for law, for government, and for government personnel.

Overall, Sutherland concludes that not only are white-collar crimes deliberate, they are also organized. Sutherland wrote 60 years ago, 'We are in transition from free competition and free enterprise toward some other system, and the violations of the anti-trust laws by large corporations are an important factor in producing this transition' (Sutherland 1949: 88). From this, he infers that persistent widespread white-collar crime undermines the ideological justification for capitalism—a lesson apparently not yet learned on Wall Street. For a recent, entertaining treatment of this topic, you may want to view the movie *The Informant*. Matt Damon plays the lead character—a truth-challenged corporate executive who decides (for personal reasons) to cooperate with the FBI to bring down a major company whose corporate culture promotes fraud, price fixing, and embezzlement.

Sutherland also argued that traditional theories about crime that focus on biological factors, poverty, lack of opportunity, personality defects, or bad family experiences—culture of poverty theories—are unable to explain white-collar and corporate crime. By contrast, his theory of *differential association* applies as well to these types of criminals as it does to poor street criminals. For white-collar and blue-collar criminals alike, 'criminal behavior

In 2007, Canadian-born magnate Conrad Black was tried and convicted of fraud in the United States. He was granted bail and released in 2010 after serving part of the sentence in a Florida prison.

is learned in association with those who define such behavior favorably and in isolation from those who define it unfavorably' (ibid).

For obvious reasons, these findings attracted a great deal of criticism, not only from the corporate world that Sutherland was attacking, but also from other sociologists. Among the latter, some criticized Sutherland for failing to state and justify how the companies in his study were selected; some said his study was methodologically not scientific enough. However, most reviews of the book were more inclined to praise than to criticize him. The first of its kind in criminology, *White-Collar Crime* was a huge success and his term 'white-collar crime' is commonly used today. Sutherland's study also developed the most influential of all sociological perspectives on criminal behaviour: the *differential association theory*.

Sutherland's study of white-collar crime was innovative because it targeted a largely unspoken issue—crime among the upper classes. Sutherland showed this kind of crime—by executives of large corporations—to be widespread.

Since Sutherland's groundbreaking work, business crime has evolved into a visible global problem. Governments around the world are putting more effort into fighting this social problem that affects the economy, government, and public. Offshore banking and bank secrecy, as historically practised through Swiss bank accounts, are widely used to launder billions of dollars stolen from people throughout the world. US treasury officials believe that 99.9 per cent of foreign criminal and terrorist money sent to the US is placed in secure accounts, making it safe from detection. Shell companies—also known as 'mailbox' companies, international business corporations (IBCs), or personal investment companies (PICs) marketed by banks and accounting firms—launder money and hide profits from income taxes.

Some experts calculate that as much as half the world's capital flows are handled in off-shore centres. For example, the International Monetary Fund (IMF) estimates that between $600 billion and $1.5 trillion of illicit money is laundered yearly through secret bank accounts. In crimes of this sort, the line is blurred between corporate crime, organized crime, and political crime.

One recent and spectacular example of business crime was contained in charges against Canadian-born magnate Conrad Black. He was found to have fraudulently misused millions of dollars from Hollinger Incorporated profit to preserve an extraordinarily lavish lifestyle. Critics said that Black had become unable to distinguish between the company's money and his personal funds. This characteristic, which Max Weber called 'patrimonial rule', was common among kings and other aristocrats before the Industrial Revolution but has been largely eliminated in companies that are publicly traded on the stock exchange. There, an expert board of directors is expected to act forcefully to protect the stockholders. In Hollinger, they did not.

Modern Forms of Capitalism

In late capitalism, a new class of people is in control of capital. It is the managers, and not the easy-to-identify bourgeois factory owners Marx theorized about, who control the fates of workers, investors, pensioners, and all their dependants. In fact, these managers are farther away from ownership and the shop floor than Marx could ever have imagined. What's more, they have more power: the economic downturn into which the world plunged in 2008 was due to the misbehaviour not of *owners* but of *managers* of the means of production. Because of mismanagement by directors, executive officers, financiers, speculators, and bankers, the economies of Canada, the US, and all the European countries are now in jeopardy.

However, the managers of capital are not the only powerful people Marx failed to consider in his analysis. Since Marx's time, other new classes have arisen that neither own the means of production nor sell their labour to capitalists but have somewhat greater influence in Canadian society than average working-class people. This includes doctors, civil servants, judges, elected officials, and other employees of organizations outside the profit sector (for example, nurses in hospitals or social workers employed by cities). Even professors of sociology fall into this category.

Typically, all of these people have expert knowledge and special skills. They also exercise authority of certain kinds without possessing or controlling wealth. The power of some of these non-capitalists (like cabinet ministers or high court judges, for instance) is sometimes even equal to that of capitalists. In an information society like Canada, knowledge and expertise, as well as capital, are important inputs into statecraft and wealth production. As a result, these people gain social importance: they carry status, prestige, even power. For that reason, many in our society consider these people to be members of the *middle class* or *upper-middle class*. Box 9.3 looks more closely at what these terms mean in a global context.

So, we can say with certainty that not all inequality in modern Canada or the US is due to exploitation in the form that Marx imagined. Some of it is a result of unregulated market forces, like inadequate laws governing the finance industry. Some is a result of the tax structure, which redistributes the national wealth from the middle class to the rich, or the middle-class to the poor. In turn, this redistribution is a result of the connection between the state and the (rich) ruling class, and the extent to which rich, powerful people can rely on elected politicians to serve their interests.

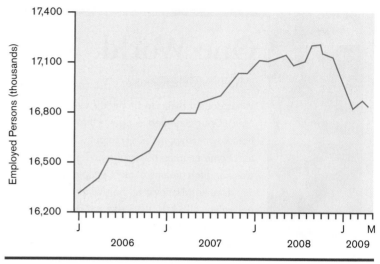

Figure 9.3 Employment, Canada

Source: Statistics Canada. *The Daily*, 11-001-XIE, Labour Force Survey May 2009, June 5, 2009. http://www.statcan.gc.ca/daily-quotidien/090605/dq090605a-eng.htm

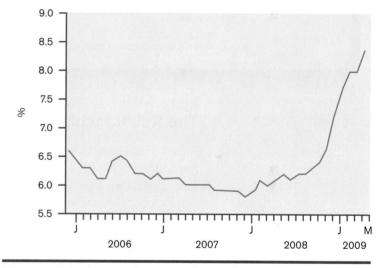

Figure 9.4 Unemployment Rate, Canada

Source: Statistics Canada. *The Daily*, 11-001-XIE, Labour Force Survey May 2009, June 5, 2009. http://www.statcan.gc.ca/daily-quotidien/090605/dq090605a-eng.htm

One World, Many Societies

BOX **9.3**

Who Is Middle-Class?

What does it mean to be middle-class, and how can middle-class status be measured? *The Globe and Mail's* Doug Saunders suggests that things like 'freedom from absolute poverty, the ability to borrow money, home ownership, the ability to put your children through school (and likely some postsecondary education) and some sources of savings and equity that could be used to start a small business' define the middle class and the dreams of most people around the world.

Branko Milanovic of the World Bank found that, by taking the median annual income of Brazil—the equivalent of $4,000 US—as the dividing line between the lower and middle class, 78 per cent of the world's population would be considered lower class, or poor. The median income of Italy—$17,000 US—separates the middle class from the upper class. By this measure, the middle and upper classes each encompass 11 per cent of the world's people.

Owning a home is thought to be a prime indicator of middle-class status. Owning property, even a mortgaged one, protects families from slipping into poverty. In the world's poorer countries, those who earn between $6,000 and $10,000 US are generally able to buy a first home. Not only does this income range agree with Milanovic's study, but it is the range often identified as middle class in much of Asia and South America.

Source: Adapted from Saunders (2007).

The Relationship Between Class and Health

An influential book by historians Richard Sennett and Jonathan Cobb, *The Hidden Injuries of Social Class* (1977 [1972]) argues that modern class warfare is usually fought without guns, instead using ideologies and legislation. However, as these authors point out, class warfare conducted in this way still injures the body and spirit, no less than physical wounds.

We know this through research on the social correlates of health and sickness. First and most important, we know that both poverty and income inequality have significantly harmful effects on people's mental health, increasing the risks of depression and anxiety. Poverty and inequality translate into surplus stress that, in turn, also translates into physical illness. It may be true that 'Money can't buy you love'—or happiness either. However, too little money, food, shelter, and safety will usually result in illness, a lowered quality of life, and a shortened lifespan. Factors associated with such insufficiencies, such as unemployment and job insecurity, predictably increase people's stress, anxiety, depression, and illness.

These risks are especially large for people who live in extreme poverty, like the urban poor discussed by Oscar Lewis or, even more so, like the urban homeless. True, many people are homeless because of earlier mental or physical health problems, conditions that rendered them jobless, socially isolated, and without money for rent. However, the street-related experiences of poverty and insecurity intensify any pre-existing mental and physical illnesses, because of exposure to violence, lack of suitable food and shelter, and poor hygiene and health care.

Similar problems are evident among people who are housed but unemployed and on welfare; who are underemployed; or who are without a stable, predictable, and sufficient income. Again, stress and anxiety—often the results of harsh economic conditions—have direct and observable effects on mental health. And even employed people are at risk of mental health problems because of workplace experiences and social inequality. Certain kinds of precarious or high-stress employment are especially likely to damage people's mental health.

Around half a million Canadian workers experience depression every year, and most say these symptoms interfere with their ability to work (Statistics Canada, 2007b; Gilmour and Patten, 2002). In addition, certain job-related factors, such as job stress, shift work (people who work at night tend to be more depressed), and hours of work (people who work too little or too much tend to be more depressed, especially those who work too little) contribute to this risk of depression. Interestingly, people in white-collar jobs are more likely than blue-collar workers to experience depression.

People with mental health problems like depression are also more likely to experience physical health problems. Two key studies have been especially informative about the link between stress, mental health, and physical health. One, by health researchers Karasek and Theorell (1990), showed that people with especially stressful jobs are far more prone to heart disease than people with less stressful and more autonomous jobs. The interesting fact about this correlation is its connection with social inequality.

Karasek and Theorell showed that many common jobs like serving in a restaurant, which carry little authority, respect, salary, or job security (given the ease with which they can be filled if vacated) are especially associated with risks of heart disease. This is because they lethally combine high job stress with low job control. Consider serving as an example. A server is at the mercy of many different people. On one side are the customers, with their whims, moods, and schedules. On the other side are kitchen and bar staff, especially chefs, who may not co-operate in speeding along the correct orders.

Defining who exactly falls into the category of 'middle class' is difficult, but one common indicator is house ownership

Conversely, the best possible job is one that lets the worker set his or her own pace and control the workflow: to decide independently what is to be done, as well as how and when it is to be done. Such a best-possible job largely eliminates the alienation of work by giving the worker more say over the work process. By this standard, professional jobs—physician, dentist, accountant, professor, or self-employed lawyer, for example—are the least alienating and healthiest—as well as being highly paid.

A large-scale series of studies conducted in Britain in the mid twentieth century arrived at a similar conclusion. These so-called 'Whitehall Studies' analyzed the health and employment records of British civil servants. (The studies are named after the block of buildings where the civil servants work.) This longitudinal project showed that a person's position in the job hierarchy is a key predictor of health and longevity. The higher a person's position, the better his or her health and prospects for a long life. This finding remained strong even after controlling for health-related lifestyle patterns. Poverty and job insecurity were *not* part of the explanation, since all the employees studied earned a regular, adequate (or better) wage.

What both these studies showed is that economic and social inequality, not merely poverty, affect people's health. Likely, they do so by affecting people's stress level—the demands made on them and their ability to deal with these demands effectively. Continued high and uncontrolled stress undermines the immune system, making the body vulnerable to a wide variety of illnesses. Intriguingly, this is the case even when lifestyle behaviours such as smoking are taken into account. High-status people who smoke fare better than low-status people who do not. Perhaps there should be a public campaign against social inequality like the public campaign against smoking! In short, social subordination damages the body and brain, causing hidden injuries of social class.

Social Class and Crime

Crime is another common response to social inequality and poverty. As Robert Merton (1957) famously said, crime is a form of 'innovation' aimed at solving the socially structured problem of a gap between ends and means. We are all socialized to desire fame and wealth, but few of us enjoy easy legal access to these rewards, and some people use illegal means to access them. To call this 'innovation' is, perhaps, to glorify crime; there is not much innovation in breaking into people's houses, stealing cars, or taking wallets at gunpoint. Most street crime by the poor is scarcely innovative at all. It is age-old and relies on stealth, threat, or violence. Even the ancient Babylonians would likely have been able to figure out how to rob a milk store.

The real innovators in crime are the corporate criminals, as shown through Sutherland's study: people like Bernie Madoff and other wealthy embezzlers, so-called Wall Street financiers and investment bankers. These innovators, aided by friendly or wilfully uninformed politicians, steal billions in ways the Babylonians could never have imagined. In fact, until 2008, many North Americans were not even aware of the possibility of such crimes, until the homes, jobs, and life savings of many of them disappeared. Criminal innovations, like other innovations, arise out of new conditions, relying on new technologies, new political opportunities, and new social and cultural formations. The largest criminal innovations are possible only in the most unequal, greedy, gullible, and risk-friendly cultures, where people are willing to believe in taking chances, believing that you can get something for nothing. Regrettably, such people—people like Bernie Madoff's investors or those who bought homes with virtually zero-interest mortgages—are gullible enough to believe that something too good to be true can actually be true.

In the late twentieth century, many people in North America, and especially in the US, forgot much of what they had known about the importance of hard work, private and public morality, and government regulation—the lessons of the Great Depression of 1929. Smitten with the glamour of inequality, they embraced a Las Vegas–style pursuit of instant fame and wealth, relying on chance and inside information. Seemingly, everyone did this: 'What happens in Vegas stays in Vegas', says the popular slogan that encourages risk-taking. It was against the cultural backdrop of fantasy and greed that we were forcefully reminded, once again, about the possible range and results of criminal innovation. The Wall Street money managers made the Mafia look penny-ante. Now that's innovation! And it relies on, creates, and preserves class inequality.

People Are Talking About . . .
GERHARD LENSKI

Gerhard Lenski was born in 1924, in Washington, DC He earned a B.A. in 1947 and a Ph.D. in sociology in 1950, both from Yale University. In 1963, he became a professor of sociology at the University of North Carolina, chairing the Department of Sociology from 1969 to 1972. His published works include *The Religious Factor* (1961), *Power and Privilege* (1966; with Jean Lenski), and *Human Societies: An Introduction to Macrosociology* (1970; with Jean Lenski).

His earliest work on social inequality was about status consistency, inconsistency, and crystallization, what he called 'non-vertical dimensions of status' (1954). Lenski notes, following Weber, that people hold a variety of social statuses—economic, educational, ethnic, and otherwise—and often these are not consistent with one another. For example, a person from an illustrious family, with a high education, may hold a low-paying job. Lenski argues that such an inconsistency in statuses produces status ambiguity, with consequences for both the individual and society, creating social tensions. Both society and the individual will have an interest in seeing these divergent statuses crystallize or converge, by lowering some (e.g., the social value of family ties) or raising others (e.g., the social value of education). In the absence of such crystallization, status inconsistency is likely to produce feelings of relative deprivation (a condition of sensed exclusion, arising from inequality) and willingness to protest the status quo.

In *Power and Privilege* (1966), Lenski describes how social stratification occurs based on how 'scarce values' are distributed among members of a society in different kinds of societies. He categorizes these societies as hunting and gathering, simple horticultural, advanced horticultural, agrarian, or industrial. In his view, technological innovation drives the evolution of society and culture, and creates the knowledge and information that permit a society to advance. Here, Lenski's work clearly builds on Durkheim's societal analysis in *The Division of Labor in Society*, discussed earlier. As a society develops new methods and technologies of communication, its economy advances and its political and social structures become more sophisticated. These changes in turn lead to uneven distribution of goods and social inequality. Like Durkheim, Lenski understands that inequality is rooted in the way society is organized for production; and its organization for production is shaped by population size, communication density, and technological sophistication.

In his later work, Lenski focuses more on the relationship between population and production'. As Thomas Malthus had argued 150 years earlier, Lenski argues that humans could reproduce in numbers beyond what Earth's resources can sustain, and that a human population will be limited by its ability to produce food for itself. Sociocultural evolution thus depends on the balance between a population and the food production that its environment can support. Due to the competition for food and the differences that exist between and among them, certain species will be more suited for survival. Variation and natural selection bring about organic and behavioural evolution, which is non-random and progresses toward the desirable traits of survival. Though Lenski seems to have shifted from sociocultural evolution to biological evolution and natural selection/survival of the fittest—including interspecies competition for resources— in fact he has merely moved from one Durkheimian variable to another: from considering what Durkheim called 'moral density' to considering population size and its effects.

Sources: Adapted from http://www.statemaster.com/encyclopedia/Gerhard-Lenski; http://www. bookrags.com/biography/gerhard-emmanuel-lenski-jr-soc/; http://www.encyclopedia.com/doc/1O88-statuscrystallization.html; and other sources.

Barnett (2004) notes Lenski's work is highly influential in examining how humans develop from hunter-gatherer groupings to post-industrial societies, differentiate, and create inequality. Many of his works are specifically about social and cultural evolution, and their effects on status consistency, power, and privilege. Even his earliest work, on religious groupings in American society, can be seen as a Weberian study of religious status-groups.

Though Durkheim is the most obvious influence, we also see the influence of Marx's and Weber's theories of economic stratification in Lenski's work. Collins (2004), for example, shows how Lenski's theory of power and privilege addresses contemporary economic stratification in the US. Collins argues that, historically, American political structures contributed to the control of the means of production. Unlike Marx, who argued the contrary position, Lenski's work on economic stratification—following Weber—argues that the concentration of power largely controls the concentration of material wealth.

Calhoun (2004) notes that sociologists of Lenski's generation often tried to apply evolutionary models—an outgrowth of nineteenth century thinking—while later sociologists have employed historical perspectives. But Lenski understood it is important that sociology be tackled from a variety of perspectives and also helped establish the historical-sociological approach in the US.

Moor, Need, and Ultee (2006) apply Lenski's theory of ecological evolution to religion—long an interest of Lenski's. They argue that as a society improves its ability to provide for its necessities, this evolution is reflected in its religion. After all, religion is one important means by which people make sense of their lives and surroundings. In a 2007 study, the same researchers examined creation myths, which are found in virtually every society, and which reflect each culture's understanding of deity, to discover whether features of the myths correlate with features of societies. They found that 'high gods' tend to be found in more advanced societies, according to Lenski's classification of the stages of technological social development. There is also a pattern in the occurrence of moral versus non-moral gods: herding and agrarian societies tend to have moral gods, while advanced horticultural societies tend to have non-moral gods. As Lenski would have predicted, these findings show a strong correlation between technological progress and religion. Later findings by the same authors (2009) show that people also use different models to think about the unknown, depending on their society's level of technology. According to Lenski's ecological-evolutionary theory, with the advance of industrial technology, decline in population growth rates, and a growing economic surplus, there is a predicted decline in the scope and influence of theistic ideologies and an increase in secular ideologies (for example, Nolan and Lenski 2009: Chapter 11). Bertoni (2009) verifies this predicted cultural shift by comparing the proportional distributions of obituaries in the New York Times in 1852, 1900, 1925, 1950, 1975, and 2000. He finds that both the number and proportion of obituaries of religious figures declines dramatically during this period, while obituaries for sports and entertainment figures increase. This confirms that a declining number of people worked in religious occupations during this time, and also that religious figures lost prestige compared to people working in sports and entertainment.

Zhang (2008) re-examines Lenski's hypothesis that status inconsistency—an outcome when income doesn't match educational attainments, for example—causes problems such as psychological stress and social isolation, and leads to a tendency to hold neo-liberal political views. As predicted, he finds support for the hypothesis in US General Social Survey data. These data show that status inconsistency causes health problems, diminishes enjoyment of life, leads people to mistrust other people—even to mistrust government and the economy; and reduces participation in social life. These effects, in turn, lead people to identify with neo-liberal politics, which further undermines social cohesion.

Lee, Toney, and Berry (2009) examine migration in light of Lenski's theory of status inconsistency. They find that highly educated people in low paying jobs are more likely to migrate in search of better jobs than people whose incomes are consistent with their educational attainment. Not surprisingly, people whose incomes are high compared with their educational attainments are least likely to leave their present surroundings. However, people of inconsistent status who live in cities are also unlikely to migrate, since cities also offer them the greatest opportunities. Only people of inconsistent status who live in rural areas are highly likely to move in search of better-paying work.

Some have deemed Lenski irrelevant to current feminist theories of inequality, but Barnett (2007) argues that Lenski's theories of status inconsistency and status crystallization presage the race–gender–class intersectionality theories of domination and subordination that achieved prominence in the 1980s and 1990s. This connection is most evident in Lenski's theory of 'status crystallization' and 'status inconsistency', which explains status ranking in multidimensional stratification systems on individual political and other behaviour. However, neither Lenski's micro nor his macro level theories have been explicitly viewed by more recent scholars as an expression of 'multidimensionality' or 'intersectionality' in explanations of inequality. Here is some important detective work to be done by new generations of sociologists.

Thus, a review of recent writings finds continued application of the work by Gerhard Lenski—nearly 50 journal articles applying Lenski's work on inequality in the last 20 years. Clearly, sociologists are talking about Gerhard Lenski. We must include Lenski in a comprehensive, fusion approach to sociology because he addresses the most basic sociological question: How do social forces and societal locations affect people's life chances, and how do these life chances change over time, with growing societal complexity?

New Insights

Despite the insecurity, hardship, and difficulty that face most people, the global economic crisis that began in 2008 does not appear to have shaken a widespread belief in the triumph of global capitalism and neo-liberal government. This means sociologists have plenty to do in studying and understanding—and perhaps even helping—the casualties of this system. But by what means should we attempt this research?

Stephen Webb (2009) suggests that postmodern analysis fails adequately to address social problems, as it typically fails to address the essential social structures. However, Sohlberg (2009) denies this and calls for more theoretical complexity today. The prevailing view is that traditional, 'modern' or 'classical' approaches to understanding inequality were too simple.

Recall that early approaches to understanding social class featured two, three or four major classes (depending on the theorist). Today, we recognize far more classes than these. As in all the other domains we have examined, new postmodern approaches have made headway in studying the domain of classes and workplaces. However, as in the other fields of sociology, debates continue to rage about the best ways to define, measure, and explain important relationships in this domain. As usual, questions remain about how to define 'class' or 'equality', and what do we know about the factors that influence their change over time.

So, for example, Grusky and Weeden (2002) reiterate the problems with conventional class analysis, noting several major theoretical and methodological questions to be answered. Conventional measures of class are statistical constructions that ignore deeply institutionalized relationships at the site of production. If we take the view that class is merely an income or educational category (for example), we gain no insight into the ways class relations are enacted in the economy or in workplaces. Instead, we might better argue that class relations are about workplace subordination and, if so, income and education are largely irrelevant. So, if we can clarify the production and boundaries of domination, class analysis can be redeemed. Doing so will mean identifying the site of 'class production' and revising class analysis so it is based on realist (that is, 'institutionalized') categories rather than nominal ones.

Related to this are issues around social mobility. Some sociologists have argued that social classes are groups that permit little entry or exit from outside, through social mobility. In short, they are products of status-based social closure, to use Weber's terms. Adams (2002), though agreeing that social closure limits mobility and contributes to social stratification, denies a conflict between these ideas and postmodernist analyses of social class. Here the problem, as so often occurs in postmodern analysis, is around the issue of definition: What do we mean by 'social class' and how do we know which social classes exist? Goldthorpe (2002) re-asserts the value of traditional Marxist-based class analyses, asserting that classes are evidently 'real social groupings' as Marx had asserted. In this respect, 'occupational closure' that hinders class mobility is only one small aspect of class formation.

In refining their method, Weeden and Grusky (2004) then test the theory that craft, professional, and service classes are 'more poorly formed' than other supposed 'big classes'. To state the problem simply, their goal is to find 'real' subclasses within these categories, with each subclass practising closure and evidencing common life-chances among its members. However, they are largely defeated in this effort. The results show that a big-class scheme, however believable—for example, an assumption that there really is a 'proletariat' or a 'service class' or even a 'professional class'—remains hard to justify, measure, and model. In other words, we are still some distance from being able to identify the true boundaries of social classes. In large part, classes remain statistical constructions, not lived, shared experiences.

Perhaps for this reason, Bidou-Zacchariasen (2004) notes that as a postmodern approach to sociology in the UK becomes increasingly popular, there is less interest in class analysis than there was from 1980 to 2000. In France, however, we see indications that sociologists may be returning to studying class, as shown by renewed interest in the traditional terminology of social classes.

Are postmodernism and Marxist class analyses in conflict, as these commentaries would seem to suggest? Charusheela (2005) thinks not, suggesting that in the postmodern era, Marxist analysis can avoid the preconceptions of modernism, Eurocentrism, and essentialism, and may even be able to provide solutions to class-based social problems.

Other commentators ignore this theoretical debate and attempt, through empirical analysis, to document the changing fortunes of the rich and poor. So, for example, Reitz (2004) looks at the political context of wealth and the causes of growing income inequality in the US. Investigating the revenue and payroll data of US manufacturing firms, he finds strong evidence of exploitation: huge differences between capitalists' return on investment and the wages paid to labourers.

Along similar lines, Kirk (2002) reviews writings of British working-class people in the last two decades of the twentieth century, when class analysis was a hot topic among British sociologists. In doing so, he challenges the recent neglect of this topic, pointing out that class combines with gender and race to create 'lived experience'. Thus it continues to be relevant to social analysis.

This leads us to ask, will class analysis stage a comeback in sociology, and will class solidarity stage a comeback in political life? Cook (2001) notes that two prominent German sociologists, Jürgen Habermas and Theodor Adorno, despite different analytical methods, both conclude it is unlikely that progressive solidarity movements will re-emerge. Habermas (whom we will discuss at length in a later chapter) claims that capitalistic political and economic power structures have taken over the 'lifeworld' and communication infrastructures. Adorno finds that class conflict is no longer a major social concern for many people, that class consciousness is pushed aside by other concerns, and that individuals are not aware of their own oppression.

Is class analysis dead, then—killed by conceptual and methodological problems and epistemological turf wars? Some sociologists say 'No'. Focusing on the Latin American peasantry, Petras and Veltmeyer (2001), use reconstituted class analysis to conclude that traditional class solidarity has produced a new kind of class struggle. Today, even peasants understand how power is deployed nationally and internationally, and use this knowledge to their advantage. At the periphery of global capitalism, class solidarity continues to wield power. Class continues to be a lived experience where the people are poorest and the stakes are highest.

Chapter Summary

We began this chapter with a look at how workplaces and work relations have changed in the last century or two, and the effect of this transformation on social class formations. People today increasingly work in service jobs with non-standard work arrangements, also known as precarious employment, and including part-time 'McJobs'.

We also paid special attention to the importance of Marx and Weber in developing our current notions of class, and focused on the role classes continue to play in present-day society. Then, we introduced Durkheim's theory about the connections between work—specifically, the division of labour—and social solidarity, noting the outcomes for workers, such as anomie and alienation. We saw that unionization has played an important role in redressing some of the inequalities and other problems associated with work. Finally, we looked at the effects of work and social class position on health and criminality.

Since most people have to earn a living, the 'problem of work' is important for sociologists and other citizens alike. For many, work is overwhelming, mentally and physically; while for others, underemployment and unemployment are also destructive—as we said, hidden injuries of social class. For Canadians, and likely for most people, at least in the developed world, work is an important part of their lives. According to Canada's first-ever work-ethic study called Workplace 2000, when asked what they would do if they won a million dollars, only 17 per cent of Canadians answered that they would quit their jobs and never work again. Among the respondents, 41 per cent stated they would remain at their current job; 17 per cent would change career paths, and 24 per cent would start their own business (Lowe, 2000: 52).

So, work is not only a source of income for people, it is also a source of meaning and identity. It shapes how people view themselves and how others view them. People who are the most satisfied with their work say it offers them a manageable challenge: enough to stimulate them, but not enough to overwhelm them. Alongside love, work has the potential of satisfying our most important life needs, giving us feelings of accomplishment, success, and worthiness, besides simply satisfying financial needs. All of us look for such jobs, and some find them.

Critical Thinking Questions

1. How do notions of class differ in Marxist and Weberian systems of thinking? What aspects of each are still applicable to the class structure of present-day Canadian society?
2. What is the importance of the managerial class in modern capitalism? How has this class emerged? How does this emergence relate to its current function? Is the managerial class effective?
3. Consider how globalization has changed the nature of social classes and workplaces around the world. How has it affected both developed and developing countries?
4. Consider unions and their role in society. Do you believe union strikes are useful or harmful? What is their impact on classes and workplaces?
5. How has the nature of work changed over time? Discuss your own experiences with work: Where did you work? What did your job entail? Did you experience alienation? How has this work experience affected your health and well-being or your view on employment?

Recommended Readings

W. Lloyd Warner, Marchia Meeker, and Kenneth Eells, *Social Class in America: A Manual of Procedure for the Measurement of Social Status* (Chicago: Science Research Associates, 1949). In this classic work, the authors undermine popular beliefs that all people have equal opportunity in a democratic society. The authors outline the typical nine-level status order of societies, from the poorest of the poor to the richest of the rich. They assert that social class permeates every aspect of our lives and influences our decisions, our experiences, and even our personal development.

Barrington Moore Jr., *Social Origins of Dictatorship and Democracy: Lord and Peasant in the Making of the Modern World* (Boston: Beacon Press, 1967). Here, the author outlines the divergent paths different societies take toward modernity, and the ways these paths influence the political outcome. Moore analyzes modern political systems—and the rise of fascism, communism, and liberal democracy—against the backdrop of their development. His main argument is that it is the evolving relationship between lords and peasants, more than any other factor, which foreshadows a country's future political orientation.

Thorstein Veblen, *The Theory of the Leisure Class* (Oxford: Oxford University Press, 2007 [1899]). This classic work, a landmark study of the 'upper class' of American society, outlined the habits and behaviours of the very rich, showing how they used all means possible to distance themselves from people who had to work to survive. Their strategies engaged fashion, beauty, animals, sports, business, religion, education, and so on. Veblen shows how many of the tactics used by the upper class were narcissistic and wasteful, exacerbating societal inequality in the process.

Richard Sennett and Jonathan Cobb, *The Hidden Injuries of Social Class* (Cambridge: Cambridge University Press, 1977 [1972]). This book introduced fascinating new theories about the effects of social class on people at the bottom of the class structure, including the effects on those who cannot find ways of improving their situation. For those who think 'class' is a trivial abstraction, this book is an eye-opener.

Ronald Inglehart, *Modernization and Postmodernization: Cultural, Economic, and Political Change in 43 Societies* (Princeton, NJ: Princeton University Press, 1997). This book contends that we can view societal development as a package of economic, social, and political trends, having great consistency and predictability. The author's argument is supported by data from the World Values survey, based on data from over 40 countries.

Vincent J. Roscigno, *The Face of Discrimination: How Race and Gender Impact Work and Home Lives* (Lanham, MD: Rowan & Littlefield, 2007). This work focuses on the prevalence, character, and consequences of racial and sexual discrimination in the workforce and their impact on aspects of personal life (for example, home life). Topics include discrimination in particular economic sectors, sexual harassment at work, and the racialization and sexualization of certain workplaces.

Websites

International Labour Organization (ILO)
www.ilo.org

Human Resources and Skills Development Canada (HRSDC)
www.hrsdc.gc.ca

Canadian Centre for Occupational Health and Safety (CCOHS)
www.ccohs.ca

Ontario Ministry of Labour
www.labour.gov.on.ca

Canadian Labour Congress (CLC)
http://canadianlabour.ca

Canadian Committee on Labour History
www.cclh.ca

10 Regions, Nation and Empires

Learning Objectives

In this chapter, you will:

> Learn to describe the balance of power between nations

> See the social and economic effects of globalization outlined

> Hear about the impacts of technology on interpersonal communication

> Come to understand the social implications of war and terrorism

> Become aware of the psychological and sociological effects of war

Chapter Outline

People live in societies, and these societies have boundaries that distinguish one from another. This chapter discusses the relationships between societies—also, between regions, nations, and empires. These living, breathing social entities shape the way we approach our everyday lives. Macro-history itself grows out of the interactions between these large social units. Conflicts among them have caused wars, revolutions, and inquisitions. Co-operation among them has led to alliances, democracies, and treaties and, in turn, to peace and prosperity. Our lives today are a result, in large part, of the historical interaction among these bounded units.

In this chapter, we will discuss the main aspects of regions, nations, and empires and the relationships among them. We will explore the ways they exercise

power, the effects of globalization on international relations, the political role of multinational corporations, and the global role of technology. Then we will examine the conflicts that sometimes occur between regions, nations, and empires. Conflict is important, because throughout history, it has been the most important source of social and political change.

Finally, we will look at the effects of such conflict on society. Some negative effects to be explored include health problems, violence, rape, and death. However, conflict can also lead to societal improvements: for example, some would argue the establishment of the United Nations and the World Court fall into this category. So we will take a closer look at the relations between regions, nations, and empires, and the ways they connect to other aspects of social life.

Everyday Observations

The corners of the world: Walking down the oldest streets of Montreal, you come face to face with an impressive array of different cultures. On the bustling streets of Chinatown, you hear the frenzied shouts of street sellers and whirr of bicycles whizzing by, and smell the delicious aroma of barbecued meat. In Greek-town, you pass by shop windows displaying beautiful laces or tantalizing baked goods, and hear music flowing out of open church doors. In more typically 'Anglo' North American parts of the city, you see tall, multi-storied malls, flashing neon advertisements, and fast food joints on every corner. How can one city have so many aspects and dimensions? What can possibly connect these different groups and the places they came from?

We know the world separates people into distinct groups. Within these groups, people are socialized to hold specific political, economic, social, and cultural views. We are thus moulded in the image of the group we belong to; as members of the particular group, we view the world from its particular standpoint. In turn, the groups to which we belong are nested within particular locales: a citizen of Winnipeg, for example, is also a resident of Manitoba, the Prairies, Western Canada, Canada, North America, the western hemisphere, and the world. Each of these locales, with its distinctive way of linking to other locales, moulds us in a particular way; so we are, in effect, citizens of multiple regions or territorial units.

This chapter is about the relationship between these different territorial units. We start by trying to define them and measure their influence on our lives. However, we will ask a great many questions and not manage to answer them all. This chapter scratches the surface of a vast, rapidly evolving topic in sociology. Perhaps this chapter will succeed best if it motivates you to dig further into the questions raised here.

Often the territories we live in compete with one another for dominance, but sometimes they make significant efforts to co-operate. These attempts at co-operation are essential in promoting peace. Moreover, co-operation between smaller territories—for example, between Western and Eastern Canada, or between Manitoba and Alberta—is what makes possible the achievement of social solidarity in the large territories—for example, in Canada as a whole. How do territorial units achieve this peaceful co-operation? Does it need diplomacy at the highest levels, or interaction and familiarity at the lowest levels? And by what mechanisms do people reach out a hand of co-operation? How, for example, does art—take music as one example—help to bridge the social distance between people in different territories? Or sports? Are the exchanges of artists or athletes better ways of brokering peaceful co-operation than political negotiation by diplomats?

Sometimes people in different territories work together to help the world at large. However, these efforts to co-operate are difficult and far from certain to succeed. So we might ask, how do territories work together to overcome common enemies (whether natural or human)? What role do global organizations, like the United Nations, play in solving international problems, and how effective are their efforts? How well does the World Health Organization, for example, succeed in reducing death and disease throughout the world?

A current version of international co-operation between territories is called 'globalization', and most people are familiar with this term. Since they hear it so often, they probably think they know what the term 'globalization' means. However, the term is complicated and not even academics and diplomats agree on what they mean by the term. So we must ask: What are the defining features of a 'global' or 'globalized' economy? What are the (related) effects of the rise of multinational organizations? Why do some people support globalization while others worry about its effects on Canada? And could globalization lead to the demise of some traditional cultures; if so, is that bad or good?

Part of globalization, as we will see, is economic; but part of it is technological. As we will see, technological innovation has helped significantly to improve co-operation between territories. Consider the role of the Internet and telephone. Today, many young people spend more time on cyberspace interactions than on face-to-face ones. But we still understand little about the social effect of this reliance on media interaction. How does such technology affect *your* social interactions? And do such electronic interactions increase global understanding and co-operation, decrease these, or have no effect whatsoever?

Despite the important role of economic and technological forces, not all efforts to promote co-operation succeed, sometimes due to prejudice—a prejudgment people in one part of the world make about people in another (for example, prejudgments Arabs make about Americans, or Americans about Arabs). We might ask: What causes such prejudice among people in different parts of the world? Do media portrayals of different regions and different cultures demonstrate prejudice and sometimes even increase it? What are current examples of such prejudice in our world?

In extreme cases, the conflicts among groups and regions lead to war. As you probably know, tens of millions of soldiers and civilians died in wars during the last century. Will this century prove to be less deadly? Will warfare become more gentle, harming fewer soldiers and fewer civilians, and have less severe psychological effects on veterans and other survivors? And consider terrorism, a particular type of warfare that is increasingly common today. What are the roots of terrorism and how does it originate? What societal factors shape and recruit terrorists? What happens when states themselves sponsor and promote terrorism?

In the last century, we became familiar with the idea of 'war crimes', and by now we realize that these crimes have a lasting effect on society. Although sometimes the perpetrators are legally punished, often they are not; so it is useful to ask what laws protect us from further war crimes. Women are especially vulnerable in times of war, especially to war crimes. For example, enemy forces often rape and kill women to disorganize and frighten their foe into submission. What are the long-term psychological and social results of such strategic rape?

This chapter will try to answer these and related questions. Ever since humans first formed separate territories (whether **regions**, **nations**, or **empires**), people have fought and died to protect their territory of birth—their Motherland, their Fatherland. In doing so, they have often used violence and promoted hatred. Nevertheless, humanity continues to try to redeem itself through peaceful co-operation. How well are we doing at this today, and why?

regions

Large land areas that may encompass portions of a country or extend over several countries. They usually share a few distinctive topographical features (e.g., mountain, flatland, or coastal terrain) and economic experiences.

nations

Large land areas where people live under the rule of a national government.

empires

Sets of nations, regions, and territories controlled by a single ruler.

Ways of Looking at . . .
REGIONS, NATIONS, AND EMPIRES

The topics of this chapter—war, peace, diplomacy, and everything in between—are macrosociological, so symbolic interactionism has little to say about them. Chiefly, we will see disagreements between the main macrosociological approaches—especially, between the functional and critical theories.

However, in most of this chapter, we will examine variants of critical theory. For example, Immanuel Wallerstein's world-systems theory (discussed in detail later in the chapter) can be considered in this light. In turn, we can trace this approach back to Karl Marx's analysis of capitalism, which set the stage for later thinking—as expressed by Russian revolutionist and Soviet ruler V.I. Lenin—that imperialism is the pinnacle of capitalism (on this, see his 1916 book, *Imperialism, the Highest Stage of Capitalism*).

According to this way of thinking, capitalism is an inherently expansionist economic system, always looking for new markets, and new, lower-cost labour and resources. This means capitalists and capitalism will always be looking to control and even conquer other societies, to manipulate their markets, populations, and, if necessary, governments. In practice, this means that the governments of leading capitalist nations—first, England, France, and Germany, then later the United States, Canada, and others—will occasionally support aggressive economic or military intrusions into foreign countries. Seen from this standpoint, it is easy to understand most wars since 1500 as extensions of the effort to capture markets, raw materials, and (eventually) consumers. Wars from this angle are merely economics at gunpoint. Certainly, the empire-building efforts that began with Spanish explorers in 1492, followed by the British, French, Dutch, and Portuguese colonial armies throughout the Americas, can be seen in this light.

Of course, capitalism did not invent imperialism: there were Egyptian, Persian, Greek, and Roman empires—complete with imperial armies and colonial wars—thousands of years before capitalism. However, the development of capitalism after 1800 intensified these colonial, imperial efforts, because of the innate expansionist tendency of capitalism mentioned earlier. In fact, many would view today's globalization as little more than the efforts by American capitalism and multinational organizations (whatever their ownership) to extend their control and wealth-gathering throughout the world. They do this by seeking ever cheaper labour and resources, and ever larger markets, even if war and espionage are needed to accomplish the task. (No wonder, then, that many view American and Russian incursions into the Middle East in recent decades—for example, the recurring wars in and around Afghanistan—as veiled attempts to capture needed oil deposits and oil transit routes in the name of democracy.)

In contrast to this critical approach, functionalists take a 'modernization approach' to understanding globalization. They focus on the spread of Western lifestyles and Western values throughout the world, and a resulting general desire for Western-style democracy and culture. This global spread of 'modernity' brings with it local desires for Americanization, including increased contact with American media, consumer items, and life choices. Purportedly, these desires, which encourage and even require the spread of Western multinational organizations, come from inside the 'less-developed countries'. In this scenario, no guns or economic threats are needed. Made aware of the modern consumer cornucopia, everyone from Lapland to Tierra del Fuego, Capetown to Kazakhstan, wants to be 'American' or, at least, Western. These Westernized 'modern' desires readily support the entry of Western capital, which provides jobs and salaries that, however meagre, permit the purchase of Western-style consumer items.

In effect, then, the debate between critical theorists and functionalists is not about whether there is a hierarchy of regions and nations. Clearly, Western capitalist societies dominate the markets of the world—although Russia, China, India, and a few others (Brazil, Nigeria, and Indonesia, for example) are quickly gaining dominance. It is about the nature of this global system—whether good or bad—and about the role of force versus choice in establishing the global order.

Classic Studies

The Modern World-System I: Capitalist Agriculture and the Origins of the European World-Economy in the Sixteenth Century

To understand global relations today, we need to grasp the historical trends that have shaped them. Therefore, we begin with the brief discussion of a classic work by Immanuel

Wallerstein, *The Modern World-System* (1974). We describe Wallerstein's life—also, his critics and influence on the field—at length toward the end of this chapter.

The Modern World-System I: Capitalist Agriculture and the Origins of the European World-Economy in the Sixteenth Century is the first book in a three-volume set that surveys economic developments in Europe from 1450 to 1640. The author argues that since the sixteenth century an important worldwide social system has developed. The basic linkages are economic and the system is organized on capitalist principles. The result is a worldwide division of labour and a global system of stratification.

Wallerstein notes that before the sixteenth century, world economies did exist but were typically parts of world empires, such as the Roman Empire. These world empires were relatively short-lived, because of the great expense needed to maintain them, politically and militarily. This changed, however, in the sixteenth century, when a new world economy emerged; based on the capitalist mode of production, this new economy did not require military or political rule to maintain itself. 'The techniques of modern capitalism and the technology of modern science . . . enabled this world-economy to thrive, produce, and expand without the emergence of a unified political structure' (Wallerstein, 1974). The capitalist mode of production built and strengthened this emerging world economy, while avoiding the massive losses and strains associated with maintaining a world empire (losses illustrated by the quick and disastrous collapse of the Spanish Empire, for example).

An important aspect of Wallerstein's model is its conception of the 'parts' that make a world system. Wallerstein divides the world's nations into three categories: **core states**, **periphery states**, and semi-periphery states. William Leiss (1977) writes that these 'shifting relationships maintained a dynamic tension that insured the growing hegemony of the system as a whole'. The value of this insight is evident when we consider the 2010 economic meltdown in Greece. At the time of this writing, the summer of 2010, not only is Greece's near-bankruptcy endangering the economies of other peripheral European debtor countries—Spain, Italy, Portugal, and Ireland—it is even endangering the economies of wealthier core nations—Germany, France, and (to a lesser degree) Britain—to whom all the peripheral nations are heavily indebted. What is threatening Europe, then, is the entire collapse of the European Economic Community, owing to this systemic relationship among countries.

Beginning in the sixteenth century, according to Wallerstein, several countries in Western Europe came to serve as the core states and the organizing base for a world economy: Spain, England, France, the Netherlands, and Portugal. Then as now, the European periphery consisted of states in eastern and southern Europe.

Historically, the differences between core and periphery states stemmed from the type of labour organization they employed. In short, the core had the most detailed and 'modern' division of labour, while the periphery had the least. In large part, it was this detailed, modern division of labour that gave the core much of its commercial and manufacturing wealth, even before the Industrial Revolution. During this period, 'wage-labor and self-employment were becoming dominant in the core, slavery and feudal relations in the periphery, and sharecropping in the semi-periphery' (Leiss, 1977). This differentiation was vital to the world system's operation. Wallerstein writes, 'The world-economy was based precisely on the assumption that there were in fact these three zones and that they did in fact have different modes of labor control. Were this not so, it would not have been possible to assure the kind of flow of the surplus which enabled the capitalist system to come into existence' (Wallerstein, 1974).

While this may sound vague and abstract, we need only remember the triangular trade relations that existed between Europe, Africa, and America from about 1500 through (roughly) 1850: from Africa to the Americas went slave labourers; from the Americas to Europe went agricultural products (like coffee, sugar, and spices) produced by slaves; from Europe to the rest of the world—Africa, Asia and the Americas—went manufactured goods

core states

The governments of industrialized, rich, powerful, and relatively independent societies; the dominant states in the world.

periphery states

The governments of less developed, relatively poor, weak societies that are subject to manipulation or direct control by core societies.

like textiles and furnishings. Core states, from the beginning, were the source of manufactured goods and the beneficiary of slave labour in the periphery.

Another distinguishing feature was the emergence of bureaucratic organizations in the core states. These bureaucratic organizations allowed the core to control and exploit the periphery more effectively. In effect, you need bureaucracy to oversee the flow of goods and control of slave peoples, local peasants, and indentured workers. Bureaucratic organization also allowed 'capitalism to maneuver freely because it allowed the economy to operate in an area that was larger than that controlled by any political entity' (Cameron 1976). Nothing was more efficient at overseeing a colonial empire than the modern army and the modern civil service, both organized bureaucratically (that is, hierarchically and according to written rules).

Reviewers have praised Wallerstein's book for its success in forging a unified historical social science—a combination of sociology, history, economics, and political science. They have also appreciated the wide and extensive historical detail presented in the book. For example, Wallerstein spells out the economic changes that followed the influx of American gold into the Spanish Empire, and he compares the relations among the bourgeoisie, the nobility, and the state in France and England. In short, *The Modern World-System* provides deep insights into the mechanics of world history, like a book by sociologist Barrington Moore we will discuss later.

Of course, the book can be criticized for its omissions: most particularly, its omission of any reference to the role of ideas and beliefs in human history. Here, it is clear that Wallerstein is much closer to the Marxist than the Weberian analysis of social change. Still, Wallerstein's theoretical account of the emergence of capitalist Europe provides a larger context for understanding international relations. Global capitalism, from this perspective, is the organizing principle behind the world's regions, nations, and empires.

Networks of Dependency

On the surface, regions, nations, and empires are merely geographic locations on a map, a matter of seemingly random borders. But as Wallerstein shows, more than geography is at stake here, since these places are also political, ecological, economic, social, and cultural units. What's more, as we have seen, they are connected in a network of interdependence and control.

This interconnection creates a tension between two sources of control: control that emanates from inside the territorial unit—from the local government and ruling class—and control that emanates from core nations outside it. Compare this to the effect of the sun on the solar system: every planet has its own orbit, its own gravity, and its own relationship to the other planets. At the same time, every planet is constantly subject to the gigantic attraction and energy of the sun. Similarly, every region, nation, or empire has its own political and legal jurisdiction—its own set of rulers and body of laws. But it is also within the orbit of much larger, imperial players—core states that are pursuing their own interests in the world. The question is, Which rulers and what body of laws will prevail in the event of a conflict? Different empires have addressed this question in different ways. The British Empire, for example, was a set of dominions, colonies, and protectorates loosely ruled from London. Within each of these territories, people were ruled by a local version of British common law, managed by local judges and magistrates. This structure of rule provided both uniformity and flexibility. Shorter-lived empires—the Spanish, Dutch and French, for example—may have failed because of insufficient uniformity and flexibility.

The purpose of imperial rule is to enrich core states—especially, capitalists in core states—at the expense of peripheral states. As noted, core states take much of the raw material, cheap labour, and economic surplus from peripheral states which are too weak to resist. Investors from the core states effectively control the economies of these peripheral states. Profits made in the periphery drain out of the local economy and flow back to the core. The world economy does not give peripheral states an opportunity to improve their situation, but rather exploits their disadvantage (Hall and Chase-Dunn, 2004). **Semi-peripheral states** (like Canada) are sometimes exploited in the same way, and sometimes serve as 'middlemen' for the core states; but they are somewhat more autonomous—more independent and self-controlling—than peripheral states. See Figure 10.1 for an illustration of how these states are related.

A core-periphery relationship can also exist between regions or between cities. Again, take the example of Canada: some believe that Central Canada—Ontario and Quebec—has historically monopolized economic and political power, acting as the country's core. Other provinces or regions, by contrast, have been the periphery. This view is easily inferred from Harold Innis's historical-geographic approach to understanding Canadian economic history; and we can see this argument developed in the classic works of historical sociology by Canadian sociologist S.D. Clark. At the same time, Canada itself has been a peripheral or semi-peripheral member of the British Empire and, later, of the American 'empire'; and Toronto and Montreal have been peripheral or semi-peripheral cities in the global networks of capital controlled out of London and New York.

The world-system perspective helps us to understand the relations between regions, nations, and empires. It also requires us to be aware of the social, historical, political, economic, and geographical context and the relationships among units. As sociologists, we must understand the extent of interdependence among nation-states, and also that this interdependence is far from equal. States have different amounts of power and influence in dealing with one another.

In fact, all regions, nations, and empires have this in common, as is evident in the world-systems theory: they are all characterized by both exchange and domination. Geographic units tied together by large-scale flows of people, goods, capital, or information effectively *become* regions, nations, or empires. Geographic units that provide other units with capital, manufactured goods, and political decisions are 'core' units; recipients of capital, manufactured goods, and political decisions are 'periphery' units. In turn, these periphery units provide labour, raw materials, and profits to the core.

Even the flow of news is dominated by this unequal balance of power and influence. News about the central or core regions is reported everywhere in the periphery, while news about the periphery is rarely reported in the centre.

For good reason, core states are often accused of engaging in imperialism, the exercise of political and economic control by one state over the territory of another. Throughout history, imperialism has often been accomplished by military means. However, as Wallerstein argues, domination—especially under capitalism—does not always require military conquest and colonization. In fact, under the right conditions, economic imperialism is far safer, less costly, and even more stable than military or political imperialism.

In networks of connected geographic units, conflicts are likely to arise for two main reasons. First, inequalities of power, wealth, and influence result in unequal exchanges. Said simply, some regions (or nations or empires) are more powerful than others, so they tend to get what they want. Second, important ecological, cultural, and social differences also divide units one from another. Often the inequalities of power and wealth are

> **semi-peripheral states**
>
> The governments of industrial or semi-industrial societies that, though prosperous, are often subject to control by core societies because of their economic or political dependency.

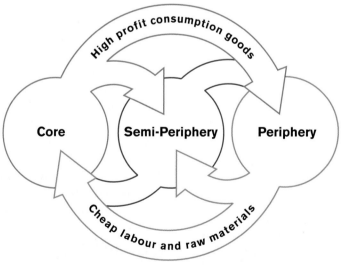

Figure 10.1 Wallerstein's World Systems Theory Model

Source: Adapted from http://img87.imageshack.us/i/gw560rf1.gif.

mistaken for, or entangled in, conflicts over social and cultural differences. Political or economic wars sometimes turn into 'culture wars', for example. Moreover, because there are so many bases of difference, it is never easy to figure out the exact reason two regions or countries or empires are in conflict with one other. War often takes people by surprise, though it is inevitable in hindsight—the result of a long buildup of threats and frustrations.

Wallerstein's discussion of global relations illustrates several key facts about the topic and about sociology. First, Wallerstein's work clearly draws on the earlier work of Marx and Weber. Like Marx, he is trying to build a theory of historical development that is driven by relations of inequality. Like Weber, however, Wallerstein understands the danger of over-simplification. The processes of change from feudalism to capitalism are complex and vary from one locale to another. More important, states, armies, and other political actors are as important as capitalist classes in bringing about this transformation. The story of how territories gain and manage the control of other territories—a topic of interest to Max Weber, for example—is central to this story.

Differentiating between Nations, Regions, and Empires

Though *empire*, *state*, and *region* are all geographic units, these names can't be used interchangeably. History shows these types of units all work quite differently, and sociologists need to recognize the differences.

For example, over the course of history, empires have varied widely, taking a range of different approaches to managing their colonies. The Roman Empire famously taxed its colonies, but did not meddle in their cultural or religious affairs; this wise decision contributed to a relatively long period of peace and stability. On the other hand, some empires, including the British, tried to convert many of the peoples it ruled to Christianity. This created hostility in many parts of the non-Christian world, and brought Britain little apparent benefit.

Nations are mainly political units that are smaller than empires. In the modern world, most national societies are (political) states and most states are national societies, as we see in Europe, which is made up of many small, medium, and large states. However, in some societies, the nation and the state do not coincide neatly—as for example, in Canada, where Quebec sovereignists and Aboriginal traditionalists demand sovereign rights for their respective 'nations'. In such societies, conflict arises and secession is threatened. Such conflicts and threats of secession are evident throughout the world. Sri Lanka is currently of interest because secessionist civil war there is causing Tamil refugees to flee to Canada. In Turkey and Iraq, the Kurds would like to create their own state, as would the Basques and Catalans in Spain and the Macedonians in Greece.

Finally, regions are variable too. Often they are merely combinations of political or jurisdictional units. However, mainly regions are geographic, ecological, and economic units. Some small nations, like the country of Andorra in the Pyrenees may have a single unified ecosystem. However, *most* nations and *all* empires span multiple ecological and geographical zones, often comprising mountains, prairies, shores, and even deserts. This ecological and economic variety is certainly characteristic of Canada, the US, China, and Russia, for example. By contrast, as we have noted, most regions are ecologically homogeneous; and their common ecology, and the common lifestyle to which it gives rise, make them into economic and cultural communities.

globalization

The development of a single world market and the accompanying trend to increased interdependence among the economies (and societies) of the world.

A Global Economy

We have so far depicted globalization as a source of control, inequality, and conflict. However, supporters of globalization view it much more positively, as a new mechanism for co-operation. Viewed this way, **globalization** is the construction of a single world market and the source of increasing interdependence among the societies of the world.

The fast food company McDonald's has extended its market all around the world as can be seen in one of its restaurants located in St. Petersburg, Russia.

The global economy as it exists today is a form of world social organization with six defining features. First, it features *global economic interdependence*, meaning that most societies trade goods and services with one another. In this system, all people are both buyers and sellers in a single world market. Second, globalization is characterized by *scientific and technological innovation*, with new methods for producing goods and services continuously developed. Third, globalization features *polycentric cultures and polities*. In this globalized world, many cultures everywhere contribute to the formation of a new global culture. Fourth, globalization leads to *homogenized human ambitions*—a 'world culture' in which values, ambitions, and ways of life fuse together, becoming more similar and familiar. Fifth, *nation-states are changing*, losing some of their influence over local culture and economy.

Sixth and finally, *corporate entities*—multinational corporations such as IBM or Toyota—and not individuals or governments are the key actors in the global economy. Because of economic globalization, today governments have less influence over the people they rule, giving way instead to multinational corporations, foreign governments, and international bodies. In the last few decades, multinational corporations (also known as *transnational corporations*) and **non-governmental organizations** (NGOs) have assumed increasingly more economic and political influence. This has reduced the historical influence of regions, nations, and empires as political actors. However, it has also provided mechanisms for sharing across regional and cultural lines.

Many people around the world are concerned about this supposed cultural sharing, and see it as the domination of American culture over all others (see Box 10.1). Through globalization, the whole world has become familiar with internationally marketed American consumer brands (like Coca Cola, McDonald's, and Nike), along with their cultural and social meanings (for example, the value of high calorie intake, fast food, and a sporty manner.) The mass media have been influential in expanding American influence through music, television, and Hollywood movies. Some have even equated this new form of domination to cultural imperialism, arguing that it brings about several consequences. These

non-governmental organizations (NGOs)

Legally constituted organizations that are independent of any national government; often, mechanisms through which different nations try to solve common problems.

One World, Many Societies

BOX 10.1

Adapting for Success on Foreign Shores

Imagine you're the CEO of a Canadian company looking to expand into the global marketplace: what's the number-one rule to keep in mind? You have to respect the local culture of the market you're trying to enter. Not to do so could cause your entire enterprise to fail, according to *Globe & Mail* business reporter Harvey Schachter. He offers some examples:

[I]n Germany, Walmart customers were offended when the greeter at the door, following Walmart policy, appeared to invade their privacy by asking, 'How are you?' This insensitivity to culture is thought to be part of the reason for the failure of Walmart's German expansion. Cultural clash is also suspected in German-based Daimler AG's failed takeover of Chrysler, 'because its disciplined, buttoned-down executives could never meld with their more freewheeling American counterparts.' North American companies can learn from McDonald's, which caters to European tastes with products developed especially for that market.

Consultants Charlene Marmer Solomon and Michael Schell, in *Managing Across Cultures*, point out that people and companies doing business in other cultures need to learn to read the cultural signals and adapt their practices accordingly. And this is also important when cultures mix in the North American head office, especially in Canada's large, multicultural cities.

Source: Adapted from Schachter (2009).

may include strong resentment, fuelling anti-Western sentiments that increase conflict and even the likelihood of war.

At the same time, supporters claim that globalization does not erase the social role of traditional cultures, nor does it reduce the number of world cultures. Instead, they say it results in cultural mixing; not only is Western culture incorporated into other cultures but the opposite also occurs. An example is the incorporation of many different cuisines into Western food tastes. We would not be surprised to hear about someone having crepes for breakfast, sushi for lunch, and tandoori chicken for dinner—especially in a multicultural city like Toronto or Vancouver. This cultural mixing, far from causing conflict, has provided a new basis for co-operation through greater cultural understanding.

Blurring Social Distance through Technology

Often, distant countries seem strange because they are unfamiliar: travel to them is hard and unusual; communication with people there is costly and rare. However, distances in time and space are easily traversed by new technology, so perhaps new technology will help to blur the social distance between different societies. One strategy for studying cross-national and cross-regional relations is to examine how technology has affected such relations in the past. To this end, consider the history of two important communication technologies: the telephone and email.

From the beginning, telephones were used mainly for long-distance calling. Commercial interests advertised the telephone as a means to link family and friends; women used it for 'kin-keeping'. The telephone also allowed people to express feelings and opinions in their own voice. Besides, the telephone was simple to use, and (once the private line replaced the party line) was as private as face-to-face communication. As a result, the telephone, widely adopted, was used to create and preserve close relations, even at a distance. No wonder people quickly became dependent on this new communication instrument!

The history of email, though shorter, is similar so far, as some of the advantages of email are similar to those of the telephone. Moreover, email is not as disruptive as the telephone, nor is it dependent on both people being available at the same time. On the other hand, unlike the telephone, email is a strictly print medium. Since it involves computer technology and some literacy, email is not as simple or inexpensive to use as the telephone. Beyond that, email carries various dangers of its own. Faceless anonymity poses the risk of indiscretion, misunderstanding, and misquoting. The shield of visual and vocal anonymity may encourage blunt disclosure and self-misrepresentation. As well, people are more likely to express themselves intemperately and thoughtlessly through email and text-messaging.

Still, the lack of temporal and spatial boundaries associated with telephone and email—let alone skyping, blogging, and twittering—frees relationships and makes new relationships possible. It also makes online relationships possible for people formerly prevented from socializing—for example, people housebound by illness or child care. One thing is certain: the telephone and email have both made cross-regional, cross-national, and cross-empire communications easier than they ever were before. By increasing national and global communication, they have increased familiarity and, in that way, increase the chance of co-operation.

However, geographic units—states and the like—and technologies are not the only actors in world history. Moreover, they may not even be the most important actors in world history. According to Karl Marx, they are only the instruments of dominant classes. So, if we are to fully understand the role of regions, states, and empires, we need to understand how they link to and articulate class interests.

Facebook is a popular global communication tool that connects both the young and old and is increasingly the most used social networking tool.

Classic Studies
The Manifesto of the Communist Party

We now address the role social classes play in world history, and the ways social classes relate to the social actors we have already discussed—cities, regions, nations, governments, multinational corporations, NGOs, and even new technologies. To do this, we will turn back the calendar to one of sociology's earliest works: the *Manifesto of the Communist Party*, published in 1848. In this famous work, Karl Marx and Friedrich Engels predict the inevitable collapse of the capitalist system of production, and consequently the end of social inequality and social strife. First, however, a few words about the authors of this earth-shaking piece of sociological analysis.

Karl Marx was born in 1818 to well-off parents in Prussia. He studied in Bonn and Berlin; in 1843, he married and moved to Paris, where he met Friedrich Engels. They both joined the Communist League and agreed to write the *Manifesto of the Communist Party* after the League in 1848 decided to put its ideas into writing. A short burst of revolutionary activity across Europe was eventually unsuccessful, and Marx and Engels moved to London. Marx's views continued to win him both admiration and persecution for the rest his life, especially after the Paris Commune in 1870. Though Marx remained influential in Communist circles, he was no political leader and spent most of his time alone, doing research in the British Museum.

Friedrich Engels was born the son of factory owner in Barmen (Prussia) in 1820. In 1842, he converted to communism. This new ideology led him to live parts of his life with working families so he would be able to understand their conditions. In 1845, he published his experiences in a shockingly descriptive book *The Condition of the Working Class in England*. The similarity of their views soon brought Marx and Engels together in a lifelong partnership, jointly publishing *The German Ideology* in 1845 and later, *The Manifesto of the Communist Party* in 1848.

In *The Manifesto of the Communist Party*, Marx and Engels proclaim the certain collapse of the capitalist system of production and thus the end to social inequality and social strife. *The Manifesto* is divided into four parts, of which the first is the most theoretically interesting. In it, they show how the capitalist system of production continually splits society into two opposing classes: the bourgeoisie and the proletariat. 'By bourgeoisie is meant the class of modern capitalists, owners of the means of social production and employers of wage labour. By proletariat, the class of modern wage labourers who, having no means of production of their own, are reduced to selling their labour power in order to live' (Marx and Engels 1948 [1848]). The antagonism between the two classes, they predict, will result in the downfall of the bourgeoisie and the end of all class conflict.

Throughout history, there has always been a struggle between the oppressed and their oppressors; but the relation between bourgeoisie and proletariat is markedly different, and the last of such struggles, they claim. First, previous ruling classes needed to conserve the existing modes of production to stay in power, but under capitalism the bourgeoisie 'cannot exist without constantly revolutionizing the instruments of production, and thereby the relations of production, and with them the whole relations of society.' It does this by expanding across the globe and exploiting its empire more efficiently. These two tactics either polarize class divisions in new areas of the world or increasingly polarize the division in already industrialized areas.

Second, in capitalist production, the worker becomes more and more an attachment to a machine, the individual character of work is lost, and payment for work is limited to the least amount that ensures the worker's continued existence. The more monotonous the work, the lower is the wage. Previous regimes rationalized exploitation with religious or other justifications, but the bourgeoisie are open in their quest for individual profit, and their increasing exploitation cannot help but outrage the worker. When the worker owns nothing, when all private property is in the hands of the bourgeoisie, when workers no longer compete, the worker has nothing to lose and can see that private property is really just bourgeoisie property. For these reasons, only abolishing private property will end class conflict.

The contribution of this approach to understanding world history is evident if we put the theory in the form of a syllogism:

Though the history of the world has always featured struggles between the oppressed and their oppressors, the struggle between bourgeoisie and proletariat is markedly different and it will be the last of such struggles for mainly three reasons:

1. To stay in power, the bourgeoisie expands across the globe and exploits existing areas more thoroughly. Likewise, the rich will increasingly exploit the poor and so too will rich nations exploit poor nations.
2. In capitalist manufacturing, the worker becomes more and more an appendage to machinery. The more mechanized the work, the more monotonous it becomes and the less it pays. Profit-making at any cost is key.

3. This exploitation can only end through the abolition of private property, which will also end alienation, inequality, oppression, and class divisions. In this way, humanity will reach the end of history—no more classes, hence no more conflict, hence no more change.

The Manifesto is generally critiqued on two major points: its materialist conception of history and its prophetic ability. The materialist conception of history is both provocative and hotly contested. Historians and sociologists, most notably Max Weber, have challenged this materialistic interpretation of history and society, pointing also to the important social role of ideas, beliefs, and religions.

One of its most glaringly wrong prophesies was the expected revolution that never happened: the failure of a mobilized, impoverished working class to overthrow a mature capitalist state. Instead, a large middle-class has emerged with more skilled jobs than ever before (Avineri, 1998:102), especially since the invention of the computer, which has required a literate and educated workforce. Though we can scarcely criticize Marx and Engels for failing to foresee the computer age, their predictions were limited because of a linear model of historical development (ibid). So, although capitalism has polarized the rich and poor in recent years, over the longer run it has produced a large middle-income class with skilled, well-paying jobs. Though perhaps a failure on humanitarian grounds, capitalism must be considered a success when judged simply by economic growth and technological development.

More directly relevant to this present chapter, Marx and Engels were correct in predicting globalization and the homogenization it entails, as well as the accompanying exploitation of poor countries by capitalists in rich countries. They also correctly predicted the cyclical crises of capitalism, of which the current crisis (beginning in 2008) is the most recent. However, they failed to predict the Keynesian strategy of protecting capitalism through regulation and strategic spending.

For this and other reasons, modern critical theorists, from Horkheimer onward, have backed away from the 'positivist' inclination of early Marxism that tried to predict the future based on universal laws of history. Even analysts whose work clearly builds on Marxian analysis—such as Braverman and Wallerstein whose work we have already examined—back away from prediction. Instead, they have sided with later Marxian works and with Max Weber's view that it is not the job of sociology (or social science) to predict the future (though we may want to influence it). Predicting the future from unique, non-reproducible historical events is impossible, on methodological grounds. Societies are not controlled experiments, with control groups or matched samples. Also, social researchers themselves are not free of biases that cloud their objectivity.

One point that is very clear in the Marxian analysis is the importance, and inevitability, of conflict in human affairs. It is to that inevitable topic that we now turn our attention.

Conflict in Society

Consider regions first; for example, think of those in Canada. No one should be surprised to discover there is a long history of regional conflict in Canada. Each Canadian province has its own government, which protects individual powers under the British North America Act. As well, the jurisdictional powers of these provinces (such as the control of health care and education) touch on the most important concerns of the twenty-first century. The provinces also have taxing powers, the right to legislate on various topics, and their own courts.

No wonder, then, that the Canadian provinces (and as we have seen, collaborations between provinces in the form of Canadian regions) have enormous importance in Canadian politics. They are constantly battling the federal government, and often enjoy

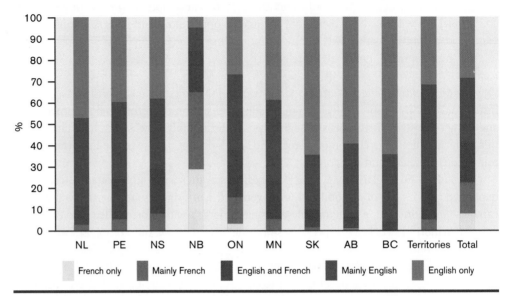

Figure 10.2 Proportion of French-speaking Adults, by the General Language Use Index, Provinces and Canada less Quebec, 2006

Source: Statistics Canada, *Minorities Speak Up: Results of Survey on the Vitality of Official-Language Minorities*, 91-548-XWE, 2007. http://www.statcan.gc.ca/pub/91-548-x/2007001/4185568-eng.htm

great success in doing so. Politics in Canada is highly regionalized, and the differences rooted in Canada's regions—geographic, ecological, economic, social, and cultural differences—explode regional conflicts onto the national political stage. Most dramatic of all is the split between French and English Canada, especially between mainly French-speaking Quebec and the mainly English-speaking rest of Canada. Language, as well as other aspects of Quebec culture, plays a significant role in the historical, never-ending conflict between English and French regions of Canada (Heller, 2007).

In general, language use varies considerably from one Canadian region to another. As Figure 10.2 shows, French is rarely used in the provinces west of Ontario. Likewise, in the Maritime provinces, except for New Brunswick where the language has actually been gaining importance, French is also rarely used (Castonguay, 2002, 2005). The recent survival and even growth of French in New Brunswick and Quebec has resulted from considerable efforts to promote French culture in Canada. English, for its part, has easily grown in use due (partly) to American influence in Ontario. Meanwhile, French use has declined in other parts of previously French-speaking Canada (ibid).

Alongside the French–English split throughout Canada, there is a split in cultural identities. Francophones in Quebec continue to identify themselves first as Québécois and only secondarily as Canadian. Francophones in Ontario, however, are likely to identify themselves as bilingual as opposed to francophone, in contrast to those who live in Quebec or New Brunswick (ibid).

Many French Canadians continue to express concern about the feared loss of French culture and language in North America, especially with continued declines in fertility in Quebec and lower levels of assimilation into French culture. Recent immigrants to Canada are more likely to choose to live in Toronto (or Vancouver, Edmonton, or Calgary) than in Quebec City, for example. This, for many, reflects a desire to assimilate into the dominant English-speaking North American culture and economy. If immigration continues at its present rate, with its present consequences, the French–English conflict is likely to disappear through lack of interest.

Even among immigrants who settle in Montreal and learn French—a provincial requirement—many take English classes as well (Grégoire, 2003). As a result, anglophone populations are growing throughout Canada, while francophone generations are declining. These patterns continue to concern French Canadian nationalists, and feature regularly in Canadian politics. Recently, some initiatives have been undertaken to counter the anglicization of Quebec—for example, offering government-funded French-language education programs for any interested students.

Conflicts about language in Quebec have led to laws proclaiming that all signs in Quebec must be bilingual, including this stop sign.

The continued contest over French- and English-language institutions lies outside the explanatory power of Marxist analysis—for example, outside the theory propounded in *The Manifesto of the Communist Party*. It also lies outside the theory of world-systems proposed by Wallerstein, discussed earlier in this chapter. However, it does offer a graphic illustration of the hardship a small culture—Quebec francophonie—faces against the assimilative tendencies of a much larger, increasingly global English-speaking, American driven culture.

Compared with regions, nations are much better able to survive and to preserve their historical culture, because they are better than regions at distinguishing themselves institutionally. One purpose of state building is to create institutions that promote the interests of one country at the expense of others. This is why sovereign countries have governments, armies, foreign policies, trade policies, tariffs, and immigration rules. It is therefore to be expected that nations will subordinate their regions. They will also conflict with other states; their core institutions depend on such conflict. Foreign conflict strengthens national solidarity. However, not all conflicts between nations have harmful outcomes. Some conflicts are mediated by international organizations (e.g., NATO and the UN) and treaties (e.g., NAFTA and the European Union), that are aimed at creating pan-national institutions with their own interests and resources.

Point/Counterpoint

BOX **10.2**

Quebec Language Police Pressure Montreal Bar over Posters

McKibbin's Irish pub in Montreal has drawn the ire of French-language activists. Quebec law prohibits English-only business signs and advertising. Pub owner Rick Fon says that his vintage posters and signs advertising beers only in English are just decorations that help make the pub look genuinely Irish. McKibbin's also provides a bilingual menu that contravenes the language law. The *Office québécois de la langue française* had ordered Fon to remove the posters, or face fines of up to $1,500 for each infraction, but after discussion it has decided to allow the posters to remain.

Even the Quebec government itself has been the subject of language complaints. Some government departments gave callers the opportunity to 'press nine' for English language service before the French instructions were given. After complaints, some of the departments now give the French instructions first.

Source: Adapted from CBC News (2008).

Some have applied Marxist analysis—for example, the theory proposed in *The Manifesto of the Communist Party*—to examine the behaviour of nation-states. For example, they have promoted the idea that national governments—politics and politicians, generally—are only mechanisms for promoting the interests of the ruling class. By this logic, the prime minister is merely a stooge for Alberta oil interests, for example; and the American president is merely a stooge for the so-called military-industrial complex. While appealing in many respects, this theory seems a little too simple. For one thing, it ignores the multiplicity of international influences on a nation's politics.

International Politics and Discrimination

Consider how politics in a country like Canada is influenced by intergroup relations: for example, between French and English, whites and Aboriginals, or Jews and Muslims. In Chapter 7, we discussed aspects of social distance, prejudice, and discrimination as they arise out of racial and ethnic differences. However, external (i.e., international) politics also exercises a major influence on intergroup relations within Canada.

Sometimes, intergroup conflict is aggravated by large-scale (largely international) conflict—for example, by war or the threat of war. The first signs of this are seen in propaganda and so-called news reporting. In wartime, as so many have noted, truth is the first casualty. Newspaper and television commentators start reporting atrocities perpetrated by one group against another. Sometimes, the reports are slanted in a way that suggests the inhumanity or moral inferiority of one group compared to another. Such messages have a huge effect on people's views of the combatants, and on their emotional reactions.

Nowhere has this been more obvious than in the current treatment of Muslims by the Western media—or for that matter, of Americans by the Islamic media. Some Western conservative commentators have tried to depict the suicide bombings in Iraq and Afghanistan and the 9/11 terrorist attacks as evidence of a 'clash of civilizations'—a 'culture war' of theocratic, backward Islamic nations against secular, progressive America. Islamic commentators, for their part, have portrayed the same acts as heroic responses to American imperialism, and have depicted the US as single-mindedly focused on securing oil, protecting Israel, supporting Arab despots, and undermining Islamic national pride and independence.

Such overgeneralized, simplistic depictions of political events—accusing all Muslims of being backward ideologues and all Americans of being venal hypocrites—increase the distance between nations and make it harder for them to resolve their differences. In Canada, such prejudiced depictions distress the uninvolved people who are vilified by mere association, especially Arab Canadians and Muslims of all nationalities and political persuasions.

Despite this situation, we have found no evidence of an increase in hate crimes in Canada related to these national depictions, nor any evidence of increased workplace discrimination. For example, there has been no upsurge of jokes at the expense of Muslims or Arabs. The main sign of tension between Islamic and Western groups in Canada has been on university campuses, around the Israel–Palestine conflict. As pollster Michael Adams has pointed out in his book *Unlikely Utopia* (2007), most Canadians seem comfortable with the presence of Muslim immigrants, and most Muslim immigrants embrace the same social, education, and economic goals as most other Canadians.

The *relative* absence of visible discrimination and prejudice in Canada suggests several things. At the risk of overstating the case, it first suggests the success of human rights legislation, which is aimed at preventing discrimination, hate crimes, and the use of derogatory language against other groups. Second, it suggests that Canadians, largely, are a moderate people who tend to avoid conflict (much more, say, than Americans do).

Finally, it suggests that American efforts to label conflicts in the Middle East as 'culture wars' have largely failed in Canada. Canadians, generally, are skeptical about the motives and claims of American foreign policy, though they may feel a strong kinship with other aspects of American society. (For example, Canadians were probably among the world's most avid supporters of Barack Obama, the first African-American presidential candidate.)

International Violence and War

It is impossible to discuss nations and empires without discussing wars, because nations and empires breed war; they thrive on war, and some would say, they are organized for war. The twentieth century was a period of continued, sporadic **war**, and the twenty-first has started out in a similar way. Figure 10.3 shows the trends in international conflict over the past 17 years. Wars (including civil wars) are raging at this moment in parts of Africa and the Middle East. Many countries even have a 'war system', in which social institutions and their economies, governments, and cultural practices promote warfare as a normal aspect of life, even if no war is being waged at a given moment. In fact, war may be necessary to the economic and political stability of many countries—part of their military-industrial complex.

Increasingly over the centuries, war (like other parts of social life) has become more technologically complex. The weapons used in present-day combat are exponentially more deadly than ever before. A single precision-guided missile released by a B-52 bomber many thousands of feet above a war zone can kill hundreds of people, soldiers and civilians alike. For innocent civilians caught in the middle, the effects of war can be devastating. Unlike soldiers, who can at least justify their participation as military personnel, civilians are rarely trained to fight. Nonetheless, they are often unwilling participants in the horrors of war.

Terrorism

New forms of warfare and organized violence have gained much public awareness in recent years. **Terrorism**, a widely discussed example, is war by other means, just as war is 'a continuation of politics by other means', as early nineteenth-century Prussian military strategist Karl von Clausewitz famously stated (Clausewitz, 1832).

war
An openly declared armed conflict between countries or between groups within a country.

terrorism
The calculated use of unexpected, shocking, and unlawful violence against civilians and symbolic targets.

Today, methods of violence and warfare extend beyond bombs and guns. Biological warfare, such as the use of the toxic bacteria anthrax, is becoming a more common, and silent, threat to society.

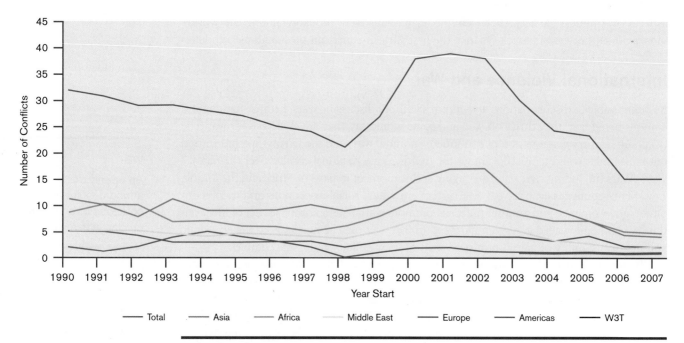

Figure 10.3 Global Conflicts, 1990–2007

Note: W3T refers to the 'Worldwide War on Terror'

Source: Adapted from Smith (2007).

A simple, dispassionate definition is difficult because 'terrorism' is an ideological and value-laden term, as well as a description of events. The roots of terrorism can be found in the religious, nationalist, political, economic, and social differences that keep people from living together in peace. There is no evidence to suggest a single motive behind the use of terrorism, but the most accepted theory is that terrorists choose violence as the best course of action after considering the alternatives. A rational cost-benefit analysis—not reckless impulse—leads people to this conclusion, often because of various frustrating or limiting social, political, and economic conditions.

Generally, terrorist acts are carried out by members of secret subnational groups, to publicize a political or religious cause. Their longer-term goal is to intimidate civilian populations and coerce governments into accepting political demands. Many of the 'terrorist' suicide bombers in the Middle East, for example, come from oppressed or relatively impoverished circumstances. Some people decide to commit suicide bombing after the promise of large payments to their families by supportive states and wealthy sympathizers.

Some terrorists—and especially their leaders, like the infamous Osama bin Laden—come from middle- to upper-class backgrounds, typically with a higher-than-average education and often with Western connections. They usually have specific skills and strong political motivation. Usually, terrorist organizations in the developing world recruit young, mostly male, members. Often, terrorists and guerrillas are the only role models available to these young people; for some, these political groups represent an opportunity for adventure, commitment, and upward mobility (like a career in the army).

Terrorism is not a new phenomenon. Indeed, a recent book by Canadian historian Ana Siljak, called *Angel of Vengeance* (2008), examines the emergence of terrorism in nineteenth-century Russia. There too, terrorist impulses drew on the alienation of young people who were impoverished, angry, and frustrated by the prevailing system of inequality. Siljak shows compellingly that, over the course of time, different groups put different interpretations on the same terrorist acts, to serve their own particular purposes of the moment. This re-imagining of events is also nothing new. However, the recent social construction of terrorism by the media has led to a general misconception that terrorism is unique to our times. It is not.

Experts today view terrorism as merely a different form of soldiering, with the usual motive: the protection of home and country. Terrorists are also motivated by personal glory, public commemoration, and supposed rewards in the afterlife. What is unique about terrorists is not their psychology so much as their degree of organization and commitment to a collective goal. Like other social movements, terrorist groups rely on existing social networks to recruit their members. And because terrorist activities are organized and carried out in secret, they rely on social networks of friendship and kinship to preserve control over recruits and to ensure their reliability. Members recruited through specific social networks of kin and friends will find it difficult to back out or betray the group, even if they change their minds. They are already embedded within the system and can't leave it easily.

State-sponsored terrorism, a variant of this, is the state-sanctioned use of terrorist groups to achieve foreign-policy objectives. In 2010, the US government had seven countries on its list of potential terrorist threats: Cuba, Iran, Iraq, Libya, North Korea, Sudan, and Syria. They were all accused of promoting terrorism abroad. Of these seven, five are Middle Eastern or other Islamic nations with mainly Muslim populations. Other governments and groups might compile different lists. In the eyes of some, the US itself might be viewed as a state that sponsors terrorism, with the aim of destabilizing foreign governments and undermining progressive political movements. Certainly, the US (through the CIA and other state organizations) is known to have played such a role in South and Central America on many occasions.

Since the 9/11 terrorist attacks and the Middle Eastern wars that followed, conflict has become a major source of conversation in our society. Thanks largely to the media, we are constantly bombarded by stories of threat, violence, and tragedy. How will this unease affect the social relationships among ordinary people? Will social life become less social as people become more fearful and start distrusting others?

Research aimed at understanding the complexities of social trust may clarify these issues. Who trusts whom, and to what extent? How are the dynamics of trust and feelings

On 11 September 2001, terrorists hijacked two planes and crashed them into the World Trade Centers in New York City.

Media Distortion

BOX **10.3**

Spy Chief Says Media Play Down Terror Threat

Are news media accurately depicting the terrorist threat to Canadians? Richard Fadden, director of the Canadian Security Intelligence Service (CSIS), doesn't think so. At a conference on security, he claimed that Canadians tend to think that 'our charm and the Maple Leafs on our backpacks are all that we need to protect us'.

Fadden believes that the media cast terror suspects in too favourable a light by, for example, publishing pictures of accused terrorists with their children and publicizing their claims to be abused by the government and by CSIS. While terrorists are single-mindedly seeking to kill their targets, and are harshly characterized by the judges who hear their cases, the media tends to portray them as 'quasi-folk heroes'.

Source: Adapted from Bronskill (2009).

of security changing along with changes in the threat level? In other words, if people no longer have confidence in the protection provided by government, will they trust other institutions or increasingly avoid situations (say, flying in airplanes) that provoke feelings of fear? These questions are being studied by sociologists all the time in relation to questions about civil society, voluntary association, and social capital. We will discuss these issues at some length in the final chapter of this book.

What is important to note in this current discussion about regions, states, and empires is that what goes on *within* societies—for example, within Canadian society—cannot be understood without reference to what goes on *between* societies. And this brings us back to Immanuel Wallerstein, and his contribution to modern sociology.

People Are Talking About . . .
IMMANUEL WALLERSTEIN

Immanuel Maurice Wallerstein was born in 1930 in New York City. He received all his degrees from Columbia University: B.A. in 1951, an M.A. in 1954 and a Ph.D. in 1959, where he subsequently taught for a time. In 1971, he was named professor of sociology at McGill University. From 1976 until his retirement in 1999, he was a distinguished professor of sociology at Binghamton University. From 1999 until 2005, he was head of the Fernand Braudel Center for the Study of Economies, Historical Systems and Civilization at Binghamton University. In 2000, he also joined the Yale Sociology department as Senior Research Scholar.

Wallerstein's earliest work was in African studies. His Ph.D. thesis used modernization theory to examine the relationship of voluntary associations to nationalist independence movements in Ghana and the Ivory Coast. In his books *Africa: The Politics of Independence* (1961) and *Africa: The Politics of Unity* (1967), Wallerstein began to develop his own approach, rather than relying on the modernization approach. He suggested that African social relationships brought about by European colonialism were inhibiting social change and economic development. He agreed with dependency theorists Samir Amin and Andre Gunther Frank that change and development would continue to be hindered by sustained Western influence in Africa.

Wallerstein is best known for world-systems theory, outlined in three books that begin with *The Modern World-System I: Capitalist Agriculture and the Origins of the European World-Economy in the Sixteenth Century* (1974) (discussed above). World-systems theory, which draws on dependency theory, encompasses the entire global economy since the sixteenth century, rather than that of one nation or continent. In a biography, Scott (in Scott, 2006: 218) notes, 'A world system is a culturally differentiated system with a single division of labour. That is, the constituent elements are culturally distinct but economically interdependent'. Unlike earlier systems (like the Roman Empire), the current world system does not need political integration any more than it needs cultural assimilation.

International capitalism, according to Wallerstein, is able to profit from the disparities in development around the world; however, nations can themselves benefit from disparity by positioning themselves advantageously in international markets. Note, however, that Wallerstein has been critical of the 'globalization' concept, which he sees as merely a variant of neo-liberalism—a cover for capitalist imperialism. In recent essays, he wrote that the ideology of neo-liberalism asserts that countries must allow corporations to transfer goods and capital across any national border they wish, that governments must not own property, and they must reduce, if not stop, social support transfer payments to their populations. Economically, he claims, this ideology has failed, since most economic markets are over-saturated. Wallerstein predicts the economic recession that began in 2008 will become a global depression with high unemployment.

Source: Adapted from *Fifty Key Sociologists: The Contemporary Theorists* (edited by John Scott, London: Routledge, 2006) and other sources.

Wallerstein's world system approach has forced sociologists to re-think their units of political analysis. For example, Cotesta (2008) describes attempts by sociologists and historians of the twentieth century to steer away from analysis based on a nation-state paradigm, by using such concepts as the clash of civilizations (Toynbee and Huntington) and world economy (Braudell and Wallerstein). He suggests that a global society paradigm is preferable, despite problems with the 'globalization' concept noted by Wallerstein.

Spohn (2008), hoping to salvage the battered 'modernity' through a judicious use of world-system thinking, highlights the structural and cultural multiplicity of forms of modernity and globalization in the emerging world society. He notes the variety of approaches that, like Wallerstein's, argue in different ways for the unity of the emerging world society. Then, he develops his own historical-comparative sociological approach that highlights the impact of culture, religion, and inter-civilizational relations in the development of a world system. His new concept of 'modernity' is more inclusive and less homogenous than ideas that prevailed before Wallerstein.

Paic (2008), for his part, hopes to salvage the concept of 'globalization' by critically reconsidering present-day globalization. He notes that any attempt at a fundamental transformation of social, political, and cultural development would require the end of 'globalization' as a neo-liberal ideology or traditional 'modernization' strategy. However, that doesn't mean we must—or can—dispense with the idea of globalization, so long as we include a more varied idea about cultural change. In every scenario we can imagine, Paic says, the complex idea of 'culture' is needed for all relevant end-of-globalization theories. Culture has become both the means and end of identity in a global age, and though we have difficulty defining both 'culture' and 'globalization', we cannot dispense with either. Both are key to our understanding of power and domination. In fact, the two concepts are necessarily related: where 'globalization' speaks to the dramatic, self-transforming impulses of the present-day world, 'culture' speaks to the stabilizing impulses. In this light, we can see culture as at least a self-organizing system of ideological hegemony.

Cultural influences are important in all processes of globalization—even in academic work. So, for example, Gunaratne (2009) applies the concepts of centre, semi-periphery, and periphery from Wallerstein's world economy theory to academic research, and the

Through the use of comparative-historical methods of analysis, Hough (2007) found that in Colombia, the banana-producing region of Uraba is controlled by a coercive form of rule. In contrast, the coffee region was characterized by a consensual form of rule and the cocoa/cattle regions were controlled by guerilla groups.

field of media and communications research in particular. Because this field originated in the European 'centre', it embodies European values and methods. Recently, however, Asian scholars have begun to formulate an alternative framework of media and communications theory, incorporating traditional Asian philosophy.

Likewise, science has globalized and universalized over the course of time. Taylor et al. (2008) see this occurring in the 'rise of modern science', and date the beginnings of this globalization back to 1450. Over time, the locations of leading scientists changed, forming four clearly defined networks that centred first in central and northern Italy (in the sixteenth century) and later in Berlin (in the nineteenth century.) In Wallerstein's world-system terms, these geographically shifting networks represented the core of a global system of scientific research.

As Marx would have predicted, the triumph of world capitalism—through globalization—has ignited bitter, forceful reactions. Carvalho (2008) notes that, according to Wallerstein's theory, anti-systemic activities are currently gaining strength. Various contradictions, conflicts, and tensions, all effects of capitalism, have fostered significant new social activities against capitalism around the world. The job for sociology today, Carvalho says, is to identify anti-systemic activities and explain how they unfold—a job not so different from the one Marx and Engels took on in the late nineteenth century, in their analysis of European capitalism.

What Marx failed to do, and sociologists need to do today, is to develop a clearer understanding of capitalist actions (and anti-capitalist reactions) in non-industrial societies. No single, simple formula describes all cases. For example, Hough (2007) compares class relations in three regions of Colombia: one that produces coffee, one that produces bananas, and one that features both cattle-ranching and coca-farming. Within each area, Hough looked at relations between the elite and subordinate classes in the mid twentieth century. He found that, in the coffee-producing region, the elites shared their power in a democratic fashion; in the banana-producing region, the elite used coercion to rule the peasantry; and in the cattle region, the elites surrendered control to guerrilla 'warlords' who began to produce coca, to be made into cocaine. As Wallerstein would have predicted, local forms of class rule varied, depending on the capacity of local elites to organize themselves and restructure their relations with the core.

However, in all three regions, these relations of control were disrupted in the 1980s and 1990s. In the coffee-producing region, neo-liberal globalization ended the democratic form of power-sharing between classes; while in the banana-producing region, more democratic class relations developed. And in the cattle/coca region, an increase in the value of the cattle ranching and continuation of the US-led 'war on drugs' returned some control to the cattle-farming elite.

Savchenko (2007) argues that we can best view Wallerstein's world system theory as a complex, flexible version of Marxist class theory. In Wallerstein's version, the economy is still a zero-sum game between capitalists and non-capitalists, based on class exploitation. However, by globalizing the canvas and adding postmodern frames of reference, Wallerstein can continue to imagine an outcome like Marx's—namely, a more peaceful, co-operative, and egalitarian world.

Thus, a review of recent writings finds continued application of the work by Immanuel Wallerstein—roughly 200 journal articles applying Wallerstein's work in the last 15 years. Clearly, sociologists are talking about Immanuel Wallerstein. Wallerstein deserves a place in our comprehensive, fusion approach to sociology because of his huge, macroscopic picture of social life: the entire world is his canvas, entire centuries his time frame. His actors are nations, ruling classes, and protest movements. He is concerned with nothing less than the distribution of power throughout the world.

New Insights

In the new sociological approaches, we see a wide variety of new political actors within the global system. Ironically, national identities—fragile and endangered—emerge despite the monopolistic policies of global dominance, according to Duman (2007). Nation-states, as modern political forms, have tried to create strong national identities by dissolving regional, ethnic, and class subidentities. However, postmodern forces, using the same strategy, have undermined this effort to construct ideological uniformity. The result is a fragmentation of national identity, and a weakening of social order through the increased emphasis on individuals and cultural subgroups. In short, Duman says, national identities may be impossible within the present-day world.

Edensor (2006) disagrees, however, suggesting that the similar daily lives and routines of citizens form a national identity, even without overarching ideologies and heroic acts. He claims that local time and space provide a more powerful basis for identity than global citizenship. This may help to explain why transnational entities have trouble gaining recognition and loyalty. Consider the European Union (EU), a relatively new political body (Hulsse, 2006). It has a complex organization, with multi-dimensional layers—much more sophisticated than the relatively homogenous nation-states that make it up. Yet people have been slow to give their loyalty to the EU, or to see themselves as meaningfully linked to this new identity. Hulsse claims the EU is perceived simply as another large nationalistic postmodern entity.

People have trouble imagining new transnational or global meanings, just as they have trouble celebrating global diversity. Kimura (2007) notes that, for the most part, international 'cultural heritage' projects assign cultural-historical meaning to largely unknown objects in other countries, in attempts to integrate them into an existing (universal) value system. However, these efforts do little more than feed a mild interest in 'ruins' and ecological beauty-spots. Neither competes strongly against the consumerism and waste of capitalist society.

Many would assign the problems of a globalized world to economic or political factors. However, modern citizenship is in crisis for cultural reasons too (Herera and Soriano Miras, 2005). States around the world face problems that are both internal and external. Usually, the internal problems arise from issues around political and cultural legitimacy, social regulation, resources and costs. The external problems, on the other hand, derive from global economic forces like recession, demographic changes like aging, and difficulties in managing social groups and social strata that are unconnected to the state: for example, multinational corporations.

The very idea of transnational or global citizenship works against the modern nation-state, in that it steers people away from national values and concerns. This leads us to ask: Is it possible to re-launch 'citizenship' as a basis for democracy, and if so, how? Doing so will likely require us to re-imagine citizenship as a complex of rights and duties that extend across national borders. In this sense, they will re-imagine civic life in terms of universal goals and universal rights. Devising this new global citizenship will, in some people's minds, be the key to a postmodern democratic state in the future.

And if the postmodern world ever comes to understand itself in a postmodern way, global cities will play a large role in this process. The reason is that, as Nisanci (2007) points out, in the context of postmodernism and globalization, cities will become the focus of democratic citizenship, just as they are (and will be) the nexus of culture, politics, and economy. Cities can play an important emancipatory (democratic) role under particular conditions; however, under other conditions they can prolong oppression and undermine citizenship. So like technology, cities are only tools for achieving social change: the rate and type of change will depend entirely on the political and class forces driving the change.

Within successful city contexts, new social groupings will continue to play an important role in the control and use of public space. While some groupings have a positive influence, others do not—especially under conditions of political conflict. Manwaring (2006) asks us to consider the role of urban 'street gangs' intent on making money: they may challenge political structures in order to operate more freely, and may even act as mercenaries for nation-states, criminal organizations, drug-traffickers, and warlords. By blurring the line between crime and war, such urban gangs become threats to national security, as well to public safety and public confidence.

One of the biggest problems in postmodern analysis is assessing the meaning and justification of rebellious, warlike, or criminal behaviour. Moral and cultural relativism makes the postmodernists reluctant to label, much less punish, rule-breakers. Yet problems of security, crime and violence remain. Here, Langman (2005) warns against cultural relativism in her review of the current debate about Islamic fundamentalism, which is viewed as a new form of totalitarian thought and practice. Langman holds present-day global capitalism partly responsible for fostering widespread antimodernist, reactionary movements throughout the Islamic world. However, the reasons are more complicated than that.

According to Langman's account, Islam emerged as a trader's religion that permitted a vast commercial empire to flourish. However, Islamic sharia law limited the rationalization of commerce, forestalled a reformation such as occurred in northern Europe, and (in these ways) weakened Islamic dominance in the face of ascendant Christendom.

It is because of these (internal) barriers to rationality and (external) interventions of capitalist imperialism that globalization has bypassed the Middle East. As a result, a powerful resentment has taken root among the marginal, disenfranchised, and otherwise powerless Muslims. They have been trained to adopt religious understandings of social problems, with religious-based actions to achieve a remedy. Fundamentalist Islamic doctrines of salvation and renewal preach authoritarian submission, hatred to outsiders (infidels), and demands for a life-and-death struggle. The fusion of eighth-century doctrines with twenty-first–century technologies (for example, Iranian access to nuclear weaponry) foreshadows greater human suffering.

This example suggests the problems associated with only partial modernization, where people have the goals of modernity but not the means, or in Iran's case, the means but not the goals. Channa (2004) claims the 'modernization project' offered many people in the less-developed countries false hope and a harsh reality. They were encouraged to adopt Western values and assured that Western science would provide all the knowledge they needed. Women in particular were characterized as oppressed, needing to be rescued by Western rationality. Even today, development continues to be seen as Westernization, even by Third World feminists. But conditions have not changed as much as people expected. Consider the crimes against women and rampant poverty in, for example, cities in India, where modern, globalized Western values have displaced traditional knowledge and values. Channa suggests that empowerment for the marginalized people of India needs to be redefined without reference to Western values.

Chapter Summary

The subject of regions, nations, and empires is important to us all. The world's political landscape has transformed the course of our history, affects our everyday lives, and will shape our future. It focuses our attention on the relationships, not just between individuals, but between larger-scale social units. Nations, regions, and empires, as we have seen, are significant historical actors, brought alive by the people, societies, laws, cultures, and organizations that locate within their boundaries.

This chapter has focused specifically on the links among these three types of entities. In the first part of the chapter, we discussed the positive links that exist among them. Topics like co-operation, globalization, multinational organizations, technology, and communication were discussed. These examples of positive relationships are possible driving forces towards global peace and unity.

In an ideal society, these positive aspects would prevail. However, in reality, there are also many negative links between regions, nations, and empires. These negative relationships are expressed through conflict: verbal, behavioural, and physical. Examples of conflicts discussed in this chapter are social distance, prejudice, discrimination, war, and terrorism. They are all harmful to society, whether on an individual level as in prejudice, or a global level as in war.

The effects of such conflict, especially of war and terrorism, are severe and traumatic. Often they have significant physical health effects, through rape, mutilation, or death; sometimes they are psychological, as in post-traumatic stress disorder; and sometimes they are environmental.

As you can see, the relationships between regions, nations, and empires are vibrant in their complexities and dramas. This everlasting struggle between peace and conflict is one driving force behind social change. However, sociologists differ in their views on whether conflict and war are unavoidable, normal, or necessary.

Critical Thinking Questions

1. What are the similarities and differences between regions, nations, and empires?
2. Do you think Canada and the United States are essentially similar or different? What is the significance of the border between them—does it separate two distinct regions, nations, or empires?
3. What is the value of the world systems perspective for understanding global capitalism? Give economic, political and cultural examples of the relationships between core states, peripheral states, and semi-peripheral states.
4. What is at issue between English and French Canada? How do these inter-cultural disagreements stem from the political, social, and economic history of Canada?
5. The twentieth century is known as the most violent century in the history of humankind, and this legacy of violence is perpetuated in the twenty-first century. What do you think is the best course of action to promote peace and co-operation and to prevent terrorism and war in our world? What are obstacles to taking such a direction?
6. Describe the importance of regional and national differences for current world conflict.

Recommended Readings

Immanuel Wallerstein, *The Modern World-System I: Capitalist Agriculture and the Origins of the European World-Economy in the Sixteenth Century* (New York: Academic Press, 1975). This seminal work develops the world-systems theory, a theoretical framework for understanding the current global capitalist economy and international relations. It outlines the important historical changes that occurred since the sixteenth century to develop the modern world. This theory allows for historically sensitive comparison between the nations of the world and their interactions.

Joel Garreau, *The Nine Nations of North America* (Boston: Houghton Mifflin, 1981). This classic work argues that the continent of North America can be divided into nine regions ('nations') according to distinctive cultural and economic features. Doing so renders the conventional state and national borders insignificant. The author asserts that these new borders are more historically relevant and provide a clearer way of understanding the development of North America.

Edward Grabb and James Curtis, *Region Apart: The Four Societies of Canada and the United States* (Toronto: Oxford University Press, 2005). This comparison between Canada and the United States explores the historical myths of each of these countries. The authors argue that the original American colonies (which developed into the United States) and English Canada were similar societies. The differences between them emerged from internal regional divisions—the English and French in Canada, and the North and South in the United States.

Ana Siljak, *Angel of Vengeance: The 'Girl Assassin,' the Governor of St. Petersburg, and Russia's Revolutionary World* (New York: St Martin's Press, 2008). This book examines 'terrorism' as it developed at the end of the nineteenth century in Russia. It began with the assassination of a prominent Russian governor by Vera Zasulich, who sought revenge for his brutal treatment of a political prisoner. Vera's trial became famous throughout Europe. After, she inspired a generation of revolutionaries who embraced violence as a means for revenge.

Eric Hobsbawm, *Age of Extremes: The Short Twentieth Century, 1914–1991* (London: Michael Joseph, 1994). This book divides the twentieth century, from the beginning of World War I to the Soviet breakdown in 1991, into three periods according to conditions of warfare and other violence: the first period is characterized by two world wars, the second by relative peace, and the last by a revival in international conflict.

Stewart Bell, *Cold Terror: How Canada Nurtures and Exports Terrorism Around the World* (Mississauga, ON: Wiley, 2005). This book, with its intriguing title, argues that Canada has become a home to terrorist organizations around the world because of its overall irresponsibility and ineptitude regarding certain laws and policies. The work has much critical acclaim and the author is an award-winning journalist. He draws his evidence from classified documents and exclusive interviews (some with the terrorists themselves) to paint a dreary picture of Canada as a locus of terrorist planning and activity.

Websites

United Nations
www.un.org

Flashpoints: Guide to World Conflicts
www.flashpoints.info/FlashPoints_home.html

Canadian Peacekeepers
www.peacekeeper.ca

Famous World Trials: The Nuremburg Trials
www.law.umkc.edu/faculty/projects/ftrials/nuremberg/nuremberg.htm

World-Systems Theory: Global Social Change in the Long Run
www.irows.ucr.edu/cd/courses/10/socchange.htm

Natural Resources Canada
www.nrcan-rncan.gc.ca/com/index-eng.php

11 Families and Socialization

Learning Objectives

In this chapter, you will:

> Learn to distinguish between good and bad parenting, and see how parenting influences a child's characteristics

> Find out how families cope differently with opportunities and crises

> See how families reproduce gender, race, ethnicity, and class identities

> Come to understand the different forms families can take and the ways 'family life' has changed over time

Chapter Outline

Almost all of us grew up in families, so we have a general idea of what a family looks like and the functions it performs. All families teach children rules for living in human society, and most children go on to be parents themselves, teaching their own children the social rules. However, the family you came from is likely different from other families that you know. That's because families are highly variable—even more variable today than in the past.

In present-day Canada, we could find a nuclear family living next door to an extended family. Down the block, you might find a cohabiting family, a single-parent family, a same-sex couple, a family with four children, and another with no children. Today, all of these families and the people in them have the same rights and are entitled to the same respect as the 'traditional' family.

This chapter is about the growth of diversity among families, and the different social processes we see in families of different types. We will discuss how families have different levels of adaptability and cohesiveness: for example, some are strict and unyielding, while others are flexible and accommodating. We will also discuss different kinds of parenting, ranging from authoritarian through permissive styles, and note that the way children are socialized makes a great deal of difference—not only to the children themselves and their families, but to society as a whole. It matters that we impose socialization on children, sometimes in harsh and damaging ways. And, as a consequence, we need to judge the satisfactoriness of families not by their forms but by their processes—the ways they do their 'family business'.

Everyday Observations

Family meets family: Fiona was going to meet her boyfriend Brian's family for the first time. She was nervous—she had spent two hours choosing just the right thing to wear, agonized over a gift to bring his parents, and worried about conversation topics. She wanted to make a good impression on Brian's family, and she knew that in her own family, to make a good impression a person had to be well-dressed, well-spoken, reserved, and polite. When she arrived at the house, Brian's mom answered the door and Fiona stuck out her arm for a handshake. His mom smiled and instead of returning the handshake, pulled Fiona in for a great big bear hug. 'It's so lovely to finally meet you, Fiona! You simply must come in and tell me all about yourself!' Brian's father and three brothers also greeted her with a hug, and then they sat down for a warm, home-cooked meal accompanied by gregarious conversation and wine. At first, Fiona was uncomfortable and not sure what to say or how to act—her family never sat down together to eat dinner, and she wasn't used to adults being this friendly with her! By the end of the night, however, she was having a great time. It would be fun to have so many siblings, she thought; but she also wondered if the noise would get to her. Compared with her small, quiet family, Brian's was like a circus—how did two such different families produce two people as compatible as her and Brian?

family

For the purpose of this chapter, any social unit, or set of social relations, that does what families are popularly imagined to do, by whatever means it does so.

Have you ever noticed how varied different families can be? Families can be different in their composition—the number, gender, and ages of parents and children in them—and in their patterns of interaction—each member's behaviour towards the others, for example. And, have you noticed how fluid and malleable, but also how basic and *necessary* the idea of **family** is in our society? Some have called family the primary unit of society, but how can this be if the term *family* applies to so many varied forms?

In present-day society, norms about what constitutes a 'family' are changing quickly and seem much more open to personal interpretation than ever before. This rapid change and social diversity sometimes creates confusion; for example, consider the furor over polygamy. In some countries, having more than one wife is common, even expected. But, in most cultures and over most of human history, monogamy has been the norm, and this is true in Canada today. Multicultural Canada supports diversity and encourages groups to retain their social values and norms, but polygamy is illegal here. Most Canadians also consider the practice sexist and exploitative, despite their support for multiculturalism. This seems contradictory. After all, in a free society that guarantees the right to follow one's own customs, how can we justify rules that exclude certain kinds of family life?

In Canada, people hold varying ideas about divorce too. In some cultures, divorce is highly discouraged—if not illegal, it is considered a moral failure. In Canada, divorce is legal, common, and considered an understandable, though sometimes unfortunate, outcome. People also hold varying ideas about family size. Today, many people put off having children until their thirties, and they tend to have fewer children than Canadians did a generation ago—something that would have seemed inexplicable a century ago, when families needed many children to help till the fields or earn incomes.

Despite their loss of certain traditional functions, families remain important in our society as agents of socialization. When we are children, our families (especially our parents) teach us how to behave and act properly. Although we continue to learn social lessons throughout our lives, our first years are the most important. In this sense, learning to share our toys is as important to society as, for example, learning to perform surgery or drive a car. When we are children, the lessons we learn from parents shape the kind of adults we become, both socially and morally.

As social norms change, so do the ways we socialize our children, and today, the social norms are more complex and confusing than ever before. Yet somehow, families continue to function and we continue to raise our children according to the social rules we understand and accept as legitimate.

Ways of Looking at . . .
FAMILY LIFE

Functionalism

Sociologists approach the study of families from different perspectives. For example, functionalists view the family as a central institution in society. They see the family as a microcosm of society, with individual family members coming together in a unified and productive whole (Lehmann, 1994). For this reason, they expect changes in the family to mirror changes in the larger society.

So, in modern industrial societies, family life is more complicated, requiring more specialization and coordination. In this respect, socialization—the manufacture of new citizens—is like any other manufacturing process in its complexity. Accordingly, Talcott Parsons and Robert Bales's functionalist analysis (1955) views the family's division of labour as the key to its success. Ideally, the husband of the household performs an instrumental role as the breadwinner, decision-maker, and source of authority and leadership, while the wife fulfills an expressive role as homemaker, nurturer, and emotional centre of the family. It is through this specialization that the family institution accomplishes several important functions, including the regulation of sexual behaviour and reproduction, the provision for the physical (food, shelter) and psychological (nurturing, learning) needs of its members, and the socialization of children. Since the 1950s, however, the roles of the husband and wife have changed and such specialization may no longer be possible or useful—especially when husbands and wives are both working for pay outside the home.

So some sociologists have revisited the questions of whether certain family forms are 'natural' or 'inevitable'. For example, psychiatrists Ronald Immerman and Wade Mackey (1999) argue that almost all marriage systems across the world support monogamy. They reason that this reduces the number of sexual partners people have—in this way limiting the transmission of sexually transmitted diseases—and reduces out-of-wedlock births, infant morbidity, violent crime, and lower educational attainment. As a result, monogamous societies tend to function better than communities that do not maintain pair bonding, so monogamy is functional in the sense it increases the survival capacity of the community.

Other present-day functionalists argue that cohabitation is inferior to traditional (legal) marriage. For example, Linda Waite (2000) argues that cohabiting relationships are often less permanent, fail to provide the economic and psychological benefits that marriage offers to both participants, are less likely to draw support from extended families, and provide less support to children and spouses during a crisis. Again, the argument is that certain traditional forms—in this case, married monogamy—contribute to the survival of society and the members of that society.

Critical Theories

Unlike functionalists, critical theorists do not look for universal truths about family life, nor do they suppose certain forms fulfill social functions better than others. Rather, they take a historical approach and focus on political and economic changes in society to explain changes in family life.

They note that with industrialization, families moved from being self-sustaining productive units (for example, farming households) to consumption units (e.g., dual-income households that purchase shelter, food, clothing, services, and luxuries). In doing so, they became dependent on outside sources of income to meet their survival needs. This meant that working-class men had to sell their labour power in exchange for an income. In this process, women gained exclusive control over (or, more accurately, were relegated to) the home, becoming responsible for child rearing, food preparation, and the provision of emotional support—for what is sometimes called the task of social reproduction.

However, as both critical and feminist theorists emphasize, women did this work without financial remuneration. Gender inequality increased with gender differentiation, and both increased under conditions of exploitive capitalism.

There are historical reasons for this change in gender relations, and for its association with the rise of industrial capitalism. Feminist theorists argue that, just as factory workers depend on capitalists for a living wage, wives depend on their husbands. In both cases, such dependence easily turns into subordination. As a result, women have endured not only economic reliance on men, but also political and social inferiority. Though these patriarchal tendencies are very old—we see strong patriarchal differentiation of men and women in many pre-literate societies—the capitalist economy affirmed them by giving men preferential access and treatment within the labour market.

These patriarchal tendencies are most common in traditionalist religions, whether within industrial or pre-industrial societies. For example, orthodox Jewish religious communities expect women to get married and start families while young, since their designated role in life is that of house workers. This traditional mentality discourages girls from pursuing higher education and meaningful employment outside the home (Longman, 2008). Some supporters of traditionalism put a positive spin on this type of arrangement. For example, evangelical feminists claim that evangelicalism is 'a strategic form of women's collective action', empowering them while also calling men to fulfill their parental responsibilities. However, in their call to unite women through a religious traditional definition of family, other women such as single mothers, working mothers, bisexuals, or lesbians are excluded (Aune, 2008).

Symbolic Interactionism

As we have seen, interactionists focus on the micro level of sociological phenomena. Symbolic interactionists study the ways members of a family interact with one another and the ways they resolve conflicts within the boundaries of their roles in the family. An important part of this process is the creation and revision of myths about family.

Social constructionists focus on the development and use of family ideologies such as the 'family values' promoted by right-wing religious leaders and conservative politicians in the United States. By appealing to people's interest in and concern about their family lives, these moral and political entrepreneurs channel popular anxieties into hostility against such groups as single mothers, gays and lesbians, and divorced people. The effect of such social constructions is to channel hostility away from exploitive employers and unresponsive governments, towards people who are most in need of support and understanding. Instead of channelling money into child care, health care, or education (for example), they channel money into policing and imprisonment.

These political initiatives undermine the welfare of minorities—for example, urban blacks in the United States or Aboriginals in Canada—that are accused of failing to lead moral family lives or instill family values in their children (McMullin, 2004). Thus, traditional ideologies are used to hurt vulnerable families, under the guise of helping to preserve family life. What is most worrisome is that the family damaged today produces the damaged citizens of tomorrow—through faulty socialization. However, even here sociologists differ in their approach to the topic.

Ways of Looking at . . . SOCIALIZATION

In sociology, there are two main views of how the socialization of children occurs: one associated with the *functionalist* perspective, and the other with the *symbolic interactionist* perspective.

Functionalists assert that socialization normally occurs from the top down, as children internalize social norms and learn to conform to the roles and expectations of society. Sociologist Talcott Parsons described this internalization process most prominently in *Family, Socialization, and Interaction Process* (1955). According to this approach, such top-down learning is necessary for society, since it creates social conformity and consensus. The more thoroughly members of society accept these norms and values, the more smoothly society will function. The ideal society is characterized by *social integration*—an outcome of internalized behavioural expectations. Supposedly, the best integrated society will function most smoothly.

Historically, this functional approach has faced various criticisms. For example, some researchers have denied that people are completely shaped by the norms and expectations of their society. To think socialization is so complete and thorough is to hold an 'oversocialized' view of human nature, according to Dennis Wrong (1961). Feminists have also criticized the functionalist perspective on socialization, since it seems to assume that the differences between men and women—as agents of socialization and objects of socialization—are natural and inevitable. By implication, the social inequalities between men and women are natural, inevitable, and justifiable.

For example, functionalists might argue that women receive lower incomes in the job market because they hold lower-paying jobs, and they hold lower-paying jobs because they were socialized as women to seek such lower-paying jobs (such as jobs in social work and child care, rather than in physics and engineering). Feminist might argue that, on the contrary, a woman socialized in the same way as her male counterparts will still face structural barriers if she pursues a male-dominated career. Thus, gendered socialization is not the only factor at play in the inequality faced by women.

Adorno and his collaborators (1950) give us a slightly different view of the topic. They show that strict, top-down socialization may indeed work well to produce conformity and conventionality. However, there are also undesirable by-products to this kind of socialization: anger, superstition, prejudice, racism, and homophobia, to name a few. So, even if the functionalists are right in asserting that top-down socialization produces social integration, the price in repression may be too high for us to pay. It may be better to have less integration, through looser socialization, if it also means less anger, prejudice, racism, and homophobia.

As well, functional theory is deficient on other grounds. Notably, it fails to address the evidence that a great deal of socialization is from the bottom up—that is, children teach themselves and one another. Peer socialization is, in some circumstances, as important as socialization by parents and teachers. The *symbolic interactionist* approach, based on this insight, is now the most accepted view of socialization in sociology. Launched by

The playground is one of the first places outside the home where children learn to socialize and their unique behaviours and attitudes begin to take form.

sociologists Charles H. Cooley and George Herbert Mead, this approach notes that people participate in their own socialization, through social interaction.

Both researchers were interested in how a child develops a sense of *self*, and in the role of the family in this development. Cooley believes children have the capacity for self-development, which they achieve through social interaction. Though parents and other adults try to train the child from the top down, through language, punishment, and other means, the child also sees and evaluates him- or herself according to how others see him or her. Cooley calls this sense of awareness the *looking-glass self*. We imagine how we appear to others and react to this with pride or embarrassment (Cooley, 1902). In adjusting ourselves to the outside world, we change our behaviour to increase our pride and decrease our embarrassment. So, the reaction of others is important for our own feelings about ourselves. But the role of others is mediated by our self-awareness, and by the importance we attach to various reference groups (including peers, mass media figures, and of course, family members).

Like Cooley, Mead (1934) was also interested in children's development. He believed the self-concept was made up of two components: the *I* and the *Me*. The *I* is one's spontaneous, creative, and unique self, while the *Me* is the self one develops for social purposes, by internalizing societal norms and values. To distinguish between the two, take the following example: suppose you love singing. Although you may belt out songs in the shower, you are less likely to do so on your subway ride down to school. The *I* is that part of your self that wants to sing; the *Me* is that socially conscious component that makes you conform to public expectations in public settings.

For children, one key public setting is the public playground; and for Mead, child's play is central to successful socialization. This play, seemingly unimportant in the eyes of adults, offers children an opportunity to practise socially learned roles and expectations. Through play and early interaction (sometimes with imaginary friends), children develop a concept of the *generalized other*, an individual's notion of the attitudes and expectations of society at large. When you imagine what other passengers on the subway might think if you suddenly burst into song, you are taking the perspective of the generalized other. On reaching the generalized-other stage of development, a child has developed a self-concept and is now able to act in a socially approved manner.

In short, family life and the socialization it provides are both deeply important for human development; although some would like to believe in universal and invariant patterns, both families and socialization have changed dramatically in the past century. The underlying pattern of change is traced out in a class study of family patterns by American sociologist William Goode.

Classic Studies
World Revolution and Family Patterns

World Revolution and Family Patterns, by William Goode (1963), reviews changes to family organization around the world in the first half of the twentieth century. In particular, Goode examines the relationship between changing family patterns and industrialization.

In doing so, he draws attention to several major cross-cultural trends. First, family patterns everywhere are moving towards the **nuclear family** model. The family unit is smaller today than it once was; now it is a self-sustaining unit of production and consumption, separate from the larger kinship group. And, with the widespread increase in contraception use and a decreased birth rate, family size has shrunk almost everywhere. Role relations within families have also changed. Individual family members today have more freedom. Parental authority over children has declined; and with the increase in women's rights, husband's control over wives has dwindled too. Gradually, dowries and bride payments are disappearing everywhere. Finally, we see everywhere an increased acceptance of changed social 'morals' and virtues, including greater acceptance of divorce, contraception, abortion, cohabitation, and premarital sexual relations.

In large part, these changes are attributable to the industrialization and urbanization of social life. These trends encourage smaller, more flexible family units. Because family units are smaller, they have more flexibility to meet industrial changes. For example, they can migrate more easily than a large family, if one or more income earners see the need to do so.

The influence of industry on family life is not one-sided, however. Family demands, such as housework and child care, act as 'barriers' to a complete takeover of family life by work. Goode notes that family systems often resist change, but changes do occur, sooner or later. Though the global trend is toward a nuclear family form, the change does not occur uniformly (at the same rate) throughout the world. Associated changes in family form and function are mediated by cultural influences that predate the Industrial Revolution. They also reflect the cultural development of ideas about what makes for an 'ideal' family. So, it is generally true to say that industrialization has produced small, flexible nuclear families throughout the world; however, in some instances, nuclear families have occurred before (even, without) industrialization, and in other instances, **extended families** have persisted despite industrialization.

In brief, the typical family structure has shifted from a 'tightly independent, patriarchal . . . institution' to a 'loose, but interdependent family group', all around the world (Cavan, 1964: 380). Where this hasn't happened, or happened completely, yet, it is on the way. Goode's work is significant because of its ambitious attempt to define the laws of family change under industrialism, and because of its ambitious data collection. In writing this book, Goode examined family patterns on a global scale, making possible cross-cultural comparisons and a review of historical trends. Only a study of this scope could permit the testing of historical theories about the societal change in family forms.

Though slightly outdated today, the study continues to play a major role in sociology of the family. Goode correctly predicted certain industrial trends and influences—specifically, that industrial growth and an emphasis on education would alter women's roles; and research has borne out these predictions. Not only, then, is this good sociological research but also it provides a good entree into the understanding of social change around the world.

As Goode might have predicted, over the last three decades, the structure of Canadian families has become increasingly diverse. Traditional nuclear families are still the norm, but among nuclear families, the number of cohabiting, single-parent, and same-sex families has increased (Statistics Canada, 2006b; Human Resources and Skills Development Canada, 2007). In 2006, married-couple families accounted for only 69 per cent of all census families, a significant decrease from the 83 per cent they formed only two decades ago (Statistics Canada, 2006b, 2007c).

As Goode would have predicted, marriage rates have been declining in Canada and elsewhere. In fact, in 2006 the number of unmarried Canadians age 15 and over outnumbered the number of legally married people for the first time ever (ibid). Just over half (52 per cent) of the population is unmarried—that is, never married, divorced, separated, or widowed (ibid). Two decades ago, this number was only 39 per cent.

nuclear family

A group that usually consists of a father, a mother, and their children living in the same dwelling. Such a family comprises no more than three relationships: between spouses, between parents and children, and between siblings.

extended family

Multiple generations of relatives living together, or several adult siblings with their spouses and children who share a dwelling and resources. More than three kinds of relationship may be present.

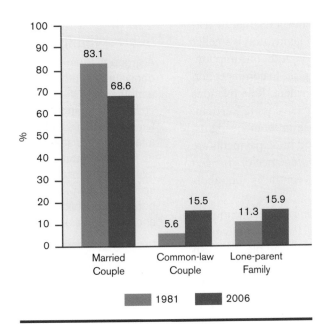

Figure 11.1 Family Structure, Canada, 1981 and 2006

Source: Human Resources and Skills Development Canada (2007). Data from Statistics Canada. *2006 Census.* (Cat. No. 97-554-XCB2006007). Ottawa, 2007.

Another change in marriage is the recognition of same-sex married couples, first enumerated in the 2006 Census after the legalization of gay and lesbian marriage in July 2005. In this tabulation, same-sex couples represent about 0.6 per cent of all couples in Canada. Of these same-sex couples, 16.5 per cent were married, and 83.5 per cent were cohabiting. Most same-sex married spouses are men, and relatively few live with children. Living with children under 24 years of age was more common among women (16.3 per cent) than among men (2.9 per cent). Half of the enumerated same-sex couples live in Canada's three largest metropolitan areas: Montreal (18.4 per cent), Toronto (21.2 per cent), and Vancouver (10.3 per cent) (Statistics Canada, 2006). Table 11.1 shows the distribution of same-sex couples by province. The percentage of same-sex couples in Canada is similar to that observed in other Western countries such as New Zealand and Australia.

Also, as Goode might have predicted, with the decline in marriage rates over the last few decades, single-parent families have increased from 11 per cent to 16 per cent, and cohabiting couples have increased from 6 per cent to 15 per cent (Human Resources and Skills Development Canada, 2007). As Figure 11.2 shows, cohabiting couples are especially common in Quebec, where one-quarter of all common-law families in Canada live.

Another well-known trend discussed by Goode is the increased rate of relationship dissolution (including divorce) in Canada and other developed countries. In part, this reflects the increased prevalence of cohabiting unions: cohabiting couples are more likely to break up than are married ones, especially for people under the age of 30 (Statistics Canada, 2006b, 2007a). In general, cohabiting unions also last for a shorter time than do legal marriages. In 2006, most people who broke up a cohabiting union had been together for only four years, compared to 14 years for the average marital breakup.

Keep in mind, however, that it is hard to accurately record cohabiting breakups, since these breakups are not documented as frequently or systematically as separations

One World, Many Societies

BOX **11.1**

Age at Marriage

Marriage is a social process that forms families. The age at which people marry, however, differs between societies, for many reasons. One CBC report tells of recent marriage trends in Canada: Statistics Canada researchers say that both men and women are increasingly older when they first marry. In 2000, first-time brides were on average 31.7 years old, while grooms were 34.3. Compare these ages to those of 1980: 25.9 and 28.5. Statistics Canada suggests two reasons for the change—women's improving career opportunities, and a growing number of people living in common-law relationships.

According to UNICEF, brides tend to be much younger outside North America. In sub-Saharan Africa and South Asia, most girls are married young, as are many of those of traditional cultures in the Middle East, North Africa, and other parts of Asia. Families may view the husband as his wife's guardian. This is often the case in conflict-ridden Northern Uganda, where a girl will be married to a man in the militia to protect her, and often her family as well, from attack.

Sources: Adapted from CBC News (2005); UNICEF (2001).

Table 11.1 Persons in Same-Sex Unions, by Broad Age Groups and Region, Canada

		Age Groups		
	Total	15–34	35–64	65 and over
Canada	90,695	22,190	65,020	3,480
Newfoundland and Labrador	615	160	430	20
Prince Edward Island	285	30	245	0
Nova Scotia	2,515	825	1,655	35
New Brunswick	1,545	305	1,180	55
Quebec	27,370	6,230	20,030	1,105
Ontario	35,020	8,730	25,095	1,195
Manitoba	1,870	500	1,300	70
Saskatchewan	1,130	375	735	25
Alberta	6,105	1,990	3,905	205
British Columbia	14,075	2,980	10,325	770
Yukon Territory	55	20	40	0
Northwest Territories	80	30	50	0
Nunavut	30	15	15	0

Source: Statistics Canada, 2007. *Families and Households Highlight Tables, 2006 Census.* Statistics Canada Catalogue no. 97-553-XWE2006002. Ottawa. Released September 12, 2007. http://www12.statcan.ca/english/census06/data/highlights/households/index.cfm?Lang=E

and divorces. For example, between 2001 and 2006, three-quarters of the couples who divorced used legal services, compared to only a quarter of couples leaving a common-law union. Divorcing people were also about twice as likely to use social services, compared to individuals who were leaving common-law unions (ibid).

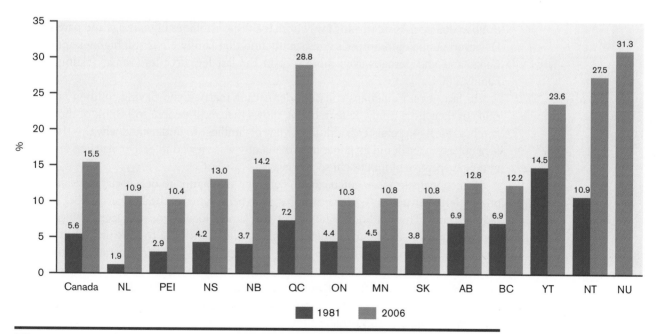

Figure 11.2 Common-Law Families, by Region, Canada,1981 and 2006

Note: For 1981, the Northwest Territories includes Nunavut. In 2001, same-sex couples are included.

Source: Adapted from Human Resources and Skills Development Canada (2007). Data from Statistics Canada. *2006 Census.* (Cat. No. 97-554-XCB2006007). Ottawa, 2007.

Table 11.2 Couple Families, by Presence of Children of All Ages in Private Households, Canada, Change from 2000 to 2006

| | Census Family Structure (%) | | | | |
| | All Couples | Married Couples | | Common-law Couples | |
		With Children	Without Children	With Children	Without Children
Canada	6.0	- 0.7	9.5	16.4	20.9
Newfoundland and Labrador	0.2	- 12.5	15.2	12.7	14.6
Prince Edward Island	2.1	- 7.4	12.7	0.3	23.6
Nova Scotia	1.5	- 8.2	8.6	7.4	22.0
New Brunswick	1.0	- 9.9	10.6	1.5	20.8
Quebec	5.0	- 10.3	10.0	19.8	20.9
Ontario	6.5	3.5	7.7	13.5	20.5
Manitoba	2.3	- 2.9	5.9	9.9	17.0
Saskatchewan	- 0.2	- 8.9	6.1	13.0	15.4
Alberta	11.5	5.8	15.4	14.6	29.3
British Columbia	7.5	2.5	10.2	18.1	18.1
Yukon Territory	5.5	- 0.4	10.2	4.0	14.5
Northwest Territories	11.5	3.5	21.2	12.3	24.4
Nunavut	7.8	1.7	28.0	11.6	9.6

Source: Statistics Canada, 2006. *Families and Households Highlight Table.* Statistics Canada Catalogue no. 97-553-XWE2006002. Accessed on July 27, 2009. http://www12.statcan.ca/english/census06/data/highlights/households/index.cfm?Lang=E

The Idea of 'Family'

Some people take the family changes described above as evidence that the family is in trouble: that people are turning away from the responsibilities of marriage and parenthood. However, public opinion polls consistently find that family life is still highly important to Canadians, and perhaps even more so over the last few decades (Vanier Institute of the Family, 2004).

In fact, most Canadians still consider getting married and having children important goals in their lives (ibid). Research also shows that most people still think of the nuclear family as ideal—a persistent traditional view of families. To understand why this traditional idea persists, we should examine how the family was viewed in earlier years, as embodied in the perspective of functional sociologists.

Functionalists, as we noted earlier, consider 'the family' to be a social institution with one preferred structure—a structure that they believe meets the largest number of social requirements. This traditional notion of the family focuses on the legal obligations of family members—on family structures that would contribute to the survival of society: for example, reproducing the population, socializing the younger generation, supporting the work force, and providing for the family's practical and financial needs. Even William Goode, whose classic analysis of worldwide changes in family life still helps us understand families today, takes the functional position that some patterns are more or less inevitable, given the demands of industrialization.

This view seemingly ignores the fact that a variety of family forms can satisfy the need for love, attachment, and understanding among the members. We can have close, intimate, and long-lasting relations within many different kinds of family arrangements.

The ideal 'golden era' nuclear family: a breadwinner father, a homemaker mother, and obedient children.

That is why we cannot afford to ignore the role of cohabiting relationships or non-nuclear families—for example, ones where several siblings live with their spouses and children. In Canada, non-nuclear, extended families are common among newly arrived immigrants to Canada, though most soon adopt local notions of family life and separate into nuclear units. Nevertheless, even when these immigrants no longer share a household with extended family members, they often live close by and rely heavily on one another. This type of family arrangement is called a *modified extended family*.

Family structures do vary. This fact is important, not only because Canadians tolerate diversity, but also because social policy needs to reflect the practices and needs of actual—not idealized—Canadians. So, for example, it needs to recognize the presence of 1.4 million lone-parent families in Canada at the last census, whether ideal or not. That said, Canadians also value the relative stability of traditional, nuclear families. Currently, many people are caught between a desire for the stability of traditional families and the greater freedom and flexibility of non-traditional families.

The **census family** devised by Statistics Canada does away with the narrow idealized definition of families, and it is practical to use because it is clearly defined and easily measured. As well, this definition tolerates diversity. As of 2006, the couple may be of opposite sexes or the same sex. Children living only with grandparents with no parents present are considered a census family, though the definition does not apparently include families with larger kin groups, including aunts, uncles, or cousins, nor does it attend to the feelings or obligations members of these families have toward each other. In other words, even the Statistics Canada definition focuses on structure or family form, although it is more inclusive than the concept of family *household* used by other agencies of the Canadian government.

The problem is this: we have traditionally assumed that social units that meet the formal or structural requirements of families—for example, those that include spouses, parents, and siblings—behave like families (e.g., reproduce the population, socialize the younger generation, support the work force, and provide for the family's practical and

census family

A household that includes two spouses—opposite or same-sex, married or cohabiting (if they have lived together for longer than one year)—with or without never-married children, or a single parent with one or more never-married children.

Table 11.3 Percentage Distribution of Census Families by Type, Canada, 2006

	%
Families without children at home	
Married couples	29.9
Common-law couples	8.5
Families with children of any age who live at home	
Married couples	38.7
Common-law couples	6.9
Female lone-parent families	12.7
Male lone-parent families	3.2
Same-sex couples as % of all couples	0.6

Source: Adapted from Vanier Institute of the Family. 2010. *Families Count: Profiling Canada's Families IV.* Data from Statistics Canada, 2006 Census of Population, Catalogue no. 97-553-XCB2006007 and 97-553-XCB2006024.

financial needs, as mentioned earlier). However, there are two problems with this assumption: first, many units that meet the structural definition do not behave like ideal families, and second, many units that behave like ideal families do not meet the structural definition.

So, in this chapter, we will focus on *family processes* instead of family forms. We will also question—call into doubt—the supposedly simple and well-known norms about families and family life. What, really, are the key social processes that define what we in Canada like to think of as 'family life'? Social groups we call 'families' ideally share a few features, and this commonality can help us understand the nature of modern families. These features include the following:

- *Dependency and intimacy*: All idealized family relations emphasize attachment and interdependency. These traits are not unique to families; most friendships also include some degree of emotional dependency, based on familiarity and exchange. Family relations are special in that they tend to include long-term commitments, both between the individual members and to the family as a social unit. In reality, many families lack these attachments and commitments, so interdependency is limited.
- *Sexuality*: Adult partners in families ideally have, or are expected to have, a long-term, exclusive sexual relationship. These sexual relations are socially 'allowed' and expected between certain members (namely, spouses) but considered abusive when they occur between other members (for example, between parents and children, or between siblings). Taboos against the sexual exploitation of children are aimed at preventing sexual relations with a family member other than a spouse.
- *Protection*: Idealized families guard their members against all kinds of internal and external dangers. Parents are supposed to keep children safe from accidents and household dangers, for example, and away from drugs, alcohol, and predators. As well, spouses are supposed to protect one another, and adult children are supposed to protect and help their parents. Once again, however, in reality some family members fail to protect each other. Moreover, some people even neglect, exploit, or abuse other family members.
- *Power*: Given the large differences in power, strength, age, and social resources among family members, ideally the more powerful members protect less powerful ones. However, this imbalance in power has made patriarchy—control of the

family by a dominant male (typically, the father)—a central fact in the history of family life in most known societies. Simply put, men have dominated because they owned and controlled more of the resources.

- *Violence*: Families—though ideally peaceful and loving—are also often marked by violence, perhaps more than any other long-lived groups. Although violence has always existed in families, it seems to have increased in the last few decades because we have been keeping records of it. Usually when violence is present, a male spouse or boyfriend assaults his partner. We mention violence here not because it is an idealized or normative aspect of family life, but because it is a common feature.

Socialization

As noted earlier, one universal feature of family life, whatever the culture or family form, is **socialization**, a process that starts at birth and continues throughout our lives. During childhood and adolescence, people experience the most intense period of socialization, known as *primary socialization*. Throughout the rest of their lives they experience *secondary socialization*.

Primary socialization usually takes place within the family context. It helps to form an individual's personality and charts the course of his or her development. In the childhood family, a youngster learns many of the social skills needed to take part in our social institutions: schools, offices, factories, public spaces, and so on. Parents (or guardians, grandparents, etc.) are important because they are usually the first people a child interacts socially with, and because they control the child's early learning environment. As such, parents have a significant influence on the formation of their child's basic character and identity.

Because primary socialization is so fundamental for both individuals and society as a whole, it interests both macrosociologists and microsociologists. For the former, primary socialization is the mechanism that integrates people into society, teaching them to fulfill socially required roles. Seen from this perspective, human babies are 'blank slates' waiting to be imprinted with socially meaningful information. It is through this effective social imprinting—for example, the teaching and learning of language—that society manages to reproduce itself into the future.

And while socialization reproduces social learning, it also perpetuates social inequality. Schools and the mass media teach people their 'place' in society and convince them that this social niche is indisputable. It is in this way that disadvantaged people learn to set their sights low, blame themselves for failing, and praise the rich for succeeding, for example. Thus, socialization contributes to the survival of inequality and preserves the advantage of dominant groups in society. We will say more about this later in the chapter.

Microsociologists, for their part, study the processes by which individual people are socialized. In particular, they focus on the social processes that shape people's self-concept—their social view of 'self'. Through these processes, people come to view themselves as good or bad, competent or inept, normal or deviant, and so on. In this connection, feminist sociologists focus especially on gender issues—how

socialization

The lifelong social learning a person undergoes to become a capable member of society, through *social interaction* with others, and in response to social pressures.

primary socialization

Learning that takes place in the early years of a person's life that is crucial to the formation of an individual's personality.

Primary socialization mainly takes place in the context of the family home.

people learn gender identities (or gendered selves) and how gendered patterns of domination and submission emerge, for example.

We stated above that socialization is a lifelong process, and that as we undergo new experiences, we change in response to them. The socialization that occurs after childhood and adolescence is **secondary socialization**. This type of socialization is less fundamental than primary socialization, since it has less of an effect on people's self-image or sense of competence than primary socialization does. Usually, it involves learning specific roles, norms, attitudes, or beliefs, and sometimes it involves self-imposed learning. Professional socialization—learning to be a doctor or lawyer, for example—falls into this category. However the concept is much broader than that. We undergo secondary socialization when we change jobs, get married, or have children, for example. Most people learn *how* to be a parent only when they become one. And often, as with socialization into parenthood, secondary socialization is a reciprocal process, with children and parents both being socialized and learning from each other through social interaction. In this particular process, children experience primary socialization while the parents experience secondary socialization.

Secondary socialization differs from primary socialization in that it often—perhaps usually—occurs outside the family, and is based on knowledge already accumulated and previous socialization. Previous experience and accumulated learning enable us to imagine and prepare for future experiences. When we prepare to play a social role we hope to enter, we are practising **anticipatory socialization**. A commonly mentioned type of anticipatory socialization occurs in medical school, first written about by sociologist Howard S. Becker and colleagues in *Boys in White: Student Culture in Medical School* (1961). This book noted that medical students not only learn about health, disease, diagnosis, and prevention—they also learn how to be a doctor *socially*. For example, they learn how to interact with patients and what to disclose about test results according to a patient's readiness to hear the information. Most important, they learn to project a sense of competence and omniscience—necessary if patients are to trust them with life and death matters.

The effectiveness of anticipatory socialization depends on whether what the person learns in anticipation corresponds with what he or she experiences in the new situation. Various means are available in our society to help people make a smooth transition from role anticipation to role acquisition. Consider examples such as orientation or 'frosh' week, which help students make the transition from high school to university life; new employee orientations and training programs for people starting new jobs; prenatal parenting courses; and even pre-retirement courses later in life. However, sometimes we cannot anticipate or prepare for life events such as being fired from a job or losing a beloved spouse, parent, or child. Such events are often sudden and we usually cannot rely on previous experience to know how to react to them.

secondary socialization

Learning that occurs after childhood, usually involving learning specific roles, norms, attitudes, or beliefs, and sometimes involving self-imposed learning.

anticipatory socialization

Learning about and preparing for future roles, built on accumulated learning.

Children display anticipatory socialization in their awareness of potential jobs and display tendencies towards the fundamental aspects of these jobs. A common question posed of children from a fairly young age is 'What do you want to be when you grow up?'

Table 11.4 Family-Related Characteristics, by Structural and Role Variations, Canada

	All (%)	Parents Together (%)		Parents Together, Dual Careers (%)	
		Yes	No	Yes	No
Teens highly value:					
Friendship	85	85	86	87	83
Family life	59	61	54	61	62
High level of enjoyment from:					
Friends	94	94	94	94	96
Mothers	71	71	71	71	75
Fathers	62	67	54	67	71
Sibling(s)	58	58	57	58	65
Grandparent(s)	54	54	53	54	56
Strongly influenced by:					
Your mother	81	81	81	81	85
Your friends	78	78	79	79	76
Your father	70	77	56	77	79
Expectations:					
Marry	88	90	86	91	91
Have children	92	92	92	92	92
Stay with same partner for life	88	91	82	92	94
Want a home like the one I grew up in	71	76	59	77	77

Note: Shading indicates a difference of more than five percentage points.

Source: Reginald Bibby, 'Canada's Teens: A National Reading on Family Life', in *Transition Magazine* 31-3 (2001). The Vanier Institute of the Family. http://www.vifamily.ca/media/node/378/attachments/Canadas_teens_Bibby.pdf

Sometimes, we learn new rules in a hurry, rapidly becoming a 'new kind of person' through a process known as **resocialization**. This may take place in a job-training course, grief counselling program, or support group. However, resocialization can also take other forms. Certain social institutions exist with the express purpose of resocializing people. Foremost among these are what sociologist Erving Goffman called *total institutions*: social institutions that are set up resocialize their 'clients' drastically, through constant surveillance and punishment where needed. In these institutions, clients' needs may vary widely. Obviously, mental patients, convicts, nuns, and military draftees are different from another. So too are asylums, prisons, monasteries, and boot camps quite different from one another. However, as Goffman points out, these institutions are the same in at least one major way: they all focus on breaking down old identities (and social patterns) and building up new ones.

The topic of top-down socialization (or resocialization, in this case) brings us to the discussion of a second classic study, which is concerned with the production of flawed or dangerous identities.

resocialization
Learning within social institutions aimed at retraining or reprogramming people.

Classic Studies
The Authoritarian Personality

Where do violent and extreme prejudices come from? Interestingly, they come from socialization, according to a classic work about the influence some families have on their children.

This finding appears in a 1950 book *The Authoritarian Personality* by Theodor Adorno and others, a book written not so much to explain socialization as to explain prejudice.

Adorno's *The Authoritarian Personality* was one of five studies commissioned by the American Jewish Committee to research the roots of prejudice and anti-Semitism. This interdisciplinary study challenged previous theories about prejudice, replacing them with a social-psychological model that centres on individual personality traits and childhood socialization experiences. The study found a close correlation between overt racism and several deep-rooted personality traits that result from faulty socialization. By measuring 'authoritarianism' using a newly created 'F-scale' (F for 'Fascism') and examining its correlates, the authors concluded that racism and anti-Semitism are associated with a wide variety of fascist tendencies. And as we eventually discover, authoritarian personalities result from socialization by authoritarian parents.

Could Nazism have developed in America?, this study started out asking. After interviewing thousands of Americans, researchers concluded that fascist—even Nazi—tendencies are present everywhere and, yes, Nazism could have arisen in the US just as it did Europe. Based on their research, Adorno et al. (1950) identified nine characteristics of the authoritarian personality that served as the basis for the F-scale. The nine component characteristics, distributed into 30 items, comprise the following:

1. *Conventionalism*: a rigid adherence to conventional, middle-class values;
2. *Authoritarian submission*: a submissive, uncritical attitude toward idealized moral authorities of the in-group;
3. *Authoritarian aggression*: a tendency to be on the lookout for, and to condemn, reject, and punish people who violate conventional values;
4. *Anti-intraception*: opposition to the subjective, the imaginative, or the tender-minded;
5. *Superstition and stereotyping*: the belief in mystical determinants of an individual's fate; the disposition to think in rigid categories;

Resocialization occurs when individuals have to be taught how to conduct themselves in society by-and-large after having been isolated from mainstream society. Here, former child soldiers from South Sudan, Kenya, are being taught job skills as part of their resocialization training.

6. *Power and 'toughness'*: a preoccupation with the dominance and submission; identification with power figures; exaggerated assertion of strength and toughness;

7. *Destructiveness and cynicism*: a generalized hostility, vilification of the human;

8. *Projectivity*: a disposition to believe that wild and dangerous things go on in the world; the projection outwards of unconscious emotional impulses; and

9. *Preoccupation with sexual goings-on*: exaggerated concern about sexual occurrences and practices.

To summarize, Adorno and his collaborators found that prejudice is a generalized tendency among authoritarian personalities: people who hate Jews also tend to hate blacks, homosexuals, immigrants, and other minorities. Second, prejudice is linked to political and social conservative attitudes of various types: for example, opposing social welfare, blaming people for their own problems, and wanting to limit the role of government in people's lives. Third, prejudice is related to a wide variety of personal beliefs (distrust of others, superstition, and fatalism, for example), and to anti-introspection (an unwillingness to explore one's own or other people's deeper feelings, anxieties, and concerns).

Anti-introspection and repression are important parts of the authoritarian personality, and they come from having grown up in families where people do not inspect or reveal their feelings. By contrast, people who are relatively unprejudiced are also more accustomed to freely debating and expressing disagreements. This tendency first appears in childhood, when they learn to argue openly with their parents, based on secure and warm relationships with these parents. While prejudiced participants are more likely to glorify their parents, they also reveal an underlying hostility and have difficulty admitting to their personal incapacities, weaknesses, or impulses. Instead, they attribute these traits to others through a process Freud called *projection*, condemning these others and identifying themselves with powerful authorities.

The argument is quite simple and follows Freud's theory of repression, which we discuss at length in a later chapter. It runs as follows: people who are forced by cruel (or unfeeling) parents to hide their fears and desires express them in veiled ways, such as in dreams, fantasies, and groundless anxieties. So, for example, people who are afraid to reveal their sexual desires project these onto other people, imagining these others are having improper sexual relations around the clock and deserve punishment for doing so. The result is an approach to the world that is fanciful, harsh, and punitive—and dangerous when it controls political power.

Some have criticized *The Authoritarian Personality* for methodological flaws and researcher bias (see, for example, Martin, 2001). In addition, from a sociological perspective, Tamotsu Shibutani notes that the study fails to 'appreciate the full significance of the social nature of man and his conduct' (1952: 528). This is to say, the study focuses more on psychological (personality) variables than on sociological (situational) variables to explain outbursts of authoritarian behaviour. Yet, despite these criticisms, the study made a significant contribution. By showing the development of prejudice through faulty socialization, *The Authoritarian Personality* gained importance for sociologists who study families. Because of evidence that relates prejudice to early family history—chiefly to cold and harsh parenting—*The Authoritarian Personality* has major interest for people who study families and children—especially parenting practices.

Thus, however unintentionally, this study addresses two themes we have already introduced. First, should socialization be imposed on children, and if so, how? Second, should we judge families by their forms or by their processes? As we have already noted, families are ideally integrative: they protect and support their members and prepare children for effective participation in society. Yet even social institutions like the family, which are essentially integrative, create inequalities and generate conflict.

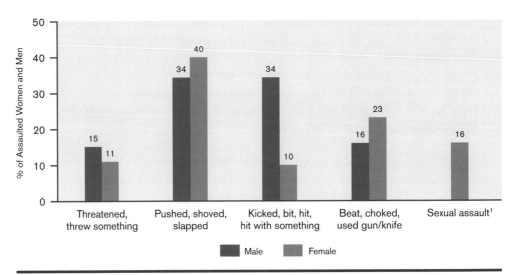

Figure 11.3 More Women than Men Experience Serious Violence

1. Data on males too unreliable to be published.

Source: Adapted from Statistics Canada (2005)

For example, we have already noted that family (or domestic) violence is far from rare. In fact, it is statistically common, although it is neither culturally normative, nor considered acceptable by most people. Often, family violence is hidden, along with other deep family secrets: addiction, mental illness, incest, infidelity, and so on. The public disclosure—or even open admission within the family—of such secrets is rare and often accompanied by shame and guilt.

As Figure 11.3 shows, women—especially, women separated from their spouses—are more likely to experience domestic violence than men (General Social Survey, 2004; Statistics Canada, 2005). Typically, their spouses are the perpetrators.

Some families experience more conflict than others, to be sure; there are sociological reasons for this. Families that are under the greatest stress—social, economic, and otherwise—are the most likely to descend into conflict. For example, unemployment—whether sudden, recurrent, or extended—is a common source of family stress and conflict. However, even given the same stresses, some families cope better than others. In general, families that are the most cohesive and adaptable (or flexible) are the best able to deal with these stresses. By 'cohesive', we mean families in which the members feel a strong personal identification with the family as a whole, and with one another. By 'adaptable', we mean those families that are most able to make changes easily, and most willing to make the needed changes.

In families, children learn how to be functioning members of adult society, and this covers a lot of territory. They learn how to be members of a family and, eventually, how to be students. But even before that, they learn how to be male or female.

Gender Socialization

Today, researchers tend to agree that most children receive *gender socialization*, and that this has a profound impact on their development of a masculine or feminine identity. Gender identities are largely absent at birth, with male and female infants showing few behavioural differences. Though more aggressiveness is eventually reported in little boys, even this can often be explained by the fact that parents, from early childhood, handle boys more roughly than girls. So, despite some evidence of genetic differences between average males and females, sociologists view the development of socially recognizable gender differences as a main social phenomenon.

This father redefines the gender stereotype of football being a predominantly boys-only sport by teaching his daughter to play the sport.

Some gendered socialization during childhood is intentional, meaning parents reinforce certain behaviour in young girls and boys according to their stereotypical expectations (into which of course, they were also socialized). However, most gender socialization is not intentional. Parents may not mean to treat girls and boys differently, but they do so without realizing it. Add to this the fact that other non-familial factors in society also contribute to this process.

For example, television ads, toy packaging, and even the organization and colour-schemes of toy departments all reinforce gender stereotypes, as do traditional practices of gift-giving by relatives (dolls and tea sets for girls; trucks and trains for boys) and designs of children's rooms and gendered names. Although research also shows that schools are highly important sites of further gender socialization, especially through the *hidden curriculum* (see Chapter 12), most gender stereotypes are well established even before children start school, mostly as a result of family influence (McHale, Crouter, and Whiteman, 2003).

Childhood experiences of gender socialization persist throughout life. They even pass from one generation to the next, with people socialized into traditional genders passing on these same assumptions to their children, and so on down the line. Such inherited assumptions perpetuate women's disadvantages at home, at school, and even in the workplace, where women continue to work in traditionally female-dominated fields. By the time children begin school, the seeds of gendering have been well planted; and since gender differences are reinforced throughout adolescence, gender distinctions are well established by adulthood.

Racial and Ethnic Socialization

The learning of racial (and ethnic) identities follows a similar pattern. What we will call *racial socialization* includes all of the ways parents shape their children's learning and understanding of race and of race relations (Hughes and Johnson, 2001). Racial and ethnic socialization occurs in many families, and it is often central to child-rearing in racial- and ethnic-minority families, where parents feel that instilling racial or ethnic pride, and transmitting group traditions, are especially important (Umana-Taylor, Bhanot, and Shin , 2006; Brown et al., 2007).

Many minority-group parents also talk to their children about the risks and experiences of discrimination, in this way solidifying a sense of separateness and difference. And, like gender socialization, racial and ethnic socialization is a repetitive process: typically, ideas and beliefs about race and ethnicity, or particular racial and ethnic groups, are communicated numerous times through social interaction. Children have these ideas drummed into them. They also learn about the meaning of race and ethnicity through discussion, observation, and imitation of significant others, usually parents (Brown et al., 2007).

Perhaps without intending to do so, parents who regularly communicate to their children messages of warning or avoidance about other ethnic groups may be promoting mistrust and setting the stage for future conflict (White and Gleitzman, 2006).

Class Socialization

Besides gender and racial or ethnic socialization, *class socialization* has an important impact on children's upbringing and important long-term effects on their lives.

In the process of class socialization, parents communicate their life experiences—especially, their experiences in the workplace—and feelings about their position in society. In this way, children learn early 'who counts' and who does not, and what their place is in the social hierarchy. By shaping the child's values and perceptions, this class socialization affects their future goals and ambitions (Hitlin, 2006). For example, a family that values independent thinking and hard work will produce children who do well at school and in the workforce. By contrast, a family that values luck and charm will teach different kinds of behaviour, with different, probably less valuable results. Generally, middle-class and immigrant families attach the highest importance to independence and hard work, suggesting these values may confer an advantage in the struggle for upward mobility.

Children who are taught the opposite—that hard work is irrelevant, school is a waste of time, and all that counts is who you know, not what you know—are less likely to get ahead. Only children who are born rich can safely afford to hold such values. No wonder the classic theorist Thorstein Veblen remarked a century ago on the likeness between the poorest and the richest members of society: neither was part of the contest for success. The

Class socialization: A son learns the skills of his father's trade at the family's upholstery shop. Often, workplace socialization means learning an outlook as well as a craft.

Media Distortion

BOX 11.2

Fathers in Popular Culture

On early TV shows, such as *Father Knows Best*, *Make Room for Daddy*, and *My Three Sons*, the dad was perfect—intelligent and reliable, respected by his family, and a good citizen. But now, on shows like *The Simpsons*, *Everybody Loves Raymond*, and *According to Jim*, we see a different dad—clownish, irresponsible, childish, sometimes selfish and dim, who will go to great lengths to avoid his family and social obligations.

These portrayals seem funny, but they could be harmful. Children might form an unrealistic or inappropriate notion of the father's role in a family—especially those children who don't have a father-figure of their own.

Source: Adapted from Media Awareness Network (N.d.).

rich would never lose their wealth and the poor would never gain it. Only people in the middle needed to mind their behaviour and mind their values. Doing so would make all the difference between success and failure.

Values like ambition and independence, responsibility and perseverance, are transformative: means by which families prepare their children for the transition to adulthood. Families shape children's occupational ambitions largely by influencing their values, and through values, their daily behaviours. As noted, middle-class American socialization is mainly concerned with ensuring that children develop high educational and occupational ambitions, stay in school, and get good grades. According to American sociologist Annette Lareau (2000), middle-class American parents stress the systematic *cultivation* of their children (stressing French immersion, extra-curricular ballet lessons, and so on). Working-class and poor families, by contrast, prefer to accomplish *natural* growth, with the children leading less scheduled and less controlled lives.

Parents also shape their children's views about inequality. In raising their children, many parents spontaneously raise the issue of fairness when discussing wealth and poverty, but many do not. As a result, many elementary school children are inclined to accept great disparities in wealth and poverty. They come to believe that people deserve their economic situation in life—whether rich or poor—and that efforts to help the poor are misguided or futile. This is particularly true of Americans, resulting from the ways Americans socialize their children. American and Spanish parents, for example, stress different values with their children—for example, placing different weight on qualities like responsibility, imagination, or perseverance. Not surprisingly, the individualistic Americans produce higher levels of ambition in their children, with resulting higher levels of economic development. They also produce a much lower sense of collective responsibility.

Of course, children often change their views over time, depending on their engagement with the news media and with voluntary associations. Adolescents who engage actively with family, peers, teachers, and the media around questions of fairness, inequality, politics, and citizenship are likely to change the most. They are not merely passive recipients of information from parents and teachers. Through the news media, social networks, and school and community volunteer activities, these adolescents learn active citizenship, and in this way, develop morally to a much higher degree than their classmates.

So, families are important sources of socialization for their children, but many families struggle to find the time for shared activities, quality time, and good parenting. This daily struggle has been central to the work of family sociologist Arlie Hochschild. However, Hochschild began her scholarly career by focusing on the topic of 'emotion work'—not a bad choice, given her interest in the gendering of labour at home and in the workplace.

People Are Talking About . . .
ARLIE HOCHSCHILD

Arlie Russell Hochschild, born in 1940 in Boston, earned her M.A. and Ph.D. from the University of California, Berkeley. As a graduate student at Berkeley, Hochschild read the writings of C. Wright Mills. Mills' argument in *White Collar*, that under capitalism we 'sell our personality', shaped Hochschild's own thinking about so-called *emotion work*.

Here, Hochschild starts with the thesis that all the ways humans feel and express emotions are largely social. Culture teaches us both what we can feel and, more important, what we should feel. Thus, we follow 'feeling rules' just as we follow other rules of behaviour. We manage our feelings according to these rules—for example, we try to be happy at a party, or sad at a funeral—and wonder whether we are normal if we cannot summon the appropriate feelings. In the ways we experience an interaction, define our feelings, and manage our expressions of feeling, we are guided by cultural and social norms.

Based on these observations, Hochschild developed her theory of 'emotional labour'—work in which someone must develop the 'right' emotion in themselves, and encourage the client or customer to also feel the 'right' emotion. People in sales and service jobs commonly do this type of work. Flight attendants, for example, must try to instill calm emotions in nervous passengers, as well as manage their own feelings when passengers cause difficulty. Hochschild describes flight attendants' emotional training in *The Managed Heart* (1983). And, as the service sector becomes increasingly important in North American economy, and the number of service jobs grows, emotional labour increases as well.

Hochschild focuses on emotion in the American family in her later work, since service and emotional management form a large part of family life. Recognizing that women who work outside the home also do much of the domestic work, in *The Second Shift* (1989) she looks at the division of both the emotional and the physical work of making a home. She explores how fairly the housework is divided, taking into account the outside demands on and expectations of family members. She also looks at how gratitude is expressed within the family for the housework done.

Her subsequent work, *The Time Bind* (1997) is based on how the work lives of couples working at a Fortune 500 company compete with their family lives. Although most of the people that Hochschild talked to said that their families took priority over their work, the demands of their jobs left them little time to spend with their families. For many people, the workplace culture, rather than their home lives, provided a sense of community, appreciation, competence, and support.

Thus in our private lives—even in our deepest emotional lives—we are pushed and pulled by social norms. We are all invited to judge our lives by ideologies (for example, about the pleasures of family life) that scarcely apply to working women.

Sources: Adapted from http://sociology.berkeley.edu/faculty/hochschild/; http://teaching.berkeley.edu/dta.html; http://socsci.colorado.edu/SOC/SI/si-hochschild.htm; http://www.asanet.org/page.ww?section=Awards&name=Public+Understanding+of+Sociology+Award; http://0-www.galenet.com.library.uor.edu/servlet/LitRC?vrsn=3&OP=contains&locID=redl79824&srchtp=athr&ca=1&c=1&ste=6&tab=1&tbst=arp&ai=U14557139&n=10&docNum=H1000046077&ST=Arlie+Hochschild&bConts=2191; http://www.genderonline.cz/view.php?cisloclanku=2007010610 'Leaving Berkeley After 35 Years: An Interview with Arlie Hochschild'.

Hochschild has given us a new, unromantic way to look at family life. Melissa Milkie et al. (2009) used Hochschild's concept of the 'second shift' to study the employment and domestic workloads of mothers with full-time jobs outside the home, whose partners also worked full-time. They particularly look at how these women—whom they call 'focal mothers'—use their time and respond to time pressures differently than do fathers and mothers not working full-time outside the home. They find that the total workload of a focal mother exceeds that of her partner by about 10 days a year, rather than the month per year that Hochschild suggested. While a focal mother has less leisure time than her partner, the housework she does is no more demanding than that done by the father, and she gets about the same amount of sleep that he does. And although a focal mother feels more time pressure than her partner does, this pressure is not very different from that experienced by other mothers of young children, although their activities as a family may be less frequent. Thus, the claims of a gendered double shift may have been exaggerated.

Similarly, Sayer et al. (2009) tracked time use by American and Australian men and women, looking for a 'gender gap' in paid and unpaid work time. Like Milkie, and in contrast to Hochschild's findings, they detected little overall difference between the genders, but some differences between different types of families. In families with pre-school-aged children, the mothers do several more hours of work per week than fathers do, and even more when the father does not work full-time. When the mother does not work outside the home, the father has significantly more hours of work than the mother.

Uhde (2009) looks at the social inequality associated with jobs in caregiving. While feminists have tried to raise the profile of caregivers in a national context, Uhde, like Hochschild, sees a need to recognize and ensure justice for the many immigrant women caregivers, who are subject to exploitation in a global capitalist system.

Emotional burnout is one result of doing the heavy emotional work identified by Hochschild (1983). In a study of Japanese care workers, Mitsuhashi (2008) finds that, among those workers who have internalized their role as emotional labourers, burnout is most likely to happen when they are *unable* to do emotional work, rather than when they actually do it. Thus, paradoxically, internalizing the emotional role can prevent burnout.

This gets into the question of the circumstances under which work does or does not make someone sick, or sickness keeps someone from working. Hansen and Andersen (2008) explore the attitudes and circumstances that influence a person's decision to work when they are unwell. They look at Danish workers, who are just as likely to go to work ('sickness presence') as they are to stay at home ('sickness absence') when sick. Supervisors or others who work long hours are most prone to sickness presence, as are those who work in small, convivial companies. Those who place a very high priority on their work, feel comfortable at work, or see absence as a weakness also tend toward sickness presence.

In *The Managed Heart* (1983), Hochschild explores how service workers' emotions are commodified, and thus how the workers are harmed (Brook, 2009), and, in this way, echoes Marx's theory of worker alienation. Some critics think the alienation of service workers is exaggerated, but Brook believes it does not go far enough.. Brook argues that Hochschild's analysis needs to extend more into the political aspects of workers' resistance to the commodifying effects of capitalism.

Ozkaplan (2009) asserts that the study of care labour, and thus emotional labour, can be considered a sociology of women's work. Emotional labour (or 'emotional intelligence', as it is often termed) is treated as a commodity in our society, although an underpaid or even unpaid commodity. It is important for feminists to reanalyze the mainstream thinking on work and call attention to a general tendency to ignore the emotional labour of women.

Emotion work is done at home and it is done in various ways in a variety of workplaces. Consider the study by Hesmondhalgh and Baker (2008) that examines the emotional labour of a television program research team. A conflictual work environment often creates stress, anxiety, and strained working relations for the television researchers attached to that program. In the precarious world of creative television work, they need to show that they can work well on a team. However, they also need to deal with the strong emotions of the performers. Like workers in other jobs and other industries, they develop unique ways of dealing with these stresses, through a frank recognition of the problems and a shared negotiation of solutions.

Blakely (2008), finally, looks at the emotional aspects of a different kind of work—wedding planning. Like other aspects of outsourced domestic activity, wedding planning has become a commodity. Blakely draws on Hochschild's research to look at how feminism relates to the buying and selling of such services, and how a wedding planner can help women balance their private and work lives. The paradox is that capitalism—a supposedly cold and exploitive system that promotes consumerism—makes it necessary for working women to need the service wedding planners provide; but it also guarantees (through market mechanisms) that these women will get what they need—will 'have it all'—if they outsource the wedding-planning process.

Thus, a review of recent writings finds continued application of the work by Arlie Hochschild—over 100 journal articles applying Hochschild's work in the last 20 years. Clearly, sociologists are talking about Arlie Hochschild. Hochschild belongs in any comprehensive, fusion approach to sociology because of the insights she brings to issues around gender, family, and work—and the intersections among these three topics. She also reminds us of the value of close empirical observation and skepticism about 'received wisdom', and calls attention to new forms of servitude, such as emotional work.

New Insights

Mann and Barnard (2002), mirroring Hochschild, note that family stability has long been part of a continued debate about 'modern families'. On one side are those who view the current trend toward diverse family forms as a serious threat to the well-being of families and society. On the other side are those who embrace diversity and see the alternative family forms as viable, inventive adaptations to social changes over the last half-century. The (conservative) American Council of Families recently raised the temperature of this debate by sponsoring a report that attacked textbooks promoting the 'diversity' view. Mann and Barnard, using a content analysis of family textbooks published in the 1990s, find that the textbooks criticized most harshly by the American Council of Families' report actually provided the most coverage of these diversity issues.

By contrast, they say, too many texts present little or no coverage of the impact of various diversifying social conditions on interpersonal relations. Especially under-discussed topics include globalization's 'shrinking' of the world and time; the massive shift from secure, unionized manufacturing jobs to insecure service jobs; the rise of new consumer patterns that replace family activities (e.g., food preparation and consumption); and the prominence of mass media in daily life.

Another aspect of the discussion of family instability concerns divorce and single parenting. Boney (2003) surveys major studies of the effects of divorce and identifies a male-focused bias in studies that negatively portray divorced single parents and their families. Postmodern studies, on the other hand, are more likely to present the positive effects of divorce, and suggest that it is possible to raise children well in families that differ from the traditional model.

Likewise, Boney (2002) notes that the negative view of single parenthood, entrenched in traditional social, legal, and religious norms, causes divorced mothers to feel guilty, and thus slows their 'recovery' from divorce. Therapy based in a postmodern perspective would enable women to move beyond the dominant modernist socio-cultural view, find the positive and empowering aspects of their new lives, and share these discoveries with each other.

A postmodern paper that tests the boundaries between families and non-families is, on its face, an exploration of brothels in early twentieth century Bombay, India (now called Mumbai). In this paper, Tambe (2006) notes that feminist theory often locates prostitution outside (or in opposition to) family institutions—indeed, as an alternative to heteronormative family life. In South Asia, women often live in brothels that resemble conventional families in their roles and structures, including those of affection, duty, and authority. In looking particularly at brothel life in 1920s Bombay, Tambe shows how joining the sex trade was encouraged by women's and girls' families, and how the family-like hierarchy of the brothel ensured that they would be loyal and obedient. In effect, brothels functioned as real homes (also, workplaces) for girls and young women, especially for those sent there by their families.

As is evident from these example, some of the exciting work in family sociology today involves testing whether Western assumptions are useful in analyzing family patterns in other parts of the world. So, for example, Pedraza Gomez (2007) finds the modern Western notion of childhood does not suit the current Third World, especially now that Western colonization has come to an end. While education took European children out of the work force in the second half of the nineteenth century, indigenous children and children of slaves in America, Africa, and Asia—those on the periphery of the world-system—continued to work alongside their families. So, many non-Western families—especially, poor and rural ones—are far from the current Western nuclear family, and so is the Western model of childhood, as a result.

Part of the difference also results from differences in values and beliefs about childhood, which evidently vary from one culture to another. Keller and Demuth (2006) try to disentangle views about 'independence' as a value for childhood socialization, for example. To do so, they interviewed grandmothers in Los Angeles and Berlin about their socialization goals and ideas of good parenting for a three-month-old baby. The researchers found that all participants set out to teach independence and interdependence; they also have a similar understanding about which caregiving practices are important.

However, caregivers differ in their views about caregiving, even between these two Western societies. German participants say they expect breastfeeding, body contact, and *Beschaftigung* ('dealing with the child') to be composed of closeness and stimulation that promotes relational closeness as well as healthy mental/psychological development. American mothers and grandmothers think of care-giving practices differently, believing that breastfeeding is for health, playing is for stimulating cognitive development, bodily closeness is for soothing. So, women in these two different societies look for different outcomes, even when they set out with the same general goals and use the same general strategies. Moreover, they differ in the extent of caregiving, in large part because of differences in contextual factors like women's participation in the labour force.

Many other researchers find Western generalizations useful in the developing world. For example, Lee (2005) notes that, in South Korea, people are spending less time working and more time with their families in leisure activities. Such family-oriented leisure activities are new to most South Korean families, who do not know what to do with their free time together. At present, most of the new family leisure involves buying things; but in time, the range of activities is likely to broaden.

Some sociologists criticize consumerism as a family leisure activity, however. For example, Kanduc (2004), a Slovenian sociologist, views present-day leisure consumerism as a type of social control through 'bread and circuses', aimed more at supporting capitalist exploitation than increasing family cohesion. The unspoken goal of the ruling class, he says, is to produce people who are productive but also gentle, adaptable, obedient, easily manipulated, isolated, and made imbecilic by the mass media. Thus, people are readied to do all that is required of them, whether as parents, workers, or consumers. They are programmed to view consumerism as a way of achieving freedom, personal growth, and life satisfaction, but this belief is merely an opiate.

Unlike open coercion (e.g., guns pointed at heads), consumerism is a kind of social control that runs from inside the individual. It colonizes people's aspirations, prescribing economically useful ways of functioning. The result is a personality type engineered to buy things—a personality with no self-defences and no self-awareness. Such socialization produces naïve children and naïve adults, people at every age willing to lead lives that are unconsidered, self-subordinating and self-humiliating (ibid).

Along these lines, Baldauf (2002) asks, Why do young people like to shop? By comparing two shopping streets, Mariahilfer Strasse in Vienna and lower Broadway in New York, the author conducts an ethnographic investigation into shoppers' motivations, which include satisfying the need for sociability, distinction, and individuality.

Shopping viewed through a 'sociology of manipulation' is seen as seductive and inducing false consciousness. Indeed, the dominant neo-liberal value system celebrates shopping as proof of the unrestrained power of the consumer. Instead, Baldauf proposes that shopping provides 'shopperedutainment'—a way of healing the wounds of capitalism by holding out the glimmers of freedom, individuality, and authenticity. Today, people don't try to answer the question 'Who am I?' by work; they do it through niche buying. 'Fashion' is their way of forming, displaying, and declaiming themselves as individuals. In the end, shopping is the result neither of pure manipulation nor of unlimited freedom. Rather, shopping involves seduction and empowerment, affirmation and intervention, pleasure and profit.

What else do families teach their children? North-Jones (2009) studied how 10 families lead their daily lives. The people studied reported feeling rushed most of the time, though children were less concerned about this, feeling their parents were able to spend enough time with them. Parents said they wanted to teach their children respect for themselves and for others, the importance of education, moral and religious values, a strong work ethic, and a good knowledge of the world around them. However, they felt frustrated in their efforts, lacking enough time to devote to this teaching.

Chapter Summary

We noted at the beginning of this chapter that everyone knows something about families and about socialization. We grew up in families, and some of us currently live in the family households where we were socialized. However, the danger of 'common knowledge'—taken-for-granted, what-everyone-knows knowledge—is that it is often wrong, because it is largely uninspected.

This applies to families: none of the sentimental myths and beliefs about family life can be taken for granted. We do not know how many Canadian families are working well by the standards stated in this chapter. The government does not study this, likely, because many Canadians would probably view such research as prying into their private lives. Also, there is the assumption that unless one practises the most extreme and visible forms of abuse, each adult is free to bear and raise children by any method judged appropriate. So family relations in many households are far from ideal.

As we have seen, the results of bad parenting are consequential for all Canadians, and for future generations of Canadians. You and everyone else pay the long-term costs of bad parenting. We pay the price as soon as poor parenting turns into mental illness, domestic violence, delinquency, dropping out of school, suicide, and anti-social behaviour of all kinds.

In some societies, parents are more socially conscious—that is, more concerned with teaching civility and good citizenship—than we are in North America. And some societies—typically, in Western and Northern Europe—are more dedicated to helping families succeed in their efforts at living together. This includes overseeing and protecting the children of vulnerable populations like the poor, and helping immigrants to assimilate culturally to national standards of ethical behaviour. However, in Canada the indiscriminate embrace of 'multiculturalism' hinders our ability to ensure this. We are too reluctant to infringe anyone's cultural freedom. What started as a plan to signal tolerance and increase social inclusion has turned into moral laziness. It is time for a national discussion of our socialization practices, if we are to build a healthy and co-operative society.

Clearly, when we compare Canada to more progressive social-democratic societies in northern and western Europe, we find many factors in our society that promote conflict and anti-social individualism. However, this is no time to give up on our families. We cannot ignore the potentially positive role that families can and must play in changing society.

Critical Thinking Questions

1. Canadian families have become much more diverse in the last few decades. What is the significance of this increased diversity?
2. What do you think were the most important values in your upbringing? What values do you expect to teach your own children, if you become a parent? Why are these values similar or different?
3. What is the key difference between the functionalist and symbolic interactionist perspective on socialization? Although not discussed in this chapter, what do you suppose critical theorists would say about socialization?
4. How do you think parents socialized into traditional gender roles should ensure they do not pass on these stereotypes to their own children? Can society do anything to prevent this reproduction of gender inequalities?

Recommended Readings

Gerald Handel (ed.), *Childhood Socialization*, 2nd edn (New Brunswick, NJ: Aldine Transaction, 2006). This book examines agents of socialization that have an impact on social learning by children. It gives an interesting account of how socialization differs in different societies and cultures.

Patrizia Albanese, *Children in Canada Today* (Toronto: Oxford University Press, 2007). This book is part of a series of works on important sociological topics with specific emphasis on Canadian issues. Albanese explores themes of childhood socialization, such as socializing agents and their impact, changes in social policy, and the relation of socialization to family and social problems.

Reginald W. Bibby, *Canada's Teens: Today, Yesterday, and Tomorrow* (Toronto: Stoddart, 2001). Canadian sociologist Reginald Bibby is well known for his surveys of adolescents and adults, as well as his studies of religion. This book historically explores the experiences of adolescents around topics like violence, sex, and drugs in relation to teenager beliefs, values, worries, and enjoyments.

Maureen Baker, *Choices and Constraints in Family Life* (Toronto: Oxford University Press, 2007). In this book, the author examines families within a historical and cross-cultural context. She argues that although we now have more choice in intimate partners, sexual behaviour, and the types of families we live in, these choices are also influenced by socio-economic context, including social policies, technology, educational opportunities, and so on. All of these must be examined to understand the changing nature of Canadian families.

Don Tapscott, *Growing Up Digital: The Rise of the Net Generation* (New York: McGraw-Hill, 1998). In this book, Tapscott argues that the children of baby boomers are part of what he calls the 'Net generation', meaning they are growing up surrounded by high-tech toys and tools from birth. This preoccupation with technology may have a significant impact on the future of these children, changing the nature of education, commerce, recreation, the workplace, government, and the family.

Susan A. McDaniel and Lorne Tepperman, *Close Relations: An Introduction to the Sociology of Families*, 3rd edn (Scarborough, ON: Pearson Educational, 2010). This is a Canadian overview of research and social theories about family life, examining topics such as the history of Canadian families, intimate relationships, parenting, stress and violence in the family context, and the future of families.

Howard S. Becker, Blanche Geer, Everett C. Hughes, and Anselm L. Strauss, *Boys in White: Student Culture in Medical School* (Chicago: University of Chicago Press, 1961). This is a classic sociological work on professional socialization. It not only explores how medical students learn about medical terms, healthcare, disease, prevention, and so on, but also focuses on how medical school socializes students into the social role of the doctor.

Websites

Vanier Institute of the Family
www.vifamily.ca

The National Longitudinal Survey of Children and Youth (NLSCY)
www.statcan.gc.ca/imdb-bmdi/4450-eng.htm

Today's Parent
www.todaysparent.com

Canadian Child Care Federation
www.cccf-fcsge.ca

Childcare Research and Resource Unit (CRRU)
www.childcarecanada.org

Public Safety Canada
www.safecanada.ca

12 Schools and Formal Education

Learning Objectives

In this chapter, you will:

> Learn about the role schools play in communities
> Come to understand the social functions of higher education
> Identify the various inequalities perpetuated by educational institutions
> Analyze how abuse or violence may take place on school grounds
> Appreciate the ability of education to foster a wholesome society

Chapter Outline

Education has proven to be one of the most valuable means of gaining a healthy, comfortable life. In the past, education was a privilege, reserved for the wealthy. Today, education is considered the right of every child. This belief is clearly expressed in the United Nations' Millennium Development Goals, which include helping children across the globe to gain a primary school education (UN, 2009).

In our society, education provides students with the knowledge and credentials they need to gain and keep paid employment. And *credentialism*, the rising need for ever more sophisticated educational qualifications, is an increasingly prominent trend in today's labour markets. In the past, a high school diploma was qualification enough for someone to get a job that could support several people. Necessary skills were, to a large extent, picked up on the job by learning the ropes from an experienced mentor. Today, employers demand far more impressive credentials. Many believe that the high school diploma is passé, and the minimum entry-level requirement today is a B.A. or college diploma.

Besides developing skills needed in the workplace, education delivers societal values. In that sense, it is a form of primary socialization. Education instills concepts such as tolerance, teamwork, and leadership in students—ideas that help them integrate into society. This learning not only benefits the student, it benefits the society as a whole. These lessons are the basis for a responsible citizenry. Education also increases people's ability to understand current events and public debates, enabling them to form sound opinions and react accordingly.

Sociologists who study education are interested in such questions as: What are the consequences of education for society? What is the influence of schooling on the social relationships between people? What types of inequalities does education create? We will explore all of these ideas in this chapter.

Everyday Observations

Starting early: Every Saturday, Liana attends a tutoring class. Her parents are paying 90 dollars per session to prepare her for an upcoming private school entrance exam. Liana and her parents enter the large, squat building and walk past classrooms where other students are prepping for the tests that schools use to select their students—everything from high school entrance exams to the MCATs and LSATs. In class, Liana finds it difficult to concentrate—she'd rather be outside, riding her bike or going swimming. After all, Liana is only six years old. Liana's parents, like the parents of 20 or so other six- and seven-year-olds in this class, have paid high fees to prepare their daughter very early on for admission to a competitive private school. They hope this will, eventually, propel her into a top university, and later, a high-income career.

Why is six-year-old Liana spending her weekends cramming for tests? Is this normal? Is it healthy? What purpose do these tests serve? Well, we all know the answers to these questions. Tests are universally used to allocate resources to people and people to positions. If Liana does well on a key test, she will get the corresponding reward. In Liana's case, the reward is a coveted spot in a top-notch educational institution.

As you probably realized while reading this scenario, many parents are unable to afford this top-notch education. But still she will try her best. If Liana gets into a prestigious university, the chances are good that she will eventually get a high-paying job, and then be able to provide the same future for her own children. This would be great for Liana and her family, but it also perpetuates social inequality. People who have more get more, and those who have less stay where they are—with less. Clearly, education isn't a level playing field and often, it doesn't even level the playing field; but stories like Liana's are far from rare. Many parents are able to pass on social advantages to their children through the mechanism of higher education, and even more parents try to do so.

Why is it that immigrants have far higher rates of educational attainment, and lower rates of school dropout, than native-born children? And among native-born Canadians, why are the dropout rates much higher in Quebec than they are in Ontario, for example? Clearly, these differences reflect different perceptions of education and what it can do for people. Some note that a lower university-attendance rate in Quebec is due to the higher value placed on skilled crafts like plumbing, carpentry, masonry, and the like. Others, however, note that people's differing perceptions, aspirations, and values tend to reflect their opportunities and role models, which suggests that through these, education continues to preserve inequalities.

In the study of **education**, some researchers stress the important of socio-economic inequality while others stress the importance of values and aspirations. In fact, both are important, as we will see.

To break the cycle of disadvantage, many societies around the world have tried to base educational systems strictly on merit, and to make a high quality education available to everyone. In a purely meritocratic system—something that doesn't exist anywhere, but is often dreamed about—opportunities like admission to a prestigious school are allocated strictly according to merit measured objectively, for example, by grades. In such a system,

education

A process designed to develop one's general capacity for thinking critically, as well as a capacity for self-understanding and self-reliance.

high grades identify the differences between applicants: they tell us which candidates are the most deserving. So, in a modern society, to get anywhere people have to get the highest grades and best degrees they can, and then put them on display like price tags, proving their personal worth.

Does such a system guarantee that people will be placed in the correct niche according to their talents and qualifications? Yes and no: the result depends entirely on the quality of the testing procedure. Tests are central in a system designed to reward people strictly according to achievement. 'Good' tests are designed to stream the right students into the right classes or levels. Some are even designed to stream students from particular high schools into particular universities, then from particular undergraduate universities to particular graduate schools. Again, we may ask, Are these tests fair, and do they work as expected? Some of the evidence suggests they don't. Some capable people are poor test takers; and on some occasions but not others, capable people perform badly. But, then, how do we improve the system?

As well, how do we improve the system of schools into which students will be admitted? Because of limited resources, educational institutions are often obliged to battle one another for resources. Schools are also the battleground over curriculum: various interest groups argue about what should be required of students and what should be optional. For example, how much sex education should students receive, at what ages, and in what format? How much information should they receive about religion, especially about Christianity versus other religions like Judaism and Islam? How much time should they spend on reading and mathematics instead of sports, music, and drama? Politicians who are responsible for education want to satisfy the voters, so they pay a lot of attention to public opinion on these issues. Often, the provincial curriculum in literature, history, social studies, and social sciences reflects a careful effort to balance the treatment of sensitive issues.

Bringing together students from different backgrounds can lead to confusion or even conflict, owing to the diversity of abilities, beliefs, and backgrounds among the students (and their parents). Sometimes, such diversity leads to conflict. More often, though, the diversity widens students' horizons, builds bridges, and engenders new respect and understanding. Students learn about other genders, races, classes, and religions by meeting classmates who are different from themselves. How does this happen? What is it about schools that can result in the formation—or destruction—of social bonds? Through the sociological study of schools and **formal education**—that is, using the tools that allow social researchers to systematically analyze societies and the way they work—we will try to find answers to some of the key questions in this domain.

formal education
Education received in accredited schools during formal teaching sessions.

informal education
The variety of ways we undertake to gain knowledge for ourselves outside institutions of formal education (e.g., schools, colleges, and universities).

Ways of Looking at . . .
EDUCATION

Functionalists focus on the *manifest* and *latent functions* of education in our society, and the degree to which schools as currently formed fulfill these functions. Manifest functions at the secondary level are designed to give all students basic skills in literacy and numeracy, and some students specific job skills. At the post-secondary level, they are designed to give some students a liberal arts training and other students an occupational **training** that prepares them for the work world. The liberal arts curriculum supposedly prepares people to be informed citizens. The professional curriculum supposedly prepares people to be valuable members of the workforce. Thus, functionalists focus on the human capital functions of education: on improving the abilities of workers to bring significant value to their jobs and workplaces through their knowledge and skills.

In recent decades, the main sociological work on education has been by critical theorists and symbolic interactionists. Critical theorists have often focused on the latent functions of

training
A process designed to identify and practise specific routines that achieve desired results.

hidden curriculum

Lessons that are not normally considered part of the academic curriculum that schools unintentionally or secondarily provide for students.

education. For example, they have studied the role of schools in warehousing unemployed (and possibly unemployable) young people, especially during times of high unemployment. In effect, they have studied the ways schools keep young people 'off the streets'. They have also studied schools as a source of **hidden curriculum** that teaches students their 'proper' place in society according to their gender and their social class. Some have even argued that the routine subordination and boredom students suffer in school is good preparation for the routine subordination and boredom they will have to endure at work.

According to this critical theory, the job of schools is not to give students 'human capital and skills' but rather to train them in patient obedience—the essential qualification for most non-professional work in our society. As well, the school promotes a meritocratic ethic, teaching students to hold themselves responsible for success and failure—an ideologically suitable message in a capitalist society. (Most schools really are meritocratic, but this doesn't prepare people for the world outside school. Though someone in school may indeed deserve the A or D received from a teacher, he or she may not always deserve the reward or punishment received from a boss at work. The world of work runs according to somewhat different rules.)

Beyond this lesson, as symbolic interactionists show, schools also teach students how to dress and behave, as befits their social role as girl or boy, middle-class or working-class person. At the higher educational levels, schools teach people how to dress for success as lawyers, doctors, managers, and so on. Thus, much of our socialization as adults, including professional socialization as doctors, lawyers, accountants, and so on begins at school, though it doesn't end there.

However, increasingly, institutions of higher education—especially universities—are taking on a new social role, not so much concerned with education (or socialization) as they are with research, also known as 'knowledge production' and 'knowledge translation'.

Classic Studies
The Academic Revolution

One of the first sociological accounts of this change was written half a century ago by Christopher Jencks and David Riesman. Their book *The Academic Revolution* (1968) looks at the historical ties between schools and societies, and examines the evolving role of higher education in modern, post-industrial society.

The Academic Revolution begins by recounting the rise to dominance of 'research universities' in the twentieth century. Reflecting the bureaucratization of American society, colleges and universities have been transformed from cohesive, often small and localized units into a single national system of higher training. In this system, which operates somewhat like a funnel, the top graduate institutions receive and train the best graduates of the best undergraduate colleges. In turn, the top undergraduate institutions receive and train the best graduates of the best secondary schools; and so on, down the line (to pre-kindergarten). This 'new' university is increasingly characterized by narrowly specialized curricula, a heavy research agenda, and an all-Ph.D. faculty. Lacking these characteristics, a college or university would be labelled sub-par, as has happened in the US to many women's, black, and religious colleges.

Thus, to escape the shame of such labels, all universities have been struggling to increase their research (and research funding), decrease their undergraduate teaching, and raise their international profile. The result is a hierarchy of research universities struggling against one another for top faculty, top students, and increased funding from government and the key research agencies.

In this transformation of the higher education system, professors have gained greater visibility and importance. They are widely known to their peers through publication,

Meritocracy: An egalitarian system of advancement where the rewards are proportioned to the accomplishment.

conferences, and grant-getting. Increasingly, these professors—primarily concerned with research and graduate teaching—determine the character of undergraduate education, which in turn defines the capacity of the workforce. Jencks and Riesman claim that professors shape the academic 'revolution' by promoting **meritocracy** and favouring a national or even international orientation in the admission process—that is, by arguing for the admission of students based on ability, not local residence. In exercising this power, professors are determining the allocation of scarce and desirable elite credentials.

Jencks and Riesman note that this revolution has been met with resistance in many quarters, which they characterize as 'generational war'. Among the people opposed to this academic revolution are the youth who resent adult authority, the locals who resent foreign students, the religious who resent secular education, and the social elite who resent upward social mobility from the lower classes.

However, the authors also recognize that this academic revolution, designed to provide every student—regardless of class, race, sex, and background—with education and a chance of upward mobility, has not succeeded fully. Positions in the top colleges and universities continue to be limited, and students from wealthy backgrounds continue to be most able to gain entry. Jencks and Riesman credit this problem to the unequal structure of American society, and propose that greater energies be directed to making American society more equal. For without equality, efforts to expand educational opportunity and achieve something closer to meritocracy are futile. Those that have will continue to get, as we said earlier; however, the failure is far from complete. Research universities have played an important role in the upward mobility of immigrants and minorities and their children, in both Canada and the United States—a goal of John Porter as we have already discussed.

More recently, the social importance of research universities has been examined in a new book by sociologist Jonathan Cole, *The Great American University: Its Rise to Preeminence, Its Indispensable National Role, Why It Must be Protected* (2009). Cole stresses the social values that underlie the work of a research university and the social and economic structures—for example, peer review and funding institutions—that underlie them. In particular, the

meritocracy

Any system of rule or advancement where the rewards are strictly proportioned to the accomplishment and all people have the same opportunity to win these rewards.

Table 12.1 Proportion of the Population Aged 25 to 64 with a University Degree, Top 10 OECD Countries

Country	%
Norway	30
United States	30
Netherlands	28
Denmark	26
Iceland	26
Australia	23
Canada	23
Korea	23
Japan	22
Sweden	21

Source: Statistics Canada (2006), Table 3, from Organization for Economic Co-operation and Development, Education at a Glance: OECD Indicators 2008 (Paris: OECD, 2008). At: http://www.oecd.org/dataoecd/23/46/41284038.pdf.

research universities have been an important source of scientific research and technological innovation. This has been possible only because the standards of excellence adopted by these research universities conform to the standards applicable to scientific research as a whole—something we will discuss in a later chapter, where we compare science with religion.

Compared to the US situation that Jencks and Riesman (and Cole) describe, conditions in Canada are similar in some respects and different in others. First, Canada has a much smaller system of colleges and universities than the US, even when measured per capita. Second, there is a much smaller range of inequality among Canada's colleges and universities, thanks largely to greater regulation and stricter accreditation. Though the best Canadian colleges and universities may not equal the very best American ones, the worst Canadian colleges and universities are not as bad as the worst American ones. This means that most Canadian students have at least one or two good universities in their own province. Perhaps for this reason, Canadians are less likely than Americans to seek a degree hundreds or even thousands of kilometres away from home.

That said, Canada has seen educational reform similar to that described by Jencks and Riesman and by Cole. This has included the growth of highly resourced research universities, the gradual decline of undergraduate teaching, students competing for entry into the top educational programs, and institutions competing for the top faculty and graduate students. Amid this scramble, and because of little growth in public funding for higher education, there has been increased reliance on private endowments and increased pressure to raise tuitions. Currently in Canada, nearly half of a university's operating costs are paid by student tuitions, and the proportion has risen steadily over the past 30 years, with no sign of stopping.

A recent book criticizing this and related tendencies is, *Higher Education? How Colleges Are Wasting Our Money and Failing Our Kids—And What We Can Do About It* by Andrew Hacker, a professor emeritus of political science at Queens College in New York. Hacker criticizes the backbreaking tuition fees at top universities and the injustice of the labour system (tenured and tenure-track professors earn most of the money and benefits, but most of the teaching is done by non-tenure-track adjuncts). Unnecessarily large graduate programs continue to pump out new Ph.D.s who can't get suitable jobs, and the main institutional concern is with funding high-status medical, scientific, and business programs. In short, the humanities are starved for funds, and students are denied legitimate learning opportunities in small classes. Students get an education they don't need and can't use, while putting themselves in debt for the next 10 or so years.

Though obviously correct in many of its general conclusions, the Jencks and Riesman study has received its share of criticisms. Some considered it a tedious read that provided no new insights into the state of American colleges and universities (Bidwell, 1969). Others noted that, in their severe criticisms of the rigid graduate curricula, the authors failed to

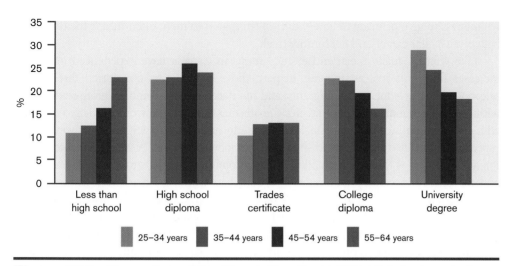

Figure 12.1   Proportion of the Population Aged 25 to 64, by Level of Educational Attainment and Age Group, Canada, 2006

Source: Statistics Canada. 2006. *Educational Portrait of Canada, 2006 Census.* 97-560-XIE2006001, March, 2008. http://www.statcan.gc.ca/bsolc/olc-cel/olc-cel?catno=97-560-XIE2006001&lang=eng

offer more than half-hearted suggestions for reform. Others felt personally attacked by Jencks and Riesman's criticisms of 'marginal colleges'—the local, black, religious, and women's colleges mentioned earlier.

Despite these criticisms, many found Jencks and Riesman's study to be 'genuinely revealing and persuasive' (Bressler, 1968: 1120). Their careful secondary analysis of various data on college and university attendance was seen as especially praiseworthy (Bidwell, 1969). Overall, *The Academic Revolution* was deemed 'subtle, complex, cultivated in irony, and enthusiastically recommended to academics' (Bressler, 1968: 1121). Most important, perhaps, this study has stood the test of time: there is nothing in important later works by (for example) Cole and Hacker that cannot be linked directly to the Jencks and Riesman study written 40 years earlier.

Educational Inequalities

Despite their failings, schools have played an important part in the lives of disadvantaged people, often levelling (or nearly levelling) the playing field. As a result, women and racial minorities are doing much better educationally than in the past. For example, as you know from Chapter 5, there has been a significant rise in women's educational attainment, with girls outperforming boys at the elementary and secondary school levels, and even at the post-secondary level. In 2003, for example, 60 per cent of the people graduating with a Canadian university degree were women (Statistics Canada, 2006).

The continuing gender differences—in salary and rank—reported each year with regularity reflect not a failure of the education system, but a reluctance of women to enter and compete in higher-paid male venues. Women continue, disproportionately, to apply to traditionally female-dominated programs like teaching and social work; they are much less likely than men to seek careers in mathematical and computer science, traditionally male-dominated programs. Women who complete the same doctoral programs as men are likely to have careers that are less varied, shorter, and less successful (Wall, 2008), but even this does not reflect a failure of the educational system.

Though some assert 'different structures of opportunities within higher education continue to perpetuate gender inequalities in the labour market' (Andres and Adamuti-Trache, 2007: 93), we know that self-selection continues to play the largest part in determining what happens to men and women at school and after graduation. Women's greater willingness to give primacy to family duties, compared to men, often means the difference between a stellar career and a 'Mommy track'.

Like women, many racial and ethnic groups in Canada have experienced important increases in educational attainment. In part, these increases have occurred through the selection of highly educated immigrants, and not necessarily by minority groups advancing within the educational system (Statistics Canada, 2006). Just like women, many racial and ethnic groups continue to face obstacles to their educational and occupational advancement, especially language difficulties and shortage of money for tuition. A factor that discourages foreign graduates is the unacceptability of many foreign credentials to Canadian employers and the often-unnecessary requirement of Canadian working experience. These requirements often force educated immigrants to take jobs for which they are highly over-qualified.

Despite these obstacles, and perhaps for these reasons, immigrants are far more likely than other Canadians to push their children to get college diplomas and university degrees. In some cases, this may represent an effort to regain a socio-economic status they held in their native country and lost on coming to Canada. However, this commitment to education also reflects a clear understanding that the investment in higher education is the best long-term investment a non-wealthy person can make. There is no better way than through formal education to work towards a comfortable and secure income, and social acceptance.

Aboriginal groups, by contrast, continue to be under-represented in Canadian colleges and universities. To some degree, this reflects a general disadvantage resulting from the harmful legacy of residential schooling and discriminatory educational policies. It also reflects the social, cultural, and economic factors that continue to hinder many minority students, especially those from rural or small-town origins and lower socio-economic status. In all of these cases a shortage of social and cultural capital reduces the likelihood of seeking and gaining higher education.

In 2006, one in three Aboriginals did not complete high school, compared to only one in eight in the non-Aboriginal population (Statistics Canada, 2006; CCL, 2008). However, the statistics are starting to improve. By 2006, 44 per cent had graduated from post-secondary education—they were as likely as their non-Aboriginal counterparts to have earned a college or trade qualification. Aboriginals are also making gains in other post-secondary education, with 8 per cent of Aboriginals reporting a university degree in 2006, far below the 23 per cent reported by the non-Aboriginal population (ibid.) but much better than a generation ago. These educational achievements are more common among Aboriginals who live in or near cities, compared with Aboriginals who live on reserves.

Table 12.2 Proportion of the First Nations People and Registered Indians Aged 25 to 64 Living On and Off Reserve, by Level of Educational Attainment, Canada, 2006

First Nations/Registered Indians	Less than High School (%)	High School Diploma (%)	Trades Certificate (%)	College Diploma (%)	University Certificate or Diploma below Bachelor Level (%)	University Degree (%)
First Nations people living on reserve[1]	50	15	13	14	4	4
First Nations people living off reserve[1]	30	24	14	20	4	9
Registered Indians[2] living on reserve	50	15	13	14	4	4
Registered Indians[2] living off reserve	31	23	13	19	4	9

1. Includes persons who reported a North American Indian identity only.
2. Includes persons who reported being Registered or Treaty Indians as defined by the Indian Act of Canada, regardless of their Aboriginal identity.

Source: Statistics Canada. 2006. Table 11 from *Educational Portrait of Canada, 2006 Census: National Picture* (Catalogue no. 97-560-X) Ottawa: Statistics Canada. http://www12.statcan.ca/english/census06/analysis/education/pdf/97-560-XIE2006001.pdf.

As noted earlier, children from poorer socio-economic backgrounds are generally less likely to gain a higher education. This inequality in educational (and later occupational) attainment begins early in life. Most children attend schools in the neighbourhoods where they live, which tend to be characterized by people of similar socio-economic status. So, children from lower-class neighbourhoods attend schools that are often not as well supplied or funded as schools in affluent neighbourhoods. Moreover, government cutbacks on educational spending have shifted this burden onto parents, many of whom cannot afford this extra load. These results come about in several ways: for example, some groups of parents are better at lobbying for discretionary spending, as well as raising money to offset funding cutbacks. As well, it is possible—though unproven—that more skilled, experienced teachers prefer the richer neighbourhoods.

A similar situation is evident in post-secondary institutions. There, rising tuition fees (increasing 37 per cent between 2000 and 2008 [CCL, 2008]), and rising costs of textbooks, technology, and supplies mean many students are unable to continue higher studies. This is especially true of students without parents who can afford to help them. Some students are also unwilling or unable to take on large loans they will have to pay back after graduation. As a result, only 60 per cent of young adults aged 18 to 24 from families earning less than $25,000 a year engaged in post-secondary education in 2006, compared with 80 per cent from families making over $100,000 a year (ibid.).

To some degree—perhaps only a small degree—the failure to continue on to post-secondary education reflects a cultural failure—the failure of our culture to support and encourage high education aspirations, especially among poor and rural native-born people. Another contributor may be the stupefying effect of 'youth culture', documented in a sociological study by James Coleman some 50 years ago. You may want to consider whether the concerns expressed in Coleman's book are still relevant today.

Classic Studies
The Adolescent Society

Since students today spend so much of their lives at school, in many ways schools have come to replace families as places where young people learn about the world. The first sociologist to look at this shift from families to schools, and the effects of this shift, was James S. Coleman, in his classic book *The Adolescent Society* (1966). We will discuss Coleman's biography, and his influence on the study of education, later in this chapter; but let's begin with one of his classic works on this topic.

Coleman based *The Adolescent Society* on a survey of US high school students at nine Midwestern schools. It studies adolescent popularity and finds that, for teenagers and young adults, academic achievement means nothing and looking good means everything. Without good looks, students are ridiculed or neglected; with good looks, they are popular. Students judge and reward one another's appearance and a few other qualities (e.g., athletic ability) according to a widely shared student code. In this ranking system, physical appearance—beauty in girls, handsomeness in boys, and good fashion sense in both—counts for more than brains. The academically successful but unattractive student not only fails to be popular with his or her peers, he or she is resented, since his or her achievement helps to uphold grading standards the other students are unable or unwilling to meet. Therefore, other students view the nerd as selfish as well as unappealing.

In this book, Coleman argues that the teenaged subculture observable in high schools, and perhaps today even in elementary schools, is largely separate from the adult world. It has a distinct set of values and its own social system of power and prestige, for example. Though in the adult world, good looks count for a lot, so do brains, hard work, and academic achievement. The adolescent way of thinking is strongly dysfunctional for society, because it discourages academic ambition and undermines the preparation of students for a workforce where knowledge is critical. Thus, Coleman says, the adolescent culture not only makes adolescents dependent on a cliquish, narrow-minded high school subculture; it also cuts them off from most parts of the adult world and fails to prepare them for adult life.

Why has this separate adolescent society developed? Coleman asserts that social changes associated with industrialization have separated adolescents from adults, leading them to seek approval from the age peers in whose company they spend most of their time at school. In this setting, a new ranking system emerges based largely on non-adult, atypical bases of evaluation. For example, athletic interests reign supreme among boys, while academia is held in low regard. In all the schools Coleman studied, he found an emphasis on athletic ability for boys and on fashion and beauty for girls in assigning social popularity and power. According to Coleman, these 'frivolous', non-adult values were seen by the group as a part of their identity—even as a means of separating themselves from what was considered a boring, meaningless adult culture. In this adolescent culture, academic success was viewed as conformity to a deadening social order, something adolescents tried to avoid.

These arguments seem to ring true even today. Yet, some critics have questioned Coleman's argument that there is a distinct adolescent subculture. They feel popularity-driven adolescents do not deviate from, but instead reflect, larger social values. In short, many parents are just as shallow as their children. By comparing values of the adolescent group with those of the larger community, we can see the adolescent value-system is largely a reflection of, or selection from, the larger society's major values. For example, like the teenage culture, the larger society also prizes athletic ability. No wonder athletic scholarships to post-secondary institutions are typically more numerous, and larger, than

The Adolescent Society: Many boys pride athletic ability over academic achievement.

academic rewards; and millions of men (especially) remain glued to their television sets on hockey nights or football Sundays.

Thus, we can read the book not only as a critique of American adolescents, but also as hidden critique of American culture and society. It seems likely this critique is as valid today as it was half a century ago. And what this further suggests is that the problems schools and educators face are indeed cultural and motivational, not merely economic. We cannot afford a society (or economy) populated by people who value nothing but sports and glamour.

As well, the adolescent society is inherently conflictual. As we saw in Chapter 3 and in Coleman's research above, clique formation—a normal part of children's development and a characteristic feature of school life—separates people and sets them against one another. In most schools, students hive off into well-recognized categories: the jocks, the nerds, the popular kids, and so on; and even within these categories, we find cliques. The tension among these groups is always high, creating unnecessary diversion from schoolwork, as well as great unhappiness among the excluded. The tension and hostility is further intensi-fied by streaming, which too conveniently identifies some students as above average ('the brains') and other students as subnormal or handicapped in some way. We shall see in detail the methods by which streaming takes place.

Ability Grouping or Streaming

Some schools minimize or control the variation between students by segregating differ-ent 'kinds' of students. One common type of segregation is *ability grouping*, more often spoken of as 'tracking' or 'streaming'. Much has been said in support of this practice. First, it ensures the best students receive the most challenging and enriched education. Second, the less-gifted students are spared the humiliation of struggling with materials they cannot master and competing against students they cannot match. Yet, in school systems all over Canada and the US a debate continues to rage over whether students, especially at the sec-ondary level (junior and senior high schools), should be segregated into classes according to academic ability.

There are three main types of ability grouping. The first, which we might call 'abil-ity grouping', is common in elementary classrooms. Here, students are divided accord-ing to their differential ability to handle new materials, for instance, as 'slow', 'average', and 'advanced' readers. The second type of grouping is termed 'setting'. Here, different classes exist in each subject, and students are assigned to classes that cover the ground more or less rapidly, according to ability in that particular subject. This system is found in North American high schools, where classes may be distinguished as 'honours', 'academic', 'applied'; or 'general' or 'vocational'; the class code often indicates the level. In the third type of grouping, variously referred to as 'tracking' or 'streaming', students move as a block from one class to another, so they take all classes within a certain level, such as all classes at the 'general' level. Sometimes, a class like this that moves around together to different courses is called a 'core group'.

The advantages of streaming have been known for generations. Streaming does all the following: allows pupils to advance according to their abilities; adapts instructional tech-niques to the needs of the group; and reduces failures and helps to preserve interest and incentive, since bright students are not bored by the sluggish participation of some others. Also, slower pupils engage more when they are not eclipsed by others who are brighter. The system also makes teaching easier, since it allows teachers to give individual instruc-tion to small groups with specific abilities. Perhaps the argument for streaming that might hold most appeal today, in an age seemingly obsessed with self-esteem, is that streaming is less likely to confront students with their inadequacy in comparison to classmates who are much more able.

Not only have the arguments *for* tracking been current for nearly 80 years, so also have been the arguments *against* it, and recently a few others have been added to the list. Some researchers claim that slow pupils need the presence of able students to stimulate and encourage them. As well, a stigma attached to low sections or classes in the school will discourage pupils who have been placed in these categories. Sometimes, tracking may even unnecessarily trap young people and prevent their advancement if their abilities are not accurately assessed. Often, students are weaker in one subject and stronger in another, or else develop later than other students. Also, teachers are often unable, or do not have time, to specify the work for different levels of ability. So, high-ability classes or groups simply receive *more* work rather than *different* work. Teachers may even object to teaching slower groups, since they would rather work with a more stimulating set of students.

As well, there is evidence that streaming or tracking reproduces existing social inequalities. Minority and lower-class students are more likely to end up in the lowest streams because they are more likely to present a lower school readiness, such as the ability to read and a general desire for learning. However, often they have not been socialized to be ambitious and do not have the same resources and experiences as students from a higher socio-economic background.

In addition, low-stream students typically receive instruction that is slower-paced, of lower quality, and even different from that available to higher-track students. These students not only cover less material, but also receive a less detailed analysis. As a result, low-stream students, who are often disproportionately poor and from minority groups, leave school with fewer of the skills necessary for employment. They also have less knowledge of how their society works and less faith in their ability to influence their own lives. In short, school has failed them. They come in with lower-than-average aspirations and little social and cultural capital, and leave with the same, having gained almost nothing from their brush with formal education.

Segregation or Distance in Schools

Not all students have the same educational experience, and in some cases, this is because some attend unconventional schools. For example, some parents choose to isolate their children in private schools where the class and ethnic or religious variety is much less than it is in secular public schools. Parents have various motives for placing their children in these schools. Some believe their children will receive a better education than in the public system, or that the private system will better prepare their children to compete for top university and occupational positions. Also, by sending their children to parochial schools, parents believe their children will be taught suitable values and religious dogma as well as academic material.

Currently, there is even a move in Toronto, Boston, and other North American cities to create special schools for children of certain racial backgrounds, such as 'black schools' where some believe black students will do better than in the mixed-race public system. The goal is to halt high dropout and failure rates among black children by building schools that meet both their academic and emotional needs. These schools would offer an alternative to the crowded and often unsafe ones with inexperienced teachers they were enrolled in before. As well, they would provide social services to help these students cope with various problems: for example, many do not have fathers at home; popular culture (such as television, movies, and music videos) often portray negative images of black people.

However, such single-race (or single-gender, or single-anything) schools minimize contact among students from different backdrops or different demographics, which decreases the familiarity with different groups that students could gain at a mixed school. As well, segregated schools limit public visibility and accountability. At the extreme, this makes children in segregated schools more vulnerable to the harm and neglect associated with total institutions. For example, horrible abuses occurred in the isolated, segregated residential schools designed for Canada's First Nations children, who were there against their will in the first place. This is not to suggest that all segregated, parochial, or private schools are abusive: only that there may be less public accountability (to students, parents, and elected officials) in such schools.

School Segregation: Wealthy parents are able to send their children to better schools.

Point/Counterpoint

BOX 12.1

Parents Spearhead Call for Action

When almost half the black kids in Toronto public schools drop out, something drastic needs to be done, says the *Toronto Star*'s Royson James. He calls it 'a crisis—a bloody disgrace'. There are those, however, are 'uncomfortable' with the idea of setting up schools just for black children, such as Ontario Premier Dalton McGuinty, and many middle-class blacks. But, according to George Dei, a sociologist at the Ontario Institute for Studies in Education, it is the alarming dropout rate that should be making the premier uncomfortable.

The politics of race is unsettling to most people, particularly blacks. But the provincial government should 'push the school board to move heaven and earth to fix the dysfunction', according to advocates.

Source: Adapted from James (2007).

Dissatisfied with both the public and private school systems, some parents choose to home-school their children. Home-schooling has been increasing in the US and Canada over the past few decades. Rather than attending a state school or registered private school, children remain at home to be taught by a parent or another relative. Many states and provinces allow children to legally be taught at home, as long as they are registered with the school system and their curriculum of study is approved. However, some opposition to home-schooling remains, and some home-schooling parents report difficulties in having their curricula approved.

Home-schoolers often see themselves as resisting this formal control. On one hand, some parents say they do not want their children 'brainwashed'; they want their children to 'think for themselves'. Many people, including schoolteachers, would wholeheartedly agree with this sentiment. Some parents, however, choose home-schooling because they do not want their children to be exposed to ideas of multiculturalism and the equality of all peoples, or to secular, scientific ideas that disagree with preferred religious beliefs. It is not evident that such educations promote the good of these children or of Canadian society.

Likewise, some parents choose to isolate their children from the opposite sex, preferring to keep their children at home or send them to boys-only or girls-only schools. There has been much research about whether girls (for example) do better in same-sex or mixed-sex schools and colleges; the evidence is still inconclusive on this point. Perhaps that is because there are strong pros and cons. On the one hand, single-sex schools reduce the degree of opposite-sex preening that Coleman reports in his 'adolescent society' book. On the other hand, segregation tends to defamiliarize the sexes with one another and lends an unnecessary, probably useless air of mystery to the opposite sex. Whatever the academic merits of segregating school-aged children—in public schools, private schools, parochial schools, same-sex schools, or at home—segregation has the social effect of separating people from others who are different socially in some ways. In this way it is likely to increase suspicion and distrust, or at the least, fail to build competence and familiarity in dealing with people who are different. Worse, it will do this among young students who may already be having trouble dealing with differential treatment based on sex, class, and races.

Nowhere is the role of the family in a child's education sketched more persuasively than in the classic work we discuss next. It is about the way a community of parents influences their children not only at home but also at school, through exercising unexpected control over the educational process.

Some parents choose to send their children to schools based on their religious faith, thus segregating them from the secular school system.

Classic Studies
Crestwood Heights

As we have already noted in this chapter, a child's family, or social origin, influences the priority given to his or her educational attainment. Equally important, a family also influences the mental health of its children. So, one might ask, What is the connection among these three variables: family life, school experience, and mental health? An early study that focused on this topic was by sociologist John R. Seeley, who created the classic book *Crestwood Heights* (1956) based on his study of a Toronto neighbourhood in the mid twentieth century.

Crestwood Heights began as a project to learn about the mental health of children in Canada, part of the National Mental Health Project, with the aim of promoting positive mental health and increasing the understanding of life in a suburb of a large Canadian city. Following World War II, this five-year project was launched by the Canadian National Committee for Mental Hygiene to study the development of Canadian children living in a suburban neighbourhood. The study began in 1950, led by chief investigator John R. Seeley, a well-known sociologist at the time with an interest in mental health, and a team of research staff from the University of Toronto.

Seeley's goal was to study 'the culture of the child under pressures for conformity'. In other words, it was a study of education, but also a study of childhood aimed at understanding the culture of the child, his values, his goals in life, and his problems. In this respect, it was similar to Coleman's study of adolescent society and the socio-psychological impact of membership in that 'society'. Seeley wanted to uncover the main guiding principles and pressures for conformity during childhood. To do so, he focused on children's lives in the Forest Hill community of Toronto. There he studied significant local institutions and the strains and conflicts in both the family and the community.

Viewed from the standpoint of parents in this community, the child is a problem to be solved, like other problems in the managerial world. Every parent wants a 'trophy child'—a child to be proud of. In Seeley's mind, this raises the question, Who *are* these parents that need a trophy child? Seeley finds they are a mixture of some 'old money' and many 'new money'—successful and upwardly mobile people, usually businesspeople or professionals. Many of the latter are the children of immigrants, with boundless energy and ambition, and high hopes for their children. Many are white and WASP, though a disproportionate number are Jewish. In this group of parents, careers are the priority and career success is important—both to the money-earning fathers and mainly stay-at-home mothers. To varying degrees, they all want their homes and personal lives to look like Hollywood movies or haute couture photo-shoots. They adorn themselves and their homes in the best money can buy.

As part of this perfect consumerism, they train their children to be 'perfect': competitive and successful in all their pursuits. For them, though they are likely unconscious of the fact, children are a consumer durable—like a car or home—that speaks volumes about the aspirations, wealth, power and 'classiness' of the parent.

So, even at a young age, they teach their children to seek success in scout groups, music lessons, hockey teams, and summer camps—also, in school! This makes the school the most important communal institution, at least where child-rearing is concerned. Parents view the school as the authority on raising children and the main place where children can prove their perfection. Parents turn their children over to the school (and to other classes, camps, and clubs), hoping that they return more mature and polished.

This concern with schooling makes the Parent–Teacher Association the neighbourhood's most significant voluntary association. At Crestwood Heights' high school, the PTA mediates between the school and the home. It retrains parents in the 'newer' ideas and techniques of child rearing, and provides oversight (and control) over the teachers and principal. School teachers become increasingly important sources of authority; parents view the teachers and administrators as experts, or at least specialists: engineers of adulthood, where their children are concerned.

Of course, the practice of expertise by teachers is complicated by stresses within the school itself. Some stresses have to do with school organization, and some with the conflicting goals of education. As industrial society increasingly bureaucratizes, child-rearing values shift from a stress on individual achievement, independence, and competition to a stress on co-operation, direction by others, and a submergence of the individual in the group. Therefore, schools can be expected to train the middle-class suburban child for 'bureaucratic crawl' and teach 'new' styles of co-operation and group orientation.

At the same time, the school continues to teach traditional values of competition and individual effort, creating academic inequalities and holding students responsible for their own successes and failure. Doing so causes tension for the students, parents, and teachers. Parents don't like their perfect children to receive grades below A. So parents press teachers for higher grades (more successes for their children)—the beginnings of grade inflation, which are still with us today. No wonder many students experience a troubled transition from high school to university, and much personal stress in both locations. The effects of bureaucratization on the jobs of teachers worsen the tension. After all, the teachers themselves are concerned about keeping their job and moving up the career ladder.

At the time of its publication, *Crestwood Heights* was criticized in several key ways. Most were concerned with the methodology Seeley employed. Bidwell (1957) points out that the small and biased size of the sample—a single community and, within that, a small sample of teachers, parents, and students—compromised the study's applicability to other North American suburbs. As well, the data analysis is mainly qualitative, with few hard, reliable statistics provided. Elkin (1957) criticized the book for being descriptively vague and for lacking a theoretical framework, though some scholars liked the anecdotal materials, which made the book an interesting read (they wanted even more anecdotes).

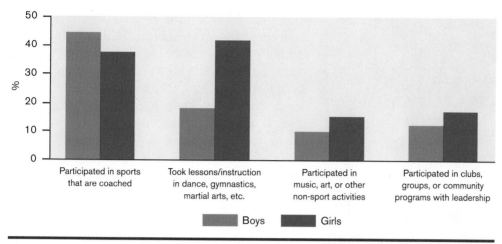

Figure 12.2 Children's Participation in Out-of-School Activities, 4- and 5-year-olds, 2002–2003

Source: Statistics Canada. *Education Matters: Insights on Education, Learning and Training in Canada,* 81-004-XIE, vol. 3 no. 3, September, 2006. http://www.statcan.gc.ca/pub/81-004-x/2006003/9341-eng.htm

But despite these criticisms, *Crestwood Heights* was praised for being a 'faithful ethnography' (Meyersohn, 1958: 331), and a 'highly stimulating book, reporting a thoughtful and sophisticated study of the community context within which the upper middle class child is socialized' (Foley, 1957: 220).

Today, more than 50 years later, the same patterns of socialization and education are evident in many urban and suburban communities. Many North American middle-class parents—perhaps especially immigrant parents—continue to drum into their children strong needs for achievement. They socialize their children to be ambitious, independent, and successful, rather than, say, dutiful, generous, or pious. They enrol their children in sports, extracurricular classes, and extra lessons to broaden their experiences and raise their test scores.

Often, the values schools promote are just an extension of values already promoted by parents, stressing ambition and advancement, especially among families of higher socioeconomic backgrounds (Lareau, 2003). As a result, children internalize the notion that in modern industrial societies, educational credentials (more than anything else) give people a foothold in the middle class. They come to expect, appropriately, that in competing for good jobs and good careers, educational credentials will largely compensate for class disadvantages at birth. As sociological data have shown repeatedly, people with the same educational credentials are roughly on the same footing when it comes to getting good jobs.

Of course, other factors matter too: for instance, *social capital* (valuable social connections) and *cultural capital* (knowledge of 'high culture', such as how to choose the best quality of wine). In Canada and the United States, as well as elsewhere in the economically developed world, these resources play a large part in securing good jobs too. In fact, research has shown that they are key influences at the highest levels of society—alongside people's B.A.s, M.B.A.s, M.D.s, Ph.D.s, and other relevant credentials. If you have little social and cultural capital, educational credentials can put you in the running for a good job and a good career. But social capital and cultural capital are the icing on the cake, especially important at the upper echelons of society.

Abuse or Violence in Schools

A source of increased concern today is bullying—especially, the use or threat of violence against children at or near school. And with the evolution of the Internet, much bullying has become psychological, rather than physical, abuse. Like everything else, bullying has become 'virtual' with the Internet, but it is no less real in its consequences.

Bullying: Children in lower grades are more likely to be victims of older bullies.

Bullies terrorize their victims, whether dominating them physically, emotionally, or socially. In face-to-face bullying, they may be bigger and stronger than the victim, or belong to a higher status within the school's social hierarchy. Often, they exploit the victim's weaknesses, and may operate in groups. Bullying can be physical or verbal. Bullies may confront their victims face-to-face, or they may use indirect means such as gossip or exclusion. Repeated bullying establishes dominance over the victim, who becomes increasingly distressed and fearful. The goal of bullying is to humiliate—to humble—another person, whether through threats, blackmail, gossip, or otherwise.

Research shows that childhood bullies are also likely to display anti-social behaviours in adulthood—30 to 40 per cent of children who are overly aggressive will have violent tendencies as adults. Generally, the motives for bullying originate at home, where children's behavioural patterns are first established. Bullies tend to have parents who are hostile, neglectful, or in conflict, or who punish their children severely. In some cases, bullies are merely imitating their parents' own social behaviour; that is, they have parents who are bullies. Sometimes, they learn that bullying is acceptable because their parents tolerate fighting in the household among siblings.

Bullies show aggression to many people: not only their peers and siblings, but also to their parents and teachers. They seek out and enjoy aggressive situations, show little empathy for people they hurt, and feel no remorse for their actions. Many have quick tempers and are hyperactive, disruptive, and impulsive. Male bullies, in particular, tend to be physically strong and use their strength to threaten and coerce others.

Like bullies, victims too have certain definable characteristics. Many display anxiety, expressed as tension, fears, and worry; low self-esteem; and depression, including sadness and withdrawal from activities. These traits are commonly reported among both boys and girls who are victimized. As they get older, children are less likely to be victims of bullies. But likely, just as bullies will continue to bully in adulthood—even if they do so in more subtle ways— so too victims will continue to be victimized, though perhaps to a reduced extent.

Most childhood bullying happens in the presence of peers. Although five out of six students say they feel uncomfortable when they see someone being bullied, peers often watch or participate in some way, whether by joining in or cheering the bully on. Peers tend to support the bully, rather than the victim, and this support can help reinforce the bully's power over the victim and his or her own social standing. Sometimes a peer will intervene to stop the bullying. Bullying by a child considered a friend can be especially upsetting. It can be difficult for the child to recognize that a friend is bullying, and for parents and teachers to identify these interactions as bullying.

Bullying is not merely a psychological pathology: it is embedded in the social norms and values common to a whole community. For example, bullying has an evident place in the 'adolescent society' Coleman described, since that society distinguishes so clearly between winners and losers in the teenage status game. Often only the students themselves—members of this adolescent society—can understand the meanings popularly

Media Distortion

BOX **12.2**

Media Fuelling School Shootings

When school or workplace violence gets wide media attention, there tend to be copycat actions. Those who are prone to perpetrating such acts, usually mentally ill, can be 'pushed over the edge' if they see extensive news coverage of an attack. University of British Columbia professor Sandra Robinson calls this phenomenon 'social contagion', and says 'When you see one of these shootings, you will see clusters of them for a time'. She notes a similar effect in teenage suicide when a well-known person, especially someone like a rock star, commits suicide.

Robinson recommends that reporters be careful not to use positive language, such as the word 'successful', when reporting school shootings, so as not to encourage copycats.

Source: Adapted from CanWest News Service (2006).

attached to bullying rumours, gossip, and threats. This is why bullying is possible even in the presence of the teacher, during classes.

Rooted in the group culture, bullying focuses on certain culturally supported stereotypes and prejudices. This includes singling out people who are handicapped (for example, deaf, blind, obese, or given to stuttering, and therefore socially isolated), unpopular, or homosexual, for example. Bullying often employs homophobic verbal taunts related to gender nonconformity—for example, calling victims 'gay'. These epithets are used even against boys who are not homosexual, the implication being that the victims are outsiders, effeminate or powerless, and worthy of ridicule. Often, this tendency is supported by aggressive, sexist, and heteronormative subcultures.

Certain hyper-masculine activities associated with contact sports like football are especially likely to encourage bullying. This tendency occurs due to the values and attitudes that circulate within these male-only (also known as 'homosocial') contexts, with their historical preference for hardiness, solidarity, and stoicism. Tensions and social anxieties around masculinity emerge in schools wherever a hyper-masculine sporting identity flourishes.

All forms of bullying—direct and indirect, and even cyber-bullying—can have important harmful effects on health and well-being that persist into adulthood. Many children do not tell anyone about their bullying experience or seek help and support. They need to be encouraged to speak out; peer support programs have already been identified as an important way to tackle and prevent bullying. These programs help by building resilience, promoting friendship, and challenging negative peer group roles.

The Integrating Power of Schools

It is in the school setting that children form and broaden their base of close friendships. Often, these turn into long-term relationships and some even turn into marriage. So, clearly, school helps to integrate people by teaching them how to live with one another.

It is paradoxical that in some ways schools bring people together, despite also (in other ways) driving them apart. The school experience increases students' familiarity with each other in various ways. In particular, it helps to wean students away from their parents and draw them closer to their peers, in dyads, cliques, teams, bands, and gangs.

What an important change this marks in children's lives. Early in life, we are most concerned about relations with our parents. Our childhood home is the culture and society we know best, and we measure everything else—including our wishes, hopes, and self-esteem—against what we have learned there. However, as we age, all this changes radically. At school, we become aware of a much larger world; the peers whom we meet there are much more varied than our parents and siblings, and often they hold different values. For the first time, we feel moral doubt. The question we face is not, 'Should I obey the rules?' but 'What *are* the rules?' As well, we must ask, 'Are the rules I follow at home inevitable, natural, and just?' In adolescence, our needs for peer acceptance increase, as we seek identities and goals of our own. We often feel torn between the conflicting goals of finding our own true selves and gaining social acceptance as just 'one of the crowd'.

Cultural norms in adolescence often invite a rejection of family life, in favour of popularity and 'fitting in'. However, as we grow older we usually reintegrate into the family, as part of a normal passage from childhood to adulthood. Teenagers rate the importance of success and comfort more highly than adults do; but this starts to change as people enter their twenties. To adults, even young adults who have formed important relationships, material success and comfort are (merely) indicators of family well-being and security. To teenagers, these attainments are the means of freeing themselves from family constraints. To adults, they are the bedrock of a new, adult identity.

Schools contribute to this evolution of independence and integration. The first and most obvious point is that schools bring together large numbers of young people, giving them an opportunity to communicate and interact easily. Like factories, schools give people occasions for interaction and sociability, as well as for work. Some of this interaction is simplified by likeness and shared beliefs. Remember that most children attend neighbourhood public schools, and most neighbourhoods are socially homogeneous—at least, more homogeneous than the city population as a whole. Even children who go to private schools are homogeneous in some respects—whether economically, ethnically, religiously, or otherwise.

Schools have the power to integrate people by helping students form friendships with one another.

Table 12.3) Erikson's Human Development Stage Theory

Age	Conflict	Resolution or 'Virtue'	Culmination in Old Age
Infancy (0–1 year)	Basic trust vs. mistrust	Hope	Appreciation of interdependence and relatedness
Early childhood (1–3 years)	Autonomy vs. shame	Will	Acceptance of the cycle of life, from integration to disintegration
Play age (3–6 years)	Initiative vs. guilt	Purpose	Humour, empathy, resilience
School age (6–12 years)	Industry vs. inferiority	Competence	Humility; acceptance of the course of one's life and unfulfilled hopes
Adolescence (12–19 years)	Identity vs. confusion	Fidelity	Sense of complexity of life; merging of sensory, logical, and aesthetic perception
Early adulthood (20–25 years)	Intimacy vs. isolation	Love	Sense of the complexity of relationships; value of tenderness and loving freely
Adulthood (26–64 years)	Generativity vs. stagnation	Care	Caritas, caring for others, and agape, empathy and concern
Old age (65–death)	Integrity vs. despair	Wisdom	Existential identity; a sense of integrity strong enough to withstand physical disintegration

Source: Dewey (2008).

Second, most children want to make friends, and going to school is a great opportunity to do so. Few people want to be isolated loners, excluded from everything that is going on. Most people would even rather be members of an unpopular group than be the member of no group whatever. This tendency to join groups is, again, part of the developmental cycle we discussed above.

Psychoanalyst Erik Erikson said that we all grow up following a predictable human life cycle, made up of eight stages of development. At each stage, we face a specific task; the successful completion of that task allows us to achieve a certain goal, and the failure to do so results may stall us at a developmental stage, unable to move forward. Two developmental stages are especially important in relation to schools.

In Erikson's Stage 4—occurring from 6 to 12 years old (also called the *latency stage*)—children learn many new skills, developing a sense of industry and competence as they do so. They also develop socially, comparing themselves to others and sometimes feeling inadequate and inferior to their peers. At these times, they may develop problems of self-esteem. Their most significant relationships are with their school, neighbourhood, and peer group. Parents, though still important, are no longer viewed as the complete authorities they once were.

This separation of young people from their family life becomes even more marked during adolescence. In Stage 5—from 12 to 19 years of age—development comes to depend mainly on what they do, not on what others do to them. Adolescents are neither children nor adults. Life gets more complex as young people try to find their own identities, struggle with social interactions, and grapple with moral issues. Their ultimate goal at this stage is to discover who they are as individuals, separate from their families of origin and as full members of a larger society.

To distance themselves from their families, many adolescents deny or ignore their family responsibilities, which Erikson calls a 'moratorium' or temporary standstill in child–family relations. Some adolescents also suffer role confusion, owing to an effort to simplify life choices. At this stage, many young people think in black-and-white, idealized terms, which are clear-cut and conflict-free—little resembling the messiness of adult reality.

Because they lack experience, adolescents substitute ideals for experience. Seeking support for their ideas, they also develop a strong devotion to friends and causes, wanting to idealize them and cling to them. At this age, their most significant relationships are often with peer groups, although families continue to be important for many.

Throughout these two key developmental stages, schools help children by providing settings where peers can watch one another and even work together on group or classroom projects. These opportunities to watch, and interact and communicate with, one another also help to develop skills for trust and conflict resolution—all unintended benefits of classroom education, whether private or public schools. In this way, schools are the primary site of peer socialization.

As we noted earlier, no one understood better than James Coleman the influence that young people exert over one another, through exclusion, gossip, jokes, and other forms of bullying.

People Are Talking About . . .
JAMES S. COLEMAN

James Samuel Coleman was born in Indiana in 1926. He joined the US Navy in 1944, after graduating from high school. He received a bachelor's degree in chemical engineering from Purdue University in 1949, followed by a Ph.D. in sociology from Columbia University in 1955. At Columbia he was influenced by Paul Lazarsfeld, a prominent European sociologist who had fled the Nazis and established a bureau of applied social research at Columbia. From Lazarsfeld, Coleman learned the value of socially relevant applied research. Coleman later taught sociology at Stanford University, the University of Chicago, and Johns Hopkins University.

Coleman was an influential figure in the sociology of education. He and several colleagues conducted one of the largest studies in history—surveying over 150,000 students—to report on equality in education in the US. Their report, Equality of Educational Opportunity, known as the 'Coleman Report', was published in 1966, and has generated debate continuously since then. In it, Coleman et al. contend that student achievement does not depend on school funding, but rather on a student's background and socio-economic circumstances.

The report's findings indicated that black students of lower socio-economic backgrounds would do better academically in racially mixed schools. The message: move the students to white schools, don't simply send more funds to black schools. These findings set in motion the trend to desegregation, with black students being bussed to schools in white neighbourhoods. In 1975, Coleman published a follow-up study in which he noted that after desegregation, many white parents withdrew their children from mixed schools—the 'white flight' phenomenon. This reaction defeated the purpose of desegregation, which was to have black students benefit from close contact with white students. Nonetheless, Coleman was right in his sociological analysis, and right in his policy recommendations.

Coleman was a prolific author, writing over 30 books and many articles. He knew that his 'worst critics' would be the best judges of the validity of his conclusions; therefore he routinely asked critics to review his work before publication. He died before finishing another large study which followed the lives and careers of 75,000 people who had graduated from high school in 1980 and 1981.

Sources: Adapted from http://www.bookrags.com/biography/james-samuel-coleman-soc/; http://www.newworldencyclopedia.org/entry/James_S._Coleman; http://social.jrank.org/pages/1661/James-S-Coleman.html; and other sources.

James S. Coleman was always interested in the ways schooling provided students with *cultural capital*—knowledge of class-significant information—and *social capital*—densely connected networks of relations. However, Lillbacka (2006) points out that, although social scientists agree that social capital is an important concept, there is little agreement on how to define and measure it, and few have tried to do so empirically. Lillbacka makes a start, finding evidence for four possible indicators of a person's social capital: (1) interpersonal trust, (2) a strong social network, (3) self-confidence, and (4) belonging to voluntary associations.

Healy (2004) too notes that the meaning and application of 'social capital' continues to be debated. Like Lillbacka, Healy mentions the problems around measuring social capital empirically. Some users of the concept have lumped together different types of social behaviour and treated these as 'social capital', regardless of the culture, institutional setting, historical context, or ruling power structure. Surely this doesn't make sense, he argues. What works as social capital in one context may not work in another. In this sense, social capital is like any other currency of exchange—e.g., Canadian dollars. You don't expect Canadian dollars to work the same way in Sri Lanka or Sardinia as they work in Saskatoon.

The author suggests these problems of context cannot be entirely resolved. However, he suggests more transdisciplinary dialogue around these issues.

To clarify the social capital concept, Barnett (2005) tests Coleman's 'Catholic school effect'—the hypothesis that Catholic schools instill more social capital in their students than do public schools, and therefore these students perform better academically. Barnett looks at students in a public high school, to see if those who attended a Catholic junior high school show more signs of social capital than those who attended a public junior high school. The results show the Catholic-schooled students do have more social capital but this does not translate into differences in academic achievement between the two groups.

Bankston (2004) asks similar questions in a study of immigrant children. He contends that, where immigrant children are concerned, we can view 'ethnicity' as social capital in determining school outcomes for immigrants. However, membership in a particular ethnic group has beneficial impacts only if that group endorses cultural values, beliefs, and expectations that are relevant to school achievement. Specifically, Bankston uses the example of academic achievement for Vietnamese American students, arguing that the investment in social relations pays off only if there is an interaction with cultural norms.

Because this is complex, it bears a little further discussion. As we know from an earlier chapter, ethnic minorities—especially, immigrants—benefit from what Raymond Breton called 'institutional completeness'. (It may be worth adding at this point that Breton was a student of James Coleman.) The argument is that students benefit from integration into their ethnic group, compared with social marginality or exclusion; and they benefit from high educational aspirations. They benefit *most* from an interaction of the two: that is, when integration into their ethnic group supports and enforces high educational aspirations.

So, for example, integration into a subculture strongly committed to postsecondary education—for example, Chinese-Canadians—will have more educational payoff than integration into a subculture less strongly committed to post-secondary education—for example, Portuguese-Canadians. Thus, the educational benefits of social capital depend on the particular ethnic group and its range of cultural 'investments'. Theories about academic achievement, therefore, must address the ways culture, social structures, and socio-economic status interact to yield sometimes unexpected outcomes.

Coleman and other sociologists of stratification have shown how socio-economic factors lead to inequalities in educational access and attainment. However, Bonikowski (2004) asserts that stratification studies like these have not considered the effect of curriculum on academic outcomes. Curriculum design, for its part, is influenced by political, economic, and organizational forces that may perpetuate social inequalities, regardless of the 'openness' of the admissions process. Thus Bonikowski argues that a wider range of variables is needed to predict educational outcomes; in this context, social capital is only one of many.

Elster (2003) offers a more fundamental criticism of Coleman's work, which he describes as perceptive but dogmatic. It could be considered dogmatic because it is rigorously empirical and parsimonious—as noted earlier, neglecting some important variables to focus on the impact of others. It also grows out of what sociologists call 'rational choice theory', a theoretical approach (somewhat like economics) that assumes people will act rationally to maximize their well-being. In this context, 'social capital' is something that is 'invested' for maximum gain in a supposedly conscious, seemingly rational way.

Elster notes that Coleman is too good a sociologist to believe in such simple-minded reasoning. After all, one can scarcely understand 'adolescent society' in terms of rational investment—the fixation on sports and glamour is much more irrational than rational. So, evidently Coleman knows there are many types of norms; but he repeatedly tries to explain them all functionally, according to the benefits they provide. Elster argues first, that some norms serve no useful purpose, but merely cause 'pointless suffering'. (This was certainly evident in the high school study Coleman did, where nerds and ugly ducklings suffered plenty.) Further, even when social norms (like the rule that 'You must not study hard') provide benefits for those who follow them—for example, benefits in the form of popularity—the causal link between these benefits and their causes remains mysterious.

Lindenberg (2003) criticizes Coleman for his apparent failure, after the Coleman Report of the 1960s, to continue producing applied sociology. Lindenberg alleges that Coleman, who thought it important that sociology produce well-designed social institutions, did very little institutional design himself. Despite recognizing that the family, the church, and the neighbourhood were all losing their prominence in the social order, Coleman proved unable to describe what new forms of institutions might take their place. Lindenberg blames this on the micro-economic theory that Coleman tried to apply to the problem, claiming that applied work needs a more complex theory.

A final word should be said about Coleman's later work—especially his work in economic sociology and mathematical sociology. This work, often abstract and without evident application, was also often hard to understand. Here, Coleman—like other mathematical sociologists—was struggling with a set of concepts and models that he hoped would provide fruitful new insights in the future. Most sociologists found these writings hard to understand, and many ignored them. Some, like Elster and Lindenberg criticized what they considered to be overly simple, overly rationalized pictures of human behaviour and interaction in Coleman's models. Likely, Coleman would have replied that abstract models are intended to provide an outline—a blueprint or skeleton of things that, in reality, are infinitely more complex and messy. All natural science has proceeded in this way, through induction, then modelling, and then back to prediction, observation, and theory testing. It seems likely that, in time, Coleman's work will be better understood and better used by new generations of sociologists. Doing so will require somewhat more theoretical and mathematical sophistication.

That said, a review of recent writings finds continued application of the work by James Coleman—over 90 journal articles applying Coleman's work in the last 20 years. Clearly, sociologists are talking about James Coleman. Coleman deserves a place in our comprehensive, fusion approach to sociology because he typifies the highest positivist/scientific rigour in his work. Trained as an engineer as well as sociologist, proficient in pure and applied social research, a master of both theory and method, Coleman brings us back time and again to basic, important questions about the ways society works—also, to the way we train our children and, in so doing, distribute social disadvantage.

New Insights

Recent writing on education is raising new questions about inclusion, advantage, and social capital. Perhaps Coleman would have embraced the conceptions of education illustrated by celebrated educators who broke new ground in teaching. So for example, Scott (2009) writes about Chris Searle, who calls his brand of teaching 'resistance education'—a way of teaching awareness and freedom to the working class. His teaching philosophy is reflected in the titles of some of his books: *Classrooms of Resistance*, *Words Unchained*, *We're Building the New School*, and *The World in a Classroom*.

Scott notes that Searle's writings, which deal with cultural colonialism, draw on his own students' lives and thoughts in the practice of critical literacy. Along similar lines, Davis (2009) tells of Searle's time spent teaching at a mostly non-white school in Sheffield in 1990, where he further developed his critical literacy curriculum. Despite racial tensions, Searle brought together Yemeni, Pakistani, and white students of various socio-economic levels, as well as involving the local community in the school. This educational practice is, perhaps, at the farthest end of a continuum with Crestwood Heights at the other end: it is not at all interested in promoting elitism and upward mobility. Nor, unlike the schools Coleman studied, is it interested in promoting juvenile sporting events or popularity contests. There are no prom queens in this scenario.

Truth is seen as the goal of inquiry of many approaches such as critical thinking and critical pedagogy. But discovering and imparting truth cannot be the goal of education from a postmodern perspective, according to Roth (2009), and a 'new critical language of education' must be based on understanding and justification.

Amatucci (2009) describes an even more nuanced notion of learning and teaching, viewing it as a personal search. She reports

> Using poetry, performative ethnography, narrative, and senses of home and heart, I engage Butler, Foucault, Baudrillard, Derrida, Marx, Deleuze, Bhabha, and others, and find myself questioning liminality and the easy answers it affords. Through stories of family and teaching high school English, I move from small town to classroom to the academy to expose contradictory and complementary versions of me at various points in time and space. I play with my hair and read Japanese poetry as I write to please an amorphous you, a 'you' who never appears but prefaces everything I have ever had to say.

Some might say Amatucci's report is a mix of bad poetry and undisciplined self-indulgence. Others might say it is a deeply personal examination of the search for learning and meaning in a fragmented world without clear boundaries. There is no doubt her report illustrates the principle that education in a postmodern age is intended—even, required—to be emancipatory.

Another emancipatory form of education is described by McNair (2009) as the 'pedagogy of porn' which the author experienced both as a student and teacher in UK universities. McNair tells how political and technological factors in the late twentieth century engendered new attitudes toward pornography. During this time, pornography became more acceptable and was seen in new forms, thanks to feminism, which encompasses those both for and against porn, the gay rights movement, and the Internet.

Schools, like other social institutions, face increasing demands for multicultural sensitivity in dealing with children (and parents) from a wide variety of backgrounds.

At the same time, schools have the responsibility to shape new identities, not only teach new skill sets.

So, for example, Klugkist (2009) describes how telling personal stories can help people 'rewrite the self'. Former students—black and coloured—of a private European school in South Africa described the process of forming identities for themselves in this multicultural school setting. By telling these stories long after they had left the school, these students were able to learn more about themselves and how their school experience led them to re-imagine lives beyond their 'boundaries'. Klugkist suggests that, within the context of South African history, telling personal stories and re-imagining a common human identity can help South Africans break free of past discourses that still influence their society.

Still, formal education takes place within schools, and there can be no understanding of education without also understanding schools. Henry (2009) takes a more traditional approach to educational research, more like Coleman's, using survey data to understand school issues—in this case, the 1999 mass murder at Columbine High School in Colorado. Before the Columbine massacre, various aspects of violence in schools were typically examined in isolation, with researchers from different disciplines focusing on different parts of the problem that suited their own discipline. The psychologist would look at the reasons why school children might become violent, for example, and the sociologist would consider whether a lack of cultural attachment and involvement were to blame. School management experts, for their part, would suggest new security measures to detect and prevent potential violence.

Treating the problem piecemeal, however, masked the complexity of the problem and hindered finding a real solution. For that reason, Henry proposes an interdisciplinary approach that synthesizes all aspects of the school experience, and simultaneously examines the community and culture in which schooling takes place. In this respect, he reminds us of the classic *Crestwood Heights* study we discussed earlier, which also situated the high school within its communal and cultural context.

Chapter Summary

In this chapter we have seen how an increased demand for highly educated workers has influenced schools and education. Post-secondary education has become a necessity, leading to the new research universities described by Jencks and Riesman. The adolescent society has morphed into something (slightly) more outward looking and career-oriented than what Coleman found 50 years ago, thanks in part to the Internet. And Canadian parents have continued to set the educational bar higher and higher, just like parents in Crestwood Heights back in the day.

A by-product of this educational development is greater inequality within society between students with a lot of social and cultural capital and those without it. Higher levels of education are not freely available to all, and access may depend on an individual's or a family's financial standing. It certainly depends on their educational aspirations. An example of the problem in Canada is a continued major disparity in the levels of education gained by Aboriginal and non-Aboriginal children. The advancement of technology, always a source of new human possibilities, has not benefitted the world equally. In fact, the so-called digital divide has hastened the opening of a knowledge gap between developed and less-developed countries.

We have looked at the segregation of students in schools and asked whether streaming and other types of segregation are good or bad. On the one hand, some parents think it is necessary for their children to attend schools that cater to their particular culture and belief system. On the other hand, this separation between people often fosters mistrust and obstructs co-operation. At best, it fails to familiarize students with other kinds of young people. If done responsibly, tracking identifies weaker students and helps them learn at a suitable pace while allowing the stronger students to learn more quickly. But evidence shows that tracking has often been implemented poorly, causing the already weak students to fall even further behind the average. In the long run, this harms the weaker students and weakens our society as well.

Stressful situations abound in schools today, such as the competition for good grades, popularity, and acceptance. These stresses may lead to overt and covert violence, including the different types of bullying we have discussed. In the long run, these experiences damage students' mental and physical well-being and undermine the educational process as well.

With diligence, we may be able to remedy the many problems found in our schools today. Fixing the problems will mean more resources—for example, smaller classes and better-trained teachers. It may also mean curriculum change, to stress principles of civility, ethics, and flexibility that can help students to continue learning productively and interact co-operatively. A good, conscientious, and responsible school not only benefits its students, but also serves the whole community by bringing people together and teaching them the skills of cooperation.

Critical Thinking Questions

1. Should high school students be taught courses on team-building and co-operation, or will these skills come naturally, as the students mature and gain familiarity with one another?
2. What is the biggest educational problem you have personally experienced, and how do you think it might be remedied?
3. Give an example of informal education that you engaged in recently. What difficulties did you experience in trying to learn outside the system of formal education?
4. How do functionalists and critical theorists view educational inequality? Which approach has provided the most useful advice for policy-makers, in your view?
5. What are the positive and negative effects of *ability grouping* (also known as *streaming* or *tracking*)? On balance, is it a good thing or bad thing?
6. What do you think is the best way of addressing the problem of bullying in schools? Why should schools be concerned with a problem that probably results from bad families?

Recommended Readings

Richard Kadison and Theresa Foy DiGeronimo, *College of the Overwhelmed: The Campus Mental Health Crisis and What To Do About It* (San Francisco: Jossey-Bass, 2004). In this book, the authors focus on the recent increase in serious mental health problems among students on campus. They examine rising incidents of depression and harmful behaviours such as binge drinking. The authors outline the school-related pressures faced by students that have an impact on their well-being and provide helpful information both for students and their parents to reduce the severity of stress-related problems.

Hugh Lauder, Phillip Brown, Jo-Anne Dillabough, and A.H. Halsey (eds), *Education, Globalization, and Social Change* (Oxford: Oxford University Press, 2006). This book outlines the relationship between education and the outcomes it is generally believed to have: economic success, the reduction of poverty, inequality, and environmental harm. However, the authors state that there are limits to education's ability to do all the above. The authors examine these limits, as well as opportunities for success, through various readings.

D.W. Livingstone, *The Education–Jobs Gap: Underemployment or Economic Democracy* (Toronto: Garamond, 2004). As the title suggests, this book, by an eminent Canadian sociologist, discusses the gap people experience between the education they receive and the skills and knowledge necessary in their occupation. The findings of this book are important for current students who are interested about what work life will be like in the future.

Neil Guppy and Scott Davies, *The Schooled Society: An Introduction to the Sociology of Education*, 2nd edn (Toronto: Oxford University Press, 2010). This book explores schooling from various perspectives, within a Canadian context. It discusses both classic and contemporary theories and theorists and links their research to educational inequality, the social organization of schooling, and the future of schooling in Canada.

James S. Coleman, with John W.C. Johnstone and Kurt Jonassohn, *The Adolescent Society: The Social Life of the Teenager and Its Impact on Education* (New York: Free Press, 1966 [1961]). As we saw earlier, this is a classic study in the sociology of education, the findings of which are still applicable in today's society. Coleman examines the distinct value system of adolescents and its implications for their academic achievement.

John R. Seeley, R. Alexander Sim, Elizabeth W. Loosley, with Norman W. Bell and D.F. Fleming, *Crestwood Heights* (Toronto: University of Toronto Press, 1956). This is a classic product of Canadian-based sociological research. An ethnographic study of an affluent Canadian suburb (Forest Hill Village in Toronto), it explores how the community school plays an important part in the lives of students, parents, and teachers, and how it impacts children's values, ambitions, and mental well-being.

Websites

Organization for Economic Co-operation and Development (OECD)
www.oecd.org

Educational Resources Information Center (ERIC)
www.eric.ed.gov

Canadian Teachers' Federation (CTF)
www.ctf-fce.ca

Canadian Council on Learning (CCL)
www.ccl-cca.ca/ccl

StudyCanada
www.studycanada.ca

Bullying.org
www.bullying.org

Toronto Star Series: Brainstorm
www.thestar.com/topic/AtkinsonSeries-Atkinson2009

13 Churches and Religion

Learning Objectives

In this chapter, you will:

> Define religion as a social phenomenon

> Recognize the role of religion today and the characteristics that define a religion

> Identify the trends of religious participation in Canada today

> Evaluate the contributions of religion to social well-being

> Understand how religion can both include and exclude others in civic relationships

Chapter Outline

In the eyes of pious people, religions consist of revealed truths—truths as solid and real as trees, but infinitely more important. After all, they convey the word of God, rendered through His prophets, recorded in holy books, and revealed in His works. Of course, that is just the Judeo-Christian take on religions; other traditions are somewhat less concrete and less prescriptive. But the point is, most religions lay claim to an almost unassailable significance and validity. So, you might wonder, what could sociologists possibly bring to the understanding of religion?

Well, sociologists of religion are not interested in whether god exists, or in other questions that scientific methods cannot answer. They do not consider religious beliefs to be unassailably true, any more than any other human beliefs with a political, economic, or cultural content: they are just beliefs. Accordingly, sociologists are interested in how people act out their religious beliefs in everyday life and how these beliefs affect their interactions with others and with society. Sociologists are concerned with how certain beliefs (and not others) are legitimized, and who in society controls this process. From a macrosociological perspective, they are interested in the rise and fall of religions, and the persistence of certain religions over centuries and even millennia; and they are interested in the effects of these long-lived belief systems on other belief systems: political, economic, or cultural.

As a social science, the stance of sociology is that religion is (merely) a social phenomenon, one of many products of social life that play an important role in society's functioning. All three founders of sociology were interested in religion, as we will see. Marx viewed it as a form of socially organized self-deception and a way that people—especially, the ruling classes—disguise their exploitation of the masses. Durkheim, on the other hand, viewed religion as an opportunity for group celebration. In his eyes, the content of religion is less important than the opportunity it presents to express social solidarity in ritualized forms. Weber, finally, viewed religion as a set of beliefs that give life meaning and purpose. These beliefs can have enormous, and sometimes positive, social consequences.

In this chapter, we will look at various definitions of religion, as well as the many roles that religion plays in a society. We will analyze the ways that people have related and continue to relate to religion, and recognize that, for many, religion still plays a central role in social life around the world. Despite a general secularization of industrial and post-industrial societies, many people still turn to spirituality for comfort and guidance; some even create new religions and new religious movements. And, although religion has historically created conflicts, it has also integrated people and continues to do so today.

Everyday Observations

Oh, Holiday Tree. For a very short time, in the year 2002, the brightly decorated fir tree in front of Toronto's city hall, usually known as a 'Christmas' tree, became a 'holiday' tree. Why did this happen? Why had the word 'Christmas' suddenly disappeared from the vocabulary of city officials? The answer is simple: Toronto city officials wanted to get out the message that the Cavalcade of Lights in Nathan Phillips Square was an inclusive celebration. The label 'Christmas tree', they thought, plainly linked the public event to a Christian holiday, and this was unacceptable in a multicultural society where Christianity is just one belief system (albeit the dominant one) among many. Nevertheless, the public reacted strongly against this move. Politicians immediately bowed to public pressure and voted to refer to the 16-metre tree in Nathan Phillips Square once again as a 'Christmas tree'.

Every year, many Canadians celebrate 'winter' festivals, attend 'holiday' concerts, and gather around 'multicultural' trees decorated with symbols from many faiths. If you have noticed this, you have probably also noticed that these celebrations are changing too. This change began in Western countries centuries ago and continues to unfold today throughout the world. As a package, the change process is often called secularization, meaning that in these celebrations and elsewhere, we continue to see the separation between religion and politics, and between sacred private beliefs and secular public practices.

One standard account of this progress goes like this: over the last few centuries, economic growth accompanied the rationalization of society and accumulation of scientific knowledge. During this period, **religion** lost much of its social relevance in the West. As a result, many came to deny the claims of traditional sacred texts and gave up attending religious ceremonies. As a result, today most people in the West are more autonomous than in past centuries and feel they no longer need the emotional support and communal solidarity religion traditionally offered.

Is this a valid description of social and cultural change over the past four centuries? That's an immense question to answer, but you can try nonetheless. In evaluating this account, begin with your personal experience. Ask yourself how large a role religion plays in your life. Do you consider yourself strongly religious? Are you even a member of a faith at all? Do you think religion plays an important part in the lives of most of the people you

religion
Any system of beliefs about the supernatural, and the social groups that gather around these beliefs.

meet every day? If you answered 'no' to all these questions you may be surprised to learn that, according to a recent study by Statistics Canada, 60 per cent of the Canadian population still consider themselves either moderately or highly religious (Statistics Canada, 2006). Although attendance at religious services has decreased over the years, many people report worshipping in their own homes. What is more, an increasing number of Canadians are turning to **new religious movements** (NRMs), which they see as better serving their spiritual needs. They have not so much given up on religion as given up on the traditional religions and traditional ways of practising their beliefs.

Given these facts, the 'holiday tree' anecdote above should give us pause. Sociologically, we understand the need for different religious faiths to coexist in a multicultural society. City officials seemed to think that such coexistence needs a neutral public sphere, one free of the symbolic predominance of any given faith. Does it follow that a multicultural society must confine all religious expressions to the private sphere—the home, the family, and the **church**? Or, does the coexistence of different faiths require that each be permitted to 'take its turn' in the public space? That too is a hard question to answer, and the answer depends in part on how much importance we attribute to religious beliefs. If we view religions as little more than organized recreational activities—like folk dancing or marathon running, for example—then they should all be treated equally in the public sphere, but never treated very seriously.

However, people who take religion seriously will fight over the amount of public attention their favourite religion gets to enjoy. They may believe, for example, that there is only one 'true' religion and all the others are erroneous or even loathsome. If so, they will scarcely want to grant the same amount of public time, resources, and attention to all religions.

Besides, can we call Canada a genuine multi-faith society, given that close to 80 per cent of all Canadians identify themselves as belonging to a Christian denomination (Statistics Canada, 2006)? The strong public outcry against the city council's decision suggests that, even in a city as multicultural as Toronto, Christianity still influences public life. Many Christians just don't want to share the public space with emblems derived from Judaism, Islam, Buddhism, or other faiths. Is it then fair, then, to say that religion and citizenship in Canada are separate? Or, are there still strong links between political power and the dominant religion?

Here's another brain teaser: Should the state condone religion or try, forcefully, to undermine its hold on people's minds? In many respects, religions are helpful and harmless, but in some respects, they are not. Consider the connection between religion and gender inequality. In most religions it is difficult, even today, for women to become religious officials. Historically, most religious institutions—especially those in the Judeo-Christian and Islamic traditions—have been patriarchal. Given that, how can we reconcile a tolerance of organized religion with our general commitment to gender equality today? On the other hand, some religious groups have changed their views and practices to adapt to new political circumstances, even if this has meant compromising its traditional doctrines. On issues like gender equality—also, sexual orientation and abortion—many religions continue to dither and only a few have made significant changes.

At a more general level, sociologists ask how religion has managed to survive despite the many developments—economic, scientific, social, and cultural—that have undermined the blind faith that religions typically require. What social and psychological forces keep such blind faith alive? What are the effects, both positive and negative, of religion's continued existence? Would society be better or worse off if all religions disappeared—if, as Max Weber said, we were able to fully 'disenchant' the world, through science and reason? As noted, these questions have preoccupied some of the greatest thinkers of the last few centuries, and it is with the views of three classic sociological theorists the next section begins.

new religious movements (NRMs)
Groups and institutions comprising people who share similar religious or spiritual views about the world but who are not part of mainstream religious institutions.

church
Any social location or building—church, mosque, synagogue, or temple—where people carry out religious rituals.

Ways of Looking at . . .
RELIGION

Émile Durkheim worked within the *functionalist* model, meaning that he was concerned with religion's role in promoting social solidarity. He wanted to know why religions are universal—found in every known society—and what functions they perform in these societies. He concluded that religion has the power to bring people together (1968 [1912]). He also noted that religion perpetuates social solidarity by continually reaffirming people's shared values. Yet, he understood the influence of religion would decline as scientific and technological thinking gradually replaced religious thinking (Thompson, 1982). This led him to wonder what would replace religion as a source of social solidarity. As we have already noted, however, most societies—even Canadian society—remain religious even to this day and will likely not become completely 'secular' any time soon. We will discuss Durkheim's views in more detail in the next section.

Karl Marx, in establishing the *critical theory* model, viewed religion largely as a form of social control and therefore as a cause of conflict (Calhoun et al., 2007). He believed that religion is part of the *dominant ideology* of society—a set of values that benefit the groups that exercise the most power in society. Therefore, he saw religion as promoting the interests of a society's ruling elites and subduing the masses. Marx spoke of religion as the 'opiate of the masses', making them submissive, uncritical, and easily manipulated. Religion, while numbing the pain of oppression, also diverted the working class's attention from injustices perpetrated by the bourgeoisie.

Like Durkheim, Marx also believed that religion would lose its importance in the future. He predicted that, after a worldwide revolution by the working class, the new socialist society would have no place for religion. Workers would identify with, and mobilize around, class concerns alone; religion would cease to be a defining force in society. As we know, Marx's prediction has so far proven incorrect; religion continues to be both a relevant social phenomenon and, therefore, an important topic in sociology. Nevertheless, religion continues to cause conflicts between people and societies, and to exert power over them; so Marxism and critical theory continue to play an important role in the sociology of religion.

Max Weber, finally, focused on the subjective meaning and personal experience of religion. He believed that people have an inner need to understand the world as 'meaningful'. Otherwise, how can we make sense of, and cope with, the fact of death and the many tragedies and injustices we witness throughout life? Thus, he concluded that religion must originate as a way of making sense of a seemingly indifferent universe, where the only human certainty is death. By allowing people to understand both happiness and suffering in the world, religion provides a measure of hope, relief, and motivation.

Weber was especially interested in the way religious doctrines shape people's world views; also, how their world views shape their secular behaviour. In his well-known book, *The Protestant Ethic and the Spirit of Capitalism* (1958 [1904]), Weber discussed the connections between the rise of capitalism and the rise of Protestantism. He argued that Protestantism, especially strict Calvinism, provided a value structure that supported the rise of capitalism in northwestern Europe. The values conducive to capitalism—a strong work ethic, strong character formation, sobriety and thrift, the organization and rationalization of work practices, and the striving towards successful business endeavours—were all present in or congruent with Calvinist belief. Calvinists were not specifically concerned with capital accumulation, but they urged their adherents to participate fully and ascetically in the everyday world of work and achievement (unlike Catholicism, which focused attention on other-worldly concerns). Through their engagement in this world, Calvinists hoped to see a divine sign of their future salvation; in fact, they organized their lives around this idea. This is the reason, Weber hypothesized, that capitalism arose in Protestant Europe, and not in ancient India, China, Israel, or Catholic southern Europe, societies that lacked the right combination of this-worldly religious doctrines—the Calvinist combination.

Now, contrast Weber's analysis of religion—which focuses on the importance of values—with Durkheim's analysis, which focuses on the importance of forms.

Classic Studies
The Elementary Forms of Religious Life

One of Durkheim's key works, and the last one he wrote—*The Elementary Forms of Religious Life* (1968 [1912])—focused on the role of religion in social life. His goal was to understand the universality of religion, and to do so, he needed to understand its emergence in the very earliest, smallest, most 'primitive' societies. However, these societies kept no records, so there is no historical account of the 'rise of religion' or its connection to the rise of another social institution like capitalism. Accordingly, the functional, and anthropological, response is to ask: How *might* religion have come into being? What problem *might* it have been devised to solve?

To answer these questions, in *The Elementary Forms of Religious Life*, Durkheim studied the phenomenon of *totemism*, the use of natural objects and animals to symbolize spirituality. He noted that small pre-literate societies adopt these objects as emblems to symbolize their faith in a higher power. An emblem—in itself, meaningless—serves as a symbol that unites all the members of society with a common belief, thus contributing to social solidarity. It does not matter if the emblem is a flag, a cross, a plant, or a lowly cockroach: all that matters is that the emblematic object denotes and evokes a sense of collective loyalty.

Around these totemic objects, rituals and ceremonies are enacted. They reinforce group solidarity and shared group beliefs in the society. They connect people, providing an opportunity to escape everyday life—which Durkheim called 'profane' life—into a higher, so-called 'sacred' plane of experience. Besides marking annual or periodic events—harvests or wars, for example—such celebratory activities may also mark important life transitions, such as marriages, births, deaths, and so on, giving the most significant life occurrences a religious significance.

However, in Durkheim's analysis, neither the ritual or totemic objects, nor the ritual activities (e.g., the ceremonies) are important or meaningful in themselves. Their meaning and significance lie only in the social cohesion they create, maintain, and celebrate. From this standpoint, people might just as well be celebrating National Cucumber Day (or Super Bowl Day) as Christ's birthday.

The reason people get excited by religion, then, is because it brings them together with other people in out-of-the-ordinary, emotionally moving rituals. Often, associated with these rituals there are strange sounds, smells, and images; strange prayers, dances, songs, and tomfoolery; even (occasional) drugs, alcohol, and sexual abandon. When people engage in such religious (that is, sacred) practices, they link themselves to each other as social beings. The totemic animals they worship are merely the pretext—merely symbols of their own society, animals widely present in their local environment. Each tribe has its own totem and its own rites and rituals. When people worship a kangaroo, plant, god, or mythical figure, they are in effect worshipping their own society—not themselves as individuals but their feeling of social connection with one another. They may even go so far as to imagine that both their ritual and their totemic deity are universally meaningful and potent: the true faith. To do otherwise is to acknowledge that one's own community is not universal and therefore open to doubt.

So, for Durkheim, religion expresses a *collective consciousness*, the sum of people's individual consciousnesses and a shared way of understanding the world. For Durkheim, the key words are 'shared' and 'symbol'. Even in present-day society, when religion is less prominent institutionally than it was a few centuries ago, many people still look for opportunities to share beliefs and celebrate this sharing. Many people still revere ritual objects and treat them with a degree of seriousness that is not inherent in the object itself. Consider, once again, the tall coniferous tree in Toronto's Nathan Philips Square and the reasons people might argue about it.

Returning to a notion he developed in his earlier classic work, *The Division of Labor in Society*, Durkheim recognized that in industrial societies, people would have a harder times subscribing to the same single set of beliefs and rituals. A diverse and interdependent (organic) society would be torn apart by religious tensions if the old, homogeneous ways of connecting with divinity remained. A diverse organic society—for example, an urban industrial society—would need a form of humanism: a worldview that lets people connect with one another around their common humanity, and not around specific religious beliefs, as was the case with mechanical solidarity.

So, Durkheim concluded that the influence of traditional religion would decline as society modernized, and scientific thinking would replace religious thinking (Thompson, 1982). The concept of 'God' would become less powerful; perhaps society would celebrate itself, instead, through nationalistic parades and events. As we shall see, this has occurred; but secular nationalistic events have come to coexist alongside more traditional religious forms. Canadian society, in many of its aspects, remains conventionally religious to this day and will likely remain so in the foreseeable future, thanks largely to the continued immigration of traditionally religious people from other parts of the world. Was Durkheim wrong then about the role of religion in society, or the likely ways it would change? We will continue to consider this question throughout the chapter.

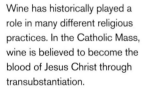

Wine has historically played a role in many different religious practices. In the Catholic Mass, wine is believed to become the blood of Jesus Christ through transubstantiation.

Definitional Problems

Part of the problem associated with making theories about religion results from the difficulty in defining 'religion'. Religion is a difficult concept to define, since it encompasses many concepts connected to spirituality and faith, and may mean different things to different people—we have already seen that in our comparison of Marx, Weber, and Durkheim. As a first approximation, McGuire (2005) suggests we can usefully distinguish between *substantive* definitions and *functional* definitions of religion. Substantive definitions focus on what religion *is*, and what does and does not count as religion; functional definitions, on the other hand, describe what religion *does* for an individual or a social group. Substantive definitions examine a religion's core elements, including the belief in a higher being and supernatural forces. By contrast, functional definitions describe how religion provides a sense of connectedness between people, while often also creating strife between religious denominations.

However, sociological theories of religion can contain both types of definition. For example, as already noted, Durkheim believed that social life could be divided into *sacred* and the *profane* (secular) parts, and that religion resided in the sacred part. Just as people need totems and rituals, so they need a portion of life that is sacred, Durkheim argued. He pointed out that we lead most of our lives in a profane world of routine social objects: everyday clothes, food, ways of speaking, ways of behaving, and so on. On special occasions, we try to shift to another way of life, a sacred plane marked by special social objects: ritual clothing, symbolic foods, unusual ways of speaking and behaving, and so on. This line of argument defines religion substantively, in terms of its core features, such as the distinction between sacred and profane activities.

According to this definition, we associate specific locations with sacred, special activities, and accept certain behaviours as suitable for these locations. That's why people behave differently in churches than they do in dance clubs, bedrooms, or school classrooms, for example. Drugs and alcohol have an ambiguous role in social life: though many people use drugs and alcohol to medicate themselves in everyday life, many religions also use drugs (e.g., peyote or magic mushrooms) and alcohol to help people shift their consciousness from sober this-worldly concerns—thrift, efficiency, and profitability—to other-worldly concerns—ecstasy, reflection, and a focus on the deeper meaning of life.

It is not accidental that, in a Catholic mass, the priest sips wine, representing Christ's blood. Wine plays a ritual part in the mass, standing in for holy blood. Cranberry juice, though the same colour, would not have the same meaning because it does not have the same 'sacred' effect. What this suggests is that religious observance is very much about shifting people's consciousness, through the use of strange sights, sounds, and chemicals to help them plug into sacred, transcendent truths.

Of course, religions vary widely in their enactment of 'the sacred' and 'the profane', and in some religions the distinction is far from easy—perhaps, nearly impossible. For example, religions that see God or the supernatural as residing in all natural objects cannot easily split the sacred from the profane. For such people, every tree, rock, bird, and animal is imbued with spiritual meaning and purpose. If so, the totemic objects Durkheim described—eagles, beavers, and trees, for example—are not entirely without substantive meaning: not entirely (and merely) functional. Westerners—including Western sociologists—have tended to rely on the Judeo-Christian tradition to define what a religion is (substantive definition) and what it does (functional definition). This bias is a challenge to sociologists today, since it may result in wrong assumptions and complicate our attempts to understand religion outside the Western tradition.

Consider the distinction between *organized religion* and *spirituality*—essentially, the separation of public and private religious belief, already hinted at earlier in this chapter. Organized religion refers to a set of social institutions: groups, buildings, resources, and

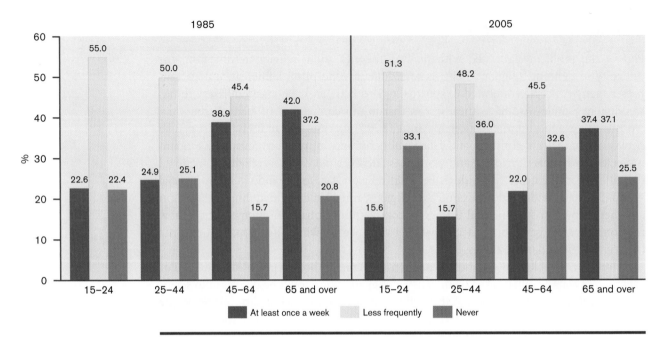

Figure 13.1 Frequency of Religious Attendance, Canada (provinces),[1] 1985 and 2005

Note: The category 'less frequently' includes: at least once a month, a few times a year, and at least once a year.

1. Canadians aged 15 and over living in the 10 provinces, not including the institutionalized population.

Source: Statistics Canada, 'Canadians attend weekly religious services less than 20 years ago.' *Matter of Fact.* 89-630-XIE, September, 2008. http://www.statcan.gc.ca/pub/89-630-x/2008001/article/10650-eng.htm

so on. Spirituality refers to a set of beliefs that, though shared, may not be enacted with other people. Such a division may be characteristic of Christianity, where typically people gather together in churches to celebrate their religion; but it is not characteristic of many other religions like Buddhism, for example. This duality also has many implications. For example, it seems to suggest that organized, communal religion is more important—more central to 'religion'—than private, spiritual devotion; and therefore, professional religious hierarchies (i.e., priests, bishops, and so on) deserve special importance.

Sociologists, increasingly aware of this bias, have tried to bridge the gap between the sacred and the profane. Recognizing the root of this bias, Goldenberg states that to many sociologists 'religions look remarkably like what Christians think of as religion' (2006: 2). Recognizing this bias is the first step in a movement toward a more inclusive view of religion in sociology. Only then can we hope to address the original questions of interest: Why do people **seek** religions? Why do they join religions? Is religious conviction declining or likely to decline?

With this in mind, we might re-orient the discussion to consider the role of religion in social altruism: in motivating people to do things for others from which they will themselves not profit. Such out-of-the-ordinary, praiseworthy behaviour may give us a different way to think about religion as both a value system and source of social cohesion.

Religion in Canada Today

An interesting sociological finding was recently reported in *The Globe and Mail* (see Box 13.1): Canadians rank highly among people of the world in terms of their charitable giving; and, research reveals, people who give more to charity tend to be happier than people who do not. Charity in Canada, the report says, is widespread and appears to make Canadians happy.

seekers

People and groups who draw on the teachings of several religions and philosophies to fulfill their needs for spirituality.

This raises several interesting questions: First, what makes some societies more charitable than others? Second, why should charitable giving make people happy? Is this a real finding, or merely a spurious one—for example, reflecting the correlation between charitable giving, personal satisfaction, and average household income? Third, is charitable giving a religious act, or is it just as validly considered a secular one, or something in between?

The report does not tell us why some societies are more charitable than others. However, we note from Table 13.1 that the most charitable societies—located mainly in Oceania and northwestern Europe—tend to be the most affluent, best educated, and (most important of all), most socially progressive societies in the world: New Zealand, Australia, Sweden, Norway, and so on. So, evidently, there is something about a commitment to social equality and social altruism that makes people happy when they give to charity. However, that raises the question of why some societies are more committed to equality and altruism than others.

Likewise, the report does not explain why charitable people are more happy or satisfied with life than less charitable people. However, the correlation between charity and happiness is similar to the correlation between religion and happiness: highly religious people tend to report being happier than less religious people. Debate continues around explanations of this finding. Some believe the happiness attributed to religion comes from a sense of meaning and fulfillment that religion provides. Others believe the happiness comes from a sense of belonging and participation in an organized, valued social enterprise. Of course, there is also the possibility that religious (and charitable) people are merely reporting themselves as 'happy' even when they are not, because they want to appear socially desirable.

Nor, finally, does the report explicitly connect charitable giving to religion or religiosity. Yet most, if not all, religions include charity as an important component of religious adherence among the faithful. Contrast this with 'science', which we will discuss later in the chapter: as an idea system or social institution, science has no more interest in charity than it has in social justice (for example). Science is concerned only with finding the laws of nature. Religion—spirituality, more generally—by contrast is concerned with promoting

Point/Counterpoint

BOX **13.1**

Canada Ranked Second-most Charitable in the World

The Charities Aid Foundation created the World Giving Index to show how willing people of 153 countries are to give money to, and volunteer for, worthy causes, and to help strangers in need. The index is based on data from an international Gallup poll, in which people are asked what charitable acts they performed in the previous month. Canada placed second in this index, tied with Ireland and just behind first-place Australia and New Zealand, with two-thirds of Canadians having both given money and having helped a stranger, and one-third having done volunteer work. Last place went to Burundi and Madagascar. Patterns of giving vary around the world, and the rankings of countries on the various measures vary widely from first to last place. Helping strangers is the most widely practised form of charity, performed by 45 per cent of the world population, followed by giving money to charity at 30 per cent, and by volunteering at 20 per cent.

The survey correlates 'life satisfaction' with giving, finding that people who report that they are happy are the ones who tend to give more. Happiness seems to have more of an effect than does wealth (based on the wealth of the nation as a whole) on people's willingness to give, leading the authors to state 'It would be reasonable to conclude that giving is more an emotional act than a rational one.'

Source: Adapted from Boesveld (2010).

Table 13.1	The World Giving Index, Top Ten and Bottom Five Rankings	

Rank	Nation	Score out of 100
1	Australia, New Zealand	57
2	Canada, Ireland	56
3	Switzerland, US	55
4	Netherlands	54
5	UK, Sri Lanka	53
6	Austria	52
7	Laos, Sierra Leone	50
8	Malta	48
9	Iceland, Turkmenistan	47
10	Guyana, Qatar	45
149	Cambodia, Pakistan, Romania, Rwanda	16
150	Bangladesh	15
151	China, Lithuania, Greece	14
152	Serbia, Ukraine	13
153	Burundi, Madagascar	12

Source: Charities Aid Foundation (2010).

ethical and charitable behaviour, and with transcendent goals: in the Christian formulation, religion is about 'faith, hope, and charity'.

Does the widespread significance of charity in Canadian society indicate a deep but hidden religiosity? Though Canada has no official state religion, religion has always played a part in our social life. Historically, Christianity was Canada's dominant religion and remains so today. About 80 per cent of Canadians still identify themselves as 'Christian'; this broad category includes Roman Catholics and different Protestant groups (such as the United Church of Canada and the Anglican Church of Canada). What's more, it includes a variety of Protestant denominations that, historically, held strikingly different views on a variety of lifestyle issues (though these differences were largely submerged in the act of church union that formed the United Church in 1925). The numbers of Roman Catholics and Protestants have been relatively equal over the last two centuries. Given the important differences between Catholicism and Protestantism in Durkheimian terms—their different rituals and ceremonial objects, for example—lumping the two together may not make sense, except to non-Christians.

Historically, Canadians have tended to remain affiliated with the religious background of their family, thus perpetuating the prevalence of Christianity in Canada. At the same time, people are ever less likely to practise their religion with the same commitment and passion as their grandparents or (even) parents may have had. Many attend church services infrequently, for example. But of course, church attendance is only one measure of religious participation and may fail to provide an accurate picture of religion in Canada (Statistics Canada, 2006). In fact, one might say that statistics on church attendance reveal as much about religious faith in Canada as statistics on divorce reveal about marital satisfaction—perhaps for similar reasons.

According to a study by Statistics Canada called *Canadian Social Trends* (Clark and Schellenberg, 2006), religion plays a more important role in the lives of Canadians than many have suggested. Only about one-third of adult Canadians go to church at least once

Table 13.2 Religions in Canada, 2001

	Number	%
Roman Catholic	12,793,125	43.2
No religion	4,796,325	16.2
United Church	2,839,125	9.6
Anglican	2,035,495	6.9
Christian, not included elsewhere[1]	780,450	2.6
Baptist	729,475	2.5
Lutheran	606,590	2.0
Muslim	579,640	2.0
Protestant, not included elsewhere[2]	549,205	1.9
Presbyterian	409,830	1.4

1. Includes persons who report 'Christian', as well as those who report 'Apostolic', 'Born-again Christian', and 'Evangelical'.
2. Includes persons who report only 'Protestant'.
Source: Statistics Canada (2007), Table 6.

a month, but more than half conduct their own private religious activities every month. These private activities may include praying, meditating, worshipping, or reading sacred texts, for example. According to an earlier study called the *Ethnic Diversity Survey* (2002), 21 per cent of the adult population carry out religious practices in their own home yet rarely or never attend public religious services. Clearly, they still attach a considerable importance to their religious beliefs.

So, church attendance on its own is not an accurate measure of religiosity in Canada. A more useful indicator used by Statistics Canada is called the 'religiosity index'. This

Table 13.3 Major Religious Denominations, Canada, 1991[1] and 2001

	1991		2001		Percentage Change 1991–2001
	Number	%	Number	%	
Roman Catholic	12,203,625	45.2	12,793,125	43.2	4.8
Protestant	9,427,675	34.9	8,654,845	29.2	-8.2
Christian Orthodox	387,395	1.4	479,620	1.6	23.8
Christian, not included elsewhere[2]	353,040	1.3	780,450	2.6	121.1
Muslim	253,265	0.9	579,640	2.0	128.9
Jewish	318,185	1.2	329,995	1.1	3.7
Buddhist	163,415	0.6	300,345	1.0	83.8
Hindu	157,015	0.6	297,200	1.0	89.3
Sikh	147,440	0.5	278,415	0.9	88.8
No religion	3,333,245	12.3	4,796,325	16.2	43.9

1. For comparability purposes, 1991 data are presented according to 2001 boundaries.
2. Includes persons who report 'Christian', as well as those who report 'Apostolic', 'Born-again Christian', and 'Evangelical'.
Source: Statistics Canada (2003).

index includes four dimensions of religiosity: affiliation, attendance, personal practices, and (stated) importance of religion. This index recognizes (and corrects) the limitations of just using church attendance to measure religiosity. Consider, for example, the person who holds the most superficial religious beliefs but, for social reasons or under family pressure, attends church every Sunday. On the other hand, consider the members of an alternative religious group who rarely practise their beliefs in public but do so regularly at home.

Using this index, we gain more accurate, reliable information about religion in Canada. According to this measure, 40 per cent of Canadians have a low degree of religiosity, 31 per cent a moderate degree, and 29 per cent a high degree of religiosity (ibid). Religiosity varies demographically: it is highest among older people, women, and people from religious families, especially families in which both parents had the same or a similar religious background (for example, where both parents were raised as Catholics).

Again, we must exercise caution, because of the variety of religious beliefs and practices among Canadians. What's more, religiosity may become harder to measure and generalize about as religious diversity increases. Non-Christian religious groups have always been present in Canada, but they have historically made up only a small fraction of the population. In recent decades however, this fraction has steadily risen with the arrival of many more immigrants with diverse religious backgrounds. Recent research shows, not surprisingly given their origins, that 41 per cent of the immigrants who arrived in Canada between 1982 and 2001 had a high degree of religiosity, compared to only 26 per cent of the people born in Canada. Not surprisingly then, immigrants are more likely to engage in both private religious practices and public religious services than the Canadian-born population (Statistics Canada, 2006).

That said, the proportion of highly religious immigrants varies with the area of the world they come from. Those with the highest levels of religiosity come from South Asia

Oftentimes recent immigrants hold on to their rituals and traditions—their religiosity—more closely than those born in Canada. Below, men hold banners and Canadian flags as they march in the parade to celebrate Vaisakhi, a holiday in the Sikh calendar, held annually by the Sikh community in Vancouver.

Table 13.4 Immigrants, by Major Religious Denominations and Period of Immigration, Canada, before 1961–2001

	Period of Immigration (%)				
	Before 1961	**1961–1970**	**1971–1980**	**1981–1990**	**1991–2001**[2]
Total immigrants	100.0	100.0	100.0	100.0	100.0
Roman Catholic	39.2	43.4	33.9	32.9	23.0
Protestant	39.2	26.9	21.0	14.5	10.7
Christian Orthodox	3.8	6.3	3.8	3.0	6.3
Christian, not included elsewhere[1]	1.3	2.2	3.8	4.9	5.3
Jewish	2.7	2.0	2.2	1.9	1.2
Muslim	0.2	1.3	5.4	7.5	15.0
Hindu	0.0	1.4	3.6	4.9	6.5
Buddhist	0.4	0.9	4.8	7.5	4.6
Sikh	0.1	1.1	3.9	4.3	4.7
No religion	11.0	13.5	16.5	17.3	21.3
Other religions	2.1	1.0	1.1	1.3	1.4

1. Includes persons who report 'Christian', as well as those who report 'Apostolic', 'Born-again Christian', and 'Evangelical'.
2. Includes data up to 15 May 2001.

Source: Statistics Canada (2003).

(e.g., Pakistan) and those with the lowest levels from East Asia (e.g., China) and western and northern Europe (ibid; Beyer, 2005). Thus, Canada's religiosity has increased with the growth in numbers of immigrants (and immigrants' children) who have come from

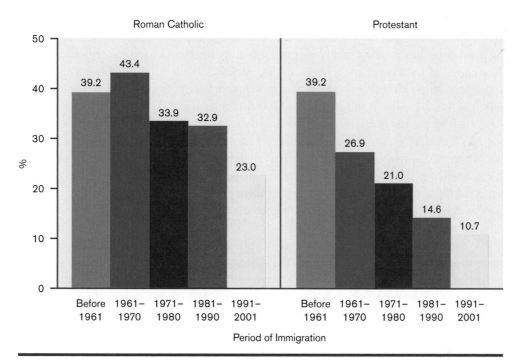

Figure 13.2 Proportion of Roman Catholic and Protestant Immigrants, by Period of Immigration, Canada, before 1961–2001

Source: Statistics Canada, *Religions in Canada*. 96F0030XIE2001015, May 2003. http://www.statcan.gc.ca/bsolc/olc-cel/olc-cel?catno=96F0030XIE2001015&lang=eng

Point/Counterpoint

BOX **13.2**

Go On, Have a Pint with the Lord

Some Canadian church groups are trying to 'blur the lines between what's a sacred space and what's a secular space', according to Ahren Summach, pastor of the Ottawa Valley Vineyard church. Meeting for theological discussion in a pub certainly fits the bill. Instead of the more common pub topics of hockey or politics, the men in Mr Summach's group are discussing 'such questions as, "Is Jesus God?" and "If God is good and all powerful, then why is there suffering in the world?"'

But some Christians are reluctant to meet in a pub, as Darryl Dash finds with the group that he runs in Toronto. And Jeff Graham, of the Roman Catholic Archdiocese of Vancouver, suggests that, in view of his Church's views on moderate alcohol drinking, these groups might be walking 'a thin line'.

Source: Adapted from Leung (2009).

traditionally religious countries. In these countries, religion has continued to maintain a strong, traditional hold on people's beliefs over centuries and even millennia. Unlike Europe, where secularization is most marked, in many of the countries from which immigrants came, there was nothing like a Protestant reformation or an Enlightenment to counteract the hold of traditional religion on people's views. Further, unlike European Protestantism and Chinese Confucianism, these traditional religions were other-worldly in their orientation.

Religion vs. Science: The Debate of the Modern Era

Our society is often called a *secular society*, meaning that people today are less religiously inclined than they were a century ago and generally throughout the history of humanity. Nowadays, as we have noted, people are less inclined to attend churches or think about the supernatural. Moreover, we have no state religion, believe in the value of religious (and ethnic) multiculturalism, and try to practise inclusion across a wide range of belief systems.

Most people today characterize our society as being, among other things, a technological, scientific, or (as Weber called it) a *rational–legal society*. These terms refer to a society in which people are 'disenchanted' or demystified about the natural world, and disinclined to explain natural phenomena by invoking supernatural causes, relying instead on scientific observation, reasoning, and evidence. Unlike pre-scientific people, modern people don't imagine lightning means the gods are angry. Even if they don't know precisely what causes lightning, they know they can find out the answer from science, not religion.

We get the clearest idea about the difference between a secular and religious society if we contrast religion with science. In fact, the science–religion debate goes back several centuries, to the Enlightenment of the seventeenth and eighteenth centuries. This debate continued into the twentieth century and included topics such as Darwin's theory of evolution. Darwin's thinking posed a significant challenge to the credibility of Christian belief in a literal interpretation of the Old Testament and, for this reason, was opposed by many religious leaders.

What we do need to consider is the big gap in thinking between science and religion, and specifically between the ways science and religion carry out their enquiries. Science, sociological speaking, is a cultural and social orientation toward the search for knowledge. Advances in technology, so important to the formation of the modern world, have come about largely through the scientific revolutions that began in Europe about five hundred years ago. These advances rest on empirical research that obeys the *norms of science* identified by Robert Merton (1976) as 'CUDO: communalism, universalism, disinterest, and organized skepticism. In short, thinking scientifically about the world is a completely different way of thinking about the world: a relatively new way, and a non-religious way.

This fact seems to draw a clear boundary between science and religion, based on several important distinctions. Science, unlike religion, advances by (somewhat combative) peer review: scholars with expertise are called on to evaluate the credibility of findings and the research methods that generated these findings. As well, science advances by independent, disinterested (unbiased) research, a public debate of findings, and the application of universal criteria of judgment. Most important of all, science demands organized skepticism. All scientific claims are critically evaluated and all conclusions are considered 'tentative', awaiting disproof.

By contrast, religion is not expected to 'advance' since it is based on timeless revealed truths. Even religious scholarship is rarely disinterested. It is often organized and funded by religious organizations or by colleges with religious affiliations. Therefore, it is unlikely that, say, a Catholic scholar will conclude the Vatican is wrong about papal infallibility or that the Gospels are a hoax. Scholars and other religious commentators who step too far outside the accepted institutional boundaries risk ridicule, exclusion, expulsion, excommunication, or even death.

Unlike debates on scientific issues, religious debates are rarely public, perhaps owing in part to a lack of public interest. Often, they are carried out 'internally', so the church can continue to present a united front toward the outside world. This is typical of a large business or governmental organization, not of an open inquiry. More important, religions do not encourage, or sometimes even approve of, organized skepticism. Churches and religions are built on faith. They do not regard their values, beliefs, and holy documents as current 'best guesses' about the supernatural. So, they are unwilling to change them.

That said, every religion has procedures for adapting their values, beliefs, and holy documents when it becomes necessary. Religions vary in their flexibility and adaptability under pressure. Like other organizations, they always have a 'Plan B'. A prime example of such adaptability is the use of *hadiths* in Islam. Hadiths are sayings and beliefs attributed to Mohammed that were not written into the Koran but are known to us through later scholars. In theory, Islam is based on a literal interpretation of the Koran. However, Islamic societies differ widely in their social, political, and economic sophistication. As a result, Islam has historically made great use of hadiths to allow flexibility in the 'interpretation' of the Koran. Typically, much effort is made to trace the genealogy, and therefore the legitimacy, of any particular hadith. For example, scholars will try to discover whether a particular commentator may have indeed spoken with Mohammed and therefore was directly exposed to a given idea.

Institutional inflexibility poses a huge problem to the survival of traditional religions. Today, for example, Catholicism continues to run a risk through its inflexible views about birth control, abortion, and premarital sex. Already, many Catholics in the West—especially, in northwestern Europe, but even in South America—have rejected Catholic teachings on these matters. Religions are most likely to loosen their grip under pressure, under especially uncomfortable situations. For example, the Roman Catholic Church did not officially admit that it was mistaken in prosecuting Galileo on his views of the solar system until 1992, three centuries after his famous trial (Lockwood, 2000). And it has been with the greatest reluctance that the Catholic Church has started to come to terms with repeated sexual abuse of children by ordained priests.

But taken as a whole, a religion can never be as flexible and adaptable as a science, because science demands no commitment whatever to traditional beliefs. Indeed, science abjures such commitments. Here's some evidence: in a religious book or textbook on theology, you will read a great deal about people who lived hundreds and even thousands of years ago. In a textbook about physics, chemistry, or astronomy, you will read next to nothing about people who lived hundreds, let alone thousands of years ago. The scientific community has left them and their ideas behind.

Consider 'phlogiston theory'—a theory about combustion advanced by J.J. Becher in the late seventeenth century and popularized by G.E. Stahl. It postulates that in all flammable materials there is present 'phlogiston', a substance without colour, odour, taste, or weight that is given off in burning. 'Phlogisticated' substances are said to be those that contain phlogiston and, on being burned, they are 'dephlogisticated'. So, only the ash of the burned material is said to be the 'true' material. This theory enjoyed strong, widespread support through much of the eighteenth century until it was disproved by the scientific work of A.L. Lavoisier in 1783. He discovered the true nature of combustion, and that there is no 'phlogiston' involved. Thus, you have probably never before heard of phlogiston theory, J.J. Becher, or G.E. Stahl.

Science is forward-looking, while religion is backward-looking. One cannot help being struck by this difference: the past orientation of religion compared with the future orientation of science. Compared to science, religion is rigid and unyielding. Religions are often convinced that they have found the eternal and everlasting truth; they are also convinced that other believers or religions are at best misguided and at worst infidels or pagans, doomed to eternal darkness. Such strong, unyielding, and exclusionary views have led to centuries, if not millennia, of hatred and bloodshed. So perhaps, it seems odd that we should even consider churches and religions as helping people to live together. Yet a case can be made for doing so, because religions clearly also bring people together, as Durkheim so aptly pointed out. By comparison, science has no important role in creating social solidarity.

Sometimes religions create benign solidarity, and other times they do not. Churches and religions continue to exert a powerful influence over political life in many parts of the world, for example. This is obvious in Islamic countries, Roman Catholic countries, Israel (the only Jewish country), and even in Protestant fundamentalist regions of the US. Religions also influence social life throughout the world—recall, once again, the Christmas tree issue mentioned at the beginning of this chapter, or the debate about turbans and burkas throughout Europe. Perhaps it would be safest and simplest to say that, institutionally, religions are committed to creating and preserving order. By contrast, sciences are committed to creating and fomenting skepticism and (in that sense) disorder.

Perhaps this notion, ultimately, is the reason people are (still) religious, given the enormous and persuasive importance of science in our lives. Religions give people a sense of meaning and purpose—a way of thinking about their lives and their sufferings—that science and other strictly rational endeavours seemingly do not. Science aside, no secular belief has been able to do the same over an extended period, although in their heyday, Russian and Chinese communism, German Nazism, and Japanese fascism were powerful competitors. (That said, it can be argued that these nationalistic belief systems also contained religious elements. German Nazism received plenty of support from national and regional religious leaders—even from the Catholic Pope in Italy. And nationalistic Japanese fascism used messianic propaganda to convince the citizenry that Emperor Hirohito was a god.)

But is science really disorderly, or is it just a different kind of social ordering—one that most non-scientists don't understand? A new area of research called 'science studies' tries to answer questions like these by studying scientific and technological human practices through the methods of sociology. Drawing in part on Thomas Kuhn's groundbreaking work, *The Structure of Scientific Revolutions* (1962), scholars in science studies examine the norms and values, called *paradigms*, which define what constitutes acceptable theoretical and experimental behaviour in the sciences (*Science Studies*, n.d.).

By doing so, researchers find some evidence that (even) science is rigid and hide-bound. Kuhn argues that even fields of scientific research go through periods of conventional, unchallenging research, punctuated by occasional paradigm shifts that challenge the most basic assumptions. Following these paradigm shifts, there is a return to 'normal science'—science premised on a set of prevailing beliefs about how nature works, and how nature should be studied. What is interesting about this is, first, the theory argues that science is sometimes orderly and sometimes disorderly. Conventional science is, for long periods, orderly; by contrast, brief and infrequent paradigm shifts are profoundly disordering. This makes science more like religion, in its conventional orderliness.

Second, the process Kuhn describes is very much like something Max Weber describes in connection with his study of religious and political movements. We will have occasion to discuss this topic at greater length in later chapters on political and social movements. For now, note that Weber observes that periods of cultural and social disruption—paradigm shifts—are typically set off by what he calls *charismatic* leadership. Afterward, cultural and social order is re-established through what he calls the *routinization of charisma*—that is, a return to conventional, institutionalized social life.

In short, in both religious institutions and scientific institutions we find an alternation between upheaval and convention (or routine). This is a second respect in which the line between these two institutions—science and religion—is blurred.

Classic Studies
Civilization and Its Discontents

For sociologists, it is natural to ask (again and again) why people keep coming back to religion, even in societies (like ours) characterized by scientific thinking and rational–legal authority. The great psychologist and social thinker Sigmund Freud provides another answer to this question in his classic work, *Civilization and Its Discontents* (1957 [1930]). In brief, Freud argues religion is little more than a symptom of neurosis, and God is an illusion that people are unable to shed, generation after generation.

To understand Freud's view of religion, we have to understand his theory of the unconscious. In short, Freud hypothesizes that we are all driven by buried desires and wishes of which we are unconscious. These include sexual desires that we must struggle to control and even repress through most of our lives. This repression explains why life in civilization is normally discontented, even neurotic. Humanity, repressed by civilized social rules, experiences a constant sense of frustration and bitterness. Repressed sexuality results in a surplus of libidinal energy that interacts with our innate aggression. Together, these impulses constantly threaten to tear civilization apart, promoting anxiety, hate, fear, and guilt.

Freud sees the monotheistic Judeo-Christian tradition as a means of atonement for collective guilt. This collective guilt results from the (imagined) slaying of the primal father, a mythologization of the wished-for death of one's actual father. So, in the end, Freud's theory is just about Judeo-Christian religions and the role of the childhood 'Oedipal struggle' with one's parents. This theory, though imaginative, does not serve well to illuminate meditative traditions, such as Buddhism which offer peace, tranquility, and other forms of escape from a harsh objective reality. Unlike Judaism, Christianity, and Islam, these more reflective and transcendent religions channel non-aggressive expressions of repressed sexuality and the death drive.

Clearly, Freud's theory asks us to assume a lot about individual psychology, not to mention instinctive drives, collective guilt, and infantile sexuality. No one can see the unconscious, and since it is assumed to express itself in a wide variety of ways—hate, fear, creativity, religiosity, and fantasy, among others—it is almost impossible to refute Freud's

The increased popularity of yoga in Western nations may suggest that people are finding ways to meet their spiritual needs outside of traditional organized religions.

theory with empirical evidence. On the other hand, it seems likely something like 'the unconscious' does exist. Like gravity, which we also cannot see, the unconscious explains a lot that we *can* see. For example, it is virtually impossible to explain paralyzing neuroses or paranoid fantasies without accepting the existence of an unconscious.

Still, critics have criticized Freud for taking a narrow view of religion that ignores its cultural and social meanings, and treats it as no more than a collective neurosis or delusion. Yet, it is a coherent theory, parts of it are testable, and they stand up well to testing. Take one example: Freud's theory would postulate that societies that are more sexually repressive will be more authoritarian and more religious. Conversely, as sexual expression is liberated, people will become less devout—more secular. Both of these have happened in the twentieth century Western world. Neither has happened in more traditional, less developed parts of the world.

The Idea of Secularization

secularization

A steadily dwindling influence of formal (institutional) religion in public life.

Durkheim and Freud both believed that, eventually, people would find a secular substitute for religion. Both theorists saw **secularization**, the steadily dwindling influence of religion in public life, as a positive development—Durkheim because it denoted a growth in tolerant diversity, Freud because it denoted a drop in repression.

However the evidence shows religion is still an important presence in even modern societies. We often hear that we live in a secular society, and many sociologists have tried to discover whether this widespread belief is true. If we look to church attendance, number of marriages, and number of baptisms, we note that these have declined. However, these measurements may not accurately reflect other forms of participation in religious practices, nor their depth of religious belief. As we saw, they do not capture the activities (and views) of people who worship shrines at home or meditate, for instance.

Secularization theory more convincingly argues that many formerly powerful religious institutions have lost their influence in society; and this is largely true. Napoleon, for example, made a point of diminishing the secular power of the Catholic Church as his armies swept through early nineteenth century Europe. Note, however, that public institutions in our society (and others) still close during Christmas and Easter holidays, though not during the holidays of other religions. So, at present, religion—especially, Christianity—remains embedded in our society, ensuring that it is not completely secular. On the other hand, many more people are finding religion irrelevant to their day-to-day lives. Even if they consider themselves Christian, they may not embrace their faith and all of its teachings. So, it is difficult to decide whether our society is secular or still relies on its religious past.

Probably the most dramatic example of secularization is provided by Quebec in the twentieth century. Historically, the Roman Catholic Church played a significant role in Quebec society: especially, in protecting traditional French-Canadian Catholic values and lifestyles against assimilation. For three centuries (from roughly 1650 to 1950), it had influenced almost every aspect of life in that province—providing education, work, medical care, and opportunities for communication and exchange. This situation was accurately documented in the sociological classic, *French Canada in Transition*, by Everett C. Hughes (2009 [1943]). In the 1960s, however, church attendance began to fall significantly and suddenly, marking the beginning of Quebec's so-called Quiet Revolution. The revolution largely removed the Church from the education business by providing an alternate secular system funded by provincial money; and virtually eliminated Church influence in provincial politics.

This seemingly sudden change was a result of many complex gradual changes that had been simmering in the province for decades (Legg, 2000). By the 1960s, Quebecers had come to regard the church as backward and oppressive. They felt it had prevented French Canadians from gaining the education they needed to succeed economically and socially in their own province, while English industries gained influence and gathered their successes (Gauvreau and Gossage, 2001).

As the example of Quebec suggests, each case of secularization is slightly different, with its own starting and ending point, and rate of change. However, a few generalizations about secularization are possible. Scholars who have studied secularization within Western industrial societies have found three common features that lead toward, or are associated with, secularization: *social differentiation*, *societalization*, and *rationalization*.

Social differentiation is the process by which a society becomes increasingly complex and diverse. In the past, churches provided centres for worship and teaching about sacred things; but they also taught children basic skills, supported people in need, cared for the sick, served as meeting places, and organized social events. In modern societies, these social roles are split among many separate institutions: schools, hospitals, government agencies, and social clubs, among others. This means the church is no longer central to daily living, but merely one institution among many.

Societalization refers to the way people increasingly connect to an abstract 'society', and not to a concrete community in which every person knows everyone else. In North America and Europe today, most people look to 'society'—a large, shapeless unit made up of organizations run on bureaucratic principles—to provide for their needs. People regularly find and work at jobs, read and watch the news, attend school, and vote in elections. All of these activities put them in contact with a society that regulates their activities, often through the state. Interaction with this society leaves little room for religion, which people increasingly view as personal (not societal) and marginal to their lives.

Rationalization represents an effort to explain the world through the logical interpretation of empirical evidence. Paradoxically, the Judeo-Christian religions themselves

Media Distortion

BOX **13.3**

Hindus Worried about Keanu Reeves Movie

American Hindu leaders are dreading the release of the film *Hanuman*. In it, Keanu Reeves will play the Hindu god Lord Vishnu, based on the sacred text known as the Ramayana. Hindus worry that the movie may present an inaccurate picture of their religion and beliefs, as many Hollywood productions do with religious themes. Rajan Zed, president of the Universal Society of Hinduism, tells celebrity news website WENN, 'If the makers of this proposed movie intend to base the storyline on the epic Ramayana and make references to it or portray Hindu gods/goddesses in the movie, we would urge the makers to stay true to the story and the spirit of the timeless epic and other Hindu scriptures'.

The Ramayana, an ancient Sanskrit text, is among the most revered of Hindu scriptures, and is believed by Hindus to bless those who read it or hear it read. It deals with Hinduism's central religious and philosophical ideas, such as the purpose of human existence and the concept of dharma, or universal justice.

Source: Adapted from IMDB/WENN News (2009).

---

encouraged the spread of rationalization, to reduce people's earlier reliance on superstition and folk-magic. For example, this emphasis on rationality stressed theology (systematic doctrinal investigation) over mythology (unsystematic leaps of faith). In most Christian denominations, church leadership still stresses philosophical inquiry into the nature of people's link with the divine, not merely a literal interpretation of Bible stories. However, secularization largely supplanted the reliance on religious texts and beliefs with a reliance on empirical evidence, scientific thinking, and non-religious 'rule of law'.

Civil Religion

civil religion

An organized secular practice that serves many of the same social functions as traditional religion, by giving people direction, explaining how the world works, and providing solidarity.

Civil religion represents an interesting mid-point between secular and sacred approaches to life; in this way, it challenges the assertion that social change is simple and one-way: namely, from religious faith to secular reasoning. Civil religion is a celebration of the state, indeed, a celebration of everyday life, complete with imposing beliefs, rituals, and sacred objects—even including persuasive versions of Heaven and Hell on earth.

The most important and widespread version of civil religion is *nationalism*. Throughout the nineteenth and twentieth centuries, nationalism provided many people with a sense of meaning and purpose. In especially patriotic countries like the US, nationalism and patriotism continue to be powerful, much more so than in Canada. In the US and elsewhere, nationalistic principles were often linked to religious beliefs—to a belief in American exceptionalism and the sense that America was God's beacon to humanity. Even today, nationalistic rituals there bring together secular, religious, and other ideological elements in vast public activities. These are evident each year in the US, in Independence Day or Memorial Day celebrations. These national celebrations are far larger and more passionate than comparable Canadian celebrations on July 1 and November 11.

On the even more secular side, consider major sporting events in the US, such as the Super Bowl, as examples of civil religion. An event like the Super Bowl—complete with thousands of die-hard fans, teams, cheerleaders, advertisements, special foods, halftime shows, and surrounding hype—is probably more important today as a ritual celebration than it is as a demonstration of sporting prowess. The Super Bowl functions as a 'religious festival' in the US, bringing together sports, politics, and a shared myth in a festival of civil religion. The 2008 Super Bowl halftime show even included symbolic militaristic and nationalistic elements during the time of the post–9/11 'war on terror'. The goal of this display was to justify the American war in Iraq by representing it in terms of 'American' values and the virtues of democratic citizenship, all in the context of sports coverage.

According to Robert Bellah et al. (1985), this kind of event provides an ethical framework for cohesiveness apart from any specific religion. People of all religions can share in the rites and rituals of Super Bowl Sunday. So, even civil religions help 'the faithful' live together—not equally or always happily, but with a feeling that they belong somewhere. This may help to explain the public outrage at singer Janet Jackson's 'wardrobe malfunction' at one Super Bowl halftime show, when her naked breasts were briefly displayed. Though breasts, naked or otherwise, are no strangers to American public entertainment, they are usually not exposed at American religious events.

Also out of sync with the claims of secularization theory is the evidence that new religious movements are surfacing all over the world.

New Religious Movements

New religious movements (NRMs), of which the Wiccans are an example, exist all over the world and have recently been gaining popularity. Some in North America and Europe are exploring their spirituality through practices based in the folk religions of Africa, America, and Europe. In Canada and elsewhere, Aboriginal groups are working to re-establish indigenous religions. Others, looking to their own background or ancestry, focus on African traditions and beliefs, or on European Celtic and Nordic folklore and mythology. Others still share an idea of the earth (Gaia) as the mother of all beings, and become promoters of environmental awareness. From this standpoint, the new environmentalism represents, for some, an effort to satisfy spiritual needs.

Wicca, a neo-pagan religion often compared to modern day witchcraft, is an example of a New Religious Movement (NRM).

Many of these groups suffer ridicule by the mainstream society, worsened by the mass media. Some are depicted contemptuously as mere 'cults', and you have likely heard of some such groups being accused of exerting 'undue influence' on their followers, 'brainwashing' and exploiting them.

However, field research by sociologists has shown that these movements or cults are mainly groups of people who share similar views about the world. To an outsider, many of their practices and beliefs may seem strange. However, members of these groups likely feel the same way about mainstream religious practices, and have therefore found an alternative religious path to fulfill their spiritual needs. Today, most researchers report that new religious movements, though unfamiliar, are not necessarily harmful.

In Canada, for example, Susan Palmer (2004) studied Raelians, a Quebec-based UFO cult who believe in divine extraterrestrial beings and claim that they have successfully cloned a human being. After years of fieldwork with the group, Palmer reports the Raelians have challenged many of the stereotypes commonly associated with NRMs. For example, fears of 'brainwashing' are unwarranted: group members make no effort to force their children into the faith, believing that personal choice is important. For this reason, baptism in this group does not occur until at least the age of 15. When a child is old enough, he or she is allowed to prove his or her faith by joining freely, without parental influence.

By now, we know what Durkheim would say: the Raelians have merely substituted UFOs for other totemic or holy objects in their practice of religion. And we know what Freud would say: the Raelians have channelled or sublimated their repressed unconscious energy into fantastic imaginings about extra-terrestrials.

Religion in the Schools?

Should religion—contested from so many angles—be taught in public schools? Educators on both sides of the Atlantic are dealing with the conflicting demands of parents who hold different views on this topic. Many say we should leave religious teaching to home and church, and use school time to build academic skills in reading, writing, and arithmetic. Others, attempting to give their children a firm basis in ethical understanding and social tolerance, look to the school system to provide guidance on these matters. Public schools aside, there are also issues about denominational or faith schools, and how these should be financed: whether they should receive public (tax) money, for example.

In Canada, education is a provincial matter, so the question of financing religious education varies from one province to another. In the nineteenth century, most schools in Canada and the US were denominational. Indeed, the idea behind establishing mass public education—secular education—was to create good citizens and responsible employees, regardless of their home religion. However, religion, an important part of society's fabric, was still to be taught in the school, to provide children with a moral basis for ideas about citizenship and social responsibility. In the early days, most schools gave a Protestant 'spin' on these moral and ethical ideas; this became a problem as Canadian society became increasingly diverse. During the twentieth century, ideas about religious education changed—especially given increased immigration to North America. Teaching just one religion (Protestant Christianity) became less acceptable. To satisfy demands for fairness, the public school system became completely secular.

However, some believe we may have gone too far in excluding religion from the school system. Even non-religious students need to understand the world views of religious people. To do so, they need a greater understanding of religion than that given in history lessons. After all, Protestant Christianity was an integral part of the creation of North America. Similarly, with Native North American issues much to the fore and controversies over issues of land claims or sacred heritage, students need to understand the basics of both Native and mainstream Christian ideas about people and land. And, modern Canadians will have little understanding of their fellow citizens if they know nothing about the Islamic, Confucian, Hindu, Buddhist, or other religious traditions from which they have originated.

Currently, in some areas of Canada, students (or their parents on their behalf) can 'opt in' to religious instruction—other areas are moving to a 'comparative religions' perspective. In the UK, religious education is mandatory, but it is moving away from 'religious instruction' in Christianity towards a comparative religion approach. In the US, religious promotion and official school prayer are not allowed, though prayer by students is permitted. Nevertheless, the boundaries between what is and is not permitted are being constantly challenged by parents' and community groups—many pushing for a restoration of school prayer and religious instruction.

Few sociologists have done more to help us understand the survival and evolution of modern religion than Robert Bellah, who embraces both Durkheimian and Weberian traditions in his understanding of the topic.

People Are Talking About . . .
ROBERT BELLAH

Robert N. Bellah was born in 1927 in Oklahoma. In 1950, he received a B.A. from Harvard University in social anthropology. (The Harvard University Press published his undergraduate thesis on 'Apache Kinship Systems'.) He received a Ph.D. from Harvard in 1955, in Sociology and Far Eastern Languages. His doctoral dissertation, *Tokugawa Religion*, was published in 1957. He did two years of postdoctoral work in Islamic Studies at McGill University in Montreal, and then began teaching at Harvard in 1957. In 1967, he became UC Berkeley Ford Professor of Sociology at University of California (Berkeley), a post he held for the next 30 years. Currently, Bellah is Elliott Professor of Sociology Emeritus at the University of California at Berkeley.

Robert Bellah's two most influential articles are 'Religious Evolution' (1964) and 'Civil Religion in America' (1967). Other published works include *Beyond Belief, Emile Durkheim on Morality and Society, The Broken Covenant, The New Religious Consciousness, Varieties of Civil Religion, Uncivil Religion, Imagining Japan,* and *The Robert Bellah Reader.* Jef Van Gerwen (1998) writes that all of Bellah's work shows his concern to see 'social science as a moral inquiry. Sociology, in his understanding, is a moral science, providing a critical reflection on the conditions of the societal projects we engage in as citizens.' Van Gerwen finds the following questions in Bellah's work: 'How can our society become and remain independent? How can it be just and fair to all its members? How can it remain innovative and democratic, true to its traditions and open to newcomers?' He continues, 'These are core issues of sociology as a moral and humanistic discipline.'

In his best-known book, *Habits of the Heart* (1985), Bellah asserts that of the three founding cultural traditions of America—republicanism, biblical religion, and individualism—the third, individualism, prevents Americans from giving proper attention to the first two. By paying too much attention to their private lives, individuals pay too little attention to the public domain: to justice, equality, social responsibility, or spiritual matters. In this respect, we forget what Durkheim taught: that the individual can only flourish under conditions of social cohesion. Bellah writes, 'We discover who we are face to face and side by side with others in work, love, and learning. All of our activity goes on in relationships, groups, associations, and communities ordered by institutional structures and interpreted by cultural patterns of meaning. Our individualism is itself one such pattern. And the positive side of our individualism, our sense of the dignity, worth, and moral autonomy of the individual, is dependent in a thousand ways on a social, cultural, and institutional context that keeps us afloat even when we cannot very well describe it . . . . Finally, we are not simply ends in ourselves, either as individuals or as a society. We are parts of a larger whole that we can neither forget nor imagine in our own image without paying a high price.'

Source: Adapted from http://www.robertbellah.com/biography.htm and other sources.

Today, many sociologists draw on Bellah's work to fashion their own analyses of modern religion. For example, Roof (2009) draws on Bellah's 'American civil religion' to examine how Americans use myths to form their national identity, and how these myths have influenced the discourse of American presidents between 1980 and 2008. The 'public faiths' of the US, which combine religious and political ideology, approximate the 'civil religion' to varying degrees and in different ways, with a clear trend toward religious nationalism. In short, they present us with a picture of religion that is both nationalistic and transcendent, sacred and profane.

Even so-called secular events are turned to religious purposes, by this reckoning. Price (1992) identified the Super Bowl as a 'religious festival' along the lines of Bellah's 'civil religion'. Butterworth (2008) takes up this theme to examine the Super Bowl XLII in

Following the death of Michael Jackson in June 2009, devoted fans began erecting shrines to honour the pop star. This type of social phenomenon is an example of what Robert Bellah refers to as 'civil religion'.

2008, which (as we noted earlier) featured several displays of national and military symbolism—deemed significant in the era of the 'war on terror'. Fox Television Network in particular promoted nationalistic themes and values, for example, in its presentation of the Declaration of Independence.

Along similar lines, Riley (2008) cites Bellah's 'civil religion' in exploring the cultural narratives, symbolism, and commemoration surrounding the site in Pennsylvania where one of the hijacked planes crashed on 11 September 2001. In the Durkheimian approach to religion, 'holy places' are like other holy (totemic) objects in providing a context for social celebration. Riley also evokes Durkheim in observing the 'sacred' and 'profane' duality of cultural symbolism and narrative.

Meizel (2006) adds American popular music to understanding the relationship between politics and religion, echoing Bellah's 1967 depiction of interrelated 'beliefs, symbols, and rituals'. Two songs in particular—'God Bless America' of World War II vintage, and 'God Bless the USA' from the time of the Iraq War—reflect the American civil religion, particularly in a globalizing world. Like holy places (shrines) and holy objects (totems), such songs provide people with 'anthems' through which they can remember and perform ritual celebration.

As in any religion, in secular religion too there are saints and sinners, gods and devils. Wender (2007) develops an analysis of religious imagery around the American 'war on terror', with the US cast as the divinely anointed deliverer of the world from the 'evil of terrorism'. Here, the evil opposition seems to confirm that American ideology is sacred, blurring the line between American foreign policy and American civil religion. The blend of democratic capitalism, liberalism, and evangelical Protestantism that form the American nationalistic ideology are supported by legislation at home and military, economic, and political policy abroad, to fuel the war on terror. The image of a holy 'civil' crusade is reinforced by the expectation that nations cleansed of terrorism will be converted to democratic liberalism.

The usefulness of this concept is further demonstrated by Swatos (2006) who imagines that, in theory, the US could have reacted in many different ways to the 9/11 attacks. The question is, Why did Americans (and their government) react so harshly and blindly by attacking Iraq, which had no connection to al Qaeda? On the one hand, the US government may have been spoiling for a war in the Middle East and Iraq promised an easy target. On the other hand, the government and citizenry may have required a decisive symbolic action, whatever its consequences. Many may have felt the US civil religion itself was under attack in 2001, so religious fervour was needed for a disproportionate response.

Appropriately, Bertin (2009) notes that Bellah originally viewed religion as unifying and stabilizing society. However, Bertin sees a crisis in American civil religion, both in its inherent contradictions and in the politically charged conflict caused by the growing power of evangelical fundamentalism and the religious Right. Increasingly, religion—including civil religion—is functioning to separate conservative and progressive Americans: separating people who are for the Iraq War from those who are against it, for example. Often, themes of loyalty and Americanism are invoked to argue for or against certain types of political action.

That said, all religion, even civil religion, continues to be under attack by various forces, including secularism, consumerism, and immigration. Hecht (2007) draws on both Bellah's 'civil religion' and the work of Will Herberg to develop the concepts of 'passive pluralism' and 'active pluralism', by looking at the *eruv*, or ritual public space, established by the Orthodox Jewish community in Los Angeles. 'Passive pluralism' was historically the norm in the United States; the mainline religions dominated the public space. This is now giving way to 'active pluralism', due to new patterns in immigration that have their roots in the 1965 changes to the Immigration Act.

Given the importance of religious socialization in competing groups, Copen and Silverstein (2007) explore how religious values and beliefs are communicated from parents to their children. A review of the literature suggests that this happens in three ways: explicitly teaching beliefs and values—socialization; living out their religion as role models—social training; and placing their children in social and economic situations that reinforce their world view—status inheritance. These mechanisms continue to be important in preserving family and minority group traditions, despite the homogenizing tendencies of 'civil religion'. Copen and Silverstein point out that Bellah and others suggest that, as families split apart through divorce, and as individualism becomes increasingly prominent in society, parents are losing the ability to pass on their values in these ways.

An understanding of the connection between religion and social cohesion goes back to work in the nineteenth century by Ferdinand Tönnies. In particular, many sociologists (following Bellah) are interested in the continued battle between the focus of traditional religions on community solidarity, and the competing claims of individualism, secularism, and consumerism (Merz-Benz, 2006). Towards the end of the nineteenth century, Tönnies clarified this modern conflict in his analysis of community and society (in the original, *Gemeinschaft* and *Gesellschaft*). Today, the sociological debate around social cohesion still involves clarifying the connection between 'me and us', the individual and the community. In principle, religion should be able to play a part in strengthening community sentiments, but (as we know from Weber's *Protestant Ethic and the Spirit of Capitalism* [1958], originally published in 1905) religion can promote individualistic acquisitiveness.

This struggle has a long history, as Turner (2005) has pointed out. In the late eighteenth century, philosopher Immanuel Kant distinguished between religion as *cult* in which people seek favours from God through prayer and offerings to bring healing and wealth, and religion as *moral action* that commands human beings to change their lives. The Kantian approach was fundamental to Max Weber's later view of the relationship between asceticism and capitalism. In turn, Talcott Parsons's early sociology of religion built on this theme in Kant and Weber; but in his later work, Parsons came to a reappraisal of Émile Durkheim. In developing his concept of the expressive revolution, Parsons followed Durkheim in studying individualism as a major transformation of society. Parsons's sociology of religion did not subscribe to the secularization thesis, but instead saw American liberalism as fulfilling Protestant individualism.

Robert Bellah was a student and protégé of Talcott Parsons and, in this sense, a direct descendant of the historic battles to conceptualize religion, incorporating the insights of Kant, Weber, Durkheim, and Parsons in an American context. Thus, Bellah's work has provided a living compendium of sociological thought on religion.

No wonder, then, that a review of recent writings finds continued application of the work by Robert Bellah—over 90 journal articles applying Bellah's work in the last 20 years. Bellah belongs in a comprehensive, fusion approach to sociology because he adopts a multi-method, cross-national, and historical approach to understanding people's belief systems, and the way these beliefs support or undermine communal life. Viewed from one angle, Bellah's goal is to promote more social attachment and, in this way, health and satisfaction. He also embodies the sociological tradition of social cohesion that began with Tönnies and Durkheim and continued through the past century in community studies and communitarianism. (In turn, Bellah viewed Durkheim as embodying and reflecting the earlier sociological concerns of important eighteenth and nineteenth French thinkers we do not have space to discuss here: Rousseau, Montesquieu, Comte, Saint-Simon, and de Toqueville.)

 **New Insights**

If we accept Bellah's idea of 'civil religion', what then are we to make of the concept of 'secularization?' Vido (2008) notes that the continued importance of religion to society appears to refute the 'secularization thesis', which predicted that the influence of religion would greatly diminish, even disappear, as modernity increasingly took hold. The relationship of modernity to religion thus appears to be more complex and ambiguous than previously thought. Perhaps for this reason, we can expect that religion in the modern and postmodern eras will be very different from its older forms.

Thus, in a review of the field, Smith (2008) contends that the sociological study of religion is going through a transition in which major issues and future goals are ambiguous. Currently, some substantive and methodological concerns clearly demand more attention from scholars. These include the new roles of beliefs, genetics, religious bodies, religious emotions, Islam, and cross-national religions. The notion of 'multiple modernities'—the notion that societies can modernize in a variety of different ways, with a variety of outcomes—needs further development in the study of religion. Clearly, we are at a turning point, where sociologists have an opportunity and a duty to increase understandings about the role of religion in social, political, economic, and cultural life.

According to Goldstein (2009), some hold that in the old paradigm of the sociology of religion, secularization is linear, while in the new paradigm it is 'revival and routinization'. In large part, this dispute reflects the disagreement between followers of Durkheim and Marx (a linear theorist) and followers of Weber (a cyclical or non-linear theorist). Still, Goldstein points out that even the Durkheimian model allows for secularization to follow patterns other than a straight line: cyclical/spiral, dialectical, and paradoxical. If we can accept a dialectical (Marxist) understanding of secularization, in which one change may challenge and overturn another, we may be able to make sense of how secularization and sacralization can occur at the same time.

What are the boundaries of the sociology of religion, then, and does religion have a central narrative today? Hornbacher and Gottowik (2008) dispute the Eurocentric version of the inevitable march of secularization behind the forces of modernity and globalization. This notion arose out of the Enlightenment dichotomy between the reason of science and philosophy, on the one hand, and religious dogmatism on the other. When faced with modern rationalism, the theory ran, religion would falter and disappear. Hornbacher and Gottowik examine how religious practices are flourishing in southeastern Asia—Indonesia, Thailand, Laos, and Vietnam—despite the unmistakable inroads of social and economic development. On this basis, they suggest that new thinking is needed on the relationship between modernity and religion.

Appropriately, sociologists continue to struggle to understand new religious contexts using the traditional ideas. As an example, consider the religious revival currently taking place in Russia. According to Mulders (2008), the revival in the Russian Orthodox church is seen not only in increased membership, but also in the presence of Orthodox discourse in public spaces, which has transformed the Russian view of religion and religious behaviour. For example, consider the teaching of Orthodox doctrine in public schools, which provides a spiritual view to set alongside the materialist view—a sign of 'postmodern ideological diversity'.

Sociologists might differ in their interpretation of this renaissance of religion in Russia. Some might argue that, though religion was suppressed by 70 years of communist government, it was never eliminated. Others might argue that the current rapid and chaotic social change in Russia has created a need for social solidarity that, in the absence of civil religion or nationalist ideology, only traditional religion can supply. Others still might attribute this re-appearance to Western influence—especially, American influence—following the disintegration of the monolithic Soviet world view since the early 1990s.

If we accept the principle of multiple modernities, and multiple roles for religion in modern societies, we can agree with Lunn (2009) that religion, spirituality, and faith need to be re-examined in connection with the theory, policy, and practice of socio-economic development. In the twenty-first century, Lunn notes, new thinking about the potential role of religion for emancipation and self-determination has begun to change this situation. In particular, sociologists have shown that religion, spirituality, and faith can help ensure that development is appropriate and sustainable. So, for example, Savagnone (2009) examines the role of the Italian Roman Catholic Church in southern Italy, which due to economic and social problems, is somewhat lagging behind the rest of the country, and suggests that the solution requires a new 'religious and civic consciousness'. The Church has, with mixed success, advocated for the people of the region, pointing out inequalities.

In some parts of the world, traditional religious rites and beliefs serve new goals of emancipation and development. For example, Horstmann (2009) considers transformation and revival of the traditional art and ancestor-worship spirituality of southern Thailand, Manooraa Rongkruu, through hybridization, fragmentation, and postmodernization. The adaptation of the traditional ways in a postmodern context help the people of Southern Thailand to adjust to a changing society and new ways of thinking. Its traditional healing practices have even been adapted to treat modern illnesses.

This new, transformative role of religion requires a strong connection with political life, and nowhere today is the link between religion and politics more evident than in Iran. Amineh and Eisenstadt (2007) note that the Iranian Islamic Revolution of 1979 produced the only modern regime founded on religious fundamentalism. The new regime incorporated modern political structures, such as a presidential–parliamentary system, and ideas, such as equality and political participation, not found in traditional Islamic thought.

Kabbalah, a form of Jewish mysticism, has reached mainstream popularity in recent years following the wave of celebrities, such as Madonna, who publicly declared themselves as followers of the faith.

Situated as it was in the globalizing modern world, it used modern media and organizational methods to promote its message and rally the people. Also, they suggest that, ironically for a fundamentalist religious movement, the Iranian Revolution and the regime it created share with postmodernism a skepticism of Western and Enlightenment ideology.

The problem of reimagining religion is not found only in southern, less-developed, or Asian countries. We find a similar development in Judaism. According to Huss (2007), in Israel, the US, and other Western countries, the Jewish mystic tradition Kabbalah has enjoyed renewed interest—its doctrines and practices, along with those of Hasidism, are widely observed, and Kabbalistic imagery has appeared in many cultural contexts. Huss places the revival of Kabbalah alongside the Western twentieth-century spiritual movements, such as the New Age movement, and notes similarities among them, suggesting that New Age themes can be found in present-day Kabbalah, in both the modern and more traditional forms. He attributes the similarities to the influence of postmodernism and the effects of globalizing capitalism.

Chapter Summary

In this chapter, we saw that even defining religion is not an easy task. Like any other sociological idea, *religion* has changed and continues to change across time and space. Besides proposing a definition of religion, we have explored a range of sociological attempts to explain the lasting significance of religion. Weber suggests that religion serves to imbue individual lives with meaning; for Durkheim, it is a source of social solidarity; Marx and Freud, in different ways, both see it as a source of malaise and oppression. One thing is certain: although religion has changed its role, it is far from unimportant and unlikely to disappear as a powerful social force in contemporary society.

Even in a time when reason trumps blind faith, people today continue to turn to spirituality. Religion, while under different guises, continues to play an essential role in society. An example is the continuing importance of ideology and civil religion. Further, people continue to use religion to include or to exclude others in civic relationships.

Today, people make their own decisions about their religious commitments. Some believe that religion and politics can be, and should be, separate. Others see them as inextricably intertwined, with religion pointing to political routes they feel obliged to take. They want the state to protect their morality, and the church to define what that morality should be. For such people, political action is a necessary result of religious belief.

Finally, as we have also seen, religion can improve or hinder collaboration across social statuses and religious divides. While religious belief has led and continues to lead to bloodshed, we should not view religion as a permanent barrier to civility. As a society, we need to learn how to harness the religious impulses that remain strong in modern societies and use them for mutual benefit.

Critical Thinking Questions

1. In your view, what is the best way to define religion? Consider your own bias when forming this definition.
2. Do you think we live in a truly secular society? If not, are some areas of life more influenced by religion than others?
3. Consider the kinds of questions that a sociologist of religion would ask about a new religious movement (NRM). Can any kind of group constitute itself as a new religious movement, or must it meet certain criteria; and if so, what criteria?
4. Give an example of the expression of civil religion in Canada. In what sense does it fall well short of expressions of traditional religion—in both emotional effect and moral uplift? In what respects does it outdo traditional religion?
5. What is the connection between religion and violence? Consider both the history of religion and recent events in your answer.
6. What do you think is the future of religion in Canadian society? Will people still be religious in the year 2500 CE?

Recommended Readings

Reginald W. Bibby, *Restless Gods: The Renaissance of Religion in Canada* (Toronto: Stoddart, 2002). In this work, well-known Canadian sociologist Bibby asserts that organized religion is increasing its influence in Canada, rather than decreasing it. He presents statistical data to support his argument and offers a guideline for mainstream Christian religious leaders to promote their spiritual causes.

Robert Choquette, *Canada's Religions: An Historical Introduction* (Ottawa: University of Ottawa Press, 2004). This book is about the history and diversity of religion in Canada and the persistent influence of religion in modern society. It also examines the connection between religion and other social institutions, including communities, the educational system, workplaces, and politics, essentially placing religion within a social context.

Meredith B. McGuire, *Lived Religion: Faith and Practice in Everyday Life* (New York: Oxford University Press, 2005). This book considers religion in contemporary society, complete with some of the diverse religious practices evident there. It argues that people today do not necessarily commit themselves to one form of organized religion but instead often find spiritual fulfillment in a mélange of religious practices. This book is useful in orienting researchers to understand religious behaviour in a new way.

Lori G. Beaman and Peter Beyer (eds), *Religion and Diversity in Canada* (Leiden; Boston: Brill, 2008). The essays that make up this book explore the many diversities of religion in Canada today, including the many different religions that come from cultures around the world and the different ways people have adopted a variety of religious practices into their everyday lives.

Lorne L. Dawson, *Comprehending Cults: The Sociology of New Religious Movements*, 2nd edn (Don Mills, ON; New York: Oxford University Press, 2006). This is a comprehensive introduction to new religious movements, also known as cults, viewed as social phenomena. Dawson summarizes major theories of cult formation, examines the type of people that are most likely to join cults, and discusses various issues surrounding cults, such as social stigma.

Susan Palmer, *Aliens Adored: Rael's UFO Religion* (New Brunswick, NJ: Rutgers University Press, 2004). This book provides an analysis of the Raelian religion, led by Claude Vorilhon. The result of 15 years of fieldwork with the Raelians, the book draws information from interviews with the leader and members, observing meetings, and witnessing rituals and religious practices.

Émile Durkheim, trans. Joseph Ward Swain, *Elementary Forms of the Religious Life* (London: Allen and Unwin, 1968 [1912]). This is a classic work in the sociology of religion, and is the last major work published by Durkheim. It is a case study of Australian Aboriginals, whose culture Durkheim believed exemplified rudimentary forms of religious practice.

Websites

Canadian Charter of Rights and Freedoms
http://laws.justice.gc.ca/en/charter

Wonder Café
www.wondercafe.ca

Thank God for Evolution!
http://thankgodforevolution.com

Info-Secte/Cult
http://infosect.freeshell.org

14 Media and Mass Communication

Learning Objectives

In this chapter, you will:

> Discuss various theoretical approaches to the media
> Recognize the role of the mass media in shaping popular opinion
> Analyze the positive and negative effects of the mass media on society
> Learn about the influence of media ownership on content
> Consider the inequalities in media access and their effects

Chapter Outline

The media have a vast effect on our everyday lives. We are exposed to media every day and in this way, become aware of things happening all around the world. The media influence our culture, ideas, ideologies, values—almost every aspect of our thinking. In this way, the media influence the ways we interact with one another, and therefore how societies change.

Sociologists who study the media ask the following questions: What role do the media play in our society? What kinds of messages do they communicate to the public? How do the public, and particular interest groups, interpret and react to these media messages? Who controls the media, and does that matter? And how are the media changing with the expansion of the Internet and cyberspace? We will discuss some of these questions in this chapter.

Everyday Observations

The mediated workplace: Isabella wakes up early for an important business meeting. She performs her daily morning routine: has some coffee while reading the newspaper, brushes her teeth, takes a shower, and briefly watches the news. Isabella then checks her cellphone: it is now 8:30 a.m. The meeting starts in a half an hour and she hasn't left the house yet, even though it normally takes her an hour to get to work. Isabella puts on her work clothes, turns on her computer, and aims her web camera. She's right on time.

mass media
The technology that makes **mass communication** possible; it includes the printing press, radio, television, photocopier, and camera, among others.

mass communication
The transmission of a message from a single source to multiple recipients at the same time.

Where once the news was confined to a limited number of mediums—television, radio, and print—it is now possible to keep up to date using cellphones and a variety of other portable electronic devices.

The media today are very different from what they were a century ago. Today, we are no longer limited to books, newspapers, and radio for sources of information about the world. In fact, paper-based news has largely become obsolete, replaced by news instantly available from online sources we can access at the click of a mouse.

Of course, printed sources like magazines and newspapers are still popular with many people. However, these traditional sources of news face an unprecedented challenge as people rely increasingly on the Internet as their primary information source. Television programs too are facing competition from media outlets like YouTube that give viewers access to a wide variety of programs and videos whenever they want, although copyright issues impose some limits on the available selection. Cellphones, for their part, have almost replaced landlines as the preferred communication device, and it is common today for people to own a cellphone but not a landline at home.

The trend today is toward more and more flexible communication devices—from television, newspapers, and radio, to the Internet, cellphones, and MP3 players. So, both as users of these media devices and as sociologists, we need to understand the historical, social, and cultural background against which these changes have occurred, and their likely consequences.

Mainstream (mass) media today often have to compete with new media sources like online blogs and popular websites. Nevertheless, the traditional (mass) media remain important, for the time being. In part, this is because we haven't figured out how to deal with all the information property issues a complete changeover would require. Whatever the media source, it is important for us to understand how the media influence our tastes, opinions, and beliefs, and how this influence affects social life. In thinking about this, consider the following questions: Do the **mass media** portray men and women similarly? Do they represent minorities fairly? Are they biased in any obvious ways? If so, what are the likely sources and causes of this bias? Do you suppose powerful groups in society use the media to spread their ideologies and beliefs? If so, how can less powerful groups respond to this dominant presence?

Modern communication has also come to rely on new technologies that, to some degree, have replaced intimate

contacts with more distant contacts. The scenario above shows this nicely. The meeting Isabella has to attend is a video conference, one of many now–widely used communication techniques that allow two or more people to interact face-to-face from distant locations. People rely on the media not only to gather information but also to remain connected with others around the world. Modern technology has made both of these functions readily available, although as we will see, inequalities still exist in the access to, and use of, media resources.

Ways of Looking at . . .
MASS MEDIA

Functionalists, as always, are interested in the way the mass media are organized and how this organization contributes to social equilibrium or stability. From this standpoint, they are interested in the role of media as a mechanism for informing, socializing, and educating the public. This point of view is especially evident in the treatment of media in developing countries.

There is a large literature that shows media literacy and mass media consumption are important factors in 'modernization'—the development of non-traditional, mainly Western, knowledge, attitudes, and practices in less-developed countries on a wide variety of topics: work, leisure, family life, consumerism, parenting, and childbearing, among others. The evidence shows that as people consume more media, whether radio, TV, videos, newspapers, videogames, or other forms, they become more knowledgeable about the world and about cultural variety. In turn, the higher they set their own sights and those of their children, the more likely they are to demand an open, democratic society. So media consumption also, indirectly, brings about social change.

Of course, there are some limitations to this process. Evidently, if people mainly consume media that are hostile to modernity or Westernization (as they view it)—for example, by exclusively receiving Arab-language, anti-Western transmissions in the Middle East—they are less likely to modernize in this way. However, one cannot underestimate the importance of information flow in and of itself. For example, despite the greatest efforts of the Soviet regime to slant and restrict information about the West, or about internal problems of the Soviet society, people got the information nonetheless and discounted what the national media told them. To a large degree, Soviet society imploded precisely because people knew lots about the Western alternative, and wanted it. In a global society, it is unlikely that anyone will, for long, remain unaware of (and unaffected by) the Hollywood dream factory and American consumerism.

This argument suggests that, as Marshall McLuhan said, 'the medium is the message'. Content aside, information flow by itself increases the appetite for more information; and more information seems to increase interest in variety and debate. At the very least, the media create and feed curiosity about the world. Increasingly, the media—even the mass media—are significant forces in social engineering through mediated health promotion, political messaging, and religious teaching. They are central, along with the Internet, in creating an international market in ideas and beliefs.

By contrast, critical theorists are interested in the ways powerful groups in society use the media they own or control to further organizational and class interests. This use of the media increases their wealth and ensures continued political hegemony. We will explore this process below in connection with the so-called **political economy perspective**, which is a variant of the critical theory.

Critical theory is also useful in understanding the use of media in politics, to manipulate public opinion about particular candidates or issues. Research has shown that media over-coverage and slanting of particular topics—for example, the extent of serious crime or

political economy perspective
A viewpoint that focuses on the ways private ownership affects what is communicated, and the ways it affects the exercise of power.

the role of black people or young people in serious crime—increases people's fearfulness, lack of trust, and desire to punish offenders. It increases their willingness to give more power to political and police officials to hire more personnel, build more prisons, and ignore civil liberties.

This notion is put forward neatly in the so-called *cultivation theory* devised by Gerbner and Gross (1976). The theory asserts that mass media—and television in particular—have become the main source of information in society today. People who watch television for four or more hours a day—'heavy television viewers'—are exposed to a great deal of violent imagery and storytelling. In this way, they are affected by the 'Mean World Syndrome'—a heightened state of insecurity, exaggerated perception of risk and danger, and a fearful propensity for hard-line political solutions to social problems. According to Gerbner, the overuse of television creates a homogeneous, almost universally fearful populace.

Television does this by normalizing violence, numbing some people to real-world violence even as it whets the appetite in others for ever higher doses. As well, some types of stories—for example, about child abductions—raise parental anxieties out of proportion to the real risk of such occurrence. The theory views audiences as passive, bringing little or no skepticism to the ideas received from the media. Since the audience is (supposedly) passive and receptive, vulnerable, and easily manipulated, ideas propagated by the media are often accepted, significantly influencing large groups into conforming. According to this theory, the mass audience is vulnerable and easily manipulated; as a result, over the long run, the media gradually build up certain false images of the world through a continued bombardment of images.

One reason for the popularity of the cultivation theory is that it is easy to apply to a wide range of texts. People who are already inclined to blame the media for excessive sex and violence in our culture find the theory appealing. A disadvantage however is that the theory denies people agency, ignoring the intelligence of audiences and their willingness to evaluate what they hear. In this respect, it ignores evidence provided in the two-step theory of communication that suggests the process of influence and opinion formation is far more complicated. In the classic study below, sociologist Herbert Gans takes an approach that is sympathetic to, but more sophisticated than, the Gerbner and Gross approach.

Classic Studies
Deciding What's News

In many domains of life where most of us have no first-hand experience—for example, in foreign affairs or warfare—the media control the way we see our world. They tell us what is going on, and we are (usually) unable to challenge their story with opposing facts. In this sense, the media act as filters, showing us some things and ignoring or even hiding others. The media organizations and journalists who work within them decide what to cover and what to ignore. Herbert J. Gans was the first researcher to look at this process through a sociological lens, in his book *Deciding What's News* (1979).

As the title suggests, this book examines the intricate way the news world works, and especially, the way what happens in the real world becomes news that we see on television or read in the newspaper. Gans began research on the book in the late 1960s, choosing four major news organizations—the CBS and NBC news networks and *Times* and *Newsweek* news journals—as his focus. To study them, he carried out extensive participant observation at the four companies, interviewing personnel at all levels and trying to find out precisely how they choose stories that become 'news'. In addition, Gans did a content analysis of nearly 3,500 news stories spanning eight years, and an in-depth review of past research on the sociology of news. So, his research method included both quantitative and qualitative data.

A journalist covers the violence between Georgia and Russia over the breakaway region of South Ossetia.

In these ways, Gans uncovered several important findings about journalism in America. First, because news reporting is concerned with gaining and keeping a mass audience, there is usually an inclination to include at least some stories that appeal to a mass audience: stories about famous people, violence and bloodshed, sex and scandal. As Gans notes, there is a tendency to report 'negative news'—as journalists say, 'If it bleeds, it leads'.

Second, Gans reports that the national news is shaped by, and in the interests of, people in high positions; so stories are chosen that will improve their reputations. After all, top journalists, top politicians, and top corporate leaders all want to look good in the news, and they all exert a direct or indirect influence on the selection process. Not surprisingly, the news is also chosen with the interests of the organization in mind. In short, most national news 'upholds the actions of elite individuals and elite institutions', Gans writes (1979: 61). News items on CBS are not going to embarrass the owners of CBS or their friends, for example; and news items on Fox are not going to embarrass the owners of Fox Network or their friends, though they may occasionally embarrass the owners of CBS and *their* friends.

That said, and despite competition, the degree of consensus among news organizations is striking. In all four organizations he studied, Gans found similar views about which ideas and values to communicate. They include the value of individualism, a belief in responsible capitalism, and a desire for social order and strong national leadership. These conventional political views—any American of either national party could endorse them—are congruent with other news choices the networks made: for example, portraying news in ways that promoted patriotism, chauvinism, and a tendency to see world events through the perspective of American culture and ideology.

Gans also finds that much of the news communicated to audiences is inaccurate or at least distorted. It is delivered in a way that benefits people with power over the media institution; the media organization does this to make friends, avoid enemies, and preserve itself. He also argues that 'the news is part of a submerged class struggle in which the middle class . . . is acting, even unknown to itself, in the interest of the elite classes' (ibid: 195).

To summarize, Gans's classic study shows that the decisions journalists make in choosing stories to cover are determined by a complex web of factors—not merely the 'newsworthiness' of the stories themselves. These factors include both internal pressures, such as the outlook of the media organization; and external pressures, such as the tastes of the audience. Yet, journalists always have choices to make in these respects, so Gans believes they hold some influence in society and bear some responsibility. Despite the constraints, they shape the views and knowledge of millions of viewers and readers.

As one of the first sociological accounts of news media, this book succeeds in carefully linking sociological theory and data to make a solid and persuasive argument (Robinson, 1980). Another commentator, Graber (1979) believes that, despite its minor flaws, the book offers valuable insights into the often-closed world of news-making and explained the rationales behind news choices. Finally, the book reveals the role of journalists and news media organizations in perpetuating the 'political status quo that they helped to create' (Robinson, 1980: 195).

Although much has changed since its publication, this book still provides a foundation on which other sociologists have built an approach to the media (M.D. Murray, 2005). Many still believe it to be the most comprehensive sociological account of the news media world and its extraordinary societal influence. So the book is a good place to start our discussion of the mass media.

Media Ownership

As already noted, media broadcasting—especially, news broadcasting—generally reflects the interests of the media owners. However, media ownership varies, so we need to look at its effects systematically. On the one hand, there are *publicly owned* media in Canada, including the Canadian Broadcasting Corporation/Société Radio-Canada (CBC/SRC) and the National Film Board of Canada (NFB). As well, various educational television broadcasters are owned and operated by provincial governments; they include Radio-Québec and TV Ontario (TVO). These public organizations use the media for public service, fulfilling social needs such as educational programming for children and providing news from a Canadian viewpoint. Usually, they are funded by the government, but may also receive advertising revenues. TVO is an exception here, since it includes no commercial breaks, is a registered charity, and is funded by memberships and donations.

Most critics believe that public media ownership is important for Canada, as a forum where Canadian citizens can voice their opinions of social issues. However, others are critical, believing that these organizations are failing to foster a united Canadian identity.

On the other hand, there are *privately owned* media in Canada. Unlike public ownership, *private* ownership is mainly concerned with profit-making; and most of the mass media in Canada are privately owned. Among the leading media organizations in Canada, only CBC/SRC is publicly owned. Historically, individuals or small groups (even families) have owned small media companies. However, over time, these small news companies have gradually combined to form massive multimedia empires, controlled by an ever smaller number of increasingly powerful players. Time Warner, for instance, is the largest media company in the world, with interests in the Internet (AOL), television (CNN, HBO, TBS, and many other networks), and film (Warner Bros.). It also controls Time Inc., the largest magazine publisher in the world, whose 115-plus titles—including *Time*, *Fortune*, *People*, and *Sports Illustrated*—reach a worldwide audience of over 300 million.

In the US, three of the four major television networks, the source of daily news for most Americans, are part of multimedia giants. ABC is owned by the Walt Disney Company (Miramax Films, Hyperion Books); and Fox Television is controlled by Rupert Murdoch's News Corporation (the *New York Post*, HarperCollins). The huge industrial conglomerate General Electric owns NBC (along with Universal Studios). CBS owns numerous other

conglomerate
A business structure that engages in several, usually unrelated business endeavours: for example, moviemaking gambling casinos, and alcoholic beverages.

media properties, including book publisher Simon & Schuster, and in turn is controlled by Sumner Redstone, who also holds the reins at Viacom, owner of Paramount Studios and MTV Networks. These companies were all controlled by Viacom until it was split into two companies several years ago: CBS Corp., which owns the TV network, also owns Simon & Schuster and various other properties. The movie business and cable networks were left with Viacom. Redstone holds a majority stake in both companies.

In Canada too, ownership is concentrated—a fact well documented over several decades. The creation of a Royal Commission (popularly known as the Kent Commission) arose out of concerns around newspaper closings in Winnipeg and Ottawa in August 1980 that eliminated direct competition between Canada's two largest newspaper chains in those cities. (An earlier government inquiry, the Davey Commission, had in fact predicted such a loss of competition.) Tom Kent, a former newspaper editor, civil servant, and academic, was chosen as chair of the Commission. In preparing its findings, the Commission collected a vast amount of information on newspapers and journalism in Canada and produced a nine-volume report outlining the structure and operation of the newspaper industry at that time.

In its 1981 report, the Kent Commission stated that 'Concentration engulfs Canadian daily news-paper publishing. Three chains control nine-tenths of French-language daily newspaper circulation, while three other chains control two-thirds of English-language circulation' (1). The report found little justi-fication for the ownership of newspaper chains by conglomerates with major interests in other sectors like television. Such **cross-ownership**, the commission felt, would comprom-ise journalism's social responsibility to the reading public and also result in lower spend-ing by newspapers on editorial content and investigative reporting. All these factors were driving good journalists out of the profession because of inadequate pay, poor newsroom management, and a concern for profit at the expense of good journalism. Further, the public (rightly) perceived that the quality of political journalism had declined, and diverse interests were less represented than they had been before.

The report praised smaller news services such as United Press Canada but expressed uncertainty that they would survive in the face of newspaper closures and mergers. These concerns proved justifiable. As well, the Commission predicted that the growth of elec-tronic publishing and telecommunication information, and the rapid development of the electronic media, could present a critical problem for the future of the newspaper industry. This, we now know, was another fully warranted concern. However, the Commission's report had little impact. Recommendations for legislation to reduce the power of con-glomerates—to solve the problems the Commission had identified—were largely ignored. Newspaper publishers fiercely opposed creating the proposed Press Rights Council, argu-ing such a Council would promote government interference. They attacked the Kent Commission's research, claiming it had not proved that chain-owned monopoly news-papers are worse than the old individually owned competitive newspapers.

CBC (Canadian Broadcasting Corporation) is the main public broadcasting network in Canada.

cross-ownership

A business structure in which one corporation owns media businesses of different types. For example, a large corporation may own newspapers, magazines, television networks, and radio channels.

For this and other reasons, interest in the Commission's findings soon faded. Some recommendations did reach the stage of draft legislation under the Liberal Trudeau government, but most disappeared during the Conservative Mulroney government that followed. As a result, the problem with Canadian media has continued unresolved. Most major media outlets are owned by large business enterprises, so the goal of producing revenue for shareholders continues to influence what gets published. The concern with two goals—immediate profit, and service to political and corporate friends—ensures that dissenting opinions and alternative voices remain marginalized—reduced to a decentralized network of activists.

Canadian Content

In Canada, the preservation and protection of Canadian culture has always been a touchy issue. The reason is that Canada is next door to the largest, richest, and most influential media machine the world has ever known. Not much can stand up to it, unless a lot of money and effort is invested to supply an attractive alternative. But private media businesses have no interest in making such an investment; the likely returns on investment are too low. So, in practice this has meant private media companies favour American content, which almost always guarantees profits, and they avoid having to invest in Canadian content (CanCon).

This has several implications. First, it means that the Canadian government, through the Canadian Radio-television and Telecommunications Commission (CRTC), has to force private media companies to include Canadian content in their programming schedule. Second, the Canadian government has to provide financial incentives to media producers to create new Canadian content. Third, it means that public broadcasters like CBC and TVO, and the NFB have to carry the weight of Canadian content programming with (usually) insufficient funds. Taken together, all of these factors serve to undermine Canadian culture in favour of American culture. They also make it increasingly difficult for Canadian media industry workers to make a living here, so many have left for the United States.

Over the years, state interventions—at different levels of government, and through varied institutions, Crown corporations, and incentive programs—have tried to ensure private media companies feature some Canadian content (Iacobucci and Trebilcock, 2007). Since 1969, the CRTC has been the key independent public authority on the regulation

Point/Counterpoint

BOX **14.1**

Media Bias: Going beyond Fair and Balanced

Some claim that US media outlets show political bias in what they choose to report and not to report. According to political scientist Tim Groeling, 'public discussions about media bias are often just 'food fights', with pundits and partisans throwing around anecdotes'. To bring the discussion into the realm of science, he examined reporting of in-house presidential approval polling by the major US television networks between January 1997 and February 2008. In conducting the study, he looked at not only the televised reports, but also the poll data itself. He found that ABC, CBS, and NBC all showed a 'pro-Democratic bias': all were more likely to report increases rather than decreases in President Bill Clinton's approval rating, but favoured reporting drops rather than gains in President George W. Bush's popularity. FOX News revealed a Republican bias, with a pattern opposite to that of the other three networks.

Source: Adapted from Martin (2008).

and supervision of Canadian media, ensuring media organizations comply with the policies and rules that have been put in place, such as Canadian content rules (Department of Justice Canada, 2009).

Canada's media are regulated by a federal Broadcasting Act, originally established in 1968 and amended in 1991. The purpose of this Act has been to strengthen Canadian culture through controls on related economic and political institutions. The Act includes a broadcasting policy for Canada, a specification of regulatory powers to be exercised by the CRTC, and a specification of how the CBC/SRC is to operate. Although these rules would seem to protect the public interest, in practice both Canada's Broadcasting Act and the CRTC also have had other responsibilities to satisfy. In general, they have shown themselves more sympathetic to private media companies than to public ones. So, in the last 30 years, neo-liberal policies have resulted in media deregulation, privatization, and concentration, showing the state's role has actually decreased. These developments have worried critics, especially those troubled by the effects of Americanization and globalization on Canadian culture.

Media and Politics

The mass media today make the news available to all interested consumers. However, the news as presented in the morning paper or evening television broadcast is not just a neutral assortment of facts. As Gans showed, the news publication or broadcast is a carefully designed product that promotes a particular political and cultural ideology. In subtle ways, the news spreads propaganda and perpetuates mainstream capitalist ideology.

News stories are coded messages about the nature of society and social life in a society. As we have seen, to achieve their ideological goal, journalists simplify and slant their news stories. During elections, political strategists—aware that voters respond best to messages delivered in simple language—advise their candidates to keep statements brief and punchy. The result is that increasingly, politicians speak in 'sound bites'. Providing the public with a true picture of current happenings no longer seems possible in the mass media. News space and time are limited and competitive, forcing editors to make choices about who and what to cover (Koenen, 2002).

In respect to political news, much journalism today is biased in favour of one political party or ideology over another. Most newspapers can be classified as either conservative or liberal, based on content analyses of their editorials and commentaries. However, as the Gans study showed, all mass media journalism is mainstream, tilting only slightly towards the left or right. None expresses radical, provocative, or anti-establishment views. Such narrow journalism erodes the quality of political debate, by blurring public opinion and oversimplifying complex issues.

As well, media coverage tends to be superficial. Increasingly, the media coverage of politics is based on polls rather than in-depth analysis of issues. This trend reflects an underlying concern with public opinion—with the so-called *vox populi*—'the voice of the people'. However, it fails to provide a

Media coverage of politics is based increasingly on polls, rather than analysis of the issues, reflecting an underlying concern with public opinion, but avoiding close examination of competing views.

close examination of competing views. Politicians give a televised speech, and it is instantly 'spun' by partisans whose views are repeated by journalists. Then, public opinion is instantly polled, to determine if the speech-maker pushed the right buttons or not. Polling, especially when used to highlight the 'horserace' aspect of a political contest, undermines the idea of democracy as a deliberative process, producing instead something closer to a popularity contest. By devoting most of the coverage to who is leading the race, news agencies increase the rates of 'bandwagonism'—people changing their views (or reporting they have changed their views) to side with the winner. Undecided voters often simply cast their ballots for the candidate who is projected to win, rather than engaging in the political debate.

Even more subtly corrosive is the media's role in 'agenda-setting', which focuses attention on some issues but not others. This is another way news organizations influence what voters think about. They also shape people's views about the candidates. A few journalists focus on policy issues but most report on the candidates' characteristics. (This tendency is particularly, and ridiculously, evident when the candidate is a woman.) A primary goal is to show the favoured candidate in a positive light and the opposing candidate in a negative one. Whether positive or negative, such media coverage influences people's views of the candidates and sets the 'tone' in which people talk about the election.

It is not only the impracticality of long stories that leads to brief or fantastic versions of the so-called news. As we already mentioned, truncation or distortion occurs mostly because the media are privately owned. The privately owned, massive mainstream news services increasingly condense the political landscape into a two-party competition, each side represented by catchy sound bites.

So, it seems that often the role of the media in politics is neither informative nor integrative. It serves the interests of the media owners and their political friends; in addition, it promotes the illusion of conflict and doubt where there is little or none. It diverts attention from important issues to trivial ones. In this way, the media reproduces—rather than changes—the existing structure of power and opinion in society.

Global Media

The same thing happens on a global scale, consolidating power in the hands of the already powerful. As you will remember from an earlier chapter, some have called globalization 'American imperialism'. The reason is that globalization often spreads American values, beliefs, and lifestyles around the world, largely through American-owned mass media. Globalization has occurred for many reasons, including the developments in media technology we have discussed, but it also results from deep economic and political motives.

Neo-liberal free-trade treaties such as the North American Free Trade Agreement (NAFTA) have increased the ease with which cultural goods (e.g., books, videos, and movies) pass through national borders. As a result, American media companies have a tremendous impact on culture worldwide. For example, consider the impact of the American film industry and the dominance of Hollywood productions around the world. Canada is a major importer of American films, which has many Canadians concerned about the impact of American culture on our own.

Leaving aside the economic consequences, many believe that constant exposure to American films and other forms of media will weaken or even destroy a distinctive Canadian culture. This is a significant concern for many Canadians. Content regulations have been effective in limiting this to some extent, but Canadians still consume a disproportionate amount of American culture. Many have come to favour it over Canadian movies, television, and music (West, 2002). And many of the movies and television programs produced in Canada, with Canadian tax subsidies for 'Canadian content', reflect American values and are set in supposedly American locales—with Vancouver, Montreal, or Toronto presented as California, New England, or New York, for example.

One result of this one-sided cultural flow—from the US to Canada, and rarely vice versa—is that Canadians are starting to pay more attention to how other countries and other media view us: how they look at our lives, our politics, and our leaders. Sometimes, we find this coverage is skewed or inaccurate. This inaccuracy is especially evident in Arab news portrayals of North American society and culture, for example.

So, recognizing the possibilities of bias, we must be equally sensitive to the way the Western media represent the world to us. Here in the West, the mass media tend to provide a pro-Western, pro-American, or pro-European bias in their coverage and understanding of the world. In keeping with the core-periphery pattern discussed in Chapter 10, media coverage continues to focus on core countries and ignore peripheral or semi-peripheral ones.

Even media coverage of human rights abuses is biased. Naturally, there is a tendency to report abuses outside the Western, capitalist world and ignore those within it. As well, according to an analysis of human rights reporting by *The Economist* (UK) and *Newsweek* (US) from 1986 to 2000, covering 145 countries, the media are more likely to report abuses when they occur in large, economically developed non-Western countries (for example, China and Russia). Poorer and less-populous countries with equally serious abuses are often ignored—think of Sudan, Myanmar, Rwanda, and the Democratic Republic of Congo as examples of such blind spots (Ron and Ramos, 2006).

Can this selective blindness be corrected? Sociologist Jürgen Habermas (2006) has famously written, 'mediated political communication in the public sphere can facilitate deliberative legitimation processes in complex societies *only if* a self-regulating media system gains independence from its social environments and if anonymous audiences grant a feedback between an informed elite discourse and a responsive civil society' (411). Simplified, this means the mass media will play a politically significant role only when it has freed itself from its current biases and preoccupations with profit-making, and when informed elites are willing to honestly discuss policy issues with an informed public.

Classic Studies
Material Girls: Making Sense of Feminist Cultural Theory

Feminist researchers were among the first to focus on the media representation of disadvantaged groups, especially women. They correctly perceived that the way the media depicted women would influence, as well as reflect, the way women were treated in society. Therefore it was important to review, critique, and change media depictions that were harmful and demeaning. Various theories about the role of the media were proposed over the last three decades. One of the most important is feminist cultural theory, outlined by Suzanna Walters in her book *Material Girls: Making Sense of Feminist Cultural Theory* (1995).

In systematically presenting feminist cultural theory, Walters begins with a look at well-known female icons in popular culture, such as the singer Madonna and the fictional lead characters in the 1991 movie *Thelma and Louise*. Using these as case studies, Walters examines the role of the media in depicting women from a variety of theoretical approaches. The book also looks at the media representation of feminism itself, and the impact of this representation on feminist thought and activism.

One of the key concepts discussed in the book is the 'male gaze' (to be discussed below), a concept that Walters did not herself invent. In respect to this 'gaze', Walters considers whether the gaze is inevitably male or whether women themselves 'gaze', and with what consequences (Walters, 1995: 88). In addition, Walters discusses concepts such as the female 'ways of seeing', as well as related themes of spectatorship, audience, subjectivity, and positioning, among others (ibid: 46). She develops these ideas with examples from popular culture and the mass media, including film, television, novels, and music.

Walters argues there is a need to integrate feminist cultural theory with other theoretical traditions, such as ethnography. The feminist cultural theorist must begin by gaining insights into the media representation of women by looking at the experiences of real women and the ways media images affect their world. Equally, the method developed for doing such research could be extended to studying other disadvantaged groups, so there would be a double benefit in following Walters' suggestions. Reviewers praised Walters' book for her systematic outline of an emerging field in feminism, and for its discussion of the experiences of different racial, class, and sexual groups as well as those of women (Starr, 1996).

The book provided a perspective from which to consider the representation and portrayal of social groups in the media, especially those who are disadvantaged by large media empires. Thus, this classic study leads naturally into our next section, which arises from the cultural studies perspective.

The Cultural Studies Perspective

cultural studies perspective
A viewpoint that focuses on the types of communication to which people are regularly exposed and especially on messages conveying the *dominant ideology*.

Cultural studies is an interdisciplinary academic field not to be confused with sociology but, like sociology, is grounded in the Frankfurt School's critical theory tradition. An interdisciplinary field, it combines insights from sociology, political economy, communication, social theory, literary theory, media theory, and other fields to study cultural phenomena in various societies. Its goal is to examine cultural themes—for example, leisure, sexuality, or technology—in terms of cultural practices and their relation to power. In Canada, Marshall McLuhan was an important figure in the development of such an interdisciplinary, cultural studies approach to media and technology, although McLuhan was no political radical and, in any event, wrote before the development of current cultural studies.

The cultural studies approach tries to understand 'culture' in all its many forms by analyzing the socio-political context in which the culture develops. Doing so is not an end in itself, but part of a larger goal of social criticism and perhaps even social action. However, the immediate purpose is to expose different 'ways of knowing'—to understand their origins and functions in relation to power. In this respect, we can see connections with the institutional ethnography of Dorothy Smith, to be discussed later. In each case, the purpose is to raise ethical, as well as analytical, questions about society, and to imagine ways of responding to issues of social inequity.

While the political economy perspective focuses on media ownership and control, the *cultural studies perspective* focuses on the ideological aspects of the media: its role in supporting and manipulating power. For example, the cultural studies approach analyzes the messages communicated in media content, the interpretation of this content by audiences, and the struggles of some groups to change mainstream media messages or else communicate their own messages in alternative media forms (Ishita, 2002).

While the cultural studies perspective can be applied to almost any topic, it is readily applicable to gender issues, since the depiction of women is an important part of women's treatment in a gendered society. And this notion necessarily brings us to a discussion of 'appearance'. Women, much more than men, are subject to appearance norms—especially beauty norms. Women, more than men, are judged, and judge one another, according to these norms. The mass media play a central role in preserving and promoting these norms.

We have already discussed some of the issues associated with beauty and appearance norms in Chapter 5, on gender. To repeat, appearance norms are shared notions about beauty that literally attract us to some people and not to others, whether as friends, mates, or merely media idols. Because these norms exist, we all (from time to time) apply sanctions like ridicule, exclusion, or disapproval to people who fail to meet our culture's standards of beauty and attractiveness.

We look at deviations from appearance norms as signs of rebellion, carelessness, or ignorance. Violations of the appearance norms may lead to mistrust, stigmatization, and exclusion. Abundant images glorify ideal men and women in the mass media, and since they vary in interesting ways, we can see different ways to meet the culture's appearance norms. By judging attractiveness based on images of 'beautiful people', our culture idealizes youth, a slender toned body, and symmetrical delicate facial features. However, few can meet the cultural ideals.

One of the results of this is the creation (and perpetuation) of social disadvantage. People with physical handicaps or disadvantages are rarely depicted on the mass media; even people who look ordinary, rather than glamorous, are ignored. This has the effect of unpreparing us for life in the real world, with other (imperfect) people. Nowhere is the role of appearance more important—as an expression of conformity or deviance—than it is in the dramaturgical approach to social life, developed by sociologist Erving Goffman. In his classic work, *The Presentation of Self in Everyday Life* (1959), Goffman uses the theatrical metaphors of stage, actors, and audiences to examine the complexities of social interaction. Appearance issues are especially well suited to this approach because physical attractiveness—like theatre—relies so much on what we can see and can't see.

Here, Goffman notes that—like actors—we all bring social expectations to any situation and these serve as scripts we feel obliged to follow. We are motivated to give believable performances, but our performances and their credibility are put at risk by discrediting or discreditable features. Of these, a flawed or deviant appearance is the most immediately visible and therefore dangerous to our successful performance. For example, a prominent black eye or facial scar invites staring, curiosity, and potentially unpleasant questions. These responses undermine the actors' performances and impede social interaction. A person who has been physically deformed may even be excluded or targeted because of his or her deformities. He or she may be reduced in our minds from a whole and usual person to a tainted and discounted one—in part because his or her appearance interrupts the smooth, easy, and conventional flow of interaction.

Any feature that has such a discrediting effect may be called a *failing*, a *flaw*, or a *handicap*. Goffman calls it a *stigma*—a brand or mark that brings disgrace. Such a mark reveals a gap between virtual and actual social identity—between the person one is pretending to be and the person one actually is. In its most general meaning, a stigma is any characteristic, behaviour, or experience that may cause the 'branded' person to be rejected by others. The stigma spoils that person's social identity, and interferes with his or her social life.

Additionally, appearance norms reflected in the mass media tend to promote appearance pathologies, especially among women. A prime example is anorexia (and related eating disorders such as bulimia). Many different disorders involve food, eating, and weight. However, in everyday conversation, the term *eating disorder* has come to mean anorexia nervosa, bulimia, binge eating, and obesity. Anorexia nervosa, one of the most common eating disorders, is characterized by a relentless pursuit of thinness and a refusal to preserve 'normal' body weight for the person's age and height. The characteristics of anorexia nervosa include a 15 per cent or more loss of body weight, the use of various strategies to lose weight, a weight phobia, body image disturbances, amenorrhea (i.e., the end of menstruation for at least three consecutive cycles), and a constant preoccupation with food.

Eating becomes ritualized, as in other obsessive-compulsive disorders; the anorexic displays strange eating habits and a division of foods into good and bad categories. People suffering from anorexia often have a low tolerance for new situations and dislike changes in their lives. Many fear growing up and assuming adult responsibilities or an adult lifestyle. About 95 per cent of anorexics are women. Young females, who feel more anxious and concerned with their body image, shape, and size, often seek a daintier body size and experience more concern with their appearance if they gain weight. Generally, anxiety about weight and a negative body image are positively correlated to the development of eating disorders.

Women with a related illness, bulimia nervosa, throw up their food after eating it. Like anorexics, bulimics believe their worth and attractiveness depends on being thin. Typically, bulimics consume large amounts of food in a short time. Their food binges often occur in secret and usually involve high-calorie, high-carbohydrate foods they can eat quickly such as ice cream, doughnuts, candy, popcorn, and cookies. Like anorexia, bulimia can be lethal. As well, the two diseases are connected; about 50 per cent of people who have been anorexic develop bulimia or bulimic patterns. Research suggests that about one out of every 25 college- or university-aged women have had bulimia. However, because people with bulimia are secretive, it is hard to know how many older people remain affected.

Because of the widespread danger anorexia and bulimia pose—especially for young women—there has been increasing interest in legislation to prevent the mass dissemination of information that might tend to encourage this behaviour. For example, a new French law—if enacted and enforced—will make the promotion of anorexia illegal and the associated behaviour even less visible and more deviant than it already is. However, the media bear a more general responsibility for this problem, by promoting images of human (physical) perfection that are absurd and virtually unattainable in real life.

Media Representation of Disadvantaged Groups

However, groups are not only misrepresented in the media; they are also selectively under-represented. Groups like women, the poor, racial and ethnic minorities, and gays and lesbians, tend to be *both* under-represented and misrepresented in mainstream media, and this significantly affects their well-being (Mahtani, 2001).

These and other disadvantaged groups are under-represented or misrepresented for various reasons—especially economic ones. Producers and advertisers favour radio and television programs that most of the population can relate to, identifying with the products and lifestyles represented. Most advertisements direct products to middle-class and upper-middle-class families, who can afford to buy them.

There are also ideological factors behind the faulty representation of subordinate groups. Dominant groups are more commonly presented in the media because they are more commonly in positions of media control. The dominant ideology is their own ideology. Alternative ideologies (and their adherents) may be misrepresented because few people in the industry have the power to push those points of view. Media content, in short, reflects the interests and concerns of people who dominate the media, as well as the concerns of people like them. People who are poor and powerless are ignored or, if presented at all, are presented in ways that are unlikely to promote admiration.

Media Portrayal of Women and Gender

Often, the mass media represent women in stereotyped and conventional ways. Historically in our culture there has been a tendency to cast women in one of two main roles: as Madonna or whore. Madonna portrayals depict women in the domestic sphere, as skillful and dedicated, but emotionally dependent and vulnerable, needing men to 'bring home the bacon' and bring the emotional chaos under control. Whore portrayals depict women in non-domestic, sexualized settings—as temptresses and hunted sex objects, or 'trophy' mates with chiefly decorative value. Both approaches preserve gender stereotypes and are likely to cause real women some performance anxieties.

Even in the newer media, such as computerized adventure games, traditional stereotypes remain. Though here we are more likely to encounter the feisty (rather than helpless) fighting woman, a woman's appeal still depends as much on her sexiness as on her competence. These media and game depictions have the effect of enforcing appearance norms and stigmatizing people who fail to conform to them.

Newspaper and television news reports, equally, describe women by their looks, age, and how many children they have, while defining men by their occupation or political affiliation. A woman whose chief interest is politics is viewed as a curiosity, as is the man who describes himself as a child-care provider. Usually, neither is depicted as a role model. For example, compare the media treatment of federal politician Belinda Stronach with that of her former boyfriend Peter MacKay: equally political yet treated differently—Stronach as sexy, MacKay as politically savvy. (Though in fairness, we should note that the media also portrayed McKay as a misogynist when their relationship ended and he compared her [unfavourably] to his dogs.)

Media advertising also tends to be gender-specific, aimed either at males or at females. Look at Saturday morning children's television—typically, cartoon shows interspersed with commercials. The products advertised are aimed directly at young girls or boys, typically matched to the type of show: Barbie dolls or male action figures. Media depictions of gender, like these, have a big impact on the later lives of women and men. It is not merely that a girl seeing another girl play with a Barbie doll on TV will choose to copy this behaviour. Rather, seeing this shapes girls' ideas about what young girls will *normally* play with. The media, in this and other spheres, shape our notions of normality; and since we strive for normality, we emulate the media.

Some branches of the media see themselves as forerunners and agents of change. They purposely present the female engineer or the male nurse not as curiosities, but as experts in their fields. These programs and magazines often show an awareness of racial and ethnic diversity too, as well as that of gender. Even so, these programs are often branded as 'educational' or 'feminist' by the rest of the media; as a result, they are watched, read, or listened to by relatively few people.

Efforts have been made to overcome the nastier and more stereotypical forms of gendered advertising. In fact, some socially conscious organizations are using commercial media (like television advertisements) to promote such change. Occasionally, we see male sports stars talking about the problems of violence against women, for example, to promote models of masculinity that are concerned, caring, and nurturing as well as strong. And, in a turnaround of traditional depictions, we sometimes see women (especially wives) presented as sensible and competent, with husbands who are inept knuckleheads. However, these gender anti-stereotypes are typically cast in the domestic realm, not in Parliament or the corporate boardroom, and they are played for humour. As a result, they simply confirm the deeply held notion that women's proper place is in the home, worrying about casserole recipes and PTA meetings.

Also, the media slant information to conform to a particular gendered approach—'the male gaze', as we briefly mentioned in the description of Walters' book. When a news story is told from a male point of view, especially a European–American male point of view, the standpoint of the reporter or editor is effectively hidden. It is assumed to be unbiased and objective, speaking on behalf of all of society. However, this 'point of view' itself subtly marks the tone of the story. The implication is that news embodies stereotypical masculine qualities of objectivity, reason, coolness, and practicality.

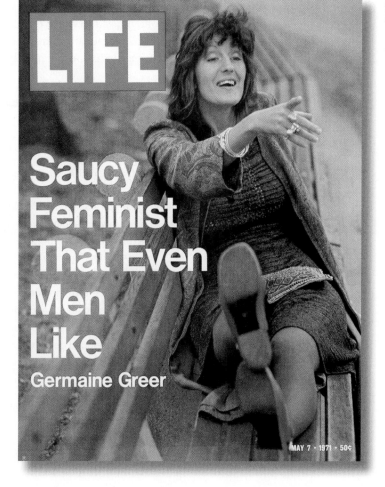

The cover of *Life* magazine features a photograph of Australian-born feminist author and journalist Germaine Greer as she sits on a park bench, accompanied by the headline 'Saucy Feminist That Even Men Like'.

Stories about women have a different tone, typically. In Canada, stories about the two most recent Governors General—Adrienne Clarkson and Michaëlle Jean—have focused on these women's style, glamour, and exoticism, while at the same time, hinting at their inexperience and inappropriateness for the role. Few, if any, male Governors General, however inept, have been treated so dismissively. Whatever the merits of these particular criticisms, and generally they are unwarranted, they remind us of a long-standing historical tendency to treat women less seriously and with less respect than men.

The continued gendering of media depiction has an effect on society. One of the oldest findings in social science is that people imitate others to gain vicarious (that is, second-hand) rewards. Certain kinds of people are more likely to be imitated than others: especially, those who are seen by audience members as similar to themselves, or those who are portrayed as powerful and important. Attractive, well-known, or admired figures in advertisements, who seem to speak directly to the viewer, are most likely to influence behaviour. We look up to these people, so we are inclined to copy their appearance and behaviour.

In short, media representations of men and women tend to reproduce conventional stereotypes and prejudices. They do so mainly by dramatizing the differences between popular conceptions of masculinity and femininity, and often as well by objectifying women as sexual commodities.

The theoretical framework that addresses this issue most carefully is feminism. Some feminists believe that women's subordination can be reduced—and gender equality can be achieved—in part through less stereotypical and more positive representation of women. Others believe that no real change is possible without a radical reorganization of society, so that women make advances in other areas of society, not only in their media depiction. And recently, feminist researchers have emphasized a comprehensive view of intersecting social inequalities, focusing not only on gender but also on the ways ethnicity, race, region, and sexual orientation shape people's experiences.

alternative media
Channels of communication used by subordinate groups to promote their own messages and points of view.

Sometimes, **alternative media** provide an outlet for these progressive views, advancing the interests of disadvantaged groups, and promoting efforts at social change. Alternative media are potentially important. Without the media depiction of the voices

One World, Many Societies

BOX **14.2**

Equal Gender Portrayal in the Media around the World

On 10 November, 2009, the Global Media Monitoring Project (GMMP) spanned the globe, as volunteers 'from Argentina to Zimbabwe, Bangladesh to Yemen, Barbados to the Solomon Islands and Australia to Canada' analyzed all forms of news reporting—thousands of stories in national newspapers, on television, radio, and the Internet—to find out how the media apportions coverage of men and women. It aims to uncover how everyday journalistic practice reinforces common perceptions of gender, and to find examples of stories that broke through the stereotypes and presented women in a fair and balanced way.

The GMMP 'is the largest research and advocacy initiative in the world on gender equality in news and journalism'. It brings together a wide range of people and organizations, from students to media professionals, who want to see 'fair and balanced gender portrayal and representation in and through the news'. In 2005, the GMMP study found that women appeared in only 21 per cent of stories, and only 10 per cent of stories were centred on women. In the 2009 survey, women appeared in 24 per cent of stories, while 16 per cent of stories focused on women.

Source: Adapted from WACC (2009, 2010).

of disadvantaged people, Canada would stop improving as a nation. Alternative media present us with true and critical understandings of the way the world is organized. They also shape the assumptions we hold about men and women, different classes, races, ethnicities, geographical regions, sexual orientations, and so on, and in this way influencing our everyday lives.

They also remind us that there are many types of people, with different interests, strengths, and weaknesses. This reminder serves to increase our understanding of reality and tolerance for diversity. However, since major corporations dominate the news, there are significant limits to the role that alternative media can play—at present.

Homogenization and Niche Marketing

Though society comprises a wide variety of people, with widely varying interests and characteristics, the mainstream media often treat the 'mass' audience as ill-defined and its members indistinguishable from one another. In the interests of making the largest possible profit, the media often play to the lowest common denominator when selecting messages to communicate to the public. By design, the mass media bring everyone down to the same intellectual level (Reinhold, 2006). The mass media—and especially television—are, as Newton Minow remarked in the 1950s, a vast wasteland. In fact, they are a wasteland with homogenizing, levelling effects.

This simplifying assumption encourages the media to approach us viscerally, at the animal or chemical level. Over 40 years ago, well-known Canadian scholar Marshall McLuhan famously stated 'the medium is the message' (McLuhan, 1964). This mystical-sounding epigram means that how people are affected by media depends largely on whether the medium is *printed* (for example, books) or *visual* (for example, television). The impact of television is much more direct and visceral, and more emotionally provocative than print media. When a mass of people receive televised communications, they are all being stimulated—massaged psychologically, if you like—in a similar, often uncritical, yet emotionally arousing way.

However, there are limits to the homogenizing effects of mass media. As noted several times, industrial societies are much more diverse than pre-industrial ones, owing to the division of labour and specialization they entail. According to Durkheim, as we pointed out in an earlier chapter, this fact creates a problem of order and conformity in modern societies. In industrial societies, social differences and inequalities separate people in important ways: by gender, age, race, ethnicity, class, region, nationality, and so on. Broadcasters and advertisers take note of these differences and use them in advertising.

This opportunity for profit through segmentation has led to a vigorous development, in the last few decades, of *niche marketing* by advertisers and broadcasters. It has even led to niche networks, like Spike and W. Today, media messages are targeted to specific demographic groupings. Think of an NFL football game: it is watched mainly by young and middle-aged men. The accompanying sports commentary and advertising strategies are all shaped with this viewing demographic in mind. In fact, *all* media 'products', whether television programs, movies, books, magazines, newspapers, or websites, target particular audiences in a range of specifically designed, artful ways. In recent decades communications technology has been influenced by increasingly sophisticated marketing research. Study after study shows that people from different demographics spend their money differently.

Of course, certain commonalities are visible. Items that were once considered luxuries have now become needs. Today almost everyone has a television, refrigerator, telephone, car, and so on. Only half a century ago most people could not afford these items; then they became commercially available and people began to adopt them. As with all innovations, the adoption pattern followed an S-shape: small numbers of adoptions by the courageous few, then a flood of adoptions, and finally, belated adoption by the cultural stragglers. Soon after buying these consumer items, most households came to value, then to *need* them: to need a second telephone, a second television, cable TV, and a VCR. And since 1980, there has been a rapid surge in the ownership of smoke detectors, clothes dryers, big-screen colour TVs, and DVD players, among other items. And, as these items became more common and their price fell, these goods also crossed the class line from luxury goods (available only to the few) to household necessities, meaning poorer people were also able to obtain them.

In general, however, the poor have less disposable income for luxury goods and leisure, so high-income families still usually own more consumer items than low-income families. People with modest incomes still spend a greater portion of their money on a small variety of goods and services, like food and rent. So, they develop distinctive spending patterns regardless of where they live. Given their lack of money and therefore lack of choice, the poor as a demographic group hold less interest for market researchers, who are more concerned with using communications technology to persuade well-off people to spend their earnings.

How then do the media respond to social diversity, and with what effect? In the influence they wield over consumers, advertisers and market researchers are 'captains of consciousness'. They mould the desires, needs, and intentions of the spending public. Market research aimed at promoting sales has become ever more sophisticated with repeated surveys of buying behaviour and the development of demographic and psychographic models. The focus is on consumer spending patterns by age, income, education, and gender across multiple market sectors. The purpose is to guess who will buy SUVs, frozen pies, Asian-style cooking sauces, vacations in the South Pacific, or Viagra, and through what inducements.

Sociologists have played a (not always glorious) part in market research. For example, to promote household products more effectively, three sociologists helped the publisher of romance magazines uncover the secret fears and desires of working-class wives (Rainwater, Coleman, and Handel, 1962). The researchers advised the publisher to play on women's fears of becoming unattractive, losing their husbands to other women, and losing the love and respect of their children.

The mass media and mass communications today have a less homogenizing effect than in the past. Media products have multiplied (consider the number of television channels available to you, for example.) This is because media products are more diverse, targeting market segments rather than everyone at once. As a result, they play a less integrative role than they once did, and reproduce the social divisions and inequalities that exist in society. This new segmentation reflects a more realistic sales strategy, not a change in the media's goals: to sell products by engaging people's aspirations and fears.

Media, Conflict, and Crime

But just how influential are the media in shaping our aspirations and fears? And do they change our behaviour, or just our ideas and attitudes? If the former, should they be praised for promoting good behaviour and blamed for promoting bad behaviour? Or do the media mainly reflect what is going on in society? We have already explored this question with respect to gendered representations of men and women; and it has also been studied at length in connection with the effects of pornography on sexual attitudes. However, nothing has received more systematic and continued attention than the supposed effect of the media on violence and aggression.

The media often portray people using violence to deal with problems. In this way, they encourage problematic handling of issues, instead of promoting peaceful and co-operative conflict resolution. As well, the mass media play a major role in setting the agenda for a public discussion of current events, and research shows they do so in a narrow, biased, and conflictual fashion. One needs only to turn on Fox News (or CNBC) to see a combative, conservative (or right-wing) portrayal of events in the United States, compared with MSNBC News, whose presentation is much more centrist or liberal, if sometimes equally combative.

Both news shows and dramas depict violence in a variety of forms, including rape, murder, gunplay, fist fights, and so on. Many efforts have been made to evaluate and measure the effect of these depictions on actual behaviour, documenting both the short- and long-term effects of media violence (Huesmann and Taylor, 2006; J.P. Murray, 2008). And experiments have strongly suggested that young people mimic violence shortly after viewing it (Bushman and Huesmann, 2006).

So, generally, researchers agree there is a short-term effect of media violence on behaviour—especially on children's behaviour. However, it has been hard to prove that long-term predispositions to violence result from long-term exposure to violent media. It is true that the media desensitize people to violence (as to pornography) and, in this way, make violent behaviour seem normal and socially acceptable. However, it is still unclear how much this media influence contributes to actual violence, compared with other social factors such as childhood trauma (e.g., parental abuse), chronic poverty and unemployment, or racial discrimination.

Boxer et al. (2009) recently addressed this issue, comparing the influence of media exposure to other potential risk factors. They found that among the many factors predicting the likelihood of violent behaviour, violent media increased the likelihood a person would involve himself in violent activities. It also heightened a person's tendency toward behavioural aggression. However, the decision to engage in violent activities may also reflect previous experiences with violence, in the family home and elsewhere (on this, see also Dodge et al., 2006). In short, it is difficult to disentangle media effects from other social influences, since different kinds of people, with different social backgrounds, expose themselves voluntarily to different kinds of media. People predisposed to violence consume violent media, and vice versa.

There is a lengthy and heated debate on this issue of circularity that goes back nearly 40 years and is summarized briefly on the website Media Awareness Network (Media Awareness Network, n.d.). It shows that a great deal of the research on media effects has been done in laboratories on small children, and as a result is tainted by the limitations of all such research. Cross-national research has presented some evidence that media causes, as well as promotes, real-life violence.

However, this conclusion is questioned in a survey of the literature by Canadian psychologist Jonathan Freedman (2002). He notes, for example, that Japanese television (and comic books) contain some of the most violent images in the world. Compare these with Disney productions to see the difference. Yet, Japan has much lower rates of murder than either Canada or the United States. This reminds us that, whatever the effects of media aggression on our arousal, cultures teach us different ways of dealing with arousal.

This discovery was made in the 1930s infamous studies of the 'frustration–aggression hypothesis', so we should have learned it by now. The original hypothesis proposed that frustration always leads to aggressive behaviour when a person is unable to attain a goal. Usually, the aggression is directed towards the cause of the frustration. When this is not possible, the aggression may be displaced onto another person or object. However, later (cross-cultural research) led to a modification of the original hypothesis. The more current version, based on social learning theory, proposes that frustration (and the resulting arousal) will lead to aggression only if the frustrated individual has been socialized to be aggressive in that kind of situation. And, if you recall from earlier chapters Robert Merton's theory of anomie, it is evident that sociologists recognize a variety of responses or adaptations to frustration, including innovation, ritualism, and rebellion.

Not surprisingly, then, Jonathan Freedman concludes that 'the scientific evidence simply does not show that watching violence either produces violence in people, or desensitizes them to it.'

Media and the Construction of Social Problems

That said, the media play an unquestionable role in 'constructing' the social problems that gain public attention. They make us pay attention to some problems (like street crime) and ignore other problems (like corporate crime), for example. As sociologist Herbert Blumer (1971) has pointed out, social problems develop in stages. The first stage is 'social recognition', the point at which a given condition or behaviour, say, drug abuse, is first identified as a potential social concern. Second, 'social legitimating' takes place. Various social institutions formally recognize that the issue poses a serious threat to social stability or well-being.

The mass media are instrumental in both raising awareness and mobilizing legitimacy for the problem, certifying that it is real. A clear example of this process is provided by the media coverage of child sexual abuse. During the 1990s, the media warned of an increase in sex offences against children. Media accounts were rife with images of sex offenders, portraying them as recidivists whose compulsive behaviour often turned violent. Yet this 'crime wave' of sexual offences was imaginary. Law enforcement data show that sex crimes against children remained stable over this period and sex crimes against adults even declined. The media coverage was part of a socially constructed panic used by policy makers to promote sex offending as a menacing social problem worthy of costly and sweeping legislation.

The most widespread, institutionalized abuse of children has been by celibate priests, and the media have largely co-operated with the Catholic Church to ignore or downplay this in favour of less politically dangerous versions of child abuse. So, for example, in 2009, a five-year investigation into sexual allegations in Cornwall, Ontario, found little objective evidence supporting the claims and accusations that police, clergy, and other leading citizens of the town had engaged in child abuse and pornography. Nonetheless, these allegations made the news, without consequence.

In a certain sense, all social problems are socially created, or 'constructed'. No problem, no matter how important, gains widespread attention and concern without social construction—the active promotion of public interest by moral entrepreneurs with access to the media. Even the most disastrous and widely obvious acts—genocidal mass murder—need reporting before we do anything about them.

This means we cannot assume that 'facts speak for themselves'. Many 'facts' in the media—for example, the 'facts' about child sexual abuse—are half-truths and distortions. Many other facts never come to our attention or are hidden for decades—again, take the example of widespread child abuse in the Roman Catholic Church (including its homes and orphanages). By contrast, bringing issues to public attention is key to the social construction of social problems and often includes the use of victim imagery, constructing horror stories, disseminating claims and accounts, and mobilizing support from public officials and private interest groups.

No one has been more creative in studying this process of information distortion than French social philosopher Jean Baudrillard, who is often hard to understand but always stimulating.

People Are Talking About . . .
JEAN BAUDRILLARD

Jean Baudrillard was born in Reims, France in 1929. He studied German at the Sorbonne University in Paris. In 1972, having finished his graduate education, he began teaching Sociology at the Université de Paris X Nanterre as a professor. From 1986 to 1990, Baudrillard was Scientific Director at the Institut de Recherche et d'Information Socio-Économique at the

Université de Paris. Between 2001 and 2007, when he died, he was a professor of philosophy of culture and media criticism at the European Graduate School in Switzerland.

Baudrillard is well-known for his work on hyperreality. He paid particular attention to Americans' construction of hyperreality—a timeless, perfect fantasy world that they believe to be real, but where nothing is authentic. Within this world, they do not experience life, but only watch performances, and are controlled by illusions.

The first Gulf War, in 1990–91, illustrates Baudrillard's use of the concept of hyperreality. Before the war began, he said that there would be no war. After the battles ceased and the American-led forces claimed that they had successfully repelled the Iraqi invasion of Kuwait, Baudrillard continued to assert that no war had taken place. He said that the war coverage people had watched on their televisions was an illusion, like a video game. Thus, the 'television war', which was how most people perceived it, was not real.

Baudrillard also engaged with Marx's concept of commodity fetishism, interested in how it relates to the fantasy aspects of consumerism. According to Marx, *commodity fetishism* arises out of the growth of commercial trade (especially) in capitalist societies, where social relationships between people come to be expressed as and transformed into objectified relationships between things (i.e., commodities and money). In short, people are dehumanized, and things assume unwarranted importance. This process tends to mystify human relations by turning things, and even people, into symbols—objects—that represent something else. Many economic phenomena—including money, consumer products, and social positions—are said to be 'fetishized' when they attain an independent power vis-a-vis ordinary people.

Even those most sympathetic to Baudrillard's approach criticize his work, finding his writing style exaggerated, sometimes chaotic, and often lacking systematic analysis. Baudrillard examined such things as televised imagery as though their importance was self-evident, and without regard for the significance of other aspects of society. In this way, he leaves himself open to Marxist critics who question the role of material factors in his analysis. Finally, he ignores contradictory evidence such as the fact that the first Gulf War *did* happen.

In his biography, William Merrin (in Scott, 2006: 17) remarks that 'His anti-empiricism, extreme and subjective analyses, his debt to radical sociological traditions and avant-garde and marginal theory . . . are problematic for sociology. So too is his methodology . . . employing an escalating 'speculation to the death'.

Nonetheless, Baudrillard is valuable in calling to our attention the way hyperreality pervades the media, and the way liberalism and Marxism have both ceased to function as overarching narratives. These processes, jointly, support and hasten the collapse of truth and rationality as relevant principles of social action. People have ceased to act either as citizens to protect their freedoms, or as proletarians yearning for the revolution. They are merely fact-consumers, and therefore the prey of 'media-fantasists'.

Source: Adapted from *Fifty Key Sociologists: The Contemporary Theorists* (edited by John Scott, London: Routledge, 2006) and other sources.

Gauthier (2009) has commemorated Baudrillard by saying that, in the thought of Jean Baudrillard, we find a seductive defiance of perception—a game played with reality—that reaches heights seldom seen before in the history of thought. The author characterizes Baudrillard's thought as a path that typifies the vigilance of the humanist thinker. It reveals the continuing struggle between the rational thinker and contemporary cultural phenomena such as consumerism, the virtual, simulation, and terrorism.

This means, in practice, rethinking every single one of our ideas, methods, and taken-for-granted assumptions. Following Baudrillard's own reasoning, Sefat and Kelly (2009) argue that nation-states, which are commonly considered to be sovereign, may not exist as such. Sefat and Kelly model this argument on Baudrillard's claim that the first Gulf War, between UN forces, led by the United States, and Iraq in 1990–91, did not take place. Baudrillard reasoned that the definition of 'war' must include the possibility of defeat for both sides. The sheer military power of the US meant that the outcome was never in doubt; thus, there was no war. Baudrillard suggests other terms such as 'domination', 'abuse', or 'discipline' to describe the event. Likewise, without a clear notion of sovereignty, sovereign nation-states may not be real.

In large part, the media are the main source and purveyor of this hyperreal fantasy world. Nowhere is this more evident than in the Western portrayals of Islam around 9/11, and the wars in Iraq and Afghanistan. Staples (2009) notes the polarization of America and Islam has been framed by the mass media in a way that stresses the symbolism of the 9/11 attacks and overlooks the global role of US power. Following Baudrillard's work on the 'binary of the Other', Staples draws on 'alternative theories of news coverage and media practice', showing how it contributes to America's 'culture of terror', justifying retaliation and further globalization by the American state.

Walters and Kop (2009) note that digital technology is not only transforming the world, it is revolutionizing people's inner lives as well as their social interactions. The authors compare digital technology's transformative effect to that of the printing press, noting, however, that the digital age is postmodern, as described by Baudrillard and others. Thus, the digital revolution is qualitatively different from the transformation brought by printing and described by McLuhan in his 1962 book, *The Gutenberg Galaxy: The Making of Typographic Man*.

The cultural impact of this new technology is enormous, and we should not underestimate the outcomes for education, including universities. Even meaning, process, and teacher–student relationships will be changed, because we are now bombarded by too much information and too much uncertainty about the meaning of this information.

Around this theme, Torikian (2009) asserts that 'postmodernism' is a dangerous philosophy because it questions whether there can (ever) be objective reality. What he considers the 'appalling' notion of hyperreality replaces the 'real world' with individually constructed illusions of reality, representing an attempt by postmodernist thinkers to discover 'the truth behind the truth'. But Torikian claims that reality must, finally, be derived from the world we perceive around us through our physical senses. The notion of hyperreality suggests that our sense perceptions need not depend on that object's inherent characteristics—that 'things are not what they seem'. (Thus, the Gulf War never happened!)

Kellner (2006) notes that events following the 11 September 2001 terrorist bombings not only revived social theorist Jean Baudrillard's interest in world events, but showed the continued relevancy of his interpretive power and analytic categories. Before 9/11, Baudrillard viewed world history as made up of 'weak events' and boring politics. After 9/11, he viewed terrorism as a sign that, with globalization and the 'war on terror', the world has entered a new world war defined by globalization's war with itself.

It is this 'war', viewed through the lens of Baudrillard's earlier theorizing, that we can understand the postmodern condition as replacing reality and truth with illusion and appearance. Thus, politics becomes nothing more than a struggle to broadcast the most compelling images and theories about present-day political and cultural 'realities'. Baudrillard's idea of 'immanent reversal' captures the process by which media images, originally intended to triumphantly present US military success and power, instead became powerful global symbols of defeat because they gave evidence of US brutality and arrogance.

In short, Baudrillard's attachment to the notion of 'hyperreality' forefronts the central problem of postmodernism, by questioning the status of 'reality' that comes to us through our senses. But how can we make sense of reality, then? (And what, in this context is to be the role of formal education?) Baudrillard is viewed as having made culture self-referential by treating 'signs' and symbols as realities in their own right, regardless of material reality (Campbell, 2008). Absolute truth, from this standpoint, is nonexistent (or at least, unknowable); and we need to consider the possibility that images are forms of resistance, not depictions of reality.

Given this conundrum about the 'reality of reality', no wonder that Rennett (2009) calls the term 'reality television' a euphemism—these programs don't show 'real life' at all. A producer begins with a story in mind, and manipulates the taping and editing of the show accordingly—for example, to create staged, rather than 'real', scenes, or to exaggerate characters' traits. So Rennett poses the question, 'If reality television does not present reality, as it claims to do, then what is it actually showing?' He quotes Baudrillard: 'reality television [gives] the illusion of a real world, an exterior world, despite the fact that each world is the exact image of the other' (Baudrillard, 2005:181).

Rennet finds that Baudrillard sees in reality TV a pretend world and a form of hyper-reality, like Disneyland. These illusions of the real world are so powerful that they can 'erase the original'. They create a normative reality for viewers just as Barbie dolls create a normative reality for little girls.

Thus, a review of recent writings finds continued application of the work by Jean Baudrillard—over 200 journal articles applying Baudrillard's work in the last 10 years. Clearly, sociologists are talking about Jean Baudrillard. Baudrillard, despite his complexity and teeming conflation of reality, unreality, and hyperreality, deserves a place in our comprehensive, fusion approach to sociology precisely because he is so disorienting and fractious. He forces us to stare unsympathetically at the patriotic weeping, the taken-for-granted, and the fakery and cheap magic, that pass for modern politics, diplomacy, and entertainment. Seemingly a joker, Baudrillard is in deadly earnest in his demand for truth, and even for Truth—however slippery that notion may be.

As the arch-empiricist Émile Durkheim might have said about Baudrillard's hyper-real sociology, parroting Dorothy in *The Wizard of Oz*, 'I've a feeling we're not in Kansas any more.'

New Insights

Like Baudrillard, Gane (2005) asserts that media technologies have become the foundation of human life. From a social viewpoint, they are the structure upon which news, propaganda, and material culture are built, and control all areas of our lives: work, politics, family, and consumption.

That said, this approach leads to new problems that become apparent when we start to question the reality (or materiality) of media themselves. Assessing the complex influence of media technology becomes extra complicated when we can't agree that reality exists outside of the media. According to Kittler, the five key figures in media research—information theorists Claude Shannon and Warren Weaver, media analyst Marshall McLuhan, psychoanalytic theorist Jacques Lacan, and postmodern sociologist Michel Foucault—all question the materiality of information technology and lead us toward a post-human, post-modern approach to media analysis.

Still, not all researchers agree on this. Rabot (2007), imagining that media still make a difference, argues against the trivialization of media imagery, noting the need to recognize their potential for deep social importance. New technologies arguably can help draw people together around images that will recreate emotional and social bonds, and aid in the 'remythologization' of society. Even alternative media, including print, online, and broadcast forms, have an important part to play in this process. To this end, Fuchs and Sandoval (2008) look at how these media relate to critical theory, believing that Marxist analysis gives the clearest understanding of these media, in providing anti-capitalist discourse.

According to Fuchs and Sandoval, these alternative media critique globalized capitalism not only through their content, but also through their organization, political and social actions, journalistic methods, financing and ownership, production, and distribution, as well as how they are received by their readers and viewers. Alternative media exemplify the 'prosumer' concept: by making people both producers and consumers, they reduce repression and increase emancipation in the process of information production.

The theoretical lines are clearly drawn in this area: postmodernists argue that reality is imaginary and the media imagine a public reality, in the form of a 'hyperreality'. The Marxist-inspired critical theorists, however, believe that reality is real and the media manipulate it, in the interests of the powerful. Thus, critical theorist Ortiz-Negron (2008) argues that the traditional lines between government, business, and media have become blurred, looking at the situation in Puerto Rico as an example. Media, especially television, influence politics and the workings of government, sometimes in direct co-operation with the state, by publicizing various social problems. Thus business and media take on some of the functions traditionally fulfilled by the state, and the state, driven by and reliant on business, uses the mass media to obscure its actual workings.

Berardi (2006) notes that over the last 15 years, Italy (like Puerto Rico) has submitted to an advanced form of control he calls 'semi-capitalism'. In this system, a government-controlled conglomerate incorporating financial, media, and cultural interests imposes 'repressive conformism' on an unwitting public, impeding democracy. However, independent media companies are working to counter the effects of this repressive organization.

In recent decades, the media have also formed new alliances with religion. Martelli (2005; Martelli and Cappello, 2005) notes that recently, two religious events have received exceptional coverage from the global media system: the funeral of Pope John Paul II and the World Youth Day. Martelli argues that currently, television favours postmodern religious expression, which has a mystical, collective flavour, in contrast to the modern ascetic, individualistic faith. He sees that not only advantages, but also risks, may accompany the Catholic Church's wider visibility through television. As we saw in the previous chapter, postmodernity brings about 'de-secularization', which erases the modern dichotomy between private faith and public life. The new media portrayals of religion help to integrate a new, more spectacular concept of religion into present-day social life.

From this point of view, the Jubilee 2000 appears as a media event typical of the global media society, which spreads religion throughout the world but does so within the limits of media (and especially television) formats.

Lyon (2006) notes a similar religious reawakening among Protestants, making use of modern media. A movement, variously called postmodern, alternative, and emerging, has been evolving over the past two decades in North America and Europe. With younger members and an urban focus, they can be seen as occupying 'social niches'. They tend to approach Christianity in non-traditional ways—informal, lively, flexible worship with rock music—albeit with an evangelical, or 'post-evangelical', perspective, and in keeping with fairly traditional doctrine and practice. And as young urban-dwellers, they make good use of the media they are familiar with: television, the Internet, cellphones, and so on. This media use, as well as their lifestyles and fashions, tend to be what sets them apart from the traditional churches. These individual congregations maintain connections with each other, as well as with the wider Christian world, through websites and blogs.

Finally, Lau (2004), contrary to Gans's earlier findings, argues that news reporting is influenced not only by outside forces, such as network ownership and relations with government and business, but also by internal forces, such as the actions and choices of journalists themselves. If TV news is to be seen as conveying reality, journalists' perspectives on values, and their professional practices, need to be considered critically and realistically. From this standpoint, the evening news is like a work of art—like Da Vinci's painting of the Mona Lisa, for example, though intentionally less enigmatic. It is not (necessarily) a picture of reality.

Chapter Summary

We have seen that the mass media play an important, though not always positive, role in our society. The media have a homogenizing effect on society; however, this effect is limited by other factors, especially by the increasing diversity of the media and the segmentation of consumer markets.

The messages and viewpoints mass media communicate are not always clear, and so we often fail to detect biases in the media. Sometimes this leads to disastrous consequences. Often, the public is misinformed when it comes to important political, social, and economic issues. Moral panics, for example, do not lead to good decision-making.

We must also remember that control over the media and its content is far from equal. In accordance with society's dominant ideology, the mass media are generally used to portray an inaccurate, and often negative, image of various groups in society, including women and minorities.

Though some media content is direct—hammering us over the head with blatant moral and commercial messages—some media portrayal is implicit, as in television talk shows. There, we learn the current standards of behaviour—what ordinary people consider deviant and normal, praiseworthy and shocking—as members of the viewing audience. Here, the program hosts are moral entrepreneurs and claims-makers; the studio audience (and home audience) serves as a court of public opinion.

We also discussed the various types of media ownership, and the impact they have on media content. In general, the media 'show what sells'. This has often meant that many Canadian media outlets prefer to import American content rather than show Canadian productions. Media ownership also affects the accuracy and objectivity of media content, since the content is likely to reflect the interests of media owners and producers.

The bottom line: in interacting with the mass media daily, we must be wary of these issues, remaining mindful of the many important dimensions of media form and message. The new media, in this context, offer new sources of information and new risks of self-delusion.

Critical Thinking Questions

1. What is the advantage of niche marketing for advertisers and broadcasters?
2. What insights on the mass media are offered by feminist sociologists? By postmodern sociologists?
3. What is the relationship between the media and politics? Do the media increase political awareness and participation, or not?
4. What is your opinion on CanCon regulations? Does it matter how much Canadian content we consume through the mass media?
5. Briefly research both a public and a private media corporation in Canada. What are the differences and similarities between the two? What are their roles in Canadian society?
6. Do you think older forms of media will lose relevance and cease to exist entirely? Collect some evidence that illustrates the decline of old media (e.g., book publishing, newspaper circulation) and the rise of new media (e.g., website hits).

Recommended Readings

Augie Fleras and Jean Lock Kunz, *Media and Minorities: Representing Diversity in a Multicultural Canada* (Toronto: Thompson Educational, 2001). This book discusses the role of mainstream media in hampering Canada's perception of multiculturalism. By promoting the dominant ideology of society and defining what is socially acceptable and desirable, it excludes many subordinate groups.

David Taras, *Power and Betrayal in the Canadian Media*, updated edn (Peterborough, ON: Broadview Press, 2001). Taras points out challenges to the Canadian media industry, including budget cuts, technological change, and ownership concentration. This book argues that these occurrences will narrow the Canadians' access to diverse and good quality information and limit our capacity to communicate with others through a vast network.

Paul Levinson, *Digital McLuhan: A Guide to the Information Millennium* (London, New York: Routledge, 1999). Marshall McLuhan was a Canadian forerunner on the subject of media in the twentieth century. He did not live to see the rise and spread of the Internet and its deep impact on societies around the world. Yet in this work, the author shows that many of McLuhan's ideas about earlier forms of media are still highly applicable in the digital age.

Jonathan Freedman, *Media Violence and Its Effect on Aggression: Assessing the Scientific Evidence* (Toronto: University of Toronto Press, 2002). Writing on a highly debated topic, Freedman disagrees with the assumption that violence has an adverse impact on children. However, he does believe that advertising has a negative impact on viewers. He considers media effects in relation to other factors with an impact on violent behaviour, such as poverty and first-hand exposure.

Elihu Katz and Paul F. Lazarsfeld, foreword by Elmo Roper, *Personal Influence: The Part Played by People in the Flow of Mass Communications* (Glencoe, IL: Free Press, 1964 [1955]). In this classic and influential work the authors put forth the idea that media messages are mediated by informal 'opinion leaders' who interpret messages and spread them as they have understood them in their informal networks.

Websites

Media Awareness Network (MNet)
www.media-awareness.ca

Canadian Broadcasting Corporation/Société Radio-Canada (CBC/SRC)
www.cbc.radio-canada.ca

National Film Board of Canada (NFB)
www.nfb.ca

Canadian Radio-television and Telecommunications Commission (CRTC)
www.crtc.gc.ca

Internet World Stats
www.Internetworldstats.com

Marshall McLuhan
www.marshallmcluhan.com

Canadian Newspaper Association (CNA)
www.cna-acj.ca

Independent Media Center (IMC)
www.indymedia.org

15 Politics and Ideologies

Learning Objectives

In this chapter, you will:

> Understand the nature of politics from a sociological perspective

> See how power is distributed in different societies

> Review and evaluate competing perspectives on democratic societies

> Discover how politics can be both an integrative and a disintegrative force

Chapter Outline

We can find politics in every aspect of social life, from personal interactions to the government of nations. This chapter is concerned with the nature of politics, the distribution of power in society, and the role of ideology in politics.

People often confuse political sociology with political science. It is true that both disciplines study politics, exploring ideas like power and authority. However, they differ in their approach. Sociologists are especially interested in studying how political power is converted into authority, for example. So, in this chapter, we will discuss different kinds of authority and the ways people obtain and hold these different kinds of authority.

The state is the chief actor in national politics, using its resources and power to control people's behaviours. Thus, it is important for sociologists to understand the nature of the state and its significance for the study of politics. As we will see in this chapter, there are different types of states around the world; for example, the Canadian state is a liberal democratic state. We will discuss several theoretical approaches towards democratic states, noting how they hold different views about the nature of democracy.

This chapter will also examine whether politics is an integrative or a disintegrative force in society. To do so, we will consider the role of ideology and its impact on people's lives.

Everyday Observations

Where do you set your standard? Elena is disillusioned with the Canadian political system. A student of environmental issues at university, she wants to vote for the Green Party, but she is sure the Green Party will lose out to the Conservatives, the Liberals, and the NDP. Even if tens of thousands of people voted for the Green Party, they might not get any seats, let alone form a government. In fact, even the big parties haven't been able to gain a majority of votes (or seats) in the last few elections. So Elena thinks the common person has little or no say in political issues. Her father, on the other hand, lived in Russia under the rule of Stalin for many years, and he thinks Canada has one of the best political systems in the world. He scolds Elena for refusing to vote, and calls her ungrateful. Do you agree?

politics

The processes by which individuals and groups act to promote their interests.

citizens

People who belong to a state. Citizenship developed out of the relative freedom of city life, granting equal treatment for all residents.

state

The set of institutions with authority to make the rules that govern a society. Weber wrote that the state 'claims a monopoly of the legitimate use of physical force within a given territory'.

By October of 2009, Canadians had experienced three elections within a span of five years. These elections cost hundreds of millions of dollars, paid for by the taxpayers. Besides the financial burden, there was a psychic cost: **politics** in the last few years have been aimed at dividing Canadians rather than bringing them together. This is obvious in the advertisements political parties use to characterize and attack their opponents. TV advertisements regularly highlight the other party's faults rather than making the public aware of a political platform. As a result, confidence in all the major parties is low, voter turnout is low, and people lack interest in the various party leaders.

To some Canadians, like Elena, the present-day political climate is disappointing. Many feel politicians are wasting Canadians' time and money. Such discontent is understandable. The question is, what can politicians do to win back the trust of **citizens**? Beyond that, how can Canadians regain some interest in the **state**—the institutional mechanism that collects and spends their taxes, makes their laws, and ultimately controls their lives?

Remembering his experiences in the former Soviet Union, Elena's father Boris feels fortunate to live in Canada. Despite all the challenges of immigration, Boris and his family enjoy freedom of speech and the legal right to vote any way they like—characteristics of a democratic government. Even so, Elena is convinced that these 'freedoms' are superficial. She believes that certain people and certain institutions ensure the state will always serve the interests of the ruling class. Is this belief justified?

By contrast, Boris thinks Canada provides equal opportunities for everyone. Having lived under an oppressive government in his youth, he feels he can now act and think freely in Canada. The Canadian government forces no ideology on him; Boris feels confident that his rights and liberties are protected by Canadian law. He can publicly criticize the government and still be treated with respect. In fact, it is illegal in Canada to discriminate against someone for their political views.

Is Boris right? Does the law in Canada protect everyone equally? And does a dominant ideology still exist in Canada, reinforced through laws and advertising? Though Canada may be better than Stalinist (or even post-Stalinist) Russia, Elena thinks there is still room for improvement. For example, in Canada there could be more women and minority-group politicians. And, do poor people ever get a say in Canadian politics? There are over 30 million people living in Canada today, yet most major political figure are drawn from the middle- and upper-middle classes. What implication does this have for our society and our political system?

Ways of Looking at . . .
POLITICS

Over the history of sociology, sociologists have analyzed politics in a variety of ways, and as usual we can put them into different categories: macrosociological versus microsociological, and functionalist versus critical theory. These differences can be illustrated with examples from classical sociology: Barrington Moore, Talcott Parsons, Seymour Martin Lipset, and George Homans.

As the leading functionalist of the mid twentieth century, Talcott Parsons, in his book *The Social System* (1964 [1951]), focused on politics as a key process in different kinds of social systems that include families, small groups, large organizations, empires, and so on. Parsons argues that all these social systems have a political process, which he labels the *goal attainment function*. This political function, or role, is necessary for the survival of the system. It is not imposed and it is not sinister. The political structure (or subsystem) is not so much committed to control and oppression (as in Marxist visions of the state) as it is to management, administration, and the promotion of citizen engagement. As its name suggests, the political system expresses and strives to achieve collective goals through debate and concerted action. Parsons assumes that people in the society usually consent to this political process and its leaders.

Parsons's approach may be criticized for being more philosophical and anecdotal than historical, and more qualitative than quantitative. However, it draws on a wide variety of evidence generally known to his readers, and its value lies in the synthesis it provides. Most important, it gives us a picture or metaphor of the political system: politics as social management. We need to view it as a provocative exploration of ideas and concepts, and underlying this exploration is the idea that politics is everywhere, and is not confined to the state.

We are more familiar with another type of political analysis based on quantitative data from political and public opinion polling. This kind of analysis is evident in American political sociologist Seymour Martin Lipset's classic work, *Political Man*. Here Lipset deals with central functionalist questions like 'What social conditions and social processes promote democracy?' This is not far from the kind of question that Parsons might ask: Under what conditions might a goal-attainment system function democratically?

Likewise, we can see similarities in the work of present-day Canadian pollster and social critic, Michael Adams of Environics—a public opinion polling firm. Adams is well known for his many books of political commentary and analysis, including *Sex in the Snow*, *Fire and Ice*, and *American Backlash*. Like Lipset, Adams wants to connect political ideas to historical events and cultural values. Like Lipset, Adams believes that clusters of demographic and psychographic (or value) features will shape the political functioning of a society. Thus, a society's politics is deeply rooted in people's beliefs and needs, as well as in their histories. Finally, like Lipset, Adams believes in the value of public awareness and public engagement in the political process.

George Homans is a type of functionalist who focuses more on the microstructure of politics, as seen in his classic work *The Human Group* (1950). In this book, Homans develops his so-called *social exchange theory*. Homans draws his data from a variety of case studies to show that small groups mainly rule themselves through processes of informal control, which we might label 'small-group politics'. They include ridiculing or excluding people who violate the group's productivity norms—those who for example, produce much more or much less than they should. Homans, like Parsons, was a functionalist, which means he too believed that groups develop and protect stable patterns. However, unlike Parsons, Homans looked for the payoff—the practical reasons people value such 'self-government' in groups. And because Homans is interested in studying the micropolitics of small groups, we could compare him fruitfully to symbolic interactionist Erving

Goffman, who in various classic works (for example, *Asylums* [1961]) does the same without drawing inferences about equilibrium.

However, most of the work we will discuss in this chapter grows out of the critical theory of sociology. A classic example of this is Barrington Moore's *Social Origins of Dictatorship and Democracy: Lord and Peasant in the Making of the Modern World* (1966), which we will discuss at length later in the chapter. Here, Moore analyzes class relations and their effects on politics—working to some extent in the traditions laid out by Marx and Weber. Moore shows that during the process of modernization, it matters whether the dominant class in society is the middle class, the peasant class, or the traditional ruling class (the landowning aristocracy, supported by military and the Church). The first scenario leads to what we know as democracy, the second to communism, and the third to fascism. Moore's theory, based on a close historical analysis of eight different societies, is important for our understanding of modernization; and it shows how politics grow out of class relations.

Classic Studies
The First New Nation

What makes Canadian society different from other societies, and what role did politics play in creating this difference? This question is largely answered in a classic sociological work, *The First New Nation*, by Seymour Martin Lipset (1967). Ironically, Lipset's real goal in that book was to answer the mirror-question: What makes American society different from other societies—indeed, exceptional—and what role did politics play in creating *that* difference?

Even before writing *The First New Nation,* Lipset was widely known in Canada for his comparative study of the politics of Saskatchewan and North Dakota. In his book *Agrarian Socialism* (1950), he discusses the rise of the NDP in Saskatchewan and tries to explain why North Dakota, next-door to Saskatchewan, did not also develop a socialist movement. In *The First New Nation*, Lipset continues his Canada–US comparison, examining the historical transformation of the United States from a British colony to an independent country.

To discover the reasons for American 'exceptionalism' or uniqueness, Lipset compares the United States to three other developed nations—Canada, Australia, and the UK—that are similarly rooted in English political (and cultural) history. He identifies several key features that made the US different from the others and made it the country that it is today. These features include a revolutionary war and a commitment to two somewhat conflicting values: equality and achievement.

Throughout its history, the US has struggled to balance these two contradictory 'American values'. For Lipset, both values are grounded in the American identity and in national development; both are the basis for such institutions as the American family, school, political party, and trade union. In a sense, both values were born in the American Revolution, which determined to set America free of England's control.

The American Revolution came to symbolize the birth of a new nation—in fact, the world's 'first new nation'. In the social and economic changes that followed, religion and the labour movement both played important roles. Religious fervour and the quest for religious independence stimulated a concern with morality, making the US a very religious country. The trade and labour union movements stimulated class consciousness and the drive for equal opportunity.

Lipset finds likenesses but also differences between the US and other developed nations that reflect important value differences. He notes, for example, that the British and, to a lesser extent the Canadians, put less emphasis on equality of opportunity because of their more elitist values, which Lipset observes in a variety of institutions. By contrast, Australia is more egalitarian and treats 'achievement' more like the US does; but because it never had a revolution, Australia is somewhat less politically populist than the US.

In this analysis, Canada is portrayed as a nation caught somewhere between the US and UK in its central values: more egalitarian than Britain but less so than the US and Australia, and certainly less concerned with achievement and opportunities for achievement than is the US. (As we noted earlier, Canada sociologist John Porter picked up this theme in his own writings, arguing for the need to extend higher education to more Canadians.) Lipset largely explains this difference by reference to the two nations' founding experiences. The US was born in blood, through a revolutionary war against England; then, its union was consolidated in blood through a civil war between the North and South. Canada, by contrast, was founded in peace, largely by pro-English Loyalists fleeing the American Revolution. Canada never had a civil war. In fact, the closest Canada ever came to bloodshed (outside of two world wars) was in the Battle of Quebec, on the Plains of Abraham in 1759; the small rebellions in Upper and Lower Canada in 1837; and the Western Riel uprising in 1885.

By applying sociological techniques to history, Lipset is able to develop an alternative interpretation of the effects of American values and the American Revolution. In this respect, Lipset rooted his study in the humanist tradition of Max Weber, using historical and comparative methods to tease out societal differences. His comparative model incidentally sheds light on the problems and prospects of newly emerging nations in Africa, Asia, and South America and helps us to generalize about evolving nations: hence, the title of the book, which speaks to the present-day concerns of 'new' nations. For example, it leads us to look for systematic differences between nations that had a revolution and those that didn't.

Although Lipset's study is well respected, McCormack criticizes Lipset's conclusions about the elitist emphasis in Canadian development, asserting that Canada may be more 'ascriptive in its status system, more diffuse and more particularistic than the US but no less stable' (McCormack, 1964: 613). We will unpack this claim later in the chapter, when we examine Talcott Parsons's 'pattern variables'. Another critic, Marcus Cunliffe, wonders 'to what extent . . . the American character [was] formed before the Revolution' (Cunliffe, 1959: 181). A third critic specifically wonders how central equality is to American identity, as compared to other values like liberty and freedom.

Regardless of such criticism, Lipset's study remains an influential work, not only for sociologists but also for political scientists and historians. Parsons, a leading American sociologist of the time and colleague at Harvard, noted that Lipset has 'succeeded in notably integrating his materials to present an impressive picture of some of the most important aspects of our (American) society' (Parsons, 1964: 374).

Political Science and Political Sociology

Noting that *The First New Nation* was of interest to both sociologists and political scientists reminds us that it is easy to confuse the sociological study of politics—political sociology—with its close neighbour, political science. We will now take a closer look at why that is, and clarify the distinction between these two fields.

Both fields study the state and both study social policy, for example. But there are some important differences between the two. *Political science* deals mainly with the machinery of government and public administration, and with elections, public opinion polling, pressure groups, and political parties. *Political sociology* is more concerned with the relations between politics, social institutions (for example, families, churches, workplaces, ethnic groups, and social classes), **ideologies**, and culture. As well, sociologists study political processes *within* social institutions, and the ways that **power** is distributed and used in different social relationships.

Political science and political sociology also differ in their methods. Political scientists tend to do more library research, more textual analysis of documents and debates, and more

ideologies

Coherent sets of interrelated beliefs about the nature of the world that imply or demand certain courses of political, social, or economic action.

power

According to Weber, 'the ability of persons or groups to achieve their objectives, even when opposed'. Said another way, power is the capacity to compel people to act in certain ways, and politics is the process by which people gain and exercise this power.

examination of laws, rules, and procedures. Their work is more often philosophical and historical. Sociologists do more survey research, and more often interview people and observe groups. Typically, sociologists are more quantitative and spend more time with living people. This quantitative tendency is not evident in Lipset's *First New Nation*, but it is evident in other of his works—for example, *Political Man*—another classic work of sociology.

Political Authority

authority
Power that is considered legitimate by the people who are subject to it.

Authority is essential to politics, and sociologists are especially interested in the social processes that justify and support authority. Max Weber was the first and most influential sociologist to analyze the workings of authority. He identified three types of authority, distinguished by the reasons those subject to it accept the authority: *traditional authority*, *charismatic authority*, and *rational–legal authority*.

Where *traditional authority* prevails, the power-holder is supported by ancient traditions and can expect obedience as long as he or she upholds these traditions. Often, the ruler holds power through dynastic inheritance; he or she inherits the legitimacy of a parent who also held power. Often, the sovereign's authority is said to descend directly from God. Varying forms of traditional authority were typical in pre-industrial societies, and were the basis of rule by monarchs such as Louis XIV of France, who, with 72 years on the throne, holds the record as the longest-ruling monarch in history. Another example is the rule by tribal chiefs and elders in pre-literate communities. Their power too is based on traditional practice, though the communities may have agreed to accept their right to rule. Traditional authority, for obvious reasons, is most secure when it is based on the belief that a ruler's power is given by God. In that case, challenging the ruler would amount to challenging God.

Unlike traditional authority, *charismatic authority* is based on the power-holder's exceptional qualities—especially, the force of his or her personality. Charisma may derive from

Although no longer a colony of the British Empire, Canada is part of the Commonwealth of Nations, made up primarily of former British colonies or dependents, and of which Queen Elizabeth II is still the head. The Queen has made 22 royal tours to Canada.

In Canada, political parties compete to hold the majority of these seats in the House of Commons. The party with the most seats at the end of a federal election forms the government.

many different characteristics, like charm and presence, and we know it by its effects, not its specific traits. Through charisma, a leader can generate feelings of excitement and anticipation, and mobilize an audience toward some goal. Charismatic leaders may provide solutions to pressing problems and promote new social values. Often, they ask followers to turn their backs on tradition and follow the leader's urging, which may be presented as a revealed truth from God. Though God is invoked here too, charismatic authority is in one sense the opposite of traditional authority: it calls on people to turn their backs on past practices and embrace new ones.

The third and final form of authority is *rational–legal authority*, the most common form of authority in modern societies today. Rational–legal authority is based on formally established rules and procedures. The right to exercise this authority is based on a person's formal position, not on traditional practices or personal magnetism. People expect that, regardless of who fills the particular position of authority, they will be treated in the way specified by the rules.

As we know from Weber's writings on the topic (1978 [1908]), rational–legal authority is also the basis of bureaucratic organization. In bureaucracies, as we saw earlier, people command other people who are designated subordinates, according to specific written rules. To do otherwise—to treat subordinates based on personal preference or whim—is considered unprofessional and improper. As we know from experience, this is an ideal that is sometimes ignored. However, Weber argues that modern states, like modern organizations (i.e., bureaucracies), are based ideally in the rule of law, which distinguishes them from societies (and organizations) that run on tradition, charm, or personal relationships. This change, however idealized, marks a major transition from traditional to modern societies, as we know them today.

Rule of law is the reason that modern states (and the people who govern them) must follow strict rules to secure and preserve public legitimacy. It gives people in authority the legitimate power over life and death in our society: for example, they have the right to call out the military, impose the death penalty, expropriate your home for a highway, and take a portion of your earnings in taxes. If these authority figures lose their legitimacy—for example, are found to be corrupt or incompetent—they can be removed from office (though in practice, this is rarely accomplished.)

The State

By common reckoning, there are three different types of modern states: *authoritarian*, *totalitarian*, and *liberal-democratic*, and it is worth spending a moment to compare them. Doing so gives us a clearer understanding of how the Canadian state, a liberal-democratic state, is different.

Authoritarian states have taken somewhat varying forms over the course of history, but we can make a few generalizations about them. Typically, they forbid public opposition and use force to ensure compliance with the written laws. Often, authoritarian leaders force citizens to display public support of the state, to prove their loyalty. Often, the authoritarian dictator exercises complete control over the country, with the co-operation of the military, the state church, and/or foreign multinational corporations. Sometimes liberal democracies (such as the US state) have propped up such dictatorships, to further their own economic and political interests in less-developed countries. Such actions were especially common throughout the history of South and Central America; however, they were not unknown in Africa and Asia.

Totalitarian states are even more extreme, and often more stable, versions of authoritarian states. The totalitarian state intervenes in both public and private life. For example, the totalitarian state illustrated in George Orwell's classic book *1984*, modelled on the Soviet Union, demands complete loyalty and compliance; it completely controls the distribution of rewards and punishments. (Orwell, who started life in the English middle class and briefly served the British government in Burma, was sympathetic to socialism and fought for the anarchist cause in the Spanish Civil War. Though he remained staunchly progressive throughout life, he came to hate and fear communism, particularly as practised in Joseph Stalin's USSR. His books *1984* and *Animal Farm* reveal his anti-communist sentiments allegorically.)

Nazi Germany under Hitler, and the Soviet Union under Stalin, are often considered the best examples of totalitarian rule. Both used the main cultural institutions (including schools and media) to promote state ideology. Both pried into the personal lives and histories of their citizens and got people to spy on one another. Both killed or exiled their opponents. No one could risk criticizing the ruler or the state, or any policies the ruler supported.

The example of Nazi Germany shows that various social and cultural factors contribute to the rise of a totalitarian society. First, the military, the landed aristocracy, the religious establishment, and the powerful corporations supported Hitler because they feared communist-inspired change far more than they feared fascist-inspired change. Unlike the communists, Hitler's Nazis didn't challenge organized religion or organized capitalism. Gradually, the people came to support Hitler, for several reasons. He promised, and delivered, jobs. He promised, and (briefly) delivered, a revival of national pride after Germany's humiliating loss in World War I. He promised, and delivered, strong government and a suppression of political dissent.

Finally, Hitler had charisma: his dynamic speeches and brilliantly stage-managed Super Bowl–like events tapped into the anger and suffering of ordinary people. He was able to motivate them to unify against their supposed enemies (especially, the Jews) and take extreme actions that included genocide. Lenin and Stalin, though less charismatic, used similar tactics to rule and unify the Soviet Union after the Russian Revolution of 1917.

Point/Counterpoint

BOX **15.1**

China Condemns International Criticism

Governments and human rights observers around the world denounced China's imprisonment of democracy activist Liu Xiaobo on 25 December 2009. Liu was sentenced to 11 years in jail for signing, along with 302 others, a document calling for China to become genuinely democratic. Salman Rushdie, Umberto Eco, and Margaret Atwood are among 300 writers from around the world who have called on China to release Liu. UN Human Rights Commissioner Navi Pillay called the sentence 'extremely harsh', and criticized this 'further severe restriction on the scope of freedom of expression in China'.

Canada's Foreign Affairs minister, Lawrence Cannon, said 'Canada deplores the sentencing of Liu Xiaobo, whom we believe is being punished for exercising his right to peaceful and non-violent freedom of expression'. But China remains defiant and refuses to entertain requests for Liu's release. According to BBC News, China's foreign ministry spokesperson Jiang Yu called the criticisms 'a gross interference of [sic] China's internal affairs'.

Source: Adapted from *Tibetan Review* (2009).

And Mao Zedong, as charismatic as Hitler, also used similar tactics to rule and unify China after the Chinese Revolution of 1949. China's so-called 'cultural revolution' was as wildly destructive in the 1960s as Hitler's rule was during the run-up to war in the 1930s.

Unlike authoritarian and totalitarian states, *liberal-democratic states* are ideally governed by citizens. These states do not monitor every action and belief, nor suppress free speech and assembly. 'Democracy' literally means 'rule by the people', though exactly how rule by the people occurs varies from one democratic society to another. The oldest type of democracy was *direct democracy*, which existed in the ancient Greek city-states—especially Athens. In this direct democracy, all the citizens discussed and voted on all the issues of importance. Clearly, this direct participation by the entire citizenry meant the citizenry had to be small; and indeed, only a small fraction of all the people who lived in Athens, say, were citizens.

During the fourth century BCE, the height of Athenian democracy, there would have been as many as 250,000 to 300,000 people living in Attica—which included Athens and the surrounding area. Of these, most were non-citizens, including resident foreigners, slaves, women, and children—none of whom were permitted to vote. Roughly 30,000 adult male citizens were eligible to vote on civic issues; sometimes the number was slightly higher.

Canada—like other democracies today—is a *representative democracy*, meaning that people express their views periodically when they elect representatives to the federal Parliament or provincial legislature. These representatives meet face-to-face and hammer out policies that they expect the electorate will support. If the electorate is not pleased, the representative can be voted out of power at the next election. Further, Canada is a *constitutional monarchy*, like Britain or Norway, which means our head of state (the Queen) inherited her position for life and is controlled by Parliament. This is in contrast to a *republic* like France or the United States, where the head of state—the president—is elected and replaced periodically.

Methods of voting also vary from one liberal democracy to another. In Canada, the country is divided into *constituencies* or *ridings*, in each of which citizens elect a representative. Each election thus consists of hundreds of mini-elections. The candidate getting the most votes in a constituency is the winner. This is called the 'first-past-the-post' method.

A problem with this method is that it tends to exclude smaller parties from representation in the legislature, even if they gain a substantial number of votes across the country. At worst, in a two-party race where the winner receives 51 per cent of the votes, 49 per cent of the voters are (by definition) unrepresented. In a three-party race where the winner receives (for example) 34 per cent of the vote, 66 per cent of the voters are (by definition) unrepresented.

To solve this problem, some countries (for example Italy, New Zealand, and Israel) use a *proportional representation* system instead. In this system, each party's votes are totalled for the entire country, and candidates are selected from a party list in proportion to the percentage of votes for each party. So if, for example, the Green Party received 10 per cent of the popular vote, it would receive 10 per cent of the seats in the legislature, regardless of whether it won a majority of votes in any one constituency. This method ensures that more parties, and a wider range of political views, are represented in the legislature. Wider representation, in turn, means that minority governments will be common, and governments will generally have to rely on multi-party alliances to gain support for their policies.

Aside from voting periodically, citizens of democratic societies organize interest and lobby groups to advance particular causes (we will talk more about different types of social movements in the next chapter). People vary widely in how politically active they are: how often they vote, whether they contribute money to political campaigns or parties, attend rallies, hand out campaign literature, or otherwise participate in elections. Typically, people's political participation can be predicted sociologically by a specified demographic, social, and psychological variables. For example, formal education is a strong predictor of political participation.

In theory, this electoral system produces a constant competition between groups, parties, and interests. According to the theory of democratic *pluralism*, in a democratic society all

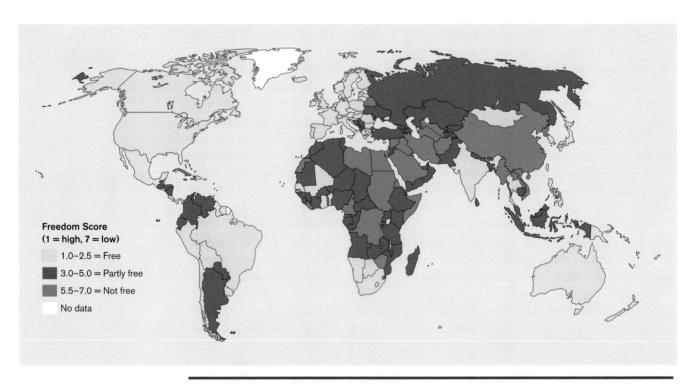

Freedom Score
(1 = high, 7 = low)

- 1.0–2.5 = Free
- 3.0–5.0 = Partly free
- 5.5–7.0 = Not free
- No data

Figure 15.1 Civil and Political Liberties, as measured by the Freedom Score Index, by Country, 2003

Source: Adapted from Freedom House, 2004; Matthews and Mock (2003), Figure 2.

citizens have the chance to voice their views and pursue their interests. The role of the state is to serve as a neutral referee, and supposedly, no one group's interests are favoured all the time. Different social groups promote their own interests, as lobby groups and political parties; as political parties, they compete to gain control of society. Even gaining control of the government doesn't give a permanent, one-sided advantage, because this control is limited by the democratic practice of periodic voting. To continue to rule, the victorious group must keep the public satisfied; thus, they are limited in what they can do. In the long term, no single group or class interest dominates, according to this theory. Democracy is protected by this competition between interests and by the constantly changing challenges society has to face.

In theory, this system is democratic because it allows many people to act politically in a lot of different ways. However, in practice, there are still problems with this system, as some groups enjoy more political influence than others. Specifically, some groups are under-represented in political offices, and some issues of importance to these groups—for example, good-quality subsidized day care, of particular interest to women—are ignored. In Canada, white males of higher socio-economic status remain the key political players in the political system.

Gender and the State

From a feminist point of view, the state is an institution permeated by gender inequality and, as a result, one that continues to subordinate women. According to McIntosh (1978), the state encourages employers to take advantage of women's free services (social reproduction) in the household to maintain low wages in the workplace. Even state policies promote women's subordination, especially when they ignore women's needs and interests (Brodie, 1996). In Canada, for example, the lack of good-quality, subsidized child care prevents many women from working outside the home (Beaujot and Ravanera, 2009). The lack of female representation in Canadian politics is important because it results in a lack of focus on concerns that matter to women more than men.

A leading concern is the significant under-representation of women in positions of political power. In most of Canada, women did not gain the right to vote until 1918, and in Quebec, not until 1940 (Library and Archives Canada, 2008). The year 1929 marked the first time women were declared 'persons' by the federal government and given the right to become members of the Senate.

Today, women make up 22.1 per cent of all members of Parliament (MPs), with 68 women sitting as MPs (Cool, 2008). This is an improvement over the past, but there is undoubtedly room for more equal representation. Many researchers have noted an unfortunate pattern in the political representation of women: the more powerful the political position, the less likely it is that a woman will occupy it (Bashevkin, 1985). So far, there has only been one female prime minister in Canada—Kim Campbell—and her time in office was brief. The major exception to this pattern is the office of Governor General, the highest position in Canadian politics, representing the Queen, which has been held by three women: Jeanne Sauvé (1984–1990), Adrienne Clarkson (1999–2005), and Michaëlle Jean (2005–2010).

Political scientist Sylvia Bashevkin (2009) argues that Canadians seem to be uncomfortable with the idea of putting a woman in a position of political power. This may be one reason why the media tend to treat women politicians less respectfully than men; or, perhaps, our discomfort is a result of this media treatment. Things can be done to change this. Bashevkin notes, for example, that where voter turnout is high, or where proportional representation is practised, more women are elected to office. Therefore, we might achieve a higher fraction of women politicians by promoting voter turnout (for example, through mandatory voting) and implementing proportional representation.

In the Canadian federal elections of 2008, of the five party leaders, only Elizabeth May was a woman.

Women's lack of participation in politics is not the result of their choice not to participate. Rather, structural and social barriers limit their efforts to follow a political career, as well as other duties, such as those related to family, that otherwise occupy their time and energy. According to Equal Voice, a non-profit organization which promotes the election of women in Canadian politics, women are less likely than men to enter politics, for various reasons. Chiefly, they suffer from financial constraints, limited access to helpful informal networks, and opposition within political party networks to their membership, which is both subtle and direct. At the same time, Equal Voice reports that according to various polls, most Canadians want more women in politics (Equal Voice, 2006b).

Compared with the rest of the developed world, Canada is significantly behind in the proportion of female politicians. Table 15.1 shows Canada is forty-fifth on the list that ranks women in legislatures.

In the last century, women made significant strides in the political sphere. However, achieving complete gender equality is a slow process and means changing a society's views of gender roles, as well as its gendered social structure. This includes altering the socialization process that maintains this gendered structure, for example. We know that this is possible, because there are examples of it: Sweden has achieved gender parity in politics (Moss, 2009). Canada has a long way to go in this domain.

Politics in Canada: A Primer

The Canadian state is a complex system in which the power of legislation—the process of making and enacting laws—is divided mainly between the federal and provincial governments, according to a formula set down in the British North America Act of 1867. This

Table 15.1 Women as Percentage of Representatives in Legislatures, Most Recent Election, Top Ten Countries and Canada, 2009

Rank	Country	Lower or Single House				Upper House or Senate			
		Election	Seats[1]	Women	% Women	Election	Seats[1]	Women	% Women
1	Rwanda	Sept. 2008	80	45	56.3	Oct. 2003	26	9	34
2	Sweden	Sept. 2006	349	164	47.0				
3	South Africa	Apr. 2009	400	178	44.5	Apr. 2009	54	16	29.6
4	Cuba	Jan. 2008	614	265	43.2				
5	Iceland	Apr. 2009	63	27	42.9				
6	Finland	Mar. 2007	200	83	41.5				
7	Netherlands	Nov. 2006	150	62	41.3	May 2007	75	26	34.7
8	Denmark	Nov. 2007	179	68	38.0				
9	Angola	Sept. 2008	220	82	37.3				
10	Costa Rica	Feb. 2006	57	21	36.8				
45	Canada	Oct. 2008	308	68	22.1	N.A.	93	32	34.4

1. Figures correspond to the number of seats currently filled in Parliament.

Source: 'Women in Parliaments: World Classification', Inter-Parliamentary Union (IPU), 31 July 2009. http://www.ipu.org/wmn-e/arc/classif310709.htm

is sociologically interesting because of important social and demographic changes since 1867. Many of the duties originally given to provinces—health, education, and welfare for example—have become very costly and important and perhaps should have been made the federal government's responsibility. As it stands, the federal government handles matters that concern the whole country (foreign affairs, the military, crime, and justice, for example), while provincial governments focus on more local issues which, however, have federal consequences. As a result, federal–provincial relations tend to dominate Canadian political discussions.

Up to 2010, only the Liberal and Conservative parties have ever governed federally. The third-largest party in terms of national electoral support is the New Democratic Party (NDP), originally the Cooperative Commonwealth Federation (CCF). The CCF was formed in 1932, modelled on labour and social democratic parties of Europe, by a coalition of socialist, farm, co-operative, and labour groups, and the League for Social Reconstruction. In 1944, it became the first socialist government in North America, in Saskatchewan; recall that Lipset studied this government in his book *Agrarian Socialism*. In 1961, the CCF was renamed the New Democratic Party. Since then it has consistently managed to win 10–20 per cent of the votes cast in federal elections, mainly from workers, farmers, educated professionals, and other citizens dissatisfied with the two major parties (Perrella, 2009). The NDP would be a prime beneficiary if proportional representation were enacted.

In the last few decades, three other new political parties emerged in Canadian federal politics. One is the Bloc Québécois, a party of mainly Quebec separatists. Another, which emerged from conservative roots in Alberta, is the Alberta Alliance; since 2002, this party has held some prominence in the West. Finally, a third party that emerged only recently is the Green Party of Canada, which focuses on environmental issues. Unlike the United States, which seems unable to field more than two parties, Canada has a history of third-party challenges to the dominant two.

Every election, citizens vote for the political party that best represents their own and their country's values.

In practice, the Canadian political process is far less representative of popular views than it might be. First, as mentioned earlier, the Canadian system elects the candidate who receives a simple plurality of the votes cast; this may be far less than 50 per cent of the votes, and in turn, far fewer than 50 per cent of the eligible voters may cast a ballot. So, our system leaves many people unrepresented. Second, constituencies or ridings each send one representative to Parliament, but ridings vary in size. Some have twice the population of others, for example; this makes some people's votes twice as influential as others, depending on where they live. Third, it is not always the party that receives the most votes overall that wins the election. It is the party with the most seats that wins, so there is a bias in favour of parties that appeal to less populated (i.e., rural or small-town) constituencies.

A party that reaches 40 per cent of the popular vote generally wins an election, but not always. Sometimes, as occurred in 2006 and 2008, no party reaches the 40-per-cent mark, and this usually results in a minority government. Another peculiarity, mentioned earlier, is that significant numbers of votes may fail to translate into seats. For example, in 2008 the Green Party won 6.8 per cent of the vote but no seats (Elections Canada, n.d.). This system makes it hard for minority parties to gain access to the federal arena and voice their concerns.

Research shows that the more visible a party is, the more support it is likely to win (Blais et al., 2009). However, over the past two decades, the Canadian public has begun to lose interest in politics, perhaps beginning to doubt that politicians will fulfill their promises (Pharr et al., 2000; Stewart, MacIver, and Young, 2008). Voter turnout has steadily decreased to about 60 per cent of eligible voters

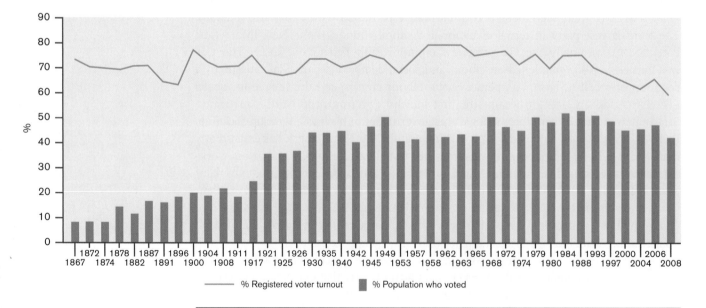

— % Registered voter turnout   ■ % Population who voted

Figure 15.2 Election Participation, Canada, 1867–2008

Source: Adapted from Heard (2009).

In the US federal elections of 2008, the Democratic leader Barack Obama managed to stir a frenzy of world-wide support, raising him to celebrity status.

(Elections Canada, 2009). Some research suggests that this drop is a result of a 'democratic deficit' in Canada, and dissatisfaction with the current system (Johnston, Krahn, and Harrison, 2006).

Throughout Canada, people of younger age groups (usually those under 30) are the least likely to vote (Adsett, 2003). Many young adults find politics boring or irrelevant to their everyday lives. However, they are not without interest in public issues. Research shows that even though young people are less likely to vote than middle-aged people, they are more likely to engage in other political activities (Statistics Canada, 2003). According to a report titled *Willing to Participate: Political Engagement of Young Adults*, people in their twenties, though about 15 per cent less likely than the middle-aged to vote, were more likely to sign petitions or attend a public meeting on political issues. This is especially true of young people with a higher education and those born in Canada. Young adults in Quebec are more likely than those in any other province to vote (ibid).

We note that, in Canada, there is usually little public interest in elections. Many people do not even vote, and those who do generally vote for the same party their parents did. No Canadian political party currently sparks the entire nation's interest, creating political fervour.

Compare this with the public response to Barack Obama in the 2008 US election. The Obama–McCain election in 2008 was a global event, sparking extreme public interest all around the world. People took time off from their everyday lives to watch the political debates; huge advertising campaigns enveloped the US; and the elections were a hot topic in the mass media. The candidates gained celebrity status, and on the night of the election, people threw election parties as they waited breathlessly in front of their TVs for the results. Canada's current leaders are failing to spark similar interest.

In short, Canada's political life is stable but, for many people, boring. It lacks the excitement found in some other liberal democracies. It also lacks the danger and oppression associated with totalitarian societies. However, classic work by Michel Foucault argues that, even in liberal democracies, the state can be dangerously powerful. Though he has nothing to say about voting or political systems, per se, Foucault teaches us plenty about styles of rule.

Classic Studies
Discipline and Punish: The Birth of the Prison

One trend in national states, over the past two centuries, has been increased surveillance and control over the citizenry. In part, this is a result of the growing bureaucratization of nation-states that began nearly two centuries ago. However, the drive towards social surveillance began, historically, not with concerns about security but with the goal of punishment. Michel Foucault documents this history of surveillance-as-punishment in his classic work, *Discipline and Punish: The Birth of the Prison* (1979), which was mentioned in chapters 1 and 3.

Punishment has a long and illustrious history, beginning perhaps with the first-known legal code, the Code of Hammurabi (1790 BCE). This code punished a great many crimes with death; other punishments included dismemberment (i.e., the removal of body parts) or exile. There were no prisons as we know them today. Even in medieval Europe, prisons were relatively unknown, so punishment had to be quick and inexpensive. Punishment then was a public spectacle, with specific rules dictating the details of torture or execution. (A contemporary comparison is the continued use of public stoning in Iran for people— particularly women—said to have committed adultery.)

However, there was also the risk of a backlash: this kind of punishment, though inexpensive, often provoked pity for the tortured criminal. Eventually, this kind of punishment came under public criticism because it was inhumane and yet it did not significantly lessen crime. Increasingly, critics argued that punishment was supposed to deter crime, not incite unrest. Yet public punishment sometimes had the opposite effect. In addition, punishment was supposed to match the offence and ensure the criminal did not repeat the crime. Yet, the punishment meted out was often far worse than the crime committed and rarely prevented a repeat of the crime. For these and other reasons, in the late eighteenth century, torture was largely eliminated and imprisonment became the standard punishment for most crimes.

Prison administrators came to think of their work as correctional, not punitive, and the punishment they doled out there was no longer publicly visible. Few could see or watch the reformative process that was to be achieved through systematic discipline and punishment.

Yet in prisons, torture of a kind continued. Discipline of the body was considered an important part of the reformation process. Physical discipline was also employed in the military, where recruits were taught how to stand, walk, hold and fire a weapon, and so on. It soon extended to other areas such as schools, which taught students how to hold a pen, sit, eat, speak, and even think. So prisons were not the only place that used these methods, but they used them more consistently, for a longer time. This bodily discipline was enforced by a focus on micro actions, through the continual correction of slight slips, and through continued testing, recording, and examination.

Record-keeping became an important part of the control-and-punishment process. People in power set about to record as much information about individuals as possible, to better regulate and examine them. By creating, codifying, and amassing ever more knowledge about individuals, they could exercise power ever more precisely. Thus, the rise of knowledge—including the social sciences—accompanied the rise of centralized power. Contrary to the beliefs and hopes of the Enlightenment, knowledge was used not to empower people but to control and disempower them.

The other main technique used to discipline was increased surveillance. Here Foucault recounts Jeremy Bentham's idea of the *Panopticon*—a prison where the guards can always see the prisoners, but prisoners cannot see the guards, and so they do not know if they are being watched. This uncertainty leads prisoners to regulate themselves. In a disciplinary society, liberal democratic or not, surveillance is everywhere.

Prisons today are just one part of an extended framework of surveillance, recording, and domination. From the moment we are born, we are disciplined in institutions: hospitals, schools, workplaces, institutions, prisons—especially in what Erving Goffman called 'total institutions'. These disciplinary institutions shape every stage of our lives. Today, someone always sees us, even if they are not actively watching and judging us. As a result, we are continually monitoring and disciplining one another. Contrary to Marx's claim that we are all isolated and estranged from one another by the alienation associated with capitalism, Foucault asserts that we are all engaged with one another, as guards and prisoners.

One consequence of this is political stability, however repressive. Through conviction and imprisonment, crime becomes de-politicized, or at least distinguished from politics and power. We come to think of the delinquent or criminal as a deviant, someone abnormal or pathological; the problem to be solved is the delinquent's behaviour, not the government's behaviour. Additionally, the class basis of punishment (and crime) is driven underground. Rule-breaking is considered pathological; rule-making and enforcement—even to extreme degrees—is considered normal. Even disadvantaged people who are disproportionately likely to receive punishment distance themselves from criminals and delinquents as a group.

The broad conclusions of *Discipline and Punish* have exposed Foucault to some criticism. For example, some observations in the book are unsupported by evidence and

Counter ideologies challenge the harm done by dominant ideologies. In this photo, Aboriginal protesters in Winnipeg, Manitoba challenge the dominant ideology by demanding jobs rather than welfare.

require a willing suspension of disbelief (Goldstein, 1979: 117). In some cases, the evidence supplied is ethnocentric and mostly of French origin, though the theory purports to describe all modern societies (Shelley, 1979: 1510; Cohen, 1978: 586). For these and other reasons, some critics have challenged Foucault's account of the reasons why public torture and execution were abandoned (Garland, 1986: 869).

Putting aside these criticisms, Foucault's theory of power is perhaps his most original and disputed contribution to sociology, though he never formulated it explicitly. The book helps develop his idea of power as progressive as well as oppressive, an idea extended in Foucault's other books. As David Garland says, 'his idea of power as positive and productive has made it easier to develop political analyses of the various agencies of health, insurance, social security, education, psychiatry, etc., that increasingly regulate our lives' (Garland 1986: 865). Foucault, in this respect, can be considered the logical successor to Max Weber, who also located power in state institutions, more than in social classes.

The Political Role of Ideology

We can readily see that politics has the power to oppress people and to frustrate them. As the Italian political philosopher Antonio Gramsci noted, capitalism maintains control not just through violence, threat, and coercion, but also through the manipulation of ideas and ideologies. By controlling a hegemonic culture, the values of the bourgeoisie become the common-sense values of all. In effect, by controlling culture, the bourgeoisie set the standards for normality and morality—a point similar to Foucault's several decades later. Thus, a culture develops in which working-class people identify their own good with the good of the bourgeoisie and, for this reason, help to maintain the *status quo* rather than overthrowing it.

To change this situation, the working class must develop a culture of its own, with its own ideas about 'natural' or 'normal' values. According to Gramsci, this culture would attract the oppressed and intellectual classes to the cause of the proletariat. Therefore, such a cultural project must precede the attainment of power; it cannot be something that is left until later, after the revolution. Any class that seeks to achieve control over its own domain would have to move beyond its own narrow economic and local interests, showing moral leadership in a variety of domains.

Whether an ideology is 'dominant' is something we can learn only through empirical research. We consider an ideology 'dominant' if the most powerful or socially dominant groups in society sponsor it, and if it supports the interests of those groups. Consider the popular belief in 'winners' and 'losers' in our society—in people getting what they deserve and deserving what they get. This ideology dominates us—disempowering the weak and empowering the already strong. The dominant ideology is also an important part of popular culture and entertainment. American culture, for example, places a high value on heroism and war. This makes it easy for American politicians to mobilize public sentiment behind activities like the Iraq War, and before that, the longstanding Cold War.

As per this ideology, most people in our society believe they are mainly responsible for their own success or failure. They think 'I am free to choose my own path; if my choice turns out badly, I have only myself to blame.' As mentioned earlier, we can relate this dominant (sometimes called 'liberal') ideology to Darwin's theory of 'survival of the fittest' and perhaps to the Calvinist theory of 'work ethic'. As you can see, ideologies 'explain' how society is organized—who gets rewarded and why. They control us from inside.

This ideology tends to focus attention away from common problems and toward individual responsibility (or blame). Some have said that this leads to 'blaming the victim' for social inequality: for example, to blame the poor for their poverty, and the unemployed for their lack of a job. By laying the blame in this way, liberal ideology affects the way people

Media Distortion

BOX **15.2**

Plans for 'Fox News North' to be Revealed in Toronto

Politics in Canada may become more polarized and combative if Pierre Karl Péladeau, a Quebec media billionaire, succeeds in establishing a news network in Canada aimed at a 'conservative-minded audience', according to Jonathan Malloy, a political scientist at Carleton University in Ottawa. The proposed network would be modelled on the US Fox News network, which is known for attaining high ratings with provocative, often controversial, programming with a right-wing bias. Péladeau's company, Quebecor Media Inc., has applied for a 'must-carry' broadcast licence, meaning that cable companies would be required to provide the channel as part of their basic offering. The network has hired such people as Kory Teneycke, who previously served as communications director for Prime Minister Stephen Harper.

Source: Adapted from Smith (2010).

behave. For one thing, it tends to make them politically inactive. It also influences which political party they will vote for and whether, for example, they will support welfare benefits for the poor or capital gains taxes for the rich. It also influences how people will react if they are thrown out of work, battered by a spouse, or mistreated by the government. In general, the dominant liberal ideology encourages people to blame themselves and support the status quo.

Yet, though it seems natural and democratic, in Canadian society, this liberal ideology is the *dominant ideology*, the ideology of the ruling class, justifying its power and wealth. Canadians are unlikely to rebel against social inequality because they have come to believe in the dominant ideology—also, to lack confidence in an alternative. We teach young people this ideology in schools, in religious institutions, and through the media; we hear it repeated throughout life. We learn to accept it, to accept inequality as natural and normal, and to live with the status quo.

Ideologies and Publics

One common approach to politics is to distinguish between the rulers and the people they rule: between the state and the citizenry, or between the elite and the public. But what is this 'public', sociologically speaking? Any given *public* is an unstructured set of people who hold certain interests in, views on, or concerns about a particular issue. Ideologies, which (as we have seen) are simplified and distorted versions of reality, help to structure this public's participation in society. Normally, members of a public do not interact with one another and are rarely aware of belonging to the same group.

Yet 'public opinion' is central to any liberal democracy, since what we mean by *democracy* is 'government by the people'. The Latin proverb *vox populi, vox dei* means 'the voice of the people is the voice of God'. This proverb *should* be the guiding principle in a democratic society, and to some degree it is, since polls accurately measure people's sentiments, and politicians follow the polls. However, polls also manipulate or shape public opinion. As well, they impute certainty (or what comedian Stephen Colbert calls 'truthiness') to opinions that often are in flux, creating something out of nothing. One tactic employed by politicians and so-called spin-doctors is to produce a unified, or apparently unified, conception of reality that the various publics can share and subscribe to.

People like being part of a group that has succeeded: they want to 'get on the band-wagon'. The bandwagon effect shows up in post-election polls, when a much larger number of voters claim to have voted for the winning candidate than actually did. After the fact, people adopt opinions that are popular *because* they are popular. They may even come to support a politician who seems likely to win (that is, according to the pre-election polls) just because they want to back a winner. Political and other public opinion polls contribute to this illusion-making, but journalists play a far larger role when they report **propaganda** under the guise of news, as we saw in the last chapter.

Not surprisingly, people are becoming more skeptical about the political information they receive and the people who control government. Survey data show that Canadians distrust politicians more than they distrust almost anyone else (including advertising executives, who have never been famous for their honesty).

propaganda

Mass communication whose purpose is to influence people's political opinions and actions.

Ideologies and Action

Unlike ideologies that support the status quo, ideologies that propose change are either radical or reformist. *Reformist ideologies* call for minor changes to the degree of inequality, without challenging the basic ground rules. In Canada, the policies that provided medicare, welfare, and unemployment insurance were all based on a reformist ideology. These innovations were intended as 'safety nets' to help people who got into trouble, and to provide a minimum level of support for everyone—not to bring about equality. However, critics argue that such reforms produce changes that are temporary and superficial. Unemployment insurance, for example, does not prevent unemployment, nor does it create jobs. It makes unemployment less painful without changing the factors that create unemployment.

Unlike reformist ideologies, *radical ideologies* call for a reshaping of society, by challenging its very foundation. This is what the CCF (the parent of today's reformist NDP) did at its founding in 1932, when it adopted the Regina Manifesto. This manifesto declared, 'No CCF government will rest content until it has wiped out capitalism and put into operation the full program of socialized planning which will lead to the establishment in Canada of the co-operative commonwealth'. One can question the wisdom of this goal, or the feasibility of trying to implement it, but no one can question its fundamental concern with inequality.

Reform and radical ideologies can both be considered *counter ideologies*— 'counter' in the sense that they challenge the bases of the dominant ideologies. They also expose the interests that dominant ideologies serve and offer people a different vision of society. Often, such counter ideologies develop out of people's responses to experiences of unequal treatment. Counter ideologies call the status quo into question and deny legitimacy to unfair ways of treating people. Feminism, for example, is a counter ideology that denies the legitimacy of sexism and traditional patriarchal ways of treating women.

Groups that promote counter ideologies get their message out to people in many ways, especially through public meetings and the media. Intellectuals and other highly educated people (called the *intelligentsia*) often play an important part in promoting counter ideologies. The Polish intelligentsia, for example, played an important role in the Solidarity movement during the early 1980s, though workers were on the front lines. And in both Poland and Hungary, the intelligentsia has helped to create a civil society since the collapse of communism. North American intellectuals, by contrast, have been much less active in criticizing the state or promoting counter ideologies.

One role of counter ideology is to challenge the harm done by the dominant ideology. According to Marxist theory, dominant ideologies promote *false consciousness*, a view of the world that is out of sync with objective reality. In a capitalist society, for example, the dominant ideology may blame workers for their own unemployment. In a feudal society, the dominant ideology may blame peasants for their sinfulness and disobedience. In a patriarchal society, the dominant ideology may blame women for any signs of insubordination or licentiousness. When people accept such views, blaming themselves even though they are victims of an unfair regime, they reveal a false consciousness of society. The job of a counter ideology is to challenge these views by asking such questions as, What really causes unemployment? Who says I'm more sinful than anyone else? Why shouldn't I be just as outspoken as my husband?

In short, ideologies serve various roles in the system of Canadian politics. What an ideology does depends entirely on its particular nature and the powerful groups that use it to serve their political goals. In this sense, ideology is just a technology—a tool of power, wielded most often by and for the powerful.

People Are Talking About . . .
JÜRGEN HABERMAS

Jürgen Habermas was born in Düsseldorf, Germany, in 1929. In the 1950s, Habermas studied philosophy at Universities in Göttingen and Bonn, followed by studies in philosophy and sociology at the Institute for Social Research under Max Horkheimer and Theodor Adorno. In the 1960s and 1970s, he taught at the University of Heidelberg and Frankfurt am Main. He was a director at the Max Planck Institute in Starnberg from 1971 to 1982. In 1980, he won the Adorno Prize, and in 1982 became a professor at the University of Frankfurt, remaining there until his retirement in 1994.

Habermas was a truly independent thinker, unable fully to embrace Marxism, critical theory, modernism, or postmodernism. He embraced the critical theory of the Frankfurt School, which, as we noted in earlier chapters, criticizes present-day Western societies for their misuse of power, including their use of rationality to increase domination through bureaucracy and other means. Habermas himself cited the way that science and technology have exploited nature as an example of this brutal tendency. Yet, like the Enlightenment thinkers whom many critical theorists criticized, Habermas valued the use of reason and logic to break free from adherence to religious rules.

In his biography, Patrick Baert (in Scott, 2006: 128) notes that Habermas criticized the positivist-inclined for failing 'to recognize that aims other than prediction can be pursued, thereby mistakenly treating empirical–analytical knowledge as the only valid type of knowledge. Other aims, such as understanding and emancipation, are [also] worth pursuing'. Though Habermas often followed Marxian thinking, he considered too narrow Marx's focus on economic progress as the measure of human development. Habermas argued the process of social learning is dynamic and unpredictable from one epoch to another, not linear and progressive as Marx had argued.

For Habermas, rationality—the ability to use logic and analysis—must go beyond the strategic calculation of resources for achieving a chosen goal. It should also seek the creation of community through communicative action that strives for agreement between groups mutually perceived as 'Other'. Only such a goal is truly 'rational' in a society. The question is how to achieve such a community of free individuals. In 1981, Habermas published *The Theory of Communicative Action*. Here, he proposed a model of communicative rationality that considers the effect power has on the situation of discourse and opposes the traditional idea of an objective and functionalist reason.

Politics and law can also be more open through communicative action. Habermas suggests that in a 'deliberative democracy', citizens would thoughtfully debate governmental policy and law. Rationality would prevail, Habermas believes, as people would be guided by a sense of the importance of the task and a desire to participate in governance. But such a process could be skewed by the inequalities and divided interests created by private ownership.

Source: Adapted from *Fifty Key Sociologists: The Contemporary Theorists* (edited by John Scott, London: Routledge, 2006) and other sources.

In the sociology of politics, as in the other domains of sociology, we see a continued debate between postmodernists like Foucault and empiricists—including critical theorists—like Jürgen Habermas. These latter sociologists, following in the footsteps of Weber and Marx, continue to examine the exercise of power in specific states under specific conditions. So, for example, Muller-Doohm (2009) notes that Habermas focuses his attention on the changing significance of the nation-state through European integration, the role of a deliberative democracy, and the controversial issue of taming world capitalism.

Jürgen Habermas's theories have received enormous attention in the public sphere as well as in sociology and political science (Pedersen, 2009). Pederson traces Habermas's interest in rational reconstruction, by describing the method's main principles and specifying how this methodology is used in Habermas's political theory. In Habermas's approach, rational reconstruction produces empirical hypotheses, though these cannot always be tested by empirical means (a problem first noted by Max Weber).

Roth (2009) notes that 'truth' is generally thought of as the goal of inquiry, whether as thinking or teaching. But he argues that the definition of 'truth' is troublesome, no matter what the approach. For this reason, Roth concludes that sociological inquiry should not aim for truth, but rather for understanding—again, in keeping with Weber's thinking a century earlier. However, he also asserts it should be used to justify political courses of action, a view more in keeping with twentieth-century critical theory.

Heath (2009) notes that the social science that underpins Marxism is obsolete, and that analytical Marxism, exemplified by the early Habermas, seeks to update the theory through analytical philosophy and positivist social science. From this perspective, Habermas in his early thinking can be seen to be an analytical Marxist, although he did not identify himself as one. However, Heath recognizes that in his later work, Habermas eventually departed from any recognizable form of Marxism, as did Foucault.

According to Keat (2008), Habermas has made a significant contribution to the effort to relate ethics to politics, embracing the supposed commitment of liberal theory to neutrality and progress, but criticizing its failure to make good on this promise. That said, Keat accuses Habermas of failing to show how political ethics can truly be the subject of rational discussion, independent of other moral and practical concerns.

Noting the concerns originally voiced by Max Weber, Hall (2009) asserts that the methods of historical sociology face research problems centred on the instability of historical referents, their historical non-independence, and the privileging of objective time of the clock and calendar. Hall proposes to solve these problems by analyzing the interplay of multiple social temporalities, attempting to distinguish social trends (for example, toward the triumph of rationalized social order) from other temporalities in the here-and-now. Overall, he finds the 'empire of modernity' is a hybrid formation that bridges diachronic and strategic temporalities. Diachronic developments tend toward what Habermas described as 'colonization of the lifeworld'—the imposition on everyday life of instrumental rationality based on bureaucracies and market-forces. Strategic temporalities reflect the durability of the here-and-now and the accretion of multiple, personal experiences.

As we saw in the previous chapter, in recent years, there has been an explosion of ambitious sociological research aiming to map and explain the dynamics of media understood not as technologies or individual organizations but rather as systems interacting with other systems. This approach has multiple roots, and Benson (2009) notes that its reach and influence have been expanded by the work of Jürgen Habermas, especially through his concept of the 'public sphere'. Habermas has been especially helpful in clarifying normative debates about democracy, and he is right to suggest that normative criteria can usefully guide empirical research. This belief in the reciprocal relationship between empirical research and public debate is central to all his work and, indeed, to all work in the Frankfort school's mode of critical theory.

However, Benson criticizes Habermas for the mistake of taking the 'media system' as a given, then orienting his analysis toward effective strategies to exert influence in the face of this supposedly invariant media 'logic'. Benson claims a new generation of researchers, influenced by Bourdieu, is moving to fill in this gap, by describing and explaining variations in media logics. Only in doing so can they hope to actively engage in shaping these logics for democratic ends.

Edwards (2009) explores how Habermas's concepts of communicative action and colonization might aid in the revival of UK public sector unions, looking specifically at the National Union of Teachers. He finds that what Habermas calls 'communicative action'—a process through which actors in society seek to reach common understanding and to coordinate actions by reasoned argument, consensus, and co-operation rather than strategic action strictly in pursuit of their own goals—has led to new ways for union members to discuss union policy, in schools, at union meetings, and online, despite efforts made by neo-liberal governments to colonize and undermine these communicative spaces through public sector restructuring. His point is, then, that Habermas provides a conceptual vocabulary for discussing political problems in new kinds of ways.

Another innovative concept Habermas developed is that of 'lifeworld', a term invented by German philosopher–sociologist Edmund Husserl in 1936. For Habermas, whose sociological approach is grounded in the analysis of communication, the lifeworld consists of informal, culturally grounded understandings and mutual accommodations, rooted in widely shared social and cultural arrangements. Wicks and Reason (2009) draw on Habermas's conceptualization to explore a theory related to communicative space. They begin by noting that the success or failure of a research project aimed at social change often depends on what happens at the beginning of the inquiry process: specifically, what matters is the way access is established, and on how participants and co-researchers are engaged early on. In particular, they show the process of opening communicative space requires group development that passes through phases of inclusion, control, and intimacy.

Along similar lines, Edwards (2009) outlines Habermas's social movement theory and reviews the critical reception of these ideas from within critical theory and social movement studies more widely. Criticism of Habermas's explanation of the new social movements has been wide-ranging and persuasive. Even critics have noted, however, the applicability of the idea of 'colonization' to twenty-first century issues around global capitalism and resistance to neo-liberal policies. As a result, there is some potential for aspects of Habermas's theory to be used in ways that make him capable of engaging in dialogue with the current concerns of social movement theory.

Thus, a review of recent writings finds continued application of the work of Jürgen Habermas—over 200 journal articles applying Habermas's work in the last three years. Clearly, sociologists are talking about Jürgen Habermas and Habermas deserves a place in our comprehensive, fusion approach to sociology. He represents the current state of Frankfurt School critical theory, as filtered through modern social science and moral philosophy. No longer on the 'left-wing' of sociology, the Frankfurt School (critical theory) exemplified by Habermas is now widely viewed as close to sociology's theoretical centre: a modern version of C. Wright Mills's 'sociological imagination'. This stance recognizes the importance of social criticism; moral engagement; and a focus on power, social change, and social action. Unlike traditional Marxism, it also recognizes the importance of reflexivity (self-awareness), contingency (historical circumstance), and multiple viewpoints in social analysis.

New Insights

Where can socio-political analysis go next, after Marx, Weber, Gramsci, Foucault, and Habermas? It seems like sociologists who study politics are currently in a consolidation phase, settling old arguments and, as yet, unready to launch dramatic new initiatives.

Perhaps the most memorable contribution of Rosemary Hunter's (2007) recent paper on politics and policy-making is its title: 'Would You Like Theory with That? Bridging the Divide between Policy-Oriented Empirical Legal Research, Critical Theory and Politics'. As we have seen in the debate around Habermas, and between Habermas and Foucault, in the political realm, debates between critical theorists and postmodern theorists are running hot and heavy. As Hunter notes, this compares oddly with the atheoretical stance of most government policy-makers. If there is to be theory with the main course (that is, with social planning), what kind of theory would we like—boiled, baked, fried, or mashed? More important, how can sociologists get policy-makers to address important social concerns if they can't explain their theories compellingly and clearly?

Zizek (2008), fittingly, writes that in this era of rapid change—as we discard old social forms and adopt new technologies—we are bombarded with injunctions to abandon (mash?) old paradigms. The New Age 'wisdom' is that this is the 'post-human era'. We seem unable to realize the New can enable the Old to survive, he writes. Instead, we should ask the difficult question posed by Blaise Pascal: 'How are we to remain faithful to the Old in the new conditions?' It is only by addressing this question that we can create something effectively New, says Zizek. We should consider what those who have gone before us have advised in essentially this same context, rather than listen to the radical academic scholars who urge us to leave the past in the dust.

Equally, one might begin by inventorying what is in the political storehouse. Cassinari and Merlini (2007) note the political, economic, and social characteristics of what is commonly referred to as the 'modern West' include free-market capitalism, individual property, democratic rule, civil society, and respect of human rights. What they find most striking about the move from modern to postmodern eras is the link to temporality. Whereas the modern identity of the West was historical, the postmodern West is ahistorical—indeed, post-historical. How will this shift affect present-day Western societies' relationship to traditional concerns like democratic representation, consumerism, information distribution and access, knowledge production, civic life, and solidarity-based wealth distribution? The renunciation of a historical time dimension—the distinguishing trait of postmodern Western identity—will, at the very least, pose problems of belonging (despite distance) and continuity (despite discontinuity).

Fives (2009) writes that postmodernists reject what they call the universalist–rationalist framework of liberalism. When they defend liberal democracy, they do so only in relativistic terms, not in absolute terms like the 'modernists'. That is, they do not see liberal democracy as a good in itself. (Perhaps they have failed sufficiently to consider—let alone experience—the Stalinist or Hitlerian alternatives.) Liberals, therefore, are right to charge postmodernism with relativism and immoralism, says Fives. Liberalism and postmodernism are incompatible and therefore they cannot join together in debates about a democratic response to oppression. Still, liberals are caught in a bind: though they insist on neutrality and open-mindedness, they also believe absolutely in the exercise of reasonableness and mutual respect as requirements of rational dialogue. In the end, then, liberals must reject postmodernism if they are conduct socially useful, change-oriented discussions.

Critical theorists have less willingness to accept a relativist position and, therefore, more willingness to reject the postmodern analysis. For example, Kurnik (2009) notes the current crisis of capitalism highlights the troubled role of labour in modern society, asserting that only a 'transformation of labour' can change the political situation. However, labour has become virtually invisible in the global political economy, even as it takes on new forms under the influence of finance capital. The current crisis can be solved only by reform or revolution, but postmodern analysis offers neither, says this author.

Nickel (2009) highlights the difficulty when theorists attempt to combine critical theory and postmodernism in political analyses of the modern welfare state. Sloganeering, which obstructs critical thinking, has no place in such important theories. Yet, only slogans are possible when theorists try to conflate postmodernism, critical theory, and pragmatism around current political concerns. This statement does not justify pragmatic, atheoretical work, let alone the modern neo-liberal welfare state; rather, it points to a deep schism in political theorizing no one has yet been able to remedy.

Rostboll (2008) notes that efforts to combine political liberalism and critical theory also obscure some important differences between the two traditions. Consider the Habermasian idea of 'internal autonomy': there is no room for this dimension of freedom in political liberalism and it has largely disappeared from the later Habermas. As a result, the theory of deliberative democracy has converged around a less critical and more pragmatic view of freedom: in effect, an acceptance of the status quo. Rastboll asserts that if we want to keep deliberative democracy as a critical theory of contemporary society, we should resist this convergence. We need to continue to criticize 'unreflective acquiescence', incorporating internal autonomy in a complex theory of freedom to which deliberative democracy should be committed.

Tassone (2008) writes that, in recent years, many critical thinkers—Habermas foremost among them—have tried to find a place for morality and ethics in a capitalist society. Some believe they have succeeded. Tassone, however, finds that these theories have failed to understand the problem of moral action in an immoral (capitalist) society. None are able to refute Adorno's assertion that 'wrong life cannot be lived rightly'. In the end, political structure will always shape and constrain people's moral conceptions and actual behaviour.

Here, consider the morality and meaning of terrorism. Baral (2008) writes that the 9/11 terrorist attacks have become part of the 'global psyche'. Academics and intellectuals have taken up the study of terrorism, to the point of developing a discourse in which all people are both potential terrorists and potential victims of terror. The events at the Abu Ghraib prison in Iraq in particular show how vague is the distinction between state and non-state terrorism. As a consequence of this and other travesties, international support for the American response to terrorism, the military actions in Afghanistan and Iraq, has lessened. Baral, reminding us of Baudrillard, argues that human degradation has become a violent spectacle in which we all participate at least as spectators. Every local, wrongful death, however minute, stands as a representative of the mass, global destruction that results from a violent exercise of state power.

Despite criticisms of the idea, Kristjanson-Gural (2008) seeks to set up a meeting of the critical and postmodern approaches. He disagrees with the common characterization of 'postmodern Marxism' as morally relativist and inadequate for systematically analyzing capitalism. Through a review of the postmodern Marxist literature in value theory, class analysis of the household and state, and class justice, he finds that postmodern Marxism offers new insights into problems of concern to Marxian theorists. In a complex technical argument, he points out that 'postmodern Marxism . . . produces an interpretation of Marx's theory of value that is logically coherent and systematic in its analysis without being structuralist in the sense of positing an inherent logic of capitalist production and exchange' (ibid.: 96). Thus, he finds in it a model for a new, pragmatic class politics, which can work toward equality through new alliances and strategies.

In the global setting, Grosfoguel (2007) suggests 'radical colonial critical theory' can provide a southern, rather than capitalist, perspective on Third World colonialism and nationalism. In this view, for example, there is no postcolonial era: the legacy of formal colonial rule lives on as 'coloniality', or continued domination by the colonial powers. Grosfoguel argues that the 'myth' of decolonization hides persistent racial and colonial hierarchies, and that new thinking is needed to complete the process of decolonization.

An important figure in resolving some of these theoretical contradictions has been Edward Said, discussed in an earlier chapter and well-known for his work on Orientalism and on the 'Other'-ing of non-Western peoples. Lima (2008), through an analysis of Said's work, sheds further light on his theoretical contributions to international politics. Beyond updating the concept of imperialism, Said's books make three other, important, relevant contributions. First, the hegemony exercised around the world by the US since the end of World War II works against the establishment of a democratic world order. Second, fights for independence and liberation tend to carry important moral risks for the national conscience in less developed countries. Third, Westerners continue to harbour stereotypical prejudices against Arabs and Muslims because they don't understand them and their culture.

Chapter Summary

We have seen that politics is a crucial part of our society. Without a good political system—featuring legitimate political authority, for example—our society would be chaotic and disordered. Life would be dangerous and frightening. A 'failed state' is not merely a poor or unfortunate state—it is a bad place for people to live. No wonder so many people emigrate, leaving failed states to take up residence in Canada and other safe places abroad.

Politics gives us social order, protection, and laws to define what is good and bad. Canada is founded on 'peace, order, and good government'—not as immediately appealing or grandiose as other national slogans, but essentially sound. Politics is one of the mechanisms that enables people to live together in states. We learned in this chapter that different forms of government run states, each upholding its unique principles. Some states are authoritarian or even totalitarian, and they achieve order but not always legitimacy; in either event, they do so at the expense of **civil liberties**. The Canadian state is liberal democratic, which is less orderly and efficient (perhaps) than totalitarianism, but more humane. However, even this kind of state can be oppressive and exploitive, as we have seen.

Governments are supported by ideologies that, like state religions, give citizens a sense of purpose and meaning. Also, governments are supported by laws. These laws ensure two important elements of a democratic society: civil liberties and **civil rights**. These liberties and rights cover the basic freedoms guaranteed to a state's residents, including the freedom of speech, freedom to practise religion, freedom of the press, and freedom to hold one's own opinion.

Despite the noble ideas that surround politics, real-life politics is sometimes corrupt, bungling, deceitful, and harmful. As we learned in this chapter, politics gives a select few the power over enormous resources, and sometimes these chosen ones ignore—even abuse—the public interest. No wonder many people have lost faith in their political leaders and have chosen not to take part in elections. Further, when voters see the politicians using propaganda to win support, they realize some leaders are more interested in gaining power than in working for the common good.

civil liberties

Freedoms that protect the individual against government. These include freedom of speech, assembly, and movement, and freedom of the press.

civil rights

Rights we consider all people deserve under all circumstances, without regard to race, ethnicity, age, sex, or other personal qualities.

Leaders may achieve power through dubious means: some through their charisma, and some through more mundane methods—making deals with other politicians, buying support with public funds, and attacking other leaders through ridicule and slander. At their best, however, political leaders unite us around commonly shared values and goals. In that sense, they integrate us—bring us together. When that happens, often under threatening national conditions like war, we feel relief and a bond with one another. We make sacrifices for one another and for our country and community. This is the ideal state of politics, perhaps rarely arrived at, perhaps ultimately unattainable.

When our leaders fail to lead, impress, or inspire us, or to pull us together, we wait for new leaders. Sometimes, we help to produce them—a topic we will discuss in the next chapter on social movements.

Critical Thinking Questions

1. What are some key differences between political science and political sociology?
2. What theoretical approaches to the democratic state make most sense to you? Why?
3. Why do you think women are under-represented in most political systems?
4. What is the role of ideologies in politics? How do these ideologies connect to religion and to mass media (discussed earlier)?
5. Choose one Canadian political party and briefly research its history. What are some of its key policies? What role does it play today in Canadian politics?
6. What is the role of politics in modern Canadian society? Provide some examples of recent political events and discuss their significance for the current political climate.

Recommended Readings

Douglas E. Baer (ed.), *Political Sociology: Canadian Perspectives* (Toronto: Oxford University Press, 2002). This is a collection of writings on political sociology in Canada. It effectively covers the basic topics of interest in this field, including political culture, the state, political movements, and more.

Barrington Moore, *Social Origins of Dictatorship and Democracy: Lord and Peasant in the Making of the Modern World* (Boston: Beacon Press, 1966). This classic work takes on a historical-comparative perspective, arguing that particular agrarian systems and ways in which industrialization occurs in societies later produces certain political systems, whether democratic, fascist, or communist.

Talcott Parsons, *The Social System* (New York: Free Press; London: Collier-Macmillan, 1964 [1951]). This classic outline of the functionalist view of society was one of Parsons's most important works.

George C. Homans, *The Human Group* (New York: Harcourt, Brace, 1950). Homans's classic work argues for the consideration and treatment of human groups as mini social systems, operating by the same principles as large societies. Here Homans provides a general theory on interpersonal relationships.

Randal Martin, *Propaganda and the Ethics of Persuasion* (Peterborough, ON: Broadview Press, 2002). This book analyzes propaganda by first providing a historical outline of its development and then discussing its rise in the twentieth century. The author aims to increase public awareness of the construction and impact of propaganda.

Louise Chappell and Lisa Hill (eds.), *The Politics of Women's Interests: New Comparative Perspectives* (London and New York: Routledge, 2006). This is a comprehensive interpretation of political issues from a feminist perspective. It examines how political institutions both shape and reflect gender issues, and the current role of women in politics around the world.

Sylvia Bashevkin, *Women, Power, Politics: The Hidden Story of Canada's Unfinished Democracy* (Oxford; New York: Oxford University Press, 2009). In this important new addition to Canadian political sociology, the author argues that Canadians are unsettled by women politicians—in fact, by women in positions of authority in general. Exploring this discomfort, Bashevkin points out the many barriers and difficulties women face in politics.

Websites

The State, by Statistics Canada
www43.statcan.ca/04/04a/04a_001f_e.htm

Freedom House
www.freedomhouse.org

Parliament of Canada
www.parl.gc.ca

Elections Canada
www.elections.ca

Canadian Election Study (CES)
http://ces-eec.mcgill.ca

Inter-Parliamentary Union (IPU)
www.ipu.org

Canadian Women in Government
www.collectionscanada.gc.ca/women/002026-800-e.html

Equal Voice
http://equalvoice.ca

16 Social Movemen and Voluntary Associations

Learning Objectives

In this chapter, you will:

› Learn how participation in voluntary associations is useful both to the individual and to society

› Consider the various theoretical perspectives on social forces that lead people to seek change and form social movements

› Recognize how people make and preserve social order, despite differences, inequalities, conflicts, and constant change

Chapter Outline

Humans are social creatures. We form social relationships—acquaintanceships, friendships, and families—that then make up the intricate social network that is 'society'. We exist within society, shape it, and are shaped by it too.

Living together in society means following certain rules—rules that give us similar expectations and behaviour patterns. To make sure people follow these rules, we have created governments—social institutions that oversee our lives and ensure social order. We rely on governments to protect us from harm, to mediate conflicts, deliver essential services, regulate markets, punish crime, and, most importantly, keep the peace. We judge the social order by how well governments perform these duties.

However, governments are not the only source of social order. Within society, we also form smaller groups. When we choose to do this, we call the resulting groups *voluntary associations*. We create these groups for practical reasons—for sociability,

play, and social support. Voluntary associations also have rules that guide and enforce our behaviours. Sometimes, they even adopt other, larger societal goals—for example, to produce change. When this happens, voluntary associations change their form and enter the political arena. Then, they become what sociologists call *social movements*. As we will see, sociologists have differing viewpoints about why social movements form. Nevertheless, social movements and the voluntary associations that produce them are an integral part of societies and their development.

In short, this chapter is about what we might think of as 'everyday life' processes, or even as 'unwashed history'. It looks at the things that motivate most people most of the time: social attachments, shared beliefs, ideas (good and bad), rumours, moral concerns, manners, etiquette, and concerns about social acceptance. It is also about informal social control and the reasons people conform, co-operate, and form groups. In the end, social order comes down to this.

Everyday Observations

As viewed from Outer Space: 'This planet has—or rather had—a problem, which was this: most of the people on it were unhappy for pretty much of the time. Many solutions were suggested for this problem, but most of these were largely concerned with the movements of small green pieces of paper, which is odd because on the whole it wasn't the small green pieces of paper that were unhappy. And so the problem remained; lots of the people were mean, and most of them were miserable . . . . Many were increasingly of the opinion that they'd all made a big mistake in coming down from the trees in the first place. And some said that even the trees had been a bad move, and that no one should ever have left the oceans'. (Douglas Adams, The Hitchhiker's Guide to the Galaxy, Prologue)

Was it a mistake for pre-humans to leave the oceans? And have we come to confuse *evolution* with *devolution*? Starting from humble origins—with their homes in caves—humans appear to have made tremendous advances, and not only in the fields of science and technology. We humans have invented cultures and built complex societies. We have created structures and more importantly, we have created order. We have invented social norms and written laws that give our actions stability and predictability.

To help us live in harmony, we have developed social codes. We have learned these rules; and most of the time we follow them faithfully. Growing up in civilized societies, we follow the social codes and expect others to do the same. You leave your house every day wearing clothes and expect to see others doing the same. You can walk in the park without fearing that someone will eat you, and for your part, you don't try to eat anyone else. It is by sharing expectations like these that we are able to live close to one another—even close to strangers.

But while certain norms remain, others change. In fact, social life is changing all the time, whether we notice it or not. And not all change is bad for us. What's more, we can change society without destroying the social order. In fact, we often work together to bring about changes, acting collectively to do so. We have seen social changes occurring at an unprecedented rate in the past few decades. We are all aware of the environmental and feminist movements, for example. And let's not forget the peace movement of the 1960s, the anti-free trade movement of the 1980s, the Black Power movement, gay and lesbian movements, and so on.

Throughout history, and certainly in the past few centuries, such **voluntary associations** and **social movements** have helped to shape the society we live in today. Often starting with a narrow goal—for example, ensuring workers a living wage, getting women the right to vote, or saving the whales—they sometimes end up transforming society. Ordinary humans make history: not gods and spirits, nor a disembodied 'spirit of the times', nor an inescapable 'logic' of economic or technological change, nor geniuses and 'great men'. They do so through complex networks of interdependence and organized co-operation.

Interdependence: The Real State of Nature

One of the fundamental features of social life, and one that contributes most to social integration, is interdependence. People need one another and benefit from each other's

voluntary association

A group formed by voluntary membership. Unlike other voluntary associations, social movements usually have a political goal.

social movements

Organized groups of people with an agenda or plan for social change, to be achieved through agitation and political pressure.

In our society, we often put a significant amount of trust in our neighbours.

existence. The more we realize this, the more likely we are to behave decently toward one another. Thus, interdependence promotes tolerance and civility, especially if the nation-state is committed to protecting tolerance and civility.

In due course, people in complex societies come to understand that they face common goals and common dangers, and even share common friends and common enemies. Beyond that, we come to see the first-hand benefits of co-operation with others, both those nearby and those faraway. This unity is sometimes hard to achieve, as Durkheim notes, but it may have become easier in the last few decades. Gradually, we come to understand we are connected in a vast, global network of exchange.

All of our interdependencies, which Durkheim felt would be important as sources of (organic) solidarity in an industrial society, are clearer today than ever before. Consider a few examples.

First, we live and work in a global marketplace. Whether your home is in Toronto, Edmonton, Halifax, Buenos Aires, Mumbai, or Moscow, you are looking for the best goods and services at the lowest prices. And our jobs and incomes depend on the outcome of this process. Shifts in buying and selling, and in capital investment shape our individual lives and national economies, and they control the balance of global economic and political power. So, when we buy and sell to one another, we are remaking the world's economy. We are also remaking world politics.

As buyers or sellers, we have an unequal influence on this process; clearly, some people are more powerful than others. However, we are all affected by the process and all have choices to make—whether to buy Canadian- or Chinese-made goods, North American or Japanese cars, for example. More important, we can choose to elect governments that are more or less friendly to the concerns of ordinary citizens and workers, rather than those of investors.

The market is sociologically interesting because it shows how multiple *dyadic* (that is, two-person) relationships between buyers and sellers can gather into complex networks of exchange that indirectly connect (and affect) millions of unseen, distant participants all around the globe. In one way, this remarkable human achievement shows that we—through interdependence—can fulfill our needs without the supervision of a Hobbesian despot. However, recent economic events have also shown the need for control of the market. Markets do not and cannot regulate themselves. It is true they create prices in response to changes in supply and demand. But, as we have seen, they are also vulnerable to distortion by insiders, monopolists, and fraudsters. Without oversight and control, markets can easily create dangerous booms and busts. In 2010, we are all currently experiencing a bust—the global financial downturn that has affected billions of people, including you.

Markets respond to our human need for interdependence, and they are self-regulating in the sense that they set prices without outside political interference. This ability to set prices independently marks the difference between a 'free market' and a 'command economy', for example. However, to repeat, markets need legally enforceable rules and regulators to enforce them, or financial frauds will steal everyone's savings (again).

Over the past 30 years, deregulation has become the prime source of increased economic instability and inequality—hollowing out the middle class and transferring wealth from the poor to the rich—in the US, and to a lesser degree in Canada. Interestingly, while governments have increasingly tried to turn our attention to the (exaggerated) dangers of criminal violence and marijuana smoking, they have stood by while banks and brokers pilfered the savings of ordinary people.

The Internet is like the market in some respects, though different in others. What is the Internet, or cyberspace, but a vast information market, in which the participants establish the value and credibility of what others display? The most commonly used Internet institutions today (Google, eBay, Craigslist, Wikipedia, Facebook, and YouTube) are the results of information exchange—a market in information—that is virtually unregulated. People continue to use these cyber-institutions because, though unregulated, they are often as useful or credible as anything else available outside cyberspace.

The most striking feature of cyberspace is its diversity, ranging from a seemingly infinite number of commercial websites to personal blogs and various group effusions. The richness of the Internet has continued to de-localize social interactions. However, this process of de-localization began much earlier with the development of high-speed transport (trains, planes, and automobiles) and communication (the public mail service, the telegraph, and the telephone). Today, few of us rely exclusively on face-to-face communications. Most of the time, we communicate in other, less direct or less immediate ways. This, as we have noted, has led to the development of large social networks. In effect, society today is a network of networks. We are all embedded in large social networks, and most of these large social networks are all connected to one another.

As a result, we live in a 'small world', as psychologist Stanley Milgram showed in a landmark study conducted in 1967. Milgram's experiment grew out of the common observation that, when two strangers meet, they often search for, and find, people they both know. So, Milgram asked, 'What is the probability that two randomly selected people would know each other?' Or, asked a slightly different way, 'In a vast social network connecting everyone to everyone else, how many links are needed to connect any two randomly chosen people?'

Milgram devised an ingenious way to answer this question. He chose random individuals in two Midwestern US cities (Omaha, Nebraska, and Wichita, Kansas) to be the starting point of a 'search'. He then named specific individuals in Boston, Massachusetts, to be the destination, target, or final recipient of small packages. He asked the randomly chosen people in Omaha and Wichita to do their best to get their package to their Bostonian counterpart only through people they knew personally, on a first-name basis.

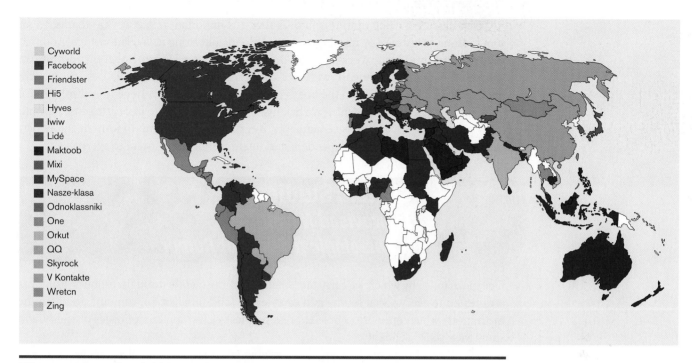

Cyworld
Facebook
Friendster
Hi5
Hyves
Iwiw
Lidé
Maktoob
Mixi
MySpace
Nasze-klasa
Odnoklassniki
One
Orkut
QQ
Skyrock
V Kontakte
Wretcn
Zing

Figure 16.1   Social Networks around the World

Source: Adapted from http://www.vincos.it/wp-content/uploads/2009/06/wmsn-06-09.png.

If, say, George Smith (the source in Wichita) knew John Brown (the target in Boston) personally, he would send the package directly to him. However, if George didn't know John personally, then he was to think of a friend or relative he knew personally (say, Alice in New York) who was more likely to know John the Bostonian. Usually, participants focused on geographic characteristics when choosing the next person in the chain, sending the package to someone who lived closer to the target. When the package eventually reached John in Boston, the researchers could examine the roster of recipients to see how many times it had been forwarded from person to person. And, for packages that never reached the destination, the incoming postcards helped identify where and when the chain was broken.

Sometimes a package would reach the target with only one or two stops, and sometimes the trip needed as many as nine or ten. Many of the packages never reached their destination at all. Of the packages that finally did reach their target, the average path length was between five and six people. This finding may be the origin of the phrase we sometimes hear today, that we are all connected by (only) 'six degrees of separation'.

Even more interesting, perhaps, was the finding reported later—sometimes called the 'small world property'—that individuals with very large and diverse networks played an especially important role in linking people and networks. When researchers first started to study social networks in the 1950s, they labelled these linking individuals 'sociometric stars'.

More recently, sociologists (like Ron Burt) have called them 'brokers' or even 'entrepreneurs', especially when they connect otherwise unconnected networks. These terms are used because these people's structural positions, as intermediaries between individuals, organizations, and networks, allows them to provide unusually valuable connective services. They are 'brokers' in the sense that they can act on behalf of others; they are 'entrepreneurs' in the usual sense of the 'go-between'. Typically, these brokers or entrepreneurs have an unusual amount of social capital, which they use to build their (and other people's) financial or political capital.

One might conclude from this finding that it is important to 'network'—that is, to set about forming networks by meeting new people and cultivating new relationships. And that strategy may occasionally work as planned. However, we need to remember that people can choose other people to network with, but they cannot choose the people *these* people will network with, and so on down the line. This means that we cannot hope to control the size or quality of the network to which we belong. At best, we can try to insinuate ourselves into other people's large and extensive networks, if we can identify them. In forming larger networks, we become more interdependent and interdependence is useful to everyone.

Classic Studies
Improvised News:
A Sociological Study of Rumor

One mechanism by which we carry out 'small world' business is through rumours. Rumours are created in every social setting and carry every kind of news. So, rumours are often the medium by which ordinary people express political views, construct images of reality, and show their social solidarity.

This view of rumours as a type of news emerges from the work of sociologist Tamotsu (Tom) Shibutani, who called rumours 'improvised news'. As Shibutani's classic study *Improvised News: A Sociological Study of Rumor* (1966) showed, rumours travel through existing networks and provide a basis for sociability among people. The information they convey is sometimes distorted but it always carries important social truths. Shibutani's work was significant for several reasons. Most important, it challenged the previously dominant notion that rumours are always inaccurate and distorted, and that people who transmit rumours are suggestible, disorganized, or psychologically unbalanced.

The characterization of rumour as pathology begins with a work called *The Psychology of Rumor* (1947) by Gordon Allport and Leo Postman. Using laboratory experiments, they simulated the children's game 'broken telephone'. In this context, they defined rumour as 'a specific (or topical) proposition for belief, passed along from person to person, usually by word of mouth, without secure standards or evidence being present' (Allport and Postman, 1947: ix). They showed that the movement of information from one person to another tends to distort the original message. The result, as heard by a large number of people most distant from the source, is often deeply flawed—even downright wrong. And such distorted information can have disastrous results; for example, it can ignite racial conflicts.

The shortcoming in this approach is that it takes rumour transmission out of its natural social context, so meanings and motives are lost. There are many important respects in which a psychology laboratory at, say, the University of British Columbia, is *not* like an Aboriginal community in the Yukon, for example. (If you remember nothing else from this book, please remember the previous sentence, for it calls attention to a key distinction between psychology and sociology.)

Shibutani offered an alternative way of thinking about rumours—one that focused on ordinary people in natural communities. Shibutani's research on rumour was shaped by his own experience at a Japanese-American relocation centre as a young man. There, he noted how an interned population made sense of its situation, using limited and often inaccurate news. Through this experience, Shibutani came to see rumour as social information with a purpose—collectively to achieve clarity on issues of common concern through repeated interaction and discussion. Rumour-formation, then, is a problem-solving strategy that relies on the pooling of resources—knowledge and intelligence—to make an informed and critical assessment of the situation. In this sense, rumours are 'improvised news': news imagined and created under conditions of hardship and confusion.

Rumours are a way of resolving ambiguity by pooling together available resources and knowledge.

As Shibutani points out in *Improvised News*, rumours typically emerge when unusual, unexpected events occur, and the normally reliable channels of communication break down. When the demand for credible, reliable news surpasses its availability, individuals rely on speculations and interpretations from others—often, from opinion leaders. Thus, reliance on rumour is not abnormal, vicious, or socially pathological, as Allport had suggested.

Shibutani also noted that rumours are not merely the result of faulty communication. In ambiguous situations, people often respond like practical problem-solvers, pooling their intellectual resources. These resources may include accurate data, guesses, beliefs, or speculation—constructing consensus from whatever sources that are available. Since much of life is ambiguous, this assessment of rumour may apply to large parts of life, well beyond what we normally think of as rumour. Many important decisions—whether personal, group, governmental, or otherwise—have to be made with inexact information. The rapid pace of social and environmental change calls for rapid decisions using a flood of inexact information. So our understanding of collective decision-making in ambiguous situations applies to a wide range of situations.

In this 'collective transaction', there are five roles to perform: messenger, interpreter, skeptic, protagonist, and decision maker. In the process of turning alleged facts into information, and information into ideas, some opinions are challenged and rejected, while others are retained. This continues until the group achieves a satisfactory interpretation of the situation. Contrary to the view of Allport and Postman that rumours grow increasingly distorted, threatening social order, Shibutani shows that rumours collaboratively gain accuracy and provide more stability (Miller, 2006).

Rumour is a form of communication, so it travels like other forms of human communication. As Shibutani saw at the relocation camps, rumours are transmitted within existing social networks. People rarely transmit them serially or randomly, indiscriminately to strangers and friends alike, as Allport and Postman seemed to suggest. According to Shibutani, rumour—as 'improvised news'—spreads within a network through a series of interpersonal communications, until they eventually reach the outskirts of the communication network.

Gradually, bits and pieces of information and opinion are combined, and through a series of deliberations an overall story gains consistency and clarity. By sharing with other members of the network, the 'improvised news' story becomes uniform across the different members.

As a result, rumour making is a powerful method of communication with the potential to strengthen and increase the solidarity of networks. Whenever reliable information is rare yet certainty is needed, 'improvised news' is created and shared within informal communication networks, often becoming the only source of information (Shibutani, 1966).

Some reviewers believed Shibutani's analysis was flawed. Shibutani had studied 60 situations and 471 rumours, and perhaps he should have based his conclusions on more (Knopf, 1975). He based his argument about the universality of rumour development on an unrepresentative sample of groups and rumours. Others believe Shibutani's theory is too simplistic and fails to consider the other forces that influence in rumour formation (Meyersohn, 1969). These might include the factors of interest to Allport: intergroup distrust, competition, and conflict, for example. As well, some reviewers think Shibutani overestimated human rationality in his study (ibid).

Nevertheless, Shibutani's work was the first comprehensive review of this topic (Knopf, 1975). It provided insight into the nature of rumour formation, altering the view of many about this topic. Shibutani showed that while some rumours are inaccurate and harmful, the vast majority are not. Most rumours come about as a way of interpreting unusual events when there is a shortage of trustworthy news.

Even more important, Shibutani offered us a positive image of human beings where Allport offered us a negative one. For Shibutani, people are trying—as rationally and creatively as possible—to deal with danger and uncertainty; rumours are the result of this. As we will see repeatedly in this chapter, ordinary people do these things and society is the result.

Voluntary Associations and Sociability

More organizationally complex than networks are voluntary associations, which address a wide variety of concerns, include alumni associations, charitable groups, fraternal orders, mutual aid societies, golf clubs, book clubs, church groups, and support groups—groups for recovering addicts, families, or prisoners, and for spouses of people with Alzheimer's disease, to name a few.

All of these groups draw on the same factors that make for social organization and integration. They promote familiarity among their members through communication and interaction. In some of these groups, intimacy, trust, and similarity develop gradually and even unexpectedly, as members work together to raise money for a charity, say, or recruit people to work on a community issue. The more people work together on a common goal, the more similar they become, and the more they find—and create—experiences they can share with each other.

These voluntary associations—though often aimed at solving a particular problem—are rooted ultimately in sociability, which some have considered a natural and universal human impulse. Sociability—as pure play—may be the most basic human inclination. The philosopher Johan Huizinga (1955 [1938]) spoke of humanity as 'homo ludens'—'man the game-player'. According to Huizinga, play has three key features that attract people: play is free, in fact, it is freedom in itself; play is a departure from 'ordinary' or 'real' life; and play occupies its own time and place. When people play, they leave themselves and enter into 'the moment'. Every society has play—even animals have play—and one might say that culture itself is a form of play (consider wordplay in the form of puns and jokes, for example). In this respect, the abstract arts like music are pure play, with no meaning beyond themselves but pleasure. Sport and other competition can be pure play, so long as they have no hidden motive (like profit).

One thing that makes playing with others fun is that different people bring different qualities and personalities to the event. People discuss politics differently, view life differently, play cards differently, play musical instruments differently, dance differently, and tell different kinds of jokes or stories. These differences make social interaction interesting and unpredictable. Yet, as Georg Simmel points out, despite these differences, play follows social forms; like fashion, play must be more than the mere expression of personal tastes and peculiarities. Otherwise, there would be no bridge between the participants; people would be playing by themselves in parallel, like toddlers, rather than really playing *with* each other.

Even in play that is free and for fun (not profit), there are social norms to obey: specifically, norms of tact. These norms, related to civility, oblige us to keep a little of ourselves back even when we are being the most open and intimate. To do otherwise would be to use a play event for some other purpose: to demand attention, support, pity, or encouragement, for example. Play is not intended to be a psychodrama.

So, when people organize voluntarily—as they do in so many domains of life, every single day—they do so in ways that are organized, but not always goal oriented. Still, goal-orientation is another important reason people come together.

The Benefits of Voluntary Associations

Not only do voluntary associations provide sociability: they bring together a diverse group of people for a common cause (Côté and Erickson, 2009). In doing so, they increase people's knowledge and social tolerance. In these associations, very different people are apt to meet voluntarily as equals, so these associations are often 'sites of positive learning' and 'schools for democracy' (ibid).

That said, voluntary associations have a somewhat unpredictable effect on social tolerance, the effect varying with the nature both of the group and its activities. For example, members of environmental groups tend to be more tolerant than average. Their ideals of global justice encourage discussions of social issues and a positive view of non-white people. On the other hand, members of sports groups tend to be less tolerant than average. The competitiveness of sports and the fixation on winning favours antagonism and hostility. Likewise, occupational groups—labour unions, business groups, and professional associations—are highly sensitive to economic competition and may therefore express hostile views towards outsiders and minority groups. The increased perception of threat discourages tolerance here and drives people further apart.

So, familiarity and sociability are important sources of tolerance, but they tend to work best under non-competitive (friendly) conditions. In this respect, trust and liking are as important as (mere) familiarity.

Trust, like familiarity, is essential in society—a key to social order, co-operation, and democracy. Trust is the set of 'socially learned and socially confirmed expectations that people have of each other, of the organizations and institutions in which they live, and of the natural and moral social orders that set the fundamental understandings for their lives' (Barber, 1983). Of course, we trust different people to different degrees, in different ways: for example, we trust close friends who keep our secrets, neighbours who serve us homemade food, babysitters who look after our children, and doctors who tend to our health care. Under some conditions, trust can also be extended to strangers or *generalized others*—for example, we trust strangers to stop at red lights (Paxton, 2007). In general, however, trust is limited and conditional. Unconditional trust is rare and, sometimes, foolhardy.

Still, trust enables us to live near one another without paralyzing fear. Trust is hard to develop between groups; doing so requires us to share rules and interpretations about the world, which increases our predictability in one another's eyes. The question then is, 'Where does trust come from and how is it increased?' Often, trust arises within voluntary associations, as an unexpected benefit. Within groups, trustworthy people are rewarded and untrustworthy people are sanctioned. This increases the likelihood that members will become more trustworthy and come to trust others.

Often, trust arises through connection as well as familiarity. Connectedness expands the category of 'we' by increasing predictability through the expansion of norms and morals. The overlapping of associations increases opportunities to meet individuals outside the group who are not immediately associated. In this way, trust is created by 'vouching', the transfer of trust to less familiar but socially connected third parties. I grant trust to someone who my friend or cousin or workmate says is trustworthy, because they say so (and I trust them). Therefore, voluntary associations that are more connected with one another help to promote generalized trust and social cohesion.

In this sense, we can think of society not so much as a network of individuals (let alone, a mere collection of individuals), but as a network of organizations.

People Control One Another Informally

As social animals, people tend to crave the good opinion of others, their company, and their approval. They even base their opinions of themselves largely on how they believe other people view them and feel punished—bruised even—when other people hint at disapproval.

In fact, most people can be made to feel guilt or shame even without enforcing social norms. This, George Mead would say, is rooted in childhood learning of the views of the 'generalized other'. Informal social control—which controls people through guilt, shame, gossip, rumour, and threatened rejection—is extremely effective under many circumstances. It is inexpensive to administer and often almost impossible to see. It seamlessly punishes the rule-breaker and silently rewards the conformist with esteem, trust and, most important, co-operation. Informal social control, then, is like a wonder drug, a miracle cure: almost free, almost painless, almost invisible, and it usually works. Compare that with imprisonment: enormously expensive, terribly painful, a blight on the society, and it almost never works.

The idea of communities enforcing their rules through informal punishments (like shaming, ridicule, and ostracism—also, gossip and rumour) has been central to social science since the beginnings of anthropology over a century ago. Some believe that control and conformity are explainable in individual terms, as self-interested behaviour. Everyone obeys the rules because each individual will gain from obeying and lose by not obeying. Others believe that altruistic rewards and punishments—'strong reciprocity'—play an important role in promoting co-operation. Societies in which people obey the rules and behave altruistically tend to survive.

That said, the wellspring of altruism is always hard to locate, and especially difficult to locate in large, complex, individualistic societies like our own as opposed to small tribal societies. All religions call for altruism and obedience, but we are increasingly a secular society. All families and communities pay homage to some measure of self-sacrifice, but real altruism is so rare that the few true altruists are widely viewed as saints. So, again by default, it is easiest to explain conformity as a reaction to social control and a self-interested obedience of social rules.

'Social control' is an idea especially at home in sociology and anthropology, yet seemingly outside the realm of other social sciences (such as political science or criminology.) The concept identifies a new realm for discussing order and regulation. Social control, defined as 'control by society or social relations', is distinct from, say, political control,

Markets are largely maintained by our interdependence.

military control, police control, or even legal control. 'Social control' identifies society as the source of control in our lives. In doing so, it calls attention to civil society as a place of importance in human lives, rather than the state (highlighted by Hobbes 1968 [1660]) or the economy (highlighted by Karl Marx.)

Viewed in this historical light, the discussion of social control in sociology is finally a discussion of the connection between sociology's two key questions: Why (and how) is social order achieved? And, why does social inequality exist (and persist)? The connections can be stated in many ways: How does social inequality affect the forces of social order?; How are the forces of social order used to preserve unequal advantages?; and so on. These, you may have noticed, are the questions around which this book was organized.

What is perhaps most remarkable about society is that it is a co-operative venture. We are all continuously engaged in social control practices. These practices do not require that we all have guns and badges to 'police' the social micro-order in which we live. By studying social control in this micro-order, we gain a better understanding of it—what it is, why it is necessary, and how it can sometimes harm us.

Sociological theories about small groups and social systems, especially by the sociologist George Homans, provide us with deeper insight into group influences—especially, into the ways in which groups protect themselves against deviant activities and deviant identities. These principles apply even to couples and families, the smallest long-standing groups.

People use many informal ways to control one another, but these mainly fall within two processes: rewarding wanted behaviour and withholding rewards for unwanted behaviour. Rewards between spouses, for example, include respect, love, sex, friendship, emotional support, and sometimes money. One thing that makes couples—and indeed all groups—unique is their shared history of good and bad experiences, including the history of rewards and punishments they have given one another. This generalization applies as readily to work groups, cliques, teams, clubs, bands, and gangs as it does to marriages and families. At ground level, among real people in real situations, shared, interlinked, mutually rewarding histories of life together are effective sources of control.

Classic Studies
The Civilizing Process

Evidently, in many situations, people can control one another informally. On the other hand, people sometimes also need the power of the state to back up their efforts to control one another. Thus, formal and informal controls work together to bring about important social changes. This is evident in a classic work on good manners and etiquette by sociologist Norbert Elias in *The Civilizing Process* (1969 [1939]).

The Civilizing Process comprises two volumes—*The History of Manners* and *Power and Civility*—with a single aim. Together, they show that polite manners and state government develop together. These developments make up the so-called 'civilizing process' which link changes in politics to changes in interpersonal relations (such as table etiquette and good manners generally).

Good manners, according to Elias, historically began with the aristocracy and spread to the bourgeoisie, who then began to teach these manners to their children. This sounds simple but it took a long time—generations and perhaps centuries. Like other fashions, good manners spread downward through emulation of the rich and powerful by people with social pretensions. Over the same period—roughly 1300 to 1600—the bourgeoisie was establishing itself in cities, through the spread of commerce and early versions of global trade. With more money and more time to spend, good manners and domesticity became important middle-class virtues.

How do we know this? In brief, Elias examined changes in the rules governing public behaviour. In the first volume of his study, he documents changes in table manners, such as the growing use of knives and forks; in excretion, such as the growing use of private places for urinating and defecating; in sexual relations, which increasingly demanded privacy too. In learning these new manners, people learn to repress their 'natural' drives. Shows of embarrassment and shame become more common with the spread of politeness norms. The spread of politeness, generated by class distinction, created even more class distinctions, with manners serving as markers of social standing. People with pretensions to the 'upper class'—or at least the middle class—were expected to show their classiness through elegant manners and a knowledge of etiquette.

The second volume of this study shows that social behaviours and social structures reinforce each other. Self-control—in the form of good manners, polite excretion, and private sexuality, for example—coincides with the rise of a strong state, since it is through the rise of this state that a national, official culture develops. Regional variations are less socially acceptable—whether in speech, dress, dining, or defecation.

Over several centuries, monarchical power grew throughout Europe. Central authorities (especially kings) came to monopolize wealth, build powerful armies, and gain a following of noble courtiers. The state became more stable and so did the rule imposed on civilians. Citizens were expected to regulate their conduct in an increasingly predictable, acceptable manner. This spread of norms set the groundwork for social complexity. As norms became more predictable, people became more secure, depended more on one another, and trusted one another despite differences. However, this also obliged them to act in socially acceptable ways.

Elias documents the changes in manners from 1400–1800, mainly in France and Germany, by examining etiquette books and other primary sources. At least one reviewer has questioned the reliability of Elias' sources, as it is unknown whether 'manners manuals were actually followed' at that time, given that most people—those who formed the lower classes—were illiterate (Seigel, 1979: 125). In addition, as this work only looked at European manners, the findings may not be generalizable to other societies (ibid). Another reviewer points out that Elias ignores other 'variables such as the emerging concepts of privacy . . . the changing status of women, [and] medical and scientific discoveries' (Bullough, 1979: 444).

Despite such limitations, this work remains important for several reasons. It was the first to give the code of manners a scholarly interpretation, which is 'crucial for an understanding of what had moved men and peoples in modern times' (Mosse, 1978: 178). Beyond that, the work showed a clear linkage between the microsociological and macrosociological realms of society: between formal and informal control, for example. As we have noted throughout this book, this linkage is fundamental to sociology and we will visit it again in the last section of this book.

As Norbert Elias shows in his study, we all exist in both large and small social settings, so we are all influenced by national life and family life, the coercive power of armies and the coercive power of ridicule. We are all socialized into this multi-dimensional reality and will always be under its influence. This is particularly true when we undertake the study of social movements and their effects on political life. As usual in sociology, there are alternative approaches to this topic.

Ways of Looking at . . .
SOCIAL MOVEMENTS AND VOLUNTARY ASSOCIATIONS

As we have said, social movements grow out of voluntary associations. And as in other subfields, sociologists vary somewhat in their approach to the study of social movements. These approaches include the *breakdown approach*, *resource mobilization approach*, *cultural approach*, and *political process approach*. As we will see, to varying degrees they reflect the influences of functionalism, critical theory, and symbolic interactionism.

The so-called *breakdown approach* builds on the work of Émile Durkheim and reflects the dominant concerns of functionalism. To repeat, functionalism assumes that social order and consensus are the basis of society. Anything that disturbs the social order will disturb the members of society, causing them to seek ways to re-establish equilibrium. So, these theorists argue that social movements form when rapid and widespread changes in society weaken the social bonds—the shared norms and values—that hold society together, causing people distress. Social movements, then, signify societal disintegration. Arising only when social equilibrium has been disturbed—whether by war, natural disaster, or economic upheaval—they are a symptom of social disorganization.

A related functionalist approach, *relative deprivation theory*, argues that people form protest movements when they believe that society is falling short of what they expect or aspire to have, even if in the past people were satisfied with less. This argument, which emerged during the 1960s (an important period for social uprisings), goes like this. During a period of stable deprivation, people may be unhappy but—given low expectations—they are peaceful and satisfied. When the society enters a period of economic and social progress, people are suddenly able to buy more goods, and the rights of citizens improve. As a result, their expectations about the quality of life rise. However, this social improvement may not continue as quickly as hoped for. There may even be periods of reversal, when prices rises, living conditions worsen, and authorities become strict, censoring the press and forbidding protest, for example (Davies, 1962). Yet, because high (new) expectations persist, a gap opens up between the newly established expectations and disappointing realities. It is this gap that gives rise to protest or even rebellion by the least-advantaged citizens.

Three kinds of critique have been levelled at relative deprivation theory and, by implication, at the functional approach. First, it is not always only the most disadvantaged members of society who are frustrated and fight for social change. Members of the middle and upper classes are more likely than poor people to lead revolutions, especially the successful ones. That is because they have access to the resources and social contacts that are needed to bring about radical social changes. Second, not all societies that experience relative deprivation try to bring about change through revolution, so another factor must be involved. Third, the relative deprivation 'theory' may be more **ideology** than theory, intended to criticize protesters who the ruling class deems impatient and irrational. This approach devalues protest as a seemingly trivial symptom of discontent.

Another functionalist theory, called *systemic theory*, also grows out of the social breakdown perspective. This approach, similar to relative deprivation theory, focuses not on the frustration of individuals but on the whole society (Smelser, 1963). It highlights the importance of groups and their dynamics, pointing out that although many individuals may feel frustrated about social issues, their frustration is effective in altering those conditions only when they mobilize as a group. For example, they must develop a common ideology and agree on a plan for change. This theory improves on relative deprivation theory by focusing on the organizational aspects of protest, making it a more sociological approach; but some assert it is ultimately based on circular reasoning (on this, see Aya, 1990).

Conversely, sociologists who take the critical theory approach call attention to flaws in these functionalist theories. Critics of the breakdown approach and theories stemming from it argue that social conflict is a natural feature of social life—not a pathology or symptom of social disorganization. Social movements are types of *organization*—not merely disorganization—and, by destroying current social arrangements, expose the conditions that perpetuate inequality. In short, most movements are not spontaneous, childish outbursts of frustration but organizations with rational goals and plans.

So, for example, *resource mobilization* theorists believe protest organizations are much like many other organizations, and just as helpful to society. Like other organizations, social movements try to spread the influence of their perspective on society through their **counter-ideology**. As well, like other organizations, social movements try to find and mobilize supporters for their position.

Resource mobilization theorists do not assume a consensus about the way society is organized. In fact, they believe just the opposite, arguing that there will always be frustrated people in society because social goods are (always) unequally distributed. So, for a resource mobilization theorist, the question is, 'Why aren't people protesting all the time?' They conclude that resource availability—money, contacts, and so on—determines the formation and actions of social movements, not goals and motivations. Given the many injustices that characterize society, there are always good reasons to protest. However, only occasionally are there adequate resources to do so.

To succeed (or even hope to succeed), protestors need at least one and (perhaps as many as) three types of power. They need *economic power*—the control over material production (for example capital, technology, labour power, materials, and so on), or at least money. They need *political power*—control over the legitimate use of violence (for example, control over the state, police, or military). Finally, they need *ideological power*—the ability to spread symbols and ideologies through social institutions like schools, churches, newspapers, and the media. Social movements arise when they gain access to at least one of these resources; they succeed if they gain more access than the forces opposing them.

Often, these protest organizations build on already-existing social forms like social networks. Informal networks of friends and colleagues within the movement provide an accessible and inexpensive set of potential supporters waiting for the right conditions (Melucci, 1989). Likewise, informal networks of outside organizations are also important, since they may provide aid and support to the social movement. Thus, the interaction between organizations is also important for our understanding of social movements.

ideology

A strategy, program, or point of view that justifies the goals and strategies of the movement: for example, it may justify demands for gender equality.

counter-ideology

An ideology that supports alternative social values and challenges the **dominant ideology**.

dominant ideology

An ideology that supports the status quo and the interests of the ruling class.

There are two different approaches to how resource mobilization occurs: the *utilitarian perspective* and the *political conflict theory*. The *utilitarian perspective* assumes that individuals join social movements to promote their own interests. No doubt there is some truth to this; people are unlikely to join movements that clearly oppose their own interests. However, movement formation cannot be explained by individual motivations alone; social incentives also motivate people to join. For example, some people join a movement simply because it is headed for success (the *bandwagon effect*). Or they may join it because they see similarities between themselves and current members, or feel pressure from friends or relatives to join.

Another critical theory, the *political conflict theory*, highlights how social classes promote the interests of their members through social movements. You will recall that Marx theorized extensively about the mobilization of the working class, and even predicted a worldwide revolution by working-class people. Researchers in this tradition have found the most important conditions for success of class-based social movements to be social ties between members, influential social contacts, and available resources. Also important is the role of the state, since it has a significant influence on whether, and how, the movement gains opportunities to voice its concerns (Mitlin, 2008; Walker, Martin, and McCarthy, 2008).

Finally, some theories reflect the influence of symbolic interactionism and the social construction approach. These *cultural approaches* to social movements stress the importance of values and beliefs in their analysis, recognizing that people react not to social situations per se, but to their interpretation and evaluation of these situations. The resource mobilization approach takes values and beliefs for granted in its analysis of social movements. However, since the 1980s, many scholars have recognized this limitation and made culture central to their analysis, noting that the goals of social movements, and the ways social movements pursue those goals, are always linked to cultural considerations.

Two cultural approaches to social movements are important: the *new social movements* (NSMs) approach and *framing theory*. The NSMs approach, which arose in Europe (Touraine, 1981; Melucci, 1989), argues that structural changes in Western society over the last century have given rise to new identities that are not class-based. In effect, they have given rise to 'identity politics'—a substitute for class-based politics (Martin, 2001). Today, identity-based movements that focus on race and ethnicity, gender, sexual orientation, age, and so on are especially important. These newer social movements are more about the particular people they speak for and the equalities they seek rather than about material resources. These groups fight for equity, dignity, and cultural recognition, as much as for economic justice. In other words, they seek the right to practise certain styles of life without prejudice or discrimination.

These movements have mainly emerged since the 1960s, fighting against what they saw as intrusion into people's private lives of citizens. Declaring his support for this way of thinking, in 1967 Prime Minister Trudeau famously said, 'There's no place for the state in the bedrooms of the nation' (CBC Archives, 1967). Identity-based social movements would surely agree with him.

Like the NSMs approach, *framing theory*, which emerged in North America, has also criticized resource mobilization theory for its lack of attention to culture (Benford and Snow, 2000). Framing theory, inspired by the symbolic interactionist tradition, is interested in how people develop and communicate cultural goals in a social movement (Andretta, 2005; Nadeem, 2008). The process by which individuals adopt ideologies and plans in a particular movement, called *frame alignment*, is necessary if a social movement is to work actively and collectively (Snow et al., 1986).

It is useful to consider some of these ideas about identity politics, social networks, and rational organization in connection with a particular social movement: in this case, the women's temperance movement that, in early twentieth-century America, succeeded briefly in banning alcoholic beverages.

Classic Studies
Symbolic Crusade

One classic study of such a social movement is *Symbolic Crusade* (1963), by Joseph Gusfield. An American sociologist, Gusfield has taught mainly at the University of California in San Francisco. He has also worked with various governmental boards on issues of alcoholism and drunk driving. Besides *Symbolic Crusade*, his other books include *The Culture of Public Problems: Drinking-Driving and the Symbolic Order* (1981), *Contested Meanings: the Construction of Alcohol Problems* (1996), and *Performing Action: Artistry in Human Behavior and Social Research* (2000).

Symbolic Crusade is about the social forces behind the rise of Prohibition legislation in the United States. In December 1917, the US Congress began debating the Eighteenth Amendment to the Constitution. This proposed Amendment banned 'the manufacture, sale, or transportation of intoxicating liquors'. The Eighteenth Amendment was passed in January 1919, and went into effect federally in January 1920. However, the law proved hard to enforce and was a boon to organized crime; so this prohibition on alcohol drinking lasted more in name than in fact for the next dozen years, becoming especially unpopular in large US cities. Finally, in March 1933, President Franklin Roosevelt signed an Amendment that once again allowed the production and sale of certain kinds of alcoholic drinks. The Eighteenth Amendment was fully repealed with confirmation of the Twenty-first Amendment in December 1933.

Symbolic Crusade outlines the role of the Women's Christian Temperance Union (WCTU)—a voluntary association—in promoting this troubled, ineffective, and short-lived legislation. From 1874 onward, the WCTU made repeated efforts to reduce or outlaw alcohol consumption in America. And for an even longer period, it had sought nationwide 'moral' improvement by educating people about the dangers of alcohol and trying to change the conditions that caused people to drink. This was linked, at some points, to other organized efforts to achieve women's rights—so-called first-wave feminism, as many married women were concerned about their husbands' drinking and the consequences of this drinking for household poverty, domestic violence, and poor parenting.

However, this battle against alcohol was also part of a larger status war. According to Gusfield, the point of Prohibition was not to make people stop consuming alcohol—that was impossible—but to affirm sobriety (the guiding goal of WCTU) as a key value in American society. This success, indirectly, would confer a morally superior status on the WCTU and its members: chiefly, small-town white Anglo-Saxon Protestant women. However, this goal would never be achieved. Industrialization, urbanization, and immigration—important forces of social change after the American Civil war—all threatened the traditional native-born WASP lifestyle, and more important, undermined traditional moral authority.

As their efforts at change faded, gradually the WCTU's educational strategies became more coercive, turning away from public education towards prohibitive legislation. The gloves were off. This was status warfare—the native-borns against the immigrants, Protestants against Catholics, small-town people against city people, women against men. In the introduction to his book, Gusfield writes: 'For many observers of American life, the Temperance Movement is evidence for an excessive moral perfectionism and an overly legalistic bent to American culture . . . . This moralism and utopianism brings smiles to the cynical and fear to the sinner. Such a movement seems at once naive, intolerant, saintly and silly.'

The Temperance Movement was more about status and the principle of sobriety than alcohol consumption.

Gusfield uses various historical sources to support his argument, including partisan writings and records of temperance organizations. In analyzing the documentary material, Gusfield focuses especially on 'Max Weber's multidimensional view of social class, with particular emphasis upon style of life' (Ullman, 1964: 154). Gusfield thus presents the temperance movement as a group for whom status is more central than (economic) class. Overall, Gusfield's study focuses on two main themes: alcohol as a symbolic social issue, and other 'non-economic' issues related to temperance reforms.

In the study, Gusfield distinguishes usefully between class politics, expressive politics, and status politics. The latter is central to his argument that 'limited use of alcoholic beverages and then total abstinence became symbolic for certain groups of their legitimate claims for high status' (1963: 27). For Gusfield, class politics 'arise out of conflicting economic interests' and are 'oriented toward the allocation of material resources' (Lang, 1964: 768). Expressive politics on the other hand are 'characterized by goalless behaviour or by pursuit of goals which are unrelated to the discontents from which the movement has its source' (Clarke, 1987: 237).

The study also examines shifts in the movement's organization, which affected the way goals for social change were pursued. Gusfield notes that initially the movement was a vehicle 'for the assertion of moral superiority' of upper class influence (Ullman, 1964). During this period, the organization pursued national 'moral' changes through assimilationist, inclusive strategies. These included working for greater access to education, attempting to change the social conditions that caused people to drink, and generally persuading people to build a better society (Zald, 1964). When these efforts failed to work, the movement adopted a shriller, more coercive approach.

This study has been criticized for various reasons. For example, one reviewer asserts the distinction between status and class politics is not as clear as Gusfield has claimed it was (Zald, 1964). Another reviewer, similarly, believes Gusfield unduly ignored 'economic

Environmental activists are often integral in promoting discussion of issues that are not only related to the planet, but also tied in with social and political arguments.

and expressive factors in favour of cultural conflicts' and neglected the self-interests of movement members (Hessel, 1964: 56). And, as another reviewer points out, the efforts of the group to change society were also a way for its members to protect their own family and community lifestyles (Rumbarger, 1989).

Despite these criticisms, Gusfield's study provides an alternative perspective on a major historical movement. His application of sociological theories and concepts to historical research yielded a new approach to studying social movements in their pursuit of social change. Clearly, his approach viewed social movements as efforts to consciously change society, not merely as symptoms of social disorganization, narrow self-interest, or class identification.

Changing Causes of Social Movement Formation

Let us return to social movements, because they provide lessons about everyday social organization and social change that can be applied to a wide variety of sociological themes. As we have seen, there are many ways to understand social movements, their motives, causes, and processes. While social movements are a mechanism for social change, they exist within a social context and therefore are affected by changes in society. So, just as society evolves, so too do social movements.

In the eighteenth and nineteenth centuries, most social movements in Europe and elsewhere were organized poorly. They lacked resources and, more important they were limited by difficulties associated with pre-industrial travel and communication. As a result, they usually targeted local issues. However, with the rise of urbanized nation-states and improved technology, social movements began to grow and gain more importance.

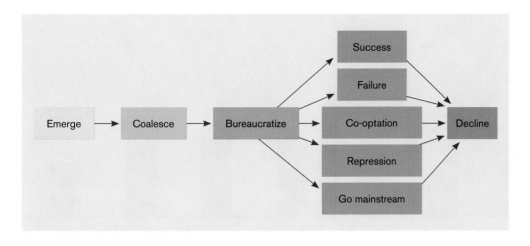

Figure 16.2   Stages of Social Movements

Source: Adapted from Answers.com (N.d.).

In the early twentieth century, they became organized by developing a complex division of labour and targeting the most pressing social issues. These movements—especially those aimed at forming workers' unions—sought to reduce economic inequality, increase political representation for working people, and redistribute the wealth that was held in upper-class hands. To achieve their goals, these early social movements began to invent new and more effective ways to protest, such as mass demonstrations, blockades, boycotts, sit-ins, and strikes.

In the second half of the twentieth century, ever more influential social movements emerged, often called *new social movements* (NSMs). They exhibited a greater awareness of the social inequalities faced by women, black people, and gays and lesbians, as well as

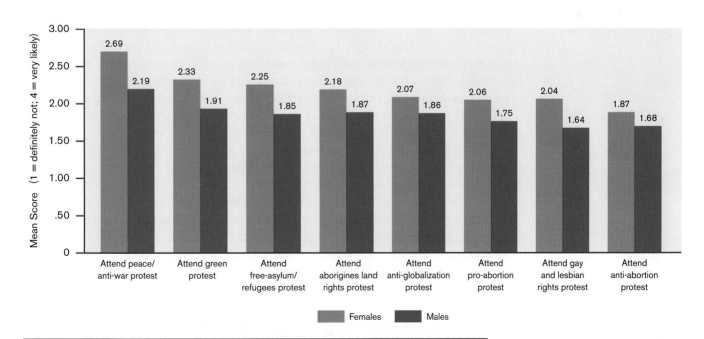

Figure 16.3   Student Willingness to Participate in Demonstrations in Support of Specific Social Movements, by Sex, Australia

Source: Adapted from Saha et al. (2005), Figure 5.

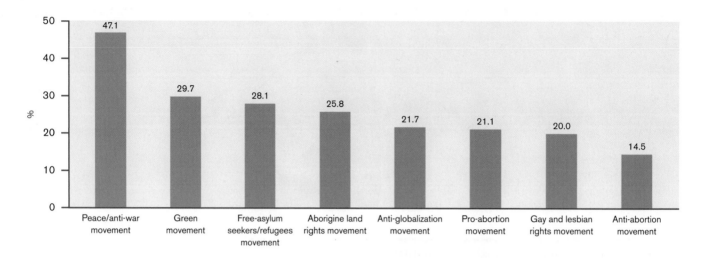

Figure 16.4   Percentage Who Would Likely or Very Likely Join Protest in Support of Movement, Australia

Source: Adapted from Saha et al. (2005), Figure 4.

working class and unemployed people. Besides aiming to redistribute wealth, these social movements fought for equity and human rights.

According to Kitschelt (1993), social movement activity has risen over the last few centuries, with movements becoming more complex and shifting their focus to societal rather than local issues. Especially in democratic countries, social movements have become larger and more common since the 1960s. However, around this general trend toward more social movement activity, we see a fluctuation. Some periods are much more active than others, with social movement activity rising and falling with changes in the social and political context.

Social movements are most likely to form and protest when political parties and other interest groups fail to satisfy public demands. Under such conditions of dissatisfaction, people are more likely to organize, mobilize available resources, and put a plan into action. However, this momentum lessens when resources become scarce, members' involvement dwindles, or the issue at hand receives more attention from political parties. Note, however, that a decline in social movement activity does not prove that the original problem has gone away or that discontent has dissipated—merely, that resources for mobilization have dried up or other institutions have channelled the popular discontent.

Social movements that gain a great deal of popular support may sometimes turn into political parties, or they may be co-opted into existing political parties. For example, the Green parties in Europe emerged out of environmental movements in the 1960s and 1970s, as did the Green Party of Canada (Green Party of Canada, 2009). When a social movement becomes a political party (by campaigning in elections), it alters its goals slightly. Parties, besides fighting for social change, are primarily concerned with winning and keeping political power (Camcastle, 2007). This pragmatism creates a party identity but sometimes disappoints members of the original social movement, alienating potential voters (Pelletier and Guerin, 2000).

Social Movements in a Globalized World

As noted earlier in the chapter, social movements have changed over the years, increasing in size and complexity; such change is likely to continue. The development of information

Media Distortion

16.1

Pageant Protest Sparked Bra-Burning Myth

The vision of feminists burning their bras entered the public imagination following media reports of a protest of the 1968 Miss America pageant—but no bras were torched, according to protest organizer Carol Hanisch. While the group had intended to burn their bras, police wouldn't allow a fire on the boardwalk outside the Atlantic City convention hall where the pageant was held. So, instead of burning their restrictive undergarments, the women tossed them into a garbage can, along with other 'instruments of female torture'—mops, girdles, pots and pans, and *Playboy* magazines. Hanisch says 'if they had called us "girdle burners", every woman in America would have run to join us'.

'Bra burning' was mentioned in a *New York Post* story on the protest—fire was a familiar element of protest in those days, as military draft cards were burned in protest of the Vietnam War.

The group decided to protest the Miss America pageant to bring attention to the oppressive beauty standards that women were expected to strive for. Hanisch recalls that they were propelled to act by a movie that highlighted the pageant's swimsuit competition. 'It got me thinking that protesting the pageant might be a good way to launch the movement into the public consciousness', Hanisch says. 'It was kind of a gutsy thing to do. Miss America was this 'American pie' icon. Who would dare criticize this?'

Source: Adapted from Greenfieldboyce (2008).

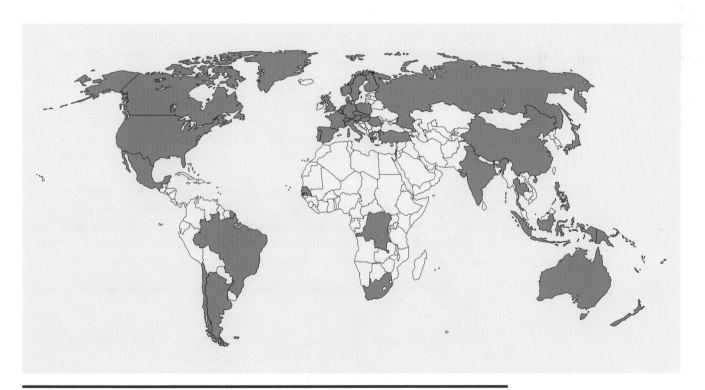

Figure 16.5   National Offices of Greenpeace, Worldwide

Source: Adapted from Artamonov (2009).

technology, and especially the global reach of the Internet, has been instrumental in this process of enlargement and increased complexity.

However, globalization also poses new problems. Globalization means the stakes, the territory, and the resources needed to advance social movements are larger and require stronger leaders and more-dedicated followers than ever before. Moreover, the easy movement of capital, people, and organizations around the world changes the political terrain, altering the opportunities for and constraints on collective action. No one has studied this dramatic, remarkable change more thoroughly or effectively than sociologist Charles Tilly.

People Are Talking About . . .
CHARLES TILLY

Charles Tilly was born in 1929 near Chicago. He studied at Harvard and Oxford universities, and received a Ph.D. in sociology from Harvard in 1958. He taught at the University of Delaware, Harvard University, the University of Toronto, the University of Michigan, The New School, and Columbia University. At the time of his death in 2009, Charles Tilly was Joseph L. Buttenwieser Professor of Social Science, Columbia University.

Tilly, an influential scholar of social movements, focused on large-scale social change in Europe since 1500, and the role played by political conflict in those changes. He showed how social protest is inevitably linked to the politics, society, and economics of its time and place. Collective violence, too, is rooted in political conflict. For his book *Popular Contention in Great Britain, 1758–1834*, Tilly examined over 8,000 'contentious gatherings'—meetings of ordinary local people making collective claims. From this he formulated his notion that social movements have their beginnings in specific events.

The social movement phenomenon originated in the West in the late eighteenth century, according to Tilly. As Western culture spread through trade, colonialism, and migration, the tendency for people to form social movements spread as well, particularly in societies that were developing democratic systems. Tilly claimed that successful social movements can aid political causes.

In his biography, Carlo Ruzzo (in Scott, 2006: 211–12) notes that Tilly often 'emphasizes the role of structural political conflict over dispositional variables, showing that political identities result from relational dynamics, not from durable psychological dispositions as many approaches to political identity instead contend'. This is perhaps best explained in his ambitious and abstract work, *Durable Inequality* (1999), which examines inequalities that persist over repeated interactions.

Finally, Tilly noted the need to distinguish between the goals of social movements and their eventual outcomes. A movement seeking democracy might defeat its own purpose and actually impede democracy; for example, a democratic movement might be disrupted by internal anarchist factions. Or, a movement against democracy, such as an anti-immigration movement, might prompt citizens and government to take up the cause of democracy in opposition.

Source: Adapted from *Fifty Key Sociologists: The Contemporary Theorists* (edited by John Scott, London: Routledge, 2006) and other sources.

Stanley (2009), advocates following the approach Tilly laid out in *Big Structures, Large Processes, Huge Comparisons* (1984) for narrative inquiry. Tilly points out that narrative inquiry is typically too narrow in paying attention to the small-scale, local matters that are the substance of the stories. Stanley agrees that analysis should place the stories in the context of contemporary, large-scale, collective issues, and look beyond the storyteller's own version of the causes and effects contained in the narrative. The analyst should look for and examine fundamental large-scale processes, their connections with each other, and how they affect social structures to show how social change takes place.

Sakai (2009) follows Tilly's model for analyzing narrative in examining trans-generational narratives. She studies stories told by people of Northern Ireland who were born after World War II. In these stories, the narrators encompass both their own experiences in living through the post-war conflicts in Northern Ireland, and those of their parents during World War II. Sakai finds that the storytellers reinterpret their own lives through the experiences of their parents, and thus place themselves within a 'macro memory framework'. In this way, the trans-generational stories show the influence of collective social cause-and-effect on individual lives, and can be seen to contribute significantly to ethnic, national, and cultural identity.

For Tilly, the job of the sociologist is to trace the 'logic of violence' in the mobilization of social change. Green and Ward (2009) agree, claiming that a 'logic of violence' is evident in Iraq following the invasion of 2003. One aspect of the 'logic of violence' that emerges as especially important in Iraq is 'dual purpose violence', which simultaneously serves two or more goals of individuals, groups and political organizations. So, for example, contenders for economic or political influence may commit crimes—using bribery, extortion, blackmail, and even assassination—to further their goals; and the (illegal) black market may be economically as important as the legal market for goods and services. This seemingly happens in many societies with unstable governments. Remedying this in the context of Iraq means not only consolidating central government power but building numerous state-like power structures at local and regional level.

Likewise, Pallister-Wilkins (2009) looks at activism surrounding the building of the West Bank barrier wall between Israeli and Palestinian territories, noting that both Israeli and Palestinian activists protest the building of the wall. The Palestinians are motivated to protest by the threat to the well-being or even survival of their communities. The Israelis, on the other hand, show that people need not feel oppressed or threatened themselves to act against perceived injustice. These activists protest the exercise of power in true post-structuralist fashion, by addressing its networks, extensions, and connections. By seeking change through direct action, they also follow the model of protest-anarchism—taking matters into their own hands rather than expecting the powerful to grant their demands.

Hockey, Meah, and Robinson (2009) look at the tension between social constraints and individual actions in the sex lives of young adults during World War II. They find that despite the collective social taboos on premarital and extramarital sex, in the historical context of general social upheaval in wartime, individual young people were forming sexual relationships outside of marriage. As with the evolution of good manners discussed earlier, neither the individualistic nor the collective approach to analyzing personal narratives alone is able to provide a satisfactory explanation, and a combination of these approaches is needed. This example also shows how the social conventions, which incorporated distinctions of class, gender, and identity, could be upheld on the collective level (as cultural notions of 'proper behaviour') yet flouted on the individual level.

Thus, a review of recent writings finds continued application of the work by Charles Tilly—over 150 journal articles applying Tilly's work in the last 15 years. Clearly, sociologists are talking about Charles Tilly.

Without doubt, Charles Tilly belongs in our comprehensive, fusion approach to sociology. Like Habermas, Tilly asks large, morally engaged questions. Like Dorothy Smith, he includes biographic materials in his investigations. Like Anthony Giddens, he wants to understand the 'rules' of history. Like James Coleman, he argues rigorously, from empirical evidence. Like Jean Baudrillard and Michel Foucault, he ranges widely over time and space, looking at the details of people's lives. Like many of the sociologists we have discussed in this book, he is interested in structures of control and domination. What makes Tilly stand out from the rest is his expertise as a historian and writer.

New Insights

It is reported the doomed Mary, Queen of Scots, soon to be beheaded, said 'In my end is my beginning'. And, in his poem, *East Coker*, T.S. Eliot famously writes, 'In my beginning is my end.' Eliot continues,

> In succession
> Houses rise and fall, crumble, are extended,
> Are removed, destroyed, restored, or in their place
> Is an open field, or a factory, or a by-pass.
> Old stone to new building, old timber to new fires,
> Old fires to ashes, and ashes to the earth
> Which is already flesh, fur and feces,
> Bone of man and beast, cornstalk and leaf.
> Houses live and die: there is a time for building
> And a time for living and for generation
> And a time for the wind to break the loosened pane
> And to shake the wainscot where the field-mouse trots
> And to shake the tattered arras woven with a silent motto.

So as we near the end of this book, we return to beginnings or starting points: to fundamental questions about the purpose of sociology, the methods of sociology, and the ways sociologists can make a difference to society and to social change—the 'rise and fall of houses' in Eliot's words.

Many of our everyday actions are conventional, even ritualistic. Roberge (2009), writing about Jeffrey Alexander's cultural sociology, notes that even secular present-day societies are 'ritual-like'—not fully ritualistic but not meaningless or wholly rationalized either. Using this particular logic, we can understand the forms of performances in the civil sphere—even in the political sphere. As Goffman told us, we are all playing parts, all presenting ourselves to audiences in everyday life. In that sense, civil society—the realm of play, voluntary association, and movement formation—is a vast staging area for socially and culturally meaningful events—events that may, in the long run, be politically meaningful.

One question that continues to interest sociologists is how to use research to inform and mobilize civil society, to bring about social change. Gustavsen (2008) notes that so-called action-research—research aimed at informing and promoting change—exists in many varieties and domains. Action-research projects may vary in the practical challenges they face, or in their different theoretical outlooks. Nonetheless, they typically have one main feature in common: an attention to whether a particular approach succeeds or fails in meeting specific practical challenges. Given this dedication to success, the role of theory is to deepen an understanding of the challenges faced and suggest what courses of action are open in each specific situation.

Consider Sarah Wakefield's (2007) experience with action research in the 'food movement', for example. In this study of critical geography—a theoretical approach to geography that builds on the insights of the Frankfurt critical theory— she uses the term 'praxis'— theory-based action intended to produce change—to describe how people live out their beliefs. People use different forms of praxis in their search for alternatives to Canada's corporate-industrial food system; these various approaches make different contributions to the quest for freedom that is at the heart of critical theory.

Likewise, in the context of organizational management, we can see similar goals under the rubric of 'critical management studies' (CMS). On this, Willmott (2008) asks, what is the point and direction of CMS? Different factions within CMS privilege different 'points' or goals. Some believe the future of CMS might include the forging of closer connection with social movements concerned with global justice—for example, with Amnesty International. Others favour a shared opposition to such practices as 'the profit imperative, patriarchy, racial inequality, and ecological irresponsibility', along with a stated 'desire to change this situation' and 'generate radical alternatives'. With these principles in mind, a valid strategy would include developing connections between CMS and activists who share similar aims and objectives. These goals of committing management—more generally, business —to social justice are interrelated and will require supranational cooperation. Therefore, they demand a global orientation to the theory and practice of social transformation.

Ross (2008) argues against relying too heavily on the role of civil society and too little on the role of the state in bringing about needed social changes. She writes that, given the atrophied version of democracy offered by neo-liberal states hemmed in by the privileges of global capital, attempts to reinvent radically egalitarian, decentralized, and participatory democratic practices are unsurprising. On the other hand, pervasive anarchist and postmodern assumptions have led to an 'anti-statism': a rejection of the possibility that state power can be used by progressive forces to create alternatives to capitalism.

Ross contests anti-statism, arguing it is rooted in an impoverished and monolithic understanding of the state. Besides, it accompanies a romanticized view of civil society as a realm of freedom and autonomy, and it results in the adoption of easily marginalized forms of resistance. She argues that an abandonment of the state as a terrain of struggle allows its continued and unhindered use by capital. Besides, it reinforces the neo-liberal mantra that the state should *not* impose social values on the market, and abandons the possibility of creating a unified, sustained, and effective counter-hegemonic political project.

It is easy to see the flaws in an over-reliance on civil society, for civil society is made up of ordinary people and their (sometimes informal) social institutions. And ordinary people often fail to take their civic duties seriously. On this, Sukhov (2008) writes that, despite concerns about political events and issues, significant factors lead people to defer taking action. Causes of deferral may include an underdeveloped capacity for independent moral judgment, or a tendency to delay or defer decisions because of the complex, uncertain conditions of modern life. A personal connection to others who already are involved in efforts to address the problem may also influence the individual to participate. Finally, the individual's own biographical availability for involvement— for example, their own previous involvement, or involvement by friends and kin—is also influential.

In studying the inactivity of his respondents, Sukhov found that behaviour that may appear non-rational, under some interpretations of what actors say and do, can be understood as rational. Often, in terms of most of the data he analyzes, the respondents' exercise of political agency is not absent, but rather deferred. The respondents appear to be no less 'active' than those who already are participating in social movement organizations or activities, and thus already are committed to a particular mode of political involvement. Simply, their time hasn't come yet.

Once again, postmodernists and critical theorists have trouble agreeing on the appropriate course of action. By turning attention away from causes and effects, and problems and solutions, postmodern theorists may be doing society a disservice—at least in the eyes of critical theorists. Soares (2007), for example, notes that postmodernism has been characterized by what Samir Amin called the 'new imperialism' and Leo Panitch and Colin Leys called the 'new' face of imperialism. That suggests it is on the same path as liberalism, capitalism, globalization, and US dominance, leading toward a higher stage of monopoly capitalism.

Soares notes that postmodernism emerged in the academy in the 1980s, an American era that saw the rise of social and political conservatism, Christian fundamentalism, extreme nationalism, and global economic expansion. It found an audience in the UK during an era of free-market economics and internal social conservatism. Intellectuals disillusioned with the collapse of the USSR, and thus with socialism, found postmodern discourse to their liking because of its more individualistic approach, which demanded nothing of capitalism and the social ills it engenders.

True, some social movements saw postmodernism as a means to effect social change. Obviously, not everyone viewed postmodernism the same way. Sukhov, however, concludes that postmodernist discourse legitimizes the social injustice brought about by capitalism and globalization.

Chapter Summary

Now we come to the end of this sociological journey. In this chapter, we looked at the connections between civil society, voluntary associations, social movements, and the broad changes in social life. In doing so, we linked the microsociological and macrosociological perspectives of sociology.

As discussed, voluntary associations are often the groups that give us sociability and common resources. These groups, and the social relationships they provide, help us to make sense of the world and change the world. For example, the sharing of rumours through reciprocal and redundant social interactions helps us to 'improvise news' at times when reliable information is scarce.

Sometimes, voluntary associations develop past providing mere interaction and sociability. Sometimes, they mobilize their resources, including funds and social contacts, to seek changes in the larger society through social action. When these voluntary associations enter the political sphere, they become social movements. Yet, just as some people may want change, others will resist it. The friction between these groups at times may threaten social order.

Perhaps the best way forward, then, is with caution, collegiality, and by means of 'bricolage'—a strategy memorialized by noted French anthropologist Claude Lévi-Strauss. 'Bricolage' is a French term for something created with 'found' materials—whatever happens to be at hand—often items used for something other than their original purpose. A 'bricoleur', thus, is a 'do-it-yourselfer' or handyman—perhaps, a person who takes the 'fusion approach', using materials close at hand. In his book *The Savage Mind* (1966 [1962]), Lévi-Strauss uses the word *bricolage* to describe thoughts and actions that spring from personal experience. 'Mythological thought' can arise from ideas already in a person's mind: for example, gods can be created from someone hearing thunder and seeing lightning. In short, bricolage creates an experience-driven culture—without master narratives and guided mainly by convenience and workability.

As we try together to fashion a picture of society and explain how it works, we need to remember—over and over again—that what we see and think is a product of our social location. This means that, as scientists and researchers, we need input from every social location—every 'kind of person'. It is only when the widely varying pictures of reality converge that we can begin to think we have a 'true picture' of reality. We are recommending this fusion approach.

In the end, this is what sociology is finally about: people making their own history. Some of the history people make is readily visible, through the work of social movements. But most of human history occurs in quiet, almost invisible, and incremental ways. One individual, then another, makes a new choice: about education, childbearing, or the environment, for example. When enough people do this, our society changes, then other societies change.

Some would say great rulers, diplomats, and politicians brought about the most important changes of the past century. Others would argue that great scientists and inventors brought them about. Still others would say that great rulers, diplomats, politicians, scientists, and inventors, as well as creative artists, philosophers, humanitarians, and saints, are all products of their time. In human history, there may have been dozens of potential Mozarts or Einsteins or Gandhis, for example. Yet they all passed through life unfulfilled and unnoticed because the time was not right. They may not have had, as Virginia Woolf said of women artists, 'a room of their own'—space and time to do what they were otherwise destined to do.

If so, this argues for the need to celebrate and nourish ordinary humanity, so all people will fulfill their human potential. Doing so may call for new social movements, to do for the still unsung what the labour movement, the women's movement, the black movement, and the gay rights movement did for ordinary North Americans in the nineteenth and twentieth centuries. It requires a culture of civility to ensure human rights and human dignity, equal protection under the law. Perhaps it will demand the social citizenship that T.H. Marshall wanted: secure jobs, housing, and health for everyone. Everyone will need 'a room of their own', if we are to find the other Mozarts and Einsteins and Gandhis.

Critical Thinking Questions

1. What are the social effects of rumours? What does this tell us about the social interaction between humans and its impact on society?
2. Have you ever engaged in a social movement? If yes, describe the experience, including your reasons for joining and the outcomes of your decision. If no, describe why or why not you would be interested in doing so.
3. What is the importance of the Internet to social movements around the world?
4. Choose one social movement and briefly research its history—what are the challenges it faced and successes it enjoyed?
5. What is the significance of the fact that we are all connected in a 'small world' of social networks?
6. What is the significance of studying sociology?

Recommended Readings

William K. Carroll (ed.), *Organizing Dissent: Contemporary Social Movements in Theory and Practice*, 2nd edn (Toronto: Garamond, 1997). This is a collection of leading articles and essays on social movements in North America. It is useful in that it applies theory to real-life examples, and shows the value of theoretical approaches when analyzing collective action.

David S. Meyer, Valerie Jenness, and Helen Ingram (eds), *Routing the Opposition: Social Movements, Public Policy, and Democracy* (Minneapolis: University of Minnesota Press, 2005). Covering various topics, the authors discuss how states and social movements intertwine and meet on issues such as public policy, social institutions and the people who make them up, and society as a whole.

Robert D. Putnam, *Bowling Alone: The Collapse and Revival of American Community* (New York: Simon & Schuster, 2000). Putnam argues that American civil society is breaking down, that people are less connected to their families, communities, and societies. He uses 'bowling alone' as a metaphor for our increasing individualization.

Donatella della Porta, Massimiliano Andretta, Lorenzo Mosca, and Herbert Reiter, *Globalization from Below: Transnational Activists and Protest Networks* (Minneapolis: University of Minnesota Press, 2006). This work analyzes the perspective on global social movements from below: that is, from the points of view of activists, organizers, and demonstrators.

Miriam Smith, *Lesbian and Gay Rights in Canada: Social Movements and Equality-Seeking, 1971–1995* (Toronto: University of Toronto Press, 1999). Smith's work analyzes the trends in social movement activity by Canadian gays and lesbians over the last few decades. The author highlights the importance of social policies, counter-ideologies, organizational strategies, and other factors that influenced how these movements have operated.

Charles MacKay, *Extraordinary Popular Delusions and the Madness of Crowds* (Wells, Vermont: Fraser Publishing Company, 1969 [1841]). This classic history of popular folly in collective action was published over 150 years ago. Nevertheless, its insight into what happens when people merge into crowds remains relevant in our society today. MacKay, a well-known figure in his time, covered many different disciplines and topics.

Talcott Parsons, *The Structure of Social Action: A Study in Social Theory With Special Reference to a Group of Recent European Writers*, 2nd edn (Glencoe, Ill: Free Press, 1949). This is a classic sociological work and the first major book by this author. It draws on the work of founding sociologists and develops a systematic theory of how and why people act collectively.

John Scott (ed.), *Fifty Key Sociologists: The Formative Theorists* (London: Routledge, 2007), and John Scott (ed.), *Fifty Key Sociologists: The Contemporary Theorists* (London: Routledge, 2007). These two books, one of which covers classical sociologists and the other contemporary ones, offer invaluable information about key sociologists over the last two centuries.

Websites

Canada's Rights Movement: A History
www.historyofrights.com/introduction.html

Global Solidarity Dialogue
www.antenna.nl/~waterman/dialogue.html

Free the Children
www.freethechildren.com

Canadian Labour Congress/Congrès du travail du Canada (CLC/CTC)
www.canadianlabour.ca

Greenpeace International
www.greenpeace.org

Greenpeace Canada
www.greenpeace.org/canada.

Voice of Women (VOW)
http://home.ca.inter.net/~vow/

Canadian Lesbian & Gay Archives (CLGA)
www.clga.ca/archives

Assembly of First Nations/Assemblée des Premières Nations (AFN/APN)
www.afn.ca

Glossary

ageism All types of prejudice or discrimination against members of society based on an individual's age, whether old or young.

alternative media Channels of communication used by subordinate groups to promote their own messages and points of view.

anticipatory socialization Learning about and preparing for future roles, built on accumulated learning.

assimilation The process by which an outsider or immigrant group becomes indistinguishably integrated into the dominant host society; similar to *acculturation*.

authority Power that is considered legitimate by the people who are subject to it.

bedroom suburb A residential area near a large city that provides housing and services for people who each day commute into the downtown urban area.

bourgeoisie According to Marx, the controlling class, which owns the means of production.

census family A household that includes two spouses—opposite or same-sex, married or cohabiting (if they have lived together for longer than one year)—with or without never-married children, or a single parent with one or more never-married children.

church Any social location or building—church, mosque, synagogue, or temple—where people carry out religious rituals.

citizens People who belong to a state. Citizenship developed out of the relative freedom of city life, granting equal treatment for all residents.

civil liberties Freedoms that protect the individual against government. These include freedom of speech, assembly, and movement, and freedom of the press.

civil religion An organized secular practice that serves many of the same social functions as traditional religion, by giving people direction, explaining how the world works, and providing solidarity.

civil rights Rights we consider all people deserve under all circumstances, without regard to race, ethnicity, age, sex, or other personal qualities.

class According to Marx, a group of people who share the same relationship to the means of production, or to capital; according to Weber, a group of people who share a common economic situation, based on (among other things) income, property, and authority.

class consciousness A group's awareness of their common class interest and their commitment to work together to attain collective goals.

cohort A set of people with a common origin or starting point; *birth cohort*—a set of people born in the same year or set of years.

conglomerate A business structure that engages in several, usually unrelated business endeavours: for example, movie-making, gambling casinos, and alcoholic beverages.

core states The governments of industrialized, rich, powerful, and relatively independent societies; the dominant states in the world.

counterculture A subculture that rejects conventional norms and values and adopts alternative ones.

counter-ideology An ideology that supports alternative social values and challenges the **dominant ideology**.

cross-ownership A business structure in which one corporation owns media businesses of different types. For example, a large corporation may own newspapers, magazines, television networks, and radio channels.

cultural capital A body of knowledge and interpersonal skills that helps people to get ahead socially, which often includes learning about and participating in high culture.

cultural integration The process whereby parts of a culture (for example, ideal culture and real culture) come to fit together and complement one another.

cultural literacy A solid knowledge of the traditional culture, which contains the building blocks of all communication and learning.

cultural studies perspective A viewpoint that focuses on the types of communication to which people are regularly exposed and especially on messages conveying the **dominant ideology**.

culture Our uniquely human environment. It includes all of the objects, artifacts, institutions, organizations, ideas, and beliefs that make up the social environment of human life.

demography The study of human populations—their growth and decline through births, deaths and migration.

dependency ratio The proportion of people who are considered 'dependants' (under 15 or over 65 years old) compared to people 15 to 64 years, who are considered of working age.

diaspora A dispersion of people through migration, resulting in the establishment and spread of same-ethnicity communities throughout the world.

diasporic group Any ethnic group that has established multiple centres of immigrant life throughout the world.

dominant ideology An ideology that supports the status quo and the interests of the ruling class.

double shift Heavy daily workloads, both at the workplace and at home, that women are far more likely than men to experience.

double standard (sexual) The notion that women are supposed to feel or behave differently from men where sexual matters are concerned.

education A process designed to develop one's general capacity for thinking critically, as well as a capacity for self-understanding and self-reliance.

empires Sets of nations, regions, and territories controlled by a single ruler.

environmental geography The systematic study of the interaction between humans and the surrounding natural world, focusing on the human impact on the environment and vice versa.

ethnic enclave A neighbourhood that is mainly or exclusively populated by people who belong to the same ethnic group.

ethnic group A set of people commonly defined as belonging to the same group by virtue of a common birthplace, ancestry, or culture.

ethnocentrism The tendency to use one's own culture as a basis for evaluating other cultures.

expectation A shared idea about how people should carry out the duties attached to a particular status.

extended family Multiple generations of relatives living together, or several adult siblings with their spouses and children who share a dwelling and resources. More than three kinds of relationships may be present.

false consciousness A willingness to believe in ideologies that support the ruling class but that are false and disadvantageous to working class interests.

family For the purpose of this book, any social unit, or set of social relations, that does what families are popularly imagined to do, by whatever means it does so.

folkways Norms based on popular habits and traditions, and ordinary usages and conventions of everyday life.

formal education Education received in accredited schools during formal teaching sessions.

gender The expectations of behaviour or appearance that we describe as *masculine* or *feminine*; a set of social expectations.

gerontology The scientific study of aging and old age.

glass ceiling Any sex-based barrier to equal opportunity for hiring and promotion.

globalization The development of a single world market and the accompanying trend to increased interdependence among the economies (and societies) of the world.

heteronormativity The social institutions, practices, and norms that support an automatic assumption that other people are or should be heterosexual.

heterosexism A belief in the moral superiority of heterosexual institutions and practices.

heterosexuality A sexual or romantic attraction to people of the opposite sex.

hidden curriculum Lessons that are not normally considered part of the academic curriculum that schools unintentionally or secondarily provide for students.

high culture   The set of preferences, tastes, and norms that are characteristic of, or supported by, high-status groups, including fine arts, classical music, ballet, and other 'highbrow' concerns.

homophobia   An overt or covert hostility toward gay and lesbian people, sometimes stemming from an irrational fear or hatred of homosexuals.

homosexuality   A sexual or romantic attraction to people of the same sex; in males, called 'homosexuality' and in females, 'lesbianism'.

homosociality   A social preference for members of one's own gender.

human capital   A skill or skill set, usually including educational attainment or job-related experiences, that enhances a worker's value on the job; the result of foregone income and a long-term investment in personal improvement.

human geography   The systematic study of the location of human enterprises and characteristics; for example, health, education, commerce and trade; closely linked to other social sciences like sociology.

ideal culture   That aspect of culture that lives only in people's minds. It is the set of values people claim to believe in, profess openly, hold up for worship and adoration, and in day-to-day life pay 'lip service' to.

identity   All the ways in which we view and describe ourselves (female/male, friend, student, attractive, unusual, etc.) and in which others perceive us.

ideologies   Coherent sets of interrelated beliefs about the nature of the world that imply or demand certain courses of political, social, or economic action.

imagined communities   Social groupings, like races or ethnic groups, that are treated as real because they are widely believed (or imagined) to be real.

informal education   The variety of ways we undertake to gain knowledge for ourselves outside institutions of formal education (e.g., schools, colleges, and universities).

institutional completeness   The degree to which a community or enclave has established services aimed at a particular ethnic community, often in their traditional language.

interaction   The processes by which, and manner in which, social actors—people trying to meet each other's **expectations**—relate to each other, especially in face-to-face encounters.

looking-glass self   A process in which people come to see (and value) themselves as others see them.

macrosociology   The study of social institutions (for example, the Roman Catholic Church or marriage) and large social groups (for example, ethnic minorities or college students).

mass communication   The transmission of a message from a single source to multiple recipients at the same time.

mass media   The technology that makes **mass communication** possible; it includes the printing press, radio, television, photocopier, and camera, among others.

material culture   The physical and technological aspects of people's lives, including all the physical objects that members of a culture create and use.

median age   The point that divides a population into two groups of equal size based on age, with half the population above that age and half below it.

megacity   A geographic locale with a large concentrated population, sometimes defined as exceeding 5 million people (also, *megalopolis* or *megapolis*).

meritocracy   Any system of rule or advancement where the rewards are strictly proportioned to the accomplishment and all people have the same opportunity to win these rewards.

microsociology   The study of the processes and patterns of personal interaction that take place among people within groups.

mores   Norms that carry moral significance. People believe that mores contribute to the general welfare and continuity of the group.

multiculturalism   A Canadian political and social policy aimed at promoting ethnic tolerance and ethnic community survival.

nations   Large land areas where people live under the rule of a national government.

negotiation The ways in which people try to make sense of one another, and make sense to one another; for example, by conferring, bargaining, making arrangements, compromising, and reaching agreements.

new religious movements (NRMs) Groups and institutions comprising people who share similar religious or spiritual views about the world but who are not part of mainstream religious institutions.

non-governmental organizations (NGOs) Legally constituted organizations that are independent of any national government; often, mechanisms through which different nations try to solve common problems.

non-material culture People's values, beliefs, philosophies, conventions, and ideologies: in short, all the aspects of a culture that do not have a physical existence.

non-standard work arrangements Dead-end, low-paying, insecure jobs, also known as *precarious employment*.

norms The rules or expectations that serve as common guidelines for behaviour in daily life, telling us what kinds of behaviour are appropriate or inappropriate in specific social situations.

nuclear family A group that usually consists of a father, a mother, and their children living in the same dwelling. Such a family comprises no more than three relationships: between spouses, between parents and children, and between siblings.

organizational culture The way an organization has learned to deal with its environment; it includes norms and values that are subculturally distinct to the organization.

paraphilia Any sexual deviation or departure from the norm.

periphery states The governments of less developed, relatively poor, weak societies that are subject to manipulation or direct control by core societies.

petit bourgeoisie The lower middle class; a group of people who own the means of production on a small scale, such as owners of small shops.

political economy perspective A viewpoint that focuses on the ways private ownership affects what is communicated, and the ways it affects the exercise of power.

politics The processes by which individuals and groups act to promote their interests.

popular (or mass) culture The culture of ordinary people. It includes those objects, preferences, and tastes that are widespread in a society.

population composition The makeup or mix of different social types in a population; for example, the different numbers of men and women, old and young people.

population pyramid A graphic depiction of the age–sex composition of a population.

pornography The explicit description or exhibition of sexual activity in literature, films, or elsewhere, intended to stimulate erotic, rather than aesthetic, feelings.

post-industrialism An economic system based more on services and information than on manufactured goods or primary production.

power According to Weber, 'the ability of persons or groups to achieve their objectives, even when opposed'. Said another way, power is the capacity to compel people to act in certain ways, and politics is the process by people gain and exercise this power.

primary socialization Learning that takes place in the early years of a person's life that is crucial to the formation of an individual's personality.

proletariat According to Marx, the subordinate class, who work for wages from the bourgeoisie.

propaganda Mass communication whose purpose is to influence people's political opinions and actions.

prostitution The provision of sexual services for reward, usually money.

race A set of people commonly defined as belonging to the same group by virtue of common visible features, such as skin colour or facial characteristics.

racial (or ethnic) socialization The process by which we learn to perceive and evaluate people (including ourselves) according to presumed racial or ethnic differences.

racial variations Differences in behaviour which some people attribute to differences in race.

real culture   The ways people dress, talk, act, relate, and think in everyday life, as distinct from their idealized or proclaimed culture.

regions   Large land areas that may encompass portions of a country or extend over several countries. They usually share a few distinctive topographical features (e.g., mountain, flatland, or coastal terrain) and economic experiences.

religion   Any system of beliefs about the supernatural, and the social groups that gather around these beliefs.

reserve army of labour   People who, because they are impoverished and often unemployed, form an easily mobilized, easily disposable workforce at the mercy of employers.

resocialization   Learning within social institutions aimed at retraining or reprogramming people.

role   The expected behaviour of an individual in a social position and the duties associated with that position.

role strain   A result of role conflict, when the demands of some roles conflict with the demands of others.

role-making   The process of creating new social roles in and through interaction.

role-set   The collection of roles any individual plays.

role-taking   The process in which we take on existing defined roles.

secondary socialization   Learning that occurs after childhood, usually involving learning specific roles, norms, attitudes, or beliefs, and sometimes involving self-imposed learning.

secularization   A steadily dwindling influence of formal (institutional) religion in public life.

seekers   People and groups who draw on the teachings of several religions and philosophies to fulfill their needs for spirituality.

semi-peripheral states   The governments of industrial or semi-industrial societies that, though prosperous, are often subject to control by core societies because of their economic or political dependency.

sex   Both the biological characteristics that define a person as male or female and the act of sexual intercourse.

sexism   The perceived superiority of one sex (most often men) over the other (usually women).

sexual infidelity   Sexual relations between a married (or cohabiting) person and someone other than his or her spouse.

sexual scripts   The guidelines that describe socially acceptable ways of behaving when engaging in sexual activities.

sexuality   Feelings of sexual attraction and any behaviours related to them.

signs   Gestures, artifacts, or words that express or meaningfully represent something other than themselves.

social institution   One kind of social structure, made up of a number of relationships (i.e., stable patterns of meaningful orientations to one another). People use institutions to achieve their intended goals, as students use schools, or patients use hospitals.

social movements   Organized groups of people with an agenda or plan for social change, to be achieved through agitation and political pressure.

social script   Guidelines that people follow to carry out interactions and fulfill role expectations as seamlessly as possible.

social structure   Any enduring, predictable pattern of social relations among people in society; the subject matter of sociology. All social structures *control us*, so that we act in a certain way in a given situation, despite personal differences; they *change us*, so we behave differently in different situations, despite our more or less fixed 'personalities'; and although they *resist* the efforts of individuals to bring about social change, they also *produce social change*.

socialization   The lifelong social learning a person undergoes to become a capable member of society, through *social interaction* with others, and in response to social pressures.

society   The largest-scale human group, whose members interact with one another, share a common geographic territory, and share common institutions.

sociological imagination An approach to sociology that situates the personal experiences of individuals within the societal context in which these experiences occur.

sociology The systematic study of social behaviour, or the study of society.

state The set of institutions with authority to make the rules that govern a society. Weber wrote that the state 'claims a monopoly of the legitimate use of physical force within a given territory'.

status A person's social position, which is associated with a role and its associated scripts.

status sequence The array of statuses we occupy over a lifetime, through which we pass in a socially recognizable order.

subculture A group that shares the cultural elements of the larger society but which also has its own distinctive values, beliefs, norms, style of dress, and behaviour patterns.

symbol A thing that stands for or represents something else, and provides a means of communication (e.g., through spoken words, written words, facial expressions, or body language).

taboos Powerful social beliefs that a particular act, food, place, etc. is totally repulsive and dangerous. Violation of the taboo is supposed to result in immediate punishment.

terrorism The calculated use of unexpected, shocking, and unlawful violence against civilians and symbolic targets.

training A process designed to identify and practise specific routines that achieve desired results.

values Socially shared conceptions of what a group or society considers good, right, and desirable.

voluntary association A group formed by voluntary membership. Unlike other voluntary associations, social movements usually have a political goal.

war An openly declared armed conflict between countries or between groups within a country.

References

Chapter 1

Becker, Howard. 1963. *Outsiders: Essays in the Sociology of Deviance*. New York: Free Press.

Berger, Peter, and Thomas Luckmann. 1966. *The Social Construction of Reality: Treatise in the Sociology of Knowledge*. Garden City, NY: Anchor.

Blumer, Herbert. 1937. 'Social Psychology', in E.P. Schmidt, ed., *Man and Society: A Substantive Introduction to the Social Sciences*. New York: Prentice-Hall, 148–98.

———. 1969. *Symbolic Interactionism: Perspective and Method*. Englewood Cliffs, NJ: Prentice-Hall and Berkeley: University of California Press.

———. 1971. 'Social Problems as Collective Behavior', *Social Problems* 18 (Winter): 298–306.

Boswell, Randy. 2009. 'Head-of-State Debate Makes for Bizarre Spectacle'. Canwest News Service, 11 October. At: http://www.canada.com/entertainment/Head+state+debate+makes+bizarre+spectacle/2092140/story.html.

Brown, Kevin Pearson. 2009. '"My Way": Karaoke and the Performance of Gender, Ethnicity, and Class', *Dissertation Abstracts International, A: The Humanities and Social Sciences* 70, 4: 1099.

Clement, Wallace. 1975. *The Canadian Corporate Elite: An Analysis of Economic Power*. Toronto: McClelland & Stewart.

Cole, Mike. 2009. 'A Response to Charles Mills', *Ethnicities* 9, 2: 281–84.

Comte, Auguste. 1856 (1844). *A General View of Positivism (Discours sur l'Esprit positif)*.

Cooky, Cheryl. 2009. '"Girls Just Aren't Interested": The Social Construction of Interest in Girls' Sport', *Sociological Perspectives* 52, 2: 259–84.

Darden, Joe. 2005. 'Black Occupational Achievement in the Toronto Census Metropolitan Area: Does Race Matter?', *Review of Black Political Economy* 33, 2: 31–54.

Dube, Rebecca. 2008. 'Mean Girls, But With Walkers', *The Globe and Mail*, 27 May. At: http://www.theglobeandmail.com/archives/mean-girls-but-with-walkers/article688076/

Durkheim, Émile. 1951 (1897). *Suicide: A Study in Sociology*, trans. John A. Spaulding and George Simpson. New York: Free Press.

———. 1958, 1964 (1895). *The Rules of Sociological Method*, trans. S. Solovay and John Mueller. New York: Free Press.

———. 1965 (1912). *The Elementary Forms of Religious Life*, trans. Joseph Ward Swain. New York: Free Press.

———. 1964 (1893). *The Division of Labor in Society*, trans. George Simpson. New York: Free Press.

Elchardus, Mark. 2009. 'Self-control as Social Control: The Emergence of Symbolic Society', *Poetics* 37, 2: 146–61.

Erdmans, Mary Patrice. 2007. 'The Personal Is Political, but Is it Academic?.' *Journal of American Ethnic History* 26, 4: 7–23.

Foucault, Michel. 1995 (1977). *Discipline and Punish: The Birth of the Prison*, trans. Alan Sheridan. New York: Vintage.

Goffman, Erving. 1959. *The Presentation of Self in Everyday Life*. Garden City, NY: Doubleday-Anchor.

———. 1961. *Asylums: Essays on the Social Situation of Mental Patients and Other Inmates*. New York: Doubleday.

———. 1963. *Stigma: Notes on the Management of Spoiled Identity*. Englewood Cliffs, NJ: Prentice-Hall.

Habermas, Jürgen. 1984. *The Theory of Communicative Action*, 2 vols, trans. Thomas McCarthy. Cambridge: Polity.

Helmes-Hayes, Rick, and James Curtis, eds. 1998. *The Vertical Mosaic Revisited*. Toronto: University of Toronto Press.

Lau, Raymond W.K. 2009. 'The Contemporary Culture of Blame and the Fetishization of the Modernist Mentality', *Current Sociology* 57, 5: 661–83.

Laub, John, and Robert J. Sampson. 2003. *Shared Beginnings, Divergent Lives: Delinquent Boys to age 70*. Cambridge, MA: Harvard University Press.

Lemert, Charles, and Ann Branaman. 1997. 'Goffman's Social Theory', in Charles Lemert and Ann Branaman, eds., *The Goffman Reader*. Malden, MA, and Oxford: Basil Blackwell.

Marx, Karl. 1956. *Selected Writings in Sociology and Social Philosophy*, ed. T.B. Bottomore and Maximilien Rubel, trans. T.B. Bottomore. New York: McGraw-Hill.

———. 1965 (1867). *Capital: A Critique of Political Economy*. New York: International Publishers.

Marx, Karl, and Friedrich Engels. 1948 (1848). *Manifesto of the Communist Party*. New York: International Publishers.

———. 1970 (1845–6). *The German Ideology*, Part I, with selections from Parts 2 and 3, trans. C.J. Arthur. New York: International Publishers.

Mead, George Herbert. 1934. *Mind, Self, and Society from the Standpoint of a Social Behaviorist*. Chicago: University of Chicago Press.

Merton, Robert. 1957 (1949). *Social Theory and Social Structure*, revised and expanded edition. New York: Free Press.

Mills, Charles. 1999. *The Racial Contract*. Ithaca: Cornell University Press.

Mills, Charles W. 2009. 'Critical Race Theory: A Reply to Mike Cole.' *Ethnicities* 9: 2, 270–81.

Mulinari, Diana, and Kerstin Sandell. 2009. 'A Feminist Re-reading of Theories of Late Modernity: Beck, Giddens and the Location of Gender', *Critical Sociology* 35, 4: 493–507.

Ogmundson, Rick. 1990. 'Perspectives on the Class and Ethnic Origins of Canadian Elites: A Methodological Critique of the Porter/Clement/Olsen Tradition', *Canadian Journal of Sociology* 15, 2: 165–77.

Olsen, Dennis. 1980. *The State Elite*. Toronto: McClelland & Stewart.

Porter, John. 1965. *The Vertical Mosaic*. Toronto: University of Toronto Press.

Preston, John. 2008. 'Protect and Survive: "Whiteness" and the Middle-Class Family in Civil Defence Pedagogies', *Journal of Education Policy* 23, 5: 469–82.

Sangster, Joan. 2007. 'Making a Fur Coat: Women, the Labouring Body, and Working-Class History', *International Review of Social History* 52, 2: 241–70.

Simmel, Georg. 1950a. 'The Metropolis and Mental Life', in Simmel (1950b: 400–27).

———. 1950b. *The Sociology of Georg Simmel*, trans. Kurt Wolff. New York: Free Press.

Slattery, David. 2008. 'Minding the Gaps in Dublin's New Light Rail System', *The International Journal of Baudrillard Studies* 5, 1 (Jan.).

Statistics Canada. 2007. 'Crime Statistics in Canada, 2006.' *Juristat: Canadian Centre for Justice Statistics* 27, 5. Catalogue no. 85-002.

At: http://www.statcan.gc.ca/pub/85-002-x/85-002-x2007005-eng.pdf.

Thomasson, Emma, and Sam Cage. 2009. 'Swiss to Tighten Assisted Suicide Rules, Consider Ban', *Reuters*, 28 Oct. At: http://www.reuters.com/article/idUSTRE59R3X820091028

Weber, Max. 1968. *Economy and Society: An Outline of Interpretive Sociology*. New York, Bedminster Press.

Chapter 2

Antweiler, Christoph. 2004. 'Urbanism and Anthropology. Current Trends and Methods of Anthropological Urban Research' ('Urbanitat und Ethnologie: Aktuelle Theorietrends und die Methodik ethnologischer Stadtforschung'), *Zeitschrift fur Ethnologie* 129, 2: 285–307.

Arantes, Pedro Fiori. 2009. 'In Search of the Urban: Marxists and the City of Sao Paulo in the 1970s' ('Em busca do urbano: marxistas e a cidade de Sao Paulo nos anos de 1970'), *Novos Estudos CEBRAP* 83: 103–27.

Bauman, Zygmunt. 2000. *Liquid Modernity*. Cambridge: Polity Press.

Beck, Ulrich. 1992 (1986). *Risk Society: Towards a New Modernity*, trans. Mark Ritter. London: Sage.

Brown, Lester. 2010. 'Data Highlights on the Global Food Supply', *Grist*. 12 Feb. At: http://www.grist.org/article/data-highlights-on-the-global-food-supply/.

Buchanan, David. 2002. 'Gendercide and Human Rights', *Journal of Genocide Research* 4, 1: 95–108.

Caldarovic, Ognjen, and Jana Sarinic. 2009. 'Contemporary Communication Technology and Urban Milieu—Space, Place and Time' ('Suvremena komunikacijska tehnologija i urbana sredina—prostor, mjesta, vrijeme'), *Socijalna Ekologija* 17, 4: 331–41.

Caldwell, John C., James F. Phillips, and Barkat-e-Khuda. 2002. 'The Future of Family Planning Programs', *Studies in Family Planning* 33, 1: 1–10.

Campbell, Martha. 2007. 'Why the Silence on Population?', *Population and Environment* 28, 4–5: 237–46.

Coale, Ansley J. 1974. 'The History of the Human Population', *Scientific American* 231 (special issue): 15–25.

Connor, Steve. 2007. 'The Real Global Warming Swindle', *The independent*, 14 March. At: http://www.independent.co.uk/environment/climate-change/the-real-global-warming-swindle-440116.html.

Devadas, Vijay. 2008. 'Protean Borders & Unsettled Interstices', *Borderlands E-Journal* 7, 1. At: http://www.borderlands.net.au/vol7no1_2008/editors_protean.htm.

Durkheim, Émile. 1964 (1893). *Division of Labor in Society*. New York: Free Press.

Erol, Pelin Onder. 2008. 'Leisure as a Commodity: A Case of Well To Do Old People in Turkey'. Paper presented at First ISA Forum of Sociology, International Sociological Association, Barcelona, Spain.

Gaard, Greta, ed. 1993. *Ecofeminism: Women, Animals, Nature*. Philadelphia: Temple University Press.

Gans, Herbert. 1982. *The Urban Villagers: Group and Class in the Life of Italian-Americans*. New York: Free Press.

———. 2009. 'Some Problems of and Futures for Urban Sociology: Toward a Sociology of Settlements', *City & Community* 8, 3: 211–19.

Gazdar, Haris. 2002. 'Pre-Modern, Modern and Post-Modern Famine in Iraq', *IDS Bulletin* 33, 4: 63–9.

Goh, Robbie B. H. 2001. 'Ideologies of "Upgrading" in Singapore Public Housing: Post-Modern Style, Globalisation and Class Construction in the Built Environment', *Urban Studies* 38, 9: 1589–604.

Grant, Bruce. 2005. 'The Traffic in Brides', *American Anthropologist* 107, 4: 687–9.

Handrahan, Lori. 2004. 'Hunting for Women: Bride-Kidnapping in Kyrgyzstan', *International Feminist Journal of Politics* 6, 2: 207–33.

Harris, Colette. 2006. 'Bride Kidnapping in Kyrgyzstan', *Slavic Review* 65, 1: 153–4.

Holter, Oystein Gullvag. 2002. 'A Theory of Gendercide', *Journal of Genocide Research* 4, 11: 11–38.

Humphrey, Matthew, ed. 2002. *Political Theory and the Environment: A Reassessment*. London: Routledge (Taylor and Francis).

Johnson, Victoria. 2009. 'The Status of Identities: Racial Inclusion and Exclusion at West Coast Ports', *Social Movement Studies* 8, 2: 167–83.

Jones, Adam. 2000. 'Gendercide and Genocide', *Journal of Genocide Research* 2: 185–211.

———. 2006. 'Why Gendercide? Why Root-and-Branch? A Comparison of the Vendee Uprising of 1793–94 and the Bosnian War of the 1990s', *Journal of Genocide Research* 8, 1: 9–25.

Knox, Hannah, Damian O'Doherty, Theo Vurdubakis, and Chris Westrup. 2009. 'Enacting Airports: Space, Movement and Modes of Ordering', *Organization* 15, 6: 869–88.

Lindner, Evelin Gerda. 2002. 'Gendercide and Humiliation in Honor and Human Rights Societies', *Journal of Genocide Research* 4, 1: 137–55.

Marin, Noemi. 2002. 'Eastern European Exile and Its Contemporary Condition', *Migration* 33–35: 155–71.

Meadows, Donella H., Dennis L. Meadows, Jørgen Randers, and William W. Behrens III. 1972. *The Limits to Growth: A Report for the Club of Rome's Project on the Predicament of Mankind*, 2nd edn. New York: Universe Books.

———, Dennis L. Meadows, and Jørgen Randers. 2004. *Limits to Growth: The 30-Year Update*. White River Junction, VT: Chelsea Green Publishing.

Miranda, Fernanda Eleonora, and Jacqeuline de Oliveira Moreira. 2006. 'Female Infertility in Post-modernity: Between Narcissism and Tradition' ('A infertilidade feminina na pos-modernidade: entre o narcisismo e a Tradicao'), *Revista de Ciencias Humanas* 39:183–97.

Mongabay.com. 2008. 'Continued Focus on Economic Growth will Doom the Planet'. Oct. 16. At: http://news.mongabay.com/2008/1015-economic_growth.html.

Morgan, Philip S. 2003. 'Is Low Fertility a Twenty-First-Century Demographic Crisis?', *Demography* 40, 4: 589–603.

Plambech, Sine. 2005. '"Mail Order Brides" in Northwestern Jutland: Transnational Marriages in the Global Care Economy', *Dansk Sociologi* 16, 1: 91–110.

Plant, Martin A. 1990. 'Alcohol, Sex and AIDS'. *Alcohol and Alcoholism* 25, 2–3: 293–301.

Population Reference Bureau (PRB). 2009. *World Population Data Sheet for 2008*. Washington: PRB.

———. N.d. 'Mean Ideal Number of Children, All Women 20–24'. At: http://www.prb.org/Datafinder/Topic/Bar.aspx?sort=v&order=d&variable=120.

Pregowski, Michael P. 2009. 'The Netiquette and Its Expectations—The Personal Pattern of an Appropriate Internet User' ('Wzor osobowy internauty: czego oczekuja od nas netykiety?'), *Studia Socjologiczne* 2 (193): 109–30.

Rosewarne, Stuart. 2004. 'Globalization and the Recovery of the Migrant as Subject: "Transnationalism from Below"', *Capitalism, Nature, Socialism* 15, 3: 37–52.

Rynbrandt, Linda, and Mary Jo Deegan. 2002. 'The Ecofeminist Pragmatism of Caroline Bartlett Crane 1896–1935', *The American Sociologist* 33, 3: 58–68.

Schoenfeld, A. Clay, Robert F. Meier, and Robert J. Griffin. 1979. 'Constructing a Social Problem: The Press and the Environment.' *Social Problem* 27, 1: 38–61.

Serbulo, Leanne Claire. 2009. '"Whose Streets? Our Streets!": Urban Social Movements and the Transformation of Everyday Life in Pacific Northwest Cities, 1990–1999', *Dissertation Abstracts International, A: The Humanities and Social Sciences* 70, 1: 376.

Simmel, Georg. 1950. 'The Metropolis and Mental Life,' in Wolff, Kurt, *The Sociology of Georg Simmel*. Glencoe, IL: Free Press.

Smith, Keith. 2001. *Environmental Hazards: Assessing Risk and Reducing Disaster*. London: Routledge (Taylor and Francis).

Statistics Finland. 2007. Figure 1, 'Population Development in Independent Finland—Greying Baby Boomers', in *Finland 1917–2007*. At: http://www.stat.fi/tup/suomi90/joulukuu_en.html.

Tjeldvoll, Arild. 2009. 'A Lao Wai's Reflections on Education Quality in East Asia—Focus: Hong Kong', *Socialiniai Mokslai* 2: 7–15.

UN Population Division. 2009. *World Population Prospects: The 2008 Revision*. New York: UN. At: http://www.un.org/esa/population/publications/wpp2008/wpp2008_highlights.pdf.

Vlahov, David, Sandro Galea, Emily Gibble, and Nicholas Greudenberg. 2005. 'Perspectives on Urban Conditions and Population Health', *Cadernos de Saude Publica* 21, 3: 949–57.

Warren, Mary Anne. *Gendercide: The Implications of Sex Selection*. Totowa, NJ: Rowman & Allanheld, 1985.

Worldometers. N.d. 'World Population Clock'. At: http://www.worldometers.info/population/. Accessed 3 Dec. 2009.

World Wildlife Fund. 'Earth Hour 2009.' *WWF: Local to Global Environmental Conservation*. 19 May. At: http://wwf.ca/earthhour.

Chapter 3

Adler, Patricia A., and Peter Adler. 2008. 'The Cyber Worlds of Self-Injurers: Deviant Communities, Relationships, and Selves', *Symbolic Interaction* 31, 1: 33–56.

Antonowicz, Dominik, and Lukasz Wrzesinski. 2009. 'Sport Fans As a Community of the Invisible Religion' ('Kibice jako wspolnota niewidzialnej religh'), *Studia Socjologiczne* 1 (192): 115–49.

Bales, Robert F. 1950. *Interaction Process Analysis: A Method for the Study of Small Groups*. Cambridge, MA: Addison Wesley.

Batiuk, Mary Ellen, James A. Boland, and Norma Wilcox. 2004. 'Project Trust: Breaking Down Barriers between Middle School Children', *Adolescence* 39, 155: 531–8.

Becker, Howard S. 1963. *Outsiders: Studies in the Sociology of Deviance*. New York: Free Press.

———. 2005. 'An Introduction to the Danish and Brazilian editions of *Outsiders*'. At: http://home.earthlink.net/~hsbecker/articles/danishintro.html.

Blain, Michael. 2009. 'Sovereignty, Bio-power, and the Global War on Terrorism', *The Discourse of Sociological Practice* 8, 2: 37–58.

Carpenter, Hutch. 2008. 'Social Media Identity: Personal vs. Professional', *I'm Not Actually a Geek*. 29 Apr. At: http://bhc3.files.wordpress.com/2008/04/social-media-personal-professional.png.

Castle, Nicholas. 2009. 'Practice Implications: A Commentary on Powell's Foucauldian Toolkit', *The Journal of Applied Gerontology* 28, 6: 683–4.

Conroy, Sean. 2007. 'The Nightmare of Clever Children: Civilization, Postmodernity, and the Birth of the Anxious Body', *Human Architecture: Journal of the Sociology of Self-Knowledge* 5, 2: 21–40.

Cooley, Charles Horton. 1902. *Human Nature and Social Order*. New York: Scribner.

Debrix, Francois, and Alexander D. Barder. 2009. 'Nothing to Fear but Fear: Governmentality and the Biopolitical Production of Terror', *International Political Sociology* 3, 4: 398–413.

Delvinia Interactive. 2009. 'Online Communities & Information Sharing'. Accessed at: http://www.delvinia.com/wp-content/uploads/2009/12/DelviniaInsights_Online_Communities_and_Information_Sharing.pdf

Evans, Bethan, and Rachel Colls. 2009. 'Measuring Fatness, Governing Bodies: The Spatialities of the Body Mass Index (BMI) in Anti-Obesity Politics', *Antipode* 41, 5: 1051–83.

Goffman, Erving. 1959. *The Presentation of Self in Everyday Life*. Garden City, NY: Doubleday-Anchor.

———. 1963. *Stigma: Notes on the Management of Spoiled Identity*. Englewood Cliffs, NJ: Prentice-Hall.

Goudreau, J., and E. Pelzak. 2008. 'Social Networking Sites: Blah, Blah, Blah', The Debate Room, BusinessWeek.com. At: http://www.businessweek.com/debateroom/archives/2007/08/social_networki.html. Accessed 21 Nov. 2009.

Granovetter, Mark S. 1974. *Getting a Job: A Study of Contacts and Careers*. Cambridge, MA: Harvard University Press.

Hay, Thorkild Holmboe. 2009. 'Enrolling Technologies of the Self in Employee/Leader Conversations', *Tidsskrift for Arbejdsliv* 11, 3: 78–92.

Heinlein, Robert. 1961. *Stranger in a Strange Land*. New York: Putnam.

Heyes, Cressida J. 2009. 'Diagnosing Culture: Body Dysmorphic Disorder and Cosmetic Surgery', *Body & Society* 15, 4: 73–93.

Lazzarato, Maurizio. 2009. 'Neoliberalism in Action: Inequality, Insecurity and the Reconstitution of the Social', *Theory, Culture & Society* 26, 6: 109–33.

Lemke, Jay. 2001. 'Discursive technologies and the social organization of meaning', Special issue: 'Critical Discourse Analysis and Cognition', *Folia Linguistica* 35, 1–2: 79–96.

Linton, Ralph. 1936. *The Study of Man: An Introduction*. New York: Appleton-Century-Crofts.

McDaniel, Susan A. 2009. 'Challenging Gerontology's Empirical Molehills: A Commentary on Powell's Foucauldian Toolkit', *The Journal of Applied Gerontology* 28, 6: 685–9.

Mead, George Herbert. 1934. *Mind, Self, and Society from the Standpoint of a Social Behaviorist*. Chicago: University of Chicago Press.

Parsons, Talcott. 1949. *Essays in Sociological Theory*. New York: Free Press.

———. 1951. *The Social System*. Glencoe, IL: Free Press.

Pew Internet. 2008. 'Adults and social network websites'. Accessed at: http://www.pewinternet.org/~/media//Files/Reports/2009/PIP_Adult_social_networking_data_memo_FINAL.pdf.pdf

Purcell, Mark. 2009. 'Hegemony and Difference in Political Movements: Articulating Networks of Equivalence', *New Political Science* 31, 3: 291–317.

Rabot, Jean-Martin. 2007. 'The Image, Vector of Society' ('L'image, vecteur de socialite'), *Sociétés* 1,19–31.

Rapoport, Anatol. 1953. 'Spread of Information Through a Population with Socio-structural Bias, I-III.' *Bulletin of Mathematical Biophysics* 15: 523–33; 15: 535–46; 16: 75–81.

Rehmann, Jan C. 2007. 'Towards a Deconstruction of Postmodernist Neo-Nietzscheanism: Deleuze and Foucault, Situations', *Project of the Radical Imagination* 2, 1: 7–16.

Salerno, Roger A. 2006. 'Alienated Communities: Between Aloneness and Connectedness', in Lauren Langman and Devorah Kalekin-Fishman, eds., *The Evolution of Alienation: Trauma, Promise, and the Millennium*. Lanham, MD: Rowman & Littlefield, 253–68.

Simmel, Georg. 1906. 'The Sociology of Secrecy and of Secret Societies', *American Journal of Sociology* 11, 4: 441–98.

Singer, Merrill. 2006. 'What Is the "Drug User Community"?: Implications for Public Health', *Human Organization* 65, 1: 72–80.

Stark, Sasha. 2009. 'The Gambling Research Community: A Preliminary Collaboration Network Analysis', unpublished report, Ontario Problem Gambling Research Centre.

Svihula, Judie. 2009. 'Gerontological Theory: A Commentary on Powell's Foucauldian Toolkit', *The Journal of Applied Gerontology* 28, 6: 690–6.

'The Social Networking Imperative'. 2007. Future Perfect Publishing, 25 June. At: http://futureperfectpublishing.com/2007/06/. Accessed 28 May 2009.

Thompson, Craig J., and Gokcen Coskuner-Balli. 2007. 'Enchanting Ethical Consumerism', *Journal of Consumer Culture* 7, 3: 275–303.

Turner, Ralph. 1962. 'Role-Taking: Process versus Conformity', in Arnold Rose, ed., *Human Behavior and Social Processes*. Boston: Houghton Mifflin, 20–40.

Wu, Charlene. 2005. 'Cultural Gestures', *Nonverbal Communication Web Project*. At: http://soc302.tripod.com/soc_302rocks/id6.html. Accessed 24 November 2009.

Yeygel, Sinem. 2006. 'A New Dimension of Marketing Is Brought by the Postmodern Society Structure: Tribal Marketing' ('Postmodern Toplumsal Tapının Pazarlamaya Getirdigi Yeni Boyut: Topluluk Pazarlaması [Tribal Marketing])'), *Bilig—Turk Dunyasi Sosyal Bilimler Dergisi* 38: 197–228.

Chapter 4

Abercrombie, Nicholas, Stephen Hill, and Bryan S. Turner. 2006. *The Penguin Dictionary of Sociology*, 5th edn. London: Penguin.

Agger, Ben. 2001. 'Are Authors Authored? Cultural Politics and Literary Agency in the Era of the Internet', *Democracy and Nature* 7, 1: 183–203.

Arvidsson, A. 2001. 'From Counterculture to Consumer Culture: Vespa and the Italian youth market, 1958–1978', *Journal of Consumer Culture* 1, 1: 47–71.

Baer, Douglas, Edward Grabb, and William Johnston. 1993. 'National Character, Regional Culture, and the Values of Canadians and Americans', *Canadian Review of Sociology and Anthropology* 30, 1: 13–36.

Becker, Sascha O., and Ludger Woessmann. 2009. 'Was Weber Wrong? A Human Capital Theory of Protestant Economic History', *Quarterly Journal of Economics* 124, 2: 531–96.

Berger, John. 1972. *Ways of Seeing*. London: British Broadcasting Corporation/Penguin.

Bishop, Ron. 2001. 'Stealing the Signs: A Semiotic Analysis of the Changing Nature of Professional Sports Logos', *Social Semiotics* 11, 1: 23–41.

Boggs, Carl, and Tom Pollard. 2001. 'Postmodern Cinema and Hollywood Culture in an Age of Corporate Colonization'. *Democracy & Nature* 7, 1: 159–81.

Bottero, Wendy. 2009. 'Relationality and Social Interaction', *British Journal of Sociology* 60, 2: 399–420.

Bourdieu, Pierre. 1984 (1979). *Distinction: A Social Critique of the Judgement of Taste*, trans. Richard Nice. Cambridge, MA: Harvard University Press.

Canada Council for the Arts. 2009a. 'Total Funding 2008–2009'. At: http://www.canadacouncil.ca/NR/rdonlyres/1638A8DC-D57A-41CD-8403-7B1BDCE79B50/0/Overview2EN.pdf.

———. 2009b. 'Who Received a Grant?'. At: http://www.canadacouncil.ca/grants/recipients/.

Castro-Gomez, Santiago. 2001. 'Traditional Theory and Critical Theory', *Cultural Critique* 49: 139–54.

Catlaw, Thomas J., and Qian Hu. 2009. 'Legitimacy and Public Administration: Constructing the American Bureaucratic Fields', *American Behavioral Scientist* 53, 3: 458–81.

Citizenship and Immigration Canada. 2009. 'Annual Report on the Operation of the *Canadian Multiculturalism Act* 2007–2008'. 11 February. At: http://www.cic.gc.ca/english/resources/publications/multi-report2008/part1.asp#diversity. Accessed 17 Apr. 2010.

———. 2010. Annual Report on the Operation of the *Canadian Multiculturalism Act* 2008–2009. March 4. At: http://www.cic.gc.ca/english/pdf/pub/multi-report2009.pdf. Accessed 16 Apr. 2010.

Collins, Randall. 1986. *Max Weber*. Beverly Hills, CA: Sage.

DiMaggio, Paul. 1982. 'Cultural Capital and School Success: The Impact of Status Culture Participation on the Grades of the US High School Students,' *American Sociological Review* 47, April: 189–201.

Dorfman, Joseph. 1961 (1934). *Thorstein Veblen and His America*. New York: Viking Press.

Durkheim, Émile. 1965 (1912). *The Elementary Forms of Religious Life*, trans. Joseph Ward Swain. New York: Free Press.

Edgell, Stephen. 2001. *Veblen in Perspective: His Life and Thought*. Armonk, NY: Myron E. Sharpe.

Engerman, Stanley. 2000. 'Capitalism, Protestantism, and Economic Development'. EH.NET. At: http://www.eh.net/bookreviews/library/engerman.shtml.

Glastra, Folke, and Paul Vedder. 2010. 'Learning Strategies of Highly Educated Refugees in the Netherlands: Habitus or Calculation?', *International Migration* 48, 1: 80–105.

Goldfarb, Jeffrey C. 2005. 'Dialogue, Culture, Critique: The Sociology of Culture and the New Sociological Imagination', *International Journal of Politics, Culture and Society* 18, 3–4: 281–292.

Gorski, Philip S. 2002. Review of *The Protestant Ethic and the Spirit of Capitalism* and *The Protestant Ethic and the Spirit of Capitalism and Other Writings*. *Social Forces* 82, 2: 833–39.

Grabb, Edward, and James Curtis. 2005. *Regions Apart: The Four Societies of Canada and the United States*. Toronto: Oxford University Press.

Gramsci, A. 1992. *Prison Notebooks*, vol. I, trans J. Buttigieg and A. Callarri. New York: Columbia University Press.

Gruner, Sabine. 2010. '"The Others Don't Want . . .": Small-Scale Segregation: Hegemonic Public Discourses and Racial Boundaries in German Neighbourhoods', *Journal of Ethnic and Migration Studies* 36, 2: 275–92.

Hall, Stuart. 1980. 'Cultural Studies: Two Paradigms', *Media, Culture and Society* 2: 57–72.

Hirsch, E.D. 1988. *Cultural Literacy: What Every American Needs To Know*. New York: Knopf Doubleday.

Horkheimer, Max. 2002 (1937). 'Traditional and Critical Theory', in Max Horkeimer, ed., *Critical Theory: Selected Essays*, trans. Matthew J. O'Connell. New York: Continuum.

Ignatow, Gabriel. 2009. 'Culture and Embodied Cognition: Moral Discourses in Internet Support Groups for Overeaters', *Social Forces* 88, 2: 643–69.

Kerr, Ron, and Sarah Robinson. 2009. 'The Hysteresis Effect as Creative Adaptation of the Habitus: Dissent and Transition to the "Corporate" in Post-Soviet Ukraine', *Organization* 16, 6: 829–853.

Kim, Kyung-Man. 2009. 'What Would a Bourdieuan Sociology of Scientific Truth Look Like?', *Social Science Information/ Information sur les Sciences Sociales* 48,1: 57–79.

Kirkpatrick, G. 2007. 'Between Art and Gameness: Critical Theory and Computer Game Aesthetics', *Thesis Eleven* 89: 74–93.

Lieberson, Stanley. 2000. *A Matter of Taste*. New Haven, CT: Yale University Press.

Lipset, Seymour Martin. 1963. *First New Nation: The United States in Historical and Comparative Perspective*. New York: W.W. Norton.

———. 1990. *Continental Divide: The Values and Institutions of the United States and Canada*. New York: Routledge.

Marshall, Gordon. 1994. *The Concise Oxford Dictionary of Sociology*. New York: Oxford University Press.

Matthews, Laurel. 2002. 'Book Review of *Gestures: The Do's and Taboos of Body Language Around the World*', *Business Credit*. All Business, January 1. At: http://www.allbusiness.com/business-finance/business-loans-business-credit/105598-1.html. Accessed 16 Apr. 2010.

Media Awareness Network. 2010. 'The Impact of Stereotyping on Young People' At: http://www.media-awareness.ca/english/issues/stereotyping/aboriginal_people/aboriginal_impact.cfm. Accessed 16 Apr. 2010.

Murdock, George. 1945. 'The Common Denominator of Culture', in Ralph Linton, ed., *The Science of Man in the World Crisis*. New York: Columbia University Press.

Peterson, Richard A. 1994. 'The Seventh Stream: The Emergence of Rocknroll in American Popular Music.' *American Journal of Sociology* 100, 1: 296–8.

Phipps, Sean. 2009. 'Canadian Culture: A Category?' *The Globe and Mail*. 3 Apr. At: http://www.theglobeandmail.com/archives/canadian-culture-a-category/article801204. Accessed 16 Apr. 2010.

Pollmann, Andreas. 2009. 'Formal Education and Intercultural Capital: Towards Attachment beyond Narrow Ethno-national Boundaries?' *Educational Studies* 35, 5: 537–45.

Qin, Dongxiao. 2004. *Crossing Borders: International Women Students in American Higher Education*. Lanham, MD: University Press of America.

Rief, S. 2008. 'Outlines of a Critical Sociology of Consumption: Beyond Moralism and Celebration', *Sociology Compass* 2, 2: 560–76.

Rossel, Jorg, and Kathi Bromberger. 2009. 'Is the Consumption of Popular Culture Structured by Cultural Capital as Well?', *Zeitschrift fur Soziologie* 38,6: 494–512.

Sapir, E. 1929. 'The Status of Linguistics as a Science', *Language* 5: 209.

Schumpeter, Joseph. 1991. *The Economics and Sociology of Capitalism*. Princeton, NJ: Princeton University Press.

Sniderman, Paul M., Peter Russell, Joseph Fletcher, and Philip Tetlock. 1996. *The Clash of Rights: Liberty, Equality, and Legitimacy in Liberal Democracy*. New Haven, CT: Yale University Press.

Stabile, Donald. 2002. 'Veblen in Perspective: His Life and Thought'. EH.NET. At: http://eh.net/book_reviews/veblen-perspective-his-life-and-thought.

Statistics Canada. 2009. 'Quick Fact'. 1 May. At: http://www.statcan.gc.ca/pub/81-004-x/2008005/chrt-graph/desc/desc-qf-eng.htm. Accessed 17 Apr. 2010.

Tawney, R.H. 1926. *Religion and the Rise of Capitalism*. Harmondsworth, UK: Penguin.

Till, Rupert. 2006. 'The Nine O'clock Service: Mixing Club Culture and Postmodern Christianity', *Culture and Religion*, 7, 1: 93–110.

Treasury Board of Canada. 2009. 'Social Affairs', in *Canada's Performance Report 2008–09: The Government of Canada's Contribution*. 7 Oct. At: http://www.tbs-sct.gc.ca/reports-rapports/cp-rc/2008-2009/cp-rc04-eng.asp. Accessed 17 Apr. 2010.

Veblen, Thorstein. 1899. *Theory of the Leisure Class: An Economic Study of Institutions*. New York: Macmillan.

Weber, Max. 1958 (1905). *Protestant Ethic and the Spirit of Capitalism*, trans. Talcott Parsons. New York: Scribner.

Weiss, M.J. 1988. *The clustering of America*. New York: Harper & Row.

White, Harrison, and Cynthia White. 1965. *Canvases and Careers: Institutional Change in the French Painting World*. Chicago: University of Chicago Press.

Wood, John Cunningham. 1993. *Thorstein Veblen: The Life of Thorstein Veblen and Perspectives on his Thought*, vol. 1. London and New York: Routledge.

Wright, April L. 2009. 'Domination in Organizational Fields: It's Just Not Cricket', *Organization* 16, 6: 855–85.

Zarycki, Tomasz. 2009. 'The Power of the Intelligentsia: The Rywin Affair and the Challenge of Applying the Concept of Cultural Capital to Analyze Poland's Elites', *Theory and Society* 38, 6: 613–48.

Chapter 5

Ammar, Nawal H. 2007. 'Wife Battery in Islam: A Comprehensive Understanding of Interpretations', *Violence Against Women* 13: 516–26.

Andres, Lesley, and Maria Adamuti-Trache. 2007. 'You've Come a Long Way, Baby? Persistent Gender Inequality in University Enrolment and Completion in Canada, 1979–2004', *Canadian Public Policy/Analyse de Politiques* 33: 93–116.

Armstrong, Pat, and Hugh Armstrong. 1994. *The Double Ghetto: Canadian Women and Their Segregated Work*, 3rd edn. Toronto: McClelland & Stewart.

Arnot, Madeleine. 2002. 'Making the Difference to Sociology of Education: Reflections on Family-School and Gender Relations', *Discourse* 23: 347–55.

Ayyub, Ruksana. 2000. 'Domestic Violence in the South Asian Muslim Immigrant Population in the United States', *Journal of Social Distress & the Homeless* 9: 237–48.

Barnett, R.C. 1994. 'Women and Work', in P. Sarrell and L. Sarrell, eds., *Realities of Midlife in Women*. London: Wells Medical, 49–54.

———, and J.S. Hyde. 2001. 'Women, Men, Work and Family: An Expansionist Theory', *The American Psychologist* 56, 10: 781–96.

Baxter, J. 2000. 'The Joys and Justice of Housework', *Sociology* 34: 609–31.

———, and M. Western. 1998. 'Satisfaction with Housework: Examining the Paradox', *Sociology* 32: 101–20.

Beaujot, Roderic, and Zenaida Ravanera. 2009. 'Family Models for Earning and Caring: Implications for Child Care and for Family Policy', *Canadian Studies in Population* 36: 145–66.

Benhabib, Seyla. 1995. *Feminist Contentions: A Philosophical Exchange*. New York: Routledge.

Bianchi, S. M., M.A. Milkie, L.C. Sayer, and J.P. Robinson. 2000. 'Is Anyone Doing the Housework?', *Social Forces* 79: 191–228.

Blum, Linda, and Vicki Smith. 1988. 'Women's Mobility in the Corporation: A Critique of the Politics of Optimism', *Signs* 13: 528–45.

Bonney, N. and E. Reinach. 1993. 'Housework Reconsidered—The Oakley Thesis 20 Years Later', *Work Employment and Society* 7: 615–27.

Boyd, Monica, and Elizabeth Grieco. 2003. 'Women and Migration: Incorporating Gender into International Migration Theory.' At: http://www.migrationinformation.org/issues_mar03.cfm. Accessed 2 June 2009.

Bradley, K. 2000. 'The Incorporation of Women into Higher Education: Paradoxical Outcomes', *Sociology of Education* 73: 1–18.

Breslauer, Helen J., and Jane Gordon. 1989. 'The Two-Gender University: Catching Up to Changes in the Clientele'. Paper presented at a meeting of the Canadian Sociology and Anthropology Association and Canadian Society for the Study of Higher Education, Quebec City, Quebec.

Bui, H.N., and M. Morash. 2007. 'Social Capital, Human Capital, and Reaching Out for Help with Domestic Violence: A Case Study of Women in a Vietnamese American Community', *Criminal Justice Studies* 20: 375–90.

Bumpass, Larry L., Teresa Castro Martin, and James A. Sweet. 1991. 'The Impact of Family Background and Early Marital Factors on Marital Disruption', *Journal of Family Issues* 12: 22–42.

Carex Canada. 2009. 'Shiftwork'. At: http://www.carexcanada.ca/en/shiftwork.pdf.

Chaykowski, R.P., and L.M. Powell. 1999. 'Women and the Labour Market: Recent Trends and Policy Issues', *Canadian Public Policy/Analyse de politiques* 25: 1–25.

Clark, W. 2001. 'Economic Gender Equality Indicators', *Canadian Social Trends* 60: 1–8.

Comber, Barbara, and Helen Nixon. 2009. 'Teachers' Work and Pedagogy in an Era of Accountability', *Discourse* 30, 3: 333–45.

Connell, R.W., D.J. Ashenden, S. Kessler, and G.W. Dowsett. 1982. *Making the Difference: Schools, Families and Social Division*. Sydney: Allen & Unwin.

Davis, Kathy. 2008. 'Intersectionality as Buzzword: A Sociology of Science Perspective on What Makes a Feminist Theory Successful', *Feminist Theory* 9, 1: 67–85.

Denton, Margaret, and Linda Boos. 2007. 'The Gender Wealth Gap: Structural and Material Constraints and Implications for Later Life', *Journal of Women & Aging* 19: 105–20.

———, Steven Prus, and Vivienne Walters. 2004. 'Gender Differences in Health: A Canadian Study of the Psychosocial, Structural and Behavioural Determinants of Health', *Social Science & Medicine* 58: 2585–600.

Edwards, Lisa, and Carwyn Jones. 2009. 'Postmodernism, Queer Theory and Moral Judgment in Sport: Some Critical Reflections', *International Review for the Sociology of Sport* 44, 4: 331–44.

Einstein, Gillian, and Margit Shildrick. 2009. 'The Postconventional Body: Retheorising Women's Health', *Social Science & Medicine* 69, 2: 293–300.

Emerson, Tiffany. 2009. 'Between Flirting and Sexual Harassment: Explaining Efficacy and Effrontery in the Workplace. *Masters Abstracts International* 47, 5: 2469.

Endler, N.S., A. Rutherford, and E. Denisoff. 1999. 'Beck Depression Inventory: Exploring its Dimensionality in a Nonclinical Population', *Journal of Clinical Psychology* 55: 1307–312.

Esfandiari, Golnaz. 2009. 'Female Genital Mutilation Said to be Widespread in Iraq's, Iran's Kurdistan'. Association for Women's Rights in Development. 10 March. At: http://www.awid.org/eng/Issues-and-Analysis/Library/A-New-Resource-Article-Radio-Free-Europe-Radio-Liberty-Female-Genital-Mutilation-Said-To-Be-Widespread-In-Iraq-s-Iran-s-Kurdistan.

Fortin, N.M., and M. Huberman. 2002. 'Occupational Segregation and Women's Wages in Canada: An Historical Perspective', *Canadian Public Policy/Analyse de politiques* 28: 11–39.

Gadalla, Tahany M. 2008. 'Gender Differences in Poverty Rates after Marital Dissolution: A Longitudinal Study', *Journal of Divorce and Remarriage* 49: 225–38.

Gazso-Windle, Amber, and Julie Ann McMullin. 2003. 'Doing Domestic Labour: Strategising in a Gendered Domain', *Canadian Journal of Sociology/Cahiers canadiens de sociologie* 28: 341–66.

Gerth, H., and C.W. Mills, eds. 1974. *From Max Weber: Essays in Sociology.* Glencoe, IL: Free Press.

Greenstein, T.N. 2000. 'Economic Dependence, Gender, and the Division of Labor in the Home: A Replication and Extension', *Journal of Marriage and Family* 62, 2: 322–35.

Hadas, Doron, Gila Markovitzky, and Miri Sarid. 2008. 'Spousal Violence Among Immigrants from the Former Soviet Union—General Population and Welfare Recipients', *Journal of Family Violence* 23: 549–55.

Haines, Victor Y., III, Alain Marchand, Vincent Rousseau, and Andree Demers. 2008. 'The Mediating Role of Work-to-Family Conflict in the Relationship between Shiftwork and Depression', *Work & Stress* 22: 341–56.

Hamlin, Cynthia Lins. 2008. 'Ontology and Gender: Critical Realism and the Method of Contrastive Explanation' (Ontologia e genero: realismo critico e o metodo das explicacoes contrastivas'), *Revista Brasileira de Ciencias Sociais* 23, 67: 71–81.

Hammond, Judith. 1977. 'Ann Oakley: The Sociology of Housework (Book Review)', *Social Forces* 55, 4: 1103–4.

Hochschild, Arlie. 1990. *Second Shift: Working Parents and the Revolution at Home*, comp. Anne Machung. London: Piatkus.

Howkins, Mary Ball. 2009. 'Teaching Cultural Competence in Print Advertising: Postmodern Ads and Multi-Race Clothing Models', *Human Architecture: Journal of the Sociology of Self-Knowledge* 7, 1: 93–8.

Hurd Clarke, Laura, and Meredith Griffin. 2007. 'The Body Natural and the Body Unnatural: Beauty Work and Aging', *Journal of Aging Studies* 21, 3: 187–201.

Ibrahim, Selahadin A., Fran E. Scott, Donald C. Cole, Harry S. Shannon, and John Eyles. 2001. 'Job Strain and Self-Reported Health among Working Women and Men: An Analysis of the 1994/5 Canadian National Population Health Survey', *Women and Health* 33: 105–24.

Jaaber, R., and S. Dasgupta. 2003. 'Assessing Social Risks of Battered Women'. Praxis International. At: http://www.praxisinternational.org/praxis_lib_advocacy.aspx.

Janzen, B.L., and Nazeem Muhajarine. 2003.'Social Role Occupancy, Gender, Income Adequacy, Life Stage and Health: A Longitudinal Study of Employed Canadian Men and Women', *Social Science & Medicine* 57: 1491–503.

Johnson, Jennifer A., and Megan S. Johnson. 2008. 'New City Domesticity and the Tenacious Second Shift', *Journal of Family Issues* 29: 487–515.

Kanter, Rosabeth. 1993 (1977). *Men and Women of the Corporation.* New York: Basic Books.

Kay, F.M., and J. Brockman, 2003. 'Barriers to Gender Equality in the Canadian Legal Establishment', in U. Schultz and G. Shaw, eds., *Women in the World's Legal Professions.* Oxford: Hard Publishing, 49–75.

Kessler, Ronald C. 2003. 'Epidemiology of Women and Depression', *Journal of Affective Disorders* 74: 5–13.

Kim-Goh, Mikyong, and Jon Baello. 2008. 'Attitudes toward Domestic Violence in Korean and Vietnamese Immigrant Communities: Implications for Human Services', *Journal of Family Violence* 23: 647–54.

Knudson-Martin, Carmen, and Anne Rankin Mahoney. 2009. 'Gendered Power in Cultural Contexts: Capturing the Lived Experience of Couples', *Family Process* 48, 1: S. 5–8.

Ladson-Billings, Gloria. 2009. 'Who You Callin' Nappy-Headed?: A Critical Race Theory Look at the Construction of Black Women', *Race, Ethnicity and Education* 12, 1: 87–99.

Lennon, M.C., and S. Rosenfield. 1994. 'Relative Fairness and the Division of Housework', *American Journal of Sociology* 100: 506–31.

Luken, Paul C. and Suzanne Vaughan. 2007. 'Institutional Ethnography and the Critique of Professional Practice'. Atlanta, Georgia: Southern Sociological Society.

———— and ————. 2008. 'Putting Theory in Its Place: An Institutional Ethnography Approach'. Paper presented at First ISA Forum of Sociology, International Sociological Association, Barcelona, Spain.

Lyons, Sean, Linda Duxbury, and Christopher Higgins. 2005. 'Are Gender Differences in Basic Human Values a Generational Phenomenon?', *Sex Roles: A Journal of Research* 53: 763–78.

MacDonald, Martha, Shelley Phipps, and Lynn Lethbridge. 2005. 'Taking Its Toll: The Influence of Paid and Unpaid Work on Women's Well-Being', *Feminist Economics* 11: 63–94.

McFarlane, Seth, Roderic Beaujot, and Tony Haddad. 2000. 'Time Constraints and Relative Resources as Determinants of the Sexual Division of Domestic Work', *Canadian Journal of Sociology/Cahiers canadiens de sociologie* 25: 61–82.

MacKinnon, Catherine A. 2000. 'Points Against Postmodernism,' *Chicago-Kent Law Review*, 687.

McMullen, Kathryn, Jason Gilmore, and Christel Le Petit. 2010. 'Women in Non-traditional Occupations and Fields of Study', *Education Matters: Insights on Education, Learning and Training in Canada*, 7, 1. At: http://www.statcan.gc.ca/pub/81-004-x/2010001/article/11151-eng.htm.

Malenfant, Romaine, Andrée Larue, and Michel Vézina. 2007. 'Intermittent Work and Well-Being: One Foot in the Door, One Foot Out', *Current Sociology* 55, 6: 814–35.

Markert, John. 2009. 'Social Eclipses and Reversion to Type: Sexual Issues Confronting Postmodern Men and Women Working in Strongly Patriarchal Societies', *Theory in Action* 2, 1: 86.

Media Awareness Network. N.d. 'Beauty and Body Image in the Media'. At: http://www.media-awareness.ca/english/issues/stereotyping/women_and_girls/women_beauty.cfm.

Merton, Robert. 1957 (1938). 'Social Structure and Anomie', in Robert Merton, ed., *Social Theory and Social Structure*, 2nd edn. New York: Free Press.

Mills, A.J. 2002. 'Studying the Gendering of Organizational Culture Over Time: Concerns, Issues and Strategies', *Gender, Work & Organization* 9, 3: 286–307.

Mirowsky, John and Catherine E. Ross. 1995. 'Sex Differences in Distress: Real or Artifact?' *American Sociological Review* 60, 3: 449–68.

Morash, Merry, Hoan Bui, Yan Zhang, and Kristy Holtfreter. 2007. 'Risk Factors for Abusive Relationships', *Violence Against Women* 13: 653–75.

Muhajarine, Nazeem, and Bonnie Janzen. 2006. 'The Health of Employed Women and Men: Work, Family, and Community Correlates', *Journal of Community & Applied Social Psychology* 16: 233–41.

Mustafa, Naheed. 1993. 'My Body Is My Own Business', *The Globe and Mail*, 29 June, A26. At: http://www.islaam.ca/index.php?option=com_content&view=article&id=213:my-body-is-my-own-business-the-hijab-freedom-or-oppression&catid=48:women-in-islam&Itemid=196.

Oakley, Ann. 1974. *The Sociology of Housework*. London: Martin Robertson.

Olofsson, Per-Olof. 2006. 'Structuration against Personal Reflexivity—Consequences of Late Modernity?' Paper presented at the World Congress of Sociology, International Sociological Association, Durban, South Africa.

Parsons, Talcott. 1955. 'The American Family: Its Relations to Personality and the Social Structure', in T. Parsons and R. F. Bales, eds., *Family Socialization and Interaction Process*. New York: Free Press.

Patten, S.B. 2000. 'Incidence of Major Depression in Canada', *Canadian Medical Association Journal* 163: 714–15. Phipps, Shelley, and Frances Woolley. 2008. 'Control over Money and the Savings Decisions of Canadian Households', *The Journal of Socio-Economics* 37: 592–611.

Phipps, Shelley and Frances Woolley. 2008. 'Control over money and the savings decisions of Canadian households.' *The Journal of Socioeconomics* 37, 2: 592–611.

Posner, Judith. 1984a. 'The Objectified Male: The New Male Image in Advertising', *Atkinson Review* 1: 17–22.

———. 1984b. 'Women, Aging and Advertising', *Canadian Woman Studies* 5, 3: 70–1.

Ronholt, Helle. 2002. '"It's Only the Sissies . . .": Analysis of Teaching and Learning Processes in Physical Education: A Contribution to the Hidden Curriculum', *Sport, Education and Society* 7: 25–36.

Rushing, Sara Lacy. 2007. 'Future Framers: Feminism, Hope and Utopia', *Dissertation Abstracts International, A: The Humanities and Social Sciences*, 68, 2: 715.

Sabo, Anne G. 2009. 'Highbrow and Lowbrow Pornography: Prejudice Prevails Against Popular Culture—A Case Study', *The Journal of Popular Culture* 42, 1: 147–61.

Shannon, M., and M.P. Kidd. 2001. 'Projecting the Trend in the Canadian Gender Wage Gap 2001–2031: Will an Increase in Female Education Acquisition and Commitment be Enough?', *Canadian Public Policy/Analyse de politiques* 27: 447–67.

Simon, R. 2002. 'Revisiting the Relationships among Gender, Marital Status and Mental Health', *American Journal of Sociology* 107: 1065–96.

Smith, Dorothy E. 2000. 'Schooling for Inequality', *Signs* 25: 1147–51.

Sonnert, Gerhard, and Gerald James Holton. 1995. *Who Succeeds in Science?: The Gender Dimension*. New Brunswick, NJ: Rutgers University Press.

——— and ———. 1996. 'Career Patterns of Women and Men in the Sciences', *American Scientist* 84: 63–71.

Spitzer, Brenda L., Katherine A. Henderson, and Marilyn T. Zivian. 1999. 'Gender Differences in Population versus Media Body Sizes: A Comparison over Four Decades', *Sex Roles* 40, 7–8: 545–65.

Spiwak, Rae, and Douglas A. Brownridge. 2005. 'Separated Women's Risk for Violence: An Analysis of the Canadian Situation', *Journal of Divorce and Remarriage* 43: 105–17.

Sprague, Joey, and Heather Laube. 2009. 'Institutional Barriers to Doing Public Sociology: Experiences of Feminists in the Academy', *The American Sociologist* 40, 4: 249–71.

Statistics Canada. 2008. *Earnings and Incomes of Canadians Over the Past Quarter Century, 2006 Census*. Censuses of Population, 1981, 1991, 2001, and 2006. Catalogue no. 97-563-X. Ottawa: Minister of Industry. At: http://www12.statcan.ca/english/census06/analysis/income/pdf/97-563-XIE2006001.pdf. Accessed 9 June 2009.

Stone-Mediatore, Shari. 2007. 'Challenging Academic Norms: An Epistemology for Feminist and Multicultural Classrooms', *NWSA Journal* 19, 2: 55–78.

Strohschein, Lisa, Peggy McDonough, Georges Monette, and Qing Shao. 2005. 'Marital Transitions and Mental Health: Are There Gender Differences in the Short-Term Effects of Marital Status Change?', *Social Science & Medicine* 61: 2293–303.

Sullivan, Oriel. 2000. 'The Division of Domestic Labour: 20 Years of Change?', *Sociology* 34: 437–56.

Tong, Rosemarie. 2007. 'Feminist Thought in Transition: Never a Dull Moment', *The Social Science Journal* 44, 1: 23–39.

Varcoe, Colleen, and Lori G. Irwin. 2004. '"If I Killed You, I'd Get the Kids": Women's Survival and Protection Work with Child Custody and Access in the Context of Woman Abuse', *Qualitative Sociology* 27: 77–99.

Walters, Vivienne, Peggy McDonough, and Lisa Strohschein. 2002. 'The Influence of Work, Household Structure, and Social, Personal and Material Resources on Gender Differences in Health: An Analysis of the 1994 Canadian National Population Health Survey', *Social Science and Medicine* 54: 677–92.

Wernick, Andrew. 1987. 'From Voyeur to Narcissist: Imaging Men in Contemporary Advertising', in Kaufman, M., ed., *Beyond Patriarchy: Essays by Men on Pleasure, Power, and Change*. Toronto: Oxford University Press.

Williams, K. 2003. 'Has the Future of Marriage Arrived? A Contemporary Examination of Gender, Marriage and Psychological Well-being', *Journal of Health and Social Behavior* 44: 470–87.

Yick, Alice G., and Jody Oomen-Early. 2008. 'A 16-Year Examination of Domestic Violence Among Asians and Asian Americans in the Empirical Knowledge Base: A Content Analysis', *Journal of Interpersonal Violence* 23: 1075–94.

Chapter 6

Adam, Barry D. 1996. 'Review: The Social Organization of Sexuality: Sexual Practices in the United States', *Gay Lesbian Quarterly* 3, 2–3: 311–16.

Adorno, Theodor W. 1950. *The Authoritarian Personality*. New York: Harper.

Allen, Louisa. 2008. 'Poles Apart? Gender Differences in Proposals for Sexuality Education Content', *Gender and Education* 20, 5: 435–50.

Artemova, Olga and Andrey V. Korotayev. 2003. 'Monopolization of Information and Female Status: A Cross-Cultural Test', *Cross-Cultural Research* 37, 1: 81–6.

Attwood, Feona. 2006. 'Sexed Up: Theorizing the Sexualization of Culture', *Sexualities* 9, 1: 77–94.

Baldick, Chris. 2008. 'Queer Theory' in *The Oxford Dictionary of Literary Terms*. Oxford: Oxford University Press, 279.

Baril, Audrey. 2007. 'Constructing from Gender to Sex: Postmodern Feminist Thesis in Judith Butler's Work', *Recherches Feministes* 20, 2: 61–90.

Baute, Nicole. 2010. 'Generation Me Employees Seek Gold Stars, Vacation Time', *Toronto Star*. 19 Mar. At: http://www.thestar. com/living/article/780859--generation-me-employees-seek-gold-stars-vacation-time. Accessed 18 Apr. 2010.

Belgrave, Faye Z., Barbara Van Oss Marin, and Donald B. Chambers. 2000. 'Cultural, Contextual, and Interpersonal Predictors of Risky Sexual Attitudes Among Urban African American Girls in Early Adolescence', *Cultural Diversity & Ethnic Minority Psychology* 6, 3: 309–22.

Boritch, Helen. 1997. *Fallen Women: Female Crime and Criminal Justice in Canada*. Toronto: ITP Nelson.

Brickell, Chris. 2005. 'Masculinities, Performativity, and Subversion: A Sociological Reappraisal', *Men and Masculinities* 8, 1: 24–43.

Broad, K. L. 2002. 'GLB+T?: Gender/Sexuality Movements and Transgender Collective Identity (De)Constructions', *International Journal of Sexuality and Gender Studies* 7, 4: 241–64.

Butler, Judith. 1984. *Subjects of Desire: Hegelian Reflections in Twentieth-century France*. New York: Columbia University Press.

———. 1990. *Gender Trouble Feminism and the Subversion of Identity*. New York: Routledge.

———. 1993. *Bodies That Matter: on the Discursive Limits of 'Sex'*. New York: Routledge.

———. 1997. *The Psychic Life of Power: Theories in Subjection*. Stanford, CA: Stanford University Press.

———. 2004. *Undoing Gender*. New York: Routledge.

Calder, Gideon. 2004. 'The Language of Refusal: Sexual Consent and the Limits of Post-Structuralism' in Mark Cowling and Paul Reynolds, eds., *Making Sense of Sexual Consent*. Aldershot, UK: Ashgate, 57–71.

Chancer, Lynn. 1995. 'Review: The Social Organization of Sexuality: Sexual Practices in the United States', *Contemporary Sociology* 24, 4: 298–302.

Cordoba Garcia, David. 2003. 'Sexual Identity and Performativity', *Athenea Digital: Revista De Pensamiento E Investigacion Social* 4: 87–96.

Cramer, R.E., B. Manning-Ryan, L. Johnson, and E. Barbo. 2000. 'Sex Differences in Subjective Distress to Violations-of-Trust: Extending an Evolutionary Perspective', *Basic and Applied Social Psychology* 22, 101–9.

Davis, Kingsley. 1979. 'The Sociology of Prostitution', in John F. Decker, ed., *Prostitution: Regulation and Control*. Littleton, CO: F.B. Rothman, 746–55.

D'Emilio, John. 1983. *Sexual Politics, Sexual Communities: The Making of a Homosexual Minority in the United States, 1940–1970*. Chicago: University of Chicago Press.

De Munck, V. and A. Korotayev. 1999. 'A Re-Analysis of Rosenblatt's Study on the Function of Romantic Love', *Cross-Culture Research: The Journal of Comparative Social Science* 33, 3: 265–77.

Diagnostic and Statistical Manual of Mental Disorders. 2000. 4th edn, revised. Washington, DC: American Psychiatric Association.

Edwards, Lisa, and Carwyn Jones. 2009. 'Postmodernism, Queer Theory and Moral Judgment in Sport: Some Critical Reflections', *International Review for the Sociology of Sport* 44, 4: 331–44.

Emig, Rainer. 2006. 'Sexing The Matrix: Gender and Sexuality In/As Cyberfiction', *Critical Studies* 29, 1: 193–208.

Espiritu, Yen Le. 2001. '"We Don't Sleep Around Like the White Girls Do": Family, Culture, and Gender in Filipina American Lives', *Signs* 26, 2: 415–40.

European Graduate School. 2010. 'Biography of Judith Butler— Hannah Arendt Professor of Philosophy. At: http://www.egs. edu/faculty/judith-butler/biography.

Family Safe Media. N.d. 'Pornography Statistics'. At: http://www. familysafemedia.com/pornography_statistics.html. Accessed 17 Apr. 2010.

Fingerson, Laura. 2000. 'Do Parents' Opinions Matter? Family Processes and Adolescent Sexual Behavior'. Paper presented to the American Sociological Association.

Foucault, Michel. 1979. *Discipline and Punish: the Birth of the Prison*, trans. Alan Sheridan. New York: Vintage.

Gauntlett, David. 1998. 'Judith Butler'. Theory.Org.UK. At: http:// www.theory.org.uk/ctr-butl.htm.

Gil Rodriguez, Eva Patricia. 2002. 'Why Do They Call It Gender When They Mean Sex? An Approach to Judith Butler's Theory of Performativity', *Athenea Digital: Revista De Pensamiento E Investigacion Social* 2: 30–41.

Green, Adam Isaiah. 2002. 'Gay but Not Queer: Toward a Post-Queer Study of Sexuality', *Theory and Society* 31, 4: 521–45.

Grindstaff, Davin. 2003. 'Queering Marriage: An Ideographic Interrogation of Heteronormative', *Journal of Homosexuality* 45, 2–4: 257–75.

Hansen, Lisa, Janice Mann, Sharon McMahon, and Thomas Wong. 2004. Sexual health. *BMC Women's Health* 4: S24. At: http:// www.biomedcentral.com/content/pdf/1472-6874-4-S1-S24. pdf. Accessed 18 Apr. 2010.

Hey, Valerie. 2006. 'The Politics of Performative Resignification: Translating Judith Butler's Theoretical Discourse and Its Potential for a Sociology of Education', *British Journal of Sociology of Education* 27, 4: 439–57.

Hines, Sally. 2006. 'What's the Difference? Bringing Particularity to Queer Studies of Transgender', *Journal of Gender Studies* 15,1: 49–66.

Hoffman, Martin. 1968. *The Gay World: Male Homosexuality and the Social Creation of Evil*. New York: Basic Books.

Humphreys, Laud. 1970. *Tearoom Trade*. Chicago: Aldine.

Hurley, Michael. 2002. On Not Getting It: Narration, Sex and Ageing', *Sexualities* 5, 4: 407–23.

Johnson, Paul J. 2001. 'The Histories of Sexuality: The Future of Debate', *Social Epistemology* 15, 2: 127–37.

Kinsey, Alfred C. 1953. *Sexual Behavior in the Human Female*. Philadelphia: Saunders.

———, Wardell Baxter Pomeroy, and Clyde E. Martin. 1948. *Sexual Behavior in the Human Male*. Philadelphia: W.B. Saunders.

Komiya, Tomone. 2009. 'The Description of Actions and Identities in Our Social Lives: A Sociological Examination of Judith Butler's Concept of Gender', *Shakaigaku Hyoron/Japanese Sociological Review* 60, 3: 192–208.

Langlois, Tish. 2009. 'Navigating Sexual Terrain: Legacies of the Sacred and the Secular in the Lives of French-Canadian Women', in Bonnie Fox, ed., *Family Patterns, Gender Relations*, 3rd edn. Toronto: Oxford University Press, 219–35.

Laumann, Edward O. 1994. *The Social Organization of Sexuality: Sexual Practices in the United States*. Chicago: University of Chicago.

Leacock, Eleanor B. 2009. 'Women in an Egalitarian Society: The Montagnais-Naskapi of Canada', in Bonnie Fox, ed., *Family Patterns, Gender Relations*, 3rd edn. Toronto: Oxford University Press, 43–54.

Marcuse, Herbert. 1955. *Eros and Civilization: A Philosophical Inquiry into Freud*. Boston: Beacon.

Martin, Karin A. 2009. 'Normalizing Heterosexuality: Mother's Assumptions, Talk, and Strategies with Young Children', *American Sociological Review* 74, 2: 190–207.

Meldrim, H. 2005. The Impact of Marital Infidelity on the Offended Spouse: How Christian Women and Men Cope. N.p.: Booksurge.

Media Awareness Network. N.d. 'Sex and Relationships in the Media'. At: http://www.media-awareness.ca/english/issues/stereotyping/women_and_girls/women_sex.cfm. Accessed 16 Apr. 2010.

Merton, Robert King. 1957. *Social Theory and Social Structure*. Glencoe, IL: Free Press.

Michalski, R.L., T.K. Shackelford, and C.A. Salmon. 2007. 'Emotional Reactions to Infidelity', *Cognition and Emotion* 14: 643–59.

Miller, Kim S., Rex Forehand, and Beth A. Kotchick. 1999. 'Adolescent Sexual Behavior in Two Ethnic Minority Samples: The Role of Family Variables', *Journal of Marriage and the Family* 61, 1: 85–98.

Mirchandani, Rekha. 2005. 'Postmodernism and Sociology: From the Epistemological to the Empirical', *Sociological Theory* 23, 1: 86–115.

Moss, Nancy. 1996. 'Review: The Social Organization of Sexuality: Sexual Practices in the United States', *American Journal of Public Health* 86, 7: 1037–9.

Murray, Stephen O. 1995. *Latin American Male Homosexualities*. Albuquerque: University of New Mexico.

———. 1996. *American Gay*. Chicago: University of Chicago.

———. 2000. *Homosexualities*. Chicago: University of Chicago.

Nathanson, Jessica. 2009. 'Bisexual Pedagogy: Bringing Bisexuality Into The Classroom', *Journal of Bisexuality* 9, 1: 71–86.

Nayak, Anoop, and Mary Jane Kehily. 2006. 'Gender Undone: Subversion, Regulation and Embodiment in the Work of Judith Butler', *British Journal of Sociology of Education* 27, 4: 459–72.

Ost, Suzanne. 2002. 'Children at Risk: Legal and Societal Perceptions of the Potential Threat that the Possession of Child Pornography Poses to Society', *Journal of Law and Society* 29: 436–60.

Pellauer, Mary D. 1995. 'Review: Social Organization of Sexuality:

Sexual Practices in the United States', *Christian Century* 112, 20: 642.

Plummer, Ken. 2003. 'Queers, Bodies and Postmodern Sexualities: A Note on Revisiting the "Sexual" in Symbolic Interactionism', *Qualitative Sociology* 26, 4: 515–30.

Powell, Jason L., and Malcolm Carey. 2007. 'Social Theory, Performativity and Professional Power—A Critical Analysis of Helping Professions in England', *Human Affairs* 17, 1: 78–94.

Reiche, Reimut. 2004. 'Regarding Judith Butler', *Zeitschrift Fur Sexualforschung* 17, 1: 11–25.

Rooke, Alison. 2007. 'Navigating Embodied Lesbian Cultural Space: Toward a Lesbian Habitus', *Space and Culture* 10, 2: 231–52.

Russell-Brown, Pauline. 2000. 'Wives' and Husbands' Contraceptive Knowledge and Beliefs and Pregnancy Planning Behavior in Rural Nigeria', *Dissertation Abstracts International, The Humanities and Social Sciences* 60, 7: 2694–A.

Sabo, Anne G. 2009. 'Highbrow and Lowbrow Pornography: Prejudice Prevails Against Popular Culture—A Case Study', *The Journal of Popular Culture* 41, 2: 147–61.

Schmidt, Gunter. 1997. 'Review: The Social Organization of Sexuality: Sexual Practices in the United States', *Archives of Sexual Behavior* 26, 3: 327–32.

Schützwohl, A. 2008. 'The Disengagement of Attentive Resources from Task-Irrelevant Cues to Sexual and Emotional Infidelity', *Personality and Individual Differences*, 44: 631–42.

Schwartzman, Lisa H. 2002. 'Hate Speech, Illocution, and Social Context: A Critique of Judith Butler', *Journal of Social Philosophy* 33, 3: 421–41.

Scoular, Jane. 2004. 'The "Subject" of Prostitution: Interpreting the Discursive, Symbolic and Material Position of Sex/Work in Feminist Theory', *Feminist Theory* 5, 3: 343–55.

Statistics Canada. 2003. 'Canadian Community Health Survey', cycle 2.1. At: http://www.statcan.gc.ca/concepts/health-sante/cycle2_1/index-eng.htm.

———. 2004. 'Canadian Community Health Survey', *The Daily*, 15 June. At: http://www.statcan.gc.ca/daily-quotidien/040615/dq040615b-eng.htm.

Stormhoj, Christel. 2003. 'The Politicized Two-Sex Model', *Grus* 24, 69: 118–37.

Tillotson, Rachel F. 2007. 'Borderland Women: Cultural Production on the Women of Juarez', *Masters Abstracts International* 45, 3: 1221.

Tyler, Melissa. 2004. Managing between the Sheets: Lifestyle Magazines and the Management of Sexuality in Everyday Life', *Sexualities* 7, 1: 81–106.

———, and Laurie Cohen. 2008. 'Management in/as Comic Relief: Queer Theory and Gender Performativity in the Office', *Gender, Work and Organization* 15, 2: 113–32.

Valverde, Mariana. 2009. 'Heterosexuality: Contested Ground', in Bonnie Fox, ed., *Family Patterns, Gender Relations*, 3rd edn. Toronto: Oxford University Press, 212–18.

Wellings, Kaye. 1995. 'Review: The Social Organization of Sexuality: Sexual Practices in the United States', *BMJ* 310.6978: 540. At: http://www.bmj.com/cgi/content/citation/310/6978/540. Accessed 17 Apr. 2010.

Whitty, M. 2005. 'The Realness of Cybercheating', *Social Science Computer Review*, 23, 1: 57–67.

Wolff, Brent, Ann Blanc, and Anastasia Gage. 2000. 'Who Decides? Women's Status and Negotiation of Sex in Uganda', *Culture, Health, and Sexuality* 2, 3: 303–22.

Youngren, Gina. 2010. 'Gay and Lesbian Rights Around the World Increase: World Acceptance of Same Gender Couples to Marry Strengthens'. Suite101.com. 16 January. At: http://gay-rights-law.suite101.com/article.cfm/progress_for_gay_rights_around_the_globe. Accessed 16 Apr. 2010.

Chapter 7

Abu-Laban, Yasmeen, and Abigail Bakan. 2008. The Racial Contract: Israel/Palestine and Canada, *Social Identities* 14, 5: 637–60.

Ahmad, Farah, Angela Shik, Reena Vanza, Angela M. Cheung, Usha George, and Donna E. Stewart. 2004. 'Voices of South Asian Women: Immigration and Mental Health,' *Women & Health* 40, 4: 113–130.

Allport, G.W., and L. Postman. 1947. *The Psychology of Rumor*. New York: Henry Holt.

Anderson, Benedict. 1983. *Imagined Communities: Reflections on the Origin and Spread of Nationalism*. London: Verso.

Anderson, Kay. 2008. '"Race" in Post-universalist Perspective', *Cultural Geographies* 15, 2: 55–171.

Barbujani, G., A. Magagni, E. Minch, and L.L. Cavalli-Sforza. 1997. 'An Apportionment of Human DNA Diversity', *Proceedings of the National Academy of Sciences* 94: 4516–19.

Bogardus, E.S. 1925. 'Measuring Social Distances', *Journal of Applied Sociology* 9: 299–308.

———. 1959. *Social Distance*. Yellow Spring, OH: The Artichild Press.

———. 1967. *A Forty-Year Racial Distance Study*. Los Angeles, CA: University of Southern California Press.

Breton, Raymond. 1964. 'Institutional Completeness of Ethnic Communities and the Personal Relations of Immigrants', *American Journal of Sociology* 70, 2:193–205.

Brown, Tony N. 2008. Race, Racism, and Mental Health: Elaboration of Critical Race Theory's Contribution to the Sociology of Mental Health', *Contemporary Justice Review* 11, 1: 53–62.

Byrnes, D. A., and G. Kiger. 1988. 'Contemporary Measures of Attitudes toward Blacks', *Educational & Psychological Measurement* 48: 107–18.

Campbell, Fiona, and A. Kumari. 2008. 'Exploring Internalized Ableism using Critical Race Theory', *Disability & Society* 23, 2: 151–62.

Canadian Council on Learning. 2007. *Survey of Canadian Attitudes Toward Learning*. At: http://www.ccl-cca.ca/CCL/Reports/CLI/2009Factsheet8.htm Accessed 2 July 2009.

Citizenship and Immigration Canada. 2006. *Facts and Figures, 2006*. At: www.atlantic.metropolis.net/events/3rd%20Retreat/SK_Atlantic__Metropolis_2.ppt. Accessed 2 Jul. 2009.

———. 2008a. *Facts and Figures, 2007*. At: http://www.cic.gc.ca/english/pdf/pub/facts2007.pdf. Accessed 2 Jul. 2009.

———. 2008b. 'Annual Report to Parliament on Immigration, 2008'. At: http://www.cic.gc.ca/english/resources/publications/annual-report2008/section3.asp. Accessed 29 June 2009.

———. 2008c. 'Canadian Multiculturalism: An Inclusive Citizenship'. At: http://www.cic.gc.ca/english/multiculturalism/citizenship.asp.

———. 2009. 'Annual Report to Parliament on Immigration (2008).' At: http://www.cic.gc.ca/english/resources/publications/annual-report2008/index.asp.

Clairmont, Donald. 1996. 'Alternative Justice Issues For Aboriginal Justice', *Journal of Legal Pluralism and Unofficial Law* 36: 125–58.

Comeau, Tammy Duerden, and Anton L. Allahar. 2001. 'Forming Canada's Ethnoracial Identity: Psychiatry and the History of Immigration Practices', *Identity* 1: 143–60.

Coser, L. 1965. *Georg Simmel*. Englewood Cliffs, NJ: Prentice Hall.

Du Bois, W.E.B. 1995 (1903). *The Souls of Black Folk*, introduction by Randall Kenan. New York: Penguin.

Figueroa, Jose Antonio. 2009. 'Realismo magico, vallenato y violencia politica en el Caribe Colombiano', *Dissertation Abstracts International, A: The Humanities and Social Sciences* 70, 3: 886.

Gorrotxategi Azurmendi, Miren. 2005. 'The Management of Cultural Diversity: Multiculturalism in a Multinational Society. French Canadian Interculturalism in the Face of Canadian Multiculturalism', *Revista de Estudios Politicos* 129: 89–136.

Green, Alan G., and David Green. 2004. 'The Goals of Canada's Immigration Policy: A Historical Perspective', *Canadian Journal of Urban Research* 13: 102–39.

Hevia, James L. 2009. '"The Ultimate Gesture of Deference and Debasement": Kowtowing in China', *Past and Present* 203, suppl. 4: 212–34.

Holyfield, Lori, Matthew Ryan Moltz, and Mindy S. Bradley. 2009. 'Race Discourse and the US Confederate Flag', *Race, Ethnicity and Education* 12, 4: 517–37.

Jung, Dietrich. 2009. 'Edward Said, Michel Foucault and the Essentialist Image of Islam' ('Edward Said, Michel Foucault og det essentialistiske islambillede'), *Dansk Sociologi* 20, 3: 33–50.

Katz, A., and P. Foley. 1974. 'Development of a Social Distance Scale'. San Diego, CA: Navy Personnel Research and Development Center.

Kymlicka, Will. 1995. *Multicultural Citizenship: A Liberal Theory of Minority Rights*. Oxford: Oxford University Press.

McLean, Lorna. 2004. 'To Become Part of Us': Ethnicity, Race, Literacy and the Canadian Immigration Act of 1919', *Canadian Ethnic Studies/Etudes Ethniques au Canada* 35: 1–28.

Media Awareness Network. N.d. 'Ethnic and Visible Minorities in Entertainment Media'. At: http://www.media-awareness.ca/english/issues/stereotyping/ethnics_and_minorities/minorities_entertainment.cfm. Accessed 25 Nov. 2009.

Melancon, Hugues. 1997. 'A Pluralist Analysis of Indigenous Legal Conceptions before the Criminal Law Courts of Canada', *Canadian Journal of Law and Society/Revue canadienne droit et societe* 12, 2: 159–86.

Moore, Harry E. 1940. 'Critiques of Research in the Social Sciences, Vol. I: An Appraisal of Thomas and Znaniecki's 'The Polish Peasant in Europe and America'. *Social Forces* 18, 4: 580–3.

Munro, Daniel. 2005. 'Is Multiculturalism on Its Deathbed?' *Immigration Watch Canada*. 18 Aug. At: http://www.immigrationwatchcanada.org/index.php?module=pagemaster&PAGE_user_op=view_page&PAGE_id=242&MMN_position=92:90. Accessed 27 November 2009.

Nugent, Amy. 2006. 'Demography, National Myths, and Political Origins: Perceiving Official Multiculturalism in Quebec', *Canadian Ethnic Studies* 38, 3: 21–36.

Ozkisi, Zeynep Gulcin. 2007. 'A Definition of "World Music": In the Context of Postmodernism and Globalization' ('Postmodernizm ve kuresellesme baglaminda: "World Music" Tanimlamasi), *Journal of Academic Studies* 9, 33: 152–64.

Park, Robert E. 1928. 'Human Migration and the Marginal Man,' *American Journal of Sociology*, 33: 881–93.

Parmar, A. 2007. 'Crime and the "Asian Community": Disentangling Perceptions and Reality'. Unpublished Ph.D. dissertation, University of Cambridge, Institute of Criminology.

Pedersen, Helena. 2007. 'The School and the Animal Other: An Ethnography of Human–Animal Relations in Education', *Dissertation Abstracts International, C: Worldwide* 68, 4: 868.

Prasad, Aarathi. 2009. 'It's a Wonderful, Mixed-Up World'. Telegraph.co.uk. 1 November. At: http://www.telegraph.co.uk/comment/6475543/Its-a-wonderful-mixed-up-world.html. Accessed 27 Nov. 2009.

Rice, Stephen K., John D. Reitzel, and Alex R. Piquero. 2005. 'Shades of Brown: Perceptions of Racial Profiling and the Intra-Ethnic Differential', *Journal of Ethnicity in Criminal Justice* 3.1–2: 47–79.

Romero, Mary. 2008. 'Crossing the Immigration and Race Border: A Critical Race Theory Approach to Immigration Studies', *Contemporary Justice Review* 11, 1: 23–37.

Spaulding, Richard. 1997. 'Peoples as National Minorities: A Review of Will Kymlicka's Arguments for Aboriginal Rights from a Self-Determination Perspective', *University of Toronto Law Journal* 35: 65–7.

Statistics Canada. 2006a. 'Canada's Ethnocultural Mosaic, 2006 Census: Findings.' 2006 Census of Canada. At: http://www12.statcan.ca/census-recensement/2006/as-sa/97-562/index-eng.cfm. Accessed 26 June 2009.

———. 2006b. *Hate Crime in Canada.* Canadian Centre for Justice Statistics. At: http://www.statcan.gc.ca/pub/85f0033m/85f0033m2008017-eng.pdf .

Thomas, William I., and Florian Znaniecki. 1918–1920. *Polish Peasant in Europe and America,* 5 vols. N.p.: Kessinger Publishing.

UN Development Program. 2004. *Human Development Report 2004.* New York: UN.

UN Refugee Agency. 2009. '2008 Global Trends: Refugees, Asylum-seekers, Returnees, Internally Displaced and Stateless Persons: Country Data Sheets'. At: http://www.unhcr.org/4a375c426.html.

Walton-Roberts, M. 2003. 'Transnational Geographies: Indian Immigration to Canada', *The Canadian Geographer* 47, 3: 235–50.

Warburton, Rennie. 1997. 'Status, Class and the Politics of Canadian Aboriginal Peoples', *Studies in Political Economy* 54: 119–41.

Chapter 8

Aries, Philippe. 1963. *Centuries of Childhood: A Social History of Family Life* (*L'Enfant et la vie familiale sous l'Ancien Regime*), trans. Robert Baldick. New York: Vintage.

Bélanger, Alain, Laurent Martel, and Éric Caron Malenfant. 2005. *Population Projections for Canada, Provinces and Territories 2005-2031,* Statistics Canada Catalogue no. 91-520

Benjamin, Cynthia. 1999. 'Review', *Canadian Journal of Criminology* 41: 420–4.

Biggs, Simon. 1999. 'The "Blurring" of the Lifecourse: Narrative, Memory and the Question of Authenticity', *Journal of Aging and Identity* 4, 4: 209–21.

Blakeborough, Darren. 2008. '"Old People Are Useless": Representations of Aging on The Simpsons', *Canadian Journal on Aging/La Revue Canadienne du Vieillissement* 27, 1: 57–67.

Cumming, E., and W. Henry. 1961. *Growing Old: The Process of Disengagement.* New York: Basic Books.

D'Agostino, A. Federico. 1998. 'Identity, Time and Death in the Postmodernity—A Triangular Perspective'. International Sociological Association.

Deshaw, Rell. 2006. 'The History of Family Reunification in Canada and Current Policy', *Canadian Issues* Spring: 9–14.

de Sousa, Janice Tirelli Ponte. 2006. 'Introduction to the Dossier: A Society Viewed through the Generations' ('Apresentacao do Dossie: A sociedade vista pelas geracoes'), *Politica & Sociedade: Revista de Sociologia Politica* 5, 8: 9–29.

Edmunds, June, and Bryan S. Turner. 2005. 'Global Generations: Social Change in the Twentieth Century', *British Journal of Sociology* 56, 4: 559–77.

Elder, Glen H. Jr. 1999. *Children of the Great Depression: Social Change in Life Experience.* Thousand Oaks, CA: Sage.

Feixa, Carles, and Carmen Leccardi. 2008. 'The Concept of Generation in Youth Theories'. Paper presented at First ISA Forum of Sociology, International Sociological Association, Barcelona, Spain.

Flesher, Mark S. 2001. 'Review', *Annals of the American Academy of Political and Social Science* 575: 239–40.

Fullmer, Elise M., Dena Shenk, and Lynette J. Eastland. 1999. 'Negating Identity: A Feminist Analysis of the Social Invisibility of Older Lesbians', *Journal of Women & Aging* 11: 131–48.

Germain, Anthony. 2009. 'Shanghai Nights', CBC News. 28 Oct. At: http://www.cbc.ca/world/story/2009/10/28/f-rfa-germain.html.

Ginn, Jay, and Sara Arber. 1995. 'Exploring Mid-Life Women's Employment', *Sociology* 29, 1: 73–94.

Goldner, Melinda, and Patricia Drentea. 2009. 'Caring for the Disabled: Applying Different Theoretical Perspectives to Understand Racial and Ethnic Variations Among Families.' *Marriage & Family Review* 45, 5: 499–518.

Hagan, John, and Bill McCarthy. 1997. *Mean Streets: Youth Crime and Homelessless.* New York: Cambridge University Press.

Havighurst, R.J., and R. Albrecht. 1953. *Older People.* New York: Longmans, Green.

Henchoz, Karine, Stefano Cavalli, and Myriam Girardin. 2008. 'Health Perception and Health Status in Advanced Old Age: A Paradox of Association', *Journal of Aging Studies* 22, 3: 282–90.

Hendrick, Harry. 1992. 'Children and Childhood.' *ReFresh (Recent Findings of Research in Economic & Social History)* 15 (Autumn): 1–4.

Hirschi, Travis. 1969. *Causes of Delinquency.* Berkeley and Los Angeles: University of California Press.

Hockey, Jenny, and Allison James. 2002. 'The Embodiment of Age. Identity and Sexual Health across the Life Course' ('L'incorporamento dell'eta. Identita e salute sessuale attraverso il corso di vita'), *Rassegna Italiana di Sociologia* 43, 3: 353–77.

Ianni, Francis A.J., and Reuss-Ianni, Elizabeth. 1972. *A Family Business: Kinship and Social Control in Organized Crime*. London: Routledge and Kegan Paul.

Johnson, David. 2003. 'Why View All Time from the Perspective of Time's End? A Bergsonian Attack on Bataillean Transience', *Time & Society* 12, 2–3: 209–24.

Kuljic, Todor. 2007. '"Problem of Generations": Origins, Content and Continuing Relevance of Karl Mannheim's Article' ('"Problem generacija": nastanak, sadrzaj i aktuelnost ogleda Karl Manhajma'), *Sociologija*. 49, 3: 223–48.

Laaksonen, Helena T., and Eriikka M. Oinonen. 2008. 'Thirty-Somethings: The First European Generation? A Comparison of Family and Gender Attitudes and Practices'. Paper presented at First ISA Forum of Sociology, International Sociological Association, Barcelona, Spain.

Matza, David. 1964. *Delinquency and Drift*. New York: John Wiley and Sons.

Mechling, Jay. 1976. 'Review', *Journal of Social History* 9, 3: 418–20.

Merico, Maurizio. 2008. 'Youth and Social Change in Karl Mannheim's Sociology'. Paper presented at First ISA Forum of Sociology, International Sociological Association, Barcelona, Spain.

Moody, Harry R. 2000. *Aging: Concepts and Controversies*. Thousand Oaks, CA: Pine Forge Press.

Ondrejkovic, Peter, and Jana Majercikova. 2006. 'Changes in Society and Changes in Family—Continuity and Change: A Contribution to the Discussion about the Character of Family in Slovakia' ('Zmeny v spolocnosti a zmeny v rodine—kontinuita a zmena. Prispevokk diskusii o charaktere rodiny na Slovensku'], *Sociologia/Slovak Sociological Review* 38, 1: 5–30.

Phillipson, Chris, and Simon Biggs. 1998. 'Modernity and Identity: Themes and Perspectives in the Study of Older Adults', *Journal of Aging and Identity* 3, 1: 11–23.

Piliavin, Irving. 1998. 'Review'. *Contemporary Sociology*, 27, 4: 414–15.

Powell, Jason L. 2009. 'A Response to Castle, McDaniel, and Svihula', *The Journal of Applied Gerontology* 28, 6: 697–701.

———, and Charles F. Longino, Jr. 2002. 'Postmodernism versus Modernism: Rethinking Theoretical Tensions in Social Gerontology', *Journal of Aging and Identity* 7, 4: 219–26.

Schwartz, Barry. 2005. 'The New Gettysburg Address: Fusing History and Memory', *Poetics* 33, 1: 63–79.

Statistics Canada. 2003. 'Canadian Community Health Survey', cycle 2.1. At: http://www.statcan.gc.ca/concepts/health-sante/cycle2_1/index-eng.htm.

———. 2006a. Health Reports: Seniors' Health Care Use', *The Daily*, 7 Feb. At: http://www.statcan.gc.ca/daily-quotidien/060207/dq060207a-eng.htm. Accessed 21 June 2009.

———. 2006b. 'New Frontiers of Research on Retirement', *The Daily*, 27 Mar. At: http://www.statcan.gc.ca/daily-quotidien/060327/dq060327b-eng.htm. Accessed 24 June 2009.

———. 2006c. 'Study: Pension Coverage and Retirement Savings of Canadian Families', *The Daily*, 26 Sept. At: http://www.statcan.gc.ca/daily-quotidien/060926/dq060926a-eng.htm. Accessed 21 June 2009.

———. 2007a. '2006 Census: Age and Sex', *The Daily*, 17 July. At: http://www.statcan.gc.ca/daily-quotidien/070717/dq070717a-eng.htm. Accessed 24 June 2009.

———. 2007b. '2006 Census Analysis Series'. At: http://www12.statcan.ca/census-recensement/2006/as-sa/97-551/figures/c1-eng.cfm.

———. 2007c. 'A Portrait of Seniors', *The Daily*, 27 Feb. At: http://www.statcan.gc.ca/daily-quotidien/070227/dq070227b-eng.htm. Accessed 23 June 2009.

———. 2007d. 'Participation and Activity Limitation Survey', *The Daily*, 3 Dec. At: http://www.statcan.gc.ca/daily-quotidien/071203/dq071203a-eng.htm. Accessed 21 June 2009.

———. 2007e. 'Portrait of the Canadian Population in 2006, by Age and Sex: Highlights.' Census of Canada. At: http://www12.statcan.ca/census-recensement/2006/as-sa/97-551/p1-eng.cfm. Accessed 19 June 2009.

Toby, Jackson. 1957. 'Social Disorganization and Stake in Conformity: Complementary Factors in the Predatory Behavior of Young Hoodlums', *Journal of Criminal Law, Criminology, and Police Science* 48, 1: 12–17.

Torres, Sandra. 2000. 'A Postmodern Ethnogerontology . . . Why Not? . . . What For?' *Contemporary Gerontology* 6, 4: 114–17.

Turcotte, Martin and Grant Schellenberg, 2007. *A Portrait of Seniors in Canada*, Statistics Canada, Catalogue No. 89-519-XIE. Feb.

Weller, Wivian, and Nicolle Pfaff. 2008. 'The Concepts of Generation and Youth in the Work of Karl Mannheim', Paper presented at First ISA Forum of Sociology, International Sociological Association, Barcelona, Spain.

World Health Organization. 2002a. *World Report on Violence and Health: A Summary*. Geneva.

———. 2002b. 'Prevention of Elder Abuse.' At: http://www.who.int/ageing/projects/elder_abuse/en/index.html. Accessed 22 June 2009.

Chapter 9

Adams, Julia. 2002 'Deconstruction and Decomposition? A Comment on Grusky and Weeden', *Acta Sociologica* 45, 3: 225–27.

Barnett, Bernice McNair. 2004. 'Introduction: The Life, Career, and Social Thought of Gerhard Lenski—Scholar, Teacher, Mentor, Leader', *Sociological Theory* 22, 2: 163–93.

———. 2007. 'Theories and Research on the Intersections of Race, Gender, and Class Inequalities: From Lenski's Status Inconsistency to Collins' Matrix of Domination and Beyond, 1954 to present'. American Sociological Association.

Bertoni, Timothy J. 2009. 'Industrialization, Wealth, and the Pursuit of Pleasure: The Rise of Celebrity in Advanced Industrial Society 1852–2000', *Masters Abstracts International* 47, 5: 2657.

Bidou-Zachariasen, Catherine. 2004. 'The Middle Classes: Definitions, Works and Controversies' ('Les classes moyennes: definitions, travaux et controverses'), *Education et Sociétés* 2, 14: 119–34.

Braverman, Harry. 1974. *Labor and Monopoly Capital: The Degradation of Work in the Twentieth Century*. New York: Monthly Review Press.

Burnham, James. 1941. *The Managerial Revolution: What is Happening in the World*. New York: John Day.

Calhoun, Craig. 2004. 'Gerhard Lenski, Some False Oppositions, and The Religious Factor', *Sociological Theory* 22, 2: 194–204.

Charusheela, S. 2005. 'Class Analysis and Politics: Pushing the Boundaries', *Rethinking Marxism* 17, 1: 19–27.

Coleman, Daniel. 1975. 'Review', *The Journal of Economic History*, 35, 3: 647–648.

Collins, Randall. 2004. 'Lenski's Power Theory of Economic Inequality: A Central Neglected Question in Stratification Research', *Sociological Theory* 22, 2: 219–28.

Cook, Deborah. 2001. 'Critical Perspectives on Solidarity', *Rethinking Marxism* 13, 2: 92–108.

Dryden, Ken. 1993. *The Moved and the Shaken*. Toronto: Penguin.

Durkheim, Émile. 1933 (1893). *The Division of Labour in Society*, trans. George Simpson. New York: Free Press.

Edwards, Richard. 1979. *Contested Terrain: The Transformation of the Workplace in the Twentieth Century*. New York: Basic Books.

Gilbreth, Frank B. 1914. *The Primer of Scientific Management*. New York: Van Nostrand.

Gilmour, Heather, and Scott B. Patten. 'Depression and Work Impairment.' Canadian Community Health Survey 18 (2002/2003). National Population Health Survey. At: http://www.statcan.gc.ca/pub/82-003-x/2006001/article/9566-eng.htm#7. Accessed 8 Jul. 2009.

Goldthorpe, John H. 2002. 'Occupational Sociology, Yes: Class Analysis, No: Comment on Grusky and Weeden's Research Agenda,' *Acta Sociologica* 45, 3: 211–17.

Grusky, David B., and Kim A. Weeden. 2001. 'Decomposition without Death: A Research Agenda for a New Class Analysis', *Acta Sociologica* 44, 3: 203–18.

—— and ——. 2002. 'Class Analysis and the Heavy Weight of Convention,' *Acta Sociologica* 45, 3: 229–36.

Human Resources and Skills Development Canada. 2007. 'Looking-Ahead: A 10-Year Outlook for the Canadian Labour Market (2006–2015).' At: http://www.hrsdc.gc.ca/eng/publications_resources/research/categories/labour_market_e/sp_615_10_06/page06.shtml. Accessed 8 July 2009.

——. 2008. *Labour Force Historical Review 2007*. At: http://www4.hrsdc.gc.ca/.3ndic.1t.4r@-eng.jsp?iid=17.

——. 2009. 'Union Membership in Canada—2009'. At: http://www.hrsdc.gc.ca/eng/labour/labour_relations/info_analysis/union_membership/index2009.shtml.

Hyman, Richard. 2002. 'The Future of Unions.' *Just Labour:* 7–15. At: http://www.yorku.ca/julabour/volume1/jl_hyman.pdf. Accessed 5 Dec. 2009.

Jackson, Andrew, and David Robinson. *Falling Behind: The State of Working Canada, 2000*. Ottawa: Canadian Centre for Policy Alternatives.

Karasek, R. and T. Theorell. 1990. *Healthy Work: Stress, Productivity and the Reconstruction of Working Life*. New York: Basic Books.

Kirk, John. 2002. 'Invisible Ink: Working-Class Writing and the End of Class', *European Journal of Cultural Studies* 5, 3: 343–62.

Lee, Ji-Youn, Michael B. Toney, and E. Helen Berry. 2009. 'Social Status Inconsistency and Migration', *Research in Social Stratification and Mobility* 27, 1: 35–49.

Lewis, Oscar. 1961. *The Children of Sanchez*. Toronto: Random House.

Lowe, Graham S. 2000. *The Quality of Work: A People-Centered Agenda*. Toronto: Oxford University Press.

Marx, Karl, and Friedrich Engels. 2008 (1848). *The Communist Manifesto*. Introduction by David Harvey. London: Pluto Press.

Media Awareness Network. N.d. 'Media Representations of the Working Classes'. At: http://www.media-awareness.ca/english/issues/stereotyping/whiteness_and_privilege/whiteness_working_class.cfm. Accessed 5 Dec. 2009.

Merton, Robert K. 1938. 'Social Structure and Anomie', *American Sociological Review* 3, 5: 672–82.

——. 1957. *Social Theory and Social Structure*. Glencoe, IL: Free Press.

Moor, Nienke, Ariana Need, and Wout Ultee. 2006. 'Comprehending the Unknown by Analogy', Paper presented at the World Congress of Sociology, International Sociological Association, Durban, South Africa.

——, Wout Ultee, and Ariana Need. 2007. 'Analogies, Subsistence Technologies and Supreme Gods in Pre-Industrial Societies', *Kolner Zeitschrift fur Soziologie und Sozialpsychologie* 59, 3: 383–409.

——, ——, and ——. 2009. 'Analogical Reasoning and the Content of Creation Stories: Quantitative Comparisons of Preindustrial Societies', *Cross-Cultural Research* 43, 2: 91–122.

Nolan, Patrick, and Gerhard Lenski. 2009. *Human Societies: An Introduction to Macrosociology*, 11th edn. Boulder, CO: Paradigm.

Petras, James, and Henry Veltmeyer. 2001. 'Are Latin American Peasant Movements Still a Force for Change? Some New Paradigms Revisited', *The Journal of Peasant Studies* 28, 2: 83–118.

Prodialing.com. N.d. 'The Debate Over Call Centre Outsourcing'. At: http://www.prodialing.com/call-center-outsourcing.html. Accessed 6 Dec. 2009.

Reitz, Charles. 2004. 'Teaching about Oppression and Exploitation: Critical Theory and the Origins of Inequality', *Cultural Logic: An Electronic Journal of Marxist Theory and Practice* 7. At: http://clogic.eserver.org/2004/reitz.html.

Saunders, Doug. 2007. 'Defining the Middle Class', *The Globe and Mail*, 24 July. At: http://www.theglobeandmail.com/news/world/article772689.ece.

Seeman, M. 1959. 'On the Meaning of Alienation', *American Sociological Review* 24, 6: 783–91.

Sennett, Richard, and Jonathan Cobb. 1977 [1972]. *The Hidden Injuries of Social Class*. Cambridge: Cambridge University Press.

Sohlberg, Peter. 2009. 'Is There Nothing Beyond Postmodernism and "the Theoretical Other"? The Need for Balancing Universalism and Diversity in Social Work', *International Journal of Social Welfare* 18, 3: 317–22.

Statistics Canada. 2004. 'Study: The Union Movement in Transition', *The Daily*, 31 Aug. At: http://www.statcan.gc.ca/daily-quotidien/040831/dq040831b-eng.htm. Accessed 8 Jul. 2009.

——. 2007a. 'Earnings and Incomes of Canadians Over the Past Quarter Century, 2006 Census: Earnings.' Census of Canada. At: http://www12.statcan.ca/english/census06/analysis/income/eicopqc07.cfm. Accessed 6 Jul. 2009.

——. 2007b. 'Study: Depression and Work Impairment', *The Daily*, 12 Jan. At: http://www.statcan.gc.ca/daily-quotidien/070112/dq070112a-eng.htm. Accessed 9 Jul. 2009.

——. 2007c. 'Study: Work Stress and Job Performance', *The Daily*, 19 Dec. At: http://www.statcan.gc.ca/daily-quotidien/071219/dq071219d-eng.htm. Accessed 8 Jul. 2009.

——. 2009a. 'Labour Force Survey, May 2009'. 5 June. At: http://www.statcan.gc.ca/daily-quotidien/090605/dq090605a-eng.htm.

————. 2009b. 'Latest release from the Labour Force Survey, Friday, July 10, 2009.' At: http://www.statcan.gc.ca/subjects-sujets/labour-travail/lfs-epa/lfs-epa-eng.htm.

Sutherland, Edwin H. 1924. *Principles of Criminology*. Chicago: University of Chicago Press.

————. 1961(1949). *White-Collar Crime*. New York: Holt, Rinehart and Winston.

Webb, S.A. 2009. 'Against Difference and Diversity in Social Work: The Case of Human Rights', *International Journal of Social Welfare* 18, 3: 307–16.

Weeden, Kim A., and David B. Grusky. 2004. 'Are There Any Big Classes at All?' *Research in Social Stratification and Mobility* 22: 3–56.

Wright, Eric O. 1997. *Class Counts: Comparative Studies in Class Analysis*. Cambridge: Cambridge University Press.

Zhang, Xiaotian. 2008. 'Status Inconsistency Revisited: An Improved Statistical Model', *European Sociological Review* 24, 2: 155–68.

Chapter 10

Adams, Michael. 2007. *Unlikely Utopia*. Toronto: Viking.

Avineri, Shlomo. 1998. 'The Communist Manifesto at 150', *Dissent* 45, 1: 101–5.

Bronskill, Jim. 2009. 'Spy Chief Says Media Play Down Terror Threat', *Toronto Star*, 30 Oct. At: http://www.thestar.com/news/canada/article/718481--spy-chief-says-media-play-down-terror-threat.

Cameron, R. 1976. 'Book Review—Untitled' [*The Modern World-System I: Capitalist Agriculture and the Origins of the European World-Economy in the Sixteenth Century*], *Journal of Interdisciplinary History* 7, 1: 140–144.

Carvalho, Giane Carmem Alves de. 2008. 'Fight for What? Thoughts about the Anti-Systemic Activity Trends' ('Lutar pelo que? Reflexoes sobre os rumos dos movimentos anti-sistemicos'), *Estudos de Sociologia* 13, 2: 153–169.

Castonguay, Charles. 2002. 'Linguistic Assimilation and Replacement of the Francophone and Anglophone Generations in Quebec and Canada', *Recherches Sociographiques* 43: 149–82.

————. 2005. 'Ruptures of Identity and Language in French Canada', *Recherches Sociographiques* 46: 473–94.

CBC News. 2008. 'Quebec Language Police Pressure Montreal Bar over Posters', 14 February. At: http://www.cbc.ca/canada/montreal/story/2008/02/14/qc-olf-0214.html.

Channa, Subhadra Mitra. 2004. 'Globalization and Modernity in India: A Gendered Critique', *Urban Anthropology* 33, 1: 37–71.

Clark, S.D. 1978. *The New Urban Poor*. Toronto: McGraw-Hill Ryerson.

Clausewitz, Karl von. 1832. *Ueber das Leben und den Charakter von Scharnhorst*.

————. 1966 (1832). *On War*, trans. J.J. Graham; comp. F.N. Maude. London: Routledge and Kegan Paul.

Cotesta, Vittorio. 2008. 'From Nation-State to Global Society: The Changing Paradigm of Contemporary Sociology', *International Review of Sociology/Revue Internationale de Sociologie* 18, 1: 19–30.

Duman, M. Zeki. 2007. 'Discussions on Identity and Multiculturalism from Modernity to Post-Modernity' ('Modernden Post-Moderne Geciste Kimlik Tartısmaları ve cokkulturluluk'), *Uluslararasi Iliskiler* 4, 13: 3–24.

Edensor, Tim. 2006. 'Reconsidering National Temporalities: Institutional Times, Everyday Routines, Serial Spaces and Synchronicities', *European Journal of Social Theory* 9, 4: 525–45.

Grégoire, Isabelle. 2003. 'L'école des nouveaux Québécois', *L'actualité* 28: 43–4.

Gunaratne, Shelton A. 2009. 'Emerging Global Divides in Media and Communication Theory: European Universalism versus Non-Western Reactions', *Asian Journal of Communication* 19, 4: 366–83.

Hall, Thomas D., and Christopher Chase-Dunn. 2004. 'Global Social Change in the Long Run.' IROWS. At: http://www.irows.ucr.edu/cd/courses/10/socchange.htm. Accessed 14 Jul. 2009.

Halsall, Paul. 1997. 'Wallerstein on World Systems'. *Modern History Sourcebook*. At: http://www.fordham.edu/halsall/mod/wallerstein.html. Accessed 16 Jul. 2009.

Heller, Monica. 2007. '"Language," "Community" and "Identity": Expert Discourse and the Issue of French in Canada', *Anthropologie et Sociétés* 31: 39–54.

Herrera Gomez, Manuel, and Rosa Soriano Miras. 2005. 'From Modern Versions of Citizenship to the Citizenship of Post-Modern Social Autonomies' ('De las versiones modernas de la ciudadania a la ciudadania de las autonomias sociales de la postmodernidad'), *Revista Espanola de Investigaciones Sociologicas* 112: 43–74.

Hough, Phillip A. 2007. 'Trajectories of Hegemony and Domination in Colombia: A Comparative Analysis of the Coffee, Banana and Coca Regions from the Rise of Developmentalism to the Era of Neoliberalism', *Dissertation Abstracts International, A: The Humanities and Social Sciences* 68, 4: 1665.

Hulsse, Rainer. 2006. 'Imagine the EU: the metaphorical construction of a supra-nationalist identity', *Journal of International Relations and Development*, 9, 4: 396–421.

Innis, Harold. 1930. *The Fur Trade in Canada: An Introduction to Canadian Economic History*. New Haven, CT: Yale University Press, 1930.

————. 1933. *Problems of Staple Production in Canada*. Toronto: University of Toronto Press.

————. 1936. *Settlement and the Mining Frontier*. Toronto: University of Toronto Press.

————. 1940. *The Cod Fisheries: The History of an International Economy*. New Haven, CT: Yale University Press.

————. 1965 (1952). *Essays in Canadian Economic History*, ed. Mary Q. Innis. Toronto: University of Toronto Press.

————. 1971. *A History of the Canadian Pacific Railway*. Toronto: University of Toronto Press.

Kimura, Shisei. 2007. 'A Critical Reconsideration of Cultural Heritage—Cultural Sociology of "Ruins"', *Soshioroji* 51, 3: 3–19.

Langman, Lauren. 2005. 'The Dialectic of Unenlightenment: Toward a Critical Theory of Islamic Fundamentalism', *Critical Sociology* 31, 1–2: 243–79.

Leiss, W. 1977. 'Book Review: Untitled.' [*The Modern World-System I: Capitalist Agriculture and the Origins of the European World-Economy in the Sixteenth Century*]. *Canadian Journal of Political Science-Revue Canadienne de Science Politique* 10: 202–3.

Manwaring, Max G. 2006. 'Gangs and Coups D'Streets in the New World Disorder: Protean Insurgents in Post-Modern War', *Global Crime* 7, 3–4: 505–43.

Marx, Karl, and Friedrich Engels. 1948 (1848). *Manifesto of the Communist Party*. New York: International Publishers.

Nisanci, Ensar. 2007. 'Cities as a Potential Spaces for Citizenship and Democracy and Pro-City Discourse' ('Vatandaslık ve Demokrasi Icin Potansiyel Mekan Olarak Sehirler ve Sehirci Soylem'), *Sivil Toplum* 5, 17–18: 21–42.

Paic, Zarko. 2008. 'After Culture—What? Theories of a Turning Point and a Turning Point of Theory in a Global Age' ('Teorije preokreta i preokret teorija u globalno doba'), *Politicka misao* 45, 1: 29–70.

Savchenko, Andrew. 2007. 'Constructing a World Fit for Marxism: Utopia and Utopistics of Professor Wallerstein', *The American Journal of Economics and Sociology* 66, 5: 1033–52.

Schachter, Harvey. 2009. 'Adapting For Success on Foreign Shores', *The Globe and Mail*, 11 November. At: http://www.theglobeandmail.com/report-on-business/adapting-for-success-on-foreign-shores/article1358845.

Siljak, Ana. 2008. *Angel of Vengeance: the 'Girl Assassin,' the Governor of St. Petersburg, and Russia's Revolutionary World*. New York: St Martin's Press.

Smith, Dan. 2007. 'Alternatives to War'. Friends Committee on National Legislation. At: http://www.fcnl.org/smith/world_war07/world_war_count.htm. Accessed 15 Jul. 2009.

Spohn, Willfried. 2008. 'World-Society, Globalizations and Multiple Modernities—Outline of a Historical-Sociological Approach'. Paper presented at First ISA Forum of Sociology, International Sociological Association, Barcelona, Spain.

Statistics Canada. 2006. *Survey on the Vitality of Official-Language Minorities*. At: http://www.statcan.gc.ca/pub/91-548-x/2007001/4185568-eng.htm. Accessed 12 Jul. 2009.

Taylor, Peter J., Michael Hoyler, and David M. Evans. 2008. 'A Geohistorical Study of "The Rise of Modern Science": Mapping Scientific Practice through Urban Networks, 1500–1900', *Minerva* 46, 4: 391–410.

Wallerstein, Immanuel. 1961. *Africa, The Politics of Independence*. New York: Vintage.

———. 1967. *Africa: The Politics of Unity*. New York: Random House.

———. 1980 (1974). *The Modern World-System I: Capitalist Agriculture and the Origins of the European World-Economy in the Sixteenth Century*. New York: Academic Press.

Chapter 11

Adorno, T.W., E. Frenkel-Brunswik, D.J. Levinson, and R.N. Sanford. 1950. *The Authoritarian Personality*. New York: Harper and Row.

Aune, Kristin. 2008. 'Evangelical Christianity and Women's Changing Lives', *European Journal of Women's Studies* 15, 3: 277–94.

Baldauf, Anette. 2002. 'Shopping: Manifestations of Consumer Practices in Youth Culture', *Dissertation Abstracts International, A: The Humanities and Social Sciences* 62, 9: 3205–A.

Becker, Howard S., Blanche Geer, Everett C. Hughes, and Anselm L. Strauss. 1961. *Boys in White: Student Culture in Medical School*. Chicago: University of Chicago.

Blakely, Kristin. 2008. 'Busy Brides and the Business of Family Life: The Wedding-Planning Industry and the Commodity Frontier', *Journal of Family Issues* 29, 5: 639–62.

Boney, Virginia M. 2002. 'Divorced Mothers' Guilt: Exploration and Intervention through a Postmodern Lens', *Journal of Divorce and Remarriage* 37, 3–4: 61–83.

———. 2003. 'Alternative Research Perspectives for Studying the Effects of Parental Divorce', *Marriage & Family Review* 35, 1–2: 7–27.

Brook, Paul. 2009. 'In Critical Defense of Emotional Labour', *Work, Employment and Society*, 23, 3: 531–48.

Brown, Tony N., Emily E. Tanner-Smith, Chase L. Lesane-Brown, and Michael E. Ezell. 2007. 'Child, Parent, and Situational Correlates of Familial Ethnic/Race Socialization', *Journal of Marriage and Family* 69, 1: 14–25.

Cavan, Ruth Shonle. 1964. 'World Revolution and Family Patterns', *Journal of Marriage and Family* 26, 3: 380–1.

CBC News. 2005. 'Marriage by the Numbers'. 9 Mar. At: http://www.cbc.ca/news/background/marriage.

Cooley, Charles Horton. 1902. *Human Nature and the Social Order*. New York: C. Scribner's Sons.

Goffman, Erving, 1961. *Asylums: Essays on the Social Situation of Mental Patients and Other Inmates*. New York: Doubleday.

Goode, William Josiah. 1963. *World Revolution and Family Patterns*. New York: Free Press of Glencoe.

Freud, Sigmund. 1964 (1928). *The Future of an Illusion*, trans. W. D. Robson-Scott, ed. James Strachey. Garden City, NY: Doubleday.

Hansen, Claus D., and Johan H Andersen. 2008. 'Going Ill to Work—What Personal Circumstances, Attitudes and Work-related Factors are Associated with Sickness Presenteeism?', *Social Science & Medicine* 67, 6: 956–64.

Hesmondhalgh, David, and Sarah Baker. 2008. 'Creative Work and Emotional Labour in the Television Industry', *Theory, Culture & Society* 25, 7–8: 97–118.

Hitlin, Steven. 2006. 'Parental Influences on Children's Values and Aspirations: Bridging Two Theories of Social Class and Socialization.' *Sociological Perspectives* 49, 1: 25–46.

Hochschild, Arlie. 1983. *The Managed Heart: The Commercialization of Human Feeling*. Berkeley: University of California Press.

———. 1989. *The Second Shift: Working Parents and the Revolution at Home*, with Anne Machung. New York: Viking Penguin.

———. 1997. *The Time Bind: When Work Becomes Home and Home Becomes Work*. New York: Metropolitan/Holt.

Hughes, Diane, and Deborah Johnson. 2001. 'Correlates in Children's Experiences of Parents' Racial Socialization Behaviors', *Journal of Marriage and Family* 63, 4: 981–96.

Human Resources and Skills Development Canada. 2007. 'Canadians in Context: Households and Families'. At: http://www4.hrsdc.gc.ca/.3ndic.1t.4r@-eng.jsp?iid=37. Accessed 21 Jul. 2009.

Immerman, R., and W. Mackey, W. 1999. 'The Societal Dilemma of Multiple Sexual Partners: The Costs of the Loss of Pair-Bonding', *Marriage & Family Review* 29, 11: 3–19.

Kanduc, Zoran. 2004. 'The Post-Modern Situation and Social Control' ('Postmoderno stanje in druzbeno nadzorstvo'), *Revija za kriminalistiko in kriminologijo* 55, 1: 3–21.

Keller, Heidi, and Carolin Demuth. 2006. 'Further Explorations of the "Western Mind": Euro-American and German Mothers' and Grandmothers' Ethnotheories', *Forum Qualitative Sozialforschung/Forum: Qualitative Social Research* 7, 1, article 5.

Lareau, A. 2000. 'Social Class and the Daily Lives of Children—A Study from the United States.' *Childhood: A Global Journal of Child Research* 7, 2: 155–71.

Lee, Hyun-Ji. 2005. 'A Conception of Post-Modern Family Leisure', *Journal of East Asian Social Thoughts* 12:161–81.

Lehmann, Jennifer M. 1994. *Durkheim and Women*. Lincoln, NE: University of Nebraska Press.

Longman, Chia. 2008. 'Sacrificing the Career or the Family? Orthodox Jewish Women in between Secular Work and the Sacred Home', *European Journal of Women's Studies*, special issue 'Questioning the Secular' 15, 3: 223–39.

McHale, Susan M., Ann C. Crouter, and Shawn D. Whiteman. 2003. 'The Family Contexts of Gender Development in Childhood and Adolescence', *Social Development* 12, 1: 125–48.

McMullin, Julie. 2004. *Understanding Social Inequality: Intersections of Class, Age, Gender, Ethnicity and Race*. Don Mills: Oxford University Press.

Mann, Susan A., and Jeanne Barnard. 2002. 'Contested or Barren Terrain? Postmodernity in Family Sociology Textbooks', Southern Sociological Society.

Martin, John Levi. 2001. 'The Authoritarian Personality, 50 Years Later: What Lessons are There for Political Psychology?', *Political Psychology*, 22, 1: 1–26.

Mead, George Herbert. 1934. *Mind, Self & Society: From the Standpoint of a Social Behaviorist*, ed. Charles W. Morris. Chicago: University of Chicago.

Media Awareness Network. N.d. 'TV Dads: Backgrounder for Teachers'. At: http://www.media-awareness.ca/english/resources/educational/teaching_backgrounders/stereotyping/tv_dads_backgrounder.cfm.

Milkie, Melissa A., Sara B. Raley, and Suzanne M. Bianchi 2009. 'Taking on the Second Shift: Time Allocations and Time Pressures of U.S. Parents with Preschoolers', *Social Forces* 88, 2: 487–518.

Mitsuhashi, Koji. 2008. 'Emotional Labor and Burnout: Does Emotional Labor Cause Burnout?' *Shakaigaku Hyoron/Japanese Sociological Review* 58, 4: 576–92.

North-Jones, Margaret A. 2009. 'Values and Time Usage in Families: Perception vs. Reality', *Dissertation Abstracts International, A: The Humanities and Social Sciences* 69, 8: 3341.

Ozkaplan, Nurcan. 2009. 'Duygusal Emek ve KadIn Isi/Erkek Isi', *Calisma ve Toplum* 2: 15–23.

Parsons, Talcott, Robert F. Bales, and James Olds. 1955. *Family, Socialization and Interaction Process*. Glencoe, IL: Free Press.

Pedraza Gomez, Zandra. 2007. 'Child Labor and the Colonial Code: Historical and Anthropological Considerations' ('El trabajo infantile en clave colonial: consideraciones historico-antropologicas'), *Nomadas* 26: 80–90.

Sayer, Liana C., Paula England, Michael Bittman, and Suzanne M. Bianchi. 2009. 'How Long Is the Second (Plus First) Shift? Gender Differences in Paid, Unpaid, and Total Work Time in Australia and the United States', *Journal of Comparative Family Studies* 40, 4: 523–45.

Shibutani, Tamotsu. 1952. 'Review of *The Authoritarian Personality*. by T. W. Adorno; Else Frenkel-Brunswik; Daniel J. Levinson; E. Nevitt Sanford', *The American Journal of Sociology* 57, 5: 527–29.

Statistics Canada. 2005. 'Family Violence in Canada: A Statistical Profile', *The Daily*, 14 Jul. At: http://www.statcan.gc.ca/daily-quotidien/050714/dq050714a-eng.htm. Accessed 25 Jul. 2009.

———. 2006a. 'Census Family', *2006 Census Dictionary*. At: http://www12.statcan.ca/english/census06/reference/dictionary/fam004.cfm. Accessed 22 Jul. 2009.

———. 2006b. *Families and Households Highlight Table*. Statistics Canada Catalogue no. 97-553-XWE2006002. At: http://www12.statcan.ca/english/census06/data/highlights/households/index.cfm?Lang=E. Accessed 27 Jul. 2009.

———. 2007a. 'General Social Survey: Navigating Family Transitions', *The Daily*, 13 June. At: http://www.statcan.gc.ca/daily-quotidien/070613/dq070613b-eng.htm. Accessed 24 Jul. 2009.

———. 2007b. *Families and Households Highlight Tables*. 2006 Census. Statistics Canada Catalogue no. 97-553-XWE2006002. Ottawa. At: http://www12.statcan.ca/english/census06/data/highlights/households/index.cfm?Lang=E.

———. 2007c. 'Families, Marital Status, Households and Dwelling Characteristics', *The Daily*, 12 Sept. At: http://www.statcan.gc.ca/daily-quotidien/070912/dq070912a-eng.htm. Accessed 21 Jul. 2009.

Tambe, Ashwini. 2006. 'Brothels as Families: Reflections on the History of Bombay's Kothas', *International Feminist Journal of Politics* 8, 2: 219–42.

Uhde, Zuzana. 2009. 'Towards a Feminist Concept of Care As a Critical Category of Social Inequality', ('K feministickemu pojeti pece jako kriticke kategorie sociallni nerovnosti'), *Sociologicky Casopis* 45, 1: 9–29.

Umana-Taylor, Adriana J., Ruchi Bhanot, and Nana Shin. 2006. 'Ethnic Identity Formation during Adolescence: The Critical Role of Families', *Journal of Family Issues* 27, 3: 390–414.

UNICEF. 2001. 'Early Marriage: Child Spouses', *Innocenti Digest* 7 (March). At: http://www.unicef-irc.org/publications/pdf/digest7e.pdf.

Vanier Institute of the Family. 2001. *Transition Magazine* 31, 3. *Youth and Identity*. At: http://www.vifamily.ca/media/node/378/attachments/313.pdf. Accessed 23 Jul. 2009.

———. 2004. 'Media Coverage Archives'. At: http://www.vifamily.ca/newsroom/media_04.html. Accessed 23 Jul. 2009.

———. 2006. 'Family Facts'. At: http://www.vifamily.ca/library/facts/facts.html. Accessed 22 Jul. 2009.

Veblen, Thorstein. 1973. *The Theory of the Leisure Class*, introduction by John Kenneth Galbraith. Boston: Houghton Mifflin.

Waite, Linda J., and Maggie Gallagher. 2000. *The Case for Marriage: Why Married People Are Happier, Healthier, and Better Off Financially*. New York: Doubleday.

White, Fiona A., and Melanie Gleitzman. 2006. 'An Examination of Family Socialisation Processes as Moderators of Racial Prejudice Transmission Between Adolescents and Their Parents', *Journal of Family Studies* 12, 2: 247–60.

Wrong, Dennis H. 1961. 'The Oversocialized Conception of Man in Modern Sociology', *American Sociological Review* 26, 2: 183–93.

Chapter 12

Amatucci, Kristi Bruce. 2009. 'Tangled Theories', *Qualitative Inquiry* 15, 7: 1225–40.

Andres, L., and M. Adamuti-Trache. 2007. 'You've Come a Long Way, Baby? University Enrolment and Completion by Women and Men in Canada 1979–2004', *Canadian Public Policy* 33, 1: 1–24.

Bankston, Carl L., III. 2004. 'Social Capital, Cultural Values, Immigration, and Academic Achievement: The Host Country Context and Contradictory Consequences', *Sociology of Education* 77, 2: 176–79.

Barnett, Mathew. 2005.'The Effects of Social Capital on the Academic Performance and Social Behavior of Students from Parochial and Public School Backgrounds', *Dissertation Abstracts International, A: The Humanities and Social Sciences* 65, 9: 3329–A.

Bidwell, Charles E. 1957. 'Reviewed Work(s): *Crestwood Heights: A Study of the Culture of Suburban Life* by John R. Seeley; R. Alexander Sim; Elizabeth Loosley,' *The Elementary School Journal* 57, 7: 404–5.

———. 1969. 'Reviewed Work(s): *The Academic Revolution* by Christopher Jencks; David Riesman,' *American Sociological Association* 34, 4: 590–1.

Bonikowski, Bart. 2004. 'Questioning Pedagogy: Reflections on the Critical Theory of Curriculum,' *The Discourse of Sociological Practice* 6, 2: 41–9.

Bressler, Marvin. 1968. 'Reviewed Work(s): *The Academic Revolution* by Christopher Jencks; David Riesman', *Science* 161, 3846, 1120–1.

Canadian Council on Learning. 2008. 'CCL: Key Findings.' At: http://www.ccl-cca.ca/CCL/Reports/PostSecondaryEducation/PSEHome/PSE2009KeyFindings.htm?Language=EN. Accessed 27 Jul. 2009.

CanWest News Service. 2006. 'Prof. Says Media Fuelling School Shootings', Canada.com. 3 October. At: http://www.canada.com/montrealgazette/news/story.html?id=4f60e188-a7b8-4f4a-a51e-f17750bbc13f&k=64809.

Cole, Jonathan. 2009. *The Great American University: Its Rise to Preeminence, Its Indispensable National Role, Why It Must be Protected*. New York: Public Affairs, Perseus Books.

Coleman, James S., John W.C. Johnstone, and Kurt Jonassohn. 1966 (1961). *The Adolescent Society: The Social Life of the Teenager and Its Impact on Education*. New York: Free Press.

Davis, Bob. 2009. 'Going in by the Front Door: Searle, Earl Marshal School and Sheffield', *Race and Class* 51, 2: 79–91.

Dewey, Russ. 2008. 'Erikson's Psychosocial Stages', in *Psychology: An Introduction*. 18 Sept. At: http://www.intropsych.com/ch11_personality/eriksons_psychosocial_stages.html. Accessed 31 Jul. 2009.

Elkin, Frederick. 1957. 'Reviewed Work(s): *Crestwood Heights: A Study of the Culture of Suburban Life*. by John R. Seeley; R. Alexander Sim; E. W. Loosley,' *Social Forces* 35, 3: 284.

Elster, Jon. 2003. 'Coleman on Social Norms', *Revue française de sociologie* 44, 2: 297–304.

Foley, Donald L. 1957. 'Reviewed Work(s): *Crestwood Heights: A Study of the Culture of Suburban Life*. by John R. Seeley; R. Alexander Sim; Elizabeth W. Loosley,' *The Public Opinion Quarterly* 21, 1: 218–20.

Hacker, Andrew and Claudia Dreifus. 2010. *Education? How Colleges Are Wasting Our Money and Failing Our Kids—And What We Can Do About It*. New York: Henry Holt/Times Books.

Healy, Tom. 2004. 'Social Capital: Old Hat or New Insight?', *Irish Journal of Sociology* 13, 1: 5–28.

Henry, Stuart. 2009. 'School Violence Beyond Columbine: A Complex Problem in Need of an Interdisciplinary Analysis', *American Behavioral Scientist* 52, 9: 1246–65.

James, Royson. 2007. 'Black Schools in Focus'. *Toronto Star*. 19 November. At: http://www.thestar.com/News/GTA/article/277427.

Jencks, Christopher, and David Riesman. 1968. *The Academic Revolution*. Garden City, NY: Doubleday.

Klugkist, Dagmar Adina Inga. 2009. 'Texts of Identity: Rewriting the Self within a Multicultural School Community', *Dissertation Abstracts International, A: The Humanities and Social Sciences* 69, 11.

Lareau, Annette. 2003. *Unequal Childhoods: Class, Race, and Family Life*. Berkeley, University of California Press.

Lillbacka, Ralf. 2006. 'Measuring Social Capital: Assessing Construct Stability of Various Operationalizations of Social Capital in a Finnish Sample', *Acta Sociologica* 49, 2: 201–20.

Lindenberg, Siegwart. 2003. 'Coleman's Problem with Institutional Design: Neglect of Social Rationality?' ('Coleman et la construction des institutions: peut-on negliger la rationalite sociale?'), *Revue française de sociologie* 44, 2: 357–73.

McNair, Brian. 2009. 'Teaching Porn', *Sexualities* 12, 5: 558–67.

Meyersohn, Rolf. 1958. 'Reviewed Work(s): *Crestwood Heights: A Study of the Culture of Suburban Life*. by John R. Seeley; R. Alexander Sim; Elizabeth W. Loosley,' *The American Journal of Sociology* 64, 3: 331–2.

Roth, Klas. 2009. 'Some Thoughts for a New Critical Language of Education', *Philosophy & Social Criticism* 35, 6: 685–703.

Scott, Jonathan, and Chris Searle. 2009. 'Funk Brother Number One', *Race and Class* 51, 2: 33–43.

Seeley, John R., R. Alexander Sim, Elizabeth W. Loosley, Norman W. Bell, and D.F. Fleming. 1956. *Crestwood Heights*. Toronto: University of Toronto.

Statistics Canada. 2006. 'Educational Portrait of Canada, 2006 Census: National Picture'. Catalogue no. 97-560-X. At: http://www12.statcan.ca/english/census06/analysis/education/pdf/97-560-XIE2006001.pdf.

———. 2008. 'Back to School Factbook' At: http://www.statcan.gc.ca/pub/81-004-x/2006003/9341-eng.htm.

Vanier Institute of the Family. 2001. *Transition Magazine* 13, 3. *Youth and Identity*. At: http://www.vifamily.ca/media/node/378/attachments/313.pdf. Accessed 23 Jul. 2009.

United Nations. 2009. 'United Nations Millennium Development Goals.' At: http://www.un.org/millenniumgoals/education.shtml. Accessed 12 Dec. 2009.

Wall, Sarah. 2008. 'Of heads and hearts: Women in doctoral education at a Canadian University,' *Women's Studies International Forum* 31, 3: 219–28.

Chapter 13

Amineh, M.P., and S.N. Eisenstadt. 2007. 'The Iranian Revolution: The Multiple Contexts of the Iranian Revolution', *Perspectives on Global Development and Technology* 6, 1–3: 129–157.

Bellah, Robert. 1967. 'Civil Religion in America', *Journal of the American Academy of Arts and Sciences* 96, 1: 1–21.

———. 1973. *Émile Durkheim: On Morality and Society, Selected Writings*. Chicago: The University of Chicago Press.

———, R. Madsen, W.M. Sullivan, A. Swidler, and S.M. Tipton. 1985. *Habits of the Heart: Individualism and Commitment in American Life*. Berkeley: University of California Press.

Bertin, Adriano. 2009. 'On the Crisis of American Civil Religion. A Theological-Political Perspective' ('Sulla crisi della religione civile americana. Una prospettiva teologico-politica'), *Fenomenologia e Societa* 32, 1: 54–76.

Beyer, Peter. 2005. 'Religious Identity and Educational Attainment among Recent Immigrants to Canada: Gender, Age, and 2nd Generation', *Journal of International Migration and Integration* 6, 2: 177–99.

Bibby, Reginald. 2002. *Restless Gods: The Renaissance of Religion in Canada*. Toronto: Stoddart.

Boesveld, Sarah. 2010. 'Canada Ranked Second-most Charitable in the World', *The Globe and Mail*, 9 September, A3.

Butterworth, Michael. 2008. 'Fox Sports, Super Bowl XLII, and the Affirmation of American Civil Religion', *Journal of Sport and Social Issues* 32, 2: 318–23.

Calhoun, C., J. Gerteis, J. Moody, S. Pfaff, and I. Virk, eds. 2007. *Classical Sociological Theory*, 2nd edn. Malden, MA: Blackwell.

Charities Aid Foundation. 2010. *The World Giving Index 2010*. At: http://www.cafonline.org/pdf/0882A_WorldGivingReport_Interactive_070910.pdf.

Clark, Warren, and Grant Schellenberg. 2006. 'Who's Religious?' *Canadian Social Trends*. Statistics Canada — Catalogue No. 11–008.

Copen, Casey, and Merril Silverstein. 2007. 'Transmission of Religious Beliefs across Generations: Do Grandparents Matter?' *Journal of Comparative Family Studies* 38, 4: 497–510.

Durkheim, Émile. 1964 (1893). *The Division of Labor in Society*, trans. George Simpson. New York: Free Press.

———. 1968 (1912). *The Elementary Forms of the Religious Life*, trans. Joseph Ward Swain. London: Allen & Unwin.

Freud, Sigmund. 1957 (1930). *Civilization and its Discontents*, trans. Joan Riviere. London: Hogarth Press.

———. 1939. *Moses and Monotheism*. New York: Random House.

Gauvreau, Danielle, and Peter Gossage. 2001. 'Canadian Fertility Transitions: Quebec and Ontario at the Turn of the Twentieth Century', *Journal of Family History* 26, 2: 162–88.

Goldenberg, N. 2006. 'What's God Got to Do With It? A Call for Problematizing Basic Terms in the Feminist Analysis of Religion.' Paper presented at the Biannual Meetings of the Britain and Ireland School of Feminist Theology, Edinburgh. July.

Goldstein, Warren S. 2009. 'Secularization Patterns in the Old Paradigm', *Sociology of Religion* 70, 2: 157–78.

Hecht, Richard D. 2007. 'Active versus Passive Pluralism: A Changing Style of Civil Religion?', *The Annals of the American Academy of Political and Social Science* 612: 133–51.

Herberg, Will. 1955. *Protestant, Catholic, Jew: An Essay in American Religious Sociology*. Garden City, NY: Doubleday.

Hornbacher, Annette, and Volker Gottowik. 2008. 'The Transformation of Religiosity. Southeast Asian Perspectives' ('Die Transformation des Religiosen. Sudostasiatische Perspektiven'), *Zeitschrift fur Ethnologie* 133, 1: 19–30.

Horstmann, Alexander. 2009. 'The Revitalisation and Reflexive Transformation of the Manooraa Rongkruu Performance and Ritual in Southern Thailand: Articulations with Modernity', *Asian Journal of Social Science* 37, 6: 918–34.

Hughes, Everett C. 2009 (1943). *French Canada in Transition*, introduction and forward by Lorne Tepperman and Nathan Keyfitz. New York: Oxford University Press.

Huss, Boaz. 2007. 'The New Age Of Kabbalah: Contemporary Kabbalah, the New Age and Postmodern Spirituality', *Journal of Modern Jewish Studies* 6, 2: 107–25.

IMDB/WENN News. 2009. 'Hindus Worried About Keanu Reeves Movie'. 8 Sept. At: http://www.imdb.com/news/ni0972905.

Kuhn, Thomas. 1962. *The Structure of Scientific Revolutions*. Chicago: University of Chicago Press.

Legg, T. David. 2000. 'A Tale of Two Nations: The Emergence and Evolution of Modern Quebec Nationalism', *Dissertation Abstracts International, A: The Humanities and Social Sciences* 61, 5: 2064–A.

Leung, Wency. 2009. 'Go On, Have a Pint With the Lord'. *The Globe and Mail*, 12 Oct. 12. At: http://www.theglobeandmail.com/life/family-and-relationships/go-on-have-a-pint-with-the-lord/article1321117.

Lindsay, Colin. 2008. 'Matter of Fact: Canadians Attend Weekly Religious Services Less than 20 Years Ago'. Statistics Canada. At: http://dsp-psd.tpsgc.gc.ca/collection_2008/statcan/89-630-X/89-630-XIE2008003.pdf. Accessed 13 Aug. 2009.

Lockwood, Robert P. 2000. 'Galileo.' *Catholic League: For Religious and Civil Rights*. http://www.catholicleague.org/research/galileo.html. Accessed 13 Aug. 2009.

Lunn, Jenny. 2009. 'The Role of Religion, Spirituality and Faith in Development: A Critical Theory Approach', *Third World Quarterly* 30, 5: 937–51.

McGuire, Meredith B. 2005. *Lived Religion Faith and Practice in Everyday Life*. New York: Oxford University Press.

Meizel, Katherine. 2006. 'A Singing Citizenry: Popular Music and Civil Religion in America', *Journal for the Scientific Study of Religion* 45, 4: 497–503.

Merton, Robert. 1976. 'The Normative Structure of Science', in Robert Merton, ed., *The Sociology of Science: Theoretical and Empirical Investigations*. Chicago: University of Chicago Press.

Merz-Benz, Peter-Ulrich. 2006. 'Beyond Individualism, the Theorem of Community and Society—Ferdinand Tonnies and Communitarianism' ('Die Uberwindung des Individualismus und das Theorem von Gemeinschaft und Gesellschaft—Ferdinand Tonnies und der Kommunitarismus'), *Schweizerische Zeitschrift fur Soziologie/Revue Suisse de sociologie/Swiss Journal of Sociology* 32, 1: 27–52.

Mulders, Joera. 2008. 'The Debate on Religion and Secularisation in Russia Today: Comments on Kyrlezhev and Morozov, with Focus on Education', *Religion, State & Society* 36,1: 5–20.

Palmer, S. 2004. *Aliens Adored: Rael's UFO Religion*. New Brunswick, NJ: Rutgers University Press.

Price, Joseph L. 1992. 'The Super Bowl as Religious Festival', in Shirl J. Hoffman, ed., *Sport and Religion*. Champaign, IL: Human Kinetics Books, 13–15.

Riley, Alexander. 2008. 'On the Role of Images in the Construction of Narratives about the Crash of United Airlines Flight 93', *Visual Studies* 23, 1: 4–19.

Roof, Wade Clark. 2009. 'American Presidential Rhetoric from Ronald Reagan to George W. Bush: Another Look at Civil Religion', *Social Compass* 56, 2: 286–301.

Savagnone, Giuseppe. 2009. 'The Church of the South Reflects on Itself' ('Le Chiese del Sud si interrogano'), *Aggiornamenti Sociali* 60, 5: 364–73.

Science Studies. N.d. At: http://www.sciencestudies.fi/. Accessed 11 Dec. 2009.

Smith, Christian. 2008. 'Future Directions in the Sociology of Religion', *Social Forces* 86, 4: 1561–89.

Statistics Canada. 2003. 'Religions in Canada'. *Census of Canada* 2001. At: http://www12.statcan.ca/english/census01/products/analytic/companion/rel/canada.cfm. Accessed 13 Aug. 2009.

———. 2004. 'Religions in Canada'. Census of Canada 2001. At: http://www12.statcan.ca/english/census01/products/analytic/companion/rel/canada.cfm. Accessed 11 Aug. 2009.

———. 2006. 'Study: Who's Religious?', *The Daily*, May 2. At: http://www.statcan.gc.ca/daily-quotidien/060502/dq060502a-eng.htm. Accessed 12 Aug. 2009.

———. 2007. *Canada at a Glance 2007: Demography*. At: http://www45.statcan.ca/2007/cgco_2007_001-eng.htm#t06. Accessed 14 Aug. 2009.

Swatos, William H., Jr. 2006. 'Implicit Religious Assumptions within the Resurgence of Civil Religion in the USA since 9/11', *Implicit Religion* 9, 2: 166–79.

Thompson, Kenneth. 1982. *Émile Durkheim*. London: Tavistock Publications.

Turner, Bryan S. 2005. 'Talcott Parsons's Sociology of Religion and the Expressive Revolution: The Problem of Western Individualism,' *Journal of Classical Sociology* 5, 3: 303–18.

Van Gerwen, Jef. 1998. 'Introduction to Robert N. Bellah', *Ethical Perspectives* 5, 1: 89.

Vido, Roman. 2008. 'Religion and Modernity in the Contemporary Sociology of Religion' ('Nabozenstvi a modernita v soucasne sociologii nabozenstvi'), *Socialni Studia* 5, 3–4: 27–51.

Weber, Max. 1958 (1904). *The Protestant Ethic and the Spirit of Capitalism*, trans. Talcott Parsons. New York: Scribner.

Wender, Andrew M. 2007. 'State Power as a Vehicle for the Expression and Propagation of Implicit Religion: The Case Study of the "War on Terrorism",' *Implicit Religion* 10, 3: 244–61.

Chapter 14

Baudrillard, Jean. 2005. *Conspiracy of Art*. New York: Semiotext(e).

Berardi, Franco (BIFO). 2006. 'Media, Politics and Collective Attention: A Constitutional Problem for Europe' ('Riflessioni varie: Riportiamo di seguito alcune riflessioni proposte, in diverse occasioni'), *Inchiesta* 36, 152: 110–15.

Blumer, Herbert. 1971. 'Social Problems as Collective Behavior'. *Social Problems* 18 (Winter): 298–306.

Boxer, Paul, L., Rowell Huesmann, Brad J. Bushman, Maureen O'Brien, and Dominic Moceri. 2009. 'The Role of Violent Media Preference in Cumulative Developmental Risk for Violence and General Aggression', *Journal of Youth and Adolescence* 38, 3: 417–28.

Bushman, Brad J., and L. Rowell Huesmann. 2006. 'Short-term and Long-term Effects of Violent Media on Aggression in Children and Adults', *Archives of Pediatrics & Adolescent Medicine* 160, 4: 348–52.

Campbell, David. 2008. 'Beyond Image and Reality: Critique and Resistance in the Age of Spectacle,' *Public Culture* 20, 3: 539–49.

Canada. 1981. *Royal Commission on Newspapers*. Hull, QC: The Queen's Printer.

Dodge, K. A., J. D. Coie, and D. Lynam. 2006. 'Aggression and Antisocial Behavior in Youth', in W. Damon and N. Eisenberg, eds., *Handbook of Child Psychology: Social, Emotional, and Personality Development*, vol. 3, 6th edn. New York: Wiley, 719–88.

Freedman, Jonathan L. 2002. *Media Violence and its Effect on Aggression: Assessing the Scientific Evidence*, Toronto: University of Toronto Press.

Fuchs, Christian, and Marisol Sandoval. 2008. 'Critical Theory and Alternative (Online) Media: Do We Need a Marxist Theory of Critical Media?'. Paper presented at First ISA Forum of Sociology, International Sociological Association, Barcelona, Spain.

Gane, Nicholas 2005. 'Radical Post-Humanism: Friedrich Kittler and the Primacy of Technology', *Theory, Culture & Society* 22, 3: 25–41.

Gans, Herbert J. 1979. *Deciding What's News: A Study of CBS Evening News, NBC Nightly News, Newsweek, and Time*. New York: Vintage.

Gauthier, Alain. 2009. 'The Singularity of Jean Baudrillard' ('La Singularite de Jean Baudrillard'), *The International Journal of Baudrillard Studies* 6, 2, Jul.

Gerbner, G., and L. Gross. 1976. 'Living with Television: The Violence Profile'. *Journal of Communication* 26, 2: 172–99.

Graber, Doris A. 1979. 'Review: *Deciding What's News: A Study of CBS Evening News, NBC Nightly News, Newsweek, and Time* by Herbert J. Gans', *Political Science Quarterly* 94, 4: 692–3.

Goffman, Erving. 1959. *The Presentation of Self in Everyday Life*. Garden City, NY: Doubleday-Anchor.

Habermas, Jürgen. 2006. 'Political Communication in Media Society: Does Democracy Still Enjoy an Epistemic Dimension? The Impact of Normative Theory on Empirical Research', *Communication Theory* 16: 411–26.

Huesmann, Rowell L., and Laramie D. Taylor. 2006. 'The Role Of Media Violence In Violent Behavior', *Annual Review of Public Health* 27: 393–415.

Iacobucci, Edward M., and Michael J. Trebilcock. 2007. 'The Design of Regulatory Institutions for the Canadian Telecommunications Sector', *Canadian Public Policy/Analyse de Politiques* 33, 2: 127–45.

Ishita, Saeko. 2002. 'Media and Cultural Studies in Japanese Sociology: An Introduction', *International Journal of Japanese Sociology* 11: 2–5.

Kellner, Douglas. 2006. 'Jean Baudrillard after Modern Philosophy: Provocations on a Provocateur and Challenger', *The International Journal of Baudrillard Studies* 3, 1 (Jan.).

Koenen, Elmar J. 2002. 'The Visibility of Politics. Newer Studies about Media Publicity of Political Communication', *Soziologische Revue* 25, 3: 258–65.

Lau, Raymond W.K. 2004. 'Critical Realism and News Production', *Media, Culture & Society* 26, 5: 693–711.

Lyon, David. 2006. 'By Their Media Shall You Know Them: 'Emerging Churches' in Urban Ontario'. Paper presented at the World Congress of Sociology, International Sociological Association, Durban, South Africa.

McLuhan, Marshall.1964. *Understanding Media*. London: Routledge.

Mahtani, Minelle. 2001. 'Representing Minorities: Canadian Media and Minority Identities', *Canadian Ethnic Studies/Etudes Ethniques au Canada* 33, 3: 99–133.

Martelli, Stefano. 2005. 'What Religiosity Emerges from Neo-Television?' ('Quale religiosita emerge dalla neo-televisione?'), *Religioni e Societa* 20, 53: 26–35.

———, and Gianna Cappello. 2005. 'Religion in the Television-Mediated Public Sphere Transformations and Paradoxes', *International Review of Sociology/Revue Internationale de Sociologie* 15, 2: 243–57.

Martin, Vivian B. 2008. 'Media Bias: Going beyond Fair and Balanced', *Scientific American*, 26 Sept. At: http://www.scientificamerican.com/article.cfm?id=media-bias-presidential-election.

Media Awareness Network. n.d. 'Research on the Effects of Media Violence'. At: http://www.media-awareness.ca/english/issues/violence/effects_media_violence.cfm.

Murray, John P. 2008. 'Media Violence', *American Behavioral Scientist* 51, 8: 1212–30.

Murray, Michael D. 2005. 'Review: *Deciding What's News: A Study of CBS Evening News, NBC Nightly News, Newsweek, and Time* by Herbert J. Gans', *American Journalism* 22, 4: 113–14.

Ortiz-Negron, Laura L. 2008. 'States of Mutation: Re-configurations of State, Business and Media'. Paper presented at First ISA Forum of Sociology, International Sociological Association, Barcelona, Spain.

Rabot, Jean-Martin. 2007. 'The Image, Vector of Society', *Sociétés*, 1: 19–31.

Rainwater, Lee, Richard P. Coleman, and Gerald Handel. 1962. *Working Man's Wife*. New York: Macfadden Books.

Ramos, Howard, James Ron, and Oskar N.T. Thoms. 2007. 'Shaping the Northern Media's Human Rights Coverage, 1986–2000', *Journal of Peace Research* 44, 4: 385–406.

Reinhold, Thomas. 2006. 'Modeling Symbolically Generalized Media', *Soziale Systeme* 12, 1: 121–56.

Rennett, Michael. 2009. 'Baudrillard and The Joe Schmo Show', *The International Journal of Baudrillard Studies* 6, 1.

Robinson, Michael J. 1980. 'Review: *Deciding What's News: A Study of CBS Evening News, NBC Nightly News, Newsweek, and Time* by Herbert J. Gans'. *The American Political Science Review* 74, 1: 194–5.

Ron, J. and H. Ramos. 2006. 'Shaping the Media's Human Rights Agenda, 1986–2000.' Paper presented at the Annual Meeting of the International Studies Association, San Diego, CA. At: http://www.allacademic.com/meta/p98157_index.html.

Sefat, Kusha, and Tene Kelly, eds. 2009. 'Saudi Arabia Does Not Exist', *The International Journal of Baudrillard Studies* 6, 2 (Jul.).

Staples, Sacha. 2009. 'Incarcerated by a Discourse of Binaries: America's Mediated Culture of Terror', *The International Journal of Baudrillard Studies* 6, 2, (Jul.).

Starr, C. 1996. 'Review: *Material Girls: Making Sense of Feminist Cultural Theory* by S.D. Walters', *Contemporary Sociology* 25, 5: 818–20.

Statistics Canada. 2001. 'General Social Survey: Internet Use', *The Daily*, 26 Mar. At: http://www.statcan.gc.ca/daily-quotidien/010326/dq010326a-eng.htm. Accessed 20 Aug. 2009.

———. 2006. 'Television Viewing', *The Daily*, 31 Mar. At: http://www.statcan.gc.ca/daily-quotidien/060331/dq060331b-eng.htm. Accessed 22 Aug. 2009.

———. 2008. 'Private radio broadcasting', *The Daily*, 25 Aug. At: http://www.statcan.gc.ca/daily-quotidien/080825/dq080825c-eng.htm. Accessed 23 Aug. 2009.

Torikian, Garen J. 2009. 'Against a Perpetuating Fiction: Disentangling Art from Hyperreality', *The International Journal of Baudrillard Studies* 6, 2, (Jul.).

WACC. 2009. 'Global Media Monitoring Project Scrutinizes Fairness and Balance in Representation of Gender in the News around the World'. 10 Nov. At:
http://www.awid.org/eng/Women-in-Action/Announcements2/WACC-Press-Release-Global-Media-Monitoring-Project-scrutinizes-fairness-and-balance-in-representation-of-gender-in-the-news-around-the-world.

———. 2010. 'Global Media Monitoring Project 2010 Preliminary Findings'. At: http://www.whomakesthenews.org/images/stories/website/gmmp_reports/2010/gmmp_2010_prelim_key_en.pdf.

Walters, Patrick, and Rita Kop. 2009. 'Heidegger, Digital Technology, and Postmodern Education', *Bulletin of Science, Technology and Society* 29, 4: 278–86.

Walters, Suzanna Danuta. 1995. *Material Girls: Making Sense of Feminist Cultural Theory*. Berkeley: University of California Press.

West, Emily. 2002. 'Selling Canada to Canadians: Collective Memory, National Identity, and Popular Culture', *Critical Studies in Media Communication* 19, 2: 212–29.

Chapter 15

Adsett, Margaret. 2003. 'Change in Political Era and Demographic Weight as Explanations of Youth "Disenfranchisement" in Federal Elections in Canada, 1965–2000', *Journal of Youth Studies* 6, 3: 247–64.

Baral, Kaialsh. 2008. 'Terrorism, Jean Baudrillard and a Death in Northeast India', *The International Journal of Baudrillard Studies* 5, 1, (Jan.).

Bashevkin, Sylvia. 1985. *Toeing the Lines: Women and Party Politics in English Canada*. Toronto: University of Toronto Press.

———. 2009. *Women, Power, Politics: The Hidden Story of Canada's Unfinished Democracy*. Toronto: Oxford University Press.

Beaujot, Roderic, and Zenaida Ravanera. 2009. 'Family Models for Earning and Caring: Implications for Child Care and for Family Policy', *Canadian Studies in Population* 36, 1–2: 145–66.

Benson, Rodney. 2009. 'Shaping the Public Sphere: Habermas and Beyond', *The American Sociologist* 40, 3: 175–197.

Blais, Andre, Elisabeth Gidengil, Patrick Fournier, and Neil Nevitte. 2009. 'Information, Visibility and Elections: Why Electoral Outcomes Differ when Voters are Better Informed', *European Journal of Political Research* 48, 2: 256–80.

Brodie, Janine. 1996. *Women and Canadian Public Policy*. Toronto: Harcourt Brace.

Cassinari, Flavio, and Fabio Merlini. 2007. 'Trunks and Roots: The Western Identity Today' ('Tronchi e radici: l'identita occidentale oggi'), *Fenomenologia e Societa* 30, 2: 7–27.

Cohen, Stanley. 1978. 'Review: The Archaeology of Power', *Contemporary Sociology* 7, 5: 566–8.

Cool, Julie. 2008. 'Women in Parliament.' Parliament of Canada, Political and Social Affairs Division. At: http://www2.parl.gc.ca/Content/LOP/ResearchPublications/prb0562-e.htm. Accessed 22 Sept. 2009.

Cunliffe, Marcus. 1959. *The Nation Takes Shape 1789-1837*, Chicago: The Chicago History of American Civilization, University of Chicago Press.

Edwards, Gemma. 2009. 'Habermas and Social Movement Theory', *Sociology Compass*, 3, 3: 381–93.Elections Canada. N.d. 'Elections Canada On-line.' At: http://www.elections.ca/home.asp.

Equal Voice. 2006a. 18 Sept. 2009. http://equalvoice.ca/.

———. 2006b. 'Women in Canadian Politics'. At: http://www.equalvoice.ca/uploads/288_46709afdcb27f.pdf. Accessed 13 Sept. 2009.

Fives, Allyn. 2009. 'Reasonable, Agonistic, or Good?: The Character of a Democrat', *Philosophy and Social Criticism* 35, 8: 961–83.

Foucault, Michel. 1979. *Discipline and Punish: The Birth of the Prison*, trans. Alan Sheridan. New York: Vintage.

Garland, David 1986: 'Review: Foucault's 'Discipline and Punish'—An Exposition and Critique', *American Bar Foundation Research Journal* 11, 4: 847–80.

Goldstein, Jan 1979: 'Review: [Untitled]', *The Journal of Modern History* 51, 1: 116–18.

Grosfoguel, Ramon. 2007. 'The Epistemic Decolonial Turn: Beyond Political-Economy Pardigms', *Cultural Studies* 21, 2–3: 211–23.

Hall, John R. 2009. 'Apocalypse in the Long Run: Reflections on Huge Comparisons in the Study of Modernity', *Sociological Research Online* 14,5. At: http://www.socresonline.org.uk/14/5/10.html.

Heard, Andrew. '2008 Canadian Election Results', *Elections*. Simon Fraser University. At: http://www.sfu.ca/~aheard/elections/results.html. Accessed 20 Sept. 2009.

Heath, Joseph. 2009. 'Habermas and Analytical Marxism', *Philosophy & Social Criticism* 35, 8, 891–919.

Homans, George Caspar. 1950. *The Human Group*. New York: Harcourt, Brace.

Hunter, Rosemary. 2007. 'Would You Like Theory with That? Bridging the Divide between Policy-Oriented Empirical Legal Research, Critical Theory and Politics', *Studies in Law, Politics, and Society* 41: 121–48.

Inter-Parliamentary Union. 2009. 'Women in Parliaments: World Classification'. *Parliamentary Democracy*. At: http://www.ipu.org/wmn-e/arc/classif310709.htm. Accessed 23 Aug. 2009.

Johnston, W.A., Harvey Krahn, and Trevor Harrison. 2006. 'Democracy, Political Institutions, and Trust: The Limits of Current Electoral Reform Proposals', *Canadian Journal of Sociology/Cahiers canadiens de sociologie* 31, 2: 165–82. At: http://muse.jhu.edu.myaccess.library.utoronto.ca/journals/canadian_journal_of_sociology/v031/31.2johnston.html. Accessed 14 Sept. 2009.

Keat, Russell. 2008. 'Social Criticism and the Exclusion of Ethics', *Analyse & Kritik* 30, 2: 291–315.

Kristjanson-Gural, David. 2008. 'Postmodern Contributions to Marxian Economics: Theoretical Innovations and their Implications for Class Politics', *Historical Materialism* 16, 2: 85–115.

Kurnik, Andrej. 2009. 'Crisis and Labor in the Constitution' ('Kriza in delo v konstituciji'), *Teorija in Praksa* 46, 5: 653–69.

Library and Archives Canada. 2008. 'Canadian Women in Government: Celebrating Women's Achievements.'At: http://www.collectionscanada.gc.ca/women/002026-800-e.html. Accessed 16 Sept. 2009.

Lima, Marcos Costa. 2008. 'Edward W. Said's Critical Humanism', Lua Nova—Revista de Cultura e Politica' 73.

Lipset, Seymour Martin. 1967. *The First New Nation: The United States in Historical and Comparative Perspective*. Garden City, NY: Doubleday, Anchor.

Matthews, Emily, and Gregory Mock. 2003.'EarthTrends Featured Topic: More Democracy, Better Environment?' At: http://earthtrends.wri.org/pdf_library/feature/gov_fea_dem.pdf. Accessed 16 Sept. 2009.

McCormack, Thelma. 1964. 'Book Review: The First New Nation by Seymour Martin Lipset', *The Canadian Journal of Economics and Political Science* 30, 4: 612–13.

McIntosh, Mary. 1978. 'The State and the Oppression of Women', in Annette Kuhn and Ann Marie Wolpe, eds., *Feminism and Materialism*. London: Routledge & Kegan Paul, 254–89.

Moore, Barrington, Jr. 1966. *Social Origins of Dictatorship and Democracy; Lord and Peasant in the Making of the Modern World*. Boston: Beacon Press.

Moss, Martha. 2009. 'Swedish EU Presidency "Must Promote Women's Rights"'. At: http://www.theparliament.com/latestnews/news-article/newsarticle/wallstroem-cautions-against-complacency-on-womens-rights/. Accessed 22 Sept. 2009.

Muller-Doohm, Stefan. 2009. 'Nation, State, Democracy, Philosophical and Political Motives in the Thought of Jürgen Habermas' ('Nationalstaat, Kapitalismus, Demokratie. Philosophisch-politische Motive im Denken von Jürgen Habermas'), *Leviathan: Zeitschrift fur Sozialwissenschaft* 37, 4: 501–17.

Nickel, Patricia Mooney. 2009. 'Liberalism, Postmodernism, and Welfare: A Critique of Martin', *New Political Science* 31, 1: 69–86.

Parsons, Talcott. 1964. 'Book Review: The First New Nation by Seymour Martin Lipset', *The American Journal of Sociology* 70, 3: 374–5.

———. 1964 (1951). *The Social System*. New York: Free Press.

Pedersen, Jorgen. 2009. 'Habermas and the Political Sciences', *Philosophy of the Social Sciences* 39, 3: 381–407.

Perrella, Andrea M.L. 2009. 'Economic Decline and Voter Discontent', *The Social Science Journal* 46, 2: 347–68.

Pharr, Susan J., Robert Putnam, and Russell Dalton. 2000. 'A Quarter-Century of Declining Confidence', *Journal of Democracy* 11: 5–25.

Rostboll, Christian F. 2008. 'Emancipation or Accommodation?: Habermasian vs. Rawlsian Deliberative Democracy', *Philosophy & Social Criticism* 34, 7: 707–36.

Roth, Klas. 2009. 'Some Thoughts for a New Critical Language of Education', *Philosophy & Social Criticism* 35, 6: 685–703.

Scott, John, ed. 2006. *Fifty Key Sociologists: The Formative Theorists.* London: Routledge.

Shelley, Louise I. 1979. 'Review: [Untitled]', *The American Journal of Sociology* 84, 6: 1508–10.

Smith, Joanne. 2010. 'Plans for "Fox News North" to be revealed in Toronto', *The Toronto Star,* 14 June. At: http://www.thestar.com/news/canada/article/823283--plans-for-fox-news-north-to-be-revealed-in-toronto.

Statistics Canada. 2003. 'The State'. At: http://www43.statcan.ca/04/04_002_e.htm. Accessed 22 Sept. 2009.

———. 2005. 'Study: Political Activity among Young Adults', *The Daily,* 6 Dec. At: http://www.statcan.gc.ca/daily-quotidien/051206/dq051206b-eng.htm.

Stewart, Kennedy, Patricia MacIver, and Stewart Young. 2008. 'Testing and Improving Voters' Political Knowledge', *Canadian Public Policy/Analyse de Politiques* 34, 4: 403–17.

Tassone, Giuseppe. 2008. 'Antinomies of Transcritique and Virtue Ethics: An Adornian Critique', *Philosophy & Social Criticism* 34, 6: 665–84.

Tibetan Review. 2009. 'China Condemns Int'l Criticism of Harsh Sentence for Democracy Activist'. 28 Dec. At: http://www.tibetanreview.net/news.php?cat=2&&id=5186.

Weber, Max. 1978 (1908). *Economy and Society: An Outline of Interpretive Sociology,* ed. Guenther Roth and Claus Wittich, trans. Ephraim Fischoff. Berkeley: University of California Press.

Wicks, Patricia Gaya, and Peter Reason. 2009. 'Initiating Action Research', *Action Research* 7, 3: 243–62.

Zizek, Slavoj. 2008.'The Prospect of Radical Politics Today', *The International Journal of Baudrillard Studies* 5, 1, (Jan.).

Chapter 16

Adams, Douglas. 1979. *The Hitchhiker's Guide to the Galaxy.* London: Pan Books.

Allport, Gordon W., and Leo Postman. 1947. *The Psychology of Rumor.* New York: Henry Holt.

Andretta, Massimiliano. 2005. 'The "Framing" of the Movement against Neoliberal Globalization', *Rassegna Italiana di Sociologia* 46, 2: 249–74.

Answers.com. N.d. 'Social Movements'. At: http://www.answers.com/topic/social-movement-1. Accessed 25 Sept. 2009.

Artamonov, Dmitry. 2009. 'Greenpeace International'. Greenpeace. 14 Jan. At: http://commons.wikimedia.org/wiki/File:Greenpeace_worldwide.svg. Accessed 27 Sept. 2009.

Aya, Rod. 1990. *Rethinking Revolutions and Collective Violence: Studies on Concept, Theory, and Method.* Amsterdam: Het Spinhuis.

Barber, Bernard. 1983. *The Logic and Limits of Trust.* New Brunswick, NJ: Rutgers University Press.

Benford, Robert D., and David A. Snow. 2000. 'Framing Processes and Social Movements: An Overview and Assessment', *Annual Review of Sociology* 26: 611–39.

Bullough, Vern. L. 1979. 'The Civilizing Process: The History of Manners, Review', *The American Historical Review* 84, 2: 444.

Burt, Ronald S. 2005. *Brokerage & Closure: An Introduction to Social Capital.* Oxford: Oxford University Press.

CBC Archives. 1967. 'The Bedrooms of the Nation.' At: http://archives.cbc.ca/politics/rights_freedoms/clips/2671/.

Camcastle, Cara. 2007. 'The Green Party of Canada in political space and the new middle class thesis', *Environmental Politics* 16, 4: 625–42.

Clarke, Allan. 1987. 'Moral Protest, Status Defense and the Anti-Abortion Campaign', *The British Journal of Sociology* 38, 2: 235–53.

Côté, Rochelle R., and Bonnie H. Erickson. 2009. 'Untangling the Roots of Tolerance: How Forms of Social Capital Shape Attitudes Toward Ethnic Minorities and Immigrants', *American Behavioral Scientist* 52, 12: 1664–89.

Davies, James C. 1962. 'Toward a Theory of Revolution', *American Sociological Review* 27, 1: 5–19.

Elias, Norbert. 1969 (1939). *The Civilizing Process*: vol. I, *The History of Manners.* Oxford: Blackwell.

———. 1982 (1939). *The Civilizing Process*: vol. II, *State Formation and Civilization.* Oxford: Blackwell.

Eliot, T.S. 1940. 'East Coker', No. 2 in *Four Quartets.* London: Faber.

Green Party of Canada. 2009. 'Our History'. At: http://www.greenparty.ca/about-us/our-history. Accessed 29 Sept. 2009.

Green, Penny, and Tony Ward. 2009. 'State-Building and the Logic of Violence in Iraq', *Journal of Scandinavian Studies in Criminology and Crime Prevention* 10, S1: 48–58.

Greenfieldboyce, Nell. 2008. 'Pageant Protest Sparked Bra-Burning Myth'. NPR, 5 Sept. At: http://www.npr.org/templates/story/story.php?storyId=94240375.

Gusfield, Joseph R. 1963. *Symbolic Crusade: Status Politics and the American Temperance Movement.* Urbana, IL: University of Illinois Press.

———. 1981. *The Culture of Public Problems: Drinking-Driving and the Symbolic Order.* Chicago: University of Chicago Press.

———. 1996. *Contested Meanings: The Construction of Alcohol Problems.* Madison, WI: University of Wisconsin Press.

———. 2000. *Performing Action: Artistry in Human Behavior and Social Research.* New Brunswick, NJ: Transaction.

Gustavsen, Bjorn. 2008. 'Action Research, Practical Challenges and the Formation of Theory', *Action Research* 6, 4: 421–37.

Hessel, Deiter. 1964. 'Review'. *Review of Religious Research* 6, 1: 56–7.

Hobbes, Thomas. 1968 (1660). *Leviathan,* ed. C.B. Macpherson. Harmondsworth, UK: Penguin.

Hockey, Jenny, Angela Meah, and Victoria Robinson. 2009. 'Fast Girls, Foreigners and GIs: An Exploration of the Discursive Strategies Through Which the Status of Pre-Marital (Hetero) sexual Ignorance and Restraint Was Upheld During the Second World War', *Sociological Research Online* 14, 5. At: http://www.socresonline.org.uk/14/5/14.html.

Huizinga, Johan. 1955 (1938). *Homo Ludens: A Study of the Play-element in Culture.* Boston: Beacon Press.

Kitschelt, Herbert. 1993. 'Social Movements, Political Parties, and Democratic Theory,' *Annals of the American Academy of Political and Social Science* 528, 1: 13–29.

Knopf, Terry Ann. 1975. *Rumors, Race, and Riots.* New Brunswick, NJ: Transaction.

Lang, Kurt. 1964. 'Review', *American Sociological Review* 29, 5: 768–9.

Lévi-Strauss, Claude. 1966 (1962). The Savage Mind. Chicago: University of Chicago Press.

Martin, Greg. 2001. 'Social Movements, Welfare and Social Policy: A Critical Analysis', Critical Social Policy 21, 3: 361–83.

Melucci, Alerbero. 1989. Nomads of the Present: Social Movements and Individual Needs in Contemporary Society. Philadelphia: Temple University Press.

Meyersohn, Rolf. 1969. 'Tamotsu Shibutani, "Improvised News: A Sociological Study of Rumor" (Book Review)', Social Research 36: 169–70.

Milgram, Stanley. 1967. 'The Small World Problem', Psychology Today 1, 1: 60–7.

Miller, Dan E. 2006. 'Rumor: An Examination of Some Stereotypes', Symbolic Interaction 28, 4: 505–19.

Mitlin, Diana. 2008. 'With and Beyond the State Co-production as a Route to Political Influence, Power and Transformation for Grassroots Organizations', Environment & Urbanization 20, 2: 339–60.

Mosse, George. 1978. 'The Civilizing Process: The History of Manners, Review', New German Critique 15, (Autumn): 178–183.

Nadeem, Shehzad. 2008. 'The Living Wage Movement and the Economics of Morality: Frames, Ideology and the Discursive Field', Research in Social Movements, Conflicts and Change 28: 137–67.

Pallister-Wilkins, Polly. 2009. 'Radical Ground: Israeli and Palestinian Activists and Joint Protest Against the Wall', Social Movement Studies 8, 4: 393–407.

Paxton, Pamela. 2007. 'Association Membership and Generalized Trust: A Multilevel Model Across 31 Countries', Social Forces 86, 1: 47–76.

Pelletier, Rejean, and Daniel Guerin. 2000. 'New Social Movements and Political Parties in Quebec: An Organizational Challenge', Politique et Sociétés 19, 1: 135–61.

Roberge, Jonathan. 2009. 'Jeffrey C. Alexander and the Ten-year Strong Cultural Sociology Program' ('Jeffrey C. Alexander et les dix ans du programme fort en sociologie culturelle'), Cahiers de recherche sociologique 47: 47–66.

Ross, Stephanie. 2008. 'The Strategic Implications of Anti-Statism in the Global Justice Movement', Labour, Capital and Society/Travail Capital et Société, 41, 1: 7–32.

Rumbarger, John. 1989. Profits, Power and Prohibition: Alcohol Reform and the Industrializing America 1800–1930. New York: Sunny Press.

Saha, Lawrence J., Murray Print, and Kathy Edwards. 2005. 'Youth, Political Engagement and Voting', Youth Electoral Study. Sydney and Canberra, Australia: University of Sydney and the Australian National University. At: http://www.aec.gov.au/pdf/publications/youth_study_2/youth_electoral_study_02.pdf.

Sakai, Tomoko. 2009. 'Trans-Generational Memory: Narratives of World Wars in Post-Conflict Northern Ireland', Sociological Research Online 14, 5 (Nov.). At: http://www.socresonline.org.uk/14/5/15.html.

Seigel, Jerrold. 1979. 'The Civilizing Process: The History of Manners, Review'. The Journal of Modern History. 51, 1: 123–6.

Shibutani, Tomatsu. 1966. Improvised News: A Sociological Study of Rumor. Indianapolis: Bobbs-Merrill.

Smelser, Neil J. 1963. Theory of Collective Behaviour. New York: Free Press.

Soares, Judith. 2007. 'Legitimizing Injustice', Peace Review 19, 4: 597–601.

Snow, David A., E. Burke Rochford Jr., Steven K. Worden, and Robert D. Benford. 1986. 'Frame Alignment Processes, Micromobilization, and Movement Participation', American Sociological Review 51, 4: 464–81.

Stanley, Liz. 2009. 'Narratives from Major to Minor: On Resisting Binaries in Favour of Joined Up Thinking', Sociological Research Online 14, 5 (Nov.). At: http://www.socresonline.org.uk/14/5/25.html.

Sukhov, Michael J. 2008. 'Political Activism and Deferred Agency', Dissertation Abstracts International, A: The Humanities and Social Sciences, 68, 11: 4869.

Tilly, Charles. 1978. From Mobilization to Revolution. Reading, MA: Addison-Wesley.

———. 1984. Big Structures, Large Processes, Huge Comparisons. New York: Russell Sage Foundation.

———. 1995. Popular Contention in Great Britain, 1758–1834. Cambridge, MA: Harvard University Press.

Touraine, Alain. 1981. The Voice and the Eye: An Analysis of Social Movements. Cambridge: Cambridge University Press.

Ullman, Albert. 1964. 'Review', Annals of the American Academy of Political and Social Science 355: 154–5.

Wakefield, Sarah E.L. 2007. 'Reflective Action in the Academy: Exploring Praxis in Critical Geography using a "Food Movement" Case Study', Antipode 39, 2: 331–54.

Walker, Edward T., Andrew W. Martin, and John D. McCarthy. 2008. 'Confronting the State, the Corporation, and the Academy: The Influence of Institutional Targets on Social Movement Repertoires', American Journal of Sociology 114, 1: 35–76.

Wilmott, Hugh. 2008. 'Critical Management and Global Justice', Organization 15, 6: 927–31.

Zald, Mayer. 1964. 'Review', The American Journal of Sociology 70, 3: 392–3.

Photo Credits

page 2: © Deco/Alamy; page 4: Dbdella/Dreamstime.com; page 7: AP Photo/Gerry Broome; page 8: © iStockphoto.com/WILLSIE; page 14: © Jonathan Ernst/Reuters/Corbis; page 16: © Bob Frid/Icon SMI/Corbis; page 18: Edward Simons/Alamy ; page 32: © iStockphoto.com/xyno; page 34: Colin Mcconnell/GetStock; page 43: Megapress/Alamy; page 52: Interfoto/Alamy; page 53: © iStockphoto.com/Andrew Penner; page 56: © iStockphoto.com/Dan Barnes; page 64: Buccina Studios/Getty; page 67: Jim Wikes/GetStock; page 69: © Ocean/Corbis; page 73: © iStockphoto.com/Nancy Louie; page 78: © iStockphoto.com/Eliza Snow; page 79: main person, cousin, co-worker, friend 1, friend 2, and sister from Comstock: Just Teens; boss, father, friend 3 from Corbis 298; neighbour from PhotoDisc 95; page 82: Peter Scholey/Getty; page 87: Paul J. Richards/Getty; page 92: Megapress/Alamy; page 95: imagebroker/Alamy; page 102: brianindia/Alamy; page 109: The Canadian Press/Jeff McIntosh; page 112: Graham Bezant/GetStock; page 113: Guiseppe Cacace/Getty; page 116: Peter Arnold, Inc./Alamy; page 120: Art Kowalsky/Alamy; page: 124: Jim Lane/Alamy; page 126: Caterina Bernardi/Getty; page 131: © iStockphoto.com/Petro Feketa; page 134: Bloomberg/Getty; page 135: Lourens Smak/Alamy; page 140: Nruboc/Dreamstime.com; page 143: © iStockphoto.com/Anthony Rosenberg; page 144: © iStockphoto.com/sturti; page 154: adrian lourie/Alamy; page157: Rglinsky/Dreamstime.com; page 159: Mike Goldwater/Alamy; page 161: Stacy Walsh Rosenstock/Alamy; page 168: © Atlantide Phototravel/Corbis; page 169: The Art Gallery Collection/Alamy; page 173: Michael Stuparyk/GetStock; page 184: © iStockphoto.com/Brian Chase; page 192: Meredith, C.P./Library and Archives Canada/C-068863; page 194: Joe Raedle/Getty; page 200: Isifa/Getty; page 201: Otnaydur/Dreamstime.com; page 202: Toronto Star/GetStock; photo 204: Mario Beauregard/CPI/The Canadian Press; page 209: © Ted Soqui/Corbis; page 216: ETCbild /Alamy; page 218: © iStockphoto.com/kzenon; page 219: CP Photo/Paul Chiasson; page 221: Frances Roberts /Alamy; page 230 © iStockphoto.com/Stephan Hoerold;

page 231: Joe McNally/Getty; page 234: Macduff Everton/Getty; page 240: © Don Mason/Corbis; page 244: © Roger Wood/CORBIS; page 253: © iStockphoto.com/ricardoazoury; page 257: Glenbow Archives NA-1197-1; page 260: ryan koopmans/Alamy; page 262: AP Photo/Jerry Lai, file; page 265: David Wei/Alamy ; page 274: © iStockphoto.com/Ju-Lee; page 283: Alex Segre/Alamy; page 285: Iain Masterton/Alamy; page 289: Fer737ng/Dreamstime.com; page 291: © Reuters/Corbis; page 293: Laperruque/Alamy; page 295: Peter Essick/Aurora Photos; page 302: Alan Oliver/Alamy; page 308: Colin Mcconnell/GetStock; page 313: ClassicStock/Alamy; page 315: © Laura Dwight/Corbis; page 316: © iStockphoto.com/Marilyn Nieves; page 318: Caro/Alamy; page 321: Beckyabell/Dreamstime.com; page 322: © Heather Hryciw/Corbis; page 332:© iStockphoto.com/Heather Nemec; page 336: Nicole Hill/Getty; page 342: © iStockphoto.com/Chad Narkchareon; page 345: CharlineXia Ontario Canada Collection/Alamy; page 347: Peter Essick/Aurora Photos; page 350: Photofusion Picture Library/Alamy; page 352: © iStockphoto.com/Daniel Laflor; page 362: Petr Svarc/Alamy; page 368: The Canadian Press/Chris Young; page 374: Gunter Marx/EV/Alamy; page 380: © iStockphoto.com/Stephan Zabel; page 383: © Floris Leeuwenberg/The Cover Story/Corbis; page 386: Art Directors & TRIP/Alamy; page 390: Jeff Greenberg/Alamy ; page 394: Iain Masterton/Alamy; page 396: jeremy sutton-hibbert/Alamy; page 399: Eddie Gerald/Alamy, page 401: Matt Harris Digital Photography/Alamy; page 403: CP Photo/Paul Chiasson; page 409: Vernon Merritt III/Getty; page 422: Jenny Matthews/Alamy; page 428: Jamieroach/Dreamstime.com; page 429: Tektite/Dreamstime.com; page 434: The Canadian Press/Tom Hanson; page 436: CP Photo/Ian Barrett; page 437: Scott Goldsmith/GetStock; page 439: CP Photo/Winnipeg Free Press-Linda Vermette; page 452: Jason Baxter/Alamy; page 455: Blend Images/Masterfile; page 459: © iStockphoto.com/ Michelle Scott; page 463: Randy Duchaine/Alamy; page 469: Peter Stackpole/Getty; page 470: Barry Lewis/Alamy

Index

ABC (television network), 402
ability grouping, 343–4
ableism, 212–13
abnormality: normality and, 85
Aboriginal peoples: age and, 227; education and, 340, 345; justice system and, 203; media and, 108; multiculturalism and, 203; position of, 193; religion and, 384
abortion, 377
Abraham, Laurie, 160
Abu Ghraib, 447
abuse: age and, 232–3, 236–7; child sexual, 169, 377, 413; gender and, 146–7, 161; racial and ethnic groups and, 208–10; schools and, 349–51; sexual, 169, 377
accidents: age and, 234
action-research, 476
activity theory, 221–2
Adams, Douglas, 454
Adams, Julia, 269
Adams, Mary Louise, 183
Adams, Michael, 290, 425
Adler, Patricia, and Peter Adler, 86
adolescence: schools and, 341–3, 352, 353–4; as subculture, 341–3, 350–1; as term, 223; see also youth
Adorno, Theodor, 18, 97–8, 120, 175, 270, 307, 318–19
advertising: gender and, 150, 409; high culture and, 113; political, 424
Afghanistan, 278
Africa: marriage in, 310; modernization theory and, 294; world-systems theory and, 279–80
African Americans, 205–6, 208–9
age: Canada, 226–7; drinking, 219; fear of, 84; gender and, 134; median, 226; population and, 44, 48; sexuality and, 159, 166; voting, 437; see also adolescence; children; elderly people; youth
age groups, 216–43; abuse and, 236–7; crime and, 233; critical theories and, 220–1; cross-national differences in, 239; feminist theories and, 222; functionalism and, 220; life course perspective and, 227–9; mental health and, 233–4; new insights into, 239–41; relations among, 225–6, 229; schools and, 230–1; symbolic interactionism and, 221–2; violence and, 236–7; workplace and, 230–1
ageism, 219, 220; health and, 234–5

'agenda-setting', 404
'agequake', 227
Agger, Ben, 119
aggression: children and, 350; media and, 412–13
agriculture, 36, 54; community supported, 87
AIDS, 163
Albanese, Patrizia, 330
Alberta Alliance, 435
alcohol: prohibition and, 468–70; religion and, 369, 376
Alexander, Jeffrey, 476
Alexander, Victoria D., 122
alienation: Marx and, 247; service workers and, 325; social constructionism and, 251; types of, 256
Allan, Kenneth, 30
Allen, Louisa, 180
Allport, Gordon, 208, 211, 458, 459, 460
altruism, 462; religion and, 370, 371
Amatucci, Kristi Bruce, 357
American Council of Families, 326
Americanization, 278, 283–4; media and, 403, 404–5
American Revolution, 426, 427
'American values', 426–7
Americas: world-system theory and, 279–80
Amin, Samir, 294, 478
Amineh, M.P., and S.N. Eisenstadt, 389–90
Anderson, Benedict, 199, 211, 214
Anderson, Kay, 212
Andres, Lesley, and Maria Adamuti-Trache, 139
animals: behaviour of, 95; humans and, 212
anomie, 7–8, 14, 413; adaptations to, 137, 163; industrial societies and, 255; Merton and, 16, 38, 163
anorexia, 407–8
anthems, 386
anthropology: cities, and, 59–60
anti-introspection, 319
anti-statism, 477
Antonowicz, Dominik, and Lukasz Wrzesinski, 87
Antweiler, Christoph, 59–60
anxiety, 88
appearance: gender and, 134–5; media and, 406–11
appropriation principle, 252
Arantes, Pedro Fiori, 57–8
archaeological approach, 83
Aries, Philippe, 222–4, 242
Armstrong, Pat, and Hugh Armstrong, 28, 142–3, 153

art: culture and, 99–100, 113
Arvidsson, A., 119
Ashley Madison, 157
Asia: religion in, 389
assimilation, 20, 199–200
Athens, 431
Attwood, Feona, 179
audience, mass, 399
Australia: indigenous people in, 212; US and, 426–7
authoritarian personality, 175, 317–20
authoritarian state, 430
authority, 19; bureaucracies and, 429; charismatic, 19, 428–9; political, 428–30; rational–legal, 19, 376, 428, 429–30; traditional, 19, 428
Axtell, Roger, 103

baby boom, 227
Baer, Douglas E., 450
Baert, Patrick, 443
Baker, Maureen, 330
Baldauf, Anette, 328
Bales, Robert, 77, 305
bands, 77–9
bandwagon effect, 404, 442, 467
banking: investment, 266; offshore, 262
Bankston, Carl L., III, 355
Baral, Kaialsh, 447
Baril, Audrey, 178
Barnett, Bernice McNair, 267, 268
Barnett, Mathew, 355
Bashevkin, Sylvia, 433, 451
Battle of Quebec, 427
Baudrillard, Jean, 414–17, 475
Baumann, 58
Beaman, Lori G., and Peter Beyer, 392
Beaulieu, Gisele, 117
Becher, J.J., 378
Beck, Ulrich, 49–50, 51
Becker, Howard, 9, 67–8, 316, 331
Belgrave, Faye Z., et al., 165
beliefs: culture and, 96–7
Bell, Stewart, 301
Bell, Vikki, 31
Bellah, Robert, et al., 383, 384–8
Bengston, V.L., et al., 242
Benhabib, Seyla, 18, 151
Benjamin, Walter, 18, 97–8, 120
Benson, Rodney, 444–5
Bentham, Jeremy, 11, 438
Berardi, Franco, 418
Berger, John, 122
Berger, Peter, and Thomas Luckmann, 23–4, 25

Bertin, Adriano, 387

Bertoni, Timothy J., 268

bestiality, 177

bias, media, 402, 405

Bibby, Reginald W., 392, 330

Bidou-Zacchariasen, Catherine, 269

Biggs, Simon, 239, 240

biology: race and, 206–7; sexuality and, 155, 178

'bio-power', 84, 85

'bisexual pedagogy', 180

Bishop, Ron, 119

Black, Conrad, 262

Blackledge, Paul, 31

black people: schools and, 344, 346

Blain, Michael, 86

Blakeborough, Darren, 241

Blakely, Kristin, 326

blame: dominant ideology and, 440–1, 442–3; sociology and, 5

Bloc Québécois, 435

Blum, Linda, and Vicki Smith, 138

Blumer, Herbert, 9, 24, 414

body: aging and, 241; discipline and, 437; standards, 135

Body Dysmorphic Disorder (BDD), 84–5

Body Mass Index (BMI), 85

Bogardus, Emory S., 189–91

Boggs, Carl, and Tom Pollard, 119

Boney, Virginia M., 326–7

Bonikowski, Bart, 355–6

Bonney, N., and E. Reinach, 130

Borgerson, Janet, 177

Boritch, Helen, 160

Bourdieu, Pierre, 60, 110–13, 445

bourgeoisie, 8, 251, 286–7

Boxer, Paul L., et al., 413

bra-burning myth, 473

Bradley, K., 139

Braverman, Harry, 251–2, 254, 287

breakdown approach, 465–6

Breton, Raymond, 200, 355

Brickell, Chris, 178–9

'bricolage', 478

British Empire, 280, 282

British National Party, 191

British North America Act, 434

Broad, K.L., 180

Broadcasting Act, 403

Brodsky, Joseph, 59

brokers: networks and, 457

Brook, Paul, 325

Brown, Kevin Pearson, 28–9

Brown, Lester, 36

Brown, Tony N., 212

Bui, H.N., and M. Morash, 147

building: technology and, 56–7

built environment, 33–4, 54, 56–7

bulimia, 407–8

bullying, 5–6, 350–1

bureaucracies, 67; authority and, 429; schools and, 348; world-systems theory and, 280

Burke, James, 122

Burnham, James, 253

Burundi, 210

Busfield, Joan, 147

Butler, Judith, 151, 163, 177–9

Butsch, Richard, 260

Butterworth, Michael, 385–6

Caldarovic, Ognjen, and Jana Sarinic, 59

Calder, Gideon, 179

Calhoun, Craig, 267

call centres, 252

Calvin, John, 105

Calvinism, 366–7, 440

Campbell, Fiona, and A. Kumari, 212–13

Campbell, Kim, 433

Canada: core and periphery and, 281; culture in, 116–17, 402–5; culture war in, 290–1; immigration policy in, 193–4; media in, 400, 401–3; religion in, 365, 370–6; universities in, 338; US and, 426–7; as vertical mosaic, 20–1

Canada Council for the Arts, 99–100

Canadian Broadcasting Corporation (CBC), 400, 402–3

Canadian Community Health Survey, 172, 235

Canadian Pacific Railway, 193

Canadian Radio-television and Telecommunications Commission (CRTC), 402–3

Canadian Security Intelligence Service (CSIS), 293

Canadian Union of Public Employees, 258

capital: criminal, 232; cultural, 110–13, 114, 349, 355; human, 44; social, 349, 355–8, 357

capitalism, 8; alternative media and, 418; alternatives to, 477; Braverman and, 251–2; consumerism and, 328; crises of, 287, 447; critical theories and, 248–9; culture and, 97–8; functionalism and, 247–8; gender and, 127, 142–3; global, 280; Habermas and, 444; ideologies and, 440; imperialism and, 277–82;

labour and, 251–3; late, 247, 262–3; neo-liberalism and, 85; postmodernism and, 88; power and, 270; Protestant ethic and, 104–5; semi-, 418; white-collar crime and, 261–2; world history and, 285–7; world-systems theory and, 278–80, 294

caregiving, 325; burden of, 236–7

Carey, Malcolm, 178

Carmel, Sara, et al., 243

Carroll, William, K., 480

carrying capacity, 36

Carson, Rachel, 51

Carvalho, Giane Carmem Alves de, 296

Cassinari, Flavio, and Fabio Merlini, 446

Castells, Manuel, 57–9

Castle, Nicholas, 84

Castro-Gomez, Santiago, 120

categories, demographic, 70

'Catholic school effect', 355

Catlaw, Thomas J., and Qian Hu, 112

CBS (television network), 398, 400–1, 402

cellphones, 396

Channa, Subhadra, 298

Chappell, Louise, and Lisa Hill, 450

Chappell, Neena, et al., 242

charisma: routinization of, 19, 379

charity, 370–2

Charusheela, S., 269–70

Cheal, David, 30

Chernobyl accident, 50

childbearing, 36, 37, 44, 45, 46–9; cost of, 226

child care, 144

children: abuse and, 236; accidents and, 234; authoritarian parents and, 317–20; in China, 225; faith schools and, 384; families and, 303–4; gender and, 131–2; history of childhood and, 222–4; interests of, 221; intergroup marriage and, 191; media and, 409, 413; older people and, 229; parents and education and, 347–9; pornography and, 167, 168–9; protection of, 223; religion and, 387; same-sex marriage and, 310; schools and, 351–4; sexual abuse and, 169, 377, 414; sexuality and, 159, 170–1, 176, 177; socialization and, 305, 307–8, 315–16; 'trophy', 348

China: cultural revolution in, 431; immigration from, 195; one-child policy in, 225; population in, 48; West and, 211

Chinese Exclusion Act, 187, 193
Chinese people, 187, 193
Choquette, Robert, 392
Christianity, 364, 365, 372; Darwin and, 376; embedded, 381; imperialism and, 191–2, 282; media and, 418; sexuality and, 161–2
'Christmas tree', 364
church, 365; attendance and, 372–4
cities, 33–5; core and periphery and, 281; critical theories and, 38; functionalism and, 37–8; 'global', 60, 297–8; immigration and, 197; as networks, 80; new insights into, 59–61; population and, 43, 54–6; rural areas and, 54–5; smaller, 55–6; symbolic interactionism and, 38; technology and, 56–7
citizens: definition of, 424; democracy and, 431
citizenship: globalization and, 297
'civil defence pedagogies', 28
civil liberties, 448
Civil Rights Act, 205
Clark, S.D., 281
Clark, W., 139
Clarkson, Adrienne, 410, 433
class, 244–73; 'big', 269; Bourdieu and, 111; crime and, 261–2, 266; critical theories and, 8, 18, 248–9; cultural capital and, 113–14; cultural studies and, 98–9; definition of, 246; dominant, 426; etiquette and, 464–5; feminist theories and, 250; gender and 127; generations and, 237–8; health and, 264–5; ideologies and, 440; intersectionality and, 28; labour and, 251–3; leisure, 109–10; media and, 399, 408; middle, 264, 265, 287; modern critical theories and, 21; new, 269, 264; new insights into, 268–70; politics and, 426; postmodernism and, 88; power and, 19–21; social movements and, 467, 468; socialization and, 322–4; terrorism and, 292; upper-middle, 263; Weber and, 252–3; working, 260, 366; world history and, 285–7
class analysis, 251–3; postmodern, 269–70
class conflict, 247; critical theories and, 248–9
class consciousness, 251; unions and, 256–7
Clausewitz, Karl von, 291
Clements, Wallace, 20

climate: environment and, 53; immigration and, 193
climate change, 33, 52
cliques, 82–3, 343; elderly, 22
clothing: gender and, 134–5; see also appearance
Club of Rome, 40–2
Coale, Ansley, 46
cocaine, 296
cohabitation, 310–11, 313; functionalism and, 305
cohort, 44
Cole, Jennifer, and Deborah Durham, 243
Cole, Jonathan, 337–8, 339
Cole, Mike, 28
Coleman, James, 341–3, 346, 354–6, 357, 361, 475
Collins, Randall, 267
Colombia, 296
colonialism: nationalism and, 448; Orientalism and, 211; race and ethnic groups and, 191–3, 213
colonization: capitalism and, 278; Habermas and, 444, 445
Comber, Barbara, and Helen Nixon, 148–9
common conscience, 38
common-law relationships: see cohabitation
'common sense': sociology and, 5–6
communication: culture and, 98–9; globalization and, 284–5; Habermas and, 443–5; modern, 394–421; non-verbal, 74, 102, 103; rumour as, 458–60; see also media
communicative action, 445
communism, 430; dominant class and, 426; religion and, 378
Communist Manifesto, 285–7
communities, 70–1; ethnic, 199, 200, 204; gay, 169, 170, 173; imagined, 199, 213; new insights into, 86–8
community supported agriculture (CSA), 87
compensation: investment and, 247–8
computer games, 120–1
computers: communication and, 285; middle-class and, 287
Comte, August, 3, 10
conflict, 17–22; critical theory and, 17–18; families and, 319–20; functions of, 17; gender and, 135–6, 146–7; media and, 412–13; modern critical theories and, 21; racial, 188, 205, 207–10; regions and nations and, 275, 281–2, 287–94; religion and, 378; see also class conflict

conformity, 70–1; children and, 347; class and, 114; crime and, 233; functions of, 14–17; informal control and, 462; youth and, 224–5
conglomerate, 400, 401
connections: social network and, 79
Connidis, Ingrid Arnet, 243
Conroy, Sean, 88
conservatism: families and, 319, 326; in US, 387
Conservative Party, 435
'conspicuous consumption', 60, 109–10
constituencies, 431
consumerism, 87–8, 110; critical theories and, 97–8; families and, 327–8; media and, 411–12; religion and, 387; sexuality and, 162
consumption: 'collective', 57–8; computer games and, 121; conspicuous, 60, 109–10
content analysis, 398–400
contraception, 165, 377
control: feminist theories and, 10; informal, 462–5; postmodernism and, 11–12; simple/technological/ bureaucratic, 250–1; theory, 15; types of, 462–3; work and, 250–2, 254, 265; world-systems theory and, 280–2
Cook, Deborah, 270
Cooley, Charles Horton, 71, 308
Cooperative Commonwealth Federation (CCF), 435, 442
Copen, Casey, and Merril Silverstein, 387
core-periphery: media and, 405; states and, 279–82
corporations: gender and, 137–8; globalization and, 283
cosmopolitism, 59
Cotesta, Vittorio, 295
countercultures, 114, 119; postmodernism and, 11
credentialism, 333
credentials: educational, 349; foreign, 340
Crestwood Heights, 347–9
crime: age and, 233; class and, 261–2, 266; corporate, 16, 261–2; family and, 231; function of, 7; functionalism and, 15–16; gender and, 136–7; globalization and, 298; hate, 290; media and, 397–8; punishment and, 437; sexual, 176–7; street, 16; war, 277; white-collar, 261–2; youth, 231–3
crime control approach, 232

criminology, 14
critical management studies (CMS), 477
critical pedagogy, 357
critical race theory (CRT), 28, 212–13
critical theories, 6, 8, 17–23, 306; age
groups and, 220–1; cities and, 38;
class and work and, 248–9; culture
and, 97–8, 120–1; current debates
and, 28–9; education and, 335–6;
environment and, 39; feminist theories
and, 9; gender and, 127, 128; language
and, 101; media and, 397–8, 417–18;
modern, 18–23; politics and, 425,
426, 443, 446–8; population and,
36–7; postmodernism and, 10, 477–8;
racial and ethnic groups and, 187–8;
regions and nations and, 277–8,
285–7; religion and, 366; sexuality
and, 158–9, 181; social movements
and, 466–7
Crozier, Michel, 91
Cuba, 293
cultivation theory, 398
cults, 383–4, 387–8
cultural approach: social movements and,
465, 467
cultural studies perspective, 98–9, 406–8
culture, 92–123; Canadian, 116–17,
402–3, 404–5; change and, 115;
conflict and, 288–9; consumerist,
88; as conversation, 98, 101; critical
theories and, 97–8, 120–1; definition
of, 94; families and, 327; functionalism
and, 96–7; global, 119; globalization
and, 283–4, 295; high, 110, 113–14;
ideal, 107; language and, 101–3;
material, 99–100; media and, 406–8;
as memory 93; new insights into,
119–21; non-material, 99–100;
non-verbal communication and, 74;
organizational, 94; popular/mass, 110,
113; postmodernism and, 119; real,
121; regional, 116–17; reproduction of,
110–13; social organization and, 94–5;
symbolic interactionism and, 24, 98;
universals and, 95; variation in, 113–15;
working-class, 440; 'world', 283
Cumming, Elaine, and William Henry, 220
Cunliffe, Marcus, 427
curriculum, 335, 355–6; hidden, 131, 321,
336

D'Agostino, A. Frederico, 239–40
Dahrendorf, Rolf, 248

Darfur, 209
Darwin, Charles, 376, 440
Darwinism: imperialism and, 192
Davey Commission, 401
Davis, Bob, 357
Davis, Kathy, 149
Davis, Kingsley, 167, 256
Dawson, Lorne L., 393
death: disasters and, 39; political causes of,
59–60
d'Eaubonne, Françoise, 40
Debrix, Francois, and Alexander D., Barder,
84
decoding, 98–9
'definition of the situation', 24–5
Dei, George, 346
delinquency, 224
della Porta, Donatella, 480
D'Emilio, John, 173
democracy, 430, 431–3; in China, 431;
'deliberative', 443, 444, 447; direct,
431; dominant class and, 426;
postmodernism and, 446; public
opinion and, 441–2; representative,
431–3
demography: definition of, 35; new
insights into, 59–61; sociology and,
42–4
De Munck, V., and A. Korotayev,166
dependency: world-systems theory and,
280–2, 294
dependency ratio, 227
depression: age and, 233–4; class and,
264–5; gender and, 144–5; *see also*
Great Depression; mental health
deprivation: aging and, 228; relative, 266,
465–6
deregulation, economic, 456
de Sousa, Janet Tirelli Ponte, 239
Devadas, Vijay, 59
development: religion and, 389; sustainable,
41–2
deviance: feminist theories and, 10;
functions of, 14–17; secrecy and,
75–6; sequential model of, 67–8;
sexual, 155, 175–7
*Diagnostic and Statistical Manual of Mental
Disorders*, 176
dictatorships, 430
differential association theory, 262–1
DiMaggio, 114
disability, 212–13; age and, 236; media and,
407; sexuality and, 162–3
disasters, 39, 49, 50

discipline: bodily, 437; Foucault and,
11–12, 83–4, 437–40
discourse theory, 211
discrimination: international politics and,
290–1; racial socialization and, 321–2
disengagement theory, 220
distance: role, 71; schools and, 344–6;
social, 189–91, 284–5
divorce, 304, 310–11, 326–7; feminist
theories and, 10; gender and, 135–6,
140
Dobkowski, Michael N., and Isidor
Wallmann, 62
'double shift', 143–4, 145
double standard, 128, 156, 164–5, 166
dramaturgical approach, 68–9, 407
dropouts, school, 334, 340, 346
droughts, 39
drugs: religion and, 369
Dryden, Ken, 246
Dube, Rebecca, 22
Du Bois, W.E.B., 205
Du Gay, Paul, 90
Duman, M. Zeki, 297
Dunlap, Riley, et al., 62
Durkheim, Émile, 3; anomie and, 7–8; class
relations and, 246–7; culture and,
96–7; deviance and, 16–17; division
of labour and, 43; industrial societies
and, 255–6; Lenski and, 267; religion
and, 106, 363, 365, 369, 380, 385,
388, 393; religious forms of life and,
367–8; social movements and, 465;
solidarity and, 38, 455; suicide and,
12–13, 14
dyadic relationships, 80
dyads, 76–7
Dyson, Tim, et al., 62

Earth Hour, 51
eating disorders, 407–8
ecofeminism, 40
ecological-evolution theory, 266, 267–8
Economist, 405
economy: boom and bust, 248; command,
456; global, 282–4
Edmunds, June, and Bryan S. Turner, 239
education, 332–61; children and, 223;
critical theories and, 335–6; definition
of, 335; emancipatory, 357–8; equality
in, 354; formal, 335; functionalism
and, 335; funding for, 338, 341, 384;
gender and, 139, 339–40; informal,
335; inter-ethnic interaction and, 199;

mandatory, 223; new insights into, 357–8; religion and, 381; 'resistance', 357; sexual, 159, 180; social change and, 238; social mobility and, 20–1; symbolic interactionism and, 336; see also schools

Edwards, Gemma, 445

Edwards, Lisa, and Carwyn Jones, 150

Edwards, Richard, 249–50

Ehrenreich, Barbara, 260

Einstein, Gillian, and Margit Shildrick, 150

Elchardus, Mark, 27

Elder, Glen H., 227–9, 232

elderly people: abuse and, 236–7; chronic conditions and, 235–6; disengagement theory and, 220; health and, 234–6; interests of, 221; mental health and, 233; stereotypes of, 222; young people and, 229

elections: in Canada, 424, 436; democratic, 431–2; voter turnout and, 436–7

Elias, Norbert, 464–5

Eliot, T.S., 476

elites, 19–21

Elkin, Frederick, 348–9

Ellis, Henry Havelock, 171

Elster, Jon, 356

email: globalization and, 284–5

Emerson, Tiffany, 150

'emotion work', 324, 325–6

empire: definition of, 277, 282; multimedia, 400; pre-capitalist, 279, 282; see also imperialism; regions, nations, and empires

employment: education and, 338, 339–40; gender and, 131, 136, 137–9, 142–3, 150; health and, 264; present-day, 253–5; racial and ethnic groups and, 188–9, 205–6; see also labour; work

encoding, 98–9

Engels, Friedrich, 285–6

English language, 288–9

Enlightenment, 3

'enterprise society', 85

entrepreneurs: ethnic, 189; markets and, 457; moral, 9, 306–7

environment: see built environment; natural environment

environmental movement, 50–1, 472

equality: as US value, 426

Equal Voice, 434

equilibrium, social, 35–7, 41

Erdmans, Mary Patrice, 28

Erikson, Erik, 353–4

Erol, Pelin Onder, 60

Espiritu, Yen Le, 165–6

essentialism, 177, 211, 212

ethics: politics and, 444, 447

ethnic enclaves, 199, 200, 204

ethnic groups: definition of, 186; education and, 339–40, 355; gender violence and, 146–7; power and, 20–1; sexuality and, 165–6, 170; socialization and, 321–2; see also racial and ethnic groups

ethnicity: race and, 207

ethnocentrism, 107–9

ethnography, institutional, 147–9, 406

etiquette, 4, 464–5

Europe: colonization and, 191–3; preferred immigrants from, 193; world-systems theory and, 279–80

European Union, 297

Evans, Bethan, and Rachel Colls, 85

'exceptionalism', 426

exclusion principle, 252

exhibitionism, 176

exile, 60

expectations, 8–9; families and, 307; roles and, 70

exploitation: critical theories and, 248–9, 252; social constructionism and, 251; work and, 247

Fadden, Richard, 293

false consciousness, 252, 442–3; shopping and, 328

families, 302–31; aggression and, 350; attitudes toward, 312–13; census, 313; as consumption units, 306, 327–8; critical theories and, 306; cross-cultural trends in, 308–10; definition of, 304; diversity of, 304, 326; education and, 346–9; extended, 309, 313; feminist theories and, 306, 307, 315–16; forms of, 309–15; functionalism and, 305, 312; gender and, 136; as group, 67; modified extended, 313; new insights into, 326–8; nuclear, 309, 313; postmodernism and, 326–7; processes of, 314–15; single-parent, 144, 145, 310, 313, 326–7; size of, 304, 309; stability of, 326; symbolic interactionism and, 306–7; traditional, 312; violence and, 234, 236, 315, 320

famines, 36–7, 59–60

fascism, 318–19; dominant class and, 426; religion and, 378

fashion, 115

fathers: paid and unpaid work and, 325; television and, 323; see also parents

fear: media and, 398; 'mobilization' of, 84

Feixa, Carles, and Carmen Leccardi, 238

female genital mutilation, 146

feminism: bra-burning myth and, 473; as counter ideology, 442; first-wave, 468; types of, 129

feminist cultural theory, 405–6

feminist theories, 6, 9–10, 28, 127; age groups and, 222; environment and, 40; families and, 306, 307, 315–16; gender and, 160–1, 177–8; intersectionality and, 149; language and, 101–2; media and, 132–4, 135, 405–6, 410–11; pornography and, 150, 168, 179–80; sexuality and, 160–1; types of, 128–9; work and class and, 250

fertility: immigration and, 193; rates of, 45, 46–9, 227

fetishism, 176; commodity, 415; consumer, 87–8

Figueroa, Jose Antonio, 211

film: postmodern, 119; in US, 404

financiers, criminal, 266

Fingerson, Laura, 166

'first-past-the-post' system, 431–2

Fives, Allyn, 446

flag, Confederate, 213

Fleras, Augie, and Jean Lock Knuz, 420

Florida, Richard, 173

'flow of spaces', 58–9

folkways, 97

food: population and, 267; supply of, 35–7, 51

food movement, 476–7

Fortin, N.M., and M. Huberman, 140

Foucault, Michel, 83–6, 240, 417, 475; discourse theory and, 211; sexuality and, 161–2, 178, 179; social control and, 11–12, 14, 27, 83–6; surveillance-as-punishment and, 437–40

'Fourth World', 59

Fox News, 386, 400, 402, 412–13; 'North', 441

framing theory, 467

Frank, Andre Gunther, 294

Frankfurt School, 18, 97–8, 120, 406; Habermas and, 445

Freedman, Jonathan, 413, 420

Freeman, Linton C., 90

French Canadians: multiculturalism and, 203–4

French language, 203, 288–9

French Revolution, 3

Freud, Sigmund, 131, 176, 319, 379–80

frotteurism, 176

frustration–aggression hypothesis, 413

'F-scale', 318–19

Fuchs, Christian, and Marisol Sandoval, 417–18

Fullmer, Elise M., et al., 241

functionalism, 6–8, 14–17; age groups and, 220; cities and, 37–8; class and work and, 247–8; culture and, 96–7; education and, 335; families and, 305, 307–8, 312; gender and, 127; language and, 101; media and, 397; natural environment and, 39; politics and, 425–6; population and, 35–6; prostitution and, 167; racial and ethnic groups and, 186–7; regions and nations and, 278; religion and, 366; roles and, 73; sexuality and, 158; social movements and, 465–6; symbolic interactionism and, 77–8

functions: latent, 7, 335; manifest, 7, 14, 335

fundamentalism, evangelical, 387

funding: Canadian content and, 402; education and, 338, 341, 384

fusion approach, 3–4, 475, 478; Bellah and, 388; Castells and, 59; Giddens and, 26–7; Habermas and, 21; Lenski and, 268; Smith and, 149

Gaard, Greta, 40

Gail, Lauren, 182

Galileo, 377

Gane, Nicholas, 417

gangs, 77–9, 298

Gans, Herbert, 38, 398–400, 403, 418

Garcia Marquez, Gabriel, 211

Gardiner, Judith Kegan, 152

Garland, David, 440

Garreau, Joel, 300

Gartner, Rosemary, 146

Gauthier, Alain, 415

gays and lesbians: identity and, 240–1; marriage and, 156, 310; see also homosexuality; sexuality

Gazdar, Haris, 59–60

Gazso-Windle, Amber, and Julie Ann McMullin, 143

Gemeinschaft/Gesellschaft, 387

gender, 124–53; abuse and, 161; adolescence and, 342; age at marriage and, 310; aging and, 222, 235; appearance and, 134–5; Butler and, 177–9; capitalism and, 127, 142–3; crime and, 136–7; critical theories and, 127; definition of, 126; education and, 139, 339–40; experiences and, 10; feminist theories and, 160–1, 177–8; functionalism and, 127, 305; Giddens and, 27; health and, 144–5, 150; homophobia and, 175; immigration and, 141–2; income and, 138–41; inequality and, 9–10; intersectionality and, 28; labour market and, 188; language and, 101–2; media and, 132–4, 135, 405–11; paid and unpaid work and, 142–5, 325; pedophilia and, 177; politics and, 433–4; population and, 43–4; postmodern theories and, 28, 29; prostitution and, 158–9; regimes and, 131; relationship dissolution and, 135–6; religion and, 365; same-sex marriage and, 310; 'sex ed' and, 180; sexuality and, 171; social constructionist approaches and, 128; socialization and, 307, 315–16, 320–1; suicide and, 13; symbolic interactionism and, 127–8; unions and, 258; violence and, 146–7, 161, 236, 320; voyeurism and, 176; wage gap and, 139–40; work and class and, 250; see also women

gendercide, 44–5

genealogical approach, 83, 86, 161

General Electric, 400

generalized other, 308, 461, 462

generations: 'boomerang', 224; differences among, 219; 'global', 239; Mannheim and, 237–8

genetics: race and, 206–7

genocide, 209–10

geography: environmental, 39; human, 53–4

Gerbner, G., and L. Gross, 398

gerontology, 239; 'Foucauldian', 240

Gerth, H., and C.W. Mills, 149

gestures, 74, 102, 103

Gettysburg Address, 238

Giddens, Anthony, 26–7, 248, 475

Gilbreth, Frank, 251–2

glass ceiling, 136

Glastra, Folke, and Paul Vedder, 112

globalization, 59, 276–7, 282–300; Canadian culture and, 403, 404–5; capitalism and, 278; characteristics of, 283; definition of, 282; media and, 404–5; social movements and, 472–4; work and, 253

Global Media Monitoring Project, 410

'global overshoot', 41

global warming, 52

goal attainment function, 425

Goddu, Jenn, 133

Goffman, Erving, 22–3, 25, 476; identity and, 68–9, 71, 76, 407; total institutions and, 317, 439

Goldenberg, N., 370

Goldfarb, Jeffrey C., 121

Goldstein, Warren S., 388–9

Goldthorpe, John H., 269

Goode, William, 308–10, 312

Goodwin, Stefan, 63

Gore, Al, 51

government: federal, 434–5; minority, 436; see also state

'governmentality', 84, 85

Governors General, 25, 410, 433

Grabb, Edward, and James Curtis, 117, 300

Graber, Doris A., 300

Gracia, Jorge J.E., 214

grades: education and, 334–5; inflation of, 348

Gramsci, Antonio, 97, 440

Granovetter, Mark, 79

Great Depression: children of, 227–9

Greater Metropolitan Area, 56

Greece, 279, 431

Green, Adam Isaiah, 180

Green, Alan G., and David Green, 194

Green, Penny, and Tony Ward, 475

Green Party of Canada, 435, 472

Greenpeace, 51

'greenwashing', 40

greetings: culture and, 74

Griffin, Nick, 191

Grindstaff, Davin, 178

Groeling, Tim, 402

Grosfoguel, Ramon, 448

groups, 66–7; 'charter', 20, 21; deviant, 67–8; diasporic, 200; interest/lobby, 432; small, 76–83; status, 8, 21, 110, 253; see also racial and ethic groups

growth ethic, 39

Gruner, Sabine, 112

Grusky, David B., and Kim A. Weeden, 269

guilt, collective, 379

Gulf War, 415–16
Gunaratne, Shelton A., 295–6
Guppy, Neil, and Scott Davies, 360
Gusfield, Joseph, 468–70
Gustavsen, Bjorn, 476
Gutenberg, Johannes, 108

Haberman, Jürgen, 18, 21, 27, 270, 475, 443–5, 447; Marx and, 21; media and, 405
habitus, 112–13
Hacker, Andrew, 338, 339
hadiths, 377
Hagan, John, and Bill McCarthy, 231–3
Haine, Victor Y., III, et al., 145
Halasz, Shane, 208
Hall, John R., 444
Hall, Stuart, 98–9
Hamlin, Cynthia Lins, 150
Hammond, Judith, 130
Hammurabi, Code of, 437
Handel, Gerald, 330
Hanisch, Carol, 473
Hansen, Claus D., and Johan H. Andersen, 325
happiness: age and, 233; religion and, 371
Hardin, Garrett, 39
Harper, Stephen, 441
Hay, Thorkild Holmboe, 85
health: age and, 233–6; class and, 264–5; gender and, 144–5, 150; population and, 44; work and, 325–6; see also mental health
health-care system, 235–6
Healy, Tom, 355
Heath, Joseph, 444
Hecht, Richard D., 387
Hegel, Georg W.F., 97
Heinlein, Robert, 73
Henry, Frances, and Carol Tator, 214
Henry, Stuart, 358
Herodotus, 5
Hesmondhalgh, David, and Sarah Baker, 325–6
heteronormativity, 170–3
heterosexism, 170
Heterosexual–Homosexual Rating Scale, 171–2
heterosexuality: as norm, 155, 170
Hevia, James L., 211
Heyes, Cressida J., 85
hijab, 141
Hinduism, 382
Hines, Sally, 180

Hirsch, E.D., 114–15
Hirschi, Travis, 224
Hitler, Adolf, 430
Hobsbawm, Eric, 301
Hochschild, Arlie, 143, 324–6
Hockey, Jenny, 241, 475
Holyfield, Lori, et al., 213
Homans, George, 256, 425–6, 450, 463
homelessness: health and, 264; youth and, 231–3
home-schooling, 346
homophobia, 173–5; schools and, 351
homosexuality, 169–75; acceptance of, 159, 173–5; in Canada, 172–3; as deviance, 155, 157; Foucault and, 162; heteronormativity and, 170–3; identity and, 240–1; incidence of, 164; pedophilia and, 177; in US, 169–70
horizontal organizational networks, 58
Horkheimer, Max, 18–19, 97–8, 120, 287
Hornbacher, Annette, and Volker Gottowik, 389
Horstmann, Alexander, 389
household: as term, 313
housework, 129–30, 142–5, 147, 324
Howarth, David, 210
Howkins, Mary Ball, 150
Hughes, Everett C., 62, 67
Huizinga, Johan, 460
human development stage theory, 353–4
Human Genome Project, 206–7
human rights: in China, 431; gender and, 136; legislation and, 290; media and, 405
Humphreys, Laud, 169
Hunter, Rosemary, 446
Huss, Boaz, 390–1
Husserl, Edmund, 445
Hutu, 209, 210
hyperreality, 415–17

I, 308
Ianni, Francis, 231
identity: adolescent, 342; age and, 239–41; current debates on, 28–9; definition of, 70; education and, 357–8; ethnic, 187; flawed, 317–20; formation of, 71; gender and, 320–1; multiple, 60; national, 202, 297; roles and, 66, 68–74; sexual, 177–9, 240–1; stigma and, 22–3; work and, 250, 254–5
ideologies, 440–3; action and, 442–3; counter, 442, 466; critical theories and, 18, 21; culture and, 97; definition

of, 427; dominant, 366, 440–1, 466; liberal, 440–1; media and, 406, 408; politics and, 440–1; postmodernism and, 10; publics and, 441–2; radical, 442; reformist, 442; religion and, 106; social movements and, 466; traditional family, 306–7
Ignatow, Gabriel, 112
'immanent reversal', 416
Immerman, Ronald, and Wade Mackey, 305
immigrants: business class, 196; education and, 334, 340; family class, 196; number of, 185
immigration: aging population and, 226; categories of, 196–7; credentials and, 189; critical race theory and, 212; employment and, 189; families and, 313; gender and, 141–2; gender violence and, 146–7; intergroup marriage and, 191; point system, 195; policy on, 193–4; population and, 44, 60; present-day, 195–7; in Quebec, 288; religion and, 374–6, 387; settlement and, 197; source countries and, 195–7
imperialism: capitalism and, 277–82; cultural, 283–4; economic, 281; new, 478; race and ethnic groups and, 191–3, 211; see also empire
'impression management', 76
India, 195
individualism: environment and, 39; gender and, 151; industrial societies and, 255; religion and, 385, 387, 388; sexuality and, 156; social control and, 84
industrialization: adolescents and, 342; families and, 306, 308–10
Industrial Revolution, 3
inequalities: Canadian mosaic and, 20–1; computer technology and, 254; critical theory and, 8, 18; current debates on, 28–9; education and, 334, 339–41; families and, 315, 319–20, 323; feminist theories and, 9–10; gender, 126–7; overpopulation and, 37; relations among, 28; sociology and, 6; streaming and, 344; universities and, 337
infidelity, marital, 157, 158, 166
information: distorted, 458–60; Internet as market for, 456; rumour as, 458–60; social networks and, 79–80
information society, 57, 58–9

Inglehart, Ronald, 273

innovation: crime as, 266; technical, 266–7

institutional completeness, 200, 355

integration: cultural, 107–9; schools and, 351–4

intelligentsia: ideologies and, 442

interaction: definition of, 8–9; *see also* symbolic interactionism

interculturalism, 203–4

interdependence, 252, 454–8

International Earth Day, 51

International Monetary Fund, 262

Internet: bullying and, 349; infidelity and, 166; information and, 58–9; as information market, 456; news and, 396

intersectionality, 10, 28, 149; Lenski and, 268

Inuit, 203, 227

inverse interdependence principal, 252

investment: compensation and, 247–8

Iran, 293; revolution in, 389–90

Iraq, 210, 293; food supply in, 59–60; violence in, 475; war in, 383

Ireland, 60

Islam: adaptability of, 377; capitalism and, 298; Iran and, 389–90; media portrayals of, 416; politics and, 378, 389–90; Said and, 211; *see also* Muslims

Islamists, 211

Israel, 210, 211, 378; protest in, 475

Italy, 389

Jackson, Janet, 383

James, Allison, 241

James, Royson, 346

Japan: fascism in, 378; violence in, 413

jazz musicians, 67–8

Jean, Michaëlle, 25, 410, 433

Jencks, Christopher, and David Riesman, 336–9

Jewish people, 193; stereotype of, 208; *see also* Judaism

Johnson, David, 240

Johnson, Jennifer A., and Megan S. Johnson, 130

Johnson, Paul J., 181

Johnson, Victoria, 58

'joker', 77

jokes: gender and, 132–3

journalism: as filter, 398–400; narrow, 403; *see also* media; news

Judaism, 390–1; politics and, 378; *see also* Jewish people

Judeo-Christian religions, 379, 381–2

Jung, Dietrich, 211

Kabbalah, 390–1

Kadison, Richard, and Theresa Foy DiGeronimo, 360

Kanduc, Zoran, 327–8

Kant, Immanuel, 387–8

Kanter, Rosabeth, 137–8, 145

Karasek, R., and T. Theorell, 265

Katz, Elihu, and Paul F. Lazarsfeld, 421

Kaufman, Michael, 153

Kay, F.M., and J. Brockman, 139

Keat, Russell, 444

Keller, Heidi, and Carolin Demuth, 327

Kellner, Douglas, 416

Kent Commission, 401–2

Kerr, Ron, and Sarah Robinson, 112

Kettler, David, and Volker Meja, 237

Keynesianism, 287

Kilbourne, Jean, 160

Kim, Kyung-Man, 112

Kimmel, Michael S., 30, 152

Kimura, Shisei, 297

Kinsey, Alfred, 164, 171–2, 173

Kipling, Rudyard, 192

Kirk, John, 270

Kirkpatrick, G., 120

Kitschelt, Herbert, 472

Kittler, Friedrich, 417

Klugkist, Dagmar Adina Inga, 358

knowledge: culture and, 114–15; embodied, 147, 149; Foucault and, 83–4; postmodernism and, 11; 'production/translation' of, 336

Knox, Hannah, et al., 58

Koedt, Anna, 172

Kosovo Muslims, 209

kowtow, 211

Krassas, Nicole, 160

Kristjanson-Gural, David, 447

Kuhn, Thomas, 378–9

Kurnik, Andrej, 446–7

Kymlicka, Will, 203

Laaksonen, Helena T., and Erükka Oinonen, 238

labelling theory, 9, 67–8, 71

labour: class and, 251–3; clerical, 251; division of, 43, 255–6; emotional, 139, 324, 325–6; family division of, 305; gendered division of, 127, 142–3, 144; modern division of, 279–80; postmodernism and, 447; reserve army of, 142, 248–9; skilled immigrant, 196

labour market: immigration and, 193; primary, 188–9; racial and ethnic groups and, 188–9; secondary, 188–9

Lacan, Jacques, 417

land claim settlements, 203

Langman, Lauren, 298

language: in Canada, 288–9; culture and, 101–3; fashion and, 115; gender-neutral, 101–2; racist, 188

Laqueur, Thomas W., 182

Lareau, Annette, 323

Latin America: West and, 211

Lau, Raymond W.K., 418–19

Lauder, Hugh, et al., 360

Laumann, Edward, et al., 163–4, 182

Lavoisier, A.L., 378

law: rule of, 429–30; *see also* legislation

Lazarsfeld, Paul, 354

Lazzarato, Maurizio, 85

leaders: charismatic, 379; groups and, 77, 78–9; social networks and, 81–2, 83

Lee, Hyun-Ji, 327

Lee, Ji-Youn, et al., 268

legislation: anorexia and, 408; capitalism and, 251; power of, 434–5

legislature, 431

Leiss, William, 279

Lemert, Charles, and Ann Branaman, 22

Lemke, Jay, 84

Lenin, V.I., 277

Lenski, Gerhard, 248, 266–8

lesbianism, 169

lesbians and gays: identity and, 240–1; marriage and, 156, 310; *see also* homosexuality; sexuality

less-developed countries: globalization and, 298; immigration from, 194, 195–7; population and, 48, 55, 60

Levinson, Paul, 420

Lévi-Strauss, Claude, 478

Lewis, Oscar, 259–61, 264

liberal-democratic state, 430, 431–3

Liberal Party, 435

Lieberson, Stanley, 115, 122

lies, 76

life course perspective, 227–9, 240, 241

life expectancy, 227

'life-story telling', 28, 148

'lifeworld', 445; colonization of, 444

Lillbacka, Ralf, 355

Lima, Marcos Costa, 448

Limits to Growth, The, 40–2
Lincoln, Abraham, 238
Lindenberg, Siegwart, 356
Linton, Ralph, 73
Lipset, Seymour Martin, 116, 425, 426–7, 428, 435
literacy, 108; cultural, 114–15
Livingstone, D.W., 360
localism, 58, 59
localization, 59
location: environment and, 53–4, 56; social, 237, 238
logos, 119
Longino, Charles F., 241
looking-glass self, 71, 308
Loyal, Steven, 26
Luckmann, Thomas, 87
Lui Xiaobo, 431
Luken, Paul C., and Suzanne Vaughan, 148
Lumb, Lionel, 208
Luther, Martin, 105
lynching, 208–9
Lyon, David, 418

McCormack, Thelma, 427
McDaniel, Susan A., 84, 331
McGuire, Meredith B., 369, 392
McIntosh, Mary, 433
'McJobs', 254
MacKay, Charles, 480
MacKay, Peter, 409
MacKinnon, Catharine, 151
McLuhan, Marshall, 397, 406, 411, 416, 417
McNair, Brian, 357
McRobbie, Angela, 122
macrosociology, 6
Madoff, Bernie, 266
magazines, 400
'male gaze', 405, 409
Malloy, Jonathan, 441
Malthus, Thomas, 35–7, 41, 59, 267
managers: capitalism and, 253, 262–3
Manifesto of the Communist Party, 285–7
Mann, Susan A., and Jeanne Barnard, 326
manners, 4, 464–5
Mannheim, Karl, 237–9
Manwaring, Max G., 298
Mao Zedong, 431
Marcuse, Herbert, 18, 97–8, 162
marijuana, 9, 67–8
Marin, Noemi, 60
marketing: niche, 411–12; postmodern, 88; research and, 412

marketplace, 455–6; control of, 456
marriage: age at, 310; functionalism and, 305; infidelity and, 158, 166–7; intergroup, 190–1; interracial, 186, 198; rates of, 309–10; same-sex, 156, 172, 174, 310; traditionalist religion and, 306; in US, 163
Marshall, T.H., 479
Martelli, Stefano, 418
Martin, Karin A., 170–1
Martin, Randal, 450
Marx, Karl, 3, 8, 18, 21; alienation and, 256; Bourdieu and, 111; class conflict and, 248–9, 251; class relations and, 246–7; *Communist Manifesto* and, 285–7; conflict and, 19, 20; culture and, 97; Lenski and, 267; religion and, 363, 366, 388; Veblen and, 110; Wallerstein and, 282
Marxism: gender and, 127, 129, 147, 151; Habermas and, 443, 444; modern, 28; postmodernism and, 88; social control and, 85; world-systems theory and, 296
masochism, sexual, 176
mass communication: definition of, 396; *see also* media
mass media: definition of, 396; *see also* media
'material density', 255
materialism: environment and, 39
material settings: society and, 32–63
Mattachine Society, 173
Matza, David, 224
Me, 308
Mead, G.H., 24, 25, 72–3, 308, 462
Meadows, Donella H., et al., 40–2
means of production, 247
'Mean World Syndrome', 398
media, 394–421; aging and, 241; alternative, 410–11, 417; Canadian content and, 402–3; colonialism and, 213; critical theories and, 417–18; culture and, 107–9, 113; current debates on, 29; distortion by, 22, 52, 404, 405, 408, 414–17; fathers and, 323; filtering and, 398–400; functionalism and, 397; gender and 132–4, 135, 405–6, 410–11; globalization and, 283–4; homogenization and, 411–12; influence of, 412–13; mainstream, 396; modern critical theories and, 21; new insights into, 417–19; new, 396,

401; ownership and, 399, 400–2, 404; paper-based, 396, 411; postmodernism and, 11, 416–17, 418; propaganda and, 290; school shootings and, 351; sexuality and, 160, 168; social problems and, 414; terrorism and, 293; under-representation and, 408; violence and, 398, 412–13; visible minorities and, 208; working class and, 260
Media Awareness Network, 413
median income, 264
media system, 445
'medium is the message', 397, 411
megacities, 55
Meizel, Katherine, 386
Meldrim, H., 166
mental health: age and, 233–4; children and, 347; class and, 264–5; *see also* depression
Merico, Maurizio, 238
meritocracy: education and, 334–5, 337
Merrin, William, 415
Merton, Robert, 14, 256; anomie and, 16, 38, 163; crime and, 266; latent/manifest functions and, 7; science and, 377; strain theory and, 137
Meyer, David S., et al., 480
microsociology, 7
Middle East, 278; globalization and, 298
Milanovic, Branko, 264
Milgram, Stanley, 456–7
Milkie, Melissa, 325
Mills, A.J., 139
Mills, C. Wright, 248, 324, 445
Mills, Charles, 28
minorities: 'middleman', 189; 'national', 203; visible, 190–1, 208; *see also* ethnic groups; racial and ethnic groups
Minow, Newton, 411
Miranda, F.E., and J. de Oliveira Moreira, 60
Mirowsky, John, and Catherine E. Ross, 91
misogyny, 168
Mitsuhashi, Koji, 325
mobility, social, 20–1, 269
mode of production, 97
modernism: postmodernism and, 10–11
modernity: late, 27; 'multiple', 388, 389; religion and, 388, 389
modernization: class and, 426; media and, 397; 'reflexive', 49–50; theory, 278, 294, 295, 298
Mohammed, 377
monarchy, constitutional, 431

money: crime and, 15–16, 262
Monière, Denis, 133
monogamy, 304
Montreal: inter-ethnic interaction and, 199
Moor, Nienke, et al., 267
Moore, Barrington, Jr, 272, 280, 425, 426, 450, 443
'moral density', 255
moral panic, 168–9
moral philosophy, 5
more-developed countries: population and, 48
mores, 97
mosaic, vertical, 20–1
mothers: children's sexuality and, 170–1; focal, 325; paid and unpaid work and, 325; see also parents
MSNBC (television network), 413
Muhajarine, Nazeem, and Bonnie Janzen, 144
Mulders, Joera, 389
Mulinari, Diana, and Kerstin Sandell, 27
multiculturalism, 185, 201–4; families and, 304; religion and, 365
murder: gender and, 137, 146; lust, 177
Murdoch, Rupert, 400
Murdock, George, 95
Murray, Stephen, 169–70
music: club, 119; religion and, 386; 'world', 213
Muslims, 141; globalization and, 298; in Iraq, 210; in Kosovo, 209; propaganda and, 290; terrorism and, 293; see also Islam
Mustafa, Naheed, 141
Myrdal, Karl Gunnar, 205–6, 210

names, first, 115
Nathanson, Jessica, 180
nation: culture and, 288–9; definition of, 277, 282; state and, 282; see also regions, nations, and empires; state
National Film Board (NFB), 400
nationalism: religion and, 106, 378, 382–3, 387
National Mental Health Project, 347
natural environment, 33, 34, 50–3; critical theories and, 39; feminist theories and, 40; functionalism and, 39; new insights into, 59–61; non-renewable resources and, 53; other species and, 51; symbolic interactionism and, 39–40
nature: cornucopia view of, 39

Nazism, 318–19, 378, 430
NBC (television network), 398, 400, 402
necrophilia, 177
negotiations, interpersonal, 24
Nelson, Claudia, and Michelle H. Martin,182
neo-liberalism, 85, 88, 294, 328; media and, 403, 404; social movements and, 477
Ness, Gayl D., and Michael M. Low, 63
'netiquettes', 59
nets, 'biased/random', 80
networks: rumour and, 458; social, 79–83, 456–8
neurosis: religion as, 379–80
'neutralization': techniques of, 224
New Democratic Party (NDP), 435
new religious movements (NRMs), 365, 383–4
news: filtering and, 398–400; 'improvised', 458–9; influence on, 398–400, 418–19; negative, 399; political, 402, 403–4; see also journalism; media
News Corporation, 400
new social movements (NSMs), 467, 471–2
newspapers, Canadian, 401–2; see also media
news services, 401
Newsweek, 398, 405
Nickel, Patricia Mooney, 447
9/11 attacks, 386, 387, 416, 447
Nine O'clock Service (NOS), 119
Nisanci, Esnar, 297–8
'no-care zones', 239
node, 80
non-governmental organizations (NGOs), 283
'normal': stigma and, 22
normality: Foucault's view of, 83–6; postmodernism and, 11, 161–3; sexuality and, 171–2
norms: appearance, 134–5, 406–7; culture and, 96–7; families and, 307; functionalism and, 7–8; science and, 377; sexual, 155, 156, 157
North American Free Trade Agreement (NAFTA), 404
North-Jones, Margaret A., 328
North Korea, 293
Northwest Territories: fertility in, 227
Nunavut, 203; fertility in, 227

Oakley, Ann, 129–30, 143
Obama, Barack, 60, 437

obesity, 135
objectivity: postmodernism and, 11
occupations: gender and, 131, 137–8, 139, 140; socialization and, 323
oil spill, 50
Olofsson, Per-Olof, 149
Olsen, Dennis, 20
Ondrejkovic, Peter, and Jana Majercikova, 239
opinion, public, 403–4, 441–2
Orientalism, 210–12
Ortiz-Negron, Laura L., 418
Orwell, George, 430
Outsiders, 67–8
overpopulation, 35–7
Ozkaplan, Nurcan, 325
Ozkisi, Zeynep Gulcin, 213

Paic, Zarko, 295
Palestine, 210, 211, 475
Pallister-Wilkins, Polly, 475
Palmer, Susan, 383–4, 393
Panitch, Leo, and Colin Leys, 478
panopticon, 11, 438
paradigms: shift in, 378–9; sociological, 3–4
paraphilia, 175–7
parents: authoritarian, 319; children and, 229; education and, 346–9; lone, 144, 145, 310, 313, 326–7; socialization and, 315–16; see also families; fathers; mothers
Parent-Teacher Association, 348
Park, Robert, 24, 198
Parliament, 431
parochialism, cultural, 192
Parsons, Talcott, 14, 256, 481; family and, 305, 307; gender and, 127; politics and, 425, 427, 450; religion and, 388; roles and, 72, 73; Weber and, 104
particularism: gender and, 151
parties: Weber's view of, 253; see also political parties
Pascal, Blaise, 446
patriarchy, 10, 127, 129, 306; pornography and, 168; religion and, 306, 365; violence and, 146–7
patriotism: religion and, 382–3
'pattern variables', 427
Pedersen, Helena, 212
Pederson, Jorgen, 444
pedophilia, 176, 177
Pedraza Gomez, Zandra, 327
Péladeau, Pierre Karl, 441
pensions, 239

performativity, 178–9
perspective: age and, 237–9
petit bourgeoisie, 252–3
Petras, James, and Henry Veltmeyer, 270
Phillipson, Chris, and Simon Biggs, 239
Phipps, Sean, 117
phlogiston theory, 378
Pinnelli, Antonella, et al., 152
Plato, 3
play: culture as, 460–1
Plummer, Ken, 180
pluralism: 'active/passive', 387; democratic, 432–3, 436
Poland: ethnic relations in, 210; immigrants from, 197–8; intelligentsia in, 442
police: racial profiling and, 207–8
political conflict theory, 467
political economy perspective, 397–8
political movements, 86
political parties, 433, 435, 471
political process approach, 465
political science: political sociology and, 423, 427–8
political system: as social management, 425
politics, 422–51; authority and, 428–30; in Canada, 434–8; class, 254–5, 469–70; critical theories and, 425, 426, 443, 446–8; definition of, 424; expressive, 469; functionalism and, 425–6; gender and, 433–4; identity, 254–5, 467–8; international, 290–1; media and, 398–9, 402, 403–4, 405; new insights into, 446–8; postmodernism and, 443, 446–8; religion and, 378; rural–urban relations and, 54; 'small-group', 425
Pollmann, Andreas, 112
polls, 403–4, 441–2
polygamy, 304
population, 33, 35–7; age and, 44; aging, 48; checks on, 35; cities and, 44, 54–6; critical theories and, 36–7; dense, 43; functionalism and, 35–6; gender and, 43; growth in, 45–9; health and, 44; history and, 44–5; limits to, 40–2; optimum, 36; production and, 267; size of, 42–3; world, 45–9
population composition, 43–4
population pyramid, 44–5
Population Reference Bureau, 52, 54
pornography, 150, 157, 167–9, 357; feminist theories and, 150, 168, 179–80
Porter, John, 20–1, 199, 214, 337, 427
positivism, 10, 26–7

post-industrialism, 253–5
Postman, Leo, 458, 459, 460
postmodernism, 6, 10–12, 27–9; aging and, 239–41; class and work and, 269–70; culture and, 119; families and, 326–7; feminism and, 129; gender and, 150–1; Giddens and, 27; media and, 416–17, 418; politics and, 443, 446–8; population and, 59–61; regions and nations and, 297–8; religion and, 388–91; risk and, 49–50; sexuality and, 161–3, 179–80; social movements and, 477–8; social structures and, 86–8
'post-queer' study, 180
poverty: cities and, 38; culture of, 259–61; 'feminization' of, 222; gender and, 140, 222; health and, 264–5; overpopulation and, 37; prostitution and, 159; terrorism and, 292
Powell, Jason, 178, 241
power: age and, 225, 229; consumption and, 110; critical theory and, 19–21; definition of, 427; families and, 314–15; Foucault and, 83–6, 437–40; postmodernism and, 11–12; regions and nations and, 281; sexuality and, 161–2; types of, 466; Weber and, 252; work and class and, 248–9, 251
'praxis', 476–7
predestination, 105
Pregowski, Michael P., 58–9
prejudice: racial and ethnic, 207–8; socialization and, 317–20
Preston, John, 28
Price, Joseph L., 385
printing, 108–9
prisons, 11–12, 83–4, 437
production of culture perspective, 99–100
'profane': sacred and, 367–8, 369, 386
professions: associations and, 256; health and, 265
professors, 336–7
progressivism: in US, 387
Prohibition, 468
projections, 319
proletariat, 8, 251, 286–7
pronatalism, 173
propaganda, 290, 442
prostitution, 157, 180; families and, 327; feminist theories and, 160; marriage and, 158, 166–7; theories and, 158–9
'prosumer' concept, 418
Protagoras, 172

protest, 474, 475; theories of, 465–8
Protestantism: in Canada, 372; media and, 418; politics and, 378; work ethic and, 104–5, 366–7, 440
Proust, Marcel, 111
provinces: age in, 226–7; conflict and, 287–9; powers of, 434–5; union membership and, 258; see also specific provinces
psychology: deviance and, 15; suicide and, 12
public, 441–2
public speaking, 66
publishers: conglomerates and, 401
punishment: capital, 208–9; Foucault and, 437–40; informal control and, 462
Purcell, Mark, 86
Putnam, Robert D., 480

Quebec, 288–9; Battle of, 427; Church and, 381; culture in, 117; education in, 334; marriage in, 310; multiculturalism and, 203–4; youth voting in, 437
queer theory, 150, 177, 178, 180
Quiet Revolution, 381

Rabot, Jean-Martin, 87, 417
race: definition of, 186; postmodern theories and, 28, 29; socialization and, 321–2
racial and ethnic groups, 184–215; abuse and violence and, 208–10; background of, 191–3; critical theories and, 187–8; education and, 339–40, 345–6; functionalism and, 186–7; interaction among, 198–200; labour market and, 188–9; new insights into, 212–13; prejudice and discrimination and, 207–8; structural theory and, 188–9; symbolic interactionism and, 188; social distance and, 189–91
racialization, 187–8, 206–7
racial profiling, 188, 207–8
racial variations, 186
racism, 186; immigration policy and, 187, 195; racialization and, 206–7; recent examples of, 191; socialization and, 317–20; in US, 205, 208–9
radical colonial critical theory, 448
Radio-Québec, 400
Raelians, 383–4
Ramayana, 382
rank: age and, 230

rape, 277

Rapoport, Anatol, 80

rational choice theory, 15–16, 356

rationality, communication, 443

rationalization: religion and, 381–2

rational–legal authority, 19, 376, 428, 429–30

rational reconstruction, 444

rebellions: in Canada, 427

recession (2008), 263, 269, 294, 456

Redstone, Sumner, 401

refugees, 196–7

Regina Manifesto, 442

region: culture and, 288–9; definition of, 277, 282

regions, nations, and empires, 274–301; conflict and, 275, 281–2, 287–94; critical theories and, 277–8, 285–7; dependency and, 280–2; functionalism and, 278; globalization and, 276–7, 282–300; international politics and, 290–1; postmodernism and, 297–8; technology and, 277, 284–5; violence and, 291–4

Rehmann, Jan C., 88

Reiche, Reimut, 179

Reitz, Charles, 270

relationship dissolution, 310–11; *see also* divorce

relations of production, 247

relativism, cultural, 107, 298

religion, 5, 362–93; adaptability and, 377; capitalism and, 104–5; civil, 382–3, 385–9; 'comparative', 384; critical theories and, 366; culture and, 106–7, 119; definition of, 106; definitional problems and, 369–70; ecological evolution and, 267–8; education and, 384; empire and, 282; forms of life and, 367–8; functionalism and, 366; gender and, 146; invisible, 87; literacy and, 108; media and, 418; meditative, 379; new insights into, 388–91; as 'opiate of the masses', 366; organized, 369–70; patriarchy and, 306, 365; politics and, 381; postmodernism and, 388–91; private practice of, 373; race and ethnic groups and, 191–3; scholarship and, 377; science and, 371, 376–9; sexuality and, 161–2; state, 376; suicide and, 12–13; in US, 426

religiosity, 373–6; index of, 373–4

Rennett, Michael, 417

representation: female, 433–4; proportional, 432

repression: authoritarian personality and, 319; sexual, 379–80

republic, 431

research, action, 476

reserve army of labour, 142, 248–9

resocialization, 317

resource mobilization approach, 465, 466–7

responsibility: risk society and, 50

retirement, 220

revolution: academic, 336–9; American, 426, 427; Chinese cultural, 431; digital, 416; French, 3; Industrial, 3; in Iran, 389–90; Quiet, 381; scientific, 378–8; working-class, 287

rewards: informal control and, 463

ridings, 431; size of, 436

Rief, S., 121

rights: civil, 205, 448; gay and lesbian, 172–4; *see also* human rights

Riley, Alexander, 386

risk: youth and, 224–5

risk society, 49–50

rituals, 476; religious, 367, 369

Roberge, Jonathan, 476

Robinson, Sandra, 351

role conflict, 74–5

role distance, 71

role embracement, 71

role exit, 71

role-making, 73

roles, 7, 66, 68–74; change in, 72–3; compartmentalization and, 75; conflicts and, 74–5; expressive, 305; groups and, 77; identity and, 70–1; instrumental, 305; new, 73; prioritizing, 75; sex, 175; 'sick', 72

role-set, 71–2

role strain, 74–5; gender and, 145

role-taking, 72

Roman Catholicism: in Canada, 372; child abuse and, 414; inflexibility of, 377; in Italy, 389; media and, 418; politics and, 378; in Quebec, 381

Roman Empire, 282

Romero, Mary, 212

Roof, Wade Clark, 385

Rooke, Alison, 178

Roscigno, Vincent J., 273

Rosewarne, Stuart, 60

Ross, Stephanie, 477

Rostboll, Christian F., 447

Roth, Klas, 357, 444

'routinization of charisma', 19, 379

rule of law, 429–30

rules: enforcers and violators of, 68; social, 67–8

rumours, 458–60

rural–urban relations, 54–5

Russell-Brown, Pauline, 165

Russia, 389

Ruzzo, Carlo, 474

Rwanda, 209

Sabo, Anne G., 150, 179–80

'sacred': profane and, 367–8, 369, 386; secular and, 376

sadism, sexual, 176

sadomasochism, 176

Said, Edward, 210–12, 448

Sakai, Lawrence J., 475

Salerno, Roger A., 88

Sampson, Robert J., and John Laub, 15

Sangster, Joan, 29

Sapir, Edward, and Benjamin Whorf, 102

Saskatchewan, 435

Satzewich, Vic, and Nikolaos Liodakis, 214

Saunders, Doug, 264

Sauvé, Jeanne, 433

Savagnone, Giuseppe, 389

Savchenko, Andrew, 296

Sayer, Liana C., et al., 325

Schachter, Harvey, 284

Schoenfeld, Clay, et al., 40

schools: adolescents and, 341–3; age groups and, 230–1; 'black', 344, 346; children and, 223; cliques and, 83; denominational, 384; distance in, 344–6; gender socialization and, 131–2; integration and, 351–4; inter-ethnic interaction and, 199; labour market and, 188; mixed, 344–5, 354; neighbourhood, 341; obedience and, 336; private, 344; religion and, 344, 384; residential, 345; segregated, 344–6; shootings at, 351, 358; single-sex, 346; violence and, 349–51, 358; *see also* education

Schwartz, Barry, 238

Schwartzman, Lisa H., 179

science: critical theory and, 18–19; globalization and, 296; norms of, 377; postmodernism and, 11, 49–50; religion and, 371, 376–9; as rigid, 379; sexuality and, 162; universities and, 338

'science studies', 378–9

scientific management, 251
Scott, John, 481
Scott, Jonathan, 357
Scoular, Jane, 180
scripts: gender, 138; sexual, 159, 163; social, 65–6, 69–70
Searle, Chris, 357
seats, Parliamentary, 436
'second shift', 324, 325
secrecy, 75–6
secular: sacred and, 376
secularism, 387
secularization, 106, 364, 380–2; patterns of, 388–9; theory of, 381, 383
security: globalization and, 298
seekers, 370
Seeley, John R., et al., 347–9, 361
Seeman, Melvin, 256
Sefat, Kusha, and Tene Kelly, 415
segregation: children and, 223; schools and, 344–6; self-, 199, 200; in US, 205
Seidman, Steven, 183
self: looking-glass, 71, 308; socialization and, 308, 315–16
self-injury, 86
Sennett, Richard and Jonathan Cobb, 264, 273
Serbulo, Leanne Claire, 58
service sector: emotional labour and, 324, 325
setting, 343
sex, 125; definition of, 131, 156; extramarital, 158, 166–7; premarital, 156, 377, 475; safe, 165
sexism, 126; pornography and, 168
sex ratio, 43–4
sex-role rigidity/confusion, 175
sexuality, 84, 154–83; changing trends in, 164–5; as continuum, 171–2; critical theories and, 158–9, 181; definition of, 156; families and, 314; female, 172; Freud and, 379–80; functionalism and, 158, 167; new insights into, 179–81; social organization of, 163–4; symbolic interactionism and, 180
sexualization, 156, 161, 181
sexual orientation: in Canada, 172; see also sexuality
'sex work', 157; feminist theories and, 160
Shannon, Claude, and Warren Weaver, 417
Shibutani, Tamotsu, 319, 458–60
shopping, 328
signs: language and, 102
Siljak, Ana, 292, 300

Siltanen, Janet, and Andrea Doucet, 152
Simmel, Georg, 24, 38, 66, 75–6, 461
Simpsons, The, 241
Singapore, 60
Singer, Merrill, 86
'six degrees of separation', 80, 457
skepticism: science and, 377, 378
skin: colour of, 192–3
slang, racist, 188
Slattery, David, 29
slavery, 205; world-systems theory and, 279–80
'small world', 456–8; social networks and, 80
Smith, Christian, 388
Smith, Dorothy, 147–9, 237, 406, 475
Smith, Miriam, 480
Soares, Judith, 477–8
sociability: voluntary association and, 460–1
social bond theory, 224–5
social change, 452–81; generations and, 238
social cohesion, 387; conflict and, 17; loss of, 255–6
social constructionism, 25–7; families and, 306–7; work and class and, 250–1
social control theory, 15
social differentiation, 381
social exchange theory, 425
social facts, 12
social field, 112–13
social forms, 65–6; groups and, 76–7
social institutions: functional theory and, 6–7, 14
social integration: families and, 307; suicide and, 12–13
socialization, 66, 74, 303, 305; anticipatory, 316; class, 322–4; culture and, 96; definition of, 315; education and, 349; faulty, 317–20; functionalism and, 305, 307; gender, 131–2, 307, 315–16, 320–1; peer, 307–8; primary, 315–16; professional, 316; prostitutes and, 159; racial/ethnic, 188, 207, 321–2; religion and, 387; secondary, 315, 316; status and, 73; symbolic interactionism and, 307–8; top-down, 307–8
socialism: in North America, 435, 442
social movements, 70, 445, 452–81; changing causes of, 470–2; critical theories and, 466–7; functionalism and, 465–6; globalization and, 472–4; labour, 471; new insights into, 476–8;

postmodernism and, 477–8; stages of, 471; symbolic interactionism and, 467; see also new social movements
social networking services, 80, 81
social problems: cities and, 37–8; critical theory and, 8; functional theory and, 7–8; media and, 414; sociology and, 3; stages of, 9, 414; symbolic interactionism and, 8–9
social structures, 64–91; new insights into, 86–8; symbolic interactionism and, 24
social systems, 77–8
'social volume', 255
social welfare approach, 232
societalization, 381
society: definition of, 5
'sociological imagination', 7, 445
sociology: current debates in, 27–9; definition of, 5; 'epistemological problem' of, 4; gender and, 148; introduction to, 2–31; market research and, 412; mathematical, 356; medical, 15; political, 14–15, 423, 427–8; present-day, 4, 27–9; urban, 57–9
'sociometric stars', 457
Sohlberg, Peter, 269
solidarity: industrial societies and, 255–6; mechanical/organic, 38, 368; new, 270; organic, 255, 455; religion and, 366, 367–8, 378
Solidarity movement, 442
Sonnert, G., and G.J. Holton, 138
sound bites, 403
Soviet Union, 430; media and, 397
'space of flows', 58–9
Spillman, Lyn, 122
'spin', 404
spirituality: religion and, 369–70, 371–2
Spitzer, Brenda, et al., 135
Spohn, Willfried, 295
sports: gender and, 150
Sprague, Joey, and Heather Laub, 148, 149
Stahl, G.E., 378
Stalin, Joseph, 430
'standpoint theory', 143, 237
Stanley, Liz, 474–5
Staples, Sacha, 416
Stark, Sasha, 80
state: civil religion and, 382–3, 385–9; class and, 263; core, 279–82; definition of, 424; etiquette and, 464–5; evolving, 427; Foucault and, 84; gender and, 433–4; nation and, 282; as oppressive, 247; periphery, 279–82; racial equality

and, 205; role of, 453; semi-peripheral, 281; sexuality and, 162; study of, 427–8; totalitarian, 430–1; types of, 430–3

Statistics Canada: elections and, 437; employment and, 254–5; families and, 313; gender and, 131; intergroup marriage and, 190–1; religion and, 365, 372–3; sexual orientation and, 172; wages and, 259

status, 18, 73; consumption and, 110; health and, 265; inconsistency and, 266, 268; master, 75; social order and, 73; temperance movement and, 468–70; work and, 247, 250

status sequence, 73

stereotypes: age and, 219, 222; cults and, 383–4; gender, 127, 321, 408, 409, 410; poverty, 250, 261; racialized, 187, 208

stigma, 22–3, 407, 408

Stone-Mediatore, Shari, 149

strain theory, 137

stratification: education and, 355–6

streaming, 335, 343–4

Stronach, Belinda, 409

structural functionalism: see functionalism

structural theory: racial and ethic groups and, 188–9

structuration theory, 26–7

subclasses, 269

subcultures: adolescent, 341–3, 350–1; cities and, 38; culture and, 98–9, 114; gay, 169, 173

suburbs, bedroom, 56

Sudan, 293

suicide: assisted, 13; bombing and, 292; egoistic/altruistic/anomic, 12–13

Sukhov, Michael J., 477

Super Bowl, 382–3, 385–6

supernatural, 106

surgery, cosmetic, 84–5

surveillance, 83, 84, 437–40

'survival of the fittest', 440

Sutherland, Edwin, 261–2

Suzuki, David, 51

Svihula, Judie, 84

Swartz, David, 111

Swatos, William H., Jr, 387

Switzerland, 13

symbolic interactionism, 6, 8–9, 22–5; age groups and, 221–2; cities and, 38; culture and, 98; education and, 336; environment and, 39–40; families and, 306–8; feminist theories and, 9–10;

functionalism and, 77–8; gender and, 127–8; key ideas of, 23–5; language and, 101; racial and ethic groups and, 188; sexuality and, 159, 180; social movements and, 467; social structures and, 66–89; work and class and, 250

symbols: language and, 102; roles and, 72

Syria, 293

systemic theory, 466

taboos, 97

Tambe, Ashwini, 327

Tapscott, Don, 330

Taras, David, 420

Tassone, Giuseppe, 447

tax: head, 187, 193; inequality and, 263

Taylor, Peter J., et al., 296

TBGs (teams, bands, and gangs), 77–9

teams, 66–7, 77–9

technologies: cities and, 56–7; communication, 306–7, 406, 417; digital revolution in, 416; globalization and, 284–5; information, 109; post-industrialism and, 253–5; postmodernism and, 49–50, 58–9; regions and nations and, 277, 284–5; science and, 376–7; social evolution and, 266–7; universities and, 338; war, 291

telephone, 396; globalization and, 284–5

television: competition and, 396; fathers and, 323; fear and, 398; homogenization and, 411; ownership of, 400–1; political bias and, 402; 'reality', 417; see also media

temperance movement, 468–70

Teneycke, Kory, 441

Tepperman, Lorne, 331

terrain: environment and, 53–4

terrorism, 86, 277, 291–4; definition of, 291–2; media and, 416; non-state, 447; state-sponsored, 293, 447

tests, 334, 335

Thailand, 389

Thomas, W.I., 24, 197–8

Thompson, Craig J., and Gokcen Coskuner-Balli, 87

Till, Rupert, 119

Tilly, Charles, 474–6

time: aging and, 239–40

Times, 398

Time Warner, 400

Toby, Jackson, 233

tokenism theory, 138

Tong, Rosemarie, 151

Tönnies, Ferdinand, 387, 388

Torikian, Garen J., 416

Toronto: inter-ethnic interaction and, 199; youth homelessness in, 231–2

Torres, Sandra, 241

torture, 437

total institutions, 317, 438

totemism, 367–8, 369

tracking, 343

traditional authority, 19, 428

'tragedy of the commons', 39

training, 335

Travers, Max, 90

triads, 76–7

Trudeau, Pierre, 467

trust, 461–2

truth: as nonexistent, 416–17

tuition, 338, 341

Turkey, 60

Turner, Bryan S., 387–8

Turner, Jonathan H., 30

Turner, Ralph, 73

Tutsi, 209, 210

TV Ontario (TVO), 400

Uhde, Zuzana, 325

Ukraine, 60

unconscious, 379–80

under-representation: politics and, 433

unemployment: capitalism and, 142; critical theories and, 248–9; in North America, 252; technology and, 254

unhappiness: age and, 233

unions, 247, 256–9; advantage of, 259; capitalism and, 251; membership decline and, 258; social movements and, 471

United Kingdom: religious education in, 384; US and, 426–7

United Nations Millennium Development Goals, 333

United States: adolescent subculture in, 341–3; African Americans in, 205–6; assimilation in, 20; Canada, Australia, UK and, 426–7; Canadian content and, 402–3, 404–5; Canadian culture and, 116–17; class socialization in, 323; culture war and, 290–1; elections in, 437; Gulf War and, 415–16; health in, 236; media in, 400–1, 402, 412–13; propaganda and, 290; race relations in, 208–9; religion in, 378, 382–3, 384, 385–8; sexuality in, 163–4; society in, 426–7; terrorism and, 293

universalism: postmodernism and, 11
universals, cultural, 95
universities: in Canada, 338; inter-ethnic interaction and, 199; research, 336–9; revolution in, 336–9
upheavals, social, 19
urban planning, 60
urban social movements, 58
utilitarian perspective, 467

values: 'American', 426–7; culture and, 95–7, 106–7; education and, 334, 349; news media and, 399
Valverde, Mariana, 170
Vancouver: inter-ethnic interaction and, 199; youth homelessness in, 231–2
Van Gerwen, Jef, 385
Veblen, Thorstein, 60, 109–10, 272, 322–3
vertical mosaic, 20–1
Viacom, 401
victimization: bullying and, 350; feminist theories and, 10; race relations and, 210
Vido, Roman, 389
violence: age groups and, 236–7; collective, 474; families and, 234, 236, 315, 320; gender and, 146–7, 161; globalization and, 298; international, 291–4; 'logic of', 475; media and, 398, 412–13; racial and ethnic groups and, 208–10; schools and, 349–51, 358
Voltaire, 5
voluntarism, 77
voluntary associations, 453, 454; benefits of, 461–2; critical theories and, 466–7; functionalism and, 465–6; sociability and, 460–1
vote: women and, 433; see also elections
voyeurism, 176

Wade, Peter, 214
wage: gender and, 138–41
Waite, Linda, 305
Wakefield, Sarah, 476–7

Wallerstein, Immanuel, 277–82, 287, 294–6, 300
Walt Disney Company, 400
Walters, Patrick, and Rita Kop, 416
Walters, Suzanna, 405–6
Walters, Vivienne, et al., 144
war, 277; Afghanistan, 416; civil, 427; 'culture', 54, 282, 290–1; economic, 282; 'generational', 337; Iraq, 383, 387, 416; 'television', 415; 'on terror', 383, 386–7, 416
Warner, W. Lloyd, et al., 272
Warren, Mary Anne, 44
'war system', 291
water: environment and, 51–3
wealth: gender and, 140
Webb, Stephen, 269
Weber, Max, 3, 4, 5, 8, 262; authority and, 19, 428–30; class relations and, 246–7, 248, 252–3; conflict and, 18, 19–20, 21; Lenski and, 267; religion and, 104–5, 106, 363–4, 365, 365–6, 379, 388; Veblen and, 110; Wallerstein and, 282; work and class and, 252–3; work ethic and, 104–5, 366–7, 440
Webster, Frank, 57
Weller, Wivian, and Nicolle Pfaff, 238
Wender, Andrew M., 386–7
West: globalization and, 298; media and, 397, 405; non-Western families and, 327; world markets and, 278
White, Harrison, and Cynthia White, 99
'Whitehall Studies', 265
White Man's Burden, The, 193
white people: immigration and, 193
'white supremacy', 28
Whitty, M., 166
Wicks, Patricia Gaya, and Peter Reason, 445
Willmott, Hugh, 477
women: education and, 339–40; emotional labour and, 324; 'fallen', 160; families and, 309; globalization and, 298; as Madonna/whore, 408; media and,

405–11; nature and, 40; as 'persons', 433; politics and, 433–4; war and, 277; see also gender
Women's Christian Temperance Union, 468–70
women's movement, 128, 151
Woolf, Virginia, 479
work, 244–73; critical theories and, 248–9; degradation of, 254, 251–2; feminist theories and, 250; full-time, 254; functionalism and, 247–8; need for, 248; new insights into, 268–70; non-standard, 254; organization of, 245, 247, 253–5; paid/unpaid, 142–5, 324–6; part-time, 254; self-employed, 254; shift, 145; see also employment; housework; labour
work ethic, 104–5, 366–7, 440
'working poor', 259–61
workplace: age groups and, 230–1; inter-ethnic interaction and, 199
Workplace 2000, 271
World Giving Index, 371–2
world-systems theory, 277–82, 294–6
'World3 model', 41–2
World Wildlife Fund, 51
Wright, April L., 112
Wright, Erik O., 248, 252
Wrong, Dennis, 307

Yeygel, Sinem, 88
youth: homeless, 231–3; mental health and, 233–4; older people and, 229; risk and, 224–5; social change and, 238; voting and, 437; see also adolescence
YouTube, 396
Yukon: fertility in, 227

Zarycki, Tomasz, 112
zero population growth (ZPG), 37
Zhang, Xiaotian, 268
Zizek, Slavoj, 446
Znaniecki, F., 197–8

STARTING POINTS
A Sociological Journey
Lorne Tepperman

President, Oxford University Press Canada
David Stover

Vice-President and Director, Higher Education Division
Sophia Fortier

Managing Editor, Higher Education Division
Phyllis Wilson

Senior Acquisitions Editor
Katherine Skene

Associate Acquisitions Editor, Sociology
Mark Thompson

Developmental Editor
Allison McDonald

Copy Editor
Leslie Saffrey

Vice-President and Director, Creative Services
Wendy Moran

Senior Production Coordinator
Steven Hall

Permissions Manager
Sandy Cooke

Permissions Coordinator
Nicole Argyropoulos

Design Manager, New Titles
Sherill Chapman

Cover and Text Design
Ellissa Glad

Formatter
Janette Thompson, Jansom

Indexer
Francesca Scalzo

Proofreader
Elaine Melnick

Senior Research Assistant
Nina Gheihman

Research Assistant
Hilary Killam

Student Advisory Team
Balsam Attarbashi
Pam Bautista
Roxy Chis
Anita Feher
Sarah Fox
Jason Jensen
Len Liu
Cathy Long
Brianna Sykes
Cindy Yi

Reviewers
Christopher J. Fries, University of Manitoba
Leanne Joanisse, McMaster University
Abdolmohammad Kazemipur, University of Lethbridge
C. Barry McClinchey, University of Waterloo
Erin Steuter, Mount Allison University
Ann Travers, Simon Fraser University

If you would like to consider *Starting Points* or another Oxford textbook for an upcoming course, please contact your OUP sales and editorial representative, or email: sales.hed.ca@oup.com.

OXFORD
UNIVERSITY PRESS

Tel: 416-441-2941 or 1-866-229-7025
Fax: 416-441-0345
E-mail: sales.hed.ca@oup.com